AN INTRODUCTION
TO
THE HINDUSTANI LANGUAGE

AN INTRODUCTION
TO
THE HINDUSTANI LANGUAGE.

COMPRISING

A GRAMMAR,

AND

A VOCABULARY, ENGLISH AND HINDUSTANI;

ALSO

SHORT SENTENCES AND DIALOGUES; SHORT STORIES IN PERSIAN AND NAGARI CHARACTERS, WITH SOME GRAMMATICAL ANALYSIS; HINDUSTANI COMPOSITION, OR FACILITIES FOR TRANSLATING ENGLISH INTO HINDUSTANI,

AND

MILITARY WORDS OF COMMAND, NAGARI AND ENGLISH.

BY JOHN SHAKESPEAR

GYAN

Published by

Gyan Publishing House
5, Ansari Road
Daryaganj, New Delhi-110002
Phone: 011-47034999, 9811692060
E-mail: books@gyanbooks.com

Distribution Network
gyanbooks.com
India, USA, Canada, UK, Australia

ISBN: 978-93-6208-098-1 (PB)
First Published, 1845

2nd Impression 2024

Printed at: Gyan Press, Delhi.

AN INTRODUCTION TO THE HINDUSTANI LANGUAGE
Author: JOHN SHAKESPEAR

AN INTRODUCTION

TO

THE HINDUSTANI LANGUAGE.

COMPRISING

A GRAMMAR,

AND

A VOCABULARY, ENGLISH AND HINDUSTANI;

ALSO

SHORT SENTENCES AND DIALOGUES; SHORT STORIES IN PERSIAN AND NAGARI CHARACTERS, WITH SOME GRAMMATICAL ANALYSIS; HINDUSTANI COMPOSITION, OR FACILITIES FOR TRANSLATING ENGLISH INTO HINDUSTANI,

AND

MILITARY WORDS OF COMMAND, NAGARI AND ENGLISH.

By JOHN SHAKESPEAR.

LONDON:

WM. H. ALLEN & Co.

BOOKSELLERS TO THE HONOURABLE EAST-INDIA COMPANY,

7, LEADENHALL STREET.

1845.

J. & H. COX, BROTHERS (LATE COX & SONS),
PRINTERS TO THE HONOURABLE EAST-INDIA COMPANY,
74 & 75, Great Queen Street, Lincoln's-Inn Fields.

TO

Sir HENRY WILLOCK, K.L.S., CHAIRMAN.

JAMES WEIR HOGG, Esq., M.P., DEPUTY CHAIRMAN.

WILLIAM ASTELL, Esq., M.P.

WILLIAM WIGRAM, Esq.

Sir ROBERT CAMPBELL, Bart.

JOHN MASTERMAN, Esq., M.P.

JOHN PETTY MUSPRATT, Esq.

HENRY ALEXANDER, Esq.

Major-Gen. Sir J. L. LUSHINGTON, G.C.B.

Sir WILLIAM YOUNG, Bart.

GEORGE LYALL, Esq., M.P.

RUSSELL ELLICE, Esq.

Sir RICHARD JENKINS, G.C.B.

WILLIAM BUTTERWORTH BAYLEY, Esq.

JOHN SHEPHERD, Esq.

FRANCIS WARDEN, Esq.

MARTIN TUCKER SMITH, Esq.

Lieut.-Col. WILLIAM HENRY SYKES.

Major-Gen. ARCHIBALD GALLOWAY, C.B.

Major-Gen. Sir JEREMIAH BRYANT, C.B.

Major-Gen. ARCHIBALD ROBERTSON.

ELLIOT MACNAGHTEN, Esq.

Major JAMES OLIPHANT.

JOHN CLARMONT WHITEMAN, Esq.

DIRECTORS

OF THE

Honourable East-India Company,

THIS

INTRODUCTION TO THE HINDUSTANI LANGUAGE,

IS,

WITH GREAT RESPECT, DEDICATED,

BY

THEIR VERY OBEDIENT,

AND VERY HUMBLE SERVANT,

THE AUTHOR.

London, 12th May, 1845.

ADVERTISEMENT.

THE conviction that great advantage is likely to accrue to Candidates for the Indian Service, from the acquisition of some elementary and grammatical acquaintance, with the most common and practically useful dialect of India, previous to their arrival in that country, is now become so prevalent, that argument seems hardly needed to extend or strengthen it. And, as in India a knowledge of the languages of that region, but especially of the Hindustani, is made indispensable to the attainment of staff, as well as of other extraordinary beneficial appointments, no opportunity—no time should be let slip or lost by those about to go thither, for commencing and continuing the study of that dialect. To facilitate this study, the author or compiler of the following sheets has before prepared and passed through the press, various editions of a Grammar, Dictionary, and two volumes of Selections, the utility of which is best proved by the uninterrupted public countenance shewn them; and, for such learners as can obtain the assistance of a fit instructor, these helps might have sufficed. From the manner, however, in which some persons are obliged, without much previous notice and with little or no instruction in the language, to proceed to India, a compendious work, made as easy as possible, has been judged still requisite for individuals thus circumstanced: and, though some little instruction from a qualified teacher is earnestly recommended where it can be obtained, to guide the reader in the pronunciation and other particulars, yet it is hoped this book may prove essentially useful to the assiduous student, whether aided by others or obliged to rely solely on his own application and discernment.

INDEX TO THE CONTENTS.

PART I.

PART II.

PART III.

PART IV.

PART V.

APPENDIX.

AN INTRODUCTION

TO THE

HINDŪSTĀNĪ LANGUAGE.

PART I.

GRAMMAR.

CHAPTER I.

Alphabets, Orthographical Signs, and Pronunciation.

THE most common dialects of India, whether that of Hindustan proper, or that of the Dakhan, are often found written in the Persian or Arabic characters, especially by the Musalman population of the country; by Hindūs, however, the Devanāgari (a word often contracted to Nāgarı), or characters allied to the Devanāgari, are usually adopted: the alphabets and other orthographical signs, therefore, made use of in each of those two systems of writing claim the earliest attention of the learner; and, will in the first place be submitted to his notice.

Persian Alphabet.*

Letters unconnected.	Names in Persian and Roman.	Usual equivalents in Roman.	Letters unconnected.	Names in Persian and Roman.	Usual equivalents in Roman.
ا	اَلِف *alif*	*a, ā, i, u.*	ص	صاد *ṣād*	*ṣ.*
ب	بي *bē*	*b.*	ض	ضاد *ẓād*	*ẓ.*
پ	پي *pē*	*p.*	ط	طوي *ṯō'ē*	*ṯ.*
ت	تي *tē*	*t.*	ظ	ظوي *ẕō'ē*	*ẕ.*
ث	ثي *s̤ē*	*s̤.*	ع	عَين *ăin*	*, *ă, ĭ, ŭ,* &c.
ج	جِيم *jīm*	*j.*	غ	غَين *ghain*	*gh.*
چ	چي *chē*	*ch.*	ف	في *fē*	*f.*
ح	حي *ḥē*†	*ḥ.*	ق	قاف *ḳāf*	*ḳ.*
خ	خي *khē*	*kh.*	ک	کاف *kāf*	*k.*
د	دال *dāl*	*d.*	گ	گاف *gāf*	*g.*
ذ	ذال *ẕāl*	*ẕ.*	ل	لام *lām*	*l.*
ر	ري *rē*	*r.*	م	مِيم *mīm*	*m.*
ز	زي *zē*	*z.*	ن	نُون *nūn*	*n.*
ژ	ژي *zhē*	*zh.*	و	واو *wā'ō*	*w, v, ū, o, au,* &c.
س	سِين *sīn*	*s.*	ه	هي *hē*‡	*h.*
ش	شِين *shīn*	*sh.*	ي	يي *yē*	*y, ī, e, ai,* &c.

* The characters of this alphabet are to be read from right to left.

† Called *ḥā'ē ḥuṯṯī* (حائي حُطي) by way of distinction from the other *hē*.

‡ Called *hā'ē hawwaz* (هائي هَوَّز) or *hā'ē mudawwara* (هائي مُدَوَّره).

The Persian characters, as above described, are used when standing alone; and, the letters ا د ذ ر ز ژ و neither admit of junction to a following one, nor are liable to any material change from another letter being prefixed: the rest of the characters, however, become apparently abridged, retaining their essential portion only or assuming some variation of form, when used in composition; as in

اب با بب بچ جد ذر رس سر شش ضر طع غف قص کا کل کک

kk kl kā kz ghf t̤ʿ zr shsh sr rs zr jd pch bb bā ab

گا لا or لا لک ما من نو یه هي نن مم وي لل ها هه يي يم

ym yē hhh hā ll wē mm nn hy yh nw mn mā lk lā gā

قعد فقط غغغ ععع ططط ضضض شست دجد ججج تتت ببب

kʿd fkt ghghgh ʿʿʿ ttt zzz shst djd jjj ttt bbb

ققق کهه للل ممم ننن ههه ههه ييي

yyy hhh hhh nnn mmm lll khh kkk

To represent some sounds peculiar to the Hindūs, additional marks are commonly assumed with a few of the Persian letters, or certain combinations may be adopted; as,

ٹ ڈ ڑ بھ پھ تھ ٹھ جھ چھ دھ ڈھ ڑھ کھ گھ مھ نھ پھب

phab nh mh gh kh ṛh ḍh dh chh jh ṭh th ph bh ṛ ḍ ṭ

ٹھب چھب دھب ڑھب کھب مھب نھب

nhab mhab khab ṛhab dhab chhab ṭhab

In uttering ٹ or ڈ or ڑ the point of the tongue is to be reverted to the palate; and the aspiration intended in بھ *bh*, &c. is to be expressed at once with the preceding consonant.

Of the letters above recited, the term حرفِ علّت *ḥarf-i-ʿillat* (infirm letter) is technically given to ا or و or ي, as that of حرفِ صحيح *ḥarf-i-ṣaḥīḥ* (sound letter) is applied to each of the rest.

The short vowels are three, namely ´ (زبر) *zabar* or (فتحه) *fat'ḥa*, to which may correspond the Roman *a*; ˏ (زير) *zēr* or (كسر) *kasr*, which may be represented by *i;* and ُ (پيش) *pēsh* or (ضم) *ẕamm,* by *u:* so, in بَد *bad;* بِد *bid;* بُد *bud.**

The long vowels and the diphthongs are formed by the adjunction of the infirm letters (ا و ي) to consonants uttered with the short vowels; yet, at the beginning of a word or syllable, each of these infirm letters may perform the office of a consonant; and, instead of writing ا ا (two *alifs*) at the commencement of a word, one of those letters with the sign ~ (مده) *madda,* is commonly adopted: so,

آب وه يه اُوب اوب اَوب با بُوت بوت بَوت جِيد جيد جَيد

jaid jē‡d jīd baut bō†t būt bā aub ō†b ūb yah wah āb

سا سِي سي سَي يا يِي يي يَي

yai yē‡ yī yā sai sē‡ sī sā

---

* These short vowels are but rarely marked by the natives in writing Hindustani; yet, for the guidance of European learners in pronunciation, they may with much convenience be frequently used; the most common of them, however, *fat'ḥa* or *zabar,* will be left generally unmarked in this work; and, must then be understood after a consonant, which is not final, nor marked with either of the other short vowels, or with *jazm.*

† For the sound here intended there is no discriminating mark in the Arabic orthography, because it is unknown in that language: and the *wā'ō* in such case termed *wāw-i maj'hūl* (unknown *wā'ō*) is left without any vowel accompanying the preceding consonant, which circumstance will sufficiently distinguish it from the *wā'ō* when following a vowel and taking another sound.

‡ The *yā-i maj'hūl* (unknown *yē*) is, for the like reason as the *wāw-i maj'hūl,* left without any vowel accompanying the foregoing consonant.

Other orthographical signs are—

ٔ (همزه) *hamza*, which is always initial in a syllable and accompanied or moved by a short vowel either written or understood; as, in أَب (*ab*), هُوئِي (*hū'ī*), عائِد (*ā'id*).

ْ or ْ (جزْم) *jazm* shews that the subscribed letter has no vowel to be sounded after it; so, in اِسْم (*ism*), فِعْل (*fi'l*), حرْف (*harf*).

ّ (تشْدِيد) *tashdīd*, which shews that the letter underneath is to be pronounced double; as, in شِدّت (*shiddat*): and the letter so marked must be distinctly twice sounded.

ٱ (وصْل) *waṣl*, which serves to join together two Arabic words, the latter having the article ال (*al*) prefixed, the vowel of which is dropped in pronunciation; as, in آخِرُ ٱلامْر (*ākhiru-l-amr*): and, the ل (*lām*) of the article becomes converted in sound to the following letter, if this be ت ث د ذ ر ز س ش ص ض ط ظ ل or ن which may then be marked with *tashdīd*, and is to be uttered as double; so, in عَوَامُّ ٱلنّاس (*āwāmmu-n-nās*).

ً ٍ ٌ (تنْوِين) *tanwīn*, giving the nasal sound to the final vowel; as, in خُصُوصٌ (*khuṣūṣun*), خُصُوصٍ (*khuṣūṣin*), خُصُوصًا (*khuṣūṣan*).

Some few words, in which the use of these letters and signs will be farther exemplified.

ابد	انْدر	آيت	اَور	بُود	بوجْه	بُودہ	جبّار	خَير	ژوله	سِدّھ
abad	*andar*	*āyat*	*aur*	*būd*	*bojh*	*būda*	*jabbār*	*khair*	*zhola*	*siddha*
شُبْهه	ضِدّ	طُرّه	عيّار	غُبّار	كاغذ	گُمبذ	لال	لاله	لاثانِي	
shubha	*zidd*	*ṭurra*	*āiyār*	*ghubbār*	*kāghaz*	*gumbaz*	*lāl*	*lāla*	*lā-sānī*	
مُذكّر	مُدّت	مغْرب	عِنْدَ ٱلْحق	أَلْحَمْدُ لِلّٰه	فِي ٱلفور					
muzakkar	*muddat*	*maghrab*	*inda-l-hakk*	*alhamdu lillāh*	*fi-l-faur*					
فِي ٱلْحقِيقت	فَورًا	حقِيقتًا	ذُو ٱلْفقار	طاؤُس	قلْعه	نُجبا	هِبه			
fi-l-hakīkat	*fauran*	*hakīkatan*	*zu-l-fakār*	*ṭā'ūs*	*kal'ā*	*nujabā*	*hiba*			

شہاب شاہنشاہ تھوڑا ٹھنڈھا ڈوبنا ڈھونڈھنا شعاع

*shuhāb shāhanshāh thoṛā ṭhanḍhā ḍūbnā ḍhūnḍhnā shu'ā**

بسم اللہ الرحمان الرحیم تنبیہ

*bismi-l-lāhi-r-raḥmāni-r-raḥīm tam*bīh*†

DEVANAGARI ALPHABET.‡

Vowels.

अ *a*, आ *ā*; इ *i*, ई *ī*; उ *u*, ऊ *ū*; ऋ *ṛi*, ॠ *ṛī*;‖ ऌ *ḷri*,‖ ॡ *ḷrī*;‖ ए *ē*, ऐ *ai*; ओ *ō*, औ *au*.

Consonants.

Gutturals,	क *ka*,	ख *kha*,	ग *ga*,	घ *gha*,	ङ *nga*.‖
Palatals,	च *cha*,	छ *chha*,	ज *ja*,	झ *jha*,	ञ *nya*.‖
Cerebrals,	ट *ṭa*,	ठ *ṭha*,	ड *ḍa*,¶	ढ *ḍha*,¶	ण *ṇa*.
Dentals,	त *ta*,	थ *tha*,	द *da*,	ध *dha*,	न *na*.
Labials,	प *pa*,	फ *pha*,	ब *ba*,	भ *bha*,	म *ma*.
Semivowels,	य *ya*,	र *ra*,	ल *la*,	व *va*.	
Sibilants and Aspirate,	श *ṣa*,**	ष *sha*,††	स *sa*,	ह *ha*.	

* The ن (*nūn*) before a ب (*be*) or پ (*pe*) becomes *m* in pronunciation.

† When ہ (*he*) sensibly expressed is preceded by a vowel, it may be thus represented to distinguish it from the *hā-ē mukhtafī* (concealed *he*) as in گہ *ga*, or from the aspirated compound as in گھ *gha*.

‡ Frequently called Nāgarī alphabet, and read from left to right.

‖ But very rarely, if ever, used in writing Hindustani.

¶ ड and ढ are often pronounced rather as *ṛa* and *ṛha* by reverting the tip of the tongue to the palate; and, to mark this variation, a point may be subscribed, as ड़ *ṛa*, ढ़ *ṛha*.

** श is a palatal sibilant; and often adopted to represent the Arabic ش (*shīn*).

†† ष is sometimes uttered as *kha*.

In addition to the above are the two characters, *anuswāra* (ं) and *visarga* (ः), the first of which placed over a letter imparts to the vowel a slight nasal sound, somewhat stronger however than the French *n* in *bon;* and the latter placed after a letter denotes a soft aspiration (not perceptible, and but rarely used in Hindustani).*

The forms of the vowels, as above described, are used when standing alone or when initial in a syllable: after consonants, however, there is no character for अ (*a*), which is to be understood in case no other vowel be noted, or no consonant be added as a compound, or no mark called *virāma* (rest) be appended, as in ग्. Yet, in Hindustani, this unwritten vowel is not to be understood at the end of a word, where indeed no vowel, unless expressly marked, is to be sounded.

After consonants, and as compounded with them, the rest of the vowels are represented by the following forms:—

ा *ā;* ि *i;* ी *ī;* ु *u;* ू *ū;* ृ *ṛi;* ॄ *ṛī;* ॢ *ḷri;* ॣ *ḷrī;* े *ē;* ै *ai;* ो *ō;* ौ *au.*

And the composition of vowels and other marks with consonants may be exemplified in

अक *aka* आका *ākā* इकि *iki* ईकी *īkī* उकु *uku* ऊकू *ūkū* ऋकृ *ṛikṛi* ॠकॄ *ṛīkṛī* ऌकॢ *ḷrikḷri* ॡकॣ *ḷrīkḷrī*

एके *ēkē* ऐकै *aikai* ओको *ōkō* औकौ *aukau* अकं *akań* अकः *akah* कंसः *kańsah* दिश् *diş*

---

* Though in repeating the alphabet, it is usual to say *a, ā, i, ī,* &c. *ka, kha, ga, gha,* &c. simply, as before noted, yet in naming the letters कार *kāra* (or *kār*) is added to the sound of each; so अकार (*akār*) the letter अ, ककार (*kakār*) the letter क.

If two or more consonants come together without the intervention of a vowel, they should coalesce and become one compound character. Such compounds are formed in various ways; either by placing the body of the subsequent consonant under the first, as in क्व *kw;* by arranging them in their usual order, omitting however the perpendicular line in all but the last, as स्म्य *smy;* or, by varying somewhat the elementary characters and blending them together, as in ज्ञ *jn*, क्ष *ksh*, द्ध *ddh*. With the semivowels य *y*, and र *r*, composition is of most frequent recurrence: the adjunction of the first to a preceding consonant does not much, if at all, change its original shape; as, in क्य *ky*, ख्य *khy*, ज्य *jy*, द्य *dy*, प्य *py*, फ्य *phy*, स्य *sy*, ह्य *hy:* but, the latter, when immediately following a consonant, usually takes the form ˏ beneath, as when preceding a consonant it is denoted by the character ˆ placed above; so, क्र *kr*, ग्र *gr*, त्र *tr*, श्र *ṣr*, स्र *sr*, ह्र *hr;* र्क *rk*, र्ग *rg*, धर्म *dharm.*

Other compounds, of most frequent use, are the following:—

क्क *kk*, क्त *kt*, क्न *kn*, क्म *km*, क्ल *kl*, घ्न *ghn*, घ्य *ghy*, च्च *chch*, च्छ *chchh*, च्छ्र *chchhr*, ज्ज *jj*, ज्म *jm*, ज्ञ्य *jny*, झ्झ *jhjh*, ट्ट *ṭṭ*, ण्ड *ṇḍ*, त्त *tt*, त्त्य *tty*, त्न *tn*, त्र्य *try*, थ्थ *thth*, थ्न *thn*, द्ग *dg*, द्द *dd*, द्ध *ddh*, द्न *dn*, द्ध्न *ddhn*, द्ध्व *ddhw*, द्भ *dbh*, द्म *dm*, द्र *dr*, द्व *dw*, ध्न *dhn*, ध्म *dhm*, ध्व *dhw*, न्न *nn*, न्न्य *nny*, न्त्र्य *ntry*, न्द्य *ndy*, प्त *pt*, प्न *pn*, प्प *pp*, प्ल *pl*, प्व *pw*, प्स *ps*, प्त्व *ptw*, ब्ब *bb*, ब्ज *bj*, ब्ल *bl*, भ्य *bhy*, भृ *bhṛi*, म्म *mm*, म्ल *ml*, रु *ru*, रू *rū*, ल्ल *ll*, व्र *wr*, वृ *wṛi*, श्च *ṣch*, श्छ *ṣchh*, श्र्य *ṣry*, श्श *ṣṣ*, ष्क *shk*, ष्ट *shṭ*, ष्ट्य *shṭy*, ष्ट्व *shṭw*, ष्ठ *shṭh*, सृ *sṛi*, स्न *sn*, हु *hu*, हू *hū*, हृ *hṛi*, हॄ *hṛī*, ह्न *h n*, ह्म *hm*, ह्य *hy*, ह्ल *hl*, ह्व *hw*.

To represent such Arabic or Persian letters as have no exact correspondents in the Nāgarī, the following characters, which approach most nearly in pronunciation, are commonly used in writing this language; and, though not the practice of the people of India, points may be adopted beneath the letters, in such cases, to shew the extraordinary use made of them: thus,

स़ for ث	स़ for ص	फ़ for ف
ह़ — ح	ज़ — ض	क़ — ق
ख़ — خ	त़ — ط	ा़ (final) ى (*alif-i maḳṣūra*).
ज़ — ذ	ज़ — ظ	न for ً (*tanwīn*).
ज़ — ز	अ़ — ع	
ज़ — ژ	ग़ — غ	

Pronunciation.

اَ	or	ـَ	for	अ	*a*, as in America.
آ	or	ـا	—	आ or ा	*ā*, as a in all.
اِ	or	ـِ	—	इ or ि	*i*, as i in fin.
اِي	or	ـِيـ	—	ई or ी	*ī*, as ee in peer.
اُ	or	ـُ	—	उ or ु	*u*, as u in pull.
اُو	or	ـُو	—	ऊ or ू	*ū*, as oo in cool.
اي	or	ـيـ	—	ए or े	*e* or *ē*, as ai in pair.
اَي	or	ـَيـ	—	ऐ or ै	*ai*, as ei in height.
او	or	ـو	—	ओ or ो	*o* or *ō*, as o in bone.
اَو	or	ـَو	—	औ or ौ	*au*, as ou in our.
ب	or	ـبـ	—	ब	*b*, as the English b.
بھ	or	ـبھـ	—	भ	*bh*, as in abhor.
پ	or	ـپـ	—	प	*p*, as the English p.
پھ	or	ـپھـ	—	फ	*ph*, as ph in up-hill.
ت	or	ـتـ	—	त	*t*, as t in tube.
تھ	or	ـتھـ	—	थ	*th*, as the last aspirated.
ٹ	or	ـٹـ	—	ट	*ṭ*, as t in true.
ٹھ	or	ـٹھـ	—	ठ	*ṭh*, as the last aspirated.

ث	or	ثـ	for	स़ *s̤*, as s in sin.
ج	or	جـ	—	ज *j*, as j in judge.
جھ	or	جھـ	—	झ *jh*, as the last aspirated.
چ	or	چـ	—	च *ch*, as ch in church.
چھ	or	چھـ	—	छ *chh*,* as the last aspirated.
ح	or	حـ	—	ह़ *ḥ*, as h in horse.
خ	or	خـ	—	ख़ *kh*, as the German ch.
د	or	د	—	द *d*, as d in dew.
دھ	or	دھ	—	ध *dh*, as the last aspirated.
ڈ	or	ڈ	—	ड *ḍ*, as d in dim.
ڈھ	or	ڈھ	—	ढ *ḍh*, as the last aspirated.
ذ	or	ذ	—	ज़ *z̤*, as z in zeal.
ر	or	ر	—	र *r*, as r in rain.
رِ	or	رِ	—	ऋ *ṛi*, as ri in river.
رِي	or	رِي	—	ॠ *ṝī*, as the last prolonged.
ڑ	or	ڑ	—	ड़ *ṛ*, as r in rim nearly.
ڑھ	or	ڑھ	—	ढ़ *ṛh*, as the last aspirated.
ز	or	ز	—	ज़ *z*, as z in zeal.
ژ	or	ژ	—	ज़ *zh*, as s in pleasure.
س	or	سـ	—	स *s*, as s in sin.
ش	or	شـ	—	श *sh*, as sh in shine.
ص	or	صـ	—	स़ *ṣ*, as s in sin.
ض	or	ضـ	—	ज़ *ẓ*, as *z* in zeal.
ط	or	ط	—	त़ *ṭ*, as t in tub.
ظ	or	ظ	—	ज़ *z̤*, as z in zeal.

* The Nagari compound च्छ is occasionally represented by چھـ, and similarly pronounced.

ع or	عـ	for	अ *ǎ, ǐ, ǔ*, as a, i, or u.*
غ or	غـ	—	ग़ *gh*, as the Northumberland r.†
ف or	فـ	—	फ़ *f*, as f in fin.
ق or	قـ	—	क़ *ḳ*, as k peculiarly uttered.‡
ک or	کـ	—	क *k*, as k in king.
کھ or	کھـ	—	§ख *kh*, as the last aspirated.
گ or	گـ	—	ग *g*, as g in give.
گھ or	گھـ	—	घ *gh*, as the last aspirated.
ل or	لـ	—	ल *l*, as the English l.
م or	مـ	—	म *m*, as the English m..
ن or	نـ	—	न *n*, as n in tint.
ن or	نـ	—	ङ *n*, as n in king.
ن or	نـ	—	ञ *n*, as n, in singe.

* With the Arabs, this letter is a guttural consonant of peculiar utterance, which is hardly attempted in Hindustani; and the mere vowel used with it is noted, in the Nagari character, when it occurs at the beginning of a syllable: so, in that character, for عَ, अ may be adopted; for عا, आ; for عِ, इ; for عِي, ई; for عَي, ऐ; for عُ, उ; for عُو, ऊ; for عَو, औ. In the Roman characters, this letter ع when initial in a syllable will be here represented by a small form of itself written over its subsequent vowel; and, when in the middle or at the end of a syllable, by the same mark placed after the vowel which precedes; so, عقل *ǎḳl*, معقول *maǎḳūl*.

† Or, as the sound *gha, gha, gha*, formed in gargling.

‡ With the root of the tongue pressed back on the throat, so as to check the voice gently and to occasion a clinking intonation.

§ The Nagari ष may occasionally be sounded like this and represented by the same Persian or Roman letters.

ن	or	ڹ	for	ण	*ṇ*, as in none.
ں	or	ڼ	—	ं	*ṅ*, a slight nasal.*
و	or	ﻭ	—	व	*v*, or *w*, as v in voice.†
ه	or	ﻫ	—	ह	*h*, as h in horse, how.‡
ي	or	ﻳ	—	य	*y*, as y in yoke.§

* The Nagari sign may be used for any nasal not initial in a syllable.

† Pronounced as *w* when compounded with some other consonant. In the Arabic orthography, moreover, this letter, subsequent to *fat'ḥa* becomes *au*; to *ẕamm*, *ū*; and, when *maj'hūl*, it is sounded *ō*, as before noted under the vowels. In some Persian words, و though written is scarcely, if at all, sounded; as in خواه (*khẉāh*) *desire*, خُوش (*khụsh*) *pleasant*. When thus used it is technically termed واوِ معدوله (*wāw-i maʿdūla*); and may in the Nagari translation be either wholly omitted, or distinguished by a point underneath, as well as in the Roman, so व़ *ẉ* or *ṿ*. In a few instances, too, of Arabic words, this letter may take the sound of *alif*; so, صلوة *ṣalāt*.

‡ When final, however, in Indian and Persian words, this letter is sometimes, but very slightly, if at all, sounded, and is then termed هاءِ مُختفي (*hā'e-mukhtafī*); in which case, it may be denoted by : (*visarga*) in the Nagari character, and omitted in the Roman. At the end of certain Arabic words, too, this letter may occur with two points marked above it, when it takes the sound of *t*, as it is often transmuted to ت; so, in خلاصة الهِند (*khulāṣatu-l-hind*).

§ In the Arabic character, however, this letter when secondary in a syllable becomes, together with the preceding vowel, if *fat'ḥa*, *ai*; if *kasr*, *ī*; and, if it be *maj'hūl*, it is sounded *ē*, as before instanced under the vowels. A final ي moreover, preceding by *fat'ḥa*, in Arabic words, is sounded as *alif*; so تعالي तआला (*ta'ālā*): but, when followed by ال (*al*), as *fat'ḥa* only; so, علي الصّباح (*ālạ-ṣ-ṣabāḥ*).

CHAPTER II.

Words may be divided into Nouns substantive or Adjective, Pronouns, Verbs comprising participles, Prepositions, Adverbs, Conjunctions, and Interjections.

Nouns Substantive.

1. Nouns substantive may be, in gender, masculine or feminine; in number, singular or plural; and for case, are frequently liable to inflection or change in the termination.

2. The gender of nouns is sometimes to be determined from the nature of the beings to which words are applied; as مرد (*mard*) *man*, عورت (*ʿaurat*) *woman*: in numerous instances, however, the distinction is conventional, and to be learned by practice in the language only; yet words terminating in ه (*a*), ا (*ā*),* ان (*āṅ*), are generally masculine, and those ending in ي (*ī*), ين (*īṅ*), ت (*t*), ش (*sh*), ن (*n*), will most commonly be found to be feminine.

a. As marked exceptions to the foregoing rule, may be noticed پاني (*pānī*) *water*, گهي (*ghī*) *clarified butter*, دهي (*dahī*) *curdled milk*, جي (*jī*) *life*, موتي (*motī*) *a pearl*, which are perhaps the only masculines, unless by nature, terminating in ي (*ī*); and, many words ending with ت (*t*), ش (*sh*), or ن (*n*) will occur in use as of the masculine gender.†

---

* Most of the pure Sanskrit and Arabic nouns ending in ا (*ā*) are feminine, as well as some of the latter tongue terminating in ه (*a*). Arabic verbal nouns of the form تفعيل (*tafʿīl*) are said to be all feminine in the Dakhni of Madras; and, in *Urdū* or proper Hindustani, to exhibit but one exception, تعويذ (*taʿwīẕ*) *an amulet*, which in this dialect is masculine.

† Some words are naturally of both genders; such as, آدمي (*ādmī*) and مانس (*mānus*) *a human being*, اسامي (*asāmī*) *a client*; whilst,

3. To form feminine nouns from masculines, such of the latter description as end in ه (*a*), ا (*ā*), or يا (*yā*), usually convert those finals to ـِي (*ī*); such as end in ان (*āṅ*), or يان (*yāṅ*), to ـِين (*īṅ*); and such as end in ـِي (*ī*) to ن (*an* or *in*): so شہزادي (*shahzādī*) *a princess*, from شہزاده (*shahzāda*) *a prince*; گھوڑي (*ghōṛī*) *a mare*, from گھوڑا (*ghōṛā*) *a horse*; پرائي (*parā'ī*), from پرايا (*parāyā*) *foreign*; ساتوين (*sātwīṅ*), from ساتوان (*sātwāṅ*) *seventh*; دھوبن (*dhōbin*) *a washerwoman*, from دھوبي (*dhōbī*) *a washerman*.

a. Masculines, ending in other letters, may either assume certain of the above-mentioned feminine terminations, or take ا (*ā*), ـِني (*nī*), اني (*ānī*), ين (*yan*), or اين (*āyan*); so ھرني (*harnī*) *a doe*, from ھرن (*haran*) *a deer*; نايکا (*nāyakā*) the female of نايک (*nāyak*) *a leader*; مورني (*mōrnī*) *a peahen*, from مور (*mōr*) *a peacock*; مِہتراني (*mihtarānī*), from مِہتر (*mihtar*) *a sweeper*; بنيااين (*banyāyan*), the wife of a بنيا (*banyā*) *shopkeeper*.

4. To form the nominative plural, masculine nouns ending in ه (*a*) or ا (*ā*) change the termination to ي (*ē*); as پيالي (*piyālē*) *cups*, from پياله (*piyāla*); بيٹي (*bēṭē*) *sons*, from بيٹا (*bēṭā*): other terminations remain unaltered; as مرد (*mard*) *a man* or *men*: چور (*chōr*) *a thief* or *thieves*.*

a. Certain nouns substantive masculine, as well as adjectives, though ending in ا (*ā*) remain unchanged in the nominative plural; such as, خدا (*khudā*) *God*, اُمرا (*umarā*) *nobles* or *a nobleman*,

---

others, like فِکر (*fikr*) *care*, جان (*jān*) *life*, may be used indifferently as masculines or feminines. On the subject of gender, indeed, considerable difference will be found to exist between the Hindustani and Dakhni; and, even speakers or writers of the same dialect are sometimes at variance.

* In Dakhni, however, ان (*āṅ*) is subjoined to such nouns; so, مردان (*mardāṅ*) *men*, چوران (*chōrāṅ*) *thieves*.

ملا (*mullā*) *a doctor,* راجا (*rājā*) *a prince,* لالا (*lālā*) *master,* بابا (*bābā*) or پتا (*pitā*) *father,* سودا (*saudā*) *melancholy,* دانا (*dānā*) *wise,* داتا (*dātā*), *liberal,* پیدا (*paidā*) *produced,* and various others.*

b. Feminine nouns ending in ي (*ī*) assume ان (*āṅ*) for the nominative plural, as those of all other terminations take يں (*ēṅ*);† so, بيٹياں (*bēṭiyāṅ*) *daughters,* from بيٹي (*bēṭī*); کتابيں (*kitābēṅ*) *books,* from کتاب (*kitāb*).

c. Persian nouns may form their plurals in ان (*āṅ*) ها (*hā*) ات (*āt*) or جات (*jāt*), or by changing a singular ه (*a*) to گان (*gāṅ*); as, ساقیان (*sāḳiyāṅ*) *cupbearers,* from ساقي (*sāḳī*); سالہا (*sālhā*) *years,* from سال (*sāl*); نوازشات (*nawāzishāt*) *favours,* from نوازش (*nawāzish*). Arabic plurals, too, of various forms may occur; as, عناصر (*ānāṣir*) from عنصر (*ūnṣur*), اخبار (*akhbār*) from خبر (*khabar*), امرا (*umarā*) from امير (*amīr*).

5. Cases of nouns, excepting the nominative, are formed in this language by the means of small words, generally placed after the nouns, whence the term postposition is conveniently applied by Europeans to these words; and, such masculine nouns as have for their final in the nominative singular ه (*a*) or ا (*ā*) mostly change it to ي (*ē*) in the other cases of that number; so, دروازي کو (*darwāzē kō*) *to the door,* from دروازه (*darwāza*), لڑکي کا (*laṛkē kā*) *of the boy,* from لڑکا (*laṛkā*), گھوڑي پر (*ghōṛē par*) *on the horse,* from گھوڑا (*ghōṛā*).

---

* In the Dakhan, وں (*ōṅ*) is usually added to nouns ending in ا (*ā*) unchangeable, to form the nominative plural; so, خداوں (*khudā'ōṅ*) *gods.*

† In Dakhni, وں (*ōṅ*) or more rarely واں (*wāṅ*) is added to feminine nouns whose singular final is ا (*ā*) to form the plural, whilst other feminines assume ان (*āṅ*) or sometimes change ي (*ī*) to ياں (*yāṅ*); so, ماوں (*mā'ōṅ*) or ماواں (*māwāṅ*) *mothers,* from ما (*mā*), نديان *naddī'āṅ* (or *naddyāṅ*) *rivers,* from ندي (*naddī*).

Masculines in ا (*ā*) which are not liable to change in the nominative plural, some of which are enumerated at paragraph 4. *a.*, as well as masculines of all other terminations, and all feminines, admit of no inflection before postpositions in the singular; so, راجا سي (*rājā sē*) *from the prince;* گهر مين (*ghar mēn̄*) *in the house;* دوا سي (*dawā sē*) *with medicine;* گهوڑي كي آگي (*ghōṛī kē āgē*) *before the mare.*

a. The inflection for the plural is, in proper Hindustani, constantly ون (*ōn̄*), though in Dakhni it is more usually ان (*ān̄*); excepting, however, the vocative, in which it is commonly و (*ō*); so, لڑكون كي تئين (*laṛkōn̄ kē ta'īn̄*) *to boys;* داناؤن كي پاس (*dānā'ōn̄ kē pās*) *near the wise;* گهوڑيون پر (*ghōṛiyōn̄ par*) *on mares;* كتابون مين (*kitābōn̄ mēn̄*) *in books.**

b. It may here be noticed that words of two syllables, the first of which has any short vowel and the second is sounded with ´ (*a*), drop the latter when any termination beginning with a vowel is affixed; so, برس (*baras*) *a year* becomes برسون (*barsōn̄*), جگه (*jagah*) *a place*, جگهون (*jag'hōn̄*): and, on the contrary, nouns ending in ا (*ā*) unchangeable may assume ي (*y*) before the affixes of the plural; as, اي مايو (*ai māyō*) *O mothers!* from ما (*mā*); دوايون سي (*dawāyōn̄ sē*) *with medicines,* from دوا (*dawā*).

6. The simple postpositions used with nouns, inflected if capable of inflection, are—

For the Genitive case, كا (*kā*) كي (*kē*) كي (*kī*) *of.*

For the Dative, or For the Accusative } كو (*kō*) كي تئين (*kē ta'īn̄*), &c., *to, for,* &c.

For the Ablative, { سي (*sē*) سين (*sēn̄*) سون (*sōn̄*) سيتي (*sitī*) *from, by, with.* پر (*par*) or په (*pa*) *on, at:* مين (*mēn̄*) *in, among.*

---

* پانو (*pān̄w*) *a foot,* becomes contracted to پاون (*pā'ōn̄*) in the inflection of the plural.

Of these postpositions, کا alone is liable to change, as above noted, to agree with the noun to which it has reference; and, most commonly this noun follows immediately the postposition: thus, before a masculine nominative singular, کا is used; as, سوداگر کا بیٹا (*saudāgar kā bēṭā*) *the merchant's son*: before a masculine singular acted upon by another postposition, or before a masculine plural in every case, کي (*kē*); as, راجا کي هاتهي پر (*rājā kē hāthī par*) *on the prince's elephant;* راني کي گهوڙي (*rānī kē ghoṛē*) *the princess's horses;* لڑکوں کي هاتهوں سي (*laṛkōṅ kē hāthōṅ sē*) *from the hands of the boys:* and before a feminine noun in every case of each number, کِي (*kī*); as نوکر کِي پگڑِي (*naukar kī pagṛī*) *the servant's turban;* گنوار کِي مُرغِیاں (*gaṅwār kī murghiyāṅ*) *the peasant's hens.* The rest of the postpositions remain unchanged; as کتّي کو (*kuttē kō*) or کُتّي کي تئِیں (*kuttē kē ta'īṅ*) *to the dog* or *the dog;* بندر سي (*bandar sē*) *by the monkey;* میز پر (*mēz par*) *on the table;* اُس عرصي میں (*us ārṣē mēṅ*) *in that space of time.**

a. Many other words, moreover, are adapted to the like postpositive use; and, as some of them generally take کي (*kē*), whilst others require کِي (*kī*) before them, they have been termed compound postpositions; so, in بادشاه کي پاس (*bādshāh kē pās*) *near the king;* در کي اُوپر (*dar kē ūpar*) *at the door;* وزِیر کي واسطي (*wazīr kē wāsṭē*) *for the vizir;* گهوڙي کي آگي (*ghoṛē kē āgē*) *before the horse;* دوست کي لِیي (*dost kē li'ē*) *for the sake of the friend;* گهر کي پِیچهي (*ghar kē pīchhē*) *behind the house;* مسجِد کِي طرف (*masjid kī ṭaraf*) *towards the mosque;* سِپاهِي کِي طرح (*sipāhī kī ṭaraḥ*) *in the manner of a soldier:* yet کي (*kē*) is sometimes omitted; as, در اُوپر (*dar ūpar*),

* تک (*tak*, or dakh. تگ *tag*), تلک (*talak*, or dakh. تلگ *talag*), لگ (*lag*), توڑِي (*toṛī*) *to, up to, near,* are also much used as simple postpositive words; so گهر تک (*ghar tak*) *up to the house.*

گھوڑي پاس (*ghōṛē pās*) : occasionally, moreover, words of this description may precede the noun or pronoun ; as, نزديک اُسکي (*nazdīk us-kē*) *near him:* and two or more of the simple postpositions may occur together ; as, گھر مين سي (*ghar mēn̐ sē*) *from within the house.* It may be noticed, too, that with pronouns, such words require an inflected masculine or a feminine genitive ; so, ميري پاس (*mērē pās*) *near me,* تيري طرف (*tērī t̤araf*) *towards thee.*

7. The vocative may be the same in form as the nominative; or, it may be denoted by some one of the signs اَي (*ai*), اي (*ē*), هي (*hē*), او (*o*), اجِي (*ajī*), ابي (*abē*), يا (*yā*), or اري (*arē*) before the noun singular, inflected if capable of inflection ; but the usual termination in the plural is و (*o*); and, to a plural with this termination one of the signs above-mentioned may be prefixed. The vocative may likewise be expressed by هوت (*hōt*), ري (*rē*), or بي (*bē*) after the noun ; but, اري (*arē*) is changed to ارِي (*arī*), as ري (*rē*) is to رِي (*rī*) if applied to a feminine : the interjectional words, moreover, اري or ارِي, and ري or رِي, are generally used in a disrespectful or contemptuous sense, and بي as well as ابي is perhaps always so applied. So, بيٹا (*bēṭā*), or اَي بيٹي (*ai bēṭē*) *O son !* اي مرد (*ē mard*) *O man !* او لڑکي (*ō laṛkē*) *O boy !* اري رمچيرا (*arē ramchērā*) *holla servant !* ارِي رنڈي (*arī ranḍī*) *O woman !* يارو (*yārō*) or اَي يارو (*ai yārō*) *O friends !*

8. With Persian and Arabic words, the construction and prepositions peculiar to those languages are frequently adopted. Thus, to shew the connexion between two substantives, or between a substantive and its following adjective, the Persian *iẓāfat* may be used ; and it is denoted, if actually written, after a consonant by ِ (*zēr* or *kasr*), after ه (*hē*) silent, or after ي (*yē*) by ٔ (*hamza*), and after ا (*alif*) or و (*wā'o*) by ي (*yē*) : so, مشيرِ خاصِ شاه (*mushīr-i khāṣṣ-i shāh*) *privy counsellor of the king ;* بندۀ خدا (*banda-i khudā*) *servant of God ;* هَواي خوب (*hawā-e khūb*) *good air ;* اثناي راه (*aṣnā-e rāh*) *midst of*

the way. And, when two Arabic substantives come together, or a substantive is followed by its adjective in the Arabic construction, the latter of the two words has the article ال (*al*) prefixed, and they become united in pronunciation, the sign *waṣl* being occasionally used in writing; so, طالِبُ ٱلعِلم (*ṭālibu-l-ïlm*) *a seeker of knowledge, a student;* لِلّٰه ٱلرَّحمان (*lillāhi-r-raḥmān*) *to the merciful God.*

9. Declension, according to the preceding remarks, may now be formally exemplified; as, with a masculine noun substantive ending in ﮦ (*hē*) silent, thus—

	Singular.			Plural.	
N.	بندہ (*banda*)	*a slave.*	N.	بندي (*bandē*)	*slaves.*
G.	بندي كا كي كِي	*of a slave.*	G.	بندون كا كي كِي	*of slaves.*
D.	بندي كو	*to a slave.*	D.	بندون كو	*to slaves.*
Ac.	بندي كو	*a slave.*	Ac.	بندون كو	*slaves.*
V.	اي بندي	*O slave!*	V.	بندو or اي بندو	*O slaves!*
Ab.	بندي سي	*from a slave.*	Ab.	بندون سي	*from slaves.*

Or, as with a masculine noun ending in ا (*ā*) liable to inflection, thus—

	Singular.			Plural.	
N.	گهوڑا (*ghōṛā*)	*a horse.*	N.	گهوڑي (*ghoṛē*)	*horses.*
G.	گهوڑي كا كي كِي	*of a horse.*	G.	گهوڑون كا كي كِي	*of horses.*
D.	گهوڑي كو	*to a horse.*	D.	گهوڑون كو	*to horses.*
Ac.	گهوڑي كو	*a horse.*	Ac.	گهوڑون كو	*horses.*
V.	گهوڑا or اي گهوڑي	*O horse!*	V.	گهوڑو or اي گهوڑو	*O horses!*
Ab.	گهوڑي سي	*from a horse.*	Ab.	گهوڑون سي	*from horses.*

And nouns ending in اں (*āṅ*), the last letter being the obscure nasal, change that termination to يں (*ēṅ*) in the inflection of the singular as well as in the nominative plural; so پانچويں (*pānchwēṅ*), from پانچواں (*pānchwāṅ*), *fifth;* or, sometimes, to ي (*ē*), as بنيي (*baniyē*), from بنيان (*baniyān*), *a trader;* and they may convert it to ون (*on*), and و (*o*) if used, in the oblique cases and vocative of the plural.

Or, as with a masculine noun ending in ا (*ā*), not liable to inflection, thus—

	Singular.		Plural.
N	راجا* (*rājā*) *a prince.*	N.	راجا* (*rājā*) *princes.*
G.	راجا كا كي كِي *of a prince.*	G.	راجاؤن كا كي كِي *of princes.*
D.	راجا كو *to a prince.*	D.	راجاؤن كو *to princes.*
Ac.	راجا كو *a prince.*	Ac.	راجاؤن كو *princes.*
V.	اَي راجا or راجا *O prince!*	V.	اَي راجاؤ or راجاؤ *O princes!*
Ab.	راجا سي *from a prince.*	Ab.	راجاؤن سي *from princes.*

And, according to this example, are declined all masculine nouns ending in a consonant, or in any vowel not liable to inflection; as, گهر (*ghar*) *a house,* گهر كا *of a house,* گهر *houses,* گهرون كا *of houses;* آدمي (*ādmī*) *man,* آدمي كا *of man,* &c.

Or, as with a feminine noun terminating in ي (*ī*), thus—

	Singular.		Plural.
N.	گهوڙي (*ghōṛī*) *a mare.*	N.	گهوڙيان (*ghoṛiyān*) *mares.*
G.	گهوڙي كا كي كِي *of a mare.*	G.	گهوڙيون كا كي كِي *of mares.*
D.	گهوڙي كو *to a mare.*	D.	گهوڙيون كو *to mares.*
Ac.	گهوڙي كو *a mare.*	Ac.	گهوڙيون كو *mares.*
V.	اَي گهوڙي *O mare!*	V.	اَي گهوڙيو *O mares!*
Ab.	گهوڙي سي *from a mare.*	Ab.	گهوڙيون سي *from mares.*

Or, as with a feminine noun having any other termination than ي (*ī*), thus—

---

* This particular word has been met with inflected like گهوڙا preceding, though this is very uncommon.

	Singular.		Plural.
N.	بات (*bāt*) *a word, an affair.*	N.	باتين (*bātēṅ*) *words.*
G.	بات كا كي كِي *of a word.*	G.	باتون كا كي كِي *of words.*
D.	بات كو *to a word.*	D.	باتون كو *to words.*
Ac.	بات كو *a word.*	Ac.	باتون كو *words.*
V.	اَي بات *O word!*	V.	اَي باتو or باتو *O words!*
Ab.	بات سي *from a word.*	Ab.	باتون سي *from words.*

And a dissyllabic noun, which drops the short vowel of the second syllable before affixes beginning with a vowel, as explained at paragraph 5. *b.*, might be exemplified in the feminine جگہ (*jagah*) *a place,* which becomes in the plural جگھين (*jag'heṅ*) *places,* جگھون كا (*jag'hōṅ kā*) *of places,* &c.

10. The affix ون (*ōṅ*), or و (*ō*), is often taken, in an emphatic as well as plural sense, by numerals, whether cardinals or aggregate, whether in the nominative or in some other case; so, دونون (*dōnōṅ*) or دونو (*dōnō*), *all two, the two, both;* تِينون (*tīnōṅ*) *all three,* لاكھون شہر (*lākhōṅ shahr*) *hundreds of thousands of cities.* And, the nouns of time, برس (*baras*) *a year,* مہينا (*mahīnā*) *a month,* دِن (*din*) *a day,* پہر (*pahar*) *a watch,* not unfrequently, and for the like purpose, assume the adjunct ون (*oṅ*); as, برسون گذري (*bursōṅ guzre*) *years* (*many*) *have elapsed;* مہينون سي (*mahīnōṅ sē*) *for* (*many*) *months,* or *months ago.*

11. Adjectives are generally liable to the same changes in their finals for gender, number, and case, as substantives: in the plural, too, they may assume the same adjuncts, with the exception of ين (*ēṅ*); yet when followed immediately by nouns in this number, the plural signs ان (*āṅ*), or ون (*ōṅ*) are usually, though not always, omitted, the substantives for the most part alone retaining them, as may be exemplified in چھوٹا لڑكا (*chhoṭā laṛkā*) *a little boy,* thus—

Singular.		Plural.	
N.	چهوٹا لڑکا	N.	چهوٹي لڑکي
G.	چهوٹي لڑکي کا کي کِي	G.	چهوٹي لڑکون کا کي کِي
D.	چهوٹي لڑکي کو	D.	چهوٹي لڑکون کو
Ac.	چهوٹي لڑکي کو	Ac.	چهوٹي لڑکون کو
V.	اَي چهوٹي لڑکي	V.	اَي چهوٹي لڑکو
Ab.	چهوٹي لڑکي سي	Ab.	چهوٹي لڑکون سي

Or, in چهوٹي لڑکي (*chhōṭī laṛkī*) *a little girl*, as—

Singular.		Plural.	
N.	چهوٹي لڑکي	N.	چهوٹي لڑکيان
G.	چهوٹي لڑکي کا کي کِي	G.	چهوٹي لڑکيون کا کي کِي
D.	چهوٹي لڑکي کو	D.	چهوٹي لڑکيون کو
Ac.	چهوٹي لڑکي کو	Ac.	چهوٹي لڑکيون کو
V.	هي چهوٹي لڑکي	V.	اَي چهوٹي لڑکيو
Ab.	چهوٹي لڑکي سي	Ab.	چهوٹي لڑکيون سي

The adjective, however, may occasionally stand alone, as when used substantively, or it may follow its substantive, in either of which cases it requires in the plural the affixes ان (*āṅ*) or ون (*ōṅ*).

12. The ordinals of numbers are declined and used as adjectives, though they seem hardly capable, like the latter, of following the substantives to which they relate; so چَوتهي بار (*chauthī-bār*) *fourth time*, تيسري دروازي پر (*tīsrē darwāze par*) *at the third door*, پانچوان بيٹا (*pānchwāṅ bēṭā*) *fifth son*, چهٹوين بيٹي سي (*chhaṭwēṅ bēṭē sē*) *from the sixth son.*

13. The comparative and superlative degrees of adjectives are denoted by means of postpositions and adverbs, or occasionally by reduplication: thus, for the comparative may be used سي *from, than,*

میں *among,* میں سے *from among,* کا *of,* after the noun to which comparison is made, as well as زیادہ (*ziyāda*) or اور (*aur*) *more,* بڑا *great,* تھوڑا (*thoṛā*) or ذرہ (*ẕarra*) *a little,* &c. before the adjective; so, لوہا تانبے سے بھاري ہے (*lohā tāmbē* se bhārī hai*) *iron from copper heavy is:* for the superlative, such adverbs as بہت (*bahut*) *much,* نہایت (*nihāyat*) or نپٹ (*nipaṭ*) or اتي (*atī*) *extremely,* حد (*ḥadd*) for ازحد (*az ḥadd*) *beyond bounds, excessively,* بسا (*basā*) *most, very,* بڑا (*baṛā*) *great,* before the adjective; or, the expression سب سے (*sab sē*) or سب کا (*sab kā*) *of all,* as well as a reduplication; so بہت اونچا (*bahūt ūnchā*) *very high;* نپٹ ہوشیار (*nipaṭ hoshyār*) *extremely prudent;* نہایت بري جگہ (*nihāyat burī jagah*) *very bad place;* سب کا بڑا (*sab kā baṛā*) or سب سے بڑا (*sab sē baṛā*) *greatest;* اچھا اچھا (*achchhā achchhā*) *very good, best.*

a. With Persian adjectives, تر (*tar*) is at times suffixed for the comparative, as ترین (*tarīn*) is for the superlative; so خوبتر (*khūbtar*) *handsomer,* خوبترین (*khūbtarīn*) *handsomest,* from خوب (*khūb*): and, Arabic forms, like اظلم (*aẕlam*) *more unjust,* ظلام (*ẕallām*) *most unjust,* from ظلم (*ẕulm*) *injustice,* may occur, though but rarely.

14. The adjunct of similitude, سا (*sā*), سے (*sē*), سي (*sī*) *like,*† varying in its termination to agree with the noun to which it has reference, is much used after other adjectives, as well as after substantives and pronouns. To adjectives, which like it must be made to accord in gender, number, and case with the governing noun, it seems often to convey but little, if any, additional meaning, though in many instances it corresponds to the English useful affix, —*ish,* and in others it imports a degree of intensity to the expression; so کھٹا سا آنب

* Observe that ن before ب or پ is pronounced as *m.*

† سریکا (*sarekā*), of similar import, sometimes occurs; and in Dakhani, سریکا (*sarīkā*) *like,* is extremely common in use.

(*khaṭṭā sā āmb*) *a sour* or *sourish mango ;* چهوٹي سي کيلي (*chhōṭē sē kēlē*) *little plantains ;* کڑوي سي دوا (*kaṛwī sī dawā*) *bitter physic ;* بہت سا پاني (*bahut sā pānī*) *much* or *very much water.*

a. Before this adjunct, substantives or pronouns become inflected, and its meaning is fully intended ; so, باگھ سا مرد (*bāgh sā mard*) *a tiger-like man ;* لڑکي سي لڑکي (*laṛkī sī laṛkī*) *a boy-like girl,* مجھ سي اچھي لڑکي (*mujh sī achchhī laṛkī*) *a good girl like me :* ايسا (*aisā*) for اِس سا (*is-sā*) *like this ;* ويسا (*waisā*) for اُس سا (*us-sā*) *like that ;* and, upon the same principle, کيسا (*kaisā*) *what-like?* جيسا (*jaisā*) *which-like?* تيسا (*taisā*) *that-like.* Sometimes, however, it is subjoined to pronominals in their uninflected form, when it has a discriminative meaning ; as کونسا (*kaun-sā*) *which? what? what sort of?* جونسا (*jaun-sā*) *whichever,* تونسا (*taun-sā*) *that,* کوئي سا (*kō'i-sā*) *some one, certain person.*

CHAPTER III.

PRONOUNS.

15. Pronouns, in Hindustani, may be personal, demonstrative, common or reflective, interrogative, relative, correlative, or indefinite. Generally they are the same for feminine as for masculine ; yet, the interrogative and indefinite exhibit each two forms, and each of these forms is, in great part, appropriated to a distinct gender. In the changes for case and number, pronouns differ essentially from nouns ; as—

First Person.

Singular.	Plural.
N. مَين (*maiṅ*) *I.*	N. هم (*ham*) *we.*
G. میرا (*mērā*), میري (*mēre*), میري (*mērī*), *of me, mine.*	G. همارا (*hamārā*), هماري (*hamārē*), هماري (*hamārī*) *of us, our.*
D. Ac. مُجهه کو (*mujh kō*), or مُجهي (*mujhē*), *to me, me.*	D. Ac. هم کو (*ham kō*), or همين (*hamēṅ*) *to us, us.*
Ab. مُجهه سي (*mujh sē*) *from me.*	Ab. هم سي (*ham sē*) *from us.*

Second Person.

Singular.	Plural.
N. تُو (*tū*), or تَين (*taiṅ*) *thou.*	N. تُم (*tum*) *ye* or *you.*
G. تیرا (*tērā*), تیري (*tērē*), تیري (*tērī*) *of thee, thine.*	G. تُمهارا (*tumhārā*), تُمهاري (*tumhārē*), تُمهاري (*tumhārī*), *of you, your.*
D. Ac. تُجهه کو (*tujh kō*), or تُجهي (*tujhē*) *to thee, thee.*	D. Ac. تُم کو (*tum kō*), or تُمهين (*tumhēṅ*) *to you, you.*
V. اَي تُو (*ai tū*) *O thou!*	V. اَي تُم (*ai tum*) *O you;*
Ab. تُجهه سي (*tujh sē*) *from thee.*	Ab. تُم سي (*tum sē*) *from you.*

Third Person.

Singular.	Plural.
N. وُه (*wuh*) *he, she, it.*	N. وي (*wē*) *they.*
G. اُس کا (*us kā*), اُس کي (*us kē*), or اُس کِي (*uskī*) *of him, her, it.*	G. اُن کا (*un kā*) اُن کي (*un kē*) or اُن کِي (*un kī*) *of them, their.*
D. اُس کو (*us kō*) or اُسي (*usē*) *to him.*	D. Ac. اُن کو (*un kō*), or اُنهين (*unhēṅ*) *to them, them.*
Ac. اُس کو (*us ko*), or اُسي (*usē*) *him.*	
Ab. اُس سي (*us sē*) *from him, &c.*	Ab. اُن سي (*un sē*) *from them.*

And the same word is declined in like manner when used for the remote demonstrative, وه *that*, in contradistinction to which is the proximate demonstrative, يهه (*yih*) *this*, declined as follows—

Singular.	Plural.
N. يهه (*yih*) *this, it.*	N. يي (*yē*) *these.*
G. اس كا (*is kā*), اس كي (*is kē*), or اس كِي (*is kī*) *of this.*	G. ان كا (*in kā*) ان كي (*in kē*) or ان كِي (*in kī*) *of these.*
D. Ac. اس كو (*is kō*), or اسي (*isē*), *to this, this.*	D. Ac. ان كو (*in kō*) or انهين (*inhēṅ*) *to these, these.*
Ab. اس سي (*is sē*) *from this.*	Ab. ان سي (*in sē*) *from these.*

COMMON OR REFLECTIVE PRONOUN.

Singular and Plural.

N. آپ (*āp*) *self, myself, thyself, himself, ourselves,* &c.

G. آپ كا (*āp kā*) آپ كي (*āp kē*) آپ كِي (*āp kī*) or اپنا (*apnā*) اپني (*apnē*) اپنِي (*apnī*) *of myself,* &c., *my own,* &c.

D. آپ كو (*āp kō*) or اپني كو (*apnē kō*) *to myself,* &c.

Ac. آپ كو (*āp kō*) or اپني كو (*apnē kō*) *myself,* &c.

Ab. آپ سي (*āp sē*) or اپني سي (*apnē sē*) *from myself,* &c.

This pronoun is applicable to each of the three persons, according to the nominative, expressed or understood, with the verb in the same sentence: آپس (*āpas*), moreover, is frequently adopted before post-positions, especially in a plural sense; so, آپس مين (*āpas mēṅ*) *among themselves.*

INTERROGATIVE PRONOUN.

This is of two forms, the one كَون (*kaun*) being generally applied, whether absolutely or adjectively, to persons, as the other كيا (*kyā*) is to actions or things; yet, كِس (*kis*) the inflection of كَون may occasionally be applied to things; and, كيا in the uninflected state only seems fitted to precede, as an adjective, the names of inanimate objects: so, تم کَون هو (*tum kaun hō*) *you who are?* کیا چاهتي هو (*kyā chāhtē hō*) *what desiring are you?* کِس چیز کو (*kis chīz kō*) *to which* (or *what*) *thing?* کیا کرنا (*kyā karnā*) *what* (*is*) *to do?* کیا چیز (*kyā chīz*) *what thing?*

Singular.	Plural.
N. کَون (*kaun*) *who? which? what?*	N. کَون (*kaun*) *who? which? what?*
G. کِس کا (*kis kā*) کِس کي (*kis kē*) کِس کِي (*kiskī*) *of whom? whose?*	G. کِن کا (*kin kā*) کِن کي (*kin kē*) کِن کِي (*kinkī*) *of whom? whose?*
D. کِس کو (*kis kō*) or کِسي (*kisē*) *to whom?*	D. کِن کو (*kin kō*) or کِنهين (*kinhēn*) *to whom?*
Ac. کِس کو (*kis kō*) or کِسي (*kisē*) *whom?*	Ac. کِن کو (*kin kō*) or کِنهين (*kinhēn*) *whom?*
Ab. کِس سي (*kis sē*) *from whom,* &c.	Ab. کِن سي (*kin sē*) *from whom,* &c.

Singular and Plural.

N. and Ac. کیا (*kyā*) *what?*
G. کاهي کا (*kāhē kā*) کاهي کي (*kāhē kē*) کاهي کِي (*kāhē kī*) *of what?*
D. کاهي کو (*kāhē kō*) *to* or *for what?*
Ab. کاهي سي (*kāhē sē*) *from what?*

RELATIVE PRONOUN.

Singular.	Plural.
N. جو (*jō*)* or جَون (*jaun*) *who, which, what.*	N. جو (*jō*) or جَون (*jaun*) *who, which, what.*

* In an indefinite sense, this pronoun may be repeated; as, جو جو (*jō jō*) *whoever, whatever;* جِس جِس کا (*jis jis kā*) *of whichever:* and, it is very frequently compounded with the indefinite pronoun; as, جو کوئي (*jō kō'ī*) *whoever;* جِس کِسِي کا (*jis kisī kā*) *of whomever;* جو کُچهه (*jō kuchh*) *whatever;* جِس کِسو کو (*jis kisū kō*) *to whatever.*

Singular.	Plural.
G. جِس کا (*jis kā*) جِس کي (*jis kē*) جِس کِي (*jiskī*) *of whom*, &c.	G. جِن کا (*jinkā*) جِن کي (*jinkē*) جِن کِي (*jin kī*) *of whom*, &c.
D. جِس کو (*jis kō*) or جِسي (*jisē*) *to whom.*	D. جِن کو (*jin kō*) or جِنھين (*jin-hēṅ*), *to whom*, &c.
Ac. جِس کو (*jis kō*) or جِسي (*jisē*) *whom.*	Ac. جِن کو (*jin kō*) or جِنھين (*jin-hēṅ*), *whom*, &c.
Ab. جِس سي (*jissē*) *from whom*, &c.	Ab. جِن سي (*jin sē*) *from whom*, &c.

CORRELATIVE.

Singular.	Plural.
N. سو (*sō*) or تَون (*taun*) *that, he*, &c.	N. سو (*sō*) or تَون (*taun*) *those, they.*
G. تِس کا (*tis kā*) تِس کي (*tis kē*) تِس کِي (*tis kī*) *of that*, &c.	G. تِن کا (*tin kā*) تِن کي (*tin kē*) تِن کِي (*tin kī*) *of those*, &c.
D. تِس کو (*tis kō*) or تِسي (*tisē*) *to that.*	D. تِن کو (*tin kō*) or تِنھين (*tin-hēṅ*), *to those*, &c.
Ac. تِس کو (*tis kō*) or تِسي (*tisē*) *that.*	Ac. تِن کو (*tin kō*) or تِنھين (*tin-hēṅ*), *those*, &c.
Ab. تِس سي (*tis sē*) *from that*, &c.	Ab. تِن سي (*tin sē*) *from them*, &c.

INDEFINITE PRONOUN.

This is of two forms; the one کوئي being more commonly applied to persons, as the other کُچھ is to things: and, for number, each form admits of no change; thus—

N. کوئي (*kō'ī*) *a, an, any, some.*	N. کُچھ (*kuchh*) *some, a little, a few.*
G. کِسي کا (*kisī kā*) کِسي کي (*kisī kē*) کِسي کِي (*kisī kī*) *of any, some*, &c.	G. کِسُو کا (*kisū kā*) کِسُو کي (*kisū kē*) کِسُو کِي (*kisū kī*) *of some*, &c.

D. کسي کو (*kisī kō*) *to any, some*, &c.	D. کسو کو (*kisū kō*) *to some*, &c.
Ac. کسي کو (*kisī kō*) *any, some*, &c.	Ac. کسو کو (*kisū kō*) *some*, &c.
Ab. کسي سي (*kisī sē*) *from any*, &c.	Ab. کسو سي (*kisū sē*) *from some.*

16. In pronouns, the genitive terminations را (*rā*) نا (*nā*) admit of inflection, like کا (*kā*), so as to agree with the nouns to which they relate; thus, ميري گهوڑي پر (*mērē ghōṛē par*) *my horse on;* تيري گهوڑي (*tērī ghōṛī*) *thy mare;* اپني دوست کي واسطي (*apnē dōst kē wāsṭē*) *on account of his friend.* When, however, any word intervenes between the pronoun and postposition, مجهه and تجهه as well as هم and تم are then used with the genitive of the succeeding word; as مجهه غريب کا (*mujh gharīb kā*) *of poor me.* کون and کوئي and کچهه too, when separated from any postposition, may remain uninflected; as, کون صاحب کا آدمي هي (*kaun ṣāhib kā ādmī hai*) *what gentleman's servant is it?* کوئي دن کو مين چلا جاونگا (*kō'ī din kō main chala jā'ūngā*) *I shall depart on some day;* کچهه چيز مين (*kuchh chīz mēn*) *in something.* To هم تم ان ان کن جن تن the plural sign ون (*ōn*) may still be subjoined, provided that no noun having the like termination immediately follows; the finals of تم ان ان کن جن تن moreover may be aspirated, when used with, or without, the affix ون (*ōn*)*; so, هم کو (*ham kō*) or همون کو (*hamōn kō*) *to us;* تم سي (*tum sē*) or تمهه سي (*tumh sē*) or تمهون سي (*tumhōn sē*) *from you;* ان or انهه لوگون مين (*un* or *unh lōgōn mēn*) *among those people.* And, by the poets, مجهه and تجهه are frequently adopted in a posses-

* The word سب (*sab*) *all,* becomes on the same principle سبهون (*sabhōn*) for the inflection of the plural.

sive sense, instead of the regular genitives; as, مُجھ دِل (*mujh dil*) *my heart*, تُجھ عِشق (*tujh ʿishk*) *thy love*.

CHAPTER IV.

VERB.

17. Verbs denote the motion or action intended in a sentence, and admit of two principal divisions; verb intransitive and verb transitive; the latter of these, moreover, may be subdivided into active and passive.

18. The most simple form of the verb, and which may be termed the root, is the imperative in the second person singular: this form, also, serves frequently as a verbal noun; so, مار (*mār*) *beat* or *a beating;* بول (*bol*) *speak* or *speech;* چاہ (*chāh*) *desire* (*thou*) or *the desire*.

19. The infinitive requires the addition of نا (*nā*) to the root; and before postpositions, when the infinitive often comes into use as a gerund or verbal noun, this نا is changed to نے (*nē*); so, from مار *beat*, comes مارنا *to beat* or *a beating;* from بول *speak*, پی (*pī*) *drink*, بولنے پر (*bolnē par*) *on speaking* or *about to speak*, پینے کو (*pīnē kō*) *for drinking:* the same inflection also takes place when the infinitive is in construction with certain verbs; as, کہنے لگا (*kahnē lagā*) *he was applied to saying* or *he began to say*. This termination, moreover, may be changed to نی (*nī*) نیں (*nīṅ*) or نیاں (*niyāṅ*) when a feminine noun, singular or plural, is the object of the verb; so, ایک زبان بولنی (*ēk zabān bolnī*) *to speak a language*.

20. The past participle is obtained by subjoining to the root, ا (*ā*) ے (*ē*) ی (*ī*) یں (*īṅ*) or یاں (*iyāṅ*) according to the gender and

number of the governing noun; so, for a masculine noun in the singular بولا (*bōlā*) and in the plural بولي (*bōlē*); for a feminine noun in the singular بولي (*bōlī*) and in the plural بولين (*bōlīṅ*) or بوليان (*bōliyāṅ*) *spoken*, from بول.

a. If the root, however, ends in ا (*ā*) or و (*ō*) the letter ي becomes inserted before a subsequent ا (*ā*); but, it may be either assumed or omitted when followed by an affix consisting of, or beginning with, ي: so, from لا (*lā*) *bring*, come لايا (*lāyā*), لايي (*layē*) or لائي (*lā'ē*), لايي (*lāyī*) or لائي (*lā'ī*), &c. *brought*; from بو (*bō*) *sow*, بويا (*bōyā*), بويي (*boyē*) or بوئي (*bō'ē*), بويي (*boyī*) or بوئي (*bo'ī*), &c. *sown*. And, when to roots ending in ي, an affix consisting of, or beginning with ي (*ī*) would regularly follow, to form the feminine of this participle, one of the long vowels is usually dropped; so, دي (*dī*), دين (*dīṅ*) or ديان (*diyāṅ*), from ديا (*diyā*) *given*; لي (*lī*) لين (*līṅ*) or ليان (*liyāṅ*), from ليا (*liyā*) *taken*; كي (*kī*) كين (*kīṅ*) or كيان (*kiyāṅ*), from كيا (*kiyā*) *made*.

b. Roots consisting of more than one syllable, having any short vowel in the penultimate and *fat'ḥa* (*a*) followed immediately by a consonant in the final syllable, drop the latter vowel before all affixes beginning with a vowel; hence, گذرا (*guẕrā*) from گذر (*guẕar*) *pass*; سمجها (*samjha*) from سمجه (*samajh*) *understand*.

c. The few anomalies are گيا (*gayā*) *gone*, from جا (*jā*); كيا (*kiyā*) *done, made*, from كر (*kar*); هوا (*hū'ā*) *been, become*, from هو (*hō*);* موا (*mū'ā*) *dead*, from مر (*mar*); ديا (*diyā*) *given*, from دي (*dē*); and, ليا (*liyā*) *taken*, from لي (*lē*).

---

* The regular forms, however, sometimes occur; but, more especially, جايا (*jāyā*) and مرا (*marā*), when used with كرنا (*karnā*) to form a species of compound; and كرا (*karā*) under other circumstances, though but very rarely.

d. When used adjectively or substantively, this participle is often followed by هوا (*hū'ā*) *been, become;* as لکھا هوا کاغذ (*likhā hū'ā kāghaz*) *the become written,* or *the written, paper;* کاٹا هوا (*kāṭā hū'ā*) *the cut.*

21. The present participle is had by affixing to the root, تا (*tā*) تي (*tē*) تي (*tī*) تين (*tīṅ*) or تیان (*tiyāṅ*), agreeable to the gender and number of the governing noun; so, from چاه (*chāh*) *wish,* come چاهتا (*chāhtā*) *he wishing,* چاهتي (*chāhtī*) *she wishing,* چاهتیان (*chāhtiyāṅ*) *they (females) wishing:* and, to adapt it for use as an adjective or even substantive, هوا *become* is frequently subjoined, like as to the past; so, مارتا هوا (*mārtā hū'ā*) *striking, the person striking.*

22. The past conjunctive participle may be the same in form as the root of the verb, or it may be formed by subjoining to the root, ي (*ē*)* كي (*kē*) كر (*kar*) كركي (*karkē*) or كركر (*karkar*); so, کہہ (*kah*) or کہکي (*kahkē*) or کہکر (*kahkar*), &c., *having said:* and, from آ (*ā*) *come,* آن (*āṅ*) or آنکي (*āṅkē*), as well as the regular آ or آکي, &c., *having come.*

23. The past indefinite tense is the same in form as the simple past participle, explained at paragraph 20; so, مين بولا (*maiṅ bōlā*) *I (a male) spoke,* وہ بولي (*wuh bōlī*) *she spoke,* هم بولين (*ham bōlīṅ*) *we (females) spoke,* اس ني مارا† (*us nē mārā*) *he* or *she struck,* ان ني مارا† (*un nē mārā*) *they (males or females) struck.*

---

* With this affix, verbs become generally the same as for the inflected past participle masculine singular; so, هوئي (*hū'ē*) from هو (*ho*), کيي (*kiyē*) from كر (*kar*), ديي (*dīyē*) from دي (*dē*), ليي (*liyē*) from لي (*lē*).

† Before transitive verbs in any past tense, viz. any tense formed with the past participle in the active voice, the particle ني (*nē*) at once follows, or is affixed to, the noun or pronoun denoting the agent, which, if not the first or second personal pronoun, is inflected before it, if capable

a. The pluperfect or past past tense is obtained by adding the auxiliary past to the past participle; as, مَین بولا تہا (*maiṅ bōlā thā*) *I had spoken*,* تُم نی دو آدمِیون کو بہیجا تہا (*tum nē dō ādmiyōṅ kō bhējā thā*) *you had sent two men.*

b. The past definite or past present tense is had by the addition of the auxiliary present to the past participle; as, تُو بولا هَی (*tū bōlā hai*) *thou hast spoken*; * بِلّي نی باگہون کو دیکہا هَی (*billī nē bāghōṅ kō dekhā hai*) *the cat has seen the tigers.*

c. The past future is obtained by the addition of the auxiliary future to the past participle; as, وُہ بولي هووی or هوگي (*wuh bōlī hōwe* or *hōgī*) *she may* (*shall* or *will*) *have spoken*, or *she might* (*should* or *would*) *speak*;* اُنہون نی رکہا هووی or هوویگا (*unhōṅ nē rakhā hōwē* or *hāwēgā*) *they may* (*shall* or *will*) *have placed*, or *might* (*could* or *would*) *place.*

---

of inflection; the verb being made to agree with its object, provided this be, as is most customary, in the nominative case: when, however, the object is placed in an oblique case, or is not a word but a sentence, the verb is then invariably constructed as the third person masculine singular. Thus, بِلّي نی چُوہا مارا (*billī nē chūhā mārā*) *the cat killed the rat*; باگہ نی گہوڑي ماري (*bāgh nē ghōṛī marī*) *the tiger killed the mare*; سوداگر نی پانچ گہوڑي بیچي (*saudāgar nē pānch ghōṛē bēchē*) *the merchant sold five horses*; باگہون نی گہوڑي کو مارا (*bāghōṅ nē ghoṛī kō mārā*) *the tigers killed the mare*; لڑکون نی پُوچہا تُم کَونسي کِتاب پڑہتي هو (*laṛkōṅ nē pūchhā tum kaun-sī kitāb paṛhtī hō*) *the boys asked*, "*what book are you* (*female*) *reading?*" In the Dakhani of Madras, however, though نی is often used, it does not interrupt the agreement of the verb with the nominative or name of the agent; whilst the dialect of Bombay conforms to that of Hindustan in this respect as well as in most other particulars.

* See note † on the foregoing page.

d. The past conditional or optative is formed by the addition of the present indefinite of the verb هو (*hō*) *be, become,* to the past participle of the verb conjugated, with a conditional or optative adverb, expressed or understood, in the same sentence; so, اگر مين بولا هوتا (*agar maiṅ bōlā hōtā*) *if I had spoken;* اگر وه آيا هوتا (*agar wuh āyā hōtā*) *if he had come;* كاش اسني مارا هوتا (*kāsh us-nē mārā hōtā*) *would to God he had struck!* It may be noticed, moreover, that when any plural feminine form of the auxiliary verb هو, terminating in ن (*ṅ*) or ان (*āṅ*), is used in construction with participles preceding, these commonly drop the like plural signs ن (*ṅ*) or ان (*āṅ*); as, هم بولي هين (*ham bōlī haiṅ*) *we (females) have spoken;* وي ماري گيي هوينگين (*wē mārī ga'ī hō'ēngīṅ*) *they (females) may have been struck:* yet, sometimes, they are retained; as, هم بوليان هين (*ham bōliyāṅ haiṅ*) *we (females) have spoken.*

24. The present indefinite tense is the same in form as the present participle, already explained at paragraph 21; so, مين دوڙتا (*maiṅ dauṛtā*) *I (a male) run;* وه آتي (*wuh ātī*) *she comes;* هم جاتي (*ham jātē*) *we (males) go;* تم بولتين (*tum bōltīṅ*) *ye (females) speak.**

a. The imperfect or present past tense is obtained by adding the auxiliary past to the present participle; as, مين لكهتا تها (*maiṅ likhtā thā*) *I (a male) was writing;* وه پڙهتي تهي (*wuh paṛhtī thī*) *she was reading;* تم بولتي تهين (*tum bōltī thīṅ*) *ye (females) were speaking.*†

---

* The present indefinite tense, moreover, with a conditional conjunction or adverb of wishing, expressed or understood, is much used to convey the sense of a past conditional or optative; as, اگر مين بولتا تو وه لكهتا (*agar maiṅ bōltā tō wuh likhta*) *if I should speak, then he would write;* yet such sentences when rendered word for word are intelligible, *if I speak, then he writes.*

† When one or more feminine participles precede an auxiliary verb in the plural, the plural sign ن (*ṅ*) or ان (*āṅ*) is generally omitted in all

b. The present definite or present present is formed by the addition of the auxiliary present to the present participle; so, مین دوڑتا هون (*maiṅ dauṛtā hūṅ*) *I (a male) am running;* تو آتي هي (*tū ātī hai*) *thou (a female) art coming.*

c. The present future is had by the addition of the auxiliary future to the present participle; so, مین پڑهتا هوون or هوونگا (*maiṅ paṛhta hō'ūṅ* or *hō'ūṅgā*) *I (a male) may (shall or will) be reading;* وه گاتي هووي or هوويگي (*wuh gātī hōwe* or *hōwēgī*) *she may (shall or will) be singing.*

25. The future indefinite or aorist* is obtained by affixing to the root, for the first, second, and third persons singular of either gender, ون (*ūṅ*) ي (*ē*) ي (*ē*), and for the like persons of the plural, ين (*ēṅ*) و (*ō*) ين (*ēṅ*); so, مین کرون (*maiṅ karūṅ*) *I may do,* تو کري (*tū karē*) *thou mayest do,* وه کري (*wuh karē*) *he* (or *she*) *may do;* هم کرين (*ham karēṅ*) *we may do,* تم کرو (*tum karō*) *ye may do,* وي کرين (*wē karēṅ*) *they may do:* and, in a more strictly future sense, by subjoining گا (*gā*) گي (*gē*) گي (*gī*) گين (*gīṅ*) or گيان (*giyāṅ*), agreeable to the gender and number of the governing noun, together with the aforementioned affixes, to the root; so, مین جاونگا (*maiṅ jā'ūṅgā*) *I (a male) will go,* وه آويگي (*wuh āwēgī*) *she will come,* هم کهينگي (*ham kahēṅgē*) *we (males) shall say,* هم کهينگين (*ham kahēṅgīṅ*) *we (females) shall say.*

---

but the final auxiliary, as above exemplified; yet, sometimes, though but rarely, the participle retains it, as هم بولتيان تهيان (*ham boltiyān thī'āṅ*).

* This form serves for a subjunctive mood, and has occasionally an indefinite present meaning; so, وه آوي تو مین جاون (*wuh āwe to maiṅ jā'ūn*) *(if) he should come, then I shall go;* خدا چاهي سو کري (*khudā chāhē so kare*) *(what) God wills, that he does.*

a. To such verbal roots, however, as end in ا (*ā*) و (*ō*) ي (*ē*) or ي (*ī*), the letter و may be optionally affixed, or not, before every future termination beginning with ي (*ē*); so, from آ *come*, may be formed آوي (*āwē*) آوين (*āwēn̈*), &c.; from بو *sow*, بوويگي (*bōwēgī*) بووينگيان (*bōwēn̈giyān̈*): and, on the contrary, verbs ending in ي (*ē*) or و (*ō*) may admit of contraction or elision; so, ديون (*dē'ūn̈*) or دون (*dūn̈*) (*I*) *may give*; ديوي (*dēwē*) or دي (*dē*) (*he* or *she*) *may give*; ديونگا (*dē'ūn̈gā*) or دونگا (*dūn̈gā*) (*I*) *shall give*; ديو (*dē'ō*) or دو (*dō*) (*ye*) *may give*; ديوين (*dēwēn̈*) or دين (*dēn̈*) (*we* or *they*) *may give*; هوون (*hō'ūn̈*) or هون (*hōn̈*) (*I*) *may be*; هووي (*hōwē*) or هوئي (*hō'e*) or هو (*hō*) (*thou* or *he* or *she* or *it*) *may become*; هووينگين (*hōwēn̈gīn̈*) or هوينگين (*hō'ēn̈gīn̈*) or هونگين ([illegible]*gīn̈*) (*we* or *they females*) *shall become*; ليون (*lē'ūn̈*) or لون (*lūn̈*) (*I*) *may take*; ليوي (*lēwē*) or لي (*lē*) (*he* or *she*) *may take*; ليو (*lē'ō*) or لو (*lō*) (*ye*) *may take.*

b. Roots of more than one syllable, having a short vowel in the penultimate and *fat'ḥa* (*a*) in the final, drop the latter vowel when the signs of the future are subjoined; so, نِكلونگا (*niklūn̈gā*) from نِكل (*nikal*) *issue*; گذريگا (*guzrēgā*) from گذر (*guzar*) *pass.*

26. The imperative for the second person singular is the mere root of the verb; and, for the second person plural, it is formed by adding و (*ō*) to the root; so, بول (*bōl*) or تو بول (*tū bōl*) *speak thou*; بولو (*bōlō*) or تم بولو (*tum bōlō*) *speak ye.* The other persons of each number may be the same as in the aorist; so, مين بولون (*main̈ bolūn̈*) *I may speak*, or (*if*) *I may speak*; وه بولي (*wuh bōlē*) (*if*) *he* or *she may speak:* yet, to express the imperative sense in these persons, the verb دي (*dē*) *give* (*thou*), or in the plural دو (*dō*), or in the respectful form دِيجيي (*dījiyē*) *be pleased to give*, or دِيجيو (*dījiyō*) *you must give*, is more commonly used, like the English "let"; so, مجهه كو بولني دي (*mujh kō bōlnē dē*) *let me speak*; اسي بولني دِيجيي (*usē bōlnē dījiyē*)

be pleased to let him (or *her*) *speak;* اُنکو بولني دِيجيو (*un-kō bōlnē dījiyō*) *you must let them speak.*

a. In this mood of the verb, moreover, and of very frequent use, is the respectful or precative form ِ يي (*iyē*) or in a future sense ِ ييگا (*iyēgā*), which some honorific term, such as آپ (*āp*) *self* (*you, Sir*), حضرت (*ḥazrat*) *the presence,* صاحب (*ṣāḥib*) *the lord* or *master*, &c., generally precedes; so, آپ بولِيي (*āp bōliyē*) *be pleased, Sir, to speak;* آپ لِيجييگا (*āp lījiyēgā*) *you, Sir, will be pleased to take:* but, the termination ِ يي (*iyē*) is at times adopted impersonally, and as an indefinite future or present; so, جو مر جاِيي تو سنسار كي دُكھ سي چھوٹِيي (*jō mar jā'iyē to sansār kē dukh sē chhūṭiyē*) *when one dies, then one escapes from the trouble of the world;* چاهِيي (*chāhiyē*) *one should desire,* (*one must*). And, to give intensity to the imperative sense, or to express command respectfully, or even with a precative or future meaning, the termination ِ يو (*iyō*) comes, also, frequently into use; as, ميرا كها مانِيو (*mērā kahā māniyō*) *mind my saying;* اُسكو ميرا پيغام بولِيو (*us-kō mērā paig͟hām bōliyō*) *speak to him my message;* ميرا يار سلامت رهِيو (*mērā yār salāmat rahiyō*) *may my friend remain in safety!;* مر جاِيو (*mar jā'iyō*) *may you die.* After words ending in ِ ي (*ī*) or و (*ō*), too, it must be noticed that the affixes ِ يي (*iyē*) or ِ ييگا (*iyēgā*) and ِ يو (*iyō*) become جِيي (*jiyē*) or جي (*jē*), جِييگا (*jiyēgā*), جِيو (*jiyō*) or جو (*jō*); so, آپ دِيجِيي (*āp dījiyē*) *be pleased, Sir, to give;* صاحب كِيجِييگا (*ṣāḥib kījiyēgā*) *the gentleman will be pleased to do;* آزما لِيجِيو (*āzmā lījiyō*) *you will take* (*and*) *try.* Before these terminations, we may add, the roots هو (*hō*) كر (*kar*) دي (*dē*) لي (*lē*) usually become هُو (*hū*) كِي (*kī*) دِي (*dī*) لِي (*lī*); so, هُوجِيي (*hūjiyē*) كِيجِيو (*kījiyō*) دِيجِيي (*dījiyē*) لِيجِيو (*lījiyō*).

b. Another way of expressing an absolute command is by the use of the infinitive; as, تُم جلدي آنا (*tum jaldī ānā*) *you* (*are*) *to come immediately*; اُسکو نه کہنا (*us-kō na kahnā*) *not to tell him.*

c. In a prohibitive sense, مت (*mat*) is generally used before the verb; as, اُسکو مت مارو (*us-kō mat mārō*) *do not beat him*; تُم کُچھ مت بولو (*tum kuchh mat bōlō*) *do you not say anything*; اُسکي بات مت سُنيو (*us-kī bāt mat suniyō*) *hear not his word:* for the like purpose, however, نه (*na*) may occasionally be adopted; so, لگا نه دل کوکہیں (*lagā na dil kō kahīṅ*) *place not the heart* (*or affection*) *anywhere.*

27. A transitive verb is formed from an intransitive, or a causal from a transitive, by the addition of ا (*ā*) or وا (*wā*), and sometimes of و (*ō*) to the root, the vowel of the primitive, if long, being frequently shortened before those additions; so, جلا (*jalā*) *burn* (transitively), جلوا (*jalwā*) *cause to burn* (by another), from جل (*jal*) *burn* (intransitively), *be burnt*; هِلا (*hilā*) *move* (transitively), هِلوا (*hilwā*) *cause to move* (by another), from هِل (*hil*) *move* (intransitively), *be moved*; بُلا (*bulā*) *call*, بُلوا (*bulwā*) *cause to call* (by another), from بول (*bōl*) *speak*; ڈُبو (*ḍubō*) *drown*, from ڈوب (*ḍūb*) *be immersed* or *drowned*; بهگو (*bhigō*) *wet, steep*, from بهيگ (*bhīg*) *be wet:* and if the primitive root end in ا (*ā*) ي (*ī*) ي (*ē*) or و (*ō*), the letter ل (*l*) is to be inserted before the transitive or causal sign, the vowel being shortened; so, کهِلا (*khilā*) *feed*, کهِلوا (*khīlwā*) *cause* (*another*) *to feed*, from کها (*khā*) *eat*; پِلا (*pilā*) *give to drink*, پِلوا (*pilwā*) *cause* (*another*) *to give to drink*, from پي (*pī*) *drink*; دِلا (*dilā*) *cause to give*, دِلوا (*dilwā*) *cause* (*another*) *to cause to give*, from دي (*dē*) *give*; دهلا (*dhulā*) *cause to wash*, دهُلوا (*dhulwā*) *cause* (*another*) *to cause to wash*, from دهو (*dhō*) *wash*.

a. In other cases, these verbs are obtained by lengthening, if short, the vowel of monosyllabic, or the last vowel of dissyllabic, roots; as, کاٹ (*kāṭ*) *cut*, from کٹ (*kaṭ*) *be cut*; چهيد (*chhēd*) *bore*, from چهِد

(*chhid*) *be bored;* گھول (*ghol*) *dissolve* (transitively), from گھل (*ghul*) *be dissolved;* جوڑ (*joṛ*) *join,* from جڑ (*juṛ*) *be joined;* نکال (*nikāl*) *make issue, expel,* from نکل (*nikal*) *issue:* yet, when the termination وا (*wā*) is used, the short vowel of the primitive remains; as, کٹوا (*kaṭwā*) *cause* (*another*) *to cut;* نکلوا (*nikalwā*) *cause to be expelled,* &c.

b. In a few instances, especially if the root be a monosyllable terminating in an aspirated consonant, either ا (*ā*) or لا (*lā*), as before described, or very rarely ال (*āl*) may be added to form the causal; so, دکھا (*dikhā*) or دکھلا (*dikhlā*) *shew,* from دیکھ (*dēkh*) *see;* سکھا (*sikhā*) or سکھلا (*sikhlā*) *teach,* from سیکھ (*sīkh*) *learn;* بٹھا (*biṭhā*) or بٹھلا (*biṭhlā*) or بیٹھال (*baiṭhāl*) *seat,* from بیٹھ (*baiṭh*) *sit;* پیٹھال (*paiṭhāl*) *cause to enter,* from پیٹھ (*paiṭh*) *enter,* the long vowel being continued in the syllable before ال (*āl*). On a principle nearly analogous, too, are formed نہلا (*nahlā*) *cause to bathe,* and نہلوا (*nahalwā*) *cause to cause to bathe,* from نہا (*nahā* or *nhā*) *bathe:* and, a very few causals seem to deviate more from analogy; as, بیچ (*bēch*) *sell,* from بک (*bik*) *be sold;* چھوڑ (*chhoṛ*) *let go,* from چھٹ (*chhuṭ*) *be let go;* پھوڑ (*phōṛ*) and پھاڑ (*phāṛ*) *break* or *burst,* from پھوٹ (*phūṭ*) and پھٹ (*phaṭ*) *be broken;* توڑ (*tōṛ*) *break,* from ٹوٹ (*ṭūṭ*) *be broken;* نبیڑ (*nibēṛ*) *finish,* from نبڑ (*nibaṛ*) *be ended.*

c. In dissyllabic roots, the short vowel of the last syllable, if it be *fat'ha* (*a*), is dropped when ا (*ā*) but not when وا (*wā*) is suffixed; so, سمجھا (*samjhā*) *inform,* from سمجھ (*samajh*) *understand;* سرکا (*sarkā*) *move,* and سرکوا (*sarakwā*) *cause to move,* from سرک (*sarak*) *be moved;* بہلا (*bahlā*) *amuse,* from بہل (*bahal*) *be amused.*

28. Compound verbs may be formed in various ways. If regard be had to the structure of the words, a compound may be obtained, firstly, by the addition of some verb, regularly conjugated, to a sub-

stantive or adjective, which remains unchanged as a masculine singular uninflected; secondly, by the addition of a verb, regularly conjugated, to the root, or the infinitive, or the past participle, or the present participle of another verb; and, thirdly, by the construction of two verbs, both admitting the usual changes of conjugation: and, verbs of this description may, according to their import in English, be arranged under particular terms, as follows:—

1st. Nominals; so, بات کرنا (*bāt karnā*) *to discourse;* شروع کرنا (*shurū'* karnā*) *to begin;* یاد رکھنا (*yād rakhnā*) *to recollect;* مول لینا (*mol lēnā*) *to purchase;* غوطه مارنا (*ghōṭa mārnā*) *to dive;* تمام کرنا (*tamām karnā*) *to finish;* پورا ہونا (*pūrā hōnā*) *to be complete.*

2nd. Intensives; as, بول دینا (*bōl dēnā*) *to declare;* دي ڈالنا (*dē ḍālnā*) *to give away;* ڈال دینا (*ḍāl dēnā*) *to throw away;* مار ڈالنا (*mār ḍālnā*) *to kill downright;* کھا جانا (*khā jānā*) *to eat up;* گر پڑنا (*gir paṛnā*) *to fall down;* توڑ ڈالنا (*toṛ ḍālnā*) *to break to pieces;* بول اٹھنا (*bol uṭhnā*) *to speak out;* آ جانا (*ā jānā*) *to come suddenly.*

3rd. Potentials, formed by the addition of سکنا (*saknā*) *to be able,* to the root of another verb; so, لکھ سکنا (*likh saknā*) *to be able to write;* چل سکنا (*chal saknā*) *to be able to walk.**

4th. Completives, formed by adding چکنا (*chuknā*) *to be finished,* to the root of another verb; as, پي چکنا (*pī chuknā*) *to have done drinking;* کھا چکنا (*khā chuknā*) *to have finished eating.*

5th. Inceptives or Inchoatives, formed by the addition of لگنا (*lagnā*) *to come in contact, to be applied, to begin,* to the inflected infinitive of a verb; as, بولني لگنا (*bōlnē lagnā*) *to begin to speak;* کهني لگا (*kahnē lagā*) *he began to say;* پڑھني لگا (*paṛhnē lagā*) *he began to*

---

* Sometimes, however, especially in Dakhani, سکنا may be constructed with an inflected infinitive, or even an uninflected one.

read: and, sometimes, though but rarely, لگا precedes; as, لگا جاني (*lagā jānē*) *he began to go.**

6th. Permissives, formed by adding دينا (*denā*) *to give, to let, to permit,* to an inflected infinitive; as, جاني دينا (*jānē dēnā*) *to permit to go;* آني دينا (*ānē dēnā*) *to let come.*

7th. Acquisitives, formed by the addition of پانا (*pānā*) *to get, to acquire,* to an inflected infinitive; as, آني پانا (*ānē pānā*) *to be allowed to come;* جاني پانا (*jānē pānā*) *to be allowed to go.*

8th. Desideratives, Requisitives, and Proximatives, formed by adding چاهنا (*chāhnā*) *to desire, to require,* regularly conjugated, to the past participle of a verb, which remains unchanged in the state of the masculine singular, whatever the gender and number of the governing noun may be; so, مرا چاها (*marā chāhā*) or مرا چاهي (*marā chāhī*) *he* or *she wished to die,* or *was about to die;* جايا چاهنا (*jāyā chāhnā*) *to wish to go, to be about to go;* لكها چاهنا (*likhā chāhnā*) *to wish to write, to be about to write.*† In this compound, the regular past forms مرا (*marā*) and جايا (*jāyā*) are preferred, as in the examples above, to the more common موا (*mū'ā*) and گيا (*gayā*).

9th. Frequentatives, formed by the addition of كرنا (*karnā*) *to do, to make,* to the past participle of a verb, which is invariably used as an uninflected masculine singular, whatever the gender and number of the governing noun may be; so, آيا كرنا (*āyā karnā*)) *to make a practice of coming;* لكها كرنا (*likhā karnā*) *to make a practice of writing;* جايا كرنا (*jāyā karnā*) *to make a practice of going.* In this compound, too, like as in the last described, جايا is preferred to گيا.

---

* In Dakhani, especially in poetry, the verbal noun in ن (*an*) may be used with لگنا; as كهولن لگيا *he began to open.*

† In Dakhani, or even in Hindustani occasionally, an inflected infinitive, or in Dakhani even an uninflected one, may precede چاهنا.

10th. Continuatives, formed by adding جانا (*jānā*) *to go*, or رهنا (*rahnā*) *to remain*, to a present participle made to agree in gender and number with the governing noun; so, بولتا جانا (*bōltā jānā*) *to go on speaking* (*a male*); جاتا رهنا (*jātā rahnā*) *to keep going, to go entirely away* (*a male*); روتي جاتي هي (*rōtī jātī hai*) *she goes on weeping*; پڙهتي جاتي هين (*paṛhtē jātē hain*) or پڙهتي رهتي هين (*paṛhtē rahtē hain*) *they* (*males*) *continue reading.*

11th. Statisticals, formed by adding a verb regularly conjugated, to a present participle used invariably as an inflected masculine singular; so, بولتي جانا (*bōltē jānā*) *to go* (*in the state of one*) *speaking*; گاتي آتي هي (*gātē ātī hai*) *she comes* (*in the state of one*) *singing*; روتي دوڙتا هي (*rōtē dauṛtā hai*) *he runs* (*in the state of one*) *weeping.*

12th. Reiteratives, formed by using together two verbs regularly conjugated; as, بولنا چالنا (*bōlnā chālnā*) *to converse*; ديكهنا بهالنا (*dēkhnā bhālnā*) *to see.*

DERIVATIVE VERBS.

29. Verbs may be derived from either substantives or adjectives, by affixing the verbal signs only in some instances; or, more commonly, by shortening the vowel of the original, if long, and inserting ا (*ā*) or يا (*iyā*) before those signs: so, چوڙانا (*chauṛānā*) *to widen*, from چوڙا (*chauṛā*) *wide*; لتيانا (*latiyānā*) *to kick*, from لات (*lāt*) *a kick*; گليانا (*galiyānā*) *to abuse*, from گالي (*gālī*) *abuse*; جتيانا (*jutiyānā*) *to beat with* جوتي (*jūtī*) *a slipper.*

PASSIVE VERBS.

30. The Passive voice is formed on the past participle of an active verb, by the addition of جانا *to go*, both parts of the compound being made to agree in gender and number with the governing noun; so, مين مارا گيا (*main mārā gayā*) *I was struck*; مين مارا جاتا هون (*main mārā jātā hūn*) *I am struck*; مين مارا جاونگا (*main mārā jā'ūngā*)

I shall be struck; لڑكي مارِي جاوِيگي (*laṛkī mārī jāwēgī*) *the girl will be struck.*

AUXILIARY VERB.

31. The auxiliaries,* used in forming the definite tenses of verbs, are to denote the

Past.

	Singular.		Plural.
† (*thā*) تها	ميں *I was.*	‡ (*thē*) تهي	هم *we were.*
	تو *thou wast.*		تم *ye were.*
	§ وه *he was.*		وي *they were.*

Present.

Singular.	Plural.
(*hūṅ*) ميں هوں *I am.*	(*haiṅ*) هم هيں *we are.*
(*hai*) تو هي *thou art.*	‖ (*hō*) تم هو *ye are.*
(*hai*) وه هي *he is.*	(*haiṅ*) وي هيں *they are.*

Aorist or *Future.*

Singular.

(*hōṅ*) هوں or, (*hō'ūṅ*) ميں هووں *I*
(*hō*) هو or, (*hō'ē*) هوئي or, (*hōwē*) تو هووي *thou*
(*hō*) هو or, (*hō'ē*) هوئي or, (*hōwē*) وه هووي *he, she*

} *may, shall, &c. be.*

---

* Which are, also, the substantive verb, answering to the English *be, am, art, is, are, was, wast, were.*

† The above is for the masculine gender: with a feminine nominative, it would be تهي (*thī*), and in the plural ‡ تهيں (*thīṅ*) or تهياں (*thī'āṅ*); in Dakhani, the latter only.

§ Dakh. وه (*wah*) or او (*ō*), &c.

‖ Dakh. تم هيں (*tum haiṅ*) as in the two other persons.

Plural.

(*hōṅ*) هون or, (*hō'ēṅ*) هوئين or, (*hōwēṅ*) هم هووين *we*
* (*hō*) هو or, (*hō'ō*) تم هوؤ *ye*
(*hōṅ*) هون or, (*hō'ēṅ*) هوئين or, (*hōwēṅ*) وي هووين *they*
} *may, shall, &c. be.*

Future.

Singular.

† (*hūṅgā*) هونگا or, (*hō'ūṅgā*) مين هوونگا *I*
(*hōgā*) هوگا or, (*hō'ēgā*) هويگا or, (*hōwēgā*) تو هوويگا *thou*
(*hōgā*) هوگا or, (*hō'ēgā*) هويگا or, (*hōwēgā*) وه هوويگا *he*
} *shall, will, &c. be.*

Plural.

‡ (*hōṅgē*) هونگي or (*hō'ēṅgē*) هوينگي or (*hōwēṅgē*) هم هووينگي *we*
§ (*hōgē*) هوگي or, *hō'ōgē* تم هوؤگي *ye*
(*hōṅgē*) هونگي or (*hō'ēṅgē*) هوينگي or (*hōwēṅgē*) وي هووينگي *they*
} *shall, will, &c. be.*

Conditional or *Optative.*

Singular.		Plural.	
(*hōtā*) هوتا	مين *I become.*	(*hōtē*) هوتي	هم *we become.*
	تو *thou becomest.*		تم *ye become.*
	وه *he becomes.*		وي *they become.*

---

* Dakh. هون or هوئين or تم هووين like as in the other two persons. Remark that the ن in all these forms is the soft nasal letter (*ṅ*).

† For the feminine, the termination گا (*gā*) becomes گي (*gī*) in the singular.

‡ For the feminine, this termination گي (*gē*) becomes گين (*gīṅ*) or گيان (*giyāṅ*) in the plural; and the latter only in Dakhani.

§ Dakh. هووينگي (*hōwēṅgē*), &c., like as in the first and third persons.

32. The intransitive verb جانا (*jānā*) *to go*, is much used in forming the passive voice of transitive verbs, as well as in other compounds and it is conjugated as follows, for the masculine gender.

Imperative for the second person singular, or *The Root.*

(*jā*) جا *go.*

Infinitive and *Gerund.*

(*jānē*) جاني or, (*jānā*) جانا *to go, going.*

Past Participle.

Singular.		Plural.	
گیا (*gayā*) or, گیا هُوا (*gayā hū'ā*)	gone.	گئي (*ga'ē*) or, گئي هُوئي (*ga'ē hū'ē*)	gone.

Present Participle.

جاتا (*jātā*) or, جاتا هُوا (*jātā hū'ā*)	going.	جاتي (*jātē*) or, جاتي هُوئي (*jātē hū'ē*)	going.

Past Conjunctive Participle.

Singular and Plural.

جا جائي جاكي جاكر جاكركي or جاكركر *having gone.*

Past Indefinite Tense.

Singular.		Plural.	
(*gayā*) گیا	مَیں *I went.*	(*ga'ē*) گئي	هم *we went.*
	تُو *thou wentest.*		تُم *ye went.*
	وُه *he went.*		وي *they went.*

Pluperfect or *Past Past Tense.*

گیا تها	مَیں *I was gone.*	گئي تهي	هم *we were gone.*
	تُو *thou wast gone.*		تُم *ye were gone.*
	وُه *he was gone.*		وي *they were gone.*

Past Definite or *Past Present Tense.*

Singular.	Plural.
مَین گیا هُون *I am gone.*	هم گئیِ هَین *we are gone.*
تُو گیا هَي *thou art gone.*	تُم گئیِ هو* *ye are gone.*
وُه گیا هَي *he is gone.*	وي گئیِ هَین *they are gone.*

Past Future Tense.

Singular		Plural	
مَین گیا هووْن *I* تُو گیا هووي *thou* وُه گیا هووي *he*	*may, shall,* or *will have gone, &c.* or *might &c. go.*	هم گئیِ هووین *we* تُم گئیِ هووُو† *ye* وي گئیِ هووین *they*	*may, shall,* or *will have gone, &c.* or *might, &c. go.*

Or,

Singular		Plural	
مَین گیا هوونگا *I* تُو گیا هوویگا *thou* وُه گیا هوویگا *he*	*shall, will,* or *may have gone;* or, *might, &c. go.*	هم گئیِ هووینگي *we* تُم گئیِ هووُگي‡ *ye* وي گئیِ هووینگي *they*	*shall, will,* or *may have gone;* or, *might, &c. go.*

Past Conditional or *Optative Tense.*

Singular		Plural	
گیا هوتا { مَین / تُو / وُه } جو، کاشکي or اگر	*If, would to God, I, &c., had gone;* or, *then I, &c., should have gone, &c.*	گئیِ هوتي { هم / تُم / وي } جو، کاشکي or اگر	*If, would to God, we, &c., had gone;* or, *then we, &c., should have gone, &c.*

---

* Dakh. تُم گئیِ هَین. † Dakh. تُم گئیِ هووي or هو. ‡ Dakh. تُم گئیِ هوگي.
But the conjugation of Dakhani verbs varies in many particulars from the proper Hindustani, as may be seen in the "Short Grammar of the Dakhani," appended to the author's more extended "Grammar of the Hindustani Language."

Present Indefinite Tense.

Singular.		Plural.	
جاتا *	مَین *I go.*	جاتي *	هم *we go.*
	تُو *thou goest.*		تُم *ye go.*
	وُہ *he goes.*		وي *they go.*

Imperfect or *Present Past Tense.*

جاتا تها	مَین *I was going.*	جاتي تهي	هم *we were going.*
	تُو *thou wast going.*		تُم *ye were going.*
	وُہ *he was going.*		وي *they were going.*

Present Definite or *Present Present Tense.*

مَین جاتا هُون *I am going.*	هم جاتي هَین *we are going.*
تُو جاتا هَي *thou art going.*	تُم جاتي هو *ye are going.*
وُہ جاتا هَي *he is going.*	وي جاتي هَین *they are going.*

Present Future Tense.

مَین جاتا هوؤن *I*	*may, shall,*	هم جاتي هووین *we*	*may, shall,*
تُو جاتا هووي *thou*	or *will be*	تُم جاتي هوؤ *ye*	or *will be*
وُہ جاتا هووي *he*	*going.*	وي جاتي هووین *they*	*going.*

Or,

مَین جاتا هوؤنگا *I*	*shall, will,*	هم جاتي هووینگي *we*	*shall, will,*
تُو جاتا هوویگا *thou*	or *may be*	تُم جاتي هوؤگي *ye*	or *may be*
وُہ جاتا هوویگا *he*	*going.*	وي جاتي هووینگي *they*	*going.*

---

* This form of the verb, if a conditional conjunction or an adverb of wishing accompanies it, may be used in the sense of a conditional or optative, like the tense immediately preceding: see paragraph 24, note *.

Future Indefinite or *Aorist.*

Singular.		Plural.	
(*jā'ūṅ*) مَین جاؤں *I*	*may, shall,* or *will go; go, &c.*	(*jāwēṅ*) هم جاوین *we*	*may, shall,* or *will go;* or, *go, &c.*
(*jāwē*) تُو جاوي *thou*		(*jā'ō*) تُم جاؤ *ye*	
(*jāwē*) وُه جاوي *he* or *she*		(*jāwēṅ*) وي جاوين *they*	

Future Indefinite Tense.

(*jā'ūṅgā*) مَین جاؤنگا *I*	*shall, will,* or *may go.*	(*jāwēṅgē*) هم جاوينگي *we*	*shall, will,* or *may go.*
(*jāwēgā*) تُو جاويگا *thou*		(*jā'ōgē*) تُم جاؤگي *ye*	
(*jāwēgā*) وُه جاويگا *he*		(*jāwēṅgē*) وي جاوينگي *they*	

Imperative.

(*jā'ūṅ*) مَین جاؤں *I may go, let me go.*	(*jāwēṅ*) هم جاوين *we may go, let us go.*
(*jā*) تُو جا *go thou.*	(*jā'ō*) تُم جاؤ *go ye.*
(*jāwē*) وُه جاوي *let him* or *her go.*	(*jāwēṅ*) وي جاوين *let them go.*

Respectful and Precative forms of the Future and Imperative.

(*jā'iyē*) جاِئِيي, or, (*jā'iyēgā*) جاِئِيگا — آپ / صاحِب / حضرت — *you, Sir,* or *your excellency, &c. may, shall,* or *will go;* or, *may you, Sir, go; may your excellency, &c. go.*

(*jā'iyē*) جاِئِيي *we may, shall,* or *will go;* or, *may we go.*

(*jā'iyō*) جاِئيو
- تُو *thou mayest, shalt,* or *wilt go;* or, *go thou.*
- وُه *he may, shall,* or *will go;* or, *may he go.*
- تُم *ye may, shall,* or *will go;* or, *go ye.*
- وي *they may, shall,* or *will go;* or *may they go.*

For the feminine gender, the masculine singular final ا (*ā*) of the infinitive, the participles, the auxiliaries, and the future, as above described, must be changed to ي (ī) in that number, and to ِين (īṅ) or ِيان (iyāṅ) for the plural; but, where two or more feminine plurals come together, it is usual for the last only to take the numerical sign ں (ṅ) or اں (āṅ), the preceding participle or participles being constructed in the feminine singular form: sometimes, however, the plural termination is repeated, as shewn at note to par. 24. *a*.

33. Conjugation of a regular transitive verb for the masculine gender, exemplified in مارنا (*mārnā*) *to beat* or *strike*.

ACTIVE VOICE.

Imperative for the second person singular, or *The Root*.
(*mār*) مار *beat, strike*.

Infinitive and *Gerund*.

(*mārnē*) مارني or (*mārnā*) مارنا *to beat, beating*.

Past Participle.

Singular.	Plural.
مارا هوا or, (*mārā*) مارا *beaten*. (*mārā hū'ā*)	ماري هوي or, (*mārē*) ماري *beaten*. (*mārē hū'ē*)

Present Participle.

مارتا هوا or, (*mārtā*) مارتا *beating*. (*mārtā hū'ā*)	مارتي or, (*mārtē*) مارتي *beating*. (*mārtē hū'ē*) هوي

Past Conjunctive Participle.
Singular and Plural.

ماركر or ماري مار ماركي ماركر ماركركي ماركر *having beaten*.

Past Indefinite Tense.

Singular.	Plural.
(*mārā*) مارا { مين ني* *I beat*.	(*mārā*) مارا { هم ني* *we beat*.
تو ني *thou beatedst*.	تم ني *ye beat*.
اس ني *he beat*.	ان ني *they beat*.

* See the note to paragraph 23, for the reason of this particle in construction with the past tenses of transitive verbs.

Pluperfect or *Past Past Tense.*

Singular.			Plural.		
مارا تها	مَين ني	*I had beaten.*	مارا تها	هم ني	*we had beaten.*
	تُو ني	*thou hadst beaten.*		تُم ني	*ye had beaten.*
	اُس ني	*he had beaten.*		اُن ني	*they had beaten.*

Past Definite or *Past Present Tense.*

مارا هَي	مَين ني	*I have beaten.*	مارا هَي	هم ني	*we have beaten.*
	تُو ني	*thou hast beaten.*		تُم ني	*ye have beaten.*
	اُس ني	*he has beaten.*		اُن ني	*they have beaten.*

Past Future Tense.

مارا هوْوي	مَين ني	*I*	*may, shall* or *will have beaten;* or, *might, &c., beat.*	مارا هوْوي	هم ني	*we*	*may, shall* or *will have beaten;* or, *might, &c., beat.*
	تُو ني	*thou*			تُم ني	*ye*	
	اُس ني	*he*			اُن ني	*they*	

Or,

مارا هوگا	مَين ني	*I*	*shall, will* or *may have beaten;* or, *should, &c., beat.*	مارا هوگا	هم ني	*we*	*shall, will* or *may have beaten;* or, *should, &c., beat.*
	تُو ني	*thou*			تُم ني	*ye*	
	اُس ني	*he*			اُن ني	*they*	

Past Conditional or *Optative Tense.*

مارا هوتا	مَين ني	جو کاش	*If, would to God, I, &c., had beaten;*	مارا هوتا	هم ني	جو کاش	*If, would to God, we, &c., had beaten;*
	تُو ني	or تو	*then I, &c., would have beaten, &c.*		تُم ني	or تو	*then we, &c., would have beaten, &c.*
	اُس ني				اُن ني		

Present Indefinite Tense.

Singular.		Plural.	
مارتا *	مَين *I beat.*	مارتي *	هم *we beat.*
	تُو *thou beatest.*		تُم *ye beat.*
	وُه *he beats.*		وي *they beat.*

Imperfect or *Present Past Tense.*

مارتا تها	مَين *I was beating.*	مارتي تهي	هم *we were beating.*
	تُو *thou wast beating.*		تُم *ye were beating.*
	وُه *he was beating.*		وي *they were beating.*

Present Definite or *Present Present Tense.*

مَين مارتا هون *I am beating.*	هم مارتي هَين *we are beating.*
تُو مارتا هَي *thou art beating.*	تُم مارتي هو *ye are beating.*
وُه مارتا هَي *he is beating.*	وي مارتي هَين *they are beating.*

Present Future Tense.

مَين مارتا هوون *I*	*may, shall or will be beating.*	هم مارتي هووين *we*	*may, shall or will be beating.*
تُو مارتا هووي *thou*		تُم مارتي هوو *ye*	
وُه مارتا هووي *he*		وي مارتي هووين *they*	

Or,

مَين مارتا هُونگا *I*	*shall, will or may be beating.*	هم مارتي هووينگي *we*	*shall, will or may be beating.*
تُو مارتا هوگا *thou*		تُم مارتي هووگي *ye*	
وُه مارتا هوگا *he*		وي مارتي هووينگي *they*	

* When a conditional conjunction or adverb of wishing precedes in the sentence, this form of the verb is often used in a past conditional or optative sense, like the tense last described: see the note to paragraph 24.

Future Indefinite or *Aorist Tense.*

Singular.		Plural.	
مَین مارُون *I*	*may, shall* or *will beat*; or, *beat, &c.*	هم مارین *we*	*may, shall* or *will beat*; or, *beat, &c.*
تُو ماري *thou*		*تُم مارو *ye*	
وُه ماري *he*		وي مارين *they*	

Future Indefinite Tense.

مَین مارُونگا *I*	*shall, will* or *may beat*; or, *beat, &c.*	هم مارینگي *we*	*shall, will* or *may beat*; or, *beat, &c.*
تُو ماريگا *thou*		*تُمماروگي *ye*	
وُه ماريگا *he*		وي مارينگي *they*	

Imperative.

مَین مارُون *I may beat, let me beat.*	هم مارین *we may beat, let us beat.*
تُو مار *beat thou.*	تُم مارو *beat ye.*
وُه ماري *he may beat, let him beat.*	وي مارين *they may beat, let them beat.*

Respectful and Precative forms of the Future and Imperative.

(*māriyē*) مارِيي or (*māriyēgā*) مارِيگا { آپ / صاحِب / حضرت } *you, Sir,* or *your excellency, &c., may, shall* or *will be pleased to beat; be pleased, Sir, to beat; may your excellency, &c., be pleased to beat.*

(*māriyē*) مارِيي *we may, shall, &c., beat; may we beat.*

(*māriyō*) مارِيو {
تُو *thou mayest, shalt* or *wilt beat*; or, *beat thou.*
وُه *he may, shall* or *will beat*; or, *may he beat.*
تُم *ye may, shall* or *will beat*; or, *beat ye.*
وي *they may, shall* or *will beat*; or, *may they beat.*
}

---

* Dakhni تُم مارین and تُم مارینگي.

PASSIVE VOICE.

Imperative for the second person singular, as *The Root.*

مارا جا *be beaten.*

Infinitive and *Gerund.*

Singular.	Plural.
مارا جانا or جاني *to be beaten, being beaten.*	ماري جانا or جاني *to be beaten, being beaten.*

Past Participle.

مارا گيا *been beaten.*	ماري گئي *been beaten.*

Present Participle.

مارا جاتا *being beaten.*	ماري جاتي *being beaten.*

Past Conjunctive Participle.

ماري جا جاكي جاكر جاكركي or جاكركر | مارا جا جاكي جاكر جاكركي or جاكركر

having been beaten.

Past Indefinite Tense.

مارا گيا	مين *I was beaten.*	ماري گئي	هم *we were beaten.*
	تو *thou wast beaten.*		تم *ye were beaten.*
	وه *he was beaten.*		وي *they were beaten.*

Pluperfect or *Past Past Tense.*

مارا گيا تها	مين *I had been beaten.*	ماري گئي تهي	هم *we had been beaten.*
	تو *thou hadst been beaten.*		تم *ye had been beaten.*
	وه *he had been beaten.*		وي *they had been beaten.*

Past Definite or *Past Present Tense.*

Singular.	Plural.
مَین مارا گیا هُون *I have been beaten.*	هم ماري گَئي هَين *we have been beaten.*
تُو مارا گیا هَي *thou hast been beaten.*	تُم ماري گَئي هو *ye have been beaten.*
وُہ مارا گَیا هَي *he has been beaten.*	وي ماري گَئي هَين *they have been beaten.*

Past Future Tense.

Singular.		Plural.	
مَین مارا گیا هوْون *I*	*may, shall* or *will have been beaten;* or, *might, &c. be beaten.*	هم ماري گَئي هوْوين *we*	*may, shall* or *will have been beaten;* or, *might, &c. be beaten.*
تُو مارا گیا هوْوي *thou*		تُم ماري گَئي هوْو *ye*	
وُہ مارا گَیا هوْوي *he*		وي ماري گَئي هوْوين *they*	

Or,

Singular.		Plural.	
مَین مارا گَیا هُونگا *I*	*shall, will* or *may have been beaten;* or, *should, &c. be beaten.*	هم ماري گَئي هونگي *we*	*shall, will* or *may have been beaten;* or, *should, &c. be beaten.*
تُو مارا گَیا هوگا *thou*		تُم ماري گَئي هوگي *ye*	
وُہ مارا گَیا هوگا *he*		وي ماري گَئي هونگي *they*	

Past Conditional or *Optative Tense.*

Singular.		Plural.	
کاش or اگر { مَین / تُو / وُہ } مارا گَیا هوتا	*If, would to God, I, &c. had been beaten;* or, *then I, &c. would have been beaten.*	کاش or اگر { هم / تُم / وي } ماري گَئي هوتي	*If, would to God, we, &c. had been beaten;* or, *then we, &c. would have been beaten.*

Present Indefinite Tense.

	Singular.		Plural.
مارا جاتا	مَین *I am beaten.*	ماري جاتي	هم *we are beaten.*
	تُو *thou art beaten.*		تُم *ye are beaten.*
	وُه *he is beaten.*		وي *they are beaten.*

Imperfect or Present Past Tense.

مارا جاتا تها	مَین *I was*	*being beaten.*	ماري جاتي تهي	هم *we were*	*being beaten.*
	تُو *thou wast*			تُم *ye were*	
	وُه *he was*			وي *they were*	

Present Definite or *Present Present Tense.*

مَین مارا جاتا هُون *I am*	*being beaten.*	هم ماري جاتي هَین *we are*	*being beaten.*
تُو مارا جاتا هَي *thou art*		تُم ماري جاتي هو *ye are*	
وُه مارا جاتا هَي *he is*		وي ماري جاتي هَین *they are*	

Present Future Tense.

مَین مارا جاتا هوُون *I may*	*&c. be being beaten.*	هم ماري جاتي هووین *we may*	*&c. be being beaten.*
تُو مارا جاتا هووي *thou mayest*		تُم ماري جاتي هوُو *ye may*	
وُه مارا جاتا هووي *he may*		وي ماري جاتي هووین *they may*	

Or,

مَین مارا جاتا هُونگا *I shall*	*&c. be being beaten.*	هم ماري جاتي هونگي *we shall*	*&c. be being beaten.*
تُو مارا جاتا هوگا *thou shalt*		تُم ماري جاتي هوگي *ye shall*	
وُه مارا جاتا هوگا *he shall*		وي ماري جاتي هونگي *they shall*	

Future Indefinite or *Aorist Tense.*

Singular.		Plural.	
مَین مارا جاؤن *I*	*may, shall* or *will be beaten*; or, *be beaten*, &c.	هم ماري جاوين *we*	*may, shall* or *will be beaten*; or, *be beaten*, &c.
تُو مارا جاوي *thou*		تُم ماري جاؤ *ye*	
وُہ مارا جاوي *he*		وي ماري جاوين *they*	

Future Indefinite Tense.

مَین مارا جاونگا *I*	*shall, will* or *may be beaten.*	هم ماري جاوينگي *we*	*shall, will* or *may be beaten.*
تُومارا جاويگا *thou*		تُم ماري جاؤگي *ye*	
وُہ مارا جاويگا *he*		وي ماري جاوينگي *they*	

Imperative.

مَین مارا جاؤن *let me be beaten.*	هم ماري جاوين *let us be beaten.*
تُو مارا جا *be thou beaten.*	تُم ماري جاؤ *be ye beaten.*
وُہ مارا جاوي *let him be beaten.*	وي ماري جاوين *let them be beaten.*

Respectful and Precative forms of the Future aud Imperative.

ماري جاِئيي or ماري جاِئيگا { آپ / صاحِب / حضرت } *you, Sir,* or, *your excellency shall, will* or *may be beaten ; be you, Sir, beaten ; may your excellency, &c., be beaten.*

ماري جاِئيي *we may, shall* or *will be beaten ; may we be beaten.*

جاِئيو { مارا { تُو *thou mayest, shalt, &c.* or *be thou beaten.*
وُہ *he may, shall, &c.* or *may he be beaten.*

ماري { تُم *ye may, shall, &c.* or *be ye beaten.*
وي *they may, shall, &c.*, or *may they be beaten.* } }

For the feminine of both the active and passive voices, the singular masculine final ا (*ā*) of the infinitive, the participles and the auxiliaries, where it occurs in conjugation, must be changed to ي (ī) in the singular, and to ين (īn) or يان (iyān) in the plural: when, however two or more words are constructed together, each of which might assume the feminine plural sign ن (n) or ان (ān), as in many of the definite tenses, whether active or passive, that sign is usually omitted in all such words but the last; so, وي جاتي هووينگيان or هووينگين *they (females) shall be going;* هم ماري جاتي هونگين or هونگيان *we (females) shall be being beaten.* Sometimes, though but rarely, the plural termination is repeated: see in paragraph 23, *d.* also paragraph 24, note †.

CHAPTER V.

INDECLINABLE WORDS.

To words of this description, answering to our prepositions, adverbs, conjunctions, and interjections, the word حرف (*ḥarf*) borrowed from the Arabic, is generally applied. The preposition, which in Hindustani usage is mostly a postposition, may be termed حرفِ جر (*ḥarf-i jarr*): and, this is of two kinds: the simple (مُفرِد *mufrid*) which follows the noun it governs without the intervention of any other word; and, the compound (مُرَكّب *murakkab*) which usually requires كي (*kē*) or كي (*kī*) to intervene between the noun and itself.

34. Of the simple postpositions some notice has already been taken at paragraph 6; to which reference may be made: and, the most usual postpositions, which become compounds by taking كي (*kē*), or the inflected masculine genitive of a pronoun, in common before them, are—

پاس *near, at the side, by.*

نزدیک *near, about, with.*

یہاں (*yahāṅ*) *at the abode, with.*

واسطي *on account, for.*

لیي (*liyē*) *on account, for.*

ماري *by reason.*

سبب *by reason.*

باعث *by reason.*

موجب *by means.*

آگي *in front, before.*

سامھني *in front, before.*

مقابل *in front, opposite.*

پیچھي *in the rear, behind.*

بعد *after* (in point of time).

أوپر *over, upon, above.*

نیچي *beneath, under, below.*

تلي *beneath, under, below.*

أندر *within, in the inside.*

باهر or باهر *without, out.*

تک
تلک } *to, up to, till.*
توڑي

لگ *near, to, as far as.*

درمیان *between, among.*

بیچ *among, in, between.*

بیچمین *among, in the midst.*

آسپاس *round about.*

برابر *equal to, opposite to.*

لائق *fit, suitable, worthy.*

قابل *capable, worthy.*

موافق *according to.*

مطابق *conformable to.*

بغیر *without, besides.*

بدون *besides, without.*

ساتھ *in company, with.*

عوض *instead.*

بدل (*badal*) *in exchange, instead.*

هاتھ *into the hand.*

پار *over, across, through.*

براي *by reason, for, to.*

سوا
سواي } *besides.*

روبرو *face to face, in the presence.*

The most usual, too, of the postpositions, which become compounds by taking كي (*kī*), or the feminine genitive of a pronoun before them, are—

طرف *on the side, towards.*	نِسْبت *in relation, in respect.*
طرح *in the manner, like.*	بابت *on the subject.*
خاطِر *for the sake, for.*	معرِفت *by means, by.*

35. Adverbs admit of various divisions; and are too numerous to be here fully detailed. The adverb of time or place is often derived from the demonstrative, interrogative, or relative pronouns, though many are of other sources; and, a few of the words before described as compound postpositions, are of frequent use as adverbs: so,—

آگي *in front, before.*	جب تک or جب تلک *till when, until.*
پِيچْهي *in the rear, back.*	جب كبْهي *whenever.*
اُوپر *up.*	جب نه تب *perpetually.*
باهِر or باهر *out.*	تَو or تو or تد or تب *then.*
اب *now.*	تب تک or تب تلک *till then, so long.*
اب تلک or اب تک *till now, yet.*	يهان *here, this place.*
كد or كب *when?*	يهِين *exactly here.*
كدْهِي or كبْهِي / كدْهو or كبْهُو *ever, sometime.*	يهان تک or يهان تلک or يهان لگ or يهان توڙي *hitherto, to this degree.*
كبْهِي كبْهِي &c. *sometimes.*	وهان *there, that place.*
كبْهِي نه كبْهِي *some time or other.*	
كب سي *since when? how long ago?*	
كبْهِي نهِين *never.*	
جو or جد or جب *when.*	

وَهِين *exactly there.*

كَهان *where?*

كَهِين *somewhere, anywhere.*

كَهِين نه كَهِين *somewhere or other.*

كَهِين نَهِين *nowhere.*

هر كَهِين *every where.*

اَور كَهِين *elsewhere.*

جَهان *where, which place.*

جَهان جَهان *wherever.*

جَهان تهان *here and there, everywhere.*

جَهان كَهِين *wherever.*

تَهان *there, that place.*

اِيدْهر or اِدْهر *here, hither.*

اُودْهر or اُدْهر *there, thither.*

كِيدْهر or كِدْهر *where? whither?*

جِيدْهر or جِدْهر *where, whither.*

تِيدْهر or تِدْهر *there, thither.*

كِدْهر سي &c. *whence?*

جِدْهر تِدْهر *here and there.*

هرگاه *every where.*

دُرون *in, within.*

بهِيتر *within.*

وَري *on this side, near.*

پَري *on that side, beyond.*

وارْپار *on both sides, across.*

آج *to day.*

كل *yesterday* or *to morrow.*

آج كل *nowadays, shortly.*

پرْسون *two days ago* or *to come.*

ترْسون *three days ago* or *to come.*

نرْسون *four days ago* or *to come.*

تڑْكي *at the dawn of day, early.*

سبيري *in the morning, early.*

هميشه *always, ever.*

نِت *always, ever.*

مُدام *always, eternally.*

گاه گاهي *some time or other.*

هنوز *yet.*

بهِي *also, too, moreover, even.*

The most common adverb of interrogation is كيُون (*kyūn̊*) or كيُونْكر (*kyūnkar*) *why? how?* or كِسْواسْطي (*kiswāstē*) *wherefore? why?*

The adverb of cause or reason, کیونکہ (*kyūṅki*) *because that*, or اِسواسطے (*iswāsṯē*) *for this reason.*

The adverb of similitude, جیسا (*jaisā*) *as, like as*, or گویا (*goyā*) *one might say, as it were.*

The adverb of explanation, جیسا کہ (*jaisā ki*) or چُنانچہ (*chunānchi*) *like as, so as*, or مثلاً (*misḻaṉ*) *for example.*

The adverb of peculiarity, هي (*hī*) or هِين (*hīṅ*, used as an affix or a separate word) or ي - (*ī*, as an affix only) *very, exactly.*

The adverb of assent, هان (*hāṅ*) or هون (*hūṅ*) or بلي (*balē*) *yes.*

The adverb of negation, نہ (*na*) or نہین (*nahīṅ*) *no, not, nay, nor, neither*, اهان (*ahāṅ*) or اُونهون (*ūṅhūṅ*) *nay, no, do not.*

The adverb of prohibition, مت (*mat*) *not, do not.*

36. The Conjunction (حرفِ جُملہ *ḥarf-i-jumla*) may be—

Conditional—جو (*jo*) *if, when*, or اگر (*agar*) *if.*

Consequential—تو (*to*) *then* (answering to the conditional).

Of exception—پر (*par*) *but, moreover*, لیکن (*lekin*) *but, yet*, مگر (*magar*) *but, unless, except*, بلکہ (*balki*) *but.*

Of explanation— کہ (*ki*) *that, because.*

Conjunctive—اَور (*aur*) or و (*ō*) *and*: or (dakh.) هور (*haur*).

Disjunctive— یا (*yā*) *or*, خواہ (*khwāh*) *whether, or*, کہ (*ki*) *that, or.*

37. The Interjection may be—

Of addressing or calling to— اَي (*ai*) or اي (*ē*) or او (*ō*) or اجي (*ajī*) *O!* اري (*arē*) or ابي (*abē*) *you fellow!* &c., لو (*lō*) *look! see! there now!*

Of astonishment or of applause— واہ (*wāh*) or واہ واہ (*wāh wāh*) *well done! bravo!* اچّها (*achchhā*) or خوب (*khūb*) *well! excellent!*

Of grief or pain—آہ (*āh*) or ہائي (*hā'ē*) or وائي (*wā'ē*) or وا (*wā*) or واويلا (*wāwailā*) or ہائي ہائي (*hā'ē hā'ē*) *wo! alas! lackaday!*

Of applause or exultation—شاباش (*shābāsh*) *bravo!* جَي جَيكار (*jai jai kār*) *huzza!*

Of blame or censure—چهي (*chhī*), تَوبه تَوبه (*tauba tauba*), اُف (*uf*), *tush! fy!*

CHAPTER VI.

NUMERALS.

38. The Cardinal numbers, from one to one hundred, with Indian, Arabic, and European figures representing them, are as follows:—

FIGURES.				FIGURES.			
Europ.	Arab.	Ind.		Europ.	Arab.	Ind.	
1	۱	१	... ... (*ēk*) ایک	9	۹	९	... ... (*nau*) نَو
2	۲	२	... ... (*dō*) دو	10	۱۰	१०	... ... (*das*) دس
3	۳	३	... ... (*tīn*) تین	11	۱۱	११	... ... (*igārah*) اِگارہ
4	۴	४	... ... (*chār*) چار	12	۱۲	१२	... ... (*bārah*) بارہ
5	۵	५	... ... (*pānch*) پانچ	13	۱۳	१३	... ... (*tērah*) تیرہ
6	۶	६	... ... (*chha*) چهه	14	۱۴	१४	... (*chaudah*) چَودہ
7	۷	७	... ... (*sāt*) سات	15	۱۵	१५	... (*pandrah*) پندرہ
8	۸	८	... ... (*āṭh*) آٹھ	16	۱۶	१६	... ... (*sōlah*) سولہ

FIGURES.				FIGURES.			
Europ.	*Arab.*	*Ind.*		*Europ.*	*Arab.*	*Ind.*	
17	١٧	१७	(*satrah*) سترہ	38	٣٨	३८	(*aṭ'htīs*) اٹھتیس
18	١٨	१८	(*aṭ'hārah*) اٹھارہ	39	٣٩	३९	(*untālīs*) انتالیس
19	١٩	१९	(*unīs*) اُنیس	40	۴٠	४०	(*chālīs*) چالیس
20	٢٠	२०	(*bīs*) بیس	41	۴١	४१	(*iktālīs*) اکتالیس
21	٢١	२१	(*ikkīs*) اکیس	42	۴٢	४२	(*bē'ālīs*) بیالیس
22	٢٢	२२	(*bā'īs*) بائیس	43	۴٣	४३	(*tētālīs*) تیتالیس
23	٢٣	२३	(*tē'īs*) تیئس	44	۴۴	४४	(*chau'ālīs*) چوالیس
24	٢۴	२४	(*chaubīs*) چوبیس	45	۴٥	४५	(*paintālīs*) پینتالیس
25	٢٥	२५	(*pachīs*) پچیس	46	۴٦	४६	(*chhī'ālīs*) چھیالیس
26	٢٦	२६	(*chhabbīs*) چھبیس	47	۴٧	४७	(*saintālīs*) سینتالیس
27	٢٧	२७	(*satā'īs*) ستائیس	48	۴٨	४८	(*aṭ'htālīs*) اٹھتالیس
28	٢٨	२८	(*aṭ'hā'īs*) اٹھائیس	49	۴٩	४९	(*unchās*) اُنچاس
29	٢٩	२९	(*untīs*) اُنتیس	50	٥٠	५०	(*pachās*) پچاس
30	٣٠	३०	(*tīs*) تیس	51	٥١	५१	(*ikāwan*) اکاون
31	٣١	३१	(*iktīs*) اکتیس	52	٥٢	५२	(*bāwan*) باون
32	٣٢	३२	(*batīs*) بتیس	53	٥٣	५३	(*tirpan*) ترپن
33	٣٣	३३	(*tētīs*) تیتیس	54	٥۴	५४	(*chauwan*) چون
34	٣۴	३४	(*chautīs*) چوتیس	55	٥٥	५५	(*pachpan*) پچپن
35	٣٥	३५	(*paintīs*) پینتیس	56	٥٦	५६	(*chhappan*) چھپن
36	٣٦	३६	(*chhattīs*) چھتیس	57	٥٧	५७	(*sattāwan*) ستاون
37	٣٧	३७	(*saintīs*) سینتیس	58	٥٨	५८	(*aṭ'hāwan*) اٹھاون

FIGURES.				FIGURES.			
Europ.	*Arab.*	*Ind.*		*Europ.*	*Arab.*	*Ind.*	
59	٥٩	५९	... (*unsaṭ'h*) اُنسٹھ	80	٨٠	८०	... ... (*assi*) اسّي
60	٦٠	६०	... ... (*sāṭ'h*) ساٹھ	81	٨١	८१	... (*ikāsī*) اِکاسي
61	٦١	६१	... (*iksaṭ'h*) اِکسٹھ	82	٨٢	८२	... ... (*bē'āsī*) بياسي
62	٦٢	६२	... (*bāsaṭ'h*) باسٹھ	83	٨٣	८३	... ... (*tirāsī*) تِراسي
63	٦٣	६३	... (*tirsaṭ'h*) تِرسٹھ	84	٨٤	८४	... (*chaurāsī*) چَوراسي
64	٦٤	६४	... (*chausaṭ'h*) چَوسٹھ	85	٨٥	८५	... (*pachāsī*) پچاسي
65	٦٥	६५	... (*painsaṭ'h*) پَینسٹھ	86	٨٦	८६	... (*chhī'āsī*) چھِياسي
66	٦٦	६६	(*chhī'āsaṭ'h*) چھِیاسٹھ	87	٨٧	८७	... (*satāsī*) ستاسي
67	٦٧	६७	... (*satsaṭ'h*) سَتسٹھ	88	٨٨	८८	... (*aṭ'hāsī*) اٹھاسي
68	٦٨	६८	... (*aṭ'hsaṭh*) اٹھسٹھ	89	٨٩	८९	... (*nau'āsī*) نَواسي
69	٦٩	६९	... (*unhattar*) اُنہتر	90	٩٠	९०	.. ... (*nauwē*) نوي
70	٧٠	७०	... ... (*sattar*) سَتّر	91	٩١	९१	... (*ikānawē*) اِکانَوي
71	٧١	७१	... (*ikhattar*) اِکہتّر	92	٩٢	९२	... (*bānawē*) بانَوي
72	٧٢	७२	... (*bahattar*) بہتر	93	٩٣	९३	... (*tirānawē*) تِرانَوي
73	٧٣	७३	... ...(*tihattar*) تِہتّر	94	٩٤	९४	(*chaurānawē*) چَورانوي
74	٧٤	७४	...(*chauhattar*) چَوہتّر	95	٩٥	९५	(*pachānawē*) پچانَوي
75	٧٥	७५	... (*pachhattar*) پچھتّر	96	٩٦	९६	(*chhī'ānawē*) چھِیانَوي
76	٧٦	७६	...(*chhihattar*) چھِہتّر	97	٩٧	९७	... (*satānawē*) ستانَوي
77	٧٧	७७	... (*sat'hattar*) ستہتّر	98	٩٨	९८	... (*aṭ'hānawē*) اٹھانَوي
78	٧٨	७८	... (*aṭ'hhattar*) اٹھہتّر	99	٩٩	९९	... (*ninānawē*) ننانَوي
79	٧٩	७९	... .. (*unāsī*) اُناسي	100	١٠٠	१००	(*sau*) سو or (*sai*) سَي

Some variations from the above occur in the dialects, even, of Hindustan and Bombay; and still more in the Dakhni of Madras: for the latter, reference may be made to the appendix of the author's Hindustani Grammar; but the most striking differences discovered in the former are here subjoined. So, گیارہ *gyārah,* 11; اٹھارا *aṭ'hārā,* 18; اُنّیس *unnīs,* 19; ایکیس *ēkīs,* 21; ایکتیس *ēktīs,* 31; تینتیس *taintis,* 33; چونتیس *chauntīs,* 34; ارتیس *artīs,* 38; اُنچالیس *unchālīs,* 39; ایکتالیس *ēktālīs,* 41; تینتالیس *taintālīs,* 43; چھتالیس *chhatālīs,* 46; ارتالیس *artālīs,* 48; ایکاون *ēkāwan,* 51; چوپن *chaupan,* 54; پچاون *pachāwan,* 55; ایکسٹھ *ēksaṭ'h,* 61; چھاچھٹ *chhāchhaṭ* or چھہ سٹھ *chha-saṭ'h,* 66; ارسٹھ *arsaṭ'h,* 68; ایکہتر *ēkhattar,* 71; ترہتر *tirhattar,* 73; چھہتر *chha-hattar,* 76; ایکاسي *ēkāsī,* 81; باسي *bāsī,* or براسي *birāsī,* 82; پنچاسي *panchāsī,* 85; چھاسي *chhāsī,* 86; نود *nauwad,* 90; ایکانوي *ēkānawē* or اکانوي *ikānauwē,* 91; بانوي *bānauwē* or برانوي *birānauwē,* 92; ترانوي *tirānauwē,* 93, &c.; پنچانوي *panchānawē,* 95; چھانوي *chhānawē,* 96; نوانوي *nau'ānawe,* 99.

a. The series after one hundred is continued thus, ایک سو ایک *ēk sau ēk,* 101; دو سو پچیس *do sau pachīs,* 225; ایک هزار اور ایک *ēk hazār aur ēk,* 1001; ایک هزار پانچ سو اکیس *ēk hazār pānch sau ikkīs,* 1521.

b. When the word ایک is immediately subsequent to another numeral or other numerals, it may convey the meaning of *near* or *about, one more or less than* such number or numbers; as, سو ایک *about a hundred;* دو سو دو ایک *near two hundred and two:* and, if a noun is used, it generally precedes the numeral, when this sense is intended; so, آدمي دس ایک *about ten men;* گھڑي دو ایک بعد *two gharīs or so afterwards.*

39. The Ordinals are—

1st. پہلا *pahlā.*	6th. چھٹھا *chhaṭ'hā* or چھٹوان *chhaṭwāṅ.*
2nd. دوسرا *dūsrā.*	7th. ساتوان *sātwāṅ.*
3rd. تیسرا *tīsrā.*	8th. آٹھوان *āṭ'hwāṅ.*
4th. چوتھا *chaut'hā.*	9th. نوان *nauwāṅ.*
5th. پانچوان *pānchwāṅ.*	10th. دسوان *daswāṅ.*

And so forth, by adding generally وان (*wāṅ*) or occasionally ان (*āṅ*) to other cardinal numbers.

40. The common aggregate or collective numbers are—

سیکڑا *saikṛā*, 100.	لاکھ *lāk'h*, 100,000.
ہزار *hazār*, 1000.	کڑوڑ *kaṛōṛ*, 10,000,000.*

41. In a distributive sense the numerals, whether cardinals or ordinals, are repeated; as, ایک ایک *one by one;* دس دس *by tens;* بارھوان بارھوان *every twelfth* Proportionals and reduplicatives are formed by adding گنا *gunā*, or, more especially with regard to the folds or rows of any material, تہا *tahā*, or لڑا *laṛā*, or پرتا *partā* to the modified forms of the cardinals as used in composition, and in some cases to the unaltered forms; so, اکتہا *single,* دولڑا *double,* تیپرتا *treble,* چوگنا *quadruple,* پچتہا *quintuple,* چھہ لڑا *sextuple,* ستپرتا *septuple,* آٹھہ گنا *octuple,* نوتہا *nine fold,* دس گنا *ten fold.* With Persian numerals,

---

* In the decimal arrangement of numbers, the rank or degree of units is termed ایکائي *ēkā'ī;* that of tens, دھائي *dahā'ī;* that of hundreds, سیکڑا *saikṛā* (or at Bombay, سینکرا *sēnkrā*); that of thousands, ہزارا *hazārā;* that of tens of thousands, دس ہزارا *das-hazārā;* that of hundreds of thousands, لکھا *lakk'hā*, &c.

چند is much used for the same purpose; as, دوچند *twofold, twice as much;* سه چند *treble;* چہار چند *quadruple;* نه چند *nine fold;* ده چند *ten fold:* whilst برابر or تہ may be subjoined in a like meaning to the simple forms of the cardinals as before given, or to the Persian nouns of number; so, دو برابر *twice as much;* تین تہ *three fold;* سات برابر or هفت تہ *seven fold.*

42. The usual terms for fractionals are—

¼	پاو *pā'ō.*	1¼	سوا *sawā* (with a quarter).
⅓	تہاي *tihā'ī.*	1½	ڈيڑه *ḍēṛh.*
⅜	ڈيڑه پاو *ḍeṛh pā'ō.*	1¾	پوني دو *paunē* (quarter less) *dō.*
½	آدها *ādhā.*	2¼	سوا دو *sawā dō.*
⅔	دو تہاي *dō tihā'ī.*	3½	ساڑهي تين *sāṛ'hē* (with a half) *tīn.*
¾	پون *paun,** or تين پاو *tīn pā'ō.*	19¾	پوني بيس *paune bīs.*

And with the aggregate numbers, these terms are used as follows—

75 پوني سو *paunē sau* (100-$\frac{100}{4}$). †	1,250 سوا هزار *sawā hazār.*
125 سوا سو *sawā sau* (100+$\frac{100}{4}$).	1,500 ڈيڑه هزار *ḍeṛh hazār.*
150 ڈيڑه سو *ḍēṛh sau* (100+$\frac{100}{2}$).	1,750 پوني دو هزار *paunē dō hazār.*
175 پوني دو سو *paunē dō sau*(200-$\frac{100}{4}$)	2,250 سوا دو هزار *sawā dō hazār.*
225 سوا دو سو *sawā dō sau*(200+$\frac{100}{4}$)	2,500 اڑهائي هزار *aṛ'hā'ī hazār.*
250 اڑهائي سو *aṛhā'ī sau.*	75,000 پوني لاكه *paunē lāk'h.*§
750 ساڑهي سات سو *sāṛhē sāt sau.*‡	125,000 سوا لاكه *sawā lāk'h.*

* At Bombay, پونا *paunā.* † At Bombay, پونا سو *paunā sau.*

‡ At Bombay, پونا هزار *paunā hazār.* § At Bombay, پونا لاكه *paunā lāk'h.*

150,000 ڈیڑھ لاکھ *ḍeṛh lāk'h.*	225,000 سوا دو لاکھ *sawā dō lāk'h.*
175,000 پونے دو لاکھ *paunē dō lāk'h.*	250,000 اڑھائي لاکھ *aṛ'hā'ī lāk'h.*

CHAPTER VII.

FORMATION OF DERIVATIVES.

43. Abstract nouns are often obtained from adjectives by subjoining

ي (ī)*	as	چوڑائي *breadth,*	from	چوڑا *broad.*
پا (pā)	„	† بڑھاپا *old age,*	„	بوڑھا *old.*
پن (pan)	„	موٹاپن *fatness,*	„	موٹا *fat.*
پنا (panā)	„	بیواپنا *widowhood*	„	بیوا *widow.*
س (s)	„	†مٹھاس *sweetness,*	„	میٹھا *sweet.*
ہٹ (haṭ)	„	کڑواہٹ *bitterness,*	„	کڑوا *bitter.*
تا (tā)	„	کوملتا *softness,*	„	کومل *soft.*
تي (tī)	„	کمتي *deficiency,*	„	کم *little.*
ن (n)	„	اونچان *height,*	„	اونچا *high.*

Sometimes, though but rarely, by subjoining to primitive nouns substantive—

ت (at)	as	آدمیت *humanity,*	from	آدمي *man.*
ایت (āyat)	„	پنچایت *a council,*	„	پانچ *five.*

---

* When the original word terminates in ہ silent, گ becomes substituted for that letter before the affix ي, (ī); so, تازگي *freshness*, from تازہ *fresh:* and, in Dakhni, اگي (āgī) or ایگي (ā'egī) occurs as an affix to form abstracts.

† A long vowel is sometimes shortened before the affixes, as in these instances.

Abstract or verbal nouns, moreover, are abundantly derived from verbs; some having the same form as the imperative in the second person singular; others resembling the past or present participle in either gender; so, بول *speech;* ڈر *fear;* مار *beating;* بولتا *the faculty of speech,* from بول *speak;* گنتي *a reckoning,* from گن *count;* کہا *a saying* or *order, dictum,* from کہہ *say.* They are, also, to be obtained from the second person singular of the imperative, by adding—

و (*ō*)	as	دباؤ *pressure,*	from	دبا *press down.*
اؤ (*ā'ō*)	,,	چڑھاؤ *ascent,*	,,	چڑھ *ascend.*
ي (*ī*)	,,	کھلاي *a feeding,*	,,	کھلا *feed.*
اي (*ā'ī*)	,,	بوائي *a sowing,*	,,	بو *sow.*
ن (*an*)	,,	جلن *a burning,*	,,	جل *burn.*
وا (*wā*)	,,	بہلاوا *deception,*	,,	بہلا *deceive.*
وٹ (*waṭ*)	,,	بناوٹ *contrivance,*	,,	بنا *contrive.*
ہٹ (*haṭ*)	,,	بلاہٹ *a calling,*	,,	بلا *call.*

And, to Persian adjectives, or to imperatives of verbs, ش (*ish*) is often added to form nouns of this description, not unfrequently used in Hindustani; so, پیدایش *production,* from پیدا *produced;* دانش *knowledge,* from دان *know.*

44. The name of the agent or doer is commonly obtained by subjoining والا (*wālā*) or ہارا (*hārā*) each liable to change for gender, number, and case, to the inflected infinitive of a verb; as, لکھنے والا *writer,* مارنیہارا *smiter:* nouns of the like use are, moreover, sometimes had from verbal roots by affixing—

ک (*ak*)	as	لیکھک *a writer,*	from	لکھ *write.*
اک (*āk*)	,,	پیراک *a swimmer,*	,,	پیر *swim.*
اہا (*āhā*)	,,	دوڑاہا *a runner,*	,,	دوڑ *run.*

وڑا (*ōṛā*)	as	بھگوڑا *a deserter*,	from	بھاگ *flee.*
ویّا (*waiyā*)	„	گویّا *a singer*,	„	گا *sing.*

And, words denoting the manager or agent in anything, are occasionally formed from nouns, by the addition of—

وال (*wāl*)	as	گھٹوال		
وار (*wār*)	„	گھٹوار } *a wharfinger*,	from	گھاٹ *a wharf.*
ھا (*hā*)	„	دُلکیھا *a trotter*,	„	دُلکي *a trot.*
ھار (*hār*)	„	چُوڑیھار *bracelet-seller*,	„	چُوڑي *bracelet.*
ار (*ār*)	„	چمار *a currier*,	„	چام *leather.*
وا (*wā*)	„	مچھوا *a fisherman*,	„	مچھ *a fish.*
و (*ū*)	„	پہرو *a watchman*,	„	پہر *a watch.*
یرا (*ērā*)	„	سنپیرا *snake-catcher*,	„	سانپ *snake.*
ي (*ī*)	„	سندیسي *a messenger*,		سندیس *a message.*
یا (*iyā*)	„	مکھنیا *butter-man*,	„	مکھن *butter.*
یارا (*iyārā*)	„	گھسیارا *grass-cutter*,	„	گھاس *grass.*
یت (*ait*)	„	بھالَیت *spearman*,	„	بھالا *spear.*
پال (*pāl*)	„	گوپال *a cowherd*,	„	گو *cow.*
وان (*wān*)	„	گاڑیوان *a carter*,	„	گاڑي *cart.*
واھا (*wāhā*)	„	ھلواھا *ploughman*,	„	ھل *a plough.*
بان (*bān*)	„	دربان *a porter*,	„	در *a door.*
بند (*band*)	„	نعلبند *a farrier*,	„	نعل *a horseshoe.*
بر (*bar*)	„	رھبر *a guide*,	„	راہ *a way.*
باز (*bāz*)	„	مرغباز *cockfighter*,	„	مرغ *a cock.*
چي (*chī*)	„	طنبورچي *a drummer*,	„	طنبور *a drum.*
دار (*dār*)	„	زمیندار *a landholder*,	„	زمین *land.*

زن (*zan*)	as تیرزن *an archer*,	from تیر *an arrow*.	
ساز (*sāz*)	„ سخن ساز *an orator*,	„ سخن *speech*.	
کار (*kār*)	„ بدکار *evildoer*,	„ بد *evil*.	
گار (*gār*)	„ گناهگار *sinner*,	„ گناه *sin*.	
گر (*gar*)	„ سوداگر *a merchant*	„ سودا *trade*.	

45. The noun of place is sometimes the same in form as the infinitive of the verb; as, in هرن کا رمناهي *it is a range* or *park for deer*; but, it is more frequently formed from substantives by affixing—

ستان (*istān*)	as قبرستان *burying-place*,	from قبر *a grave*.	
ستان (*stān*)	„ هندوستان *India*,	„ هندو *Indian*.	
ستهان (*sthān*)	„ ديوستهان *a temple*,	„ ديو *a god*.	
ستهل (*sthal*)	„ ديوستهل *a temple*,	„ ديو *a god*.	
الا (*ālā*)	„ سوالا *Siva's temple*,	„ سو *Siva*.	
ل (*al*)	„ ديول *a temple*,	„ ديو *a god*.	
باڙي (*bāṛī*)	„ پهولباڙي *a flower-garden*,	پهول *a flower*.	
واڙي (*wāṛī*)	„ پهولواڙي *a flower-garden*,	پهول *a flower*.	
سال (*sāl*)	„ گهڙسال *a stable*,	„ گهوڙا *a horse*.	
سالا (*sāla*)	„ گاوسالا *a cow-house*,	„ گاو *a cow*.	
پور (*pūr*)	„ غازيپور *city of Ghāzī*,	„ غازي	*proper names*.
نگر (*nagar*)	„ احمدنگر *city of Aḥmad*,	„ احمد	*proper names*.
اباد (*ābād*)	„ حيدراباد *city of Haidar*,	„ حيدر	*proper names*.
دان (*dān*)	„ قلمدان *a pen-case*,	„ قلم *a pen*.	
زار (*zār*)	„ لالهزار *a tulip-bed*,	„ لاله *a tulip*.	
شن (*shan*)	„ گلشن *a rose-bower*,	„ گل *a rose*.	
گاه (*gāh*)	„ آرامگاه *a resting-place*,	„ آرام *rest*.	

46. The noun of instrument may be the same in form as the infinitive of a verb; or, it may be obtained by adding ن (*an*) or نِي (*nī*) to the second person singular of an imperative; so, بيلنا or بيلن *a rolling-pin,* from بيل *roll*; كترني *a pair of scissors,* from كتر *clip.* In the instance of گولا *a ball,* this noun seems formed from the adjective گول *round,* by the addition of ا (*ā*): and, from substantives it may be had by affixing—

ال (*āl*) as گھڑيال *an hour-bell,* from گھڑي *gharī.*
يل (*ēl*) „ نكيل *a camel's nose-stick* ناك *a nose.*
ه (*a*) „ دسته *a handle,* „ دست *a hand.*
انه (*āna*) „ انگشتانه *a thimble,* انگشت *a finger.*
ك (*ak*) „ چشمك *spectacles,* „ چشم *an eye.*

47. A diminutive noun is obtained from the common noun by adding—

ا (*ā*) as بٹيا *a little daughter,* from بيٹي *a daughter.*
يل (*ēl*) „ بگھيل } *a tiger's whelp,* „ باگھ *a tiger.*
يلا (*ēlā*) „ بگھيلا }
ِيا (*iyā*) „ كھٹيا *a small bedstead,* „ كھاٹ *a bedstead.*
وا (*wā*) „ مردوا *a manikin,* „ مرد *a man.*
ك (*ak*) „ توپك *a musket,* „ توپ *a cannon.*
ِيچه (*īcha*) „ باغيچه *a little garden,* „ باغ *a garden.*
چه (*cha*) „ ديگچه } *a kettle,* „ ديگ *a caldron.*
چي (*chī*) „ ديگچي }

Or, by changing a final ا (*ā*) to ي (*ī*); as, رسي *a string,* from رسا *a rope*; گولي *a bullet, a pill,* from گولا *a ball.*

48. Adjectives may be formed from substantives by prefixing—

ا (*a*)	as	اپھل *fruitless,*	from	پھل *fruit.*
ان (*an*)	,,	انہونا *impossible,*	,,	هونا *to be, being.*
نا (*nā*)	,,	نااُمّید *hopeless,*	,,	اُمّید *hope.*
لا (*lā*)	,,	لاچار *helpless,*	,,	چاره *help.*
نِ (*ni*)	,,	نِڈر *fearless,*	,,	ڈر *fear.*
نِر (*nir*)	,,	نِرادر *disrespectful,*	,,	آدر *respect.*
بِ (*bi*)	,,	بِمل *undefiled,*	,,	مل *filth.*
بي (*bē*)	,,	بیخبر *incautious,*	,,	خبر *care.*
بد (*bad*)	,,	بد ذات *ill-bred,*	,,	ذات *nature.*
کم (*kam*)	,,	کم بخت *wretch,*	,,	بخت *fortune.*
هم (*ham*)	,,	هم آهنگ *concordant,*	,,	آهنگ *sound.*
سُ (*su*)	,,	سُروپ *well-formed,*	,,	روپ *form, shape.*
کُ (*ku*)	,,	کُڈھنگ *ill-mannered,*	,,	ڈھنگ *manners.*

Or, by affixing—

ـي (*ī*)	as	بازاري *of the market,*	from	بازار *market.*
ـين (*īn*)	,,	چوبين *wooden,*	,,	چوب *wood.*
ـينه (*īna*)	,,	ريشمينه *silken,*	,,	ريشم *silk.*
ـيانه (*iyāna*)	,,	ساليانه *annual,*	,,	سال *year*
ـيلا (*īlā*)	,,	رسيلا *juicy,*	,,	رس *juice.*
يلا (*ēlā*)	,,	گھريلا *domestic,*	,,	گھر *house.*
ـَيل (*ail*)	,,	دنتيل *tusked,*	,,	دنت *a tooth.*
مند (*mand*)	,,	دَولتمند *wealthy,*	,,	دَولت *wealth.*
مان (*mān*)	,,	بدّهمان *wise,*	,,	بدّه *wisdom.*
ونت (*want*)	,,	بلونت *powerful,*	,,	بل *power.*
لُو (*lū*)	,,	جھگڑالو *quarrelsome,*	,,	جھگڑا *quarrel.*

ا (*ā*)	as	بھوکھا *hungry,*	from	بھوکھ *hunger.*
ہ (*a*)	,,	دوسالہ *biennial,*	,,	دوسال *two years.*
´ ہلا (*ahlā*)	,,	سونہلا *golden,*	,,	سونا *gold.*
لا (*lā*)	,,	پچھلا *hindermost,*	,,	پیچھا *the rear.*
و (*ū*)	,,	دیدارو *sightly,*	,,	دیدار *view.*
کا (*kā*)	,,	اکا *single,*	,,	ایک *one.*
نا (*nā*)	,,	دونا *double,*	,,	دو *two.*
را (*rā*)	,,	تیسرا *third,*	,,	تین *three.*
وان (*wāṅ*)	,,	دسوان *tenth,*	,,	دس *ten.*
ها (*hā*)	,,	پنیہا *aquatic,*	,,	پاني *water.*
جوگ (*jōg*)		بیاهني جوگ *marriageable,*	,,	بیاهنا *marrying.*
وار (*wār*)	,,	سوگوار *grievous,*	,,	سوگ *grief.*
بند (*band*)	,,	هتهیار بند *armed,*	,,	هتهیار *arms.*
مند (*mand*)	,,	عقلمند *intelligent,*	,,	عقل *intelligence.*
انہ (*āna*)	,,	طفلانہ *childish,*	,,	طفل *a child.*
دار (*dār*)	,,	وفادار *faithful,*	,,	وفا *fidelity.*
سار (*sār*)	,,	کوهسار *mountainous,*	,,	کوہ *a mountain.*
گین (*gīn*)	,,	غمگین *sorrowful,*	,,	غم *sorrow.*
ناک (*nāk*)	,,	هولناک *terrible,*	,,	هول *terror.*
ور (*war*)	,,	نامور *renowned,*	,,	نام *a name.*
آور (*āwar*)	,,	زوراور *strong,*	,,	زور *strength.*
زا (*zā*)	,,	ولایتزا *foreign-born,*	,,	ولایت *foreign country.*
زادہ (*zāda*)		نجیب زادہ *noble-born,*	,,	نجیب *noble (man).*
گون (*gūn*)	,,	نیلگون *blue-coloured,*	,,	نیل *blue, indigo.*

فام (*fām*) as زعفران فام *saffron-coloured,* from زعفران *saffron.*
مايل (*mā'il*) „ زردي مايل *yellowish,* „ زردي *yellowness.*
كونا (*kōnā*) „ چوكونا *four-cornered,* „ چو in comp. *four.*
گوشه (*gōsha*) „ شش گوشه *hexagonal* „ شش *six.*

49. Adjectives of intensity may be obtained from verbs, by affixing to the second person singular of the imperative اك (*āk*) اكا (*ākā*) or انكا (*āṅkā*) or ويا (*waiyā*); as, دوڑاك *a great runner,* from دوڑ *run;* لڑانكا *quarrelsome,* from لڑ *fight;* گويا *eloquent,* from گو *speak.*

50. Adjectives, as well as adverbs, of which latter some notice has already been taken at par. 35, may be derived from pronouns in various ways; and, like their originals, they are used demonstratively, interrogatively, or relatively: so, from يهه (or Dakh. يهه *yah*) *this,* are deduced اتنا or ايتنا or اتا or ايتا *this-much, so much, so many;* ايسا *this-like, such;* يوں or يونكر *in this manner, thus:* from وه (or Dakh. وه *wah*) *that,* اتنا or اتا or ويتنا or ويتا *that-much, so many;* ويسا *that-like, so;* ووں or وونكر *in that manner, so:* from كون *who? what? which?* كتنا or كيتنا or كتا or كيتا *how much? how many?* كي *how many?* كيسا *what like? what sort of? how?* كيوں or كيونكر *how? in what manner? why?* كهيں *somewhere, anywhere:* from جو or جوں *who, what, which,* جتنا or جيتا *what quantity, as much as, as many as;* جي *as many;* جيسا *what-like, as;* جوں or جيوں or جيونكر *as, like as:* and, from سو or توں *that,* come تتنا or تيتا *so much, so many;* تي *so many;* تيسا *such, so;* توں or تيوں or تيونكر *so, in that manner.*

51. Transitive and causal verbs have been already noticed at paragraph 27. They are generally formed from other verbs by the interposition or addition of ا or و or ي or وا or لا. The letter ا is frequently inserted after the first consonant of the root; and sometimes, though but rarely, it follows the second; in other cases, it is added to the

last: so, کاٹنا *to cut,* from کٹنا *to be cut;* نکالنا *to take out,* from نکلنا *to issue;* بچانا *to save,* from بچنا *to escape:* و and ي are used immediately before the last consonant of the root; as, کھولنا *to open,* from کھلنا *to be opened;* پیسنا *to pound* or *grind,* from پسنا *to be ground:* and وا or لا is always subjoined to the root; so, ڈروانا *to cause to frighten,* from ڈرنا *to fear;* دلانا *to cause to give,* from دینا *to give.* When the root, moreover, is a monosyllable ending in ا or و or ي, the last letter is commonly dropped and ل inserted before the causal sign ا or وا; as, کھلانا and کھلوانا *to feed* and *to cause to feed,* from کھانا *to eat;* سلانا and سلوانا *to cause to sleep* and *to cause to put to sleep,* from سونا *to sleep;* سلانا and سلوانا *to cause to sew* and *to cause to be sewed,* from سینا *to sew.*

CHAPTER VIII.

SYNTAX.

52. The terms usually applied to grammar are صرف و نحو (*ṣarf o naḥw*) which may be translated *inflection* or *accidence* and *syntax:* the first has already been treated of, in Chapters II., III., and IV. especially; and the latter, with which practice in the language will give the best acquaintance, seems not to require here any very minute or lengthened explanation.

53. The noun in the genitive case usually precedes that with which it is constructed, as does the adjective its substantive: with these exceptions, and unless a conjunction occurs, a relative pronoun, an interjection or vocative, or some word which by way of especial distinction or of emphasis takes the lead, the nominative case to the verb generally presents itself first in a sentence; nouns in other cases if required, a participle or adverb, may follow almost promiscuously;

but, the verb generally finishes the whole: so, اِس قِصّي کا فايِدہ يِہہ هَي کِہ کم ذاتون کِي صُحبت آزاد کو غُلام اَور غُلام کو خراب کرتِي هَي *of this story the advantage this is, that of the low bred the society (makes) the free born a slave, and the slave ruined makes.* In poetry, however, but little regard is sometimes had to this arrangement: as, ' سُخن کِي طلبگار هَين عقلمند ' سُخن سي هَي نامِ نکويان بُلند ' *studious of language are the intelligent; by language is the name of the good exalted.*

54. Nouns of various genders, coming together in a sentence, require the adjective, verb, or participle, governed in common by them, to have the masculine form; as, اُس کي ماتا پِتا بهاي تِينون اُسکِي شادِي کِي فِکر مين تهي *her mother, father, brother (all) the three in the meditation of the marriage of her were.* With regard to inanimate beings, however, the adjective or participle usually agrees in gender with the noun, nearest which it is placed; so, تُمهاري بيتي کِي کِتاب و کاغذ يهان پڑي هَين *your son's book and paper are lying here.*

55. Two nouns, having reference to the same person or thing, may stand in apposition without any word intervening; as, اُس کا بهاي بِکرم *his brother Bikram.*

56. Notice has already been taken, at par. 6, of the changes to which the postposition کا is liable in construction: and, though this particle serves generally to link together words of various import, yet on certain occasions it seems to be idiomatically dropped, and especially after a noun of weight or measure; so, گنگا تِير پر *Ganges-bank-on;* هزار تولي سونا *a thousand tolas (of) gold:* and, on the contrary, its use in some cases may appear to us redundant; as, in فِکر کا لفظ *fikr's word,* or *the word fikr.* This postposition, moreover, is adopted to denote purpose, worth, size, possibility, totality, &c., as well as mere relationship; so, کهاني کِي کوٹهري *an eating room;*

بڑي سِر کا چھوکڑا *of a large head a boy*; دو سَو رُپَي کا گھوڑا *of two hundred rupees a horse*; يِہہ جِيني کِي نہِين *this (female) cannot live*; کھيت کا کھيت *the whole field*; سب کا سب *all together*; چِتر کا چِتر *all a picture*; رات کِي رات مين *in the dead of the night*; بات کِي بات مين *in the mere word*; چھِپي کا چھِپا *totally concealed.*

57. The nominative case is very often used when it is the object to a transitive verb; and, indeed, no inflection of a noun, except for the nominative case plural, can take place without a postposition or preposition immediately expressed or understood; the latter circumstance, however, not unfrequently occurs, there being many expressions which from use are become idiomatical without the postposition: so, اِس کا نام تو بتاؤ *do tell me the name of this*; گھر جا *house go, go home*; نہ آنکھون ديکھا نہ کانون سُنا *neither seen (with) eyes nor heard (with) ears*; گنگا کِناري *Ganges bank (on)*; اچھِي طرح *(in) a good manner*; اُس کي دو بيٹِي تھِين *(at the abode) of him were two daughters*, an ellipsis of some word, perhaps يہان occurring in this and generally in similar sentences. The nominative case, moreover, supplies the place of the accusative, when another word with the dative postposition occurs in the same sentence; unless both words happen to be pronouns, when each may be followed by its casual sign: so, تُو اپنِي لڑکِي ميري پُتر کو دي *thou thy own daughter to my son give*; مَين اُسي تم کو دُونگا *I will give him to you.*

58. When two or more words in the same oblique case are used together, the postposition is usually subjoined to the last only; as, سوني روپي تانبي لوھي و غيرہ کِي کھانين *mines of gold, silver, copper, iron,* &c.: and, if they are in an oblique case of the plural, though even a conjunction intervene, the plural sign may be omitted in all such words but the last; so, گوزن اَور ھرنون کِي کيا دِيجي شرح *how shall we give a description of the elks and deer?*

59. The simple postpositions follow immediately the nouns they govern; but, such nouns, participles, or adverbs, as are in common use postpositively, may sometimes precede the words with which they are constructed: so, ساتھ اُسكي or اُس كي ساتھ *with him;* مارے دھشت كي or دھشت كي مارے *through fear (stricken of fear);* گھوڑے كي پاس or پاس گھوڑے كي *near the horse.*

60. Adjectives, if immediately preceding or following the substantives they qualify, must be made to agree with them in gender, case, and number; but, when separated by any other word, they may be used in the uninflected form of the masculine singular, whatever the state or gender of the substantives may be; as, اُس كي مُنھ كو كالا كرو* *make his face black.*

61. With numerals, the singular form of a noun, whether in the nominative or any other case, is generally preferred to the plural; so, تِين سِپاهِي نے چار مرد كو مارا *three soldiers beat four men;* هزار گھوڑے سے كُچھ كم هوگا *there may be something less than a thousand horse:* yet masculine nouns capable of inflection usually take the nominative plural form, as feminine nouns may occasionally take the latter, when more than one in number is to be denoted; so, تِين گھوڑے *three horses;* چار بيٹياں *four daughters.*

62. When the feminine genitive of a pronoun or adjective, or even some feminine form of a verb, is used without any noun expressed, such common word as بات *affair, matter,* is generally understood; so, نه اپني كهتا نه اَور كي سُنتا *he neither mentions his own (affair) nor attends to (that) of others;* جوكُچھ هوني تھي سو هُوئي *whatever was to be, that (has) happened.*

63. In speaking of one's self with another, it is customary to give

---

* Yet كالا كرو may be regarded as a compound (nominal) verb: see par. 28.

the first person the precedence, and, for that person even the plural is often adopted, though an individual only is intended; so, مَین تَین or هم تُم جاوینگي *I and you will go.*

64. If the saying of a third person be reported, the same pronouns and the same words, in every respect, are commonly retained, as were used by the first speaker; so, اُس نے کہا کہ مَین نہ جاونگا *he said that I shall not go,* meaning in our idiom, *that he should not go;* راجا چاہا کِہ کھانڈا مار مرون *the king wished that striking the sword I will die,* meaning, *that he would die.*

65. The second personal pronoun is rarely used in the singular, unless from motives of adoration, endearment, familiarity, or contempt: in speaking respectfully to any one, the plural of this person at least must be adopted; but, when a dependant addresses his superior, or a great degree of deference is intended, آپ *self,* صاحِب *master,* حضرت *the presence,* مہاراج *great prince,* or some other such term of honour, must be used, and generally with a verb in the third person plural. In mentioning a third person, moreover, respectfully, the plural is substituted for the singular, as it is not unfrequently done in the first person; yet, when any one speaks of his own actions or circumstances with humility to a superior, or seeks even to address his friend with great respect, it is customary to substitute such words as بندہ or غُلام *slave,* فِدوِي *devoted,* عاجز *weak,* فقیر *beggar,* عاصِي *sinner,* &c.; or, in the latter case, دوستدار *friendly,* مُخلِص *sincere,* خَیرخواہ *wellwisher,* &c. for the first personal pronoun.

66. When a possessive pronoun, referring to the same person or thing as the subject of the sentence or the nominative case before the verb, is required, the common or reflective اپنا &c. must then be used; as, اپنا نام بتا *tell thy name;* راج پُتّر اپنے جِي مین کہنے لگا *the prince began to say in his own mind:* and this reflective possessive may even

be used substantively; as, جو اپنون هین کومارو گي تو کرو گي کس کي رکّهوالي *if you shall kill your very own, then the protection of whom will you make?* In a second member of a sentence, however, the peculiar possessive, and not the common, must be adopted; as, مَین اَور میرا باپ *I and my father.*

67. If used in a respectful sense merely, as noted at paragraph 65, the word آپ does not admit of inflection before postpositions; so, آپ کي چِرنجیو رَهني سي مُجهي سُکه هي *I have pleasure, Sir, in your living a long life:* and, to آپ when used as a term of respect, the Persian خُود (*khud*), of similar meaning, is at times subjoined; or, even the word لوگ *people,* or لوگون if plurality be intended.

68. The interrogative, کیا *what? which?* seems not immediately applicable to persons. It is often used by way of scorn, as well as to express satisfaction, astonishment, or desire: and, in these senses it may be followed by the appellations of human beings; so, کیا حرامزاده *what a scoundrel!* It may be, also, adopted discriminatively; as, کیا هِندو کیا مُسلمان *whether Hindū or Musalmān.*

69. The interrogative adverbs کَهان and کب are very emphatically used to denote non-existence, dissimilitude, or difference; as, کَهان وُه راجا کَهان وُه راني *where (is) that prince? where that princess?* meaning, that they exist not; کَهان راجا بهوج کَهان گنگا تیلي *where is king Bhoj? where Ganga the oilman?* importing that there is no resemblance between them.

70. Though the indefinite pronoun کوئي is generally applied to animate beings, as کُچه is to inanimate, yet this distinction is not always observed; as, in کوئي چیز *any thing,* کُچّه آدمي *some man.*

71. The verb commonly agrees in gender and number with the nominative or subject of the sentence; except, however, that to a number of irrational beings, taken collectively, a singular verb may be attributed; and, that in general a plural verb is used with such

terms of honour or respect in the singular as are often substituted for the second personal pronoun: so, وُہ چَوکي دِيا کرتا *he makes a practice of guarding*; لڑکي سبق پڑھتي تھي *the girl was reading a lesson*; سو گھوڑي آئي or سو گھوڑا آيا *a hundred horse* or *horses came*; مہاراج آپ بڑي مِحنت کرکي ھماري واسطي آئي ھين *your majesty has with great labour come on my account*. And, when two or more nominatives of different genders come together in the same member of a sentence, the verb and participles usually accord with the masculine in this particular, as exemplified at paragraph 54.

72. Transitive verbs in any past tense of the active voice, in construction with which the particle ني must follow the subject or agent,* if actually expressed, are made to agree in gender and number with the object of the sentence, provided that it is a noun, either understood, or stated as is most usual in the nominative case; but if the object be placed in the oblique case, or if it be a member of a sentence, the verb has invariably the form of the third person singular masculine. In this construction, the subject or agent, if actually expressed, is generally inflected by ني if capable of inflection; the first and second personal pronouns being the only words liable to change for case, that retain the form of the nominative, whether in the singular or plural, before this affix.† With the verb لانا *to bring*, however, which is in fact compounded of لي *take* and آنا *to come*, or with بولنا *to speak*, though the former seems in all cases to convey a transitive meaning and the latter sometimes so, this construction is never admitted; as, کوئي جَوبي مارو بينگن خريد لايا *a Brāhman purchased (and) brought an egg-plant*; وُہ بولا کہ *he said that*—.

---

* These remarks do not apply to the Dakhni, in which dialect the particle ني does not interrupt the usual concord of the verb with the nominative case.

† See, moreover, the note to paragraph 23.

73. The form of the infinitive serves for the gerund or verbal noun, and in many cases for the noun of instrument or of place, as has before been noticed: but, it is also not unfrequently used as an imperative, and imports the absolute necessity of the action intimated; so, اُس سي غافِل مت رهنا *(it is necessary) not to remain neglectful of him;* تم جلدي پهنچنا *you (must) arrive quickly;* مين تمهاري نهين مانني كا *I can by no means obey your (word);* يهه نهين رهني كا *this (is under the absolute necessity) of not remaining.*

74. The past and present participles, whether in the simple form or compounded with هوا, are much used in the state of the inflected masculine singular, whatever the gender or number of the governing noun may be, to denote some action incidental with, or preceding, that which the subsequent verb declares; as, اُسكي لِيي *(in the) taken of him* or *for his sake;* جِسكي ماري *(in the) stricken of which* or *by reason of which;* سب سازِ ايك سُرمين مِلائي هُوئي ناچتي تهي *having made to accord all the instruments in one tone (she) was dancing;* وُه چلتي هُوئي كهه گيا تها كِه اِس پرسوارهوتي نه كوڑا كِيجو نه ايڑ مارِيو *on going away he had kept saying that (on) becoming mounted on this do not use the whip nor strike the spur.* With هي the adverb of peculiarity or identity, or with وقت *time,* subjoined, the simple present participle, too, is thus very frequently brought into use; as, وُه ديكهتي هِي بهچك سي ره گيي *immediately on seeing that she remained as one aghast.*

75. Both the past and present simple participles, moreover, are often used absolutely, and sometimes substantively, in the invariable state of the inflected masculine singular, when constructed with a preceding noun, or even with a postposition or preposition, or with a genitive case; so, شام هُوئي *(on) the become evening;* صُبح هوتي *(on) the becoming morning;* پل مارتي *(in) the striking an eyelid;* بِنا سمجهي

without having understood; بِنا بات سُني *without having heard a word;* ميري رهتي (*in*) *the remaining of me* or *before me;* جِنكي ديكهي (*at*) *the sight of which;* سب كي ديكهتي (*in*) *the sight of all;* ايك دم بي سوچي مكر كي نه رهتا *one moment without the meditation of deceit he rests not.* It should be remarked, too, that both these participles are occasionally used as nouns in either gender: and, by the repetition of a participle, continuance of the action is frequently denoted.

76. The indefinite future or aorist may not only convey a present meaning, but it may be constructed with an auxiliary verb as a present participle even; yet, when used in the latter way, it may be often understood as retaining its future sense: so, اِس مين كوسون نِكل گيا ديكهي تو شام هوگيي *in this* (*space of time*) *he went forth* (*many*) *kos,* (*when*) *he looks then evening is become;* نه ٹهنڈا رُچي هَي نه گرم *neither cold nor hot pleases;* كهولُون هون *I am opening,* or *I am about to open.*

77. The adverb of prohibition مت as well as that of negation نه or نهين may be used either before, or after, verbs; but, نهين though unfit for construction with an imperative, is more emphatical and in more general use than نه with other forms of the verb; so, مت پوچهو *do not ask;* بهولِيو مت *by no means forget;* نه جانِيو *do not suppose.* And, when the emphatic نهين is adopted, it frequently supplants the present of the substantive verb at the end of a sentence; as, تيري شان كي ظُلم لايِق نهين *acts of cruelty* (*are*) *not becoming thy dignity.*

78. The conjunctions كه and جو *that,* are used at the beginning of one member of a sentence, which explains the object or reason of another generally preceding. The conjunction كه too may be used in the way of comparison or distinction; as, ايك آدمي مري بِهتر كه

اسکو کہ اسکو تمام شہر *(that) one man die is better than a whole city;* تو لیوي *thou mayest take either this or that:* it may, also, convey the sense of *saying that;* as, یہہ کہکر سنگھاسن منگایا اور پان تلک دیکر اس پر بٹھایا کہ تم اب اجیت هوي *saying this, he called for the throne, and having given him pān and tilak seated (him) on it, (saying) that you are now become invincible.* At times, though but rarely, کہ may be adopted as the relative pronoun, after the idiom of the Persians: and, in some cases, the application of it seems intended merely to connect the members of a sentence, the meaning in other respects appearing redundant.

79. The conditional conjunction اگر or جو *if* requires the consequential تو or پس *then* in the following member of the sentence; as, اگر کوئي اس مین تجھي پکڑي تو اسي میري پاس لي آنا *if any one should interrupt thee in this, then (fail not) to bring him to me:* yet, the conditional is sometimes idiomatically omitted; so, اس ني کہا مہاراج دوگي تو کیون نہ کہاونگا *this (person) said, Sir, (if) you will give, then why shall I not eat?*

80. The adverb جون or جیون must in general be answered by the correlative تون or تیون and جون جون by تون تون; in like manner, the emphatic adverb of time جونہین is followed by ونہین; so, جونہین کتي ني کہایا ونہین چھٹپٹاکي مر گیا *as soon as the dog ate it, at that very moment he tossing about expired.* As adverbs of manner جیون and تیون frequently assume کر; so, ‘ مین کہون جیونکر ’ ‘ تیونکر تین تیري هي کرنا کام *as I may say, so it is incumbent on thee to perform the business.*

81. The usual term of affirmation or assent is هان *(hāṅ) yes;* but, this may be understood, and قبلہ گاہ or پیرو مرشد or صاحب or some other appellation of respect only be expressed, especially in the reply of a servant to his master, or of an inferior to his superior.

82. The residence of any one is often denoted by یہاں and, if more than one place is mentioned, وہاں may be used distinctively for a similar purpose; as صاحِب کي یہاں جاؤ صاحِب کي وَہاں نہِین *go to the gentleman's house here, not to that there.* Sometimes, however, the mere genitive case is adopted, the adverb being understood; and the postposition پاس may be applied in the same manner as یہاں: so, نوکر چاکر جو اُس کي دَوڑي تو اُس کو اُس کي پاس سي پکڑ لیگَیي *the servants, who ran to her house, seized and took her away from it.*

83. Two words of similar meaning, which resemble each other in sound, are often brought into use where one alone might have sufficed, as in the instance of نوکر چاکر exemplified in the last paragraph: one of such words, however, seems frequently to have little or no meaning, and to be adopted for the sake of the sound chiefly; so, جھوٹھ موٹھ *falsehood,* کھُسر پھُسر *a whisper.* By a repetition, moreover, of nouns or pronouns, as well as of some other words, individuality may be intended; as, هر ایک آدمي ایک ایک گھڑا دُودھ کا بھرکر *each man having filled each a pitcher of milk;* اپني اپني بِدیا آزماوین *let us each try his own skill:* and, when two past participles of the same transitive verb come together, the latter of them being in the feminine gender, reciprocity of action is intended; so, کھینچا کھینچي *pulling and hauling;* کہا کہي *altercation;* مارا ماري *scuffle;* دیکھا دیکھي *competition, emulation.* Here, too, may be noticed such idiomatical repetitions of participles as بنا بنایا *ready made;* پکا پکایا *ready cooked;* بیٹھي بِٹھاي مین *in sitting still:* or, of nouns; as, بِیچون بیچ *in the very midst;* راتون رات *in the dead of the night;* کانون کان *with all (his) ears.*

84. To the names of different classes or sects of men, different appellatives are by way of distinction prefixed or subjoined; thus Brāhmans take چوبي or تِواري or دوبي or پانڈي; Musalmān Fakīrs

are addressed with شاه or صُوفي or پير ; Hindū devotees or religious people, with گُرُو or بهگت or گوسائِين or سائِين ; Rājpūts, with ٹهاکُر ; or Rājpūts and Sikhs, with راي or سِنگّهه ; Moghuls, with مِرزا before the proper name, or بيگ after ; Saiyids, with مير or سيّد ; Shaikhs, with شَيخ ; Pathāns, with خان ; Doctors, with پنڈِت or مَولَوي or مُلّا ; Merchants or Bankers, with ساه or سيٹهه ; Ladies, with خانم or بيگم or خاتُون or خاتُو or صاحِبه or بِبي , which are placed after the proper name, as امينه خانم , زينب صاحِبه : and, some of the most common terms of respectful address, used generally, are جهان پناه or مهاراج or قبلهٔ عالم *your Majesty!* پيرومُرشِد or خُداوَنّد *Sire!* صاحِب or مِيان or جِي or ٹهاکُر or لالا or بابُو *Sir! Master!* غرِيب پرور *cherisher of the poor!*

PART II.

VOCABULARY, ENGLISH AND HINDUSTANI.

NOUNS.

Celestials.

God, Deity, خُدا *khuda*, پرميسّوَر *paramēswar*, الله *allāh*.

Lord, ايسْور *īswar*, ربّ *rabb*.

Creator, خالِق *khālik*, كرْتار *kartār*, آفرِيدْگار *āfrīdgār*.

Godhead, Divinity, خُدائِي *khudā'ī*, اِيسْوَرْتا *īswartā*, اِلٰهِيّت *ilāhīyat*.

A god, a deity, ديو *dēv*, سُر *sur*, ديوْتا *dēvtā*.

Goddess, ديوِي *dēwī*, ديبِي *dēbī*, ديوتِن *dē'ōtin* (f.).*

Angel, فِرِشْتَه *firishta*, ملک *malak*, دُوت *dūt*, هاتِف *hātif*.

Heaven, سوَرگ *swarg*, آسْمان *āsmān*, بِہِشْت *bihisht* (f.).

Sky, Firmament, Atmosphere, آكاس *ākās* (or اكاس *akās*), آسْمان *āsmān*, فلک *falak*.

Infernals.

Devil, Satan, شَيطان *shaiṭān*, اِبْلِيس *iblīs*.

---

* For the convenience of the learner, feminine words not terminating in ي (ī) will be marked (f.) generally; as masculines ending in ي (ī) will be marked (m.).

Demon, اسر *asur*, ديو *dēv*, عِفرِيت *ʻifrīt*.

Ghost, Goblin, Fiend, بهوت *bhūt*, بهتنا *bhutnā*, پريت *prēt*.

Hell, جهنم *jahannam*, دوزخ *dōzakh*, نرك *narak*.

Fabulous beings.

One of the Genii, جن *jinn*.

Fairy, پري *parī*.

Some general Terms.

Thing, چيز *chīz* (f.), شي *shai* (f.), بست *bast*, درب *darb*.

Mode, Manner, ڈهب *ḍhab*, طور *ṭaur*, اسلوب *uslūb*, وضع *waẓʻ* (f.).

Kind, Species, جنس *jins* (f.), نوع *nauʻ*, قسم *ḳism*, ذات *ẕāt* (f.).

Whole, جمله *jumla*, جمع *jamʻ* (f.), سب *sab*.

Part, جز *juz*, حصه *ḥiṣṣa*, انس *ans*, کانڈ *kānḍ*, کهنڈ *khanḍ*.

Cause, سبب *sabab*, موجب *mūjib*, کارن *kāran*, باعث *bāʻiṣ*.

Nature, ذات *ẕāt* (f.), پرکرت *prakrit* (f.), بهاو *bhāv*, نهاد *nihād*.

Essence, جوهر *jauhar*, ذات *ẕāt* (f.), ماهيت *māhiyat* (f.), ست *sat*.

Element, عنصر *ʻunṣur*, تت *tat*, (proper sphere) ٹهکانا *ṭhikānā*.

Fortune, Lot, نصيب *naṣīb*, بهاگ *bhāg*, قسمت *ḳismat* (f.), بخت *bakht*.

Fate, Destiny, لکها *likhā*, قضا *ḳaẓā* (f.), تقدير *taḳdīr*, قسمت *ḳismat* (f.).

Beginning, ابتدا *ibtidā* (f.), پهل *pahal*, آغاز *āghaz*, شروع *shurūʻ*.

End, انت *ant*, آخر *ākhir*, انتها *intihā* (f.), نهايت *nihāyat* (f.).

Time, زمان *zamān*, کال *kāl*, سمي *samai*, وقت *waḳt*, دهر *dahr*.

Space (absolute), ادهر *ad'har*, آکاس *ākas*.

Order, تدبير *tadbīr* (f.), ڈهب *ḍhab*, ترتيب *tartīb* (f.).

Number, عدد *ādad*, تعداد *ti'dād* (f.), سنکهیا *sankhyā* (f.).

Form, Figure, صورت *ṣūrat* (f.), شکل *shakl* (f.), هیأت *hai'at* (f.).

Matter, هیولا *hayūlā*, جوهر *jauhar*, مادّه *mādda*.

Body, جسم *jism*, کاٹهی *kāṭhī*, بدن *badan*, دیه *dēh* (f.).

World, سنسار *sansār*, عالم *ālam*, جهان *jahān*, دنیا *dunyā* (f.).

East, پورب *pūrab*, مشرق *mashriḳ*, شرق *sharḳ*.

West, پچهم *pachchham*, مغرب *maghrab*, غرب *gharb*.

North, اتر *uttar*, شمال *shamāl* (or *shimāl*).

South, دکهن *dakhan* or دکّهن *dakkhan*, جنوب *janūb*.

Spirit, Soul, روح *rūḥ* (f.), نفس *nafs*, جان *jān* (m. f.).

Life, جي *jī* (m.), حیات *ḥayāt* (f.), جان *jān* (m. f.), پران *prān* or *parān*.

Light, اجالا *ujālā*, نور *nūr*, جوت *jōt* (f.), روشنائي *roshnā'ī*.

Darkness, اندهیرا *andhērā*, تاریکي *tārīkī*, ظلمت *ẓulmat* (f.).

Heat, حرارت *ḥarārat*, تپن *tapan* (f.), گرمي *garmī*.

Cold, Coldness, ٹهنڈ *ṭhanḍ* (f.), سردي *sardī*, جاڑا *jāṛā*.

The Elements.

Ether, آکاس *ākās* (or *akās*), اثیر *aṣīr*.

Fire, آگ *āg* (f.), آتش *ātash* (f.).

Air, هوا *hawā* (f.), پون *pawan* or *paun* (f.), باؤ *bā'ō* (f.).

Water, آب *āb*, جل *jal*, پاني *pānī* (m.), نیر *nīr*.

Earth, زمین *zamīn* (f.), مٹي *miṭṭī*, خاک *khāk* (f.), بهوم *bhūm* (f.).

Heavenly bodies, signs, appearances, &c.

Sun, سورج *sūraj*, آفتاب *āftāb*, خورشید *khurshaid*.

Moon, چاند *chānd*, ماہ *māh*, قمر *ḳamar*, چندر *chandar*.

New Moon, بالاچاند *bālā-chānd*, ہلال *hilāl*, نیا چاند *nayā chānd*.

Full Moon, بدر *badr*, پنم *punim*, پورن ماسی *pūran-māsī*.

Star, تارا *tārā*, ستارہ *sitāra*, نجم *najm*.

Constellation, اختر *akhtar*, کوکب *kaukab*.

Planet, سیارہ *saiyāra*.

Saturn, سنیچر *sanīchar*, زحل *zuḥal*, کیوان *kaiwān*.

Jupiter, برہسپت *brihaspat*, مشتری *mushtarī*.

Mars, منگل *mangal*, مریخ *mirrīkh*.

Venus, سکر *sukr*, سوک *sūk*, زہرہ *zuhra* (f.), ناہید *nāhīd*.

Mercury, بدھ *budh*, عطارد *uṭārid*.

Comet, جھاڑو *jhāṛū* (m. f.), کیت *ket*, دم کا تارا *dum kā tārā*.

Meteor, شہاب *shihāb*.

Falling Star, لک *luk*, شہاب *shihāb*.

Zodiac, راس چکر *rās-chakr*, منطقة البروج *minṭaḳatu-l-burūj*.

Sign of the Zodiac, برج *burj*, راس *rās*.

Aries, the Ram, برج حمل *burj-i-ḥamal*, میکھ *mēkh*.

Taurus, the Bull, برج ثور *burj-i-ṣaur*, برکھ *brikh*.

Gemini, the Twins, برج جوزا *burj-i-jauzā*, متھن *mithun*.

Cancer, the Crab, برج سرطان *burj-i-saraṭān*, کرک *kark*.

Leo, the Lion, برج اسد *burj-i-asad*, سنگھ *singh*.

Virgo, سنبلہ *sumbula*, کنیا *kaniyā* (f.).

Libra, the Balance, میزان *mīzān* (f.), تلا *tulā* (f.).

Scorpio, the Scorpion, عقرب *aḳrab*, بچهو *bichchhū*.

Sagittarius, the Centaur, قوس *ḳaus* (f.), دهن *dhan* or *dhanu*.

Capricornus, the Goat, برج جدي *burj-i-jadī*, مکر *makar*.

Aquarius, برج دلو *burj-i-dalv*, کنبه *kumbh*.

Pisces, the Fish, برج حوت *burj-i-ḥūt*, مين *mīn*.

Milky way, Galaxy, کهکشان *kahkashān*.

Mansion of the Moon, نچهتر *nachhattar*, منزل *manzil*.

Zenith, سمت الراس *samtu-r-ras*, سمت النظر *samtu-n-naẓar*.

Nadir, نظير السمت *naẓīru-s-samt*, نظير الرجل *naẓīru-r-rijl*.

Sunshine, دهوپ *dhūp* (f.), گهام *ghām* (f.), شعاع *shu'ā'* (f.).

Moonshine, چاندني *chāndnī*, ماهتاب *māhtāb*.

Eclipse, گهن *gahan*, (of the sun) کسوف *kusūf*, (of the moon) خسوف *khusūf*.

Rainbow, قوس قزح *ḳaus-i-ḳuzaḥ* (f.), بورو *bōrō*.

Cloud, ابر *abr*, بادل *bādal*, ميغ *mēgh* (m. f.).

Rain, مينه *mēṅh*, باران *bārān*, بارش *bārish* (f.), (dakh.) مهيون *mhyūṅ*.

Shower, جهڙي *jhaṛī*, جهيسي *jhīsī*, دونگڙا *daungṛā*, جهپاس *jhapās* (f.).

Fog, Mist, کوهر *kohar*, کوهرا *kohrā*, کهاسا *kuhāsā*.

Vapour, غبار *ghubār*, بخار *bukhār*.

Lightning, بجلي *bijlī*, برق *barḳ* (f.).

Thunder, گرج *garj* (f.), تندر *tundar*, رعد *ra'd*.

Dawn, Daybreak, پوه *pōh* (f.), تڙکا *taṛkā*, بهور *bhōr* (f.), ارن *arun*, صبح *subḥ* (f.).

Twilight (evening), گودهولي *gōdhūlī*, شفق *shafak*, منهہ اندهيرا *muṅh-andherā*.

Things relating to Fire.

Flame, شعله *shu*la*, لهب *lahab*, (of a fire) آنچ *ānch*, (of a candle or lamp) تيم *ṭem* (f.).

Flash, لهک *lahak* (f.), بهبهک *bhabhak* (f.), چمک *chamak* (f.).

Blaze, بهبهوکا *bhabhūkā*, بهڑک *bhaṛak* (f.): see Flame.

Spark, چنگاري *chingārī*, چنگي *chingī*, پرکاله *parkāla*, شراره *sharāra*.

Smoke, دهواں *dhū'āṅ*, دهوم *dhūm*, دود *dūd*.

Soot, سونرا *sauṅrā*, کالک *kālik*, دوده *dūda*, سواد *sawād*.

Ashes, راکهہ *rākh* (f.), چهار *chhār* (f.), بهسم *bhasam* (f.), خاکستر *khakistar* (f.).

Cinders, (cold) کويلا *kō'ēlā*, (hot) انگارا *angārā*.

Embers, بهوبهل *bhūbhal*, انگارا *angārā*.

Firebrand, سوخته *sokhta*, لوکٹي *lūkṭī*, (dakh.) کولتي *kōltī*.

Fireworks, آتش بازي *ātash-bāzī*.

Firewood, Fuel, هيزم *hēzam* (f.), ايندهن *īndhan*, هيمه *hīma*.

Coal, Charcoal, کويلا *kō'ēlā*, زغال *zughāl*.

Things relating to Air.

Wind, باؤ *bā'ō* (f.), باد *bād* (f.), هوا *hawā* (f.)

Gale, Storm, Squall, Tempest, Hurricane, } آندهي *āndhī*, طوفان *ṭūfān*, جهکڑ *jhakkaṛ*.

Whirlwind, گِرد باد *gird-bād* (f.), بگُولا *bagūlā*, بَوَنڈر *bawanḍar*.

Stormy Wind, بادِ تُند *bād-i-tund* (f.).

Hot pestilential Wind, سمُوم *samūm* (f.), بادِ سمُوم *bād-i-samūm*.

Gust, Blast, Breeze, جھکورا *jhakōrā*, جھوکا *jhōkā*, پھُونک *phūnk*.

Fair or favourable Wind, بادِ مُراد *bād-i-murād* (f.).

Contrary or adverse Wind, بادِ مُخالِف *bād-i-mukhālif*.

Zephyr, morning breeze, بادِ صبا *bād-i-ṣabā* (f.)

Things relating to Water.

Drop, بُوند *būnd* (f.), قطْرہ *ḳaṭra*, (of rain) ٹپکا *ṭapkā*.

Bubble, بُلبُلا *bulbulā*, بُلّا *bullā*, حُباب *ḥubāb*.

Foam, Froth, Scum, پھین *phēn*, کف *kaf* (f.).

Vapour, steam, بُخار *bukhār*, باپھ *bāph* (f.), بھاپھ *bhāph* (f.).

Dew, اوس *ōs* (f.), شبنم *shabnam* (f.), سِیت *sīt* (f.).

Fog, Mist, کوھر *kohar*, کُوھرا *kūhrā*, بُخار *bukhār*, کُھاسا *kuhāsā*.

Frost, Hoar-frost, پالا *pālā*, ٹھار *ṭhār*.

Snow, برف *barf* (m. f.), پالا *pālā*, ٹھار *ṭhār*.

Hail, اولا *ōlā*, ژالہ *zhāla*, تگرگ *tagarg*.

Ice, یخ *yakh*, برف *barf* (m. f.).

Wave, Billow, موج *mauj* (f.), موجہ *mauja*, لہر *lahar* (f.).

Ocean, سمُندر *samundar*, سمُدر *samudr*, بحرِ مُحِیط *baḥr-i-muḥīṭ*.

Sea, بحر *baḥr*, سمُندر *samundar*, دریا *daryā*, ساگر *sāgar*.

Lake, جھِیل *jhīl* (f.), سرور *sarwar*, تالاب *tālāb*, پوکھر *pōkhar*.

Bay, Gulf, کول *kōl*, بحر *baḥr*, خلیج *khalīj*.

Creek, Cove, کول *kōl.*

Abyss, Gulf, قعر *ḳaʿr*, گرداب *girdāb*, لجه *lujja.*

River, ندي *naddī*, دريا *daryā*, رود *rūd*, سرتا *sartā* (f.).

Rivulet, Brook, Canal, نهر *nahr* (f.), نالا *nālā.*

Pool, Pond, كنڈ *kunḍ*, تالاب *tālāb.*

Deluge, طوفان *ṭūfān*, طغياني *ṭughyānī.*

Inundation, آهلا *āhlā*, سيلاب *sailāb* (f.): see Deluge.

Whirlpool, Eddy, Vortex, گرداب *girdāb*, بهنور *bhaṅwar*, (dakh.) بهونرا *bhauṅrā.*

Harbour, Haven, Port, بندر *bandar.*

Tank, تالاب *tālāb*, سرور *sarwar*, حوض *ḥauẓ.*

Quagmire, دلدل *daldal* (f.), پانک *pānk*, دهسن *dhasan* (f.).

Bog, Slough, پانک *pānk*, دلدل *daldal* (f.).

Fen, Marsh, جهابر *jhābar* (f.), (dakh.) مڑو *maṛū.*

Spring, Fountain, چشمه *chashma*, سوتا *sōtā*, كنڈ *kunḍ.*

Well, كوا *kū'ā*, چاه *chāh*, (large one of masonry) اندارا *indārā*, باولي *bā'ōlī.*

Pit, چاه *chāh.*

Ditch, Moat, كهائي *khā'ī*, خندق *khandaḳ* (m. f.).

Shore, Strand, Beach, Coast, Bank, تير *tīr*, كناره *kināra*, لب *lab*, ساحل *sāḥil.*

Things relating to the surface of the Earth.

Land, Ground, Soil, بهوم *bhūm* (f.), مٹي *miṭṭī* or مٹي *maṭṭī*, زمين *zamīn* (f.), بوم *būm.*

Dry land, خُشْکِي *khushkī* (in opposition to تِري *tarī*, water).

Island, ٹاپو *ṭāpū*, دِيپ *dīp*, جزِيره *jazīra*.

Peninsula, جزِيره *jazīra*, دِيپ *dīp*.

Plain, Level, مُسطح *musaṭṭah*, ميدان *maidān*.

Field, کهيت *khēt*, ميدان *maidān*.

Park, Chase, رمْنه *ramna*, شِکار گاه *shikār-gāh*.

Mountain, پهاڑ *pahāṛ*, کوه *kōh*, جبل *jabal*, پربت *parbat*, (dakh.) ڈونگر *ḍongar*.

Hill, Mount, ٹِيلا *ṭīlā*, تل *tall*, پهاڑِي *pahāṛī*, کوه *kōh*, (dakh.) ڈونگرِي *ḍongrī*.

Hillock, ٹِيلا *ṭīlā*, تل *tall*, (dakh.) ٹيکڑا *ṭekṛā*, ٹينکڑِي *ṭēnkṛī*.

Rock, سِل *sil* (f.), پهاڑ *pahāṛ*, کوه *kōh*.

Stone, پتهر *patthar*, سنگ *sang*, حجر *ḥajar*, (dakh.) پهتر *phattar*.

Block of Stone, چٹان *chaṭān* or *chaṭṭān* (f.).

Pebble, سنگريزه *sang-rēza*, گول سنگريزه *gōl sangrēza*.

Gravel, Grit, پتهرِي *patthrī*, کنکر *kankar*: see Pebble.

Sand, ريت *rēt* (f.), بالو *bālū* (f.), ريگ *rēg* (f.), رمل *raml*.

Mould, Loam, مِٹِّي *miṭṭī* or مٹِّي *maṭṭī*: see Clay.

Chalk, کهڑِي *khaṛī* or کهڑِي مِٹِّي *khaṛī-miṭṭī*, چهوئِي *chhū'ī*.

Clay, گِل *gil* (f.), چِکنِي مِٹِّي *chiknī-miṭṭī*.

Mud, Mire, Dirt, کِيچر *kīchar* (f.), کِيچ *kīch*, چهلا *chahlā* or *chihlā*, پانک *pānk*.

Dust, دهول *dhūl* (f.), دهور *dhūr* (f.), گرد *gard* (f.).

Turf, چاڑ *chāṛ* (f.), چکتا *chaktā*.

Clod, ڈھیلا *ḍhēlā*, کُلوخ *kulūkh*, ڈلا *ḍalā*, پنڈا *pinḍā*.

Minerals, Metals, &c.

A Metal, Mineral, Ore, دھات *dhāt*, فلز *filizz*.

Gold, سونا *sōnā*, زر *zar*, کنچن *kanchan*, طلا *ṭilā*.

Silver, رُوپا *rūpā*, سیم *sīm*, چاندنی *chāndnī*, نقرہ *nukra*.

Tin, قلعی *ḳala'ī*, رانگا *rāngā*, ارزیز *arzīz*, رصاص *raṣāṣ*.

Copper, تامبا *tāmbā*, مس *mis*.

Brass, پیتل *pītal*, برنج *birinj*.

Pewter, جست *jast*, رُوپجست *rūp-jast*, رانگا *rāngā*.

Lead, سیسا *sīsā*, سرب *surb*, رصاص *raṣāṣ*.

White Lead, سفیدا *safēdā*.

Black Lead, کالی مِٹّی *kālī miṭṭī*.

Red Lead, سیندور *sēndūr*, اینگر *īngur*.

Iron, لوہا *lōhā*, آہن *āhan*, حدید *ḥadīd*.

Untempered Iron, کچلوہی *kach-lōhī*.

Steel, فولاد *fūlād* (or *faulād*).

Zinc, Tutanag, Lapis calaminaris, دستا *dastā*.

Lapis lazuli, لاجورد *lājaward*.

Mercury, Quicksilver, سیماب *sīm-āb*, پارا *pārā*.

Salt, لون *lōn*, نمک *namak*, نون *nōn*.

Saltpetre, Nitre, شورہ *shōra*.

Brimstone, Sulphur, گوگرد *gogird*, کبریت *kibrīt*.

Coal (fossil), پتھر کا کویلا *patthar kā kō'ēlā*, کویلا *kō'ēlā*.

Alum, پھِٹکرِی *phiṭkarī* (m.), زاجِ سُفَید *zāj-i-sufaid.*

Amber, کَہرُبا *kah-rubā.*

Lime, چُونا *chūnā,* (quicklime) آہک *āhak.*

Marble, مرمر *marmar,* سنگِ مرمر *sang-i marmar,* رُخام *ruk͟hām.*

Alabaster, رُخام *ruk͟hām.*

Porphyry, سنگِ سُماق *sang-i sumāḳ.*

Ochre, پِیلی مِٹّی *pīlī miṭṭī,* گیرُو *gērū.*

Loadstone, Magnet, سنگِ مِقناطِیس *sang-i miḳnaṭīs,* مِقناطِیس *miḳ-nāṭīs,* آہن رُبا *āhan-rubā,* چُمبک *chumbak,* چُمّک *chummak.*

Jewel, Gem, جَوہر *jauhar,* جَواہِر *jawāhir,* من *man,* رتن *ratan.*

Diamond, ہِیرا *hīrā,* الماس *almās.*

Ruby, لعل *laʻl,* یاقُوت *yāḳūt,* مانِک *mānik.*

Garnet, یاقُوت *yāḳūt:* see Ruby.

Carbuncle, شبچِراغ *shab-chirāg͟h.*

Emerald, زُمُرُّد *zumurrud,* پنّا *pannā.*

Sapphire, نِیلم *nīlam,* نِیل من *nīl mani,* سفِیر *ṣafīr.*

Topaz, پُکھراج *pukhrāj,* زبرجد *zabarjad.*

Turkois, Beryl, فِیروزہ *fīrōza.*

Amethyst, جبلقُوم *jabalḳūm.*

Agate, Onyx, سنگِ سُلَیمانی *sang-i sulaimānī.*

Jasper, Agate, سنگِ یشم *sang-i yashm.*

Opal, دُودھِیا پتّھر *dūdhiyā patthar* (?).

Cornelian, عقِیق *ākīḳ.*

Corundum stone, کُرنڈ *kuranḍ.*

Crystal, بِلّور *billaur*, پھٹک *phaṭak.*

Glass, شيشه *shīsha*, كانچ *kānch.*

Talk, Mica, ابرق *abraḳ* or ابرک *abrak*, طلق *ṭalḳ*, هوڑل *hoṛal*, بھوڑل *bhūṛal.*

Arsenic, زرنيخ *zarnīkh*, سمّ الفار *sammu-l-fār.*

Orpiment, زرنيخ *zarnīkh*, هرتال *hartāl.*

Cinnabar, Vermilion, شنگرف *shangarf*, دردر *dardar.*

Blue Vitriol, Tutty, توتيا *tūtiyā.*

Naphtha, Bitumen, نفط *nafṭ* or نِفط *nifṭ.*

Red Earth or Ochre, گيرو *gērū.*

Armenian Bole, گِلِ ارمني *gil-i armanī*, مُلتاني مِٽي *multānī maṭṭī.*

Natron, سجّي *sajjī.*

Trees, Shrubs, Plants, and Herbs.

Tree, درخت *daraḵẖt*, پيڑ *pēṛ* (f.), گاچھ *gāchh*, (dakh.) جھاڑ *jhāṛ.*

Shrub, جھاڑ *jhāṛ*, بوٹا *būṭā*, جھاڑي *jhāṛī.*

Plant, Herb, نبات *nabāt* (f.).

Oak, بلوط *balūṭ.*

Chesnut, شاه بلوط *shāh balūṭ.*

Cypress, Cedar, سرو *sarv.*

Pine, Fir, صنوبر *ṣanaubar.*

Willow, بيد *bēd* (f.).

Poplar or Plane Tree, چنار *chanār.*

(Oak to Poplar or Plane Tree:) Trees, foreign to India; and, bearing foreign names.

Teak tree, Tectona grandis, ساگون *sāgaun* (f.) or ساگوان *sāgwān* (f.).

Bassia latifolia, مهوا *mahū'ā.*

Mesua ferrea, ناگ کیسر *nāg-kesar.*

Nauclea orientalis, کدم *kadam* or کدمب *kadamb.*

Xanthyocymus pictorius, تمال *tamāl.*

Dalbergia Sisu, سیسو *sīsū.*

Lagerstroemia regina or Flos regina, *Roxb.* جارل *jāral.*

Mango tree, Mangifera Indica, آم *ām,* آنب *āmb.*

Embryopteris glutinifera, *Roxb.* گاب *gāb.*

Melia Azedirachta, نیم *nīm,* نیمب *nīmb.*

Melia sempervirens, بکاین *bakāyan.*

Michelia Champaca, چنپک *champak.*

Cratæva Tapia, or Capparis trifoliata, برن *barun,* برنا *barnā.*

Amyris Agallocha, گوگل *gūgal.*

Mimosa Arabica, ببول *babūl* (f.), ببور *babūr* (f.)

Mimosa natans, روٹھني *rūṭhnī,* لجالو *lajālū.*

Mimosa pudica, لجالو *lajālū.*

Mimosa scandens, گیلا *gēlā.*

Mimosa Seris, سرس *siris.*

Mimosa Suma, سمي *samī.*

Dillenia Indica, چلتا *chaltā.*

Echytes caryophyllata, مالتي *mālatī.*

Shorea robusta, سال *sāl,* شال *shāl.*

Ficus glomerata, ادمبر *udumbar.*

Ficus Guleria, گولر *gūlar* (f.).

Ficus Indica, بٹ *baṭ,* بڑ *baṛ.*

Ficus religiosa, پیپل *pīpal.*

Ficus venosa (or infectoria), پاکڑ *pākaṛ*.

Zizyphus Jujuba, بيري *bērī*.

Laurus Cassia, Cassia or wild Cinnamon, تج *taj*.

Salvadora Persica (also, in the Dakh. Careya arborea), پيلو *pīlū*.

Mimusops Elengi, مولسري *maulsarī*.

Mimusops Kauki, کهرني *khirnī*.

Cedrela Toona, تن *tun*, or تون *tūn*.

Celastrus (staff-tree) مالکنگني *mālkangnī*.

Morinda citrifolia, آل *āl*.

Uvaria longifolia, ديبدار *dēbdār*, ديودارو *dēvdārū*, اسوگ *asog*.

Webera tetrandra, کارا *kārā*.

Butea frondosa, پلاس *palās*, ڈهاک *ḍhāk*.

Tamarix Indica, جهاو *jhā'ū*.

Acanthus ilicifolius, هڑکت *haṛkat*.

Terminalia alata or glabra, ارجن *arjun*.

Terminalia alata or tomentosa, آسن *āsan*.

Terminalia Belerica, Beleric Myrobolan, بهيڑا *bahēṛā*.

Phœnix sylvestris, wild Date, کهجور *khajūr*.

Justicia Adhatoda, ارس *arus*.

Justicia Gandarussa, باکس *bākas*.

Justicia nasuta, پالک جوهي *pālak jūhī*.

Achyranthes aspera, چرچرا *chirchirā*, آگاڑا *āgāṛā*.

Tamarindus Indica, املي *imlī*, تنتڑي *tintiṛī*.

Ægle Marmelos, بلب *bilb*.

Æschynomene paludosa, شولا *sholā*.

Æschynomene Sesban, جيت *jait.*

Hyperanthera Morunga, سهجنا *sahajnā,* بان *bān.*

Jack fruit tree, Artocarpus integrifolia, كٹهل *kaṭ'hal.*

Chironjia sapida, چرونجي *chirōnjī,* پيال *piyāl.*

Plantain or Banana tree, Musa sapientum, موچا *mochā,* كيلا *kēlā.*

Bombax heptaphyllum, سيمل *sēmal,* سينبل *sēmbal.*

Bauhinia variegata, كچنار *kachnār,* كچنال *kachnāl.*

Palm or Toddy tree, Borassus flabelliformis, تاڑ *tāṛ,* بل تاڑ *bal-tāṛ.*

Pinus longifolia, سرل *saral.*

Sappan wood, Cæsalpinia Sappan, بقم *baḳam.*

Papaw tree, Carica Papaya, پپيا *papaiyā.*

Cane, Ratan, Calamus Rotang, بيت *bēt* (f.).

Creeper, بيل *bēl* (f.), لتا *latā* (f.).

Agrostis linearis, دوب *dūb,* جنيوا *janēwā.*

Alangium hexapetalum, اكول *akōl.*

Aloe perfoliata, گهيكوار *ghīkuwār.*

Alpinia Galanga, Galangal, خولنجان *khōlinjān.*

Andropogon muricatum, خس *khas* (f.), اسير *usīr* (f.).

Anethum Sowa, Fennel, سوا *sō'ā.*

Annona squamosa, آت *āt.*

Argemone Mexicana, بهربهانڈ *bharbhānḍ.*

Artemisia vulgaris, مروا *marū'ā.*

Arum campanulatum, اول *ōl.*

Arum Colocasia, اروي *arwī,* كچو *kachchū.*

Arundo tibialis, نركٹ *narkaṭ.*

Asclepias gigantea, Swallow-wort, اُرک *ark*, اکوند *akwand*.

Asclepias rosea, دُودهي *dūdhī*.

Barleria longifolia, تال مکهانا *tāl makhāna*.

Boerhavia diffusa, گدها پورنا *gadhā-pūrnā*.

Bryonia grandis, *Linn.*, Momordica monodelpha, *Roxb.*, بنب *bimb*.

Callicarpa Americana, بسترا *bastarā*.

Cannabis sativa, Hemp plant, گانجها *gānjhā*, بهانگ *bhāng*.

Carissa Carandas, Corinda or Caronda, کروندا *karōndā*.

Cassia alata, داد مردن *dād-mardan*.

Cassia fistula, املتاس *amaltās*.

Cassia Tora, چکوندا *chakaundā*, (or obtusifolia?) پنوار *panwār*.

Cassia Sophera, کسوندي *kasaundī*.

Chrysanthemum Indicum, گلِ داؤدي *gul-i-dā'ūdī*.

Cissus quadrangularis, هاڑجوڑا *hāṛ-joṛā*.

Cleome Viscosa, هرهر *hurhur*.

Clitoria ternatea, اپراجتا *aparājitā*.

Cordia latifolia, بڑا لسوڑا *baṛā lasoṛā*.

Cordia Myxa, لسوڑا *lasōṛā*.

Crinum Asiaticum and Zeylanicum, سکهدرسن *sukhdarsan*.

Crotalaria juncea, سن *san* (whence, a kind of flax).

Cucumis Colocynthis, اندراين *indrāyan*.

Cucumis Madraspatanus, سيند *sēnd* (f.).

Cucumis momordica, پهوٹي *phūṭī*, پهوٹ *phūṭ* (f.)

Cucumus sativus, کهيرا *khīrā*.

Cucumis utilissimus, ککڑي *kakṛī.*

Cucurbita citrullus, تربوز *tarbūz.*

Cucurbita lagenaria, کدو *kaddū,* گهيا *ghiyā.*

Cucurbita Melopepo, ميٹهي کدو *mīṭhī kaddū.*

Cucurbita Pepo, کديمه *kadīma,* کمڑها *kamṛhā.*

Curcuma reclinata or Zerumbet, کچور *kachūr.*

Curcuma Zedoaria, نربسي *nirbisī,* جدوار *jadwār.*

Curcuma Zerumbet, زرنباد *zurumbād,* کچور *kachūr.*

Cuscuta reflexa, Air plant or Dodder, آکاس پون *ākās-pawan.*

Cyperus pertenuis or juncifolius, ناگر موتها *nāgar-mōthā.*

Cyperus rotundus, موتها *mōthā.*

Dolichos biflorus (kind of pulse), کرتهي *kurthī* or کلتهي *kulthī.*

Dolichos pruriens (Cowitch or Cowach), کوانچ *kiwānch* or کيوانچ *kēwānch.*

Dolichos Sinensis (kind of bean), لوبيا *lōbiyā.*

Echinops echinatus, Globe thistle, کٹارا *kaṭārā* or اونٹ کٹارا *ūnṭ-kaṭārā.*

Echites caryophillata, مالتي *mālatī.*

Eclipta prostrata, بهرنگراج *bhringrāj.*

Elæocarpus serratus, جلپائي *jalpā'ī.*

Epidendrum tessellatum, Mistletoe, باندا *bāndā,* بندا *bandā,* بنڈا *banḍā.*

Euphorbia antiquorum, سيهنڈ *sēhunḍ,* تدهارا *tidhārā.*

Euphorbia hirta and thymifolia, دُدّھِي *duddhī.*

Euphorbia neriifolia, تھُوھر *thūhar.*

Euryale ferox, مکھانا *makhānā.*

Feronia elephantum, کَيت *kait.*

Flacourtia cataphracta, پنيالا *paniyālā.*

Gærtnera racemosa, مادھولتا *mādhōlatā,* مالتي لتا *māltī latā.*

Gardenia florida, گندھراج *gandhrāj.*

Gardenia latifolia, پاپڑا *pāpṛā.*

Gossypium herbaceum, Cotton plant, کپاس *kapās.*

Grewia Asiatica, پھالسا *phālsā.*

Grislea tomentosa, دھاري *dhārī.*

Hedysarum Alhagi, جَواسا *jawāsā.*

Helianthus annuus, Sunflower, سُورج مُکھي *sūraj-mukhī.*

Helicteres Isora, مروڑ پھلي *marōṛ-phalī.*

Hibiscus Phœniceus, سداسُہاگن *sadāsuhāgan.*

Hibiscus Populneoides, پارس پيپل *pāras-pīpal.*

Jasminum auriculatum, جُوھي *jūhī.*

Jasminum grandiflorum, great flowered jasmine, جاتي *jātī.*

Jasminum Zambac, بيلا *bēlā.*

Jatropha Curcas, بگرينڈي *bagrēnḍī.*

Jonesia Asoca, اسوک *asok* or اشوک *ashōk.*

Ixora undulata, پالک جُوھي *pālak-jūhī.*

Kæmpferia rotunda, بھُوں چنپا *bhūṅ-champā.*

Lawsonia inermis, مينھدي *mēṅhdī,* حنا *ḥinnā* (f.).

Linum usitatissimum, اتسِي *atasī*, تِيسِي *tīsī*.

Luffa acutangula, جهينگا *jhīngā*.

Luffa pentandra, گهيا تورئي *ghiyā-tōra'ī*.

Lycopodium imbricatum, هاتها جوڑي *hāthā-jōṛī*.

Menispermum glabrum, گرچ *gurch* (f.), گڑچ *guṛach*, گلو *gilau*.

Menispermum hirsutum, فرِيد بوٹِي *farīd-būṭī*.

Menyanthes Indica or cristata, كمودِني *kamōdinī* (or *kamōdanī*).

Momordica Charantia, كريلا *karēlā*.

Myrtle (Myrtus communis) آس *ās* (in Arab.), مرد *murd* (Gilch.).

Nelumbium Speciosum, Lotus, پدم *padam*, كمل *kamal*, كنول *kaṅwal*.

Nerium odorum, sweet scented Rosebay, كنير *kanēr* (f.), كنيل *kanēl* (f.).

Nerium oleander, Oleander or Rosebay, خر زهره *khar-zahra*.

Nyctanthes arbor-tristis, سِنگار هار *singār-hār*.

Nymphæa Lotus, كوئِي *kō'ī*, سارنگ *sārang*, نِيلوفر *nīlōfar*, كمل *kamal*, كنول *kaṅwal*, امبج *ambuj*.

Ocimum basilicum, sweet Basil, سبزه *sabza*, سبزِي *sabzī*.

Ocimum pilosum, مروا *marū'ā*, رِيحان *rīḥān*, نازبو *nāzbō*.

Ocimum sanctum, تلسِي *tulsī*, برِندا *brindā*, كالِي تلسِي *kālī tulsī*.

Oldenlandia biflora, پِت پاپڑا *pit-pāpṛā*, شاه تره *shāh-tara*.

Orange tree, كونلا *kauṅlā*.

Origanum Majorana, مروا *marwā* (?).

Ovieda verticillata, بامن هتِي *bamān-haṭṭī*.

Pedalium murex, بڑا گوكهرو *baṛā gōkhrū*.

Pharnaceum Mollugo, گوما *gūmā*.

Phyllanthus Emblica, Emblic Myrobalan, آملا *āmlā*.

Physalis flexuosa, اسگندھ *asgandh*.

Piper Betle, Betel plant, ناگ بیل *nāg-bēl*.

Piper Cubeba, Cubebs, کباب چینی *kabāb chīnī*, کبابه *kabāba*.

Piper longum, long pepper, پیپل *pīpal*, پپلي *piplī*.

Plumbago Zeylanica, چتا *chittā*.

Poa Cynosuroides, کش *kush*, داب *dāb* (f.).

Pteris lanulata, پرسیاوشان *parisiyāwashān*.

Rhus coriaria, سماق *sumāḳ* (prop. سمّاق *summāḳ*).

Ricinus communis, ارنڈ *aranḍ*, انڈ *anḍ*, رینڈي *rēnḍī*, رنڈ *ranḍ*.

Rosa Chinensis, کٹھگلاب *kaṭhgulāb*.

Rottlera Indica, پنڈالو *pinḍālū*.

Rubia Manjith, مجیٹھ *majīṭh* (f.), منجیٹ *manjīṭ* (f.).

Ruellia longifolia, گوکھرو *gōkhrū*.

Rumex vesicarius, چوکا *chūkā*.

Saccharum cylindricum, الو *ulū*, اولو *ūlū* (f.).

Saccharum Munja, مونج *mūnj*.

Saccharum officinarum, اوکھ *ūkh*.

Saccharum procerum, سرپت *sarpat*.

Saccharum Sara, سر *sar*, سینٹھا *sēnṭhā*, سینٹھي *sēnṭhī*.

Santalum album, Sandal wood or tree, چندن *chandan*.

Serratula anthelmintica, بکچي *bakchī*.

Sesamum orientale, تل *til*.

Sinapis dichotoma, a species of mustard, سرسون *sarsōn.*

Solanum Jacquini, بهت کٹائي *bhaṭ-kaṭā'ī.*

Solanum melongena, بينگن *baiṅgan,* بيگن *baigan.*

Solanum nigrum, Nightshade, مکو *makō,* طوليدون *ṭūlīdūn.*

Sonchus, کامراج *kāmrāj.*

Sphæranthus Indicus, منڈي *muṇḍī.*

Strychnos nux-vomica, کچلا *kuchlā.*

Symplocas racemosa, لودھ *lōdh.*

Thymus, Thyme, اپار *ipār.*

Trapa natans, سنگهارا *singhārā.*

Trianthema pentandra, بس کهپرا *bis-khaprā.*

Trichosanthes dioica, پرور *parwar,* پلول *palwal.*

Trigonella fœnugræcum, ميتهي *mēṭhī.*

Trophis aspera, سيوڑا *sē'ōṛā.*

Typha (a species ?), گوندني *gōndnī :* (elephantina) هوگلا *hūglā.*

Valeriana Jatamansi, Spikenard, مانسي or جتا ماسي *jatā-māsī* or *-māṅsī.*

Vallisneria spiralis or octandra, سوار *siwār.*

Vangueria spinosa, مدن *madan.*

Verbesina prostrata or scandens, بهرنگراج *bhringrāj,* بهنگڑا *bhangṛā.*

Vitex Negundo, اندراني *indrānī,* سمالو *samālū.*

Vitex trifolia, سمالو *samālū.*

Volkameria infortunata, بهانٹ *bhānṭ.*

Urtica interrupta, stinging Nettle, بچهاتا *bichhātā,* انجرہ *anjira* (?).

Xanthium Indicum, گهاگهرا *ghāghrā.*

Esculent Roots and Vegetables.

Potato, آلو *ālū.*

Yam, آلو *ālū,* رتالو *ratālū.*

Sweet Potato, شکر قند *shakar-ḳand.*

Turnip, شلغم *shalg͟ham.*

Carrot, گاجر *gājar* (f.).

Radish, مولي *mūlī.*

Onion, پياز *piyāz* (f.), کاندا *kānda* (?), بصل *baṣal* (f.), گٹھا *gaṭṭhā.*

Leek, گندنا *gandanā.*

Garlick, لهسن *lahsan,* سير *sīr.*

Beet, چچنڈا *chichinḍā,* چقندر *chuḳundur.*

Ginger in the undried state, ادرک *adrak.*

A Vegetable, ترکاري *tarkārī.*

Egg-plant, بيگن *baigan,* بينگن *baiṅgan,* بهانٹا *bhānṭā.*

Greens, ساگ *sāg* or ساگ پات *sāg-pāt,* بهاجي *bhājī.*

Cabbage, کرم کلا *karam-kallā,* کوبي *kōbī.*

Cauliflower, پهول کوبي *phūl-kōbī.*

Cucumber, کهيرا *khīrā.*

Gourd, Pumpkin, کدو *kadū.*

Pea, مٹر *maṭar,* (dakh.) بٹانا *baṭānā.*

Bean, باقلا *bāḳlā.*

Kind of bean (Dolichos Sinensis) لوبيا *lōbiyā.*

Spinage, پالک *pālak.*

Mint, پودينه *podīna.*

Parsley, اَجْمُود *ajmūd*.

Endive, كاسْنِي *kāsnī*, هِنْدْبا *hindbā*.

Lettuce (Lactuca sativa) كاهُو *kāhū*.

Portulaca oleracea, Purslain, لونا *lonā*, لونيا *loniyā*, نونيا *noniyā*, كانْڈْلِي *kānḍlī*, خُرْفَه *khurfa*.

Cresses (garden), تره تيزك *tara-tezak*, چنْسُر *chansur*, هالِم *hālim*.

Cresses (water), لوت پُوتِيا *lōṭ-pūṭiyā*, ديوكانْڈر *dē'ōkānḍar*.

Arum campanulatum (root), سُورن *sūran*.

Arum Colocasia (root), كچالُو *kachālū*, گهويان *ghōyān*.

Amaranthus Gangeticus, لال ساگ *lāl-sāg*.

Amaranthus oleraceus, مرسْا *marsā*.

Amaranthus polygamus, چولائِي *chaulā'ī*.

Basella alba and nigra, پوئي *pō'ē*.

Chenopodium album, بتهُوا *bathū'ā*.

Convolvulus repens, كلْمِي *kalmī*.

Dioscorea fasciculata (root of), سُوتهْني *sūthnī*.

Dolichos Sinensis (kind of bean from), لوبيا *lōbiyā*, رَوانْس *rawāns*.

Hibiscus esculentus, بهِنْڈِي *bhinḍī*, رام ترُئِي *rām-tura'ī*.

Hyperanthera morunga (the root used for horseradish), سهجْنا *sahajnā*.

Lathyrus sativus, كِسارِي *kisārī*.

Flowers.

Althea rosea, گُلِ خَيرا *gul-i-khairā*.

Arghawān, ارْغوان.

Bassialatifolia (flowers of), گل چکان *gul chikān.*

Chāndnī, چاندنی.

Chrysanthemum Indicum, گلِ داؤدی *gul-i-dā'ūdī.*

Clitorea ternatea, کوا تھینتھی *kawwā-ṭhēnṭhī.*

Cockscomb flower, Amaranthus cruentus, گلکیش *gul-kēsh,* تاجِ خروس *tāj-i-kharōs.*

Globe Amaranth, Gomphrena globosa, گلِ مخمل *gul-i-makhmal.*

Hibiscus mutabilis, گلِ عجائب *gul-i-ajā'ib.*

Hibiscus rosa Sinensis, جوا *jawā.*

Hibiscus Syriacus, گڑھل *guṛhal.*

Impatiens Balsamina, گل مہندی *gul-mihndī.*

Jasmine, یاسمن *yāsmin* or یاسمین *yāsmīn.*

Jasmine (white), a lily or an Iris (?), زنبق *zambak.*

Jasmine (a sort of), نواڑی *niwāṛī.*

Jasminum auriculatum, جوهی *jūhī.*

Jasminum grandiflorum, چنبیلی *chambēlī.*

Jasminum multiflorum or pubescens, کٹھ بیلا *kaṭh-bēlā.*

Jasminum Zambac, بیل *bēl.*

Jasminum Zambac, var. β, موتیا *motiyā.*

Jasminum Zambac, var. γ, موگرا *mogrā.*

Kapūr, کپور.

Lily, سوسن *sōsan* (f.), (of the valley) سمن *saman.*

Linum trigynum, جعفری *ja'farī,* گلِ اشرفی *gul-i-ashrafī.*

Madan bān, مدن بان.

Mango-tree (blossom of), مور *maur*.

Marigold, گيندا *gēndā*.

Michelia Champaca, چنپا *champā*.

Mimusops Elengi, مولسري *maulsarī*.

Mirabilis Jalapa, Marvel of Peru, گلِ عبّاس *gul-i-ābbās*.

Nāfarmān, نافرمان.

Narcissus, Narcissus Tagetes, نرگس *nargis* (f.), نرگسِ شهلا *nargis-i-shahlā*.

Nelumbium speciosum, Lotus, پدم *padam*, کمل *kamal*, کنول *kaṅwal*.

Nerium odorum, sweet-scented Rosebay, کنير *kanēr* (f.), کنيل *kanēl* (f.).

Nerium Oleander, common Rosebay or Oleander, خر زهره *khar zahra*.

Nyctanthes arbor-tristis, هرسنگار *harsingār* or هارسنگار *hārsingār*.

Nymphæa Lotus, کوئي *kō'ē*, کنول *kaṅwal*, سارنگ *sārang*, نيلوفر *nīlōfar*.

Pandanus odoratissimus, کيوڙا *kē'oṛā*, کيتکي *kētakī*.

Pantapetes Phœnicea, دپهريا *dupahriyā*.

Plumeria, گلاچين *gul-āchīn*.

Poinciana pulcherrima, گلِ طرّه *gul-i-ṭurra*.

Polianthes tuberosa, گلِ شبّو *gul-i shab-bō*, or شب بو *shab-bō*.

Rā'ē-bēl, رائي بيل.

Ratan-mālā, رتن مالا.

Ratan-manjarī, رتن منجري.

Rosa centifolia, گلاب *gulāb*, گل *gul*.

Rosa chinensis, کٹهگلاب *kaṭhgulāb*.

Rosa glandulifera, سيوتي *sē'ōtī*, صد برگ *ṣad-barg*, نسترن *nastaran*.

White Rose of India, Rosa glandulifera (?), نسترن *nastaran*, نسرین *nasrīn*.

Sinapis ramosa, سرسون *sarsōn*.

Sunflower, Helianthus annuus, سورج مکھی *sūraj-mukhī*.

Tagetes patula, گل جعفری *gul-i-ja*ʿ*farī*.

Tulip, لاله *lāla*, شقایق *shaḳā'iḳ*.

Vinca rosea, گل فرنگ *gul-i farang*.

Violet, بنفشه *banafsha* (f.).

Zizyphus Jujuba (flower of), کھچڑی *khichṛī*.

Fruits.

Mango, آم *ām*, آنب *āmb*.

Plantain (fruit), کیلا *kēlā*, کدلی *kadalī*, موز *mauz*.

Custard apple, سیتا پھل *sītā-phal*, آتا *ātā*, شریفه *sharīfa*.

Annona reticulata (fruit of), لونا *lōnā*, نونا *nonā*.

Jack fruit, کٹھل *kaṭhal*.

Baṛhal, بڑھل.

Rose apple, جامن *jāman*.

Hog Plum, امرا *amrā*.

Guava, امروت *amrūt*, سفری آم *safrī ām*.

Date, چھہارا *chhuhārā*, خرما *khurmā*.

Pomegranate, انار *anār*, نار *nār*, داڑم *dāṛim*.

Pineapple, انناس *anannās*.

Cocoa-nut ناریل *nāriyal*, نارجیل *nārjīl*.

Lemon or Lime, لِيمُو *līmū*, نِيمُبو *nīmbū*.

Orange, نارنگي *nārangī*, نارنج *nāranj*, کَولا *kaulā* or کَونلا *kaunlā*, سنگتره *sangtara*.

Citron, تُرُنج *turunj*, گلگل *galgal*, کرنا *karnā*.

Pompelmoose, Shaddock, چکوتره *chakōtara*.

Fig, انجير *anjīr*.

Grape, انگور *angūr*, عنب *ʿinab*.

Mulberry, شهتُوت *shahtūt*, تُوت *tūt*.

Musk Melon, خربُوزه *kharbūza*, جمالي *jamālī*, بِطِّيخ *biṭṭīkh*.

Water Melon, تربوز *tarbūz*.

Kind of Melon (Cucumis Momordica), پهُوٹِي *phūṭī*, پهُوٹ *phūṭ*.

Gourd (Cucurbita Pepo) کمڑها *kamṛahā*, کونڈها *kōnḍhā*.

Gourd (Cucurbita lagenaria), کدُو *kadū*, or کدُّو *kaddū*, لَوکا *laukā*.

Gourd (of uncertain species), پيٹها *pēṭhā*, پروَر *parwar*, ڈهينڑس *ḍhēṅṛas*.

Apple, سيب *sēb*, سيو *sēv*.

Pear, ناشپاتِي *nāshpātī*.

Quince, بِهِي *bihī*, بِه *bih*, سفرجل *safarjal*.

Peach, شفتالو *shaftālū*, آڑُو *āṛū*, آلو بُخارا *ālū-bukhārā*.

Apricot, زرد آلُو *zard ālū*.

Cherry, شاه آلُو *shāh ālū*.

Almond, بادام *bādām*, لَوز *lauz*.

Olive, زَيتُون *zaitūn*, جلپائِي *jalpāʾī*.

Betel nut, from Areca Catechu, سُپارِي *supārī*.

Cashew nut, fruit of Anacardium orientale, كاجو *kājū*.

Nut جوز *jauz*. Filbert, فندق *funduḳ* (f.). Pistachio, پسته *pista*.

Tamarind, تمرِ هندي *tamr-i hindī*.

Emblic Myrobalan, آملا *āmlā*.

Rottlera Indica (fruit of), پنڈالو *pinḍālū*.

Scytalia Litchi (fruit of), ليچي *līchī*.

Vangueria spinosa (fruit of), مين پهل *main-phal*.

Jujube, Zizyphus Jujuba (fruit), بير *bēr*.

Phyllanthus Cheramela (fruit of), هرپهاريوڑي *harphārē'oṛī*.

Cordia Myxa (fruit of), لسوڑا *lasōṛā*.

Cordia latifolia (fruit of), بڑا لسوڑا *baṛā lasōṛā*.

Averrhoa Carambola (fruit of), كمرکه *kamrakh*.

Mimusops Kauki (fruit of), کهرني *khirnī*.

Chironjia sapida (nut of), چرونجي *chirōnjī*.

Flacourtia cataphracta (fruit of), پنيالا *paniyālā*.

Grains, Seeds.

Rice (in the husk), دهان *dhān*.

Rice (cleared of the husk), چانول *chāṅwal*, برنج *birinj*, تنڈل *tanḍul*.

Wheat, گيهون *gēhūṅ*, گندم *gandum*, (dakh.) گهيون *ghyauṅ*.

Barley, جو *jau*.

Holcus Sorghum, جوار *jō'ār*, جونڈري *jaunḍrī*, (dakh. also) جاري *jārī*, جواري *jō'ārī*.

Maize, Zea Mays, Indian corn, بهٹا *bhuṭṭā*, کوکري *kūkrī*, (dakh.) مکي جاري *makkī jārī*.

Rāgee, Elusine Coracana, منڑوا *manṛū'ā*, or منڑوي *manṛū'ī*, (dakh. TEL.) راگي *rāgī*.

Millett (kind of), Panicum Italicum, چينا *chēnā*, كنگني *kangnī*, (dakh.) رالا *rālā*.

Millett (kind of), Panicum colonum, شاما *shāmā*.

Millett (kind of), Panicum frumentaceum, سانوا *sāṅwā*, شاما *shāmā*.

Millett (kind of), Panicum miliaceum (?), چينا *chainā*.

Millett (kind of), Panicum pilosum, ارزن *arzan*.

Millett (kind of), Panicum spicatum, باجرا *bājrā*, لہرا *laharrā*.

Pulse, Vetches, دال *dāl*.

Vetches, Lentils, موٹھ *mōṭh*.

Vetch or Pulse, مسين *masīn*.

Pulse (kind of), Ervum hirsutum, مسور *masūr*.

Pulse (kind of), Cicer arietinum, چنا *chanā*.

Pulse (kind of), Phaseolus Mungo, مونگ *mūng* (f.).

Vetch (kind of), Phaseolus radiatus, ماش *māsh*.

Vetch (kind of), Dolichos biflorus, كلتهي *kulthī*, كرتهي *kurthī*.

Vetch (kind of), Vicia sativa, انكري *ankrī*.

Coriander seed, دهنيا *dhaniyā*, كشنيز *kishnīz*.

Cumin seed, زيره *zīra*, جيرا *jīrā*, كمون *kammūn*.

Anise seed, انيسون *anīsūn*, سونف *saunf* (f.).

Cardamoms, الاچي *ilāchī*, قاقله *ḳāḳula*.

Serratula anthelmintica (seed of), سومراج *somrāj*.

Sinapis ramosa (seed of), رائي *rā'ī*.

Food in general for Animals.

Grass, Hay, Straw, گهاس *ghās* (f.), گیاہ *giyāh* (f.).

Leaf, پتي *pattī*, بناسپتي *banāspattī*, برگ *barg*.

Root, کند *kand*, آلو *ālū*.

Flower, پهول *phūl*, گل *gul*.

Fruit, پهل *phal*, میوہ *mēwa*, فواکه *fawākih*.

Grain, Corn, غله *ghalla*, اناج *anāj*, دانه *dāna*.

Milk, دودھ *dūdh*, شیر *shīr*, چهیر *chhīr*, گورس *gō-ras*.

Honey, شہد *shahd*, عسل *ăsal*, مدھ *madh*.

Sugar, شکر *shakar* (f.).

Insects, Reptiles, Grubs, Worms, کیڑي *kīṛē*, کیڑي مکوڑي *kīṛē makōṛē*.

Fish, مچهلي *machhlī*.

Fowl, پرنده *paranda*, جانور *jānwar*.

Flesh, مانس *māṅs*, ماس *mās*, گوشت *gosht*.

Worms, Reptiles, Insects, Spiders.

Worm, Grub, Maggot, Reptile, Insect, کیڑا *kīṛā*, کرم *kirm*, کیڑا مکوڑا *kīṛā makōṛā*.

Earth-worm, کینچوا *kēnchwā*.

Small Worm, کرمک *kirmak*, کیڑا *kīṛā*.

Snail, گهونگا *ghōngā*, اینٹا *ainṭā*.

Leech, جونک *jōnk* (f.), زالو *zālū* (f.), جلوکا *jalaukā* (f.).

Snake, Serpent, سانپ *sāmp*.

Kind of Snake, گوهونه *gōhūna*, کریت *karait*, ڈونڑ *ḍoṅr*, دهامن *dhāmin*, سنکاتر *sunkātar*, بروت *barwat* (f.).

Boa constrictor, اجگر *ajgar.*

Coluber Naja, ناگ *nāg.*

Dragon, اژدر *azhdar,* اژدها *azhdahā.*

Viper, افعي *af'ī* (m.), سانپ *sāmp,* ناگ *nāg.*

Lizard, چهپکلي *chhipkalī,* چلپاسه *chilpāsa,* گرگٹ *girgiṭ.*

Tortoise, کچھوا *kachhū'ā,* باخا *bā<u>kh</u>ā,* سنگ پشت *sang-pusht.*

Crocodile, گھڑيال *ghaṛiyāl,* کمھير *kumhīr,* نهنگ *nihang.*

Alligator, مگر *magar,* گراه *grāh,* مگر مچهه *magar-machh,* گوه *gōh.*

Chameleon, گرگٹ *girgiṭ,* بوقلمون *buḳalamūn.*

Frog, مينڈک *mēṅḍak* or *mēṅḍuk,* دادر *dādur,* غوک *<u>gh</u>ūk.*

Toad, کٹهه بروکي *kaṭh-birūkī,* غوک *<u>gh</u>ūk.*

Salamander (fabulous inhabitant of fire), سمندر *samandar.*

Centipede, کنکهجورا *kankhajūrā,* گوجر *gōjar.*

Beetle, گوبرونڈا *gōbarōndā,* گبروتا *gubrautā.*

Fire-fly, Glowworm, جگني *jugnī.*

Grasshopper, ٹڈا *ṭiḍḍā,* پهنگا *phangā.*

Locust, ٹڈي *ṭiḍḍī,* ٹيڈي *ṭīḍī,* ٹيڑي *ṭīṛī,* جراد *jarād.*

Bug, کهٹمل *khaṭmal,* کاٹهه کيڑا *kāṭh-kīṛā,* نينايا *nīnāyā.*

Bug (green), گندهي *gandhī.*

Cricket, جهينگر *jhīngur,* جهلي *jhillī.*

Mole Cricket, Gryllus gryllotalpa, گهرگهرا *ghurghurā.*

Butterfly, تيتري *tītrī,* پروانه *parwāna.*

Moth, پتنگا *patangā,* پروانه *parwāna.*

Caterpillar, جهانجها *jhānjhā*, كيڑا *kīṛā*.

Silkworm, پاٹ كرم *pāṭ-kirm*, كرم پيله *kirm-i-pēla*.

Hornet, زنبور *zambūr*, (dakh.) ڈكوڑي *ḍikōṛī* : see Wasp.

Wasp, برني *birnī*, بر *barr* (f.), هڈا *haḍḍā*.

Bee (honey), مماكهي *mumākhī* or مدهماكهي *madhumākhī*, شهد مكهي *shahd-makkhī* or شهد كي مكهي *shahd kī makkhī*.

Bee (humble or large black), بهرنگي *bhringī*.

Bee (large black), بهنور *bhanwar* or بهنورا *bhanwrā* or بهونرا *bhaunrā*, الي *alī*, بهرنگ *bhring*.

Ant, Pismire, مور *mōr*, نمل *naml*.

Ant (black), چيونٹا *chyūnṭā*, (large) پيلك *pīlak*, (small) چيونٹي *chyūnṭī*.

Ant (large), چونٹا *chūnṭā*, مكوڑا *makoṛā*, (dakh.) مكهوڑا *makhoṛā*.

Ant (small), چونٹي *chūnṭī*, چينٹي *chīnṭī*.

Ant (white), ديمك *dīmak* (f.), ديوك *dīwak* (f.).

Fly, مكهي *makkhī*, مگس *magas* (f.).

Gadfly or large Mosquito, ڈانس *ḍāns*, (dakh. gadfly) گوماچي *gōmāchī*.

Mosquito, Gnat, Midge, مچهر *machchhar*, پشه *pashsha*, كتكي *kutkī*.

Midge (that flies into the eyes at night), آنكه پهوڑا *ānkh-phōṛā*.

Louse, جوں *jūṅ* (f), چلڑ *chillaṛ* (f.). Lice, جوئيں *jū'eṅ*, &c.

Nit, ليكه *līkh*, (f.).

Flea, پسو *pissū*, پيهو *pīhū*, كيك *kaik*.

Weevil (small insect in rice, corn, &c.), سونڈا *sūnḍā*, پتاري *pitārī*, گهن *ghun*.

Spider, مکڑي *makṛī*, مکڑا *makṛā*.

Scorpion, بِچّھو *bichchū*, بِرِشچِک *brischik*, کژدم *kazhdum*.

Fishes.

Fish, مچھلي *machhlī*, مچّھي *machchhī*, ماهي *māhī*, مين *mīn*, حُوت *hūt* (f.).

Eel, بام *bām*.

Lamprey, تنبو مچھلي *tambū machhlī*.

Mango fish, Polynemus paradiseus, تپسي مچھلي *tapassī* (or *tapsī*) *machhlī*.

Biktī, بھِکٹھِي *bhikṭhī*.

Species of Herring, Clupea alosa, هِلسا *hilsā* (f.).

Species of Herring, Clupea cultrata, چلوا *chalwā*.

Cyprinus denticulatus, روهو *rōhū* (f.).

A species of Silurus, ٹينگرا *ṭēngrā*.

Silurus pelorius, مگُري *magurī*.

Silurus pungentissimus, سِينگي *sīngī*.

Silurus sagittatus, پنگاس *pangās*.

Mullet, پڑهِن *paṛhin* (f.).

Porpoise, سوسمار *sūsmār*, سُوس *sūs*.

Sprat, or fish resembling a sprat, کهَيرا *khairā*.

Prawn or Shrimp, جهِينگا *jhīngā* (f.).

Crab, کيکڑا *kēkṛā*, گيگٹا *gēgṭā*.

Oyster, کستُورا *kastūrā* (f.).

Muscle, سِيپي کا کِيڑا *sīpī kā kīṛā* (*shell-worm*).

Birds.

Phœnix (fabulous), هما *humā*, عنقا *ănḳā*, ققنس *ḳuḳnus.*

Griffin (fabulous), سيمرغ *sīmurgh.*

Eagle, عقاب *ăḳāb.*

Vulture, گدھ *giddh*, گيدھ *gīdh*, کرگس *kargas*, نسر *nasr.*

Falcon (species of), جره *jurra* or جرا *jurrā* (male of باز *bāz*).

Falcon (royal white), شاهين *shāhīn.*

Falcon (female), باز *bāz.*

Falcon (Falco calidus), بهري *bahrī* or بحري *baḥrī.*

Hawk, باز *bāz*, شكره *shikra*, جهگڙ *jhagaṛ.*

Hawk (Falco cristatellus), کوهي *kōhī.*

Hawk (Falco fasciatus or dubius), ترمتي *turmatī.*

Hawk (Sparrow), باشا *bāshā*, موش گير *mūsh-gīr.*

Kite (Falco Cheela), چيل *chīl* (f.), زغن *zaghan* (f.)

Owl, الو *ullū*, الاغ *ulāgh*, بوم *būm*, چغد *chughd*, پيچا *pēchā.*

Sparrow, گوريا *gauriyā* (f.), چرا *chirā*, (hen) چڙيا *chiṛiya* (f.).

Lanius Boulboul (Nightingale of Persia, &c.), بلبل *bulbul.*

Turdus salica or Gracula religiosa (Moina), سارکا *sārikā.*

Swallow, ابابيل *abābīl.*

Swallow (Hirundo apus Batassia), سوپابينا *sūpābīnā.*

Lark, بهدرا *bhadrā*, اگن *agin*, (Alauda Aggia) اگيا *agiyā.*

Starling (kind of), سارو *sārō* (f.).

Raven, جنگلي کوا *janglī kawwā*, ڈهڙ کوا *ḍhaṛ-kawwā.*

Crow, کَوا *kawwā*, کاگ *kāg*, غُراب *ghurāb*.

Rook, Jackdaw, کَوّا *kawwā*, کاگ *kāg*: see Crow.

Coracias Bengalensis, نِیلکَنٹھ *nīl-kanṭh*.

Hoopoe, Upupa, هُدهُد *hudhud*, شانه سر *shāna-sar*.

Hornbill, Buceros, دهنیس *dhanēs*.

Woodpecker, کَٹھ پھوڑا *kaṭh-phoṛā*, پتّھر پھوڑ *patthar-phōṛ*.

Cuckoo (the black or Indian), کوکِل *kōkil* (f.), کویَل *kōyal* (f.), پِک *pik*.

Cuculus castaneus, مہوکھا *mahōkhā*.

Cuculus melanoleucos, چاتک *chātak*.

Parrot, توتا *tōtā*, سُوا *sū'ā*, سُک *suk*, طُوطِي *ṭūṭī*, نُورِي *nūrī*.

Paroquet, سُوا *sū'ā*, سُوگا *sūgā*, طُوطِي *ṭūṭī*, هِیرامن *hīrāman*.

Domestic Cock, کُکُّٹ *kukkuṭ*, کُوکْڑا *kūkṛā*, مُرغا *murghā*.

Domestic Hen, کُکْڑِي *kūkṛī*, مُرْغِي *murghī*.

Peacock, مور *mōr*, برْهِي *barhī*, طاؤس *ṭā'ūs*.

Peahen, مورْنِي *mōrnī*. Peachick, مُریلا *murēlā*.

Fowl, مُرْغ *murgh*, ماکِیان *mākiyān*.

Turkey, پیرو *pērū*, فِیل مُرْغ *fīl-murgh*.

Pheasant, تدْرو *tadarv*.

Partridge (Perdix francolinus), تِیتر *tītar*, دُرّاج *durrāj*.

Partridge (unknown species), دُرّاج *durrāj*, کبْک *kabk*.

Quail (kind of. Perdix olivacea), بٹیڑ *baṭēṛ*.

Quail (kind of. Perdix Chinensis), لَوا *lawā*.

Pigeon, Dove, کپوت *kapōt*, پریوا *parēwā*, کبُوتر *kabūtar*.

Pigeon (green. Columba Hurriala), هريل *hariyal.*

Pigeon (tumbler), منڈليا *manḍaliyā.*

Ortolan (Emberiza hortulana?) برگيل *bargēl,* پرگيري *pargīrī.*

Ostrich, شتر مرغ *shutur-murgh.*

Sort of Bustard (Otis Bengalensis), چرز *charz.*

Crane, كلنگ *kulang,* كونج *kūnj* : see Heron.

Heron (Ardea torra and putea), بگلا *baglā* or بگلا *bagulā,* بک *bak,* بوتيمار *būtīmār.*

Heron (Ardea Antigone), سارس *sāras.*

Heron (Ardea Argala), Adjutant Bird, هڑگيلا *haṛgīlā,* كهگيس *khagēs,* گروڑ *garuṛ.*

Heron (Ardea Indica), جانگهل *jānghal.*

Bittern (Ardea stellaris), چمر بگلي *chamar-baglī,* بوتيمار *būtīmār.*

Stork, لگلگ *laglag,* لقلق *laḳlaḳ.*

Sandpiper (Tringa Goensis, *Lath.*), ٹٹري *ṭaṭirī,* ٹٹيهري *ṭaṭīhrī.*

Waterfowl, مرغابي *murghābī.*

Coot or Diver, پنڈبي *panḍubī.*

Flamingo, راج هنس *rāj-hans* (?).

Pelican, حواصل *ḥawāṣil,* (Pelecanus onocrotalus) گگن بهيڑ *gagan-bhēṛ.*

Swan, هانس *hāṅs,* راج هنس *rāj-hans.*

Goose, Duck, هنس *hans,* بط *baṭ* (f.), قاز *ḳāz.*

Gander, Drake, بطا *baṭā,* قاز نر *ḳāz-nar.*

Beasts.

Beast, حيوان *ḥaiwān,* چرنده *charanda,* پسو *pasū.*

Horse, گھوڑا *ghōṛā*, اسپ *asp*, فرس *faras*.

Mare, گھوڑي *ghōṛī*, مادِيان *mādiyān* (f.), (dakh. also) مادوان *mādwān*.

Foal, Filly, بچھيري *bachhērī*.

Colt, بچھيرا *bachhērā*, ناکند *nā-kand*, کُرّه *kurra*.

Pony, Galloway, يابُو *yābū*, ٹٹّو *ṭaṭṭū*, ٹانگھن *ṭānghan*.

Gelding, آخته *ā<u>kh</u>ta*, کُوٹيا *kūṭiyā*.

Mule, خچّر *<u>kh</u>achchar*, استر *astar*.

Ass, گدھا *gadhā*, (she Ass) گدھي *gadhī*, خر *<u>kh</u>ar*, حِمار *ḥimār*.

Wild Ass, Onager, Zebra, گورخر *gōr-<u>kh</u>ar*, خرِدشتي *<u>kh</u>ar-i-dashtī*.

Camel, اُونٹ *ūnṭ*, شُتُر *shutur*, اُشتُر *ushtur*.

Camel (female), اُونٹني *ūnṭnī*, سانڈني *sānḍnī*, (dakh. also) سارني *sārnī*.

Dromedary, سانڈني *sānḍnī*.

Camelus Bactrianus (camel with two humps) دوکوھا *dō-kōh-ā*.

Stag, باره سِنگا *bārah-singā*, کندسار *kandsār*, هرنا *harnā*.

Elk, Moose, سانبر *sāmbar*, گوزن *gawazn* : see Stag.

Spotted Deer of India (Cervus axis), چيتل *chītal*.

Deer, مِرگ *mirg*, هرن *haran*, آهو *āhū*, کاليهر *kālīhar*.

Buck, Hart, هرنا *harnā*, هرن *haran*.

Doe, Hind, هرني *harnī*.

Fawn, هرنوٹا *harnauṭā*, آهو بره *āhū-bara*.

Camelopard, or Giraffe (from Arab. زرافه *zarrāfa*), گاو پلنگ *gāw-palang*.

Antelope, هرن *haran*, چِکارا *chikārā* : see Deer.

Antelope (painted or white-footed. Antilope picta), روجه *rōjh*.

Goat (Capper ægagrus), بکرا *bakrā*, (fem.) بکري *bakrī*, چھاگل *chhāgal*, (dakh.) چھیلا *chhēlā*, (fem.) چھیلي *chhēlī*.

Kid, میمنا *mēmnā*, بزغاله *buzghāla*, حلوان *ḥalwān*.

Sheep, بھیڑ *bhēṛ* (f.), گوسپند *gōspand* (f.), گاڈر *gāḍar* (f.), (dakh.) بکرا *bakrā*.

Ewe, بھیڑ *bhēṛ* (f.), بھیڑي *bhēṛī*, (dakh.) بکري *bakrī*.

Ram, مینڈھا *mēnḍhā*, بھیڑا *bhēṛā*, میش *mēsh*, (dakh.) بکرا *bakrā*.

Lamb, بھیڑ کا بچه *bhēṛ kā bachcha*, لیلا *lēlā*, بره *bara*.

Cow, گاي *gā'ē* (f.), گاو *gāw* (f.), (cow or one of the cow kind) گو *gō*.

Bull, آنڈو بیل *ānḍū-bail*, برد *barad*, نرگاو *nar gāw*, ثور *ṣaur*.

Ox, Bullock, بیل *bail*, بدھیا *badhiyā*.

Calf, بچھرا *bachhrā* or بچھڑا *bachhṛā*, باچھا *bāchhā*, (female) بچھیا *bachhiyā*, (dakh.) پاڑا *pāṛā*, (fem.) پاڑي *pāṛī*.

Heifer, کلور *kalōr*, اوسر *ōsar* (f.).

Steer, young bullock, دوھان *dōhān*, کھیلا *khailā*.

Buffalo (male), بھینسا *bhaiṅsā*, میہکا *maihikā*, گاو میش *gāw-mēsh*.

Buffalo (female), بھینس *bhaiṅs* (f.), میہکي *maihikī*, گاو میش *gāw-mēsh*.

Buffalo, (wild, male), ارنا *arnā*, (female) ارني *arnī*.

Buffalo (calf), پاڑھي *pāṛhī*, کاڑا *kāṛā*, سونگرا *sūngrā*, پاڑا *pāṛā*.

Bos grunniens, Yāk, سره گاي *sara-gā'ē* or سره گاو *sara-gā'ō*.

Hog (wild), بڑھیلا *baṛhēlā* or برھیلا *barhēlā*.

Boar, Hog, سوار *sū'ar*, باراه *bārāh*, خوک *khūk*, سوکر *sūkar*.

Sow, سواري *sū'arī*.

Pig, گهينٹا *ghēṅṭā*, (female) گهينٹي *ghēṅṭī*: see Hog, Sow.

Rhinoceros, گينڈا *gainḍā*, كرگدن *kargadan*.

Elephant, هاتهي *hāthī* (m.), (female) هتهني *hathnī*, فيل *fīl*.

Elephant (large) كنجل *kunjal*, (small) كميديا *kumēdyā*.

Hare, Rabbit, لمكنا *lamkanā*, لمها *lamhā*, خرگوش *khar-gosh*, كهرها *kharhā*.

Porcupine, ساهي *sāhī*, ساهل *sāhil*, خار پشت *khār-pusht*.

Rat, چوها *chūhā*, موسا *mūsā*, ايندر *īndur*.

Bandicote Rat, Mus giganteus, *Hardw.*, گهوس *ghūs*, گهوسا *ghūsā*.

Musk Rat, Sorex cærulescens, چهچهوندر *chhuchhūndar*.

Mouse, چوهي *chūhī*, موسري *mūsrī*, موش *mūsh*.

Squirrel, گلهري *gilahrī*, چيكهر *chīkhur*, روكهي *rūkhī*, (dakh.), گليري *gilīrī* (?).

Cat, بلا *billā*, (fem.) بلي *billī*, بلاو *bilā'o*, (fem.) بلائي *bilā'ī*, گربه *gurba*, منجار *manjār*, مانو *mānō*, (dakh. also) بلاوڑ *bilāwaṛ*.

Kitten, بلي كا بچه *billī kā bachcha*.

Lion, سنگه *singh*, كيسري *kēsarī*, كيهري *kēharī*, شير *shēr*, اسد *asad*.

Lioness, سنگهني *singhinī*, شيرني *shērnī*.

Tiger, باگه *bāgh*, شير *shēr*, ببر *babar*, ناهر *nāhar*.

Tigress, باگهن *bāghan* or باگهني *bāghnī*, شيرني *shērnī*.

Tiger's Whelp, بگهيلا *baghēlā*, ڈانورو *ḍāṅwrū*, (dakh.) بور *bōr* (?).

Panther, چيتا *chītā*, يوز *yūz*, پلنگ *palang*.

Leopard, Lynx, تيندوا *tēndū'ā*, پلنگ *palang*, (small hunting) چيتا *chītā*.

Persian Lynx (Felis Caracal), سیاه گوش *siyāh-gosh.*

Hyena, گرر *girir,* لکڑا *lakṛā,* کفتار *kaftār.*

Ichneumon or Mongoose, بِیجی *bījī,* راسُو *rāsū,* نیول *newal,* (dakh.) مُنگوس *mungūs.*

Dog, کُتّا *kuttā,* کُوکر *kūkar,* سگ *sag,* سوان *swān.*

Fox, لومڑي *lōmṛī,* روباه *rōbāh* (f.).

Wolf, بھیڑیا *bheṛiyā,* لانڈگا *lānḍgā,* گُرگ *gurg,* هُنڈار *hunḍār.*

Jackal, گیدڑ *gīdaṛ,* شغال *shaghāl,* سِیال *siyāl.*

Otter, اُودبلاو *ūd-bilā'ō,* ماهي گیر *māhī-gīr.*

Weasel, Ferret, Fitchat, Marten, نیول *newal,* راسُو *rāsū.*

Polecat, کھٹاس *khaṭās,* کٹار *kaṭār.*

Bear, رِیچھ *rīchh,* بھال *bhāl,* بھالو *bhālū,* خِرس *khirs.*

Mole, چھچھوندر *chhuchhūndar* (which is the musk rat).

Hedge-hog, خار پُشت *khār-pusht,* سِینھ *sīṅh.*

Bat, چمگیدڑ *chamgīdaṛ,* بادُر *bādur,* شب پره *shab-para.*

Monkey, Ape, بندر *bandar,* (fem.) بندري *bandrī,* بوزنه *bōzna.*

Baboon, لنگور *langūr,* مَیمُون *maimūn* : see Monkey.

Man.

Man, human being, مانُس *mānus,* آدمي *ādmī,* جن *jan,* اِنسان *insān,* پُرُش *purush.*

Man (in opposition to woman), مرد *mard.*

Man (servant), نوکر *naukar,* نفر *nafar.*

Woman, رنڈي *ranḍī,* عورت *ʻaurat,* اِستري *istrī,* بائیکو *bā'īkō,* زن *zan.*

Old man, بُوڑھا *būṛhā,* پِیر *pīr,* شَیخ *shaikh,* (dakh. also) بُڈّھا *buḍḍhā.*

Old woman, بڑھیا *buṛhiyā* (f.), پِیرزن *pīr-zan,* (dakh. also) بُڈّھِیا *buḍ-hiyā* (f.), بُڈّھِی *buḍḍhī* or بُڈّي *buḍī.*

Young man, نَو جَوان *nau jawān,* گبرو *gabrū.*

Young woman, جُوَتي *juvatī,* كُواري *kū'ārī,* چهوكري *chhōkrī.*

Maid, Virgin, باكِره *bākira,* كُوارِي *kū'ārī,* دوشِيزه *dōshīza,* كورِي *kōrī.*

Boy, Lad, لڑكا *laṛkā,* چهوكرا *chhōkrā,* (servant) لَونڈا *launḍā.*

Girl, لڑكي *laṛkī,* چهوكري *chhōkrī,* دُختر *dukhtar,* (servant) لَونڈي *launḍī.*

Child, Babe, Infant, بچّه *bachcha,* (fem.) بچّي *bachchī,* بالك *bālak,* طِفل *ṭifl,* فرزند *farzand.*

Giant, دانو *dānav,* عِفرِيت *ʿifrīt:* see Tall, Big.

Dwarf, بَونا *baunā,* (fem.) بَوني *baunī,* ناٹا *nāṭā,* (dakh.) ٹهینگو *ṭhēngū.*

A Human being by relationship may be—

Husband, خصم *khaṣam,* شَوهر *shauhar,* زوج *zauj.*

Wife, جورو *jōrū,* زَوجه *zauja* (f.), زن *zan.*

Father, باپ *bāp,* بابا *bābā,* باوا *bāwā,* پِتا *pitā.* پِدر *pidar.*

Grandfather, (paternal) دادا *dādā,* آجا *ājā,* (maternal) نانا *nānā,* جدّ *jadd.*

Great Grandfather, (paternal) پردادا *par-dādā,* (maternal) پرنانا *par-nānā.*

Father-in-law (husband's or wife's father), سسر *sasur* (or *susar*), سُسرا *susrā,* خُسر *khusar.*

Adopted Father or God-father, دهرم باپ *dharm-bāp.*

Mother, ما *mā*, ماں *māṅ*, ماتا *mātā*, مادر *mādar*, والدہ *wālida*.

Grandmother, (paternal) دادي *dādī*, (maternal) ناني *nānī*.

Great Grandmother, (paternal) پردادي *par-dādī*, (maternal) پرناني *par-nānī*.

Mother-in-law (husband's or wife's mother), ساس *sās*, خوش دامن *khush-dāman*.

Step-mother, بيمات *bēmāt*, ميبھا *maibhā*.

Brother, بھائي *bhā'ī* (m.), برادر *birādar*, بير *bīr*.

Own brother, سگا بھائي *sagā bhā'ī*, سہودر بھائي *sahōdar bhā'ī*.

Brother-in-law (sister's husband), بہنوئي *bahnō'ī*, بہنيو *bahnē'ō*.

Brother-in-law (husband's elder brother), جيٹھ *jēṭh*.

Brother-in-law (husband's younger brother), ديور *dēwar*.

Brother-in-law (wife's brother), سالا *sālā*.

Brother-in-law (husband's sister's husband), نندوئي *nandō'ī*.

Brother-in-law (wife's sister's husband), ساڑھو *sāṛhū*, ہم زلف *ham-zulf*.

Step-brother (brother by the father only), سوتيلا بھائي *sautēlā bhā'ī*.

Step-sister (sister by the father only), سوتيلي بہن *sautēlī bahin*.

Son, بيٹا *bēṭā*, پوت *pūt*, پسر *pisar*.

Son-in-law (daughter's husband), داماد *dāmād*, جمائي *jamā'ī*.

Adopted Son or God-son, دھرم بيٹا *dharm-bēṭā*.

Step-son (son by a former husband), ربيب *rabīb*, (or dakh.) ربيب بيٹا *rabīb bēṭā*.

Daughter, بيٹي *bēṭī*, دختر *dukhtar* (f.), پتري *putrī*, دھي *dhī*.

Daughter-in-law (son's wife), بہو *bahū*, بدھو *badhū*, پتوہ *patōh*.

Step-daughter, ربیبه *rabība*, (or dakh.) ربیبه بیٹی *rabība bēṭī*.

Sister, بہن *bahin* or *bahan*, بھگنی *bhaginī*, بوبو *būbū*.

Sister-in-law (wife's sister), سالی *sālī*.

Sister-in-law (husband's sister), نند *nand* (f.).

Sister-in-law (husband's elder brother's wife), جیٹھانی *jēṭhānī*.

Sister-in-law (husband's younger brother's wife), دیورانی *dē'ōrānī*.

Sister-in-law (brother's wife), بھاوج *bhāwaj* (f.), بھوجی *bhaujī*.

Sister-in-law (younger brother's wife), بھیہو *bhaihū*, بھاوہ *bhāwah* (f.).

Grandson (son's son), پوتا *pōtā*, (daughter's son) نواسا *nawāsā*.

Grandaughter (son's daughter), پوتی *pōtī*, پوتری *pautrī*.

Grandaughter (daughter's daughter), ناتن *nātin*, نتنی *natnī*, (dakh. also) ناتی *nātī*, نواسی *nawāsī*.

Great Grandson, پر پوتا *par-pōtā*, پر پوترا *par-pōtrā*.

Great Grandaughter, پر پوتی *par-pōtī*, پر پوتری *par-pōtrī*.

Uncle (father's elder brother), تاؤ *tā'ū*, (dakh.) تایا *tāyā*.

Uncle (father's younger brother), چچا *chachā* (or dakh.) چچا *chichā*.

Uncle (father's sister's husband), پھوپھا *phūphā*, پھوپھو *phūphū*.

Uncle (mother's brother), مامو *māmū*, ماما *māmā*, ماتل *mātul*.

Uncle (mother's sister's husband), خالو *khālū*.

Aunt (father's sister), پھوپھی *phūphī*, (or dakh.) پھوپی *phūpī*, پھوا *phū'ā* (f.).

Aunt (mother's sister), موسی *mausī*, خالا *khālā* (f.).

Aunt (father's elder brother's wife), تائی *ta'ī*.

Aunt (father's brother's wife, or father's younger brother's wife), چچي *chachī* or چچّي *chachchī*, (dakh.) چچاني *chachānī.*

Aunt (mother's brother's wife), مامي *māmī*, مُماني *mumānī.*

Nephew (brother's son), بهتيجا *bhatījā*, برادر زاده *biradar-zāda.*

Nephew (sister's son), بهانجا *bhānjā*, خواهر زاده *khwāhir-zāda.*

Niece (brother's daughter), بهتيجي *bhatījī.*

Niece (sister's daughter), بهانجي *bhānjī.*

Cousin (dakh. father's elder brother's son), تايرا بهائي *tā'ērā bhā'ī.*

Cousin (dakh. father's elder brother's daughter), تايري بهن *tā'ērī bahan.*

Cousin (father's brother's son), * چچيرا بهائي *chachērā bhā'ī.*

Cousin (father's brother's daughter), † چچيري بهن *chachērī bahan.*

Cousin (father's sister's son), ‡ پهپهيرا بهائي *phuphērā bhā'ī.*

Cousin (father's sister's daughter), § پهپهيري بهن *phuphērī bahan.*

Cousin (mother's brother's son), مميرا بهائي *mamērā bhā'ī.*‖

Cousin (mother's brother's daughter), مميري بهن *mamērī bahan.*¶

---

* In Dakhni, said to be "father's younger brother's son."

† In Dakhni, said to be "father's younger brother's daughter."

‡ Dakh. پهپيرا بهائي *phupēra bha'ī.*

§ Dakh. پهپيري بهن *phupērī bahan.*

‖ Dakh. مَوليرا بهائي *maulērā bhā'ī.*

¶ Dakh. مَوليري بهن *maulērī bahan.*

Cousin (mother's sister's son), موسیرا بهائي *mausērā bhā'ī.**

Cousin (mother's sister's daughter), موسیري بهن *mausērī bahan.*†

The Body and what belongs to the body.

Body, سریر *sarīr,* بدن *badan,* دیه *dēh* (f.).

Limb, Member, Joint, عضو *āzv,* انگ *ang,* ٹکڑا *ṭukṛā.*

Sense, حس *ḥiss* (plur. حواس *ḥawāss,* senses).

Sight, درشٹ *drishṭ* (f.), بینائي *bīnā'ī,* بصارت *baṣārat* (f.), قوتِ باصره *ḳūwat-i-bāṣira,* نظر *naẓar.*

Hearing, قوتِ سامعه *ḳūwat-i-sāmi'a,* سماعت *samā'āt* (f.).

Smell, قوتِ شامه *ḳūwat-i-shāmma,* شامه *shāmma.*

Taste, ذایقه *ẕā'iḳā,* قوتِ ذایقه *kūwat-i-ẕā'iḳa.*

Touch or Feeling, لامسه *lāmisa,* قوتِ لامسه *kūwat-i-lāmisa,* لمس *lams.*

Voice, Speech, ناطقه *nāṭiḳā,* قوتِ ناطقه *kūwat-i-nāṭiḳa,* آواز *āwāz.*

Colour, رنگ *rang,* لون *laun.*

Stature, قد *ḳadd,* قد و قامت *ḳadd o ḳāmat,* ڈیل *ḍīl.*

Skin, Hide, پوست *pōst,* کهال *khāl* (f.), چمڑا *chamṛā,* جلد *jild* (f.).

Cuticle, Pellicle, Membrane, جهلي *jhillī,* پرده *parda.*

Pore, مسام *masām,* (Pores) مسامات *masāmāt.*

Flesh, مانس *māns,* گوشت *gōsht,* هيڑا *hērā.*

Bone, هڈي *haḍḍi,* هاڑ *hāṛ,* استخوان *ustuk͟hwān,* عظم *āẓm.*

---

* Also, خلیرا بهائي *k͟halērā bhā'ī.*

† Also, خلیري بهن *k͟halērī bahan.*

Blood, لوهو *lōhū*, لہو *lahū*, (dakh.) لہو *lhau*, رکت *rakat* or *rakt*, خون *khūn*.

Chyle, کیلوس *kailūs*, کیموس *kaimūs*.

Humour (of the body), خلط *khilt*, رس *ras*.

Serum, مانج *mānj*, پاني *pānī*.

Saliva, Spittle, تهوک *thūk*, رال *rāl* (f.), تف *tuf*, لعاب *lu'āb*.

Urine, پیشاب *pēshāb*, بول *baul*, موت *mūt*, شاش *shāsh*.

Sweat, پسینا *pasīnā*, پسیو *pasē'ō*, عرق *ārak*.

Phlegm, بلغم *balgham*, کف *kāf* (f.), کپه *kaph* (f.).

Bile, Gall, پت *pit*, صفرا *ṣafrā* (f.), پتا *pittā*.

Milk, دوده *dūdh*, شیر *shīr*, چهیر *chhīr*.

Marrow, گودا *gūdā*, مغز *maghz*.

Muscle, Tendon, پٹها *paṭṭhā*, پي *pai*, نس *nas* (f.).

Nerve, Sinew, عصب *āṣab*, پٹها *paṭṭhā*, پي *pai*, نس *nas* (f.).

Fibre, ریشه *rēsha*, رگ *rag* (f.), آنس *āns* (f.).

Membrane, کهلڑي *khalṛī*, (of the fœtus) جهلي *jhillī*, پرده *parda*.

Artery, شریان *shiryān* (f.), رگ *rag* (f.).

Vein, رگ *rag* (f.), نس *nas* (f.).

Great vein in the arm, vena basilica, باسلیق *bāsalīk*, شهرگ *shahrag*, هفت اندام *haft-andām*.

Gristle, Cartilage, کري *kurrī*, غضروف *ghuṣrūf*.

Gland, گلٹي *giltī*, غدد *ghudud*, گٹهلي *guṭhlī*.

Joint, گانٹه *gānṭh* (f.), بند *band*, جوڑ *jōṛ*, گره *girih* (f.).

Hair of the head, بال *bāl*, کیس *kēs* (f.), مو *mū*.

Hair, small of the body, روان *rō'ān*, روم *rōm*, لوم *lōm*, پشم *pashm* (f.).

Feather, پر *par*, پنکھ *pankh*.

Head, سر *sir*, منڈ *muṇḍ*, سیس *sīs*, سر *sar*, کلّه *kalla*.

Crown of the head, چاندي *chāndī*, ٹٹري *ṭaṭrī*, تارق *tārak*, مفرق *mafriḳ*.

Skull, Pate, Pericranium, کھوپري *khōprī*, کاسهٔ سر *kāsa-e-sar*.

Face, منھ *munh*, مکھ *mukh*, (dakh.) مون *mūn*, چہره *chihra*, رخ *rukh*.

Forehead, Front, ماتھا *māthā*, بهال *bhāl* (f.), پیشاني *pēshānī*, جبین *jabīn* (f.).

Horn, سینگ *sīng*, شاخ *shākh*, قرن *ḳarn*.

Brain, بهیجا *bhējā*, گودا *gūdā*, مغز *maghz*, دماغ *dimāgh*.

Pia mater, پردهٔ مغز *parda-i-maghz*.

Temple (of the head), کنپٹي *kanpaṭī*, شقیقه *shaḳīḳa*.

Occiput, back of the head, قفا *ḳafā* (f.).

Eye, آنکھ *ānkh*, نین *nain* or *nayan*, چشم *chashm*, دیده *dīda*.

Eyebrow, بهون *bhaun* (f.), ابرو *abrū* (f.), بهرکٹي *bhirkuṭī*.

Eyelid, پوٹا *pōṭā*, پلک *palak* (f.).

Eyelash, مژه *mizha* (plur. مژگان *mizhgān*), برني *baranī*.

Pupil of the eye, پتلي *putlī*, مردمک *mardumak*, مردمِ چشم *mardum-i-chashm*.

Tear, آنسو *ānsū*, آنجھو *ānjhū*, اشک *ashk*, لور *lōr*.

Nose, ناک *nāk* (f.), ناسکا *nāsikā* (f.), بیني *bīnī*.

Nostril, نتھنا *nathnā*, منخر *minkhar* (f.)

Bridge of the nose, بانسا *bānsā*.

Snot, Mucus, پونٹا *pōnṭā* or پوٹا *pōṭā*, رینٹا *rēnṭā*, نیٹا *nēṭā*, لعاب *lu'āb*.

Mouth, منھ *munh*, مکھ *mukh*, دهن *dahan*, آنن *ānan*.

Roof of the mouth, Palate, تالو *tālū*, کام *kām*, مذاق *mazāķ*.

Tongue, جیبھ *jībh* (f.), (dakh.) جیب *jīb*, زبان *zabān* (f.), لسان *lisān* (f.).

Breath, دم *dam*, سانس *sāns* (f.), نفس *nafas* (f.).

Tooth, دانت *dānt*, دندان *dandān*, دسن *dasan*.

Gums, مسوڑا *masūṛā*, لثه *lisa*.

Lip, هونٹھ *hōnṭh*, لب *lab* (m. f.).

Beard, داڑهی *dāṛhī*, ریش *rīsh* (f.), خط *khatt*.

Ear, کان *kān*, گوش *gōsh*, سرون *srawan*.

Lobe or tip of the ear, بنا گوش *binā-gōsh*, نرمهٔ گوش *narma-e-gōsh*.

Drum of the ear, Tympanum, کان کا پرده *kān kā parda*.

Cheek, گال *gāl*, رخسار *rukhsār*, کپول *kapōl*.

Jaw, جبڑا *jabṛā*, جبھڑا *jabhṛā*, (jaws) کلا *kallā*.

Chin, ٹھڈی *ṭhuḍḍī*, (dakh.) تھڈی *thuḍḍī*, ذقن *zaķan*, زنخ *zanakh*.

Pit or dimple in the chin, زنخ *zanakh*, زنخدان *zanakhdān*, چاهِ غبغب *chāh-i-ghabghab*.

Dewlap, غبغب *ghabghab*.

Throat, گلا *galā*, حلق *halķ*, حلقوم *halķūm*.

Larynx, Throttle, Windpipe, Gullet, نرکھڑی *narkhaṛī*, ٹینٹوا *ṭēnṭū'ā*, نرکسی *narkasī*, نلی *nalī*, گلو *gulū*, گلا *galā*.

Neck, گردن *gardan* (f.), گلا *galā*, گریوا *grīwā* (f.), گھنچ *ghanch*.

Nape of the neck, گدی *guddī*, قفا *ķafā* (f.).

Shoulder, کاندّھا *kāndhā*, مونڈّھا *mōnḍhā*, دوش *dōsh*, (dakh.) مُنڈّا *munḍā*.

Shoulder blade, شانہ *shāna*, کتِف *katif*.

Wing, پر *par*, پنکّھ *pankh*, پچھ *pachh*, بازو *bāzū*.

Arm, بانہ *bāṅh*, ہاتّھ *hāth*.

Arm (from the shoulder to the elbow), بازُو *bāzū*, بھج *bhuj*, ڈنڈ *ḍanḍ*.

Arm (from the elbow to the wrist), پہُنچا *pahunchā*.

Wrist, کلائي *kalā'ī*, پہنچا *pahunchā*, (dakh.) منگٹ *mangaṭ*.

Hand, ہاتھ *hāth*, دسْت *dast*, چنگل *changul*, (extended) پنجہ *panja*.

Palm of the hand, ہتھیلي *hathēlī*, کفّ *kaff* (f.), کفِ دسْت *kaff-i-dast*.

Fist, مٹّھي *muṭṭhī*, مُشت *musht*.

Thumb, انگوٹّھا *angūṭhā*, انگشتِ نر *angusht-i-nar*, ابہام *ibhām*.

Finger, اُنگلي *unglī* or انگلي *anglī*, انگشت *angusht* (f.).

Forefinger, انگشتِ شہادت *angusht-i-shahādat*, کلمي کِي اُنگلي *kalmē kī unglī*, سبّابہ *sabbāba*.

Middle finger, بیچ کِي اُنگلي *bīch kī unglī*.

Ring finger, (dakh.) شہادت کِي انگلي *shahādat kī anglī*.

Little finger, (Gilch. کان انگلي *kān anglī?*), چھنگلي *chhingulī* (?).

Tips of the fingers, انامِل *anāmil*.

Nail of the finger, &c., ناخُن *nā<u>kh</u>un*, نکّھ *nakh*, نہ *nah*.

Claw, چنگل *changul*, پنجہ *panja*, ناخُن *nā<u>kh</u>un*.

Elbow, کُہنِي *kuhnī*, مِرفق *mirfak*, کوہنِي *kōhnī*.

Knuckle, اُنگلیوں کِي گانٹھ *unglīyōṅ kī gānṭh*, بند *band*.

Armpit, بغل *baghal* (f.), ككهري *kakhrī.*

Breast, Bosom, چهاتي *chhātī,* سينه *sīna.*

Pap, Nipple, Teat, Dug, سرِ پستان *sar-i-pistān,* بهتني *bhiṭnī,* ججيا *jijiyā* (f.), چونچي *chūnchī.*

Breast-bone, سر سينه *sar-sīna.*

Back, پيٹھ *pīṭh* (f.), پشت *pusht* (f.).

Backbone, ريڑه *rīṛh* (f.), ڈانڈ *ḍānḍ,* (dakh.) پيٹھ كا بانس *pīṭh kā bāns.*

Side, Ribs, پانجر *pānjar,* پسلي *paslī.*

Bosom, گود *gōd* (f.), كولا *kaulā,* كنار *kanār* or *kinār* (f.), آغوش *āghōsh* (f.).

Belly, پيٹ *pēṭ,* شكم *shikam.*

Stomach, معده *mi‘da,* جهوجه *jhōjh,* اوجه *ōjh.*

Maw, Craw, Crop, حوصله *ḥauṣila,* پوٹا *pōṭā.*

Point of the sternum or ensiform cartilage, كوڑي *kauṛī.*

Navel, ناف *nāf* (f.), نابه *nābhi* (f.), توندي *tōndī.*

Bowels, Intestines, انتڑي *antṛī,* or plur. انتڑياں *antṛiyāṅ,* آنتيں *āntēṅ* (f.).

Mesentery, انتڑيوں كي تهيلي *antṛiyōṅ kī thailī.*

Heart, هردا *hirdā,* قلب *ḳalb,* دل *dil.*

Liver, كليجه *kalēja,* جگر *jigar,* كبد *kabid.*

Lungs, Lights, ريه *riya,* or plur. ريات *riyāt* (f.), شش *shush,* پهيپهڑي *phēphṛē* (?), (dakh.) پهيپسا *phēpsā.*

Spleen, Milt, تلي *tillī,* طحال *ṭiḥāl* (f.), سپرز *supurz.*

Pluck, حَیوان کا انتریا کلیجه *ḥaiwān kā antar yā kalēja.*

Pancreas, لبلبه *lablaba.*

Kidney, گُردہ *gurda.*

Bladder, پهکنا *phuknā* or پھُوکنا *phūknā*, مثانه *maṣāna.*

Gall-bladder, Gall, Bile, پِتّا *pittā*, زهره *zahra.*

Abdomen, پیٹ *pēṭ*, شِکم *shikam*, کوکھ *kōkh* (f.), کوکھا *kōkhā* (f.).

Loins, Waste, کمر *kamar* (f.), مِیان *miyān* (f.). کٹ *kaṭ* (f.).

Flank, کوکھ *kŏkh* (f.), بغل *ba*g*h*al (f.); see Loins.

Pelvis (lower part of the belly), پیڑُو *pēṛū*, کوکھا *kōkhā.*

Private parts, اندامِ نِهانی *andām-i nihānī*, ستر *satr.*

Hip, Buttock, Ham, Haunch, Rump, کُولا *kūlā*, چُوتڑ *chūtaṛ*, سُرِین *surīn* (f.), پُوٹھ *pūṭh*, پٹّھا *puṭṭhā.*

Thigh, ران *rān* (f.), جانگھ *jāngh* (f.), جنگھا *janghā* (f.).

Knee, گھٹنا *ghuṭnā*, زانُو *zānū*, ٹھیونا *ṭhē'ōnā.*

Kneepan, کھُرِیا *khuriyā*, چکّی *chakkī*, آئِینه *ā'īna.*

Lap, گود *gōd* (f.), زانُو *zānū.*

Leg, ساق *sāḳ* (f.), پانو *pāṅw*, گوڑ *gōṛ*, پھِلّی *phillī.*

Calf of the leg, پِنڈلی *pinḍlī*, تِیلی *tīlī*, (dakh.) پِنڑی کا گوشت *pinṛī kā gōsht.*

Shin, Shin-bone, پھِلّی کی هڈّی *phillī kī haḍḍī*, (dakh.) پِنڑی کی نلّی *pinṛī kī nallī.*

Ankle, گھوٹی *ghūṭī*, کعب *ka'b*, شِتالنگ *shitālang*, (joint) ٹخنا *ṭa*kh*nā.*

Pastern (of a horse), ٹھیونا *ṭhē'ōnā*, گھُوٹی *ghūṭī.*

Heel, ایڑی *ēṛī*, پاشنه *pāshna.*

Instep, پشتِ پا *pusht-i pā.*

Foot, پانو *pañw,* پا *pā,* پیر *pair,* پگ *pag,* چرن *charan.*

Sole of the foot, تلوا *talū'ā* or تلوا *talwā,* کفِ پا *kaff-i pā.*

Toe, پانو کی اُنگلی *pāñw kī unglī,* (great) انگشتِ نر *angusht-i nar.*

Hoof, سم *sum,* کھر *khur.*

Hurts and Diseases of the Body.

Blow, Stroke, Stripe, چپیٹ *chapēṭ* (f.), ضرب *ẓarb* (f.), وار *wār,* مار *mār* (f.).

Blow with the fist, مشت *musht,* مکی *mukkī,* گھوسا *ghūsā.*

Bruise, Blow, Hurt, چوٹ *chōṭ* (f.).

Sprain, Strain, موچ *mōch,* (dakh.) موڑا *mōṛā.*

Cut, Slash, چیرا *chīrā,* زخم *zakhm.*

Scratch, small wound, چرکا *charkā.*

Wound, Sore, زخم *zakhm,* گھاو *ghā'ō,* گھائی *ghā'ē,* جراحت *jarāḥat* (f.), ریش *rēsh.*

Ulcer, Abscess, ناسور *nāsūr,* قرحه *ḳarḥa,* پھوڑا *phōṛā.*

Fistula, ناسور *nāsūr.*

Issue, Running sore, بندرکھت *bandarkhat.*

Gangrene, Mortification, خورا *khōrā,* سڑن *saṛan.*

Imposthume, Bile, Blain, دمل *dummal,* پھوڑا *phōṛā.*

Whitlow, Felon, چھلوری *chhalōrī.*

Pimple, Pustule, small Bile, بلتوڑ *baltōṛ,* پھنسی *phunsī,* چھالا *chhālā,* پنسا *pansā* (f.).

Blister, پھپھولا *phaphōlā,* چھالا *chhālā,* پھلکا *phulkā,* آبله *ābila.*

Kibe, Chap on the foot, Chilblain, بِوائِي *biwā'ī.*

Scar, Cicatrix, Mark, داغ *dāgh,* چِنْھ *chinh,* چِتّي *chittī,* چکْتا *chaktā.*

Bump, گُومْڑا *gūmṛā,* گٹْھیا *gaṭhiyā,* (from the bite of an insect) ددوڑا *dadoṛā.*

Swelling, Tumour, دُمّل *dummal,* ورم *waram,* آماس *āmās,* سُوج *sūj* (f.), پھُولاو *phūlā'ō.*

Wen, گُومْڑا *gūmṛā,* (dakh.) رسُولِي *rasūlī.*

Bronchocele, Goitre, گھیگا *ghēgā,* گھیگْھا *ghēghā.*

Scrofula, King's evil, کنْٹھ مالا *kanṭh mālā,* خنازِیر *khanāzīr.*

Cancer, سرطان *saraṭān,* ھزارچشْمہ *hazār-chashma.*

Chancre, ٹانْکِي *ṭānkī,* چٹ *chaṭ* (f.).

Wart, Excrescence, مسّا *massā,* مسْبِرْد *masbird,* اِلّا *illā.*

Pain, Ache, Ail, دُکْھ *dukh,* درْد *dard,* پِیر *pīr* (f.), بیدن *bēdan.*

Sickness, Illness, Disease, Disorder, Distemper, بِیمارِي *bīmārī,* مرْض *marz* or مرض *maraz,* آزار *āzār,* روگ *rōg.*

Contagion, Infection, سرایت *sarāyat* (f.).

Sickness at Stomach, Nausea, اوک *ōk* (f.), هِیک *hīk,* متْلائِي *matlā'ī.*

Indigestion, بد هضْمِي *bad-hazmī,* اجِیرن *ajīran.*

Fainting, Swoon, غش *ghash,* غشِي *ghashī,* مُورچّھا *mūrchhā* (f.).

Fit, بِیمارِي کِي جڑّھتِي *bīmārī kī chaṛhtī,* نوبت *naubat* (f.).

Headach, درْدِ سر *dard-i-sar,* صُداع *sudā',* (dakh.) سِر پھوڑِي *sir-phōṛī.*

Vertigo, Giddiness, Swimming in the head, دورانِ سر *daurān-i-sar.*

Ear-ach, درْدِ گوش *dard-i-gosh* (?).

Toothach, دنْت پِیر *dant-pīr* (f.), درْدِ دنْدان *dard-i dandān.*

Ophthalmia, آشوبِ چشم *āshōb-i chashm*, آنکھ کا مرض *ānkh kā maraẓ*.

Quinsy, خناق *khunāḳ*.

Sore throat, گلے کا درد *galē kā dard*.

Ringworm, Herpes, داد *dād*, بھینسیا داد *bhainsīyā-dad*.

Cold, ٹھنڈ *ṭhanḍ* (f.), سردي *sardī*, زکام *zukām*.

Catarrh, Rheum, نزله *nazla*, زکام *zukām*.

Cough, کھانسي *khānsī*, سرفه *surfa*, (dakh.) ڈھانس *ḍhāns*.

Hiccough, Hickup, ھچکي *hichkī*.

Hoarseness, گرفتگي آواز *giriftagī-āwāz* (f.).

Fever, تپ *tap* (f.), تاپ *tāp* (f.), جر *jar*, حرارت *ḥarārat* (f.).

Ague, تپ لرزه *tap-i-larza*, جوڑي *jūṛī*.

Ague, quartan, حماي ربعي *ḥummā-e rib'ī*.

Ague, tertian, تجاري *tijārī*, تپ غب *tap-i ghibb*.

Intermittent fever, انتريا *antriyā*, تپ نوبت *tap-i naubat*.

Hectick fever, تپ دق *tap-i diḳḳ*, سل *sill*.

Quotidian fever, تپ مواظبه *tap-i muwāẓaba*.

Burning fever, تپ محرق *tap-i muḥriḳ*.

Madness, Phrenzy, ديوانگي *dīwānagī*, سودا *saudā*, سڑ *siṛ* (f.).

Consumption, Phthisis, سل *sill*, چھي روگ *chhai-rōg* (or, vulg. *chha'i-rōg*).

Dropsy, Hydropsy, جلندھر *jalandhar*, استسقا *istisḳā*.

Anasarca, استسقاي زقي *istisḳā-i ziḳḳī*.

Tympany, استسقاي طبلي *istisḳā-i ṭablī*.

Pleurisy, ذاتُ آلجَنْب *ẕātu-l-jamb*, جِرْسام *jirsām*, برْسام *barsām*.

Plethora, اِفْراطِ اخلاط *ifrāṯ-i akhlāṯ*, اِفْراطِ خُون *ifrāṯ-i khūn*.

Asthma, سانْك *sānk* (f.), ضِيقُ آلنّفس *ẕīḳu-n-nafas*, دمه *dama*.

Palsy, ستنْگ *sitang*, (or hemiplegia) فالِج *fālij*, ادْهنْگ *adhang*.

Paralysis, لقْوه *laḳwa*, رعْشه *ra sha* : see Palsy.

Gout, نِقْرِس *niḳris* (improp. *naḳris*), (dakh.) گٹْهِيا بائِي *gaṯhiyā-bā'ī*.

Rheumatism, بائِي *bā'ī* or *bā'ē* (f.), بات *bāt* (m.), وجعِ مفاصِل *waja'i mafāṣil*, (dakh.) جهنكْوائِي *jhanakwā'ī*.

Jaundice, كَنْول *kańwal* or كَنْول باد *kańwal-bād*, يرْقان *yarḳān*.

Gravel, Stone, سنْگِ مثانه *sang-i maṯāna*.

A stone in the bladder, Calculus, پتّهرِي *patthrī*.

To have a palpitation of the heart, جِي دهڙكنا *jī dhaṛaknā*.

Smallpox, سِيتلا *sītalā* (f.), ماتا *mātā* (f.) or (dakh.) ماتْها *māthā*, گوٹِي *gōṯī*, چيچك *chēchak* (f.). A Pock, گوٹِي *gōṯī*.

Measles, گرْمِيدانه *garmī-dāna* (?), پنْگوٹِي *pangōṯī* (Gilch. ?).

Chincough, كهانْسِي *khāńsī*, (dakh.) كهنْگ *khang*.

A sty on the eyelids. آنْكه انْجنِي *ānkh anjanī*, انْجنْهارِي *anjanhārī*.

Gripes, Colic, پيچِش *pēchish* (f.), مروڙا *maroṛā*, قُولنْج *ḳūlinj*.

Tenesmus, هگاس *hagās* (f.), پيچِش *pēchish* (f.), سُور *sūr*.

Vomiting, اُبْكائِي *ubkā'ī* قَي *ḳai*, (f.), اِسْتِفْراغ *istifrāgh*.

Cholera, هيضه *haiẕa*, وبا *wabā* (f.).

Piles, Hemorhoids, بَواسِير *bawāsīr*.

Stoppage of the nose, Coryza, سُدّه *sudda*.

Hemorrhage, (from the nose) رُعاف *ru'āf*, (from other part) سَيلُ الدَّم *sailu-d-dam.*

Polypus, Inflammation in the nose, ناكڑا *nākṛā.*

Obstruction of the liver, سُدّۂ جِگر *sudda-i jigar.*

Diarrhœa, Flux, Dysentery, اتسار *atisār*, سِيترس *sītras*, اِسہال *is'hāl*, جِريانِ شِكم *jiryān-i shikam.*

Constipation, Costiveness, قبض *ḳabẓ* (f.), قبضِيت *ḳabẓiyat* (f.) بستگي *bastagī.*

Venereal, باؤ *bā'ō* (f.), بادِ فرنگ *bād-i farang*, آتشک *ātashak* (f.).

Gonorrhoea, سوزاک *sōzāk*, پرميو *parmē'ō*, پرميه *pramēh.*

Diabetes, سِلسِلِ بَول *silsil-i baul.*

Dysury, Strangury, حبسُ البَول *ḥabsu-l-baul*, عسرُ البَول *ʿusru-l-baul.*

Epilepsy, مِرگي *mirgī*, اپسمار *apasmār.*

Rupture, Hernia, باد خايه *bād khāya*, فتق *fatḳ.*

Leprosy, كوڑه *kōṛh*, جُذام *juẕām*, پيس *pēs*, سُفيدي *sufaidī.*

Elephantiasis, فيل پا *fīl-pā*, مہا كوڑه *mahā kōṛh.*

Plague, Pestilence, وَبا *wabā* (f.), مري *marī.*

Epidemic, مہامار *mahā-mār*, مرضِ عام *maraẓ-i-ʿāmm.*

Famine, قحط *ḳaḥṭ*, قحط سالي *ḳaḥṭ-sālī*, كال *kāl*, دُبهك *dubhuk.*

Hunger, بهوكه *bhūkh* (f.), گُرسنگي *gursinagī*, جُوع *jūʿ.*

Thirst, پياس *piyās* (f.), تراس *trās* (f.), تِشنگي *tishnagī*, عطش *ʿaṭash* (f.).

Persons employed in curing diseases.

Physician, حكيم *ḥakīm*, طبيب *ṭabīb*, بَيد *baid.*

Surgeon, جرّاح *jarrāḥ.*

Apothecary, Druggist, عطّار *āṭṭār*, دواساز *dawā-sāz*, پنساري *pansārī* (m.).

Phlebotomist, رگ زن *rag-zan*, فصّاد *faṣṣād.*

Cupper, حجّام *ḥajjām*, سينگي والا *sīngī-wālā.*

Bonesetter, كمانگر *kamān-gar.*

Medical means.

Medicine, Drug, دَوا *dawā* (f.), دارُو *dārū* (f.), اَوشدھ *aushadh* (f.).

Remedy, Cure, علاج *ilāj*, چاره *chāra.*

Emetic, مُقيّي *mukaiyī*, قَي كِي دَوا *kai kī dawā.*

Purge, جُلّاب *jullāb*, جھاڑ *jhāṛ.*

Bleeding, فصد *faṣd* (f.).

Electuary, معجون *ma'jūn*, نوش دارُو *nōsh-dārū.*

Ointment, مرهم *marham*, ليپ *lēp.*

Plaster, Salve, مرهم *marham*, ليپ *lep*, ضماد *ẓamād* (f.).

Fomentation, سينک *sēnk*, كِماد *kimād.*

Embrocation, تتار *tatār* (f.), ضماد *ẓamād* (f.), طِلا *ṭilā.*

Poultice, لوپڑي *lopṛī*, ٹِكور *ṭikōr.*

Bandage, ضماد *ẓamād* (f.), پٹّي *paṭṭī.*

Clyster, حُقنه *ḥukna.*

The Mind and its Attributes or Affections.

Mind, من *man*, بُوجھ *būjh* (f.), مُدرِكه *mudrika*, هوش *hōsh.*

Intellect, Understanding, عقل *āḳl* (f.), هوش *hōsh*, بدّھ *budh* (f.), فہم *fahm.*

Reason, عقل *åḳl* (f.); reasoning faculty, نطق *nuṭḳ*.

Will, Wish, ارادہ *irāda*, اچھا *ichchhā* (f.), بچار *bichār*.

Desire, شوق *shauḳ*, چاہ *chāh* (f.), ہوس *hawas* (f.), خواہش *khwā-hish* (f.).

Avarice, لالچ *lālach*, بخل *bukhl*, حرص *ḥirṣ* (f.).

Ambition, ہوس *hawas* (f.), امنگ *umang* (f.), حوصلہ *ḥauṣila*.

Affection, محبت *muḥabbat* (f.), پیار *piyār*, نیہ *nēh* (f.), درد *dard*.

Love, عشق *i̊shḳ*, چاہ *chāh*, پیار *pyār*, ہوا *hawā* (f.).

Hatred, Dislike, Aversion, نفرت *nafrat* (f.), بد خواہی *bad-khwāhī*, گریز *gurēz*.

Disgust, Abhorrence, کراہیت *karāhiyat* (f.), نفرت *nafrat* (f.), گھن *ghin*, (f.), بیزاری *bēzārī*.

Anger, Passion, Rage, کرودھ *brōdh*, خشم *khashm*, غصہ *ghuṣṣa*, غضب *ghaẓab*, رس *ris* (f.), طیش *ṭaish* (f.).

Pleasure, Joy, Mirth, Gladness, خوشی *khushī*, عیش *åish*, فرحت *farḥat* (f.), بلاس *bilās*, آنند *ānand*, سرور *surūr*, خرمی *khurramī*.

Happiness, Felicity, کامرانی *kāmrānī*, آنند *ānand*, خوشوقتی *khush-waḳtī*.

Hope, امید *ummēd* (f.), آس *ās* (f.), آسا *āsā* (f.).

Reliance, Faith, Trust, آس *ās* (f.), اعتماد *i̊timād*, بھروسا *bhrōsā*, تکیہ *takiya*, اعتبار *i̊tibār*.

Fear, Dread, Apprehension, ڈر *ḍar*, وسواس *waswās*, بھی *bhai*, سنکا *sankā* (f.).

Doubt, Suspicion, شک *shakk*, سندیہ *sandēh*, دبدھا *dubdhā* (f.), شبہہ *shubha*.

Courage, Valour, جُرأت *jur'at* (f.), هِمّت *himmat* (f.), دِليرِي *dilērī.*

Cowardice, بي هِمّتِي *be-himmātī,* نا مرْدِي *nā-mardi.*

Shame, Bashfulness, Modesty, شرْم *sharm* (f.), لاج *lāj* (f.), حَيا *ḥayā* (f.).

Jealousy, ظنّ *ẓann,* جهل *jhal* (f.), ڈاہ *ḍāh* (f.), شكّ *shakk.*

Spite, Malice, Grudge, Envy, بُغْض *bughẓ,* رشْك *rashk,* كِينه *kīna.*

Animosity, Enmity, بَير *bair,* لاگ *lāg* (f.), عداوت *ʿadāwat* (f.).

Vengeance, Revenge, اِنْتقام *intiḳām,* بَير *bair,* بدْلا *badlā.*

Mercy, Compassion, Pity, رحْم *raḥm,* دَيا *dayā* (f.), پِير *pīr* (f.).

Patience, صبر *ṣabr* (f.), صبُورِي *ṣabūrī,* دهِيرج *dhīraj.*

Morals, moral and immoral Actions.

Morals, Manners, سِيرت *sīrat* (f.), اخْلاق *akhlāḳ,* ادب *adab.*

Ceremonies, Custom, Etiquette, آداب *ādāb,* رسْم *rasm* (f.), چال (f.).

Politeness, good manners, خُلْق *khulḳ,* مُرُوّت *murūwat* (f.).

Civility, سُلُوك *sulūk,* خُلْق *khulḳ,* اِنْسانِيَت *insāniyat* (f.).

Honesty, Probity, سچّائِي *sachchā'ī,* راسْتِي *rāstī,* سچَوتِي *sachautī.*

Immorality, Dishonesty, بدمعاشي *bad-ma'āshī,* ادْهرْم *adharm.*

Knavery, Treachery, دغابازِي *daghā-bāzī,* بي اِيمانِي *be-īmānī.*

Falsehood, Deceit, جهُوٹه *jhūṭh,* مكْر *makr,* دروغ *darōgh.*

Temperance, Sobriety, پرْهيز *parhēz,* سنْجم *sanjam,* ورَع *waraʿ.*

Intemperance, Extravagance, بد پرْهيزِي *bad-parhēzī,* فضُولي *fazūlī.*

Prodigality, Waste, اِسْراف *iṣrāf,* ور خرْچِي *war-kharchī,* تلف *talaf.*

Niggardliness, Stinginess, كنْجُوسِي *kanjūsī,* تنْگدِلي *tangdilī.*

Liberality, Generosity, سخاوت *sak͟hāwat* (f.), جود *jūd*, كرم *karam*.

Beneficence, احسان *iḥsān*, اپكار *upakār*, فيض *faiẓ*.

Friendship, Kindness, مهرباني *mihrbānī*, كرپا *kirpā* (f.).

Professions, Occupations.

Theology, Divinity, فقه *fiḳh* (f.), علمِ الهي *ʿilm-i ilāhī*.

Medicine (practice of), Physic, طبابت *ṭabābat* (f.), طب *ṭibb* (f.).

Law, Jurisprudence, فقه *fiḳh* (f.), عدالت *ʿadālat* (f.), شرع *sharʿ*.

Military Profession, سپاه گري *sipāh-garī*.

Agriculture, Husbandry, سير *sīr*, كشتكاري *kishtkārī*, زراعت *zirāʿat* (f.).

Merchandise, Commerce, تجارت *tijārat* (f.), سوداگري *saudāgarī*, بيپار *baipār*, بنج *banij*, سودا *saudā*.

Servitude, Slavery, بندگي *bandagī*, چاكري *chākarī*, نوكري *naukarī*, غلامي *g͟hulāmī*, ٹہل *ṭahal* (f.).

People of Professions, Occupations, or Trades.

Theologian, فقيه *faḳīh*, اهلِ معرفت *ahl-i maʿrifat*, اچارج *achāraj*.

Lawyer, فقيه *faḳīh*, عدالت كا وكيل *ʿadālat kā wakīl*.

Soldier, سپاهي *sipāhī*, سپاهي پيشه *sipāhī pēsha*, لشكري *lashkarī*.

Physician, طبيب *ṭabīb*, بيد *baid*, حكيم *ḥakīm*.

Author (writer), مؤلف *mu'allif*, گرنتھ كار *granth-kār*, مصنف *muṣannif*.

Cultivator, Husbandman, كسان *kisān*, دهقان *dihḳān*, مزارع *muzāriʿ*.

Merchant, Trader, سوداگر *saudāgar*, تاجر *tājir*, بيپاري *baipārī* (m.).

Grain-merchant, بنجارا *banjārā*, غله فروش *g͟halla-farōsh*.

Banker, Moneychanger, مہاجن *mahājan*, صرّاف *ṣarrāf*, سیٹھ *sēṭh*.

Broker, Salesman, دلّال *dallāl*, مُقِیم *muḳīm*.

Artificer, Artisan, کارِیگر *kārīgar*, کسْبِي *kasbī* (m.), پیشہور *pesha-war*.

Draper, Linen-draper, Mercer, Cloth-merchant, بزّاز *bazzāz*.

Silk-mercer, أبْرِیشْمِینہ فروش *abrēshmīna-farōsh*, حرِیر فروش *ḥarīr-farōsh*.

Weaver, جُلاها *julāhā*, تانْتِي *tāntī* (m.), بافِندہ *bāfinda*.

Embroiderer, زردوز *zar-dōz*, چِکن دوز *chikan-dōz*.

Carpet-weaver, شطْرنْجِي باف *shaṭranjī-bāf*.

Tailor, درْزِي *darzī* (m.), سُوجِي *sūjī* (m.), خیّاط *khaiyāṭ*.

Shoemaker, Cobbler, موچِي *mōchī* (m.), کفْشْدوز *kafshdōz*.

Saddler زِینگر *zīngar*, موچِي *mōchī* (m.), سرّاج *sarrāj*.

Tanner, Currier, چمار *chamār*, دبّاغ *dabbāgh*, ڈبْگر *ḍabgar*.

Grocer, بقّال *baḳḳāl*, پنْسارِي *pansārī*, عطّار *ʿaṭṭār*.

Druggist, Apothecary, پنْسارِي *pansārī* (m.), عطّار *ʿaṭṭār*.

Ironmonger, آهن فروش *āhan-farōsh*.

Blacksmith, لوهار *lōhār*, آهنگر *āhangar*, حدّاد *ḥaddād*.

Farrier, نعْلْبنْد *naʿl-band*, سالوتِرِي *sālōtarī*: see Horse-doctor.

Coppersmith, Brasier, Tinker, مِسْگر *misgar*, کسیرا *kasēra*, ٹهٹهیرا *ṭhaṭhērā*.

Jeweller, جَوهرِي *jauharī*, جڑِیا *jaṛiyā*, زیور فروش *zēwar-farōsh*.

Goldsmith, Silversmith, سُنار *sunār*, زرگر *zargar*.

Cutler, کاردْگر *kāradgar*, لوهار *lōhār*.

Needle-maker, سوزنگر *sōzan-gar*.

Arrow-maker, تِیرگر *tīr-gar*.

Cartwright, Carpenter, Cabinet-maker, بڑهيي *barha'ī* (m.), كهاتي *khātī* (m.), نجّار *najjār*, درودگر *darōdgar*.

Cook, باورچي *bāwarchī* (m.), رسوئيا *rasō'iyā*, طبّاخ *ṭabbākh*.

Sutler, Innkeeper, بهٹهيارا *bhaṭhiyārā*.

Baker, نانبائي *nānbā'ī* (m.), نانپز *nānpaz*, طبّاخ *ṭabbākh*.

Butcher, قصّاب *ḳaṣṣāb*, قصائي *ḳaṣā'ī* (m.), ذابح *zābiḥ*.

Poulterer, مرغبان *murghbān*, مرغيوالا *murghīwālā*.

Fishmonger, ماهي فروش *māhī-farōsh*, مچهلي والا *machhlī-wālā*.

Green-grocer or -seller, تره فروش *tara-farōsh*, كنجڑا *kunjṛā*.

Gardener, مالي *mālī*, باغبان *bāghbān*, (dakh.) باغوالا *bāghwālā*.

Architect, Builder, Mason, Bricklayer, معمار *mi*'*mār*, تهوئي *thawa'ī* (m.), راج *rāj*, راز *rāz*.

Stonecutter, سنگ فروش *sang-farōsh*.

Brickmaker, خشت پز *khisht-paz*, اينٹ والا *īnṭ-wālā*.

Potter, كمهار *kumhār*, كلال *kulāl*, كسگر *kas-gar*.

Plasterer, كسگر *kas-gar*.

Accountant, Cashier, Clerk, Writer, متصدّي *mutaṣaddī*, محرّر *muḥarrir* ليكهك *lēkhak*.

Village Accountant, كرمچاري *karamchārī* (m.).

Steward, بكاول *bakāwal*, بهنڈاري *bhanḍārī* (m.), ديوان *dīwān*.

House-Steward, Butler, خانسامان *khānsāmān*, خدمتگار *khidmatgār*, بهنڈاري *bhanḍārī*, مودي *mōdī*.

Brewer, بوزاگر *bōzā-gar*.

Printer, چهاپےوالا *chhāpē-wālā*, (of cloth) چھیپي *chhīpī*, نقّاش *naḳḳāsh*.

Engraver, قلم کار *ḳalam-kār*, کنده کار *kanda-kār*.

Carver, Sculptor, Statuary, کنده کار *kanda-kār*, نقّاش *naḳḳāsh*.

Painter, Draftsman, چتر کار *chitr-kār*, مُصوِّر *muṣauwir*, نقّاش *naḳḳāsh*.

Actor, Mimic, Player, بهانڈ *bhānḍ*, سوانگي *swāngī*, بہُروپِیا *bahurūpiyā*, نقّال *naḳḳāl*.

Adjutant, Aide de camp, نقِیب *naḳīb*, مُصاحِب *muṣāḥib*.

Administrator, Executor (of a will), وَصِي *waṣī*.

Advertiser, Reporter, Intelligencer, مُخبِر *mukhbir*, خبر دار *khabar-dār*, شہر خبرا *shahr-khabrā*.

Alchymist, مُہوّس *muhawwis*, کِیمیاگر *kīmiyāgar*.

Amanuensis, کاتِب *kātib*, لِکھني داس *likhnī-dās*, لیکھک *lēkhak*.

Ambassador, Envoy, ایلچِي *ēlchī*, وکِیل *wakīl*, دُوت *dūt*, سفِیر *safīr*.

Angler, بنسِي باز *bansī-bāz*.

Annotator, مُفسِّر *mufassir*, شارِح *shāriḥ*.

Appraiser, Valuer, Assizer, نِرخي *nirkhī*, مُقِیم *muḳīm*.

Arbitrator, Umpire, ثالِث *ṣāliṣ*, حکم *ḥakam*, مُنصِف *munṣif*.

Archer, تِیر انداز *tīr-andāz*, کماندار *kamān-dār*, دھنک دھر *dhanuk-dhar*.

Arithmetician, مُحاسِب *muḥāsib*, گنک *ganak*, سِیاق دان *siyāḳ-dān*.

Armourer, صیقل گر *ṣaiḳal-gar*.

Artist, دست کار *dast-kār*, اُستاد *ustād*, کارِیگر *kārīgar*.

Ascetic, تپسي *tapsī* (m.), گوشه نِشِین *gōsha nishīn*.

Assassin, قاتل *ḳātil*, سفاک *saffāk*, ٹهگ *ṭhag*.

Assayer (of coins), ناقد *nāḳid*, نقاد *naḳḳād*, پركهيا *parakhaiyā*.

Assistant (in office), پيش دست *pēsh-dast*, پيش كار *pēsh-kār*.

Astrologer, Astronomer, منجم *munajjim*, جوتكهي *jōtikhī* (m.), نجومي *nujūmī*.

Attorney, نايب *nā'ib*, وكيل *wakīl*.

Auctioneer, نيلام كرني والا *nilām karnē-wālā*.

Auditor (of accounts), مستوفي *mustaufī* (m.), محاسب *muḥāsib*.

Augurer, شگونيا *shugūniyā*.

Barber, حجام *ḥajjām*, ناپت *nāpit*, استا *ustā*.

Bearer (of a letter, &c.), حامل *ḥāmil*, (porter) حمال *ḥammāl*, موٹيا *moṭiyā*, قلي *ḳulī*, (chairman) مهرا *mahrā*, كهار *kahār*, بهوي *bhō'ī*.

Beggar, بهكهاري *bhikhārī* (m.), فقير *faḳīr*, گدا *gadā*, سايل *sā'il*.

Bell-founder, جرس ساز *jaras-sāz*.

Binder (of a book), جلد گر *jild-gar*, صحاف *ṣaḥḥāf*.

Bird-catcher, مير شكار *mīr-shikār*, چڑيمار *chiṛīmār*, صياد *ṣaiyād*.

Boatman, ملاح *mallāḥ*, كشتيبان *kishtībān*, مانجهي *mānjhī*, (rower) ڈانڈي *ḍānḍī* (m.).

Bookkeeper, حساب نويس *ḥisāb-nawīs*, محرر *muḥarrir*.

Bookseller, صحاف *ṣaḥḥāf*, كتاب فروش *kitāb-farōsh*.

Bootmaker, موزه گر *moza-gar*.

Bowmaker, كمانگر *kamāngar*.

Boxer, مشت زن *musht-zan*, مال *māl*, مل *mall*.

Bracelet-maker, چوڑیہار *chūṛī-hār.*

Buffoon, مسخره *maskhara,* بهانڈ *bhānḍ.*

Burnisher, صیقل گر *ṣaiḳal-gar.*

Butterman, مکهنیا *makhaniyā.*

Calenderer, کندیگر *kundī-gar.*

Camel driver or keeper, ساربان *sārbān,* شتربان *shutur-bān.*

Cardmaker, گنجیفه ساز *ganjīfa-sāz.*

Carman, Carter, Coachman, گاڑیوان *gāṛīwān,* گاڑیبان *gāṛībān.*

Carpet-maker, شطرنجي باف *shaṭranjī-bāf.*

Cashier, تحویلدار *taḥwīl-dār,* فوطه دار *fōṭa-dār,* روکڑیا *rokaṛiyā.*

Cavalier, سوار *sawār,* سوارکار *sawār-kār,* بهل گهوڑیا *bhal-ghōṛiyā.*

Chairman (president), میر مجلس *mīr-majlis:* (bearer) see Bearer.

Chandler, شمع ساز *sham*'*-sāz.*

Charioteer, رتهبان *rath-bān,* سارتهي *sārathī* (m.).

Cheesemonger, پنیر فروش *panīr-farōsh.*

Chess-player, شطرنجباز *shaṭranj-bāz,* شاطر *shāṭir.*

Chiromancer, سمدرکي *samudrakī* (m.).

Chronologer, Chronicler, مورخ *mu'arrikh.*

Chymist, کیمیاگر *kīmiyā-gar,* رساینی *rasāyanī* (m.).

Clockmaker, ساعت ساز *sā'at-sāz.*

Coiner, ضراب *ẓarrāb,* (counterfeiter, forger) تغلبي *taghallubī* (m.).

Collector (tax-gatherer), تحصیل دار *taḥṣīl-dār,* باجدار *bāj-dār.*

Colonel, هزاري *hazārī* (m.), سالار *sālār.*

Comedian, بہرُوپیا *bahu-rūpiyā*, سَوانگي *sawāngī*, نقّال *naḳḳāl*.

Commander, سرْدار *sardār*, سالار *sālār*, حاکِم *ḥākim*, امِیر *amīr*.

Commentator, مفسِّر *mufassir*, شارِح *shāriḥ*, ٹیکا کار *ṭīkā-kār*.

Commissary, سرْبراہ کار *sarbarāh-kār*, داروغہ *dārōgha*.

Commissioner, امِین *amīn*, مُخْتار کار *mukhtār-kār*, مہْتمِم *muhtamim*.

Compiler, مؤلِّف *mu'allif*, گرنْتھ کار *granth-kār*, جامِع *jāmi'*.

Composer, مُصنِّف *muṣannif*, اِنْشا پرْداز *inshā-pardāz*.

Conductor, راہ نما *rāh-numā*, راہ بر *rāh-bar*, اگْوا *agwā*.

Confectioner, حلْوائي *ḥalwā'ī*, مِٹْھائي گر *miṭhā'ī-gar*.

Conjurer, جادُوگر *jādūgar*, ٹونْھا *ṭōnhā*, حاضِراتي *ḥāẓirātī*, جان *jān*.

Consul, وکِیل *wakīl*: see Commissioner.

Contractor, مُسْتاجِر *mustājir*.

Controller, داروغہ *dārōgha*, (of accounts) مُسْتَوفي *mustaufī*.

Cooper, پیپا بناني والا *pīpā banānē-wālā*.

A Corporal, نایک *nāyak*.

Counsellor, مُشِیر *mushīr*, مُدبِّر *mudabbir*, منْتْري *muntrī* (m.).

Courier, پیک *paik*, قاصِد *ḳāṣid*, ہرْکارہ *harkāra*.

Courtier, دربْاري *darbārī*, حضُوري *ḥuẓūrī*, اہْلِ مجْلِس *ahl-i majlis*.

Cow-herd, Cowkeeper, گوپال *gōpāl*, گوال *gwāl* or گوالا *gwālā*, اہِیر *ahīr*.

Crier, ڈھنْڈھوریا *ḍhanḍhoriyā*, مُنادي *munadi*.

Critic, حرْف گِیر *ḥarf-gīr*, مُو شِگاف *mū-shigāf*.

Cuirassier, بکْتر پوش *baktar-pōsh*.

Cupbearer, ساقِي *sāḳī*, بکاول *bakāwal*.

Darner, رفُوگر *rafū-gar.*

Dervis, درویش *darwēsh,* فقِیر *faḳīr.*

Devotee, زاهِد *zāhid,* عابِد *ābid,* رِیاضتِي *riyāẓatī,* جوگي *jōgī.*

Dier, صبّاغ *ṣabbāgh,* رنْگ ریز *rang-rēz.*

Digger, بیلْدار *bēl-dār,* کودْگر *kōdgar.*

Director (manager), کار پرْداز *kār-pardāz,* کار کُن *kār-kun,* مُخْتار کار *mukhtār-kār.*

Disciple, سِکھ *sikh,* شاگِرْد *shāgird,* چیلا *chēlā,* تلْمِیذ *talmīẕ.*

Distiller, آبْکار *āb-kār,* کلار *kalār,* سُونْڑِي *sūnṛī* (m.), (dakh.) کلال *kalāl.*

Diver, غوّاص *ghawwāṣ,* مرْجِیا *marjiyā,* غوطه خور *ghoṭa-khōr.*

Diviner, غیب دان *ghaib dān,* شُگُونِیا *shugūniyā :* see Astrologer.

Doctor, عالِم *ālim,* مولوِي *maulawī* (m.), پنْڈِت *panḍit :* see Physician.

Doorkeeper, دربْان *darbān* or درْوان *darwān,* ڈیوڑْھِي دار *dē'ōrhī-dār.*

Drover, بلْدِیا *baldiyā,* گلّه بان *galla-bān.*

Drudge, ٹہلْوا *ṭahlū'a,* مِحْنتِي *miḥnatī* (m. f.).

Drummer, ڈھولِیا *ḍhōliyā,* طنْبُورْچِي *ṭambūr-chī,* طبْل نواز *ṭabl-nawāz.*

Embroiderer, چِکن دوز *chikan-dōz,* زردوز *zar-dōz.*

Enameller, مِینا کار *mīnā-kār.*

Enchanter, جادُوگر *jādū-gar,* افْسُون گر *afsūn-gar,* ساحِر *sāḥir.*

Executioner, جلّاد *jallād,* بدْھِک *badhik.*

Factor, Agent, گُماشْته *gumūshta,* کار پرْداز *kār-pardāz,* کار گُذار *kār-guẕār.*

Falconer, بازْدار *bāz-dār,* شاهِین پرْور *shāhīn-parwar.*

Farmer, کِسان *kisān,* مِلْکِي *milkī,* چاسِي *chāsī,* زمِین دار *zamīn-dār.*

Fencer, Cudgeller, پٹي باز *paṭē-bāz,* لکڑباز *lakaṛ-bāz.*

Ferryman, گُذربان *guẕar-bān,* پٹني *paṭnī,* نيّا *naiyā.*

Fiddler, سارنگيا *sārangiyā,* سارنگي نواز *sārangī-nawāz.*

Fisherman, ماهي گير *māhī-gīr,* مچهوا *machhwā,* جليا *jaliyā.*

Footpad, راه زن *rāh-zan,* بٹ پار *baṭ-pār* : see Robber.

Forester, بن باس *ban-bās* : see Ranger.

Fortuneteller, سمُدرکي *samudrikī* (m.), رمّال *rammāl,* نُجومي *nujūmī* (m.).

Founder, Caster, کسيرا *kasērā,* (dakh.) کسار *kasār* : see Coppersmith.

Friar, فقير *faḳīr,* زاهد *zāhid,* قلندر *ḳalandar* : see Monk.

Fruiterer, ميوه فروش *mewa-farōsh.*

Furbisher, Polisher, صيقل گر *ṣaiḳal-gar.*

Furrier, سمور فروش *samūr-farōsh.*

Fusileer, زنبورچي *zambūr-chī,* بندوقچي *bandūḳ-chī.*

Gambler, Gamester, جواري *jwārī* (m.), پهڑ باز *phaṛ-bāz,* قمار باز *ḳimār-bāz.*

General, سالار *sālār,* سپاه سالار *sīpāh-sālār,* سردار *sardār.*

Generalissimo, سيناپت *sēnāpat,* اميرالامرا *amīru-l-umarā.*

Geometrician, مهندس *muhandis,* هندسه دان *handasa-dān.*

Gilder, طلا کار *ṭilā-kār,* کوفت گر *kōft-gar.*

Glass-maker, شيشه گر *shīsha-gar.*

Glazier, شيشه جڑني والا *shīsha jaṛnē-wālā.*

Governess (female teacher), آتو *ātū* (f.).

Governor, حاکم *ḥākim,* عامل *āmil,* ناظم *nāẓim,* سردار *sardār.*

Grammarian, صرف نحودان *ṣarf-naḥv-dān*, بياكرني *byākaranī*.

Grass-cutter, گهسيارا *ghasiyārā*.

Grave-digger, گورکن *gōr-kan*.

Grazier, چرواها *charwāhā*, چراني والا *charānē-wālā* : see Shepherd.

Groom, سائيس *sā'īs*, نفر *nafar*, سيس *sa'īs*.

Gunner, گولنداز *gōlandāz*, گلچلا *gulchalā*, بندهاني *bandhānī*.

Haberdasher, بساطي *bisāṭī* or بساتي *bisātī*, پٹوا *paṭwā* : see Pedler.

Harper, چنگي *changī*, بربط نواز *barbaṭ-nawāz*.

Helmsman, مانجهي *mānjhī* (m.), سکاني *sukkānī* (m.): see Steersman.

Herald, منادي *munādī*, ڈهنڈهوريا *ḍhanḍhōriyā*.

Herdsman, گله بان *galla-bān*, بلديا *baldiyā*, چرواها *charwāhā*.

Hermit, گوشه نشين *gōsha-nishīn*, خلوت نشين *khalwat-nishīn*.

Highwayman, راه زن *rāh-zan*, قزاق *kazzāk* : بٹ پار *baṭ-pār*.

Historian, مورخ *mu'arrikh*, راوي *rāwī*.

Horsebreaker, چابک سوار *chābuk-sawār*, شهسوار *shah-sawār*.

Horse-doctor, سالوتري *sālōtarī*, بيطار *baiṭār*.

Horseman (trooper), سوار *sawār*, بارگير *bārgīr*, ترک سوار *turk-sawār*.

Hosier, موزي باف *mōzē-bāf*, موزي فروش *mōzē-farōsh*.

Hostler, بهٹهياري خاني کا سائيس *bhaṭhiyārī khānē kā sā'īs*.

Housebreaker, سيندهيا *sēndhiyā*, نقب زن *nakb-zan*.

Hunter, Huntsman, شکارباز *shikār-bāz*, صياد *ṣaiyād*.

Jailer, بندي خاني کا نگهبان *bandī-khānē kā nigahbān*.

Jester, مسخره *mūskhara*, (funny fellow) ٹهٹهي باز *ṭhaṭhē-bāz*.

Inlayer, مُنبّت‌کار *munabbat-kār.*

Innkeeper, بهٹھیارا *bhaṭhiyārā,* کلار *kalār,* (dakh.) کلال *kalāl.*

Interpreter, ترجمان *tarjumān,* دوبھاشیا *dō-bhāshiyā.*

Jockey, چابُک سوار *chābuk-sawār,* سوار *sawār,* شہسوار *shah-sawār.*

Joiner, بڑھیی *baṛha'ī,* ستار *sutār:* see Cartwright, Carpenter.

Judge, قاضي *ḳāẓī* (m.), حاکِم *ḥākim,* مُنصِف *munṣif,* مُفتي *muftī.*

Juggler, حُقّه‌باز *ḥukḳa-bāz,* ڈیٹھ بند *dīṭh-band,* بٹّي‌باز *baṭṭē-bāz.*

Justice (of the peace), قاضي *ḳāẓī:* see Judge.

Keeper, رکھوالا *rakh-wālā,* نگاهبان *nigāh-bān.*

Labourer, مزدور *mazdūr,* محنتي *miḥnatī* (m. f.), قُلي *ḳulī.*

Land-steward, پٹوار *paṭwār,* سزاوِل *sazāwal.*

Land-surveyor or -measurer, جریب‌کش *jarīb-kash.*

Language-master, مُنشي *munshī,* آخون *ākhun,* اُستاد *ustād.*

Lecturer, مُدرِس *mudarris:* see Professor, Preacher.

Lexicographer, لُغت‌نَویس *lughat-nawīs.*

Librarian, کتاب‌خاني کا داروغه *kitāb-khānē kā dārōgha.*

Lighterman, بهڑوالا *bhaṛ-wālā,* بهڑ کا ملّاح *bhaṛ ḳā mallāḥ.*

Limner, صورت‌گر *ṣūrat-gar,* مُصوِّر *muṣauwir:* see Painter.

Mace-bearer, چوبدار *chōb-dār,* سونٹي‌بردار *sōnṭē-bardār.*

Machinist, کل‌ساز *kal-sāz,* صنعت‌گر *ṣan'at-gar* (?).

Magician, جادوگر *jādū-gar,* افسونگر *afsūn-gar,* بهوکس *bhōkas.*

Magistrate, فوجدار *faujdār,* قاضي *kāẓī,* حاکِم *ḥākim:* see Judge.

Major-domo, کُلکلان *kulkulān,* سربراه کار *sarbarāh-kār.*

Manager, کارگذار *kār-guẕār*, پیشکار *pēshkār:* see Director.

Manufacturer, کاریگر *kārīgar*, دستکار *dast-kār:* see Artificer.

Mariner, ملاح *mallāḥ*, کشتیبان *kishtī-ban:* see Sailor.

Mathematician, ریاضي دان *riyāẓī-dān*, مهندس *muhandis.*

Mechanic, کاریگر *kārīgar*, اهل حرفه *ahl-i-ḥirfa*, پیشه‌ور *pēsha-war.*

Mendicant, گدا *gadā*, درویش *darwēsh*, فقیر *faḳīr*, جنگم *jangam.*

Messenger, قاصد *ḳāṣid*, هرکاره *harkāra*, دوت *dūt*, سندیسي *sandēsī.*

Midwife, داي جناي *dā'ī-jānā'ī.*

Milkman, دودهوالا *dūdh-wālā:* Milkmaid, دودهوالي *dūdh-wālī.*

Miller, پیسنهارا *pīsan-hārā.*

Minister (of state), وزیر *wazīr*, پردهان *pardhān:* see Priest.

Mint-master, تکسال کا داروغه *ṭaksāl kā dārōg͟ha.*

Monk, درویش *darwēsh*, فقیر *faḳīr*, زاهد *zāhid*, بیراگي *bairāgī.*

Muleteer, خچربان *k͟hachchar-bān.*

Musician, مطرب *muṭrib*, مغني *mug͟hannī*, کلاونت *kalāwant.*

Mustermaster, عارض *ʿāriẓ*, کروڑا *karoṛā*, جایزه گیر *jā'iza-gīr.*

Musketeer, برقنداز *barḳandāz*, بندوقچي *bandūḳchī.*

Navigator, ملاح *mallāḥ*, کشتیبان *kishtībān*, مانجهي *mānjhī* (m.).

Necromancer, جادوگر *jādūgar*, ٹوني باز *ṭōnē-bāz*, ساحر *sāḥir.*

Needle-maker, سوزن گر *sōzan-gar.*

Notary, دبیر *dabīr.*

Nurse (of a sick person), بیماردار *bīmār-dār.*

Nurse (of a child), انّي *annī*, دادا *dādā* (f.), داي *dā'ī.*

Nurse (wet), داۓي پلاۓي *dā'ī-pīlā'ī*, (dry) داۓي کهلاۓي *dā'ī-khilā'ī*.

Nurse (male), دايا *dāyā*, انّا *annā*.

Oculist, كحّال *kaḥḥāl*, ستهيا *sathiyā* (?).

Officer, منصب دار *manṣab-dār*, عهده دار *ūhda-dār*, سردار *sardār*.

Oilman, Oil-merchant, تيلي *tēlī*, روغن فروش *raughan-farosh*.

Ostler, سائيس *sā'īs*, چرواادار *chirwādār* (?): see Groom.

Overseer, كروڑا *karōṛā*, داروغه *dārōgha*, اهتمامچي *ihtimāmchī*.

Palmister, سمدركي *samudrikī*, بهدري *bhadrī* (m.).

Papermaker, كاغذي *kāghazī*, كاغذ گر *kāghaz-gar*.

Parcher of grain, بهڑبهونجا *bhaṛbhūnjā*.

Pastor, گلّه بان *galla-bān*, چوپان *chaupān*, پاسبان *pāsbān*, (spiritual guide) گرو *gurū*, هادي *hādī*, مرشد *murshid*.

Pastry-cook, حلواۓي *ḥalwā'ī*: see Confectioner.

Patcher, پاره دوز *pāra-doz*, پيوند كار *paiwand-kār*.

Paver, Pavier, فرش بند *farsh-band*.

Pawn-broker, بندهكگير *bandhak-gīr*, مرتهن *murtahin*: see Banker.

Paymaster, خزانچي *khazān-chī*, بخشي *bakhshī*, (general) مير بخشي *mīr-bakhshī*.

Pedler, بساطي *bisāṭī* (m), دست فروش *dast-farōsh*, پهڑيا *phaṛiyā*.

Penman, خوش نويس *khush-nawīs*, خطّاط *khaṭṭāṭ*.

Perfumer, گندهي *gandhī* (m.), عطّار *āṭṭār*, عطر فروش *āṭr-farōsh*.

Pewterer, كسيرا *kasērā*: see Brasier.

Philosopher, فيلسوف *failsūf*, فلسفي *falsafī* (m.), حكيم *ḥakīm*.

Physiognomist, سمُدرِكي *samudrikī*, قِيافه دان *ḳiyāfa-dān*.

Pickpocket, جيب كترا *jēb-katrā*, كِيسه بُر *kīsa-bur*.

Pilgrim, اتيت *atīt*, جاتري *jātrī* (m.), سيّاح *saiyāḥ*, (to Mecca) حاجِي *ḥājī* (m.).

Pilot, مُعلِّم *mu'allim*, اركاتي *arkāṭī*, كرن دهار *kārn-dhār*.

Pioneer, لُونِيا *lūniyā*, بيلدار *bēl-dār*.

Pirate, ڈكيت *ḍakait*, ڈاكُو *ḍākū*: see Robber.

Plaiter, اُتُّوگر *uttū-gar*, اُرتُوگر *urtū-gar*.

Planter, كويڑي *kō'ēṛī* (m.), نخلبند *nakhlband*: see Gardener.

Plasterer, كسگر *kasgar*.

Player (stage), نقّال *naḳḳāl*, پيكهنِيا *pēkhniyā*, سوانگِي *swāngī* (m.).

Ploughman, هل جوتا *hal-jōtā*, هلواها *halwāhā*, جوتار *jōtār*.

Plumber, سِيسي كا كام كرنيوالا *sīsē kā kām-karnēwālā*.

Poet, شاعِر *shā'ir*, كب *kab*, كبِيشر *kabīshar*, سُخن سنج *sukhan-sanj*.

Polisher, صَيقل گر *ṣaiḳal-gar*, جِلاگر *jilā-gar*, گهوٹنہا *ghōṭan-hār*.

Porter, (carrier) باربردار *bārbardār*, موٹيا *mōṭiyā*, قُلِي *ḳulī*: see Door-keeper.

Postman, ڈاكيا *ḍākiyā*, قاصِد *ḳāṣid*, (dakh.) ٹپّالوالا *ṭappāl-wālā*.

Potter, كُمهار *kumhār*, كسگر *kasgar*, (dakh.) كُنبار *kuṅbār*.

Poulterer, مُرغِيوالا *murghī-wālā*, مُرغ فروش *murgh-farōsh*.

Preacher, واعِظ *wā'iẓ*, وعظگو *wa'ẓ-go*, خطِيب *khaṭib*.

Preceptor, اُستاد *ustād*, آخُون *ākhun*, مُعلِّم *mu'allim*.

Prefect, حاكِم *ḥākim*: see Governor.

Prelate, Primate, اِمام *imām*, مُجتهِد *mujtahid*.

President, بالا نشين *bālā-nishīn*, مير مجلس *mīr-i majlis*.

Priest, گرو *gurū*, پير *pīr*, پروهت *purōhit*: see Preacher, Prelate.

Professor (teacher), مدرس *mudarris*, پاٹهک *pāṭhak*, معلم *mu'allim*.

Prophet, نبي *nabī* (m.), پيغمبر *paighambar*, رکه *rikh*.

Pursuivant, يساول *yasāwal*, چوبدار *chōb-dār*.

Purveyor, بهنڈاري *bhanḍārī*, سربراه‌کار *sarbarāh-kār*.

Quarter-master, مير منزل *mīr-i manzil*, مير تزک *mīr-i-tuzuk*.

Ranger (of a forest), قراول *ḳarāwal*, مير شکار *mīr-shikār*.

Recorder, سررشته‌دار *sar-rishta-dar*, دفتر نويس *daftar-nawīs*.

Renter, بهڑيتي *bhaṛaitī*, اجاره‌دار *ijāra-dār*, کرايه‌دار *kirāya-dār*.

Retailer, خورده‌فروش *khurda-farōsh*, پهڑيا *phaṛiyā*.

Robber, چور *chōr*, چوٹا *chōṭṭā*, ڈکيت *ḍakait*, راه‌زن *rāh-zan*.

Ropedancer, بازيگر *bāzī-gar*, نٹوا *naṭwā*, رسن‌باز *rasan-bāz*.

Ropemaker, رسن‌ساز *rasan-sāz*.

Rower, ڈانڈي *ḍānḍī*, کهيوٹ *khēwaṭ*, کهيوک *khēwak*.

Ruler, حاکم *ḥākim*, عامل *'āmil*, ناظم *nāẓim*, (or dakh.) نظام *niẓām*.

Sailor, ملاح *mallāḥ*, جهازي *jahāzī* (m.), خلاصي *khalāṣī* (m.).

Salt-maker, لونيا *lūniyā*, ملنگي *malangī*, نونيا *nōniyā*.

Sawyer, اره‌کش *arra-kash*, کرانتي *karāntī*.

Scarifier, حجام *ḥajjām*.

Scholar, سکه *sikh*, شاگرد *shāgird*: see Disciple, Student.

Schoolmaster, آخون *ākhun*, مياں‌جي *miyān-jī* (m.), ملا *mullā*.

Schoolmistress, ملاني *mullānī*, آتو *ātū* (f.), (dakh.) آتون *ātūn*.

Scullion, دیگ‌شو *dēg-shō*.

Sculptor, بُت‌تراش *but-tarāsh*, نقّاش *nakkāsh*, سنگ‌تراش *sang-tarāsh*.

Secretary, مُنشي *munshī* (m.), مِیر مُنشي *mīr-munshī*, دبِیر *dabīr*.

Sentinel, Sentry, پاسبان *pāsbān*, پہرِیا *pahriyā*, چَوکِي‌دار *chaukī-dār*.

Servant, نوکر *naukar*, چاکر *chākar*, خِدمتگار *khidmat-gār*.

Shaver, حجّام *ḥajjām*, ناپِت *nāpit* : see Barber.

Shepherd, بھیڑِیہارا *bhēṛīhārā*, گلّہ‌بان *galla-bān*, (dakh.) دھنگر *dhangar*.

Shoemaker, موچِي *mōchī*, کفش‌دوز *kafsh-dōz*, چمار *chamār*.

Shopkeeper, بنِیا *baniyā*, دُوکان‌دار *dūkān-dār*, دُوکانِي *dūkānī* (m.).

Skinner, پوست‌کن *post-kan*, سلّاخ *sallākh*, چمار *chamār*.

Slave, بندہ *banda*, غُلام *ghulām*, چیلا *chēlā*, لَونڈا *launḍā*, داس *dās*.

Slave (female), باندِي *bāndī*, لَونڈِي *launḍī*, کنِیزک *kanīzak* (f.).

Slave merchant, بردہ‌فروش *barda-farōsh*.

Smuggler, گھاٹمار *ghaṭ-mār*, چَوکِي‌مار *chaukī-mār*.

Snake-catcher, مارگِیر *mār-gīr*, گُنِي *gunī* (m.).

Snake-keeper, سنپیرا *sampērā*.

Soap-boiler or -maker, صابُون‌گر *ṣābūn-gar*.

Soothsayer, آگم بکتا *āgam-baktā*, کاهِن *kāhin*, رمّال *rammāl*.

Sophist, بت بنا *bat-banā*, حُجّتِي *ḥujjatī* (m.), صُوفِي *ṣūfī*.

Sorcerer, افسُون‌گر *afsūn-gar*, بھوکس *bhōkas*, جادُوگر *jādū-gar*.

Sorceress, جادُوگرنِي *jādū-garnī*, کنکالِن *kankālin*, ٹونہائِي *ṭōnhā'ī*.

Spearman, برچھیت *barchhait*, نیزہ بردار *nēza-bardār*.

Spinner, Spinster, چرخ‌زن *charkh-zan*, کاتنہارِي *kātanhārī* (f.).

Sportsman, شکار باز *shikār-bāz*, شکاري *shikārī*, اهيريا *ahēriyā*.

Standardbearer, نشان بردار *nishān-bardār*, بيرقي *bairaḳ-ī* (m.).

Stationer, کاغذي *kāghazī* : see Bookseller.

Steersman جهينگت *jhīngāt*, کنڈاري *kanḍārī* (m.): see Helmsman.

Steward خانسامان *khānsāmān*, بهنڈاري *bhanḍārī* (m.), بکاول *bakāwal*.

Steward (agent), کارباري *kārbārī* (m.), ديوان *dīwān* : see Factor.

Stonecutter, سنگ تراش *sang-tarāsh* : see Carver, Sculptor.

Student, طالبُ العِلم *ṭālibu-l-ʿilm* or طالبِ عِلم *ṭālib-i ʿilm*.

Sugar-boiler, کاندو *kāndū*. Sugar-seller, شکر فروش *shakar-farōsh*.

Sutler, بهٹهيارا *bhaṭhiyārā*, (dakh.) بهٹيارا *bhaṭē'ārā*.

Sweeper, مهتر *mihtar*, جهاڑوکش *jhāṛū-kash*, جاروب کش *jārūb-kash*.

Swimmer, پيراک *pairāk*, شناور *shināwar*.

Swordman, Swordplayer, شمشيرزن *shamshēr-zan*, تلوريا *talwariyā*.

Targetier, ڈهليت *ḍhalait*.

Tavern-keeper, کلار *kalār*, کلوار *kalwār*, بهنگيرا *bhangērā*.

Tax-gatherer, باجدار *bāj-dār*, تحصيلدار *taḥṣīldār*.

Tenant, کرايه دار *kirāya-dār*, رعيت *ra'āiyat*, بهڑيتي *bharaitī* (m.).

Tent-maker, خيمه دوز *khaima-dōz*, پاره دوز *pāra-dōz*.

Testator, موصي *mūṣī*. Testatrix, موصيه *mūṣiya*.

Thatcher, چهپر بند *chhappar-band*, چهويا *chhawaiyā*, گهرامي *gharāmī* (m.).

Thief, چور *chōr*, چوٹا *chōṭṭā*, دزد *duzd*, تسکر *taskar*.

Thief-catcher, نظر باز *naẓar-bāz*, دزد گير *duzd-gīr*.

Thrasher, دهانویا *dhānwaiyā.*

Tiler, کهپري بند *khaprē-band.*

Timber-merchant, لکڑهارا *lakaṛhārā,* هیزم فروش *hēzam-farōsh.*

Tinman, قلعي گر *kal'ī-gar,* رصّاص *raṣṣāṣ.*

Tirewoman, مشّاطه *mashshāṭa* (f.), پهراوني *paharā'ōnī.*

Tobacconist, تنباکو گر *tambākū-gar,* تنباکو فروش *tambākū-farōsh.*

Toll-gatherer, ڈنڈیا *ḍanḍiyā :* see Tax-gatherer.

Torchbearer, مشعلچي *mash'āl-chī,* فلیته بردار *falīta-bardār.*

Toyman, بازیچه فروش *bazīcha-farosh,* رانگبهرا *rāngbharā.*

Trader, Tradesman, سوداگر *saudāgar,* بیپاري *baipārī :* see Artificer.

Translator, ترجمه نویس *tarjuma-nawīs,* مترجم *mutarjim.*

Traveller, مسافر *musāfir,* سیّاح *saiyāḥ,* بٹوهي *baṭōhī* (m.).

Treasurer, خزانچي *khazānchī* (m.), روکڑیا *rōkaṛiyā,* تحویل دار *taḥwīl-dār.*

Trooper, سوار *sawār,* گهڑ چڑها *ghuṛ-chaṛhā,* ترک سوار *turk-sawār.*

Tumbler, بازیگر *bāzīgar,* نٹ *naṭ,* کلا باز *kalā-bāz,* کوتکي *kautukī* (m.).

Turner, خرادي *kharādī* (m.), خراطي *kharrāṭī* (m.), خراط *kharrāṭ.*

Tutor, اتالیق *atālīḳ,* آخون *ākhun,* (patron) مربّي *murabbī* (m.) : see Professor.

Varnisher, لکهیرا *lakhērā.*

Vicegerent, قایم مقام *ḳā'im maḳām,* نایب مناب *nā'ib manāb.*

Viceroy, صوبه‌دار *ṣūba-dār,* نوّاب *nawwāb :* see Vicegerent.

Victualler رسد کا داروغه *rasad kā dārōgha :* see Purveyor, Sutler.

Vintner, مي فروش *mai-farōsh* : see Distiller.

Usher, عرض بيگي *ărz̤-bēgī* : see Mace-bearer.

Waiter, پروسيا *parōsaiyā*, خدمتگار *khidmatgār*.

Warden, دروازي *darwāzī* (m.), داروغه *darōgha* : see Keeper.

Warrior, جنگي *jangī* (m.), مبارز *mubāriz*, بهادر *bahādur*.

Washer-man, دهوبي *dhōbī* (m.), رجك *rajak*, گاذر *gāz̤ur*.

Washer-woman, دهوبن *dhobin* (f.), بريٹهن *barēṭhan*.

Watchman, چوكيدار *chaukīdār*, پاسبان *pāsbān*, پهرو *pahrū*.

Water-carrier, بهشتي *bihishtī* (m.), آبكار *ābkār*, سقا *saḳḳā*.

Water-cooler, آب دار *āb-dār*.

Waterman, كهيوٹ *khēwaṭ*, ملاح *mallāḥ* : see Water-carrier.

Wharfinger, گهٹوار *ghaṭwār* or گهٹوال *ghaṭwāl*.

Wiredrawer, تاركش *tār-kash*.

Wizard, بهوكس *bhōkas*, جنتري *jantrī* : see Magician.

Wood-cutter, لكڑهارا *lakaṛ-hārā*, هيزم كش *hēzam-kash*.

Woodmonger, هيزم فروش *hēzam-farōsh*, لكڑهارا *lakaṛ-hārā*.

Workman, كاريگر *kārīgar*, كميرا *kamērā*, دستكار *dastkār*.

Wrestler, كشتي گير يا گر *kushtī-gīr* or *-gar*, كشتي باز *kushtī-bāz*.

Writer, محرر *muḥarrir*, ليكهك *lēkhak*, كاتب *kātib*, راقم *rāḳim*.

Writer (one in the Company's service), متصدي *mutaṣaddī*.

Writingmaster, خوش نويس *khush nawīs* : see Master.

Of Meats and Drinks.

Food, Victuals, كهانا *khānā*, خوراك *khurāk* (f.), غذا *ghiẕā* (f.), بهوجن *bhōjan*, رسوئي *rasōʼī*, آهار *āhār* (or vulg. اهار *ahār*), قوت *ḳūt*.

Drink, شُرب *shurb.* Meat and Drink, اکل و شُرب *akl ō shurb,* کھانا پینا *khānā pīnā,* دانه پانی *dāna pānī.*

Fodder, چاره *chāra,* گھاس *ghās,* گھاس پات *ghās-pāt.*

Grain, Corn, غلّه *ghalla,* اناج *anāj,* دانه *dāna,* تُخم *tukhm.*

Rice (cleared of the husk, but not cooked), چاول *chāwal,* چانول *chāṅwal,* بِرنج *birinj,* تنڈل *tandul.*

Rice (boiled), بھات *bhāt,* خُشکه *khushka.*

Rice-milk, کھیر *khīr* (f.), فِرنی *firnī,* هوِکھ فِرنی *hawikh-firnī.*

Wheat, گیہوں *gēhūṅ,* گندم *gandum,* (dakh. also) گھیَوں *ghyauṅ.*

Flour, Meal, آٹا *āṭā,* آرد *ārd,* سُوجی *sūjī,* پِسان *pisān.*

Flour of Wheat, گیہوں کا آٹا *gēhūṅ kā āṭā.*

Flour of pulse (especially of چنا Cicer arietinum), بیسن *bēsan.*

Flour, fine or twice sifted, میده *maida.*

Bread, روٹی *rōṭī,* نان *nān* (f.).

Thick Bread, Loaf, روٹ *rōṭ,* روٹی *rōṭī.*

Small loaf of bread, Cake, ٹِکّی *ṭikkī,* گِرده *girda,* کُلیچه *kulīcha.*

Parched grain, لاوا *lāwā,* کھیل *khīl* (f.), چبینا *chabēnā,* ٹھُڈّی *ṭhuḍḍī.*

Parched grain, reduced to meal and made into a paste, ستّو *sattū.*

Parched grain of جوار *jō'ār* or باجرا *bājrā,* پرِمل *parimal.*

Milk, دُودھ *dūdh,* شِیر *shīr,* پَی *pai,* گورس *gōras,* چھیر *chhīr.*

Butter, مکّھن *makkhan,* ماکھن *mākhan,* مسکه *maska,* نیَون *nē'ūn.*

Butter clarified by boiling and straining, گھی *ghī* (m.).

Buttermilk, چھاچھ *chhāchh* (f.), مٹّھا *maṭṭhā,* دوغ *dōgh.*

Thick sour coagulated Milk, دہی *dahī* (m.).

Cream, ملائي *malā'ī*, ساري *sārī*.

Whey, ماءُ الجُبن *mā'u-l-jubn*, دُودھ کا پاني *dūdh kā pānī*, تورٌ *tōṛ*.

Curd, چکا *chakkā*, چھينا *chhēnā*.

Cheese, پنير *panīr*. Round (of a cheese), چکتي *chaktī*.

Meat, Flesh, گوشت *gōsht*, مانس *māṅs*, (dakh. also) هيڑا *hēṛā*.

Broth, Soup, شوربا *shōrbā* or شوروا *shōrwā*, جُوس *jūs*, پريه *parēh*.

Porridge, Pottage, لپسي *lapsī*, آش *āsh* (f.): see Broth.

Flummery, فالُوده *fālūda*: see Porridge, Rice-milk.

Gravy, آب گوشت *āb-i-gōsht*, آب‌جوش *āb-jōsh*, يخني *yakhnī*.

Roast meat, کباب *kabāb*, سيخيا کباب *sīkhiyā kabāb*.

Stew (of meat), دم پُخت *dam-pukht*, يخني *yakhnī*.

Curry (said to be from the Arab. قليه), سالن *sālan*, سالنا *sālnā*.

A certain dish made of flesh and rice, پُلاؤ *pulā'ō*.

Meat dressed dry with onions, دوپيازه *dōpiyāza*.

Minced meat, Hash, قيمه *ḳīma*.

Pie, سنبوسه *sāmbōsa*, سموسه *samōsa*.

Forced meat, پلڑي *pilṛī*. Pounded meat, کوفته *kōfta*.

Beef, گاي کا گوشت *gā'ē kā gosht*, گاؤ گوشت *gā'ō gōsht*.

Mutton, بھيڑ کا گوشت *bhēṛ kā gōsht*.

Veal, بچھڑي کا گوشت *bachhṛē kā gōsht*.

Pork, سُوأر کا گوشت *sū'ar kā gōsht*.

Ham, ران *rān* (f. m.).

Lamb, Kid, حلوان کا گوشت *ḥalwān kā gōsht*.

Venison, ہرن کا گوشت *haran kā gōsht.*

Hare, Rabbit, خرگوش *khargōsh,* لمبھا *lambhā.*

Fish, مچھلي *machhlī.*

Fowl, مرغ *murgh.*

Wild fowl, جنگلي مرغ *janglī murgh.*

Turkey, فيل مرغ *fil murgh,* پيرو *pērū.*

Peacock, مور *mōr.* Peachick, مريلا *murēlā.*

Goose, هانس *hāns.*

Duck, Waterfowl, مرغابي *murghābī.*

Partridge, تيتر *tītar.*

Pigeon, كبوتر *kabūtar,* كپوت *kapōt.*

Vegetables (esculent), Greens, ترکاري *tarkārī,* بهاجي *bhājī.*

Sausage, کلما *kulmā,* لنگوچا *langūchā,* قلمه *ḳulma.*

Pastry, Pasty, سنبوسه *sambōsa,* پراٹها *parāṭhā,* کهاجا *khājā.*

Sweet cakes fried in butter, &c., گلگلا *gulgulā.*

Confection, Conserve, Jam, Preserve, مربه *murabba.*

Sweetmeat, مٹهائي *miṭhā'ī,* حلوا *ḥalwā,* لڈو *laḍḍū.*

Egg, انڈا *anḍā,* بيضه *baiẓa.*

Omelet, خاگينه *khāgīna.*

Rice-water, Rice-gruel, پيچھ *pīchh* (f.), (dakh.) گنجي *ganjī.*

Barley-water, Watergruel, آش جو *āsh-i-jau.*

Water, پاني *pānī* (m.), آب *āb,* جل *jal.*

Wine, Spirituous liquors, شراب *sharāb* (f.), مي *mai* (f.), مد *mad.*

Arrack (from the Arab. عرق *ʿarak*, juice, spirit), تاڑي *tāṛī* (toddy), سيندهي *sēndhī*.

Beer, بوزا *bōzā* or بوزه *bōza*.

Tea, چا *chā* (f.).

Coffee, قهوه *ḳahwa*, (unground) بن *bun*.

Breakfast, حاضري *ḥāẓirī*, نانِ نهاري *nān-i-nahārī*, ناشتا *nāshtā*.

Luncheon, Tiffin, cold meat, كليوا *kalēwā*, ناشته *nāshta*, چاشت *chāsht* (f.).

Dinner, كهانا *khānā* (eating), خاصّه *k͟hāṣṣa*.

Supper, بياري *byārī*, عشا *ʿasha*, رات كا كهانا *rāt kā khānā*.

Spices, Condiments.

Spices, Condiment, Seasoning, مصالح *maṣaliḥ*, بگهار *baghār*.

Salt, لون *lōn*, نمك *namak*, (rock) سيندها *sēndhā*.

Pepper, مرچ *mirch* (f.), فلفل *filfil* (f.).

Pepper, black, گول مرچ *gōl mirch* (f.), كالي مرچ *kālī mirch*, مرچ *mirch* (f.).

Pepper, red or Capsicum, لال مرچ *lāl mirch* (f.).

Ginger (dry), سونٹه *sōnṭh* (f.), زنجبيل *zanjabīl* (f.).

Ginger (undried), ادرك *adrak* (f.), آدا *ādā*.

Clove, لونگ *laung* (f.), قرنفل *ḳaranfal*.

Mace, جاوتري *jāwatrī* or جاوِتري *jāwitrī*, بسباسه *basbāsa*.

Cinnamon, دارچيني *dārchīnī*.

Nutmeg, جائي پهل *jāʾe phal*, جوز *jauz*.

Allspice, Jamaica pepper, Myrtus pimenta, سِيتل چيني *sītal chīnī*.

Turmeric, هلدي *haldī*, زرد چوب *zard chōb* (f.), پيترس *pītras*.

Saffron, كيسر *kēsar* (f.), زعفران *zaʻfarān* (f.).

Anise-seed, سونف *saunf* (f.), انيسون *anīsūn*.

Cumin-seed, جيرا *jīrā*, زيرا *zīrā*, كمون *kammūn*.

Mustard-seed, رائي *rāʼī*, خردل *khardal*, سرشف *sarshaf*, توري *tōṛī*.

Pickles, آچار *āchār*. Pickle (brine), نمكين پاني *namkīn pānī* (m.).

Apparel, Dress.

Apparel, Clothes, Dress, كپڑا *kapṛā*, لباس *libās*, پوشاك *pōshāk* (f.).

Hat, ٹوپي *ṭōpī*, كلاه *kulāh* (f.).

Cap, كلاه *kulāh* (f.), تاج *tāj*, ٹوپي *ṭōpī*.

Turban, پگڑي *pagṛī*, پاگ *pāg* (f.), چيرا *chīrā*, دستار *dastār* (f.).

Tiara, Diadem, Crown, تاج *tāj*, مكٹ *mukuṭ*, افسر *afsar*.

A kind of Turban, عمامه *ʻāmāma*.

Ornaments for the turban, منديل *mandīl* (f.), سرپيش يا پيچ *sar-pēsh* or *-pēch*, گوش پيچ يا واره *gōsh-pēch* or *-wāra*, جيغه *jīgha*, كلغي *kalghī*, طره *ṭurra*.

Veil (woman's), برقع *burkaʻ*, گھونگھٹ *ghūnghaṭ* (f.), مقنع *maknaʻ*.

Veil or woman's cloak, اوڑھني *ōṛhnī*.

Handkerchief, رومال *rūmāl*, انگوچھا *angōchhā* : see Neckcloth.

Neckcloth, گلوبند *gulūband*.

Necklace, مالا *mālā*, كنٹھي *kanṭhī*, هار *hār*, كنٹھ مالا *kanṭh-mālā*.

Shirt, Chemise, قميص *kamīṣ*, كرته *kurta*.

Long vest resembling a shirt, جبه *jubba*.

Waistcoat, چولي *chōlī*, انگرکها *angarkhā*, فتوحي *fatūḥī*.

Bodice, Stays, چولی *chōlī*, انگيا *angiyā* (f.), محرم *maḥram*.

Coat, کرتي *kurtī*, انگا *angā*, انگرکها *angarkhā*.

Cloak, Great-coat, فرغول *farghūl* (f.), باراني *bārānī*, لباده *lubāda*.

Gown (female's), پيشواز *pēshwāz* (f.), تلک *tilak* (f.).

Gown (male's), Robe, جامه *jāma*, پيراهن *pairāhan*.

Frock, جهگلا *jhagulā*, کرتا *kurtā*, دغلا *daghlā*.

Jacket, مرزا'ي *mirzā'ī*, انگا *angā*, کرته *kurta*, انگرکها *angarkhā*.

Mantle, لباده *lubāda*, پٿو *paṭṭū*: see Cloak.

Drawers, Trousers, Pantaloons, پايجامه *pā'ējāma*, تنبان *tumbān* or *tambān*, شرعي *shar'ī*, شلوار *shilwār*, ازار *izār* (f.), سروال *sirwāl*.

Garter, موزه بند *mōza-band*, پٿي *paṭṭī*.

Girdle, کمربند *kamarband*, پٿکا *paṭkā*.

Breeches (short), جانگهيا *jānghiyā*, کچهنا *kachhnā*, چرنا *charnā*.

Breeches (that reach below the knees, and fit tight), (dakh.) گرگي *gurgī*.

Cloth worn round the waist and passing between the legs, لنگ *lung*, لنگي *lungī*, ته بند *tah-band*, لنگوٿي *langōṭī*.

Belt round the loins, to which the *langōṭī* is attached, تسمه *tasma*, دوالي *dū'ālī*.

Petticoat, لهنگا *lahangā* or لهنگا *lhangā*, گهگهرا *ghaghrā*, سايه *sāya*.

Night-clothes, شب خوابي *shab-khwābī*.

Stocking or Sock, جراب *jurrāb*, پايتابه *pā'ētāba*.

Shoe, Slipper, جوتا *jūtā*, جوتي *jūtī*, پاپوش *pāpōsh* (f.), کفش *kafsh* (f.).

Boot, موزه *mōza*, چکمه *chakma*: (leg of) پوائي *pawā'ī*.

Glove, دستانه *dastāna*.

Ear-ring, گوشواره *gōshwāra*: (kind of), کرن پهول *karn-phūl*, جهومکا *jhūmkā*.

Ring, (worn on the finger) انگشتري *angushtarī*, (on the thumb) انگشتانه *angushtāna*.

Ring, (worn in the nose) نته *nath*, نتهني *nathnī*, بلاق *bulāḳ*, بيسر *bēsar* (f.).

Bracelet, چوري *chūrī*, کنگن *kangan*, بازوبند *bāzū-band*.

Button, تکمه *tukma*, گهنڈي *ghunḍī*.

Buckle, چپراس *chaprās* (f.): (tongue of) بکسوا *baksū'ā*.

Clasp, چپراس *chaprās*, بند کرني کي آنکڑي *band karnē kī ānkṛī*.

Buildings.

A Building, Edifice, عمارت *ʿimārat* (f.).

Wall, ديوار *dīwār* (f.), بهيت *bhīt* (f.), ديوال *dīwāl* (f.).

Roof, چهت *chhat* (f.), چهان *chhān* (f.), (of thatch) چهپر *chhappar*.

Arch, Vault, Dome, Cupola, طاق *ṭāḳ*, گنبذ *gumbaẕ*, قبه *ḳubba*.

House, Mansion, گهر *ghar*, حويلي *ḥawēlī*, کوٹهي *kōṭhī*, محل *maḥall*.

Dwelling, Abode, مکان *makān*, مسکن *maskan*, ٹهکانا *ṭhikānā*.

Cottage, Cot, Hut, جهونپڑي *jhōmpṛī*, کٹي *kuṭī*.

Palace, دولتخانه *daulat-khāna*, قصر *ḳaṣr*, راجمندر *rājmandir*.

Castle, Fort, قلعه *ḳalʿa* (Hind. *ḳilʿa*), گڑه *gaṛh*, حصار *ḥiṣār*.

Tower, Bastion, Bulwark, برج *burj*.

Obelisk, Steeple, Minaret, لاٹ *lāṭ* (f.), لاٹه *lāṭh* (f.), مينار *mīnār*.

Pillar, Column, كهنبه *khambh*, ستون *satūn*, تهوني *thūnī*, ركن *rukn*.

Temple (Mahommedan), مسجد *masjid* (f. a mosque), معبد *ma*ʿ*bid*.

Temple (Hindū), ديول *dēwal*, مندر *mandir*, ديهرا *dēhrā*.

Shrine, درگاه *dargāh* (f.), مزار *mazār* (m. f.).

Altar, بيدي *bēdī*, قربان گاه *ḳurbān-gāh* (f.), مذبح *mazbiḥ*.

Church, Chapel, كليسه *kalīsa*, گرجه *girja*, معبد *maʿbid*.

Bridge, پل *pul*, سيت *sēt*.

Inn, سرائي *sarā'ē* (f.), مسافر خانه *musāfir-khāna*.

Storehouse, Magazine, Granary, مخزن *makhzan*, كوٹهي *kōṭhī*.

Cow-house, گوساله *gausāla*, سار *sār*, كهرك *kharak*, كوٹها *kōṭhā*.

Stable, گهڑسال *ghuṛsāl*, اصطبل *iṣṭabal*, طويله *ṭawēla*.

Elephant stable, فيلخانه *fīl-khāna*.

Shop, Warehouse, دوكان *dūkān* (f.), هاٹ *hāṭ* (f.), دكان *dukān* (f.).

Workshop, كارخانه *kār-khāna*, كارگاه *kār-gāh* (f.), دوكان *dūkān* (f.).

Gate, Door, پهاٹك *phāṭak*, دروازه *darwāza*, پوري *paurī*.

Gateway, Porch, Threshold, دهليز *dahlīz* (f.), ڈيوڑهي *dēwṛhī*, (dakh.) ديوڑي *dē'ōṛī*.

Window, Casement, كهڑكي *khiṛkī*, جهروكها *jharōkhā*.

Floor, زمين *zamīn* (f. ground), (of cement) گچ *gach*, (of plank) تخته بندي *takhta-bandī*.

Chamber, Room, Apartment, كمرا *kamarā*, كوٹهري *koṭhrī*, حجره *ḥujra*.

Closet, Cabinet, خلوتخانه *khalwat-khāna*, حجره *ḥujra*, گوشه *gōsha*.

Cell, حجره *ḥujra*, گوشه *gōsha*, كلبه *kulba*, كوٹهري *kōṭhrī*.

Hall, دالان *dālān*, ايوان *aiwān*, (of entrance) دردالان *dar dālān*.

Dining room, مهمان خانه *mihmān-khāna*.

Hall of audience, دربار *darbār*, ديوان خانه *dīwān-khāna*.

Kitchen, باورچي خانه *bāwarchī-khāna*, مطبخ *maṭbakh*.

Balcony, Gallery, بالا خانه *bālā-khāna*, شه نشين *shah-nishīn*.

Verandah, برامده *bar-āmada*.

Garret, طبقه بالا *ṭabka bālā*, مكان كي اوپر كي كوٹهري *makān kē ūpar kī kōṭhrī*.

Theatre, Playhouse, تماشا گاه *tamāshā-gāh* (f.), نقل خانه *nakl-khāna*.

Brick, اينٹ *īnṭ* (f.), خشت *khisht* (f.).

Tile, كهپرا *khaprā*, نريا *nariyā*, خشت *khisht* (f.).

Stone, پتهر *patthar*, پكهان *pakhān*, سل *sil* (f.), سنگ *sang*.

Mortar, Plaster, گچ *gach*, ريخته *rēkhta*.

Thatch, گهاس *ghās* (f.), كهرهـ *kharh* (f.).

Glass, كانچ *kānch*, شيشه *shīsha*: (pane of) پركاله *parkāla*.

Beam, Bar, شهتير *shahtīr*, كڑي *kaṛī*, لٹها *laṭhā*.

Rafter, Spar, كڑي *kaṛī*, كانڈي *kānḍī*, كورو *kōrō*, ترك *tarak* (f.).

Chimney, دهونوارا *dhūṅwārā*, دودكش *dūd-kash*.

Fire-place, چولها *chūlhā*, آتش دان *ātash-dān*, ديگدان *dēg-dān*.

Oven, تنور *tanūr*, تندور *tandūr*, بهٹ *bhaṭ* (f.).

Shutter or fold of a door, كيواڑ *kēwāṛ*, پلا *pallā*, پٹ *paṭ*.

Palisade, Balustrade, Railing, كٹهرا *kaṭharā*.

Plate or clamp of metal, پتر *pattar*.

Hinge, قلابه *kulāba*, چول *chūl* (f.), قبضه *kabẓa*.

Pivot on which a door turns, چول *chūl* (f.).

Lock, قفل *ḳufl*, تالا *tālā*.

Key, كنجي *kunjī*, كليد *kilīd* (f.), چابي *chābī*.

Bolt, بلي *billī*, چهتكني *chhiṭkanī*, دربند *dar-band*.

Bar of a door, هڑكا *huṛkā*, دربند *darband*, اڑدنڈا *aṛdanḍā*.

Staple (of a lock), سكري *sikrī*, قلابه *ḳulāba*.

Hasp, قلابه *ḳulāba*.

Hook, انكڑي *ankṛī*, قلاب *kullāb* : see Hasp.

Stair, Step, Ladder, سيڑهي *sīṛhī*, نردبان *nardbān*, زينه *zīna*.

Stairs, Steps, زينه *zīna*. Staircase, Steps, نرد بان *nard-bān*.

Bedchamber, Dormitory, خوابگاه *khwāb-gāh* (f.), سوني كي كوٹهري *sōnē kī kōṭhrī*.

Cellar, Vault, ته خانه *tah-khāna*, بهونگهرا *bhōngharā*.

Well, كوا *kū'ā*, (large one of masonry) اندارا *indārā*, باولي *bā'ōlī*

Cistern, Reservoir, حوض *ḥauẓ*, چهبچه *chahbachcha*.

Household Furniture.

Table, ميز *mēz* (f.), ميز كا تخته *mēz kā takhta*.

Tablecloth, دسترخوان *dastar-khwān*, سفره *sufra*, چدر *chaddar* (f.).

Chair, Stool, كرسي *kursī*, چوكي *chaukī*, صندلي *ṣandalī*.

Footstool, مونڈها *mōnḍhā*, موڑها *mōṛhā*.

Shelf, طاق *ṭāk*, طبقه *ṭabḳa*, تختي *takhtī*, پٹرا *paṭrā*.

Trivet, Tripod, سه پايه *si-pāya*, سپائي *sipā'ī*, ترپد *tirpad*.

Clock, گهڑي *ghaṛī*, گهڑيال *ghaṛiyāl*, ساعت *sā'at* (f.).

Carpet, فرش *farsh*, قالين *ḳālīn*, قاليچه *ḳālīcha*, شطرنجي *shaṭranjī*.

Carpet, (to sit or pray on) آسن *āsan*, (to pray on) سجّاده *sajjāda*.

Carpet (to clean the feet on), پا انداز *pā-andāz*.

Cloth spread over a carpet, چاندني *chāndnī*.

Cushion, گدّي *gaddī*.

Bed, Couch, سيج *sēj* (f.), بچهونا *bichhaunā*, كهاٹ *khāṭ* (f.).

Bedstead, چارپائي *chārpā'ī*, پلنگ *palang*, كهاٹ *khāṭ* (f.).

Bedding, بچهونا *bichhaunā*, فرش *farsh*, بستر *bistar*.

Mattress, توشک *tōshak* (f.), سوزني *sōznī*, بچهونا *bichhaunā*.

Pillow, Bolster, تكيه *takiya*, بالش *bālish*, اُسيسا *usīsā*.

Coverlet, Quilt, Counterpane, بالاپوش *bālā-pōsh*, پلنگ پوش *palang-pōsh*.

Sheet, چادر *chādar* (f.), چدّر *chaddar* (f.), اوڑهنا *ōṛhnā*.

Blanket, كمّل *kammal*, كملي *kamlī*, لوئي *lō'ī*.

Curtain, پرده *parda*, (of a bed, against mosquitos) مسهري *masahrī*.

Looking-glass, Mirror, آئينه *ā'īna*, درپن *darpan*, مرآت *mir'āt* (f.).

Picture, تصوير *taṣwīr* (f.), چتر *chitr*, نقش *naḳsh*.

Wash-hand bason, چلمچي *chilamchī*, هاته دهوني كا باسن *hāth dhōnē kā bāsan*.

Goglet, Ewer, Water-jug, آفتابه *āftāba*, آفتاوا *āftāwā*.

Towel, رومال *rūmāl*, دستمال *dastmāl*, منديل *mindīl* (f.).

Comb, كنگهي *kanghī*, شانه *shāna*.

Brush, (English) برش *barash*, كونچي *kūnchī*.

Box, Chest, Trunk, Coffer, صندوق *ṣandūḳ* (m. f.), پيٿي *pēṭī.*

Small box, Casket, صندوقچه *ṣandūḳcha,* بٿا *baṭṭā,* ڏبا *ḍibbā.*

Basket, ٿوکرا *ṭōkrā,* ٿوکري *ṭōkrī,* ڏليا *ḍaliyā,* پٿارا *piṭārā.*

Bellows, دهونکني *dhaunknī,* کهال *khāl* (f.), دمه *dama.*

Spit (for roasting meat), سيخ *sīkh,* (smaller) سيخچه *sīkhcha.*

Caldron, Boiler, Copper, ديگ *dēg* (f.), هنڏا *hanḍā,* کڙاه *kaṛāh.*

Kettle, Pot, ديگچه *dēgcha,* تتهرا *tatahrā,* هانڏي *hānḍī,* تسلا *taslā.*

Lid, Potlid, ڏهکنا *ḍhaknā,* ڏهپنا *ḍhapnā,* سرپوش *sarpōsh.*

Chafing dish, انگيٿهي *angēṭhī,* آتشدان *ātash-dān.*

Trivet or fireplace (for a kettle, &c.), ديگدان *dēgdān.*

Fryingpan, کڙاهي *kaṛāhī,* ماهي توه *māhī-tawa,* تابه *tāba.*

Ladle, Wooden spoon, ڏوئي *ḍō'ī,* کرچها *karchhā,* چمچه *chamcha.*

Skimmer, کف گير *kaf-gīr,* جهرنا *jharnā,* (of iron) کرچهني *karchhanī.*

Dish, Platter, Salver, تهالي *thālī,* قاب *ḳāb* (f.), سهنک *sahnak* (f.), طبق *ṭabaḳ.*

Plate, رکابي *rikābī,* رکيبي *rikēbī,* برتن *bartan,* سهنک *sahnak* (f.).

Plate (silver), ظروفِ سيمي *ẓurūf-i-sīmī,* ظروفِ نقرئي *ẓurūf-i-nuḳra'ī.*

Spoon, چمچه *chamcha,* کرچهي *karchhī:* see Ladle.

Knife, چهري *chhurī,* کارد *kārd* (f.), (pen) قلم تراش *ḳalam-tarāsh* (f.).

Clasp knife, چکو *chakkū,* بکيا *bakiyā* (f.).

Fork, کانٿا *kānṭā.*

Saltcellar, نمکدان *namak-dān.* Cruet, سرکداني *sirka-dānī.*

Bowl, طاس *ṭās,* طشت *ṭasht,* جام *jām,* (of brass) کٿورا *kaṭōrā.*

Jug, Goblet, کلهڑا *kulhṛā*, کاسہ *kāsa*, کوزہ *kūza*, طاس *ṭās*.

Bottle, Flagon, شیشہ *shīsha*, صراحي *ṣurāḥī*, گلابي *gulābī*.

Cup, Glass, Can, پیالہ *piyālā*, جام *jām*, طاس *ṭās*, کاسہ *kāsa*.

Phial, small Glass, شیشي *shīshī*.

Decanter, مینا *mīnā*, شیشہ *shīsha*, آبگینہ *ābgīna*.

Water-pot, Pitcher, Jar, گهڑا *ghaṛā*, سبو *sabū*, مٹکا *maṭkā*.

Porringer, میٹا *mīṭā*, بادیہ *bādiya*: see Cup.

Pan, Bason, باسن *bāsan*, برتن *bartan*: see Fryingpan, Bowl.

Funnel, چونگا *chōngā*, نلي *nalī*, (dakh.) پرني *purnī* (?).

Tub, کٹهرا *kaṭhrā*, تغار *taghār*, تغاري *taghārī*, گملا *gamlā* (?).

Pail, Bucket, کٹهوتي *kaṭhautī*, تغار *taghār*, (milkpail) دوهني *dōhnī*.

Milkpan, دوده هنڈي *dūdh-hanḍī*.

Churn, متهنیا *mathaniyā* (f.), مهاني *mihānī*.

Cask, Barrel, Pipe, پیپا *pīpā*.

Tray, خوان *khwān*, خوانچہ *khwāncha*, کٹهرا *kaṭhrā*.

Trough, کٹهرا *kaṭhrā*, ڈونگي *ḍōngī*, ناند *nānd*: see Tub.

Besom, Broom, جهاڑو *jhāṛū* (f.), جاروب *jārōb*, بهاري *buhārī*.

Sieve, Riddle, چلني *chalnī*, غربال *ghirbāl*, پیزنہ *pēzna*, آکها *ākhā*.

Mortar, هاون *hāwan*, اوکهلي *ōkhlī*, کونڈي *kūnḍī*.

Pestle, کوتک *kūtak*, موسل *mūsal*, دستہ *dasta*, سونٹا *sōnṭā*, لوڑها *lōṛhā*.

Lamp, چراغ *chirāgh*, دیا *diyā*, دیپ *dīp*, دیپک *dīpak*.

Oil, تیل *tēl*, روغن *raughan*.

Candle, بتي *battī*, شمع *sham'* (f.), (of wax), موم بتي *mōm battī*.

Chandelier, Lustre, جهاڑ *jhāṛ*.

Shade (for a candle), فانوس *fānūs* (f.), قندیل *ḳandīl* (f.).

Candlestick, شمعدان *sham'dān*.

Lantern, فانوس *fānūs* (f.), قندیل *ḳandīl* (f.).

Torch, Flambeau, مشعل *mash'al* (f.), ڈامر *ḍāmar*.

Snuffers, گلگیر *gul-gīr*, گلتراش *gul-tarāsh*.

Country and Country Affairs.

Country (not Town), دیہات *dīhāt*, بیرونجات *bērūnjāt*, مفصل *mufaṣṣal*.

Village, گانو *gāṅw*, بستي *bastī*, گرام *grām*, دیہ *dīh*.

Field, کهیت *khēt*, میدان *maidān*, چهیتر *chhētr*.

Farm, چک *chak*, اجارہ *ijāra*, (dakh. also) گتا *guttā*: see Field.

Garden, Orchard, باغ *bāgh*, باري *bārī*, (small) باغچہ *baghcha*, باغیچہ *bāghīcha*.

Flower garden, پهلواري *phulwārī*, گلستان *gulistān*.

Forest, Wood, جنگل *jangal*, بن *ban*, دشت *dasht*.

Heath, Copse, Brushwood, جهاڑي *jhāṛī*, جهاڑ *jhāṛ*.

Hedge, باڑ *bāṛ*, جهاڑبندي *jhāṛ-bandī*, گهیرا *ghērā*.

Meadow, Mead, Marsh, ترائي *tarā'ī*, مرغزار *marghzār*.

Pasture, Meadow, چراگاہ *charāgāh*, علفزار *'alafzār*.

Park, Chase, رمنہ *ramna*, شکارگاہ *shikār-gāh* (f.), مرگ سالا *mirg-sālā*.

Agriculture, Husbandry, سیر *sīr*, کشتکاري *kishtkārī*, زراعت *zirā'at* (f.).

Cart, Waggon, گاڑي *gāṛī*, چهکڑا *chhakṛā*, عرابہ *'arāba*.

Plough, هل *hal*, قلبہ *ḳulba*, ناگل *nāgal*, نانگل *nāṅgal*.

Harrow, هينگا *hēngā*, مَيي *ma'ī*, سراون *sarāwan*.

Spade, Shovel, بيل *bēl*, كُدالي *kudālī*, پهاوڑا *phā'ōṛā*.

Hoe, كُدالي *kudālī*, بيلچه *bēlcha*, پهاوڑا *phā'ōṛā*.

Dibble, كهنتي *khantī*, كُدالي *kudālī*.

Mattock, Pick, Pickaxe, كُدال *kudāl*, كُدرا *kudrā*, پهاوڑا *phā'ōṛā*, گينتي *gaintī*.

Ploughshare, چو *chau*, توڑا *tōṛā*, حرث *ḥarṡ*, هل كا پهل *hal kā phal*.

Pitchfork, جندرا *jandrā*.

Axe, Hatchet, كُلهاڑي *kulhāṛī*, تبر *tabar*.

Sickle, Scythe, هنسوا *hansū'ā*, درانتي *darāntī*, داس *dās*.

Sieve, چلني *chalnī*, غربال *ghirbāl*, پيزنه *pēzna*, آكها *ākhā*.

Society and Government.

People, Nation, لوگ *lōg*, قوم *ḳaum* (f.), خلق *khalḳ* (f.), گروه *gurōh*.

Family, Tribe, كُل *kul*, قوم *ḳaum* (f.), قبيله *ḳabīla*.

Family, Household, كُنبا *kumbā*, كُتم *kutum*, گهرانا *gharānā*.

A Country, Region, ديس *dēs*, مُلك *mulk*, ديپ *dīp*, ديار *diyār*.

Territory, سرزمين *sar-zamīn* (f.), ديس *dēs*, كشور *kishwar*.

Province, صوبه *ṣūba*, سركار *sarkār* : see Country.

King, Sovereign, Monarch, Potentate, بادشاه *bādshāh*, راجا *rājā*, مها راجا *mahā-rājā*, فرمان روا *farmān-rawā*.

Queen, Empress, ملكه *malika*, راني *rānī*, مها راني *mahā-rānī*.

Prince, كُنوار *kuṅwār*, راج كُنور *rāj-kuṅwar*,, شهزاده *shahzāda*.

Princess, شاهزادي *shāh-zādī*, راجكُماري *rāj-kumārī*, راني *rānī*.

Chief, Ruler, Prince, راجا *rājā*, والي *wālī*, رَئِيس *ra'īs*.

Minister (of state), وزير *wāzīr*, منترِي *mantrī* (m.), دستور *dastūr*.

Secretary (of state), منترِي *mantrī* (m.), دِيوان *dīwān*.

Officer (military), Commander, سردار *sar-dār*, منصب دار *manṣab-dār*.

Officer (civil) اهلِ خدمت *ahl-i khidmat*, منصب دار *manṣab-dār*.

Judge, قاضِي *ḳāẓī*, حاكِم *ḥākim*, نيايك *nyāyak*.

Magistrate, chief officer of police, كوتوال *kōtwāl*, فوجدار *faujdār*.

Nobleman, Grandee, امير *amīr*, (or plur.) اُمرا *umarā*, عمده *ūmda*.

Of noble birth, شرِيف *sharīf*, اشرف *ashraf*, كُلِين *kulīn*.

Landholder, زميندار *zamīndār*, جاگِيردار *jāgīrdār*.

Plebeian, Commoner, كمِينه *kamīna*, عام آدمِي *āmm ādmī*.

Townsman, Citizen, شهرِي *shahrī*, قصباتِي *ḳaṣbātī*.

Villager, Peasant, گنوار *ganwār*, گرامِين *grāmīn*, دِهقانِي *dihḳānī*.

War, Military Affairs.

War, جنگ *jang*, رن *ran*, حرب *ḥarb* (f.), لڑاي *laṛā'ī*, جدل *jadal*.
Battle, لڑاي *laṛā'ī*, جده *judh*, جنگ *jang*, محاربه *muḥāraba*.
Peace, صلح *ṣulḥ* (f.).
Dissension, Discord, بگاڑ *bigāṛ*, فتنه *fitna*, پهوٹ *phūṭ* (f.).
Pacification, Reconciliation, ملاپ *milāp* (f.), مصالحه *muṣālaḥa*.
Enemy, Foe, دشمن *dushman*, درجن *durjan*, دشٹ *dushṭ*.
Adversary, Antagonist, حرِيف *ḥarīf*, بيرِي *bairī* (m.), غنيم *ghanīm*.
Friend, Ally, پچهي *pachchhī*, كمكي *kumakī* (m.), متر *mitr*, رفِيق *rafīḳ*.
Stratagem, حيله *ḥīla*, چهل بل *chhal-bal*, فن و فريب *fann ō fareb*.
Slaughter, Carnage, قتل *ḳatl*, خونريزي *khūn-rēzī*.
Massacre, see Slaughter : (general) قتل عام *ḳatl-i-āmm*.
Victory, Conquest, جي *jai*, فتح *fatḥ* (f.), جيت *jīt* (f.), ظفر *ẓafar*.

Triumph, جي جي كار *jai-jai-kār*, جي *jai*, بجي *bijai*, فتح *fatḥ*.

Defeat, Discomfiture, Loss, شكست *shikast* (f.), هار *hār* (f.).

Flight, هزيمت *hazīmat* (f.), بهاگڑ *bhāgaṛ* (f.), گريز *gurēz* (f.), فرار *firār*.

Pursuit, پيچها *pīchhā*, تعاقب *ta'āḳub*, پيروي *pairau'ī*.

Pillage, Plunder, لوٹ *lūṭ* (f.), غنيمت *ghanīmat* (f.), لوٹ پاٹ *lūṭ-pāṭ* (f.).

Onset, Attack, Assault, Charge, حمله *ḥamla*, چڑهاي *chaṛhā'ī*.

Incursion, Inroad, Invasion, تاخت *tākht* (f.), چڑهاي *chaṛhā'ī*.

Devastation, Depredation, تاخت تاراج *tākht-tārāj*, پايمالي *pā'ēmālī*.

Destruction, هلاكي *halākī*, خرابي *kharābī*, مسماري *mismarī*.

Army, لشكر *lashkar*, سينا *sēnā* (f.), سپاه *sipāh* (f.), فوج *fauj* (f.).

Battalion, پلٹن *palṭan*, فوج كا ايک حصه *fauj kā ēk ḥiṣṣa*.

Brigade, Squadron, دسته *dasta*, غول *ghōl*.

Troop, Corps, جوق *jauḳ*, غول *ghōl*, (of horse), رساله *risāla*.

File, صف *ṣaff* (f.), قطار *ḳaṭār* (f.), پانت *pānt* (f.).

Rank, پانت *pānt* or *pānti* (f.), صف *ṣaff* (f.).

Centre or main body (of an army), قلب *ḳalb*.

Wing or Flank (of an army), پهلو *pahlū*, جناح *jaṇāḥ* (f.).

Right wing, ميمنه *maimana*. Left wing, ميسره *maisara*.

Watch, Sentinel, پهرا *pahrā*, پهريا *pahriyā*, چوكيدار *chaukīdār*.

Guard, Patrole, پهرا *pahrā*, پهروا *pahrū'ā*, پهريا *pahriyā*, شبگرد *shab-gard*.

Soldier, سپاهي *sipāhī* (m.), لشكري *lashkarī* (m.).

Foot soldier, پياده *piyāda*. Infantry, پيدل *paidal*, پيادي *piyādē*.

Horse soldier, سوار *sawār*, گهڑ چڑها *ghuṛ-chaṛhā*.

Pioneer, بيلدار *bēldār*.

Ensign, Standard, Colours, نشان *nishān*, جهنڈا *jhanḍā*, بيرق *bairaḳ*.

Ensign-bearer, نشان بردار *nishān-bardār*, علم بردار *ālam-bardār*.

Hostage, يرغمال *yarghamāl*, كفيل *kafīl*, اول *ōl*.

Captive, Prisoner, اسير *asīr*, گرفتار *giriftār*, قيدي *ḳaidī*.

Parade, قواعد گاه *ḳawā'id-gāh* (f.), صفگاه *ṣaff-gāh* (f.), ميدان *maidān*.

Muster, گنتي *gintī*, موجودات *maujūdāt* (f.), فوج كا تعليقه *fauj kā ta'līḳa*.

Arms, هتهيار *hathyār* or *hathiyār* (m. f.), سلاح *silāḥ* (f.).
Sword, تلوار *talwār* (f.), کهانڈا *khānḍā*, شمشير *shamshēr*, تيغ *tēgh*.
Dagger, خنجر *khanjar*, کٹار *kaṭār*, چهرا *chhurā*.
Spear, بهالا *bhālā*, برچهي *barchhī*, نيزه *nēza*, بلم *ballam*.
Bow, دهنک *dhanuk* (f.), کمان *kamān* (f.), قوس *ḳaus* (f.).
Arrow, تير *tīr*, بان *bān*, سر *sar*, خدنگ *khadang*.
Quiver, ترکش *tarkash*, تکش *tukkash*, تون *tūn*, نکهنگ *nikhang* (f.).
Bowstring, چلا *chillā*, زه *zih* (f.).
Sling, گوپهن *gōphan* (f.), فلاخن *falākhun* (f.), گوپهنا *gophnā* (f.).
Poleaxe, گنڈاسا *ganḍāsā*, پهرسا *pharsā*, بيلچه *bēlcha*.
Shield, Target, ڈهال *ḍhāl* (f.), سپر *sipar* (f.), پهري *pharī*.
Helmet, خود *khōd*, ٹوپ *ṭōp*, مغفر *mighfar*.
Coat of mail, جهلم *jhilam*, بکتر *baktar*, چهل ته *chihal-tah*.
Cuirass, جوشن *jaushan*, بکتر *baktar*, (f.), چار اينه *chār-ā'īna*.
Musket, Firelock, بندوق *bandūḳ* (f.), تپک *tupak* (f.).
Swivel, large Musket, wall-piece, جزايل *jazā'il*.
Barrel, Bore, Chase (of a gun), نال *nāl*, نلي *nalī*.
Chamber (of a gun), کوٹهي *kōṭhī*, خزانه *khazāna*.
Pistol, تمنچه *tamancha*, تبنچه *tabancha*.
Bayonet, سنگين *sangīn* (f.).
Pike, نيزه *nēza*, کانٹا *kānṭā*.
Flint, (for striking fire) سنگ چقمق *sang-i-chakmak*.
Powder, باروت *bārūt* (f.), بارو *bārū* (f.), دارو *dārū* (f.).
Ball, Bullet, (for a musket) گولي *gōlī*, (for a cannon) گولا *gōlā*.
Cartridge, ٹونٹا *ṭōnṭā*, کارتوس *kārtūs*.
Match, (for a gun) توڑا *tōṛā*, فليته *falīta*, (brimstone) ديا سلاي *diyā-salā'ī*.
Cannon, Gun, piece of Ordnance, توپ *tōp* (f.).
Ordnance, توپين *tōpēṅ* (f. plur.).
Fieldpiece, رهکلا *rahkalā*, سفري توپ *safarī tōp* (f.).
Park of Artillery, توپ خانه *tōp-khāna*.
Arsenal, سلاح خانه *silāḥ-khāna*, توپ خانه *tōp-khāna*.

Gun carriage, ارابه *arāba.*

Cannoneer, Gunner, توپ انداز *tōp-andāz,* گولنداز *gōlandāz.*

Bomb, Mortar, Shell, غباره *ghubāra,* (small mortar) گرنل *garnal.*

Bombardier, توپچي *tōp-chī* (m.), گولنداز *gōlandāz.*

Fusileer, Musketeer, بندوقچي *bandūkchī,* برقنداز *barkandāz.*

Fort, Fortress, Castle, گڑھ *gaṛh,* کوٹ *kōṭ,* قلعه *kal'ā.*

Redoubt, قلعچه *kil'ā-cha,* گڑھي *gaṛhī:* see Fort.

Bastion, Bulwark, برج *burj,* مرحله *marhala.*

Battery, مورچه *mōrcha,* دمدمه *damdama,* مرحله *marhala.*

Embrasure, رنده *randa,* توپ کا جهروکها *tōp kā jharōkhā.*

Ditch, Trench, Fosse, Moat, خندق *khandak,* کهاي *khā'ī.*

Trenches, Lines, مورچال *mōrchāl* (f.), سنگر *sangar,* کهاي *khā'ī.*

Wall or intrenchments round a town, شهرپناه *shahr-panāh* (f.).

Walls of a city, شهربند *shahr-band.*

Rampart, Breast-work, Parapet, فصيل *faṣīl* (f.), کنگره *kangara.*

Ponton (bridge of boats), کشتي کا پل *kishtī kā pul.*

Tent, Pavilion, ديرا *dērā,* خيمه *khaima,* تنبو *tambū.*

Camp, Encampment, لشکرگاه *lashkar-gāh* (f.), پڑاو *paṛā'ō.*

Decampment, March, کوچ *kūch.*

Halt, place of residence or encamping, مقام *mukām,* رهاو *rahā'ō.*

Field of battle, رزم گاه *razm-gāh* (f.), معرکه *ma'raka.*

Drill, قواعد فوج *kawā'id-i-fauj.*

Furlough, رخصت *rukhsat* (f.), چهٹي *chhuṭṭī,* اجازت *ijāzat* (f.).

Drum, ڈهول *ḍhōl,* طبل *ṭabl,* ڈهولک *ḍhōlak.*

Kettledrum, نقاره *nakkāra,* ڈنکا *ḍankā,* کوس *kōs.*

Trumpet, تورهي *tōrhī* or ترهي *turhī,* سنگا *singā,* نفير *nafīr* (f.).

Clarion, قرناي *karnā'ī* or *karnā'ē,* بوق *būk,* شهناي *shahnā'ī.*

Bugle, Horn, نرسنگا *narsingā,* صور *ṣūr* (f.): see Trumpet.

Hautboy, سرناي *surnā'ē.*

Flute, Flagelet, Fife, Pipe, الغوزه *alghūza,* بانسري *bānsrī,* مرلي *murlī,* پونگي *pūngī,* بنسي *bansī* ني *nai* (f.).

Naval Affairs.

Navy, Fleet, بحر *bahr* (f.), جہازوں کي فوج *jahāzōṅ kī fauj.*

Ship, جہاز *jahāz*, کشتي *kishtī*, وان *wān*, واهن *wāhan.* (Roebuck.)

Ship (or Man) of war, جنگي جہاز *jangī jahāz.*

Merchant-ship or -man, سوداگري جہاز *saudāgarī jahāz.*

Boat, کشتي *kishtī*, ناو *nā'ō* (f.), ترني *tarnī*, مچوا *machwā.* (Roeb.)

Barge, بجرا *bajrā*, نواڑا *niwāṛā*, مورپنکهي *mōr-pankhī.*

Barge, large Boat, Lighter, بهڑ *bhaṛ*, بهر *bhar.* (Roeb.)

Brig, دو دولي جہاز *dō-dōlī jahāz.* (Roeb.)

Rudder, Helm, سکان *sukkān*, پتوار *patwār* (f.), کنهر *kanhar.*

Prow, Head of a ship, ماتها *māthā*, سر *sir*, مانگ *māng.* (f.)

Stern, دبوسا *dabūsā*, پچهل *pichhil.* (Roeb.)

Poop, چهتري *chhatrī.* (Roeb.)

Deck, تخته *takhta*, منزل *manzil* (f.), تتک *tutak.* (Roeb.)

Quarter deck, دور کي پاس کا تتک *daur kē pās kā tutak.* (? Roeb.)

Main deck, اوپر کا بيچ کا تتک *ūpar kā bīch kā tutak.* (? Roeb.)

Forecastle, پهنا *phanā*, اگل فنا *āgal-fanā* (Roeb.), (dakh.) اگل *āgal* (?).

Mast, دول *dōl*, مستول *mastūl.* (Roeb.)

Afore, اگل *āgil*, اگل *āgal.* (Roeb.)

Abaft, Aft, Astern, پيچهل *pīchhil*, پچهوارا *phichwārā.* (Roeb.)

Ahead, اگل *āgil*, اگل *āgal.* (Roeb.)

Aloft, اوپر *ūpar*, دول پر *dōl par.* (Roeb.)

Amidships, بيچابيچ *bīch-a-bīch*, بيچ ميں *bīch mēṅ.* (Roeb.)

Anchor, لنگر *langar*, ننگر *nangar.* (Roeb.)

Anchorage, لنگر کرني کي جگہ *langar karnē kī jagah*, لنگرگاه *langar-gāh.* (f.)

Ashore, کناري *kināre*, (aground) کناري پر *kinārē par.*

Ballast, نيرم *nīram*, نيلم *nilām*, ليلم *līlam.* (Roeb.)

Bank or Shoal, چر *char*, خرابه *kharāba.* (Roeb.)

Beam, بيم *bīm*, اڑا *āṛā.* (Roeb.)

Bell, گهڑي *ghaṛī.* (Roeb.)

Between decks, تتک كي بيچ *tutak ke bīch*. (Roeb.)

Birth, جگهہ *jagah* (f.), مکان *makān*.

Boatswain, سرهنگ *sarhang*, بوسمان *bōsmān*, بوچمان *bōchmān*. (Roeb.)

Bottom (part of the ship in the water), پيٹهہ *pīṭh*. (f.)

Bore or Boar in the Ganges, هما *hummā*, همبا *humbā*, بان *bān*.

Broadside, Volley, شلخ *shalkh* (f.), سلک *salak*. (Roeb.)

Bucket, بالدي *bāldī*, بالتي *bāltī*. (Port. *balde*: Roeb.)

Cabin, کامرا *kāmarā* (Port. *camara*: Roeb.), دبوسا *dabūsā*.

Cable, همار *hamār*. (Port. *amarra*: Roeb.)

Call (boatswain's), سيتي *sītī*. (Roeb.)

Callipers, ماپ *māp*, کوپاس *kūpās* or کومپاس *kūmpās*. (Roeb.)

Can (jug), لوٹا *lōṭā*, پات *pāt* (from Eng. *pot*: Roeb.).

Cannon, توپ *tōp* (f.): to cannonade, توپان مارنا or توپ *tōp* or *topāṅ mārnā*.

Cap (for the head), ٹوپي *ṭōpī* or توپي *topī*. (Roeb.)

Cape, تيک *tēk*, تينک *tēnk*, پونت *pōnt*, سيس *sīs*. (Roeb.)

Captain, (European) کپتان *kaptān*, (Indian, &c.) ناخدا *nākhudā*.

Cargo, بهرتي *bhartī*, بار *bār*, بوجهاي *bōjhā'ī*. (Roeb.)

Carpenter, مستري *mistrī* (m.), ستار *sutār*, برهي *barhai*. (Roeb.)

Carriage (of a gun), توپ كي گاڑي *tōp kī gāṛī*.

Cartouch, توسدان *tōsdān*.

Cartridge, کارتوس *kārtūs*, توتا *tōtā* or تونتا *tōntā*. (Roeb.)

Case shot, چهينتا گولا *chhīntā golā*. (Roeb.)

To be cast away, (a person) تواي کهانا *tawā'ī khānā*, (a ship) ٹوٹ جانا *ṭūṭ jānā*, مارا جانا *mārā jānā*. (Roeb.)

Catamaran, کتمرال *katmarāl*, کتمرام *katmarām*, پرانچا *parānchā*.

To Caulk, کال پتي کرنا *kāl pattī karnā*. (Roeb.)

Centry or Sentry, سنتري *santrī*, پورا دار *pōrā dār*. (Roeb.)

Chain, زنجير *zanjīr*, سانکل *sānkal*, سانکر *sānkar*. (Roeb.)

Chain pump, زنجير کا بنبا *zanjīr kā bambā*. (Port. *bomba*: Roeb.)

Chain shot, زنجيري گولا *zanjīrī gōlā*.

Channel, دهار *dhār*. Mid-channel, منجدهار *manjdhār*. (Roeb.)

Chest, پيٿي *pēṭī*, صندوق *ṣandūḳ*, (for arms) بندوق كي پيٿي *bandūḳ kī pēṭī.*

To clear for action, لڙني كو تيار كرنا *laṛnē kō taiyār karnā.*

Coboose, چلدان *chuldān.* (Roeb.)

Cockswain, كاكسين *kāksēn.* (Roeb.)

Coil (of a rope), سانكلا *sānklā.* (Roeb.)

Colours, ووتا *vautā*, بوتا *bautā*, نشان *nishān.* (Roeb.)

Compass, حقه *ḥuḳḳa*, كومپاس *kūmpās.* (Roeb.)

Cook, بهانداري *bhāndārī*, باورچي *bāwarchī.* (Roeb.)

Cooking place, Galley, چلدان *chuldān*, باورچي خانه *bāwarchī-khāna.*

Cooking kettle, ديگ *dēg.* (Roeb.)

A Cot, كهات جولي *khāt jōlī* : see Hammock. (Roeb.)

A Crane, كتري *katrī.* (Roeb.)

Crew, جهازي *jahāzī*, لسكر *laskar.* (Roeb.)

Cuddy (in E. I. ships), كپتان كهانا كهاني كي جگهه *kaptān khānā khānē kī jagah.*

To Discharge (unload), اتارنا *utārnā*, (a gun) چهوڑنا *chhōṛnā*, مارنا *mārnā*, داغنا *dāghnā.* (Roeb.)

Discipline (regulation), بندوبست *bandōbast*, (punishment) سزا *sazā* (f.), سجا *sajā*, مارپيٿ *mār-pīṭ.* (f.)

Dismasted, لنڈبنڈ *lunḍ bunḍ*, ننگا بونگا *nangā būngā.* (Roeb.)

Dock, گودي *gōdī.* Dock yard, گودي كا بنسار *godī kā bansār*, گودي كا بنسال *gōdī kā bansāl.* (Roeb.)

Double headed shot, دنڈي والا گولا or دانڈي *dānḍī* or *danḍī wālā gōlā.*

To Dress (a ship), سنگارنا *singārnā.*

To Drop anchor, ننگر ڈالنا *nangar ḍālnā*, لنگر كرنا *langar karnā.*

East, پورب *pūrab*, اگمن *ugman*, مشرق *mashriḳ.* (Roeb.)

Ebb-tide, بهاٿها *bhāṭhā.*

Eddy, بهونري *bhaunrī*, گهمري *ghumrī*, گهمتا پاني *ghumtā pānī.*

Ensign, Flag, نشان *nishān*, بوتا *bautā*, ووتا *vautā.* (Roeb.)

Fair (as wind), سيدها *sīdhā*, موافق *muwāfiḳ*, جاهوم *jāhōm.* (? Roeb.)

Fair (not cloudy), پهرچها *pharchhā*, ساف *sāf*, كهلاسا *khulā-sā.* (Roeb.)

To Fall in with, ملنا *milnā,* ملاقات كرنا *mulāḳāt karnā.* (Roeb.)

False fire or blue flames, مهتاب *mahtāb,* مورم *mōram,* مورام *mōrām.* (Roeb.)

To Fasten, مزبوت كرنا *mazbūt karnā,* بند كرنا *band karnā,* باندهنا *bāndhnā.* (Roeb.)

Fathom, وام *wām,* بام *bām.* (Roeb.)

Flag, see Ensign. Flagstaff, ووٹا كاتي *wauṭā kātī,* چهڙبانس *chhaṛ bāns.* (Roeb.)

Fleet, پهليت *philīt,* قافله *ḳāfila,* بهار *bhār,* بحر *baḥr.* (Roeb.)

Float (of a fishing line), ترندا *tarindā,* ترنڈا *tirinḍā.* (Roeb.)

Flood-tide, the flow, جوار *jawār,* بهرتي *bhartī.* (Roeb.)

Fore, اگل *āgil,* اگل *āgal.* Fore and aft, اگل پيچهل *āgil pīchhil.* (Roeb.)

Foreland, تيک *tēk,* تينک *tēnk.* (Roeb.)

Fore mast, ترکت دول *trikat* (or *tirkat*) *dōl.* (Roeb.)

Fore sail, ترکت *trikat.* (Roeb.)

Freight (hire), نول *naul,* نول *nuwal,* کرايا *kirāyā.* (Roeb.)

Freight (cargo), نول کا مال *nuwal kā māl.* (Roeb.)

Fresh water, ميٹها پاني *mīthā pānī.* (Roeb.)

Gale of wind, توفان *tūfān,* اندهي *āndhī.*

Quarter gallery, کنديل *kandīl.* (Roeb.)

Stern gallery, دبوسه *dabūsa.*

Gangway, گانگوئي *gāngwa'ē.* (Roeb.)

Glass (hour), گهڙي کي شيشي *ghaṛī kī shīshī.*

Glass (spy or telescope), دوربين *dūrbīn* or دورمين *dūrmīn.* (Roeb.)

Glass (spy or telescope for night), رات کا دورمين *rāt kā dūrmīn.* (Roeb.)

Grape shot, گيرب چهانت *gērab chhānt.* (Roeb.)

A gun-shot, گولي کا تپا *gōlē kā tappā.* (Roeb.)

Gun tackles, توپ کا لپتي *tōp kā laptī.* (Roeb.)

Gunnel (of a boat), ميز *mēz* or مينچ *mēnch.* (Roeb.)

Gust, جهپيٹا *jhapēṭā,* دهپا *dhapā.*

To Hail, بونگل سي بات کرنا *būngal sē bāt karnā.* (Roeb.)

Half pike, بهالا *bhālā,* برچهي *barchhī.*

Hammock, جولي *jōlī,* جهولي *jholī,* جهولي *jhūlī.* (Roeb.)

All hands, سب ادمي *sab ādmī,* سب خلاسي *sab khalāsī.* (Roeb.)

Hand pump, چهوٹا بمبا *chhōṭā bambā,* هاتهه بنبا *hāth bambā.*

Handspike, هانسپيک *hānspīk.*

Harbour, بندر *bandar* or *bindar,* گهاٹ *ghāṭ.* (Roeb.)

Harpoon, ايک دانت والا کاوڑ *ēk dānt wālā kāwaṛ.* (Roeb.)

Hatch or Hatch way, پهالکا *phālkā* or فالکا *fālkā.* (Roeb.)

Hatches, پهالکي کا کيواڑ *phālkē kā kēwāṛ,* فالکي کا دروازه *fālkē kā darwāza.*

Hatchet, کواڑي *kuwāṛī,* کڑالي *kuṛālī.* (Roeb.)

Head (ornamented figure), پتلا *putlā,* مورت *mūrat.* (Roeb.)

To Heave the lead, پرم ڈالنا *prum ḍālnā.* (Roeb.)

A heavy sea, اکهري دريا *ākhrī daryā,* گرم دريا *garm daryā.*

Heel, سکان کي دهار *sukān kī dhār.* (Roeb.)

Helmsman, Steersman, سکاني *sukkānī.*

Hold, کهن *khan,* کهنڑ *khanṛ.* (Roeb.)

Hook (for fish), گل *gal.* (Roeb.)

Horizon, اسمان کا دهار *āsmān kā dhār.* (Roeb.)

Hoy, مچهوا *machwā:* see Boat.

Hull, منڈا جهاز *munḍā jahāz,* لنڈا منڈا جهاز *lunḍā munḍā jahāz.*

Jib, جيب *jīb.* (Roeb.) Jib boom, جيب بوم *jīb būm.*

Insurance, بيما *bīmā,* ويما *vīmā.* (Roeb.)

Jolly boat, جالي بوٹ *jālī bōt.* (Roeb.)

Journal, جهاز کا روز نامه *jahāz kā rōz-nāma.*

Island, Isle, ٹاپو *ṭāpū,* جانجيرا *janjīrā* (for جزيره *jazīra:* Roeb.).

Jury mast, پهالتو ڈول *phāltū ḍōl,* فالتو ڈول *fāltū ḍōl.* (Roeb.)

Keel, پٹهان *paṭhān,* ايراب *ērāb,* ايراف *ērāf.* (Roeb.)

Key, Quay, دنکا *dankā,* باندهيلا گهاٹ *bāndhēlā ghāṭ,* پکا گهاٹ *pakā ghāṭ.* (Roeb.)

Ladder, سيڑهي *sīṛhī.* Stern ladders, دبوسي کي سيڑهي *dabūsē kī sīṛhī.*

Land, کناره *kināra,* تڑ *taṛ.* (Roeb.)

Lantern, فانوس *fānūs,* or پھانوس *phānūs.* (Roeb.)

Larboard, داوا بوردو *dāwā būrdū.* (Roeb.)

Lascar, خلاسي *khalāsī,* کھاروا *khārwā* or *khārū'ā.* (Roeb.)

To Launch, جهاز اتارنا *jahāz utārnā.*

Lead (used to heave), پرم *prum.* To heave the lead, پرم ڈالنا *prum ḍālnā.*

League, ديڑھ کوس *dēṛh kōs* (one and a half *kōs:* Roeb.).

Leak, سلاک *sulāk,* چهيد *chhēd.*

To spring a leak, گامت هونا *gāmat hōnā,* بونبا هونا *būmbā hōnā.* (Roeb.)

Lee-side, بهاري ترف *bhārē taraf,* بهاري بوردو *bhārē būrdū.* (Roeb.)

Lee-shore, بهاري مين کناره *bhārē mēn kināra.* (Roeb.)

A Light (candle), بتي *battī.*

Light-house, کنديليا *kandīliyā,* بتي کا موناره *battī kā mūnāra.* (Roeb.)

Fishing Line مچهي کا ڈور *machhī kā ḍōr,* گل کي ڈوري *gal kī ḍōrī.* (Roeb.)

To Load (a gun) توپ بهرنا *tōp bharnā,* (a ship) جهاز بهرنا *jahāz bharnā.*

Log, تپ *tap.* Log-book, تپ نامه *tap-nāma.* Log-line, تپ کا لين *tap kā lēn.* (Roeb.)

Low water, کايم پاني *kā'im* (for قايم *ḳā'im*) *pānī;* (if in a river) سار بهاٹها *sār bhāṭhā.* (Roeb.)

Lubbers hole, پانجري کا گالا *pānjrē kā gālā.* (Roeb.)

Magazine, باروت خانه *bārūt-khāna.*

Magnet, چمک پتهر *chamak pathar,* جيتا لوها *jītā lōhā.* (Roeb.)

To Make sail, سيره کرنا *sērh karnā.* (Roeb.)

To Make stern way, پيچهي پڙنا *pīchhē paṛnā,* پيچهي هٹنا *pīchhe haṭnā.*

Mallet, موگري *mōgrī,* مونگري *mōngrī.* (Roeb.)

Marines, جهاز کي سپاهي *jahāz kē sipāhī* (lit. ship soldiers: Roeb.).

Mast, دول *dōl,* (by landsmen called) مستول *mastūl.* (Roeb.)

Main mast, بڑا دول *baṛā dōl.* Fore mast, ترکت دول *tirkat* or *trikat dōl.* Mizzen mast, کلمي دول *kilmī dōl* or کلمي دول *kalmī dōl.*

Mate (of a ship), مالم *mālam* (for Arab. معلم *mu'allim:* Roeb.).
Midshipmen, بيچمين *bīchmēn,* ميچلمين *mīchilmēn.* (Roeb.)
Midships, جهاز کا بيچ *jahāz kā bīch.*
Mortar, هواي *hawā'ē,* اوکهلي *ūkhlī,* توپ کوٿهي *kōṭhī tōp.* (Roeb.)
Muster, گنتي *gintī,* حاضري *hāẓirī,* هاجري *hājirī.* (Roeb.)
Mutineer, دنگئي *danga'ī,* فسادي *fasādī,* متفرني *mutfarnī.* (Roeb.)
Mutiny, دنگا *dangā,* بغاوت *bag͟hāwat* (f.), فساد *fasād,* آشوب *āshōb.*
Neap tides, بهانگ کا جوار *bhāng kā jawār,* مرکتال *markatāl.* (Roeb.)
North, اوتر *ūttar,* گاي *gā'ī,* شمال *shimal.* (Roeb.)
Oakum, گهني *gahnī,* (Roeb.) استوب *istūb,* استپ *istap.* (Port. *estopa.*)
Oar, هليسا *halēsā,* ڈانڈ *ḍānḍ* (Roeb.), چپو *chappū.*
Officer (of a ship), مالم *mālam:* see Mate.
Over board, دريا مين گرا *daryā meṅ girā.*
To out sail, سرس چلنا *saras chalnā,* زياده چلنا *ziyāda chalnā.* (Roeb.)
Packet, پاکيت *pākēt,* قاصد کا جهاز *ḳāṣid kā jahāz.* (Roeb.)
Paddle هاته هليسا *hāth-halēsā,* چمچه *chamcha,* پنگي *pangai.* (Roeb.)
Pass or Passport, رواني *rawāna,* پروانه *parwāna.*
Passage boat, تري پار هوني کا مچوا *tarī pār hōnē kā machwā.* (Roeb.)
Pig of ballast, (if of iron) کيتلي *kētlī,* (if of lead) پات *pāt.* (Roeb.)
Pike (spear), برچهي *barchhī,* بهالا *bhālā.*
Pilot, ارکاٿي *arkāṭī,* (at Surat) دونگوي *dūṅgvī,* (with Arabs) روبان *rūbān.*
Pirate (ship), دکيت کا جهاز *dakait kā jahāz,* چور کا جهاز *chōr kā jahāz.*
Pitch, دامر *dāmar,* پيچه *pīchh.* (Roeb.)
Pistol, تبانچه *tabancha,* پستول *pistaul.* (Roeb.)
Plank, تخته *tak͟hta,* پاتيون *pātiyūṅ.* (Roeb.)
Pleasure boat, سواري کا مچوا *sawārī kā machwā.*
Pole axe, کوهاري *kūhārī,* تبر *tabar.* (Roeb.)
Priming, رنجک *ranjak,* کان *kān.* (Roeb.)
Privateer, چور کا جهاز *chōr kā jahāz,* چنچيا کا گلوت *chanchiyā kā galwat.* (Roeb)
Prize, قيدي جهاز *ḳaidī jahāz,* پکڑيلا جهاز *pakaṛēlā jahāz.* (Roeb.)

Pump, بنبا *bambā* (from Port. *bomba:* Roeb.).

Punt, دونگا *dūngā,* تهاپرا *thāparā,* دينگي *dīngī.* (Roeb.)

Purser, جهاز کا کراني *jahāz kā kirānī,* پسر *pasar.* (Roeb.)

Quadrant, Sextant, کمان *kamān.* (Roeb.)

Quicksand, چور بالو *chōr bālū,* دلدل زمين *daldal zamīn.* (Roeb.)

Raft, پرانچا *parānchā,* ترايا *trāpā.* (Roeb.)

Reel, چرخي *char<u>kh</u>ī.*

Rocket, هواي *hawā'ī.*

Bread Room, روٿي خانه *rōṭī <u>kh</u>āna.*

Spirit Room, شراب خانه *sharāb <u>kh</u>āna.*

Ropes, الات *ālāt.* (Roeb.)

Rowers, هليسي والا *halēsē wālā.* (Roeb.)

Sail, سيره *sērh,* سيڑه *seṛh,* سر *sar.* (Roeb.)

To set sail, سيره کرنا *sērh karnā.* (Roeb.)

Salute (from a ship or fort), سلامي *salāmī.*

Scull, هولي کا هليسا *hōlī kā halēsā,* چهوٿا هليسا *chhōṭā halēsā.* (Roeb.)

Sheet, دامن *dāman,* دامان *dāmān,* دمان *damān.* (Roeb.)

To Ship (put on board a ship), جهاز پر چڑهانا *jahāz par chaṛhānā.*

To ship a sea, موج کهانا *mauj khānā.*

Shipping, جهاز کا بهار *jahāz kā bhār,* جهاز کا قافله *jahāz kā ḳāfila.*

Shipwright, جهاز کا مستري *jahāz kā mistrī.* (Roeb.)

Shoal, بالو چرا *bālū charā.* (Roeb.)

Shore, کناره *kināra,* دارا *dārā.* (Roeb.)

To shot the guns, توپون مين گولا بهرنا *tōpōṅ mēṅ gōlā bharnā.*

Shrouds, لبران *labrān.* (Roeb.)

Sick birth, ازاري کا تهکانا *āzārī kā thikānā.* (Roeb.)

Side, بردو *burdū,* بوردو *bōrdū.* (Roeb.)

Signals, سيکنيل *sīknēl,* ستنيل *sitnēl,* اشاره *ishāra.* (Roeb.)

Skiff, کاغذي مچوا *kā<u>gh</u>zī machwā.* (Roeb.)

Slack water, نرم پاني *naram pānī.* (Roeb.)

Sloop, سلوپ *salūp,* سلپ *salup.* (Roeb.)

Smuggler, ماهسول کا چٿا *māhsūl kā chuṭṭā.* (Roeb.)

South, دکهن *dakhan*, جنوب *janūb*, سولي *sūlī*. (Roeb.)
Speaking trumpet, بنگل *bungal*, بهنگل *bhungal*. (Roeb.)
Spring tide, بڑا جوار *baṛā jawār*, بڑا کتال *baṛā katāl*. (Roeb.)
Sponge, پينچي *pīnchī*, سنبها *sumbhā* (Roeb.), (of a gun) پچهارا *puchhārā*.
Squadron, جهاز کا تولي *jahāz kā tōlī*. (Roeb.)
Staff, چهوٹا بوتا کاتهي *chhōṭā bautā kāthī*, چهوٹا ووتا کاتهي *chhōṭā wautā kāthī*.
Ensign staff, بڑا ووتا کاتهي *baṛā wautā kāthī*. (Roeb.)
Jack staff, جاک ووتا کاتهي *jāk wautā kāthī*. (Roeb.)
A flag staff, اوپر کا ووتا کاتهي *ūpar kā wautā kāthī*. (Roeb.)
Stage (for carpenters or caulkers, &c.), پرانچا *parānchā*. (Roeb.)
Starboard, جمنا بردو *jamanā burdū*, اوجا بردو *ūjā burdū*. (Roeb.)
To Steer, سکان پکڑنا *sukān pakaṛnā*, جهاز چلانا *jahāz chalānā*.
Stern ports, دبوسي کي باري or باريان *dabūsē kī bārī* or *bāriyāṅ*. (Roeb.)
Steward, استور *istūr* or *istōr*. (Roeb.)
Stores (naval), جهازي سرنجام or سرمجام *jahāzī sarinjām* or *saramjām*.
Store-keeper, بنسار کا صاحب *bansār kā ṣāḥib*. (Roeb.)
Stowage, کهمال *khamāl*, سمال *samāl*. (Roeb.)
A strait, گالا *gālā*, کهچ *khuch*. (Roeb.)
Studding sail, دستور *dastūr*, (lower) نيچي دستور *nīchē dastūr*. (Roeb.)
Supercargo, (if an Englishman) ترني *tarnī*, تني *tannī*, (if a Musalman) ناخدا *nā-khudā*, (if a Parsee) کراني *kirānī*, گماشته *gumāshta*.
Surf, لير *lēr*. (Roeb.) Surge, موج *mauj*, موجه *mauja*.
Surgeon, داکتر *dāktar*, دکتر *daktar*, حکيم *hakīm*. (Roeb.)
Swivel, جمبوره *jambūra*, زنبوره *zambūra*. (Roeb.)
Tar, الکترا *alkatarā* (for Port. *alcatram*), تار *tār*. (Roeb.)
Teak (wood), ساگوان *sāgwān*. (Roeb.)
Tide, پاني کا تان *pānī kā tān*. Tide way, دهار *dhār*. (Roeb.)
Tier, تهر *thar*, هار *hār*. (Roeb.)
Tiller (of a ship), بکرا *bakrā*, سکان کا لاٹ *sukān kā lāṭ*. (Roeb.)
Tilt, چهتري *chhatrī*. (Roeb.)
Tonnage, بوجهاي کا وزن or وجن *bojhā'ī kā wazan* or *wajan*. (Roeb.)

Trade winds, موسمي هوا *maumī hawā*, موسمي هوا *mausamī hawā*. (Roeb.)

Trousers, پاجامه *pā-jāma*, اجار *ijār*, ازار *izār*. (Roeb.)

Trunnions, توپ كي موت *tōp kī mūt*, توت كا كان *tōp kā kān*. (Roeb.)

Turn of the tide, تان كا پهير *tān kā phēr*. (Roeb.)

Vane, بينده *bēndh*, بين *bēn*, كتواي *katwā'ī*. (Roeb.)

To Unmoor, ايك ننگر پر رهنا *ēk nangar par rahnā*. (Roeb.)

To Unship, نكالنا *nikālnā*, بار كرنا *bār karnā*. (Roeb.)

Upper deck, اوپر كا تتك *ūpar kā tutak*. (Roeb.)

Watch, پور *pōr*, چوكي *chaukī*. Dog watch, چهوٹا پور *chhōṭā pōr*. Middle watch, دوسرا پور *dūsrā pōr*, بيچلا پور *bīchilā pōr*. Morning watch, گوريا پور *gōriyā pōr*, گهريا پور *ghariyā pōr*, گهريا پور *ghuriyā pōr*. (Roeb.)

Fresh water, ميٹها پاني *mīṭhā pānī*. (Roeb.)

Salt water, كهارا پاني *khārā pānī*, نونا پاني *nōnā pānī*. (Roeb.)

Way (of a ship), روس *rūs*, چال *chāl*, رو *rav*, چرك *chark*. (Roeb.)

Weather, موسم *mausim* : see Wind.

Weather or Weathergage (windward), واو پر *wā'ō par*, باو پو *bā'ō par*.

To weigh anchor, ننگر اٹهانا *nangar uṭhānā*, ننگر اترنگ كرنا *nangar atrang karnā*. (Roeb.)

Wharf, گهاٹ *ghāṭ*, دهكا *dhakā*. (Roeb.)

Wheel of the helm, سكان كا چرخي *sukān kā charkhī*. (Roeb.)

West, مغرب *maghrab*, پچهم *pachham*, قبلئي *ḳibla'ī*. (Roeb.)

Wind, هوا *hawā* (f.), واو *wā'ō*, باو *bā'ō*. (f.) Fair wind, ياهوم هوا *yāhōm hawā*, جاهوم هوا *jāhōm hawā*, با مراد هوا *bā murād hawā*. Side wind, چوگوسي هوا *chau gōsī hawā*, چارگوسي هوا *chār gōsī hawā*. Head wind, گوساتي هوا *gosātī hawā*, منه پر هوا *muṅh par hawā*. Wind's eye, هوا كا گهر *hawā kā ghar*. (Roeb.)

Windlass, چيناٸي دوڑ *chīnā'ī dauṛ*, دهيگلي *dhīglī*. (Roeb.)

To windward, واو پر *wā'ō par*, هوا كا منه *hawā kā muṅh*. (Roeb.)

Worm-eaten, گهن كهائلا *ghuṇ-khā'ēlā*, گهن كا كهاديلا *ghun kā khādēlā*. (Roeb.)

Wreck, كهوكهرا *khōkhrā*, كهوكهيرا *khōkhērā*, ٹوٹيلا جهاز *ṭuṭēlā jahāz*.

Yacht, سواري کا مچوا *sawārī kā machwā*. (Roeb.)
Yard (for a sail), پروان *parwān*, پرمن *pirman*. (Roeb.)
Zenith, کپال کي اوپر *kapāl kē ūpar*. (Roeb.)

Divisions of Time.

A moment, لمحه *lamḥa*, پلک *palak*, نمکھ *nimikh*, پل *pal*, دم *dam*.
Minute, دقيقه *daḳīḳa*.
A twenty-four minutes (Indian hour), گهڙي *ghaṛī*, گهنٹا *ghanṭā*.
Hour (may be denoted by the Arab.) ساعت *sā'at*. (f.)
Watch (term of three hours), پهر *pahar*, پاس *pās*.
Day, دن *din*, روز *rōz*, يوم *yaum*, (in oppos. to night) دن *din*, نهار *nahār*.
Night, رات *rāt* (f.), شب *shab* (f.), ليل *lail* (f.), رين *rain*. (f.)
Midnight, ادهي رات *ādhī rāt* (f.), نيم شب *nīm shab*. (f.)
Morning, Morn, صبح *ṣubḥ* (f.), فجر *fajar*. (f.)
Dawn of day, بهور *bhōr* (f.), تڑکا *taṛkā*, سحر *saḥar* (f.), ارن *arun*.
Forenoon, اول دوپهر *awwal-i-dō pahar*.
Midday, Noon, دو پهر *dō-pahar* (f.), دو پهر دن *dō pahar dīn*, نصف النهار *misfu-n-nahār*, نيم روز *nīm-rōz*.
Afternoon, سه پهر *si-pahar*, دو پهر سي شام تک *dō pahar sē shām tak*.
Evening, سانجه *sānjh* (f.), شام *shām* (f.), سر شام *sar-i-shām*.
Twilight, گودهولي *gōdhulī*, منه اندهيرا *muṅh-andhērā*.
Week, اٹهواره *aṭhwāra*, هفته *hafta*.
Decade, عشره *ashara*.
Fortnight, دو هفته *dō-hafta*, پکه *pakh* or پچه *pachh*.
Month, مهينا *mahīnā*, ماس *mās*, ماه *māh*, شهر *shahr*.
Year, برس *baras*, سال *sāl*, سن *san*, سنه *sana*.
Age (period, cycle), عصر *aṣr*, عهد *ahd*, جگ *jug*.
To day, اج *āj*, (adv.) اج کي دن *āj kē din*.
To night, اج کي رات *āj kī rāt* or اج رات *āj-rāt*.
Yesterday, کل *kal*, ديروز *dīrōz*, پچهلا دن *pichhlā din*.
Last night, کل کي رات *kal kī rāt*, دوش *dōsh*.
Day before yesterday, or day after to morrow, پرسون *parsōṅ*. (adv.)

Three days ago, or to come, ترسوں *tarsōṅ*. (adv.)

Four days ago, or to come, نرسوں *narsōṅ*. (adv.)

To morrow, کل *kal*, فردا *fardā* (adv.), بہان *bihān*.

Spring, بسنت *basant* (f.), بہار *bahār* (f.), ربیع *rabiʿ*. (f.)

Summer, گرما *garmā*, گریکھم *girēkham*, تابستان *tābistān*, صیف *ṣaif*.

Autumn, پت جھڑ *pat-jhaṛ* (f.), خزان *khizān* (f.), خریف *kharīf*. (f.)

Winter, جاڑا *jāṛā*, سرما *sarmā*, زمستان *zamistān*, شتا *shitā*.

Other useful Nouns alphabetically arranged.

Abatement, گھٹتي *ghaṭṭī*, کمي *kamī*, کمتي *kamtī*, تخفیف *takhfīf*. (f.)

Abbreviation, اختصار *ikhtiṣār*, اقتصار *iḳtiṣār*, سنچھیپن *sanchhēpan*.

Abdication, تیاگ *tyāg*, ترک *tark*.

Abhorrence, نفرت *nafrat* (f.), کراهیت *karāhiyat*. (f.)

Ability, مقدور *maḳdūr*, طاقت *ṭāḳat* (f.), دست رس *dast-ras*. (f.)

Ablution, غسل *ghusl*, سنان *snān* or اسنان *asnān*, وضو *wazū*.

Abode, ٹھکانا *ṭhikānā*, مکان *makān*, بود باش *būdbāsh* (f.), ٹھور *ṭhaur*. (f.)

Abroad, باهر *bāhir*, پردیس *pardēs*, بدیس *bidēs*.

Absence, بیوگ *biyōg*, غیر حاضري *ghair-ḥāẓirī*; (in the) پیچھي *pīchhē*.

Abstinence, Abstemiousness, ریاضت *riyāẓat* (f.), پرهیزگاري *parhēz-gārī*.

Abstract (abridgment), مجمل *mujmal*, خلاصه *khulāṣa*.

Absurdity, بیهودگي *bēhūdagī*, اوٹ پٹانگ *ūṭ-paṭāng*, یاوه گوي *yāwa-gōʾī*.

Abundance, افراط *ifrāṭ*, بہتات *bahutāt* (f.), کثرت *kaṣrat*. (f.)

Abuse (contumely), گالي *gālī*, زبان درازي *zabān-darāzī*.

Abyss (cavern), غار *ghār*, ڈهک *ḍahak*, کهوه *khōh*, گڑها *gaṛhā*.

Acacia, (gum) اقاقیا *aḳāḳiyā*, (tree) کیکڑ *kīkaṛ*, مغیلان *mughailān*.

Academy, مدرسه *madrasa*, چٹ سال *chaṭ-sāl*, مکتب *maktab*.

Accent, لهجه *lahja*, سر *sur*, ضرب *ẓarb* (f.), دهرن *dhaṛan*.

Acceptation (of a word), معني *maʿnī*, لفظ کي مروج معني *lafẓ kī murauwaj maʿnī*.

Accessary, Accomplice, مددگار *madad-gār*, شریک *sharīk*, ساتهي *sāthī*.

Accident, اتفاق *ittifāḳ*, حادثه *ḥādiṣa*, سنجوگ *sanjōg*.

Account, accompt, حساب *ḥisāb*, محاسبه *muḥāsaba*, (narration) بيان *bayān*, خبر *khabar* (f.), (value) شمار *shumār*, (sake, cause) واسطي *wāsṭē*, سبب *sabab*, بابت *bābat*. (f.)

Accusation, نالش *nālish* (f.), دعوي *daʿwā*, برامد *bar-āmad*. (f.)

Ace, (at dice) پو *pau* (f.), (at cards or dice) نكا *nakkā*, (at cards) تاس كا يكا *tās kā yakkā*.

Acquaintance, (familiarity) واقفيت *wāḳifiyat* (f.), اشنائي *āshnā'ī*, (associate) اشنا *āshnā*, چنهار *chinhār*, رو شناس *rū-shinās*.

Acquisition, تحصيل *taḥṣīl* (f.), كسب *kasb*, كماي *kamā'ī*.

Act, Action, كام *kām*, كاج *kāj*, كرتب *kartab*, فعل *fiʿl*.

Addition, اضافه *iẓāfa*, (in arithmetic) ميزان *mīzān*. (f.)

Address, (skill) چالاكي *chālākī*, (of a letter) سر نامه *sar-nāma*.

Adjective, صفت *ṣifat* (f.), اسم صفت *ism-i-ṣifat*, نعت *naʿt*. (f.)

Adjustment (settlement), فيصله *faiṣala*: see Arrangement.

Admonition, نصيحت *naṣīḥat* (f.), وعظ *waʿẓ*, اپديس *upadēs*.

Adoration, عبادت *ʿibādat* (f.), پوجا *pūjā* (f.), پرستش *parastish*. (f.)

Advantage, (gain) لابه *lābh*, نفع *nāfʿ*, فايده *fā'ida*, (superiority) غلبه *ghalaba*, چڙهتي *chaṛhtī*, جيت *jīt*. (f.)

Adverb, ظرف *ẓarf*, حرف *ḥarf*, حرف تميز *ḥarf-i-tamīz*.

Adversary, حريف *ḥarīf*, مخالف *mukhālif*: see Enemy.

Adversity, بپت *bipat* (f.), بد بختي *bad-bakhtī*, فلاكت *falākat*. (f.)

Advertisement, اشتهار *ishtihār*, اشتهار نامه *ishtihār-nāma*.

Advice, نصيحت *naṣīḥat* (f.), اپديس *upadēs*, صلاح *salāh*. (f.)

Adulation, خوش امد *khush-āmad* (f.), چاپلوسي *chāplūsī*.

Adultery, زنا *zinā* (f.), زناكاري *zinā-kārī*, چهنالا *chhinālā*.

Affair, كام *kām*, بات *bāt* (f.), معامله *muʿāmala*, مقدمه *muḳaddama*.

Affection, پريم *prēm*, الفت *ulfat* (f.), محبت *muḥabbat*. (f.)

Affliction, سوگ *sōg*, رنج *ranj*, دكه *dukh*, تصديع *tasdīʿ*. (f.)

Age (time of life), عمر *ʿumr* (f.), ايربل *āyurbal*: see Time.

Agent, (doer) فاعل *fāʿil*, كرتا *kartā*, (deputy) وكيل *wakīl*: see Factor.

Agility, چالاكي *chālākī*, چستي *chustī*, پهرتي *phurtī*, چابكي *chābukī*.

Agreement, (concord) اتفاق *ittifāḳ*, (compact) شرط *sharṭ*, قباله *ḳabāla*.

Aid, کمک *kumak* (f.), مدد *madad* (f.), دستگیري *dast-gīrī*.

Alacrity, شوق *shauḳ*, دلدهي *dildihī*, چالاکي *chālākī*.

Alien, پردیسي *pardēsī*, اجنبي *ajnabī*, اوپري *ūprī*.

Alliteration, تجنیس *tajnīs*. (f.)

Almanac, تقویم *taḳwīm* (f.), پترا *patrā*.

Almighty (the), القادر *al-ḳādir*, پرمیشور *paramēshwar*: see God.

Alms, بهیکه *bhīkh* (f.), خیرات *k͟hairāt* (plur. f.), دان *dān*.

Aloes, (gum) ایلوا *ēlwā*, مصبر *muṣabbar* (f.), (wood) اگر *agar*, عود *ʿūd*.

Alphabet, الف بي *alif bē* (f.), حروف تهجي *ḥurūf-i-tahajjī*.

Amber, کهربا *kah-rubā*. Ambergris, عنبر *ʿambar*.

Amount, جمله *jumla*, جمع *jamʿ* (f.), گٹهري *gaṭhrī*, موٹه *mōṭh*. (f.)

Amusement, تماشا *tamāshā*, تفرج *tafarruj*, کهیل *khēl*.

Ancestor, پرکها *purkhā*, جد *jadd*.

Ancestors, ابا اجداد *abā-ajdād*, پرکهي *purkhē*.

Ancients, متقدمین *mutaḳaddimīn*, پراني *purānē*. (plur.)

Angle, کهونٹ *khūnṭ*, کونه *kōna*, گوشه *gōsha*, زاویه *zāwiya*.

Anguish, عذاب *azāb*, اذیت *azīyat*, (f.), الم *alam*, کشٹ *kashṭ*.

Animal, جانور *jānwar*, حیوان *ḥaiwān*, پسو *pasū*.

Answer, اتر *uttar*, جواب *jawāb*, اتارا *utārā*.

Anvil, نهاي *nihā'ī*, سندان *sindān*. (f.)

Anxiety, اندیشه *andēsha*, فکر *fikr*, تردد *taraddud*, اداسي *udāsī*.

Appellation, نام *nām*, لقب *laḳab*, (plur. القاب *alḳāb*): see Name.

Appointment, تعین *ta'ʿaiyun*, (office) عهده *ʿuhda*, (promise) وعده *waʿda*.

Argument, بحث *baḥs*, مناظره *munāzara*, دلیل *dalīl*. (f.)

Arithmetic, گنت *ganit* (f.), سیاق *siyāḳ*, فن سیاق *fann-i-siyāḳ*.

Arrangement, ترتیب *tartīb* (f.), بند و بست *band-o-bast*.

Art, هنر *hunar*, علم *ʿilm*, فن *fann*, صنعت *ṣan'ʿat*. (f.)

Artifice, مکر *makr*, حیله *ḥīla*, چهل *chhal*, فن فریب *fann-farēb*.

Ashes, راکه *rākh* (f.), چهار *chhār* (f.), خاکستر *k͟hākistar*. (f.)

Assafœtida, هینگ *hīng*, انگوزه *angūza*, حلتیت *ḥiltīt*.

Assembly, مجمع *majmaʿ*, مجلس *majlis* (f.), محفل *maḥfil*. (f.)

Assessment, خراج *k͟hirāj*, محصول *maḥṣūl*, باج *bāj*.

Assistance, مدد *madad* (f.), اپکار *upakār*, سہایتا *sahāyatā*. (f.)
Assistant, مددگار *madadgār*, کمکي *kumakī*, سہائي *sahā'ī*. (m.)
Astonishment, حيراني *ḥairānī*, تعجب *ta'ajjub*, تحير *taḥaiyur*.
Astrolabe, اصطرلاب *uṣṭurlāb*.
Attendant, خدمتگار *khidmatgār*, ملازم *mulāzim*.
Attention, هوشياري *hoshyārī*, سرت *surt* (f.); (to a guest) تواضع *tawāẓu'*.
Attraction, کهينچ *khainch* (f.), کشش *kashish* (f.), جذب *jazb*.
Attribute, صفت *ṣifat* (f.), وصف *waṣf*, خاصيت *khāṣṣiyat*. (f.)
Auction, نيلام *nīlām*, هراج *harrāj*, بکري *bikrī*.
Authority, اختيار *ikhtiyār*, حکومت *ḥukūmat*. (f.)
Awe, ڈر *ḍar*, رعب *ru'b*, گهور *ghōr*, هيبت *haibat*. (f.)
Axis, axle, axle-tree, دهري *dhurī*; (pole of the earth) قطب *ḳuṭb*.
Babbler, باوبهک *bā'ōbhak*, باوجهک *bā'ōjhak*, ياوہگو *yāwa-gō*.
Babe, baby, بچه *bachcha*, لڑکا *laṛkā* (m.), لڑکي *laṛkī*. (f.)
Backbiter, چغل خور *chughul-khor*, غماز *ghammāz*.
Badge, چپراس *chaprās*, نشان *nishān*, علامت *'alāmat*. (m.)
Bag, تهيلي *thailī*, خريطه *kharīṭa*, (sack to carry grain) گون *gōn*. (f.)
Baggage, اسباب *asbāb*, چيزبست *chīz-bast* (f.), (slut) بيحيا *beḥayā*.
Bail, (surety) ضامني *ẓāmin-ī*, (person) ضامن *ẓāmin*.
Balance, ميزان *mīzān* (f.), ترازو *tarāzū*. (f.), (of account) باقي *bāḳī*.
Bale, گٹهر *gaṭhar*, موٹه *moṭh* (f.), گانٹه *gānṭh*. (f.)
Ball, گولا *gōlā*, گولي *gōlī*, (for play) گيندا *gēndā*, (dance) ناچ *nāch*.
Bamboo, بانس *bāṅs*.
Band, (bandage) پٹي *paṭṭī*, بند *band*, (company) گروه *gurōh*. (f.)
Bane, زهر *zahr*, بس *bis*, خرابي *kharābī*, نقصان *nuḳṣān*.
Banishment, ديس نکالا *dēs-nikālā*, جلاوطن *jilā-waṭan*.
Bank (of a river, &c.), کناره *kināra*, تير *tīr*.
Bank (for money), صراف خانه *ṣarrāf-khāna*, بنک *bank*.
Bankruptcy, ديوالا *dēwālā*, ناداري *nā-dārī*, افلاس *iflās*.
Banquet, ضيافت *ẓiyāfat* (f.), دعوت *da'wat*. (f.)
Bard, بهاٹ *bhāṭ*, کڑکهيت *kaṛkhait*, برديت *bardait*.
Bargain, عهد *'ahd*, قول قرار *ḳaul-ḳarār*, شرط *sharṭ*. (f.)

Bark (of a tree), چهال *chhāl,* چهلكا *chhilkā,* پوست *pōst.*

Barm, خمير *khamīr.*

Barter, لين دين *lēn dēn,* ادلا بدلا *adlā-badlā,* مبادله *mubādala.*

Bastard, حرام زاده *ḥarām-zāda,* حرامي پلا *ḥarāmī pillā.*

Bdellium, گوگل *gūgal,* مقل *muḳl.*

Bead, گريا *guriyā* (f.), مالا كا دانه *mālā kā dāna,* منكا *mankā.*

Beak, چونچ *chōnch* (f.), نوك *nōk* (f.), منقار *minḳār.* (f.)

Beauty, خوبصورتي *khūbṣūratī,* سندرتا *sundartā* (f.), جمال *jamāl.*

Beginning, ارمبه *ārambh,* شروع *shurū*ʿ, ابتدا *ibtida.* (f.)

Behalf, كارن *kāran,* خاطر *khāṭir* (f.), حق *ḥakk,* ليے *liyē.*

Behaviour, چال *chāl* (f.), چال ڈهال *chāl-ḍhāl* (f.), ڈهنگ *ḍhang.*

Being, هستي *hastī,* وجود *wujūd,* جاندار *jāndār.*

Belch, ڈكار *ḍakār* (f.), اروغ *ārōgh.*

Belief, عقيده *ăḳīda,* ايمان *īmān,* باور *bāwar.*

Believer, معتقد *mu*ʿ*taḳid,* ايمان‌دار *īmān-dār,* مومن *mūmin.*

Bell, گهنٹا *ghanṭā,* جرس *jaras,* (small) گهنگهرو *ghunghrū.*

Belt, بند *band,* (girdle) پيٹي *pēṭī,* كمر بند *kamar-band,* (sword) پرتلا *partalā.*

Bench, چوكي *chaukī,* تخته *takhta,* (of justice) محكمه *maḥkama.*

Bend, خم *kham,* ٹيڑهائي *ṭēṛhā'ī,* (twist) بل *bal,* پيچ *pēch.*

Benediction, اسيس *asīs* (f.), دعا *du'ā* (f.), اشيرباد *āshīrbād.*

Benefaction, انعام *in'ām,* احسان *iḥsān,* بخشش *bakhshish.* (f.)

Benefit, فايده *fā'ida,* احسان *iḥsān,* (profit) نفع *naf*ʿ.

Benevolence, خيرخواهي *khair-khwāhī,* نكوي *nikō'ī,* كرپا *kirpā.* (f.)

Berry, دانه *dāna,* داني كي صورت كا پهل *dānē kī ṣūrat kā phal.*

Betel-nut, سپاري *supārī* or سپياري *supyārī.*

Betel-leaf, پان *pān,* تنبول *tambōl.*

Bier, جنازه *janāza,* تابوت *tābūt.*

Biestings, پيوسي *pē'ōsī,* پهينس *phēnus,* پيوس *pēyūs.*

Bill, (of parcels) بيجك *bījak,* سياها *siyāhā,* (of exchange) هنڈي *hunḍī,* (account) حساب *ḥisāb,* ليكها *lēkhā,* (of a bird) see Beak, (instrument) داو *dā'ō.*

Billet (note), چتهي *chiṭṭhī*, رقعه *ruḳ'ā*, پاتي *pātī*.
Billet (of wood), چيلا *chailā*, کنده *kunda*.
Bin, کوٹهي *kōṭhī*, کوٹهري *kōṭhrī*.
Binding (of a book), جلد *jild* (f.), جز بندي *juz-bandī*.
Bird, چڑيا *chiṛiyā* (f.), پکهيرو *pakhērū*, پرند *parand*, مرغ *murgh*.
Birth, جنم *janam*, پيدايش *paidā'ish* (f.), تولد *tawallud*.
Birthday, سالگره *sāl-girih* (f.), برس گانٹه *baras-gānṭh*. (f.)
Biscuit, کاک *kāk*, کليچه *kulīcha*, تکي *ṭikkī*.
Bit, (piece) ٹکڑا *ṭukṛā*, ذره *zarra*, پرزه *purza*.
Bit (of a bridle), دهانه *dahāna*, لگام *lagām*. (f.)
Bitch, کتي *kuttī*, کتيا *kutiyā* (f.), کوکري *kūkarī*.
Bitterness, کڑواهٹ *kaṛwāhaṭ* (f.), تلخي *talkhī*.
A black (negro), حبشي *ḥabshī*, زنگي *zangī* (m.), هندو *hindū*.
Blackguard, لچا *luchchā*, شهدا *shuhdā*, رند *rind*.
Blade, (of grass) پتا *pattā*, (of a sword) پهل *phal*, (a fellow) بانکا *bānkā*.
Blame, دوس *dōs*, دوکه *dōkh*, مذمت *mazammat* (f.), الزام *ilzām*.
Blank book, بياض *bayāz*, سفينه *safīna*.
Blemish, داغ *dāgh*, کلنک *kalank*, کهوٹ *khōṭ* (f.), عيب *'aib*.
Blessing, دعا *du'ā* (f.), اسيس *asīs* (f.), برکت *barakat* (f.), نعمت *ni'mat*. (f.)
Blindman's buff, انکه موندورا *ānkh mūndaurā*.
Blindness, اندهلاپن *andhlāpan*, کوري *kōrī*, نابينائي *nā-bīnā'ī*.
Block, (of wood) کنده *kunda*, کاٹه *kāṭh*, (of stone) چٹان *chaṭān*.
Blockhead, بيوقوف *be-wuḳūf*, احمق *aḥmaḳ*, گاودي *gāwdī*.
Bloodshed, خون ريزي *khūn-rēzī*, قتل *ḳatl*.
Bloom, شگوفه *shigūfa*, پهول *phūl*, (of youth) نوجواني *nau-jawānī*.
Blossom, پهول *phūl*, کلي *kalī*, (of the mango) مور *maur*.
Blot, داغ *dāgh*, چهيٹ *chhīṭ* (f.), چنه *chinh*.
Bludgeon, لاٹهي *lāṭhī*, سونٹا *sōnṭā*, ڈنڈا *ḍanḍā*.
Blueness, نيلائي *nīlā'ī*, کبود *kabūd*.
Blunder, دهوکها *dhōkhā* or دهوکا *dhōkā*, چوک *chūk*. (f.)

Board, تخته *ta<u>kh</u>ta*, (table) ميز *mēz* (f.), (food) كهانا پينا *khānā pīnā*.

Board-wages, خوراكي *<u>kh</u>urākī*, خوراكي كي دام *<u>kh</u>urākī kē dām*.

Boast, boasting, لاف زني *lāf-zanī*, بڑائي *baṛā'ī*, تفاخر *tafā<u>kh</u>ur*.

Boaster, خود فروش *<u>kh</u>ud-farōsh*, لاف زن *lāf-zan*.

Boldness, دليري *dilērī*, جرات *jur'at* (f.), ڈهٹهائي *ḍhiṭhā'ī*.

Bond, (fastening) بند *band*, بندهن *bandhan*, (written obligation) تمسك *tamassuk*, دستاويز *dast-āwēz*.

Bondsman, ضامن *ẓāmin*, كفيل *kafīl*.

Book, پوتهي *pōthī*, كتاب *kitāb* (f.), صحيفه *ṣaḥīfa*.

Boon, بر *bar*, بخشش *ba<u>kh</u>shish* (f.) : see Bounty.

Boor, گنوار *gaṅwār*, جنگلي *janglī* (m. f.), دهقاني *dihḳānī*. (m. f.)

Booty لوٹ *lūṭ* (f.), غنيمت *<u>gh</u>anīmat* (f.), يغما *ya<u>gh</u>mā*.

Borax, سوهاگا *sōhāgā*, تنكار *tinkār*, بورق *būraḳ*.

Border, (side) كناره *kināra*, چهور *chhōr*, (edging) قور *ḳōr*.

Botany, علم نبات *ʿilm-i-nabāt*, بوٹوں كا علم *būṭōṅ kā ʿilm*.

Bottom, تلا *talā*, تلي *talī*, تهاه *thāh* (f.), پيندا *pēndā*.

Bough, ڈالي *ḍālī*, ڈال *ḍāl* (f.), شاخ *shā<u>kh</u>*. (f.)

Bound, (leap) كود *kūd* (f.), (boundary) حد *ḥadd* (f.), سر حد *sar-ḥadd* (f.), (limit, end) انتها *intihā* (f.), كناره *kināra*.

Bounty, فيض *faiẓ*, كرپا *kirpā* (f.), كرم *karam*, عنايت *ʿināyat*. (f.)

Bow (obeisance), كورنش *kōrnish* (f.), تسليم *taslīm*. (f.)

Boyhood, لڑكپن *laṛakpan*, لڑكائي *laṛkā'ī*.

Brand, (burning stick) سوخته *sō<u>kh</u>ta*, لوكٹي *lūkṭī*, (mark) داغ *dā<u>gh</u>*.

Brat, لونڈا *launḍā*, چهوكرا *chhōkrā*, گرگا *gurgā*, طفل *ṭifl*.

Bravery, دليري *dilērī*, همت *himmat* (f.), بهادري *bahādurī*.

Brawl, جهگڑا *jhagṛā*. Brawler, جهگڑالو *jhagṛālū*, لڑاكا *laṛākā*.

Breach, پهوٹ *phūṭ* (f.), درار *darār*, (quarrel) بگاڑ *bigāṛ*, خلل *<u>kh</u>alal*.

Breadth, چوڑائي *chauṛā'ī*, پهنائي *pahnā'ī*, (of cloth or a river) پاٹ *pāṭ*.

Breech of a gun, بندوق كي كوٹهي *bandūḳ kī kōṭhī*.

Breed, نسل *nasl* (f.), ذات *ẕāt* (f.), اصل *aṣl* (f.), قسم *ḳism*. (f.)

Breeding, (education) تربيت *tarbiyat* (f.), (manners) چلن *chalan*.

Bribe, رشوت *rishwat* (f.), گهوس *ghūs*, منه بهري *muṅh-bharī*.

Brickbat, روڙا *rōṛā*. Brickdust, سرخي *surkhī*.

Brick-kiln, پزاوا *pazāwā* (f.), پجاوه *pajāwa*.

Bride, دلهن *dulhan* (f.), عروس *ărūs*. (f.) Bridegroom, دولها *dūlhā*.

Bridle, لگام *lagām* (f.), باگ *bāg* (f.), عنان *ĭnān*. (f.)

Brightness, روشني *roshnī*, اجالا *ujālā*, چمک *chamak*. (f.)

Brim, Brink, کناره *kināra*, لب *lab*, کڙاڙا *kaṛāṛā*.

Brine, نمکين پاني *namkīn pānī*, کهارا پاني *khārā pānī*.

Bristle, سوار کي پيٿه کا بال *sū'ar kī pīṭh kā bāl*.

Brushwood, جهاڙي *jhāṛī*, جهاڙ *jhāṛ*, جهاڙ بوٿا *jhāṛ būṭā*.

Brute, حيوان *ḥaiwān*, وحشي *waḥshī*, جانور *jānwar*.

Bud, کلي *kalī*, کونپل *kōnpal* (f.), غنچه *ghuncha*.

Bulk, موٿائي *mōṭā'ī*, بڙائي *baṛā'ī*, ڈيل *ḍīl*.

Bunch, (of fruit) گچهه *guchchha*, خوشه *khōsha*, (of ribbons) پهول *phūl*.

Bundle, گٿهري *gaṭhrī* (m.), موٿري *mōṭrī*, بقچه *bukcha*.

Bung, ڈهٿها *ḍhaṭṭhā*.

Burden, بوجه *bōjh*, بار *bār*, حمل *ḥaml*: see Grief.

Bush, جهاڙي *jhāṛī*, جهاڙ *jhāṛ*, بوٿا *būṭā*, شاخ *shākh*.

Business, کام *kām*, کاج *kāj*, (avocation) see Calling.

Butt, (mark) هدف *hadaf*, نشانه *nishāna*.

Buying and Selling, خريد فروخت *kharīd-farōkht*. (f.)

Cage, پنجرا *pinjrā*, قفس *ḳafs*, (large) کٿهرا *kaṭahrā*.

Calamity, آفت *āfat* (f.), بپت *bipat* (f.), بلا *balā*. (f.)

Calculation, حساب *ḥisab*, گنتي *gintī*, شمار *shumār*.

Calendar, پترا *patrā*, تقويم *taḳwīm*. (f.)

Calling, پيشه *pēsha*, دهندها *dhandhā*, بيوهار *byōhār*.

Camphor, Camphire, کپور *kapūr*, کافور *kāfūr*.

Cane, (stick) چهڙي *chhaṛī*, بيد *bēd* (f.), (sugar) اوکه *ūkh* (f.), گنا *gannā*.

Canon, قانون *ḳānūn*, قاعده *ḳā'ida*, آئين *ā'īn*.

Canopus, سهيل *suhail*.

Canopy, سايبان *sāyabān*, شاميانه *shāmiyāna*, چتر *chatr*.

Canter (pace), پويه *pōya*. To canter, پويون چلنا *pōyōn chalnā*.

Canvass (cloth), ٹاٹ *ṭāṭ*, اجاڑ *ajāṛ*, ولايتي ٹاٹ *wilāyatī ṭāṭ*.

Capacity, (space) گنجايش *gunjā'ish* (f.), (ability) قابليت *kābilī-yat*. (f.)

Capital, (city) تختگاه *takht-gāh* (f.), (sum) پونجي *pūnjī*.

Caprice, capriciousness, وهم *wahm*, تلون مزاجي *talauwun-mizājī*.

Captive (prisoner), قيدي *ḳaidī*, اسير *asīr*, گرفتار *giriftār*.

Caravan, كاروان *kārwān*, قافله *ḳāfila*, (car) گاڑي *gāṛī*.

Caravansary, كاروان سرا *kārwān-sarā*, سراي *sarā'ē*. (f.)

Carcass, لاش *lāsh* (f.), لوتھ *lōth* (f.), مرده *murda*, ميت *maiyit*. (f.)

Card (visiting), سلام كا رقعه *salām kā ruḳ'a*, ورق *waraḳ*.

Cards (playing), تاس *tās*, كھيلني كا تاس *khēlnē kā tās*.

Care, چنتا *chintā* (f.), فكر *fikr*, انديشه *andēsha*, پروا *parwā*. (f.)

Carefulness, خبرداري *khabardārī*, هوشياري *hōshyārī*.

Carelessness, غفلت *ghaflat* (f.), بيخبري *bēkhabarī*, سستي *sustī*.

Carnage, قتل *ḳatl*, قتال *ḳitāl* (f.), خونريزي *khūnrēzī*.

Carriage, بهل *bahal* (f.), see Cart, (carrying) باربرداري *bārbardārī*.

Carrion, مردار *murdār* : see Carcass.

Cascade, جھرنا *jharnā*, اب شار *āb-shār*, چادر *chādar*. (f.)

Case, (covering) غلاف *ghilāf*, كھول *khōl* : see State, Condition, Box.

Case, (in grammar) حالت *ḥālat* (f.), كارك *kārak*.

Cash, پيسا *paisā*, نقد *naḳd*, روكڑ *rōkaṛ*. (f.)

Cast, (throw) پھينك *phēnk* (f.), (form) نقشه *naḳsha*, (tribe) ذات *zāt*. (f.)

Catalogue, فهرست *fihrist* (f.), سياها *siyāhā*, (list) بيجك *bījak*.

Cattle, مواشي *mawāshī*, ڈهور *ḍhōr*, گائي گورو *gā'e-gōrū*.

Cave, cavern, كھوه *khōh*, غار *ghār*, گپھا *guphā* (f.), كهف *kahf*.

Caution, احتياط *iḥtiyāṭ* (f.), حذر *ḥazar*, هوشياري *hōshyārī*.

Celebrity, ناموري *nāmwarī*, شهرت *shuhrat* (f.).

Celerity, چالاكي *chālākī*, چستي *chustī*, شتابي *shitābī*.

Celibacy, كوارپنا *kū'ār-panā*, ناكتخدائي كي حالت *nā-katkhudā'ī kī ḥālat*.

Cell, گوشه *gōsha*, حجره *ḥujra*, كلبه *kulba*, كوٹھري *kōṭhrī*.

Censure, الزام *ilzām*, طعن *ta*n*, ملامت *malāmat* (f.), نندا *nindā.* (f.)
Cent, (hundred) سو *sau*, (or, per cent.) سيكڑا *saikṛā.*
Centre, مركز *markaz*, درميان *darmiyān.*
Certificate, دست اويز *dast-āwēz* (f.), وثيقه *waṣīḳā.*
Cessation, توقف *tawaḳḳuf*, فراغت *farāg͟hat* (f.), مهلت *muhlat.* (f.)
Chaff, بهوسي *bhūsī*, پهوكڑ *phōkaṛ.*
Chain, زنجير *zanjīr* (f.), سانكر *sānkar* (f.), سلسله *silsila.*
Champion, پهلوان *pahlawān*, سور *sūr.*
Chance, (accident) اتفاق *ittifāḳ*, (fortune) قسمت *ḳismat.* (f.)
Change, تبديل *tabdīl* (f.), تغير *tag͟haiyur*, بدل *badal.*
Change (small money), ريزگي *rēzgī*, پيسا كوڑي *paisā kauṛī.*
Chaplet, سهرا *sihrā*, (rosary) تسبيح *tasbīḥ.* (f.)
Chapter, باب *bāb*, ادهيايه *adhyāya*, فصل *faṣl.* (f.)
Character, (mark) نشان *nishān*, حرف *ḥarf*, (writing) دست خط *dast-k͟hatt*, رقم *raḳam* (f.), (reputation) اعتبار *i*tibār*, نام *nām.*
Charcoal, كويلا *kō'ēlā*, زغال *zug͟hāl*, انكشت *ankisht.*
Charge, (care, custody) حواله *ḥawāla*, ذمه *ẕimma*, امانت *amānat* (f.), (office) خدمت *k͟hidmat* (f.), (expense) خرچ *k͟harch*, لاگت *lāgat* (f.), (assault) حمله *ḥamla*, (accusation) الزام *ilzām*, دوكه *dōkh.*
Chariot, گاڑي *gāṛī*, گهڑبهل *ghuṛ-bahal* (f.), رته *rath.* (f.)
Charity, (benevolence) خير انديشي *k͟hair-andēshī* : see Alms.
Charles's Wain, دب اكبر *dubb-i-akbar*, سپتركه *saptarikh.*
Charm, (spell) جادو *jādū*, منتر *mantar*, (amulet) تعويذ *ta*wīẕ*, ٹوٹكا *ṭōṭkā.*
Chart, نقشه *naḳsha*, دريا كي كناري كا نقشه *daryā kē kinārē kā naḳsha.*
Charter, سند *sanad* (f.), فرمان *farmān*, عهد نامه *ahd-nāma.*
Chase, (hunting) شكار *shikār*, (park) رمنه *ramna* : see Pursuit.
Chastisement, سزا *sazā* (f.), گوشمالي *gōshmālī*, تاديب *tādīb.* (f.)
Chastity, پاكدامني *pākdāmanī*, پاكيزگي *pākīzagī*, عصمت *aṣmat.* (f.)
Chat, گپ *gap* (f.), بك *bak* (f.), بي تكلف گفتگو *bē takalluf guftgū.*
Cheat, دغا *dag͟hā* (f.), چهل *chhal*, (cheater) دغا باز *dag͟hā-bāz*, ٹهگ *ṭhag.*

Cheer, مسرت *masarrat* (f.), خرمي *khurramī*, (food) بهوجن *bhōjan*.

Chess, شطرنج *shaṭranj*. (f.) Chess-board, شطرنج كي بساط *shaṭranj kī bisāṭ*. Chess-man, مهره *muhra*, نرد *nard*, گوٹ *gōṭ*. (f.) King at chess, شاه *shāh*, بادشاه *pādshāh*. Queen, فرزين *farzīn*, وزير *wazīr*. Castle or rook, رخ *rukh*, اونٹ *ūnṭ* (?). Bishop, پيل *pīl*, هاتهي *hāthī*. Knight, اسپ *asp*, گهوڑا *ghōṛā*. Pawn, پياده *piyāda*, بيدق *baidaḳ*.

Chick, chicken, چوزه *chūza*, چنگني *chingnī*.

Chief, chieftain, سردار *sardār*, مير *mīr*, رييس *ra'īs*.

Chisel, ٹانكي *ṭānkī*, روكهاني *rūkhāni*, چهيني *chhēnī*.

Chitchat, گپشپ *gapshap*, بات چيت *bāt-chīt* (f.), بول چال *bōl-chāl*. (f.)

Choice, (will) اختيار *ikhtiyār*, (selection) انتخاب *intikhāb*.

Christianity, نصرانيت *naṣrānīyat* (f.), عيسوي مذهب *ʻīsawī maẕhab*.

Chronicles, تواريخ *tawārīkh*.

Chronology, علم تواريخ *ʻilm-i-tawārīkh*.

A Churl, گنوار *ganwār*, دهقاني *dihḳānī*, (miser) بخيل *bakhīl*.

Chymistry, كيميا *kīmiyā*, كيمياگري *kīmiyā-garī*, رساين *rasāyan*.

Cipher, (in numbers) صفر *ṣifr*, سنا *sunnā*, (letter) حرف *ḥarf*, انك *ānk*.

Circle, كنڈل *kunḍal*, دايره *dā'ira*, گهيرا *ghērā*, حلقه *ḥalḳa*.

Circuit, دور *daur*, چكر *chakkar*, گردش *gardish* (f.), احاطه *iḥāṭa*.

Circumference, گرد *gird*, گهيرا *ghērā*, پهير *phēr*, محيط *muḥīṭ*.

Circumstance, حالت *ḥālat*, كيفيت *kaifīyat* (f.), چگونگي *chigūnagī*.

Citizen, شهري *shahrī*, اهل شهر *ahl-i-shahr*, اهل پيشه *ahl-i-pēsha*.

City, شهر *shahr*, نگر *nagar*, بلده *balda*, مدينه *madīna*.

Civet, زباد *zabād*.

Civility, انسانيت *insānīyat* (f.), مروت *murūwat*. (f.)

Claim, دعوي *daʻwā*, استحقاق *istiḥḳāḳ*, حق *ḥaḳḳ*.

Clamour, شور *shōr*, غوغا *ghaughā*, غل *ghul*.

Clamp, پتر *pattar*, (of bricks) پجاوه *pajāwa*.

Clap, (blow) چميٹا *chamēṭā*, كهٹكا *khaṭkā*, (of hands) تالي *tālī*.

Clasp-knife, چاقو *chāḳū*, چكو *chakkū*, بكيا *bakiyā*. (f.)

Class, (division) فرقه *firḳa*, قسم *ḳism*, (degree) درجه *darja*.
Clause, (sentence) فقره *fiḳra*, جمله *jumla*, (condition) شرط *sharṭ*. (f.)
Clearness, صفائي *ṣafā'ī*, شفافي *shaffāfī*, اجلائي *ujlā'ī*.
Cleaver, (butcher's) بغدا *bughdā*, کهانڈا *khānḍā*.
Cleft, رخنه *rukhna*, درز *darz*, درار *darār*, شق *shaḳḳ*.
Climate, clime, اقليم *iḳlīm*, ديس *dēs*, آب وهوا *āb-o-hawā*. (f.)
Cloth, کپڑ *kapaṛ*, کپڑا *kapṛā*, بستر *bastar*, پارچه *pārcha*.
Clown, گنوار *gaṅwār*, دهقاني *dihḳānī*, انچهيلا *anchhīlā*.
Club, سونٹا *sōnṭā*, عصا *āṣā*, لاٹهي *lāṭhī*, گدا *gadā*.
Cluster, خوشه *khōsha*, گچهه *guchchha*, (crowd) جماو *jamā'ō*.
Coach, گاڑي *gāṛī*, بهل *bahal* (f.), گهڑبهل *ghuṛ-bahal*. (f.)
Cobweb, مکڑي کا جالا *makṛī kā jālā*.
Cochineal, قرمز *ḳirmiz*, کرم دانه *kirm-dāna*.
Coffin, کفن *kafan*, صندوق *ṣandūḳ*, تابوت *tābūt*.
Coil, کنڈلي *kunḍlī*, بل *bal*, پهير *phēr*, خم *kham*.
Complaint, نالش *nālish* (f.), فرياد *faryād* (f.), ناله *nāla*: see Disease.
Coin, سکه *sikka*, ضرب *ẓarb* (f.), مدرا *mudrā*. (f.)
Collection, اجتماع *ijtimā'*, مجمع *majma'*, (sum) جمع *jam'*.
College, مدرسه *madrasa*, پاٹه سالا *pāṭh-sālā*. (f.)
Collusion, بندش *bandish* (f.), سازش *sāzish* (f.), سٹا بٹا *saṭṭā baṭṭā*.
Collyrium, انجن *anjan*, کحل *kuḥl*, سرمه *surma*.
Colour, رنگ *rang*, برن *baran*, (pretext) جا *jā*, بهانه *bahāna*.
Column, ستون *sitūn*, لاٹه *lāṭh* (f.), پيل پايه *pīl-pāya*.
Combat, لڑائي *laṛā'ī*, محاربه *muḥāraba*: see Battle, Fight.
Combination, ميل *mēl*, ملاپ *milāp* (f.), اتفاق *ittifāḳ*.
Comfort, دلاسا *dil-āsā*, سکهه *sukh*, آرام *ārām*.
Command, Commandment, حکم *ḥukm*, آگيا *āggyā*, امر *amr*.
Commencement, ابتدا *ibtidā* (f.), شروع *shurū'*, آغاز *āghāz*.
Comment, Commentary, شرح *sharḥ* (f.), ٹيکا *ṭīkā* (f.), حاشيه *ḥāshiya*.
Commission, (warrant) سند *sanad* (f.), (acting) ارتکاب *irtikāb*.
Committee, پنچايت *panchāyat* (f.), مجلس *majlis*. (f.)
Commodity, جنس *jins* (f.), مال *māl*, چيز *chīz* (f.), بست *bast*. (f.)

Common shore, بدر رو *badar-rau*, (f.), پرنالہ *parnāla*.

Commotion, (tumult) بلوا *balwā*, فتنہ *fitna*: see Motion.

Community, (whole people) جمہور *jamhūr*: see Society.

Compact, قول قرار *ḳaul ḳarār*, شرط *sharṭ* (f.), عہد *ʿahd*.

Companion, ساتھي *sāthī* (m.), رفيق *rafīḳ*, مصاحب *muṣāḥib*.

Company, (society) سنگت *sangat* (f.), رفاقت *rifāḳat*, (assembly) مجلس *majlis* (f.), (guests) مہمان *mihmān*, (partnership) شراکت *sharākat* (f.), (body of people) گروہ *guroh*. (f.)

Compass, گھيرا *ghēra*, احاطہ *iḥāṭa*, پھير *phēr*: see Circuit.

Compasses (pair of), پرگار *pargār* (f.), or (dakh.) پرکار *parkār*.

Compassion, درد *dard*, پير *pīr* (f.), ديا *dayā* (f.), رحم *raḥm*.

Compensation, تلافي *talāfī*, بدلا *badlā*, جزا *jazā*. (f.)

Complaint, (lament) فرياد *faryād* (f.), نالش *nālish*: see Disease.

Complexion, (colour) رنگ *rang*, چہري کا رنگ *chihrē kā rang*.

Compliment, (salutation) سلام *salām*, (service) بندگي *bandagī*.

Computation, محاسبہ *muḥāsaba*, تعداد *tiʿdād*. (f.)

Concern, (care) پروا *parwā* (f.), انديشہ *andēsha*: see Affair.

Concord, (agreement) ميل *mēl*, موافقت *muwāfaḳat* (f.), ملاپ *milāp* (f.), (harmony) ہم آہنگي *ham-āhangī*, سما *samā*.

Concourse, ہجوم *hujūm*, بھيڑ *bhīṛ* (f.), (meeting) ملاپ *milāp*. (f.)

Condition, حال *ḥāl*, حالت *ḥālat* (f.), (stipulation) شرط *sharṭ*. (f.)

Conduct, چلن *chalan*, سلوک *sulūk*, اطوار *aṭwār*.

Confidence, بھروسا *bharōsā*, اعتقاد *iʿtiḳād*, دليري *dilērī*.

Congratulation, مبارک بادي *mubārak-bādī*, تہنيت *tahniyat*. (f.)

Conquest, فتح *fatḥ* (f.), ظفر *ẓafar*, تسخير *taskhīr*. (f.)

Conscience, ضمير *ẓamīr* (f.), سمجھ *samajh* (f.), ايمان *īmān*.

Consent, رضامندي *raẓā-mandī*, قبول *ḳabūl*, ميل *mēl*, اتفاق *ittifāḳ*.

Consequence, نتيجہ *natīja*, (moment) مضايقہ *muẓāyaḳa*, پروا *parwā*. (f.)

Conserve of roses, گل قند *gul-ḳand*, گل شکري *gul-shakarī*.

Consideration, دھيان *dhyān*, بچار *bichār*, فکر *fikr*.

Consolation, تسلي *tasallī*, دلاسا *dilāsā*, ڈھاڑس *ḍhāṛas*.

Conspiracy, بندش *bandish* (f.), گوشٹ *gōshṭ* (f.), سازش *sāzish*. (f.)

Consternation, گهبراهٹ *ghabrāhaṭ* (f.), حيرت *ḥairat.* (f.)

Constitution, مزاج *mizāj*, طبعيت *ṭab'īyat*, جبلت *jibillat* (f.), سرشت *sirisht.* (f.)

Consultation, صلاح خواهي *ṣalāḥ-khwāhī*, مشورت *mashwarat.* (f.)

Contemplation, تامل *ta'ammul*, دهيان *dhyān*, غور *ghaur*.

Contempt, حقارت *ḥikārat* (f.), اپمان *apamān*, اهانت *ihānat.* (f.)

Content, contentment, خوشي *khushī*, قناعت *kanā'at.* (f.)

Contract, قول قرار *kaul karār*, عهد *ahd*, هوڑ *hōṛ.* (f.)

Contrivance, ايجاد *ījād*, حکمت *ḥikmat* (f.), تدبير *tadbīr.* (f.)

Controversy, بحث *baḥs* (f.), ردبدل *radd-badal* (f.), قضيه *kaẓiya.*

Conversation, گفتگو *guftgū* (f.), بات چيت *bāt-chīt.* (f.)

Copy, نقل *nakl* (f.), نسخه *nuskha*, (first or foul) مسوده *musauwada.*

Coquetry, ناز *nāz*, نخرا *nakhrā*, ادا *adā* (f.), چوچلا *chōchlā* جهانولي *jhāṅwlī.*

Coquette, نخراباز *nakhrā-bāz*, عشوه‌گر *ashwa-gar.*

Coral, مونگا *mūngā*, مرجان *marjān*, (child's) چوسني *chūsnī.*

Cord, رسي *rassī*, ڈور *ḍōr* (f.), جيوڑا *jē'ōṛā.*

Cork, (plug) ڈهٹها *ḍhaṭṭhā*, ٹهينٹهي *ṭhēnṭhī.*

Corner, کونا *kōnā*, گوشه *gōsha*, کهونٹ *khūnṭ*, کنج *kunj.*

Corpse, مرده *murda*, لاش *lāsh* (f.), لوتهه *lōth* (f.), مرتک *mirtak.*

Correction, (amending) تصحيح *taṣ'ḥīḥ* (f.), (punishment) سزا *sazā.* (f.)

Correspondence, (by letter) خط کتابت *khaṭṭ-kitābat* (f.): see Relation.

Cost, مول *mōl*, قيمت *kīmat* (f.), بها *bahā*, خرچ *kharch.*

Cotton, (undressed) کپاس *kapās*, (dressed) روئي *rū'ī*, پنبه *pumba.*

Covenant, عهد نامه *ahd-nāma*, قول *kaul*, شرط *sharṭ.* (f.)

Cover, ڈهکنا *ḍhaknā*, سرپوش *sar-pōsh*, (shelter) پناه *panāh.* (f.)

Covetousness, لالچ *lālach*, لوبه *lōbh*, حرص *ḥirṣ.* (f.)

Coulter, نسي *nasī*, پهار *phār.*

Council, مجلس *majlis* (f.), سبها *sabhā* (f.), پنچايت *panchāyat.* (f.)

Counsel, نصيحت *naṣīḥat* (f.), پند *pand*: see Counsellor, Attorney.

Countenance, چهره *chihra*, منهه *muṅh*, (favour) توجه *tawajjuh.* (f.)

Country, (region) سرزمین *sar-zamīn* (f.), بهوم *bhūm* (f.), ملك *mulk*, دیس *dēs*, (opposed to town) دیہات *dīhāt*, مفصل *mufaṣṣal*, (native land) وطن *waṭan*, جنم بهوم *janam-bhūm*.

Countryman, (of the same country) هم وطن *ham-waṭan*, دیس بهائي *dēs-bhā'ī*, (peasant) دهقاني *dihḳānī*, گنوار *ganwār*.

County (division of a country), ضلع *zil'*, پرگنه *pargana*.

Couple, دو *dō*, جوڑا *jōṛā*, جفت *juft*.

Couplet, بیت *bait* (f.), دوها *dōhā*.

Course, دوڑ *dauṛ* (f.), دپٹ *dapaṭ* (f.), (race-course) گهڑ دوڑ *ghuṛ-dauṛ*.

Court, (of justice) عدالت *'adālat* (f.), کچهري *kachahrī*, (yard) صحن *ṣaḥn*, (hall of audience) دربار *darbār* : see Palace.

Cracker, (squib) پٹاخا *paṭākhā*, (boaster) لاف زن *lāf-zan*.

Cradle, هنڈولا *hinḍōlā*, گہوارہ *gahwāra*, مہد *mahd*.

Crane, (for raising goods) دمکلا *damkalā*, (dakh.) ملسوت *malsūt*.

Crease, شکن *shikan* (f.), چین *chīn* (f.), چنٹ *chunaṭ*. (f.)

Creation, آفرینش *āfrīnish* (f.), پیدائش *paidā'ish* (f.) : see World.

Creature, مخلوق *makhlūḳ*, (irrational) حیوان *ḥaiwān*.

Credit, اعتبار *i'tibār*, بهرم *bharam*, ساکه *sākh* (f.) : see Reputation.

Creditor, قرض خواہ *ḳarẓ-khwāh*, بیوهریا *byōhariyā*.

Crew, بهیڑ *bhīṛ* (f.), جماعت *jamā'at* (f.), (ship's) اهل جهاز *ahl-i-jahāz*.

Crime, تقصیر *taḳṣīr* (f.), گناہ *gunāh*, پاپ *pāp*, جرم *jurm*.

Criminal, تقصیروار *taḳṣīr-wār*, گناهگار *gunāh-gār*.

Crisis of a disease, بحران *buḥrān*.

Critic, واقف کار *wāḳif-kār*, نکته دان *nukta-dān*, علامه *'allāma*.

Crop, (harvest) فصل *faṣl* (f.), (produce) حاصل *ḥāṣil* : see Maw, Craw.

Cross, صلیب *ṣalīb*, چلیپا *chalīpā*.

Crowd, بهیڑ *bhīṛ* (f.), جماعت *jamā'at* (f.), هجوم *hujūm*.

Crumb, (particle of bread) روٹي کا ٹکڑا *rōṭī kā ṭukṛā*, (soft) گودا *gūdā*.

Crush, دباؤ *dabā'ō*, (shove, push) دهکا *dhakkā*, ٹکر *ṭakkar*. (f.)

Crust, (shell) چهلکا *chhilkā*, (of bread) پوست *pōst*, پپڑا *papṛā*.

Crutch, لاٹهي *lāṭhī*, بیساکها *baisākhā*, عصا *'aṣā*, پهاوڑي *phā'ōṛī*.

Cry, پکار *pukār* (f.), شور *shōr*, (lament) واويلا *wāwailā*.
Cub, بچه *bachcha*, پلا *pillā*.
Cube, کعب *kaʿb*, ششدر *shashdar*.
Cubit, هاتهہ *hāth*, هاتهہ بهر ماپ *hāth bhar māp*, دست *dast*.
Cuckold, ديوث *daiyūṣ*, زنجلب *zan-jalab*, قلتبان *ḳaltabān*.
Cud, جگالي *jugālī*, پاگر *pāgur*.
Cudgel, لاٹهي *lāṭhī*, لکڑ *lakaṛ*, ٹهينگا *ṭhēngā*.
Cupping glass, سينگي *sīngī*. Cupper, سينگي والا *sīngī-wālā*.
Curd, چکا *chakkā*, چهينا *chhēnā*, دهي *dahī*. (m.)
Curl, کاکل *kākul* (f.), گيسو *gēsū*, زلف *zulf* (f.): see Bend.
Currency, (of money) رواج *rawāj*, چلن *chalan*.
Currycomb, کهرهرا *kharahrā*.
Curse, سراپ *sarāp*, لعنت *laʿnat* (f.): see Calamity.
Custody, حواله *ḥawāla*, نگهباني *nigah-bānī*: see Imprisonment.
Custom, چال *chāl* (f.), چلن *chalan*, عادت *ʿādat* (f.), دستور *dastūr*, (tax) محصول *maḥṣūl*.
Custom-house, چبوتره *chabūtara*, پرمٹگهر *parmiṭ-ghar*.
Customer, گاهک *gāhak*, خريدار *kharīdār*.
Cut, (gash) کاٹ *kāṭ* (f.), زخم *zakhm*, (shape) ڈول *ḍaul*.
Cut-throat, خونريز *khūn-rēz*, ٹهگ *ṭhag*, بٹپار *baṭ-pār*.
Cycle, دور *daur*, دائره *dāʾira*, دوران *daurān*: see Circle.
Dalliance, راوچاو *rāʾō-chāʾō*, نازونياز *nāz-ō-niyāz*: see Delay.
Dam, (bank) باندهہ *bāndh*, پل *pul*: see Mother.
Damage, خسارت *khisārat* (f.), نقصان *nuḳṣān*, خرابي *kharābī*.
Damask, (silk) مشجر *mushajjar*, (cloth) جامداني *jāmdānī*.
Dance, dancing, ناچ *nāch*, رقص *raḳṣ*.
Dancing girl, کنچني *kunchunī*: (band of) طوائف *ṭawāʾif*. (f.)
Danger, خطره *khaṭra*, ڈر *ḍar*, جوکهم *jōkhim*. (f.)
Darning (s.), رفو *rafū*.
Date (time), تاريخ *tārīkh* (f.), تتهہ *tith* (f.), متي *mitī*.
Day-book, روزنامچه *rōz-nāmcha*, کهسرا *khasrā*.
Dearth, اکال *akāl*, قحط *ḳaḥṭ*, تنگي *tangī*, کمي *kamī*.

Death, موت *maut* (f.), مرگ *marg* (f.), فوت *faut* (f.), اجل *ajl.* (f.)
Debate, بحث *bahs* (f.), قضيه *kaziya*, مباحثه *mubāhasa*.
Debauchery, اوباشي *aubāshī*, رندي *rindī*, خمار *khumār*.
Debt, دين *dain*, ادهار *udhār*, قرض *karz*, وام *wām*.
Debtor, قرضدار *karz-dār*, ديندار *dain-dār*, رنيا *riniyā*.
Deceit, فريب *farēb*, دغا *daghā* (f.), جل *jul*, چهل *chhal*.
Decision, انفصال *infisāl*, رفع *raf'*, نپٹارا *niptārā*.
Decree, حكم *hukm*, فتوى *fatwā*, انفصال *infisāl*.
Deed, كام *kām*, فعل *fi'l*, (written) دستاويز *dast-āwēz*. (f.)
Defect, قصور *kusūr*, عيب *'aib*, گهٹتي *ghattī*.
Defence, حفاظت *hifāzat* (f.), پناه *panāh* (f.), روك *rōk*. (f.)
Defendant, (in law) مدعى عليه *mudda'ā 'alaihi*, اسامي *asāmī*.
Deficiency, كمتي *kamtī*, گهٹتي *ghattī*, قصور *kusūr*.
Defile, (narrow pass) ناكا *nākā*, گلي *galī*, گهاٹي *ghātī*.
Definition, بكهان *bakhān*, حد *hadd* (f.), تعريف *ta'rīf*. (f.)
Degree, درجه *darja*, مرتبه *martaba*, قدر *kadr* (f.), رتبه *rutba*.
Delay, دير *dēr* (f.), ديري *dērī*, بلمب *bilamb*, آڑ *ār*. (f.)
Deliberation, تامل *ta'ammul*, فكر *fikr*, سوچ *sōch*, غور *ghaur*. (f.)
Delight, آنند *ānand*, خوشي *khushī*, خرمي *khurramī*.
Delirium, بيهوشي *bē-hōshī*, بيخودي *bē-khudī*, سڑ *sir*. (f.)
Deliverance, delivery, نجات *najāt* (f.), بچاؤ *bachā'ō*: see Birth.
Delusion, دهوكها *dhōkhā*, فريب *farēb*, دغا *daghā*. (f.)
Demand, (claim) دعوا *da'wā*, (question) طلب *talab*. (f.)
Demolition, انهدام *inhidām*, خراب‌آبادي *kharāb-ābādī*.
Den, (lion's, &c.) تهر *thar*, ماند *mānd* (f.): see Cave.
Denial, انكار *inkār*, نفي *nafī* (m.), تنافي *tanāfī*.
Dependant, متعلق *muta'allik*, دامن گير *dāman-gīr*, پربس *parbas*.
Depth, عمق *'umuk*, گهراؤ *gahrā'ō*, (dakh.) ڈونگان *dōngān*.
Deputy, گماشته *gumāshta*, پيش دست *pēsh-dast*, نائب *nā'ib*.
Derision, ٹهٹهولي *thathōlī*, طعنه *ta'na*, ٹهٹها *thatthā*.
Derivation, اشتقاق *ishtikāk*, استخراج *istikhrāj*.
Descendant, بنس *bans*, سنتان *santān*, (plur.) اولاد *aulād*.

Desert, جنگل *jangal*, بیابان *bayābān*, بادیه *bādiya*.
Deserter, بهگوڑا *bhagōṛā*, فراري *firārī*, تارک *tārik*.
Design, (purpose) منصوبه *manṣūba*, اراده *irāda*: see Plan.
Desire, چاه *chāh* (f.), خواهش *khwāhish* (f.), هوس *hawas*. (f.)
Despair, ناامیدي *nā-ummēdī*, یاس *yās* (f.), نراسي *nirāsī*, مایوسي *mā-yūsī*.
Destiny, تقدير *takdīr* (f.), قضا *kazā* (f.), قسمت *kismat*. (f.)
Destruction, پایمالي *pā'ēmālī*, اهلاک *ihlāk*, خرابي *kharābī*.
Detail, تفصیل *tafṣīl* (f.), (in detail) مفصل *mufaṣṣal*.
Determination, قصد *kaṣd*, عزم *azm*, تجویز *tajwīz*. (f.)
Detestation, کره *karh* (f.), نفرت *nafrat* (f.): see Abhorrence.
Detraction, غیبت *ghībat* (f.), بد گوئي *bad-gō'ī*, تهمت *tuhmat*. (f.)
Detriment, نقصان *nukṣān*, مضرت *mazarrat* (f.), ٹوٹا *ṭōṭā*.
Devastation, غارت *ghārat* (f.), پایمالي *pā'ēmālī*, تباهي *tabāhī*.
Deuce (at cards, dice, &c.), دوا *dū'ā*, (dakh.) دوگا *dōgā*.
Device, (contrivance) حکمت *ḥikmat* (f.), (on a shield, &c.) نشان *nishān*.
Devotion (worship), عبادت *ibādat* (f.), پوجا *pūjā* (f.): see Prayer.
Dexterity, دست کاري *dast-kārī*, چالاکي *chālākī*.
Dialect, بولي *bōlī*, بهاکها *bhākhā*: see Language, Idiom.
Dialogue, گفتگو *guftgū* (f.), جواب سوال *jawāb suwāl*.
Diameter, قطر *kuṭr*, دائرے کي بیچ کا خط *dā'irē kē bīch kā khaṭṭ*.
Diary, روز نامه *rōz-nāma*, روزنامچه *rōznāmcha*, آوارجه *āwārja*.
Dice, پاسے *pāsē* (plur. of پاسا *pāsā*, a die), (dakh.) پهانسے *phānsē*.
Dice-board, بساط *bisāṭ*. (f.)
Dictionary, فرهنگ *farhang* (f.), لغت *lughat* (f.), کوش *kōsh*.
Die (colour), رنگ *rang*, (stamp) سکه *sikka*, ٹهپا *ṭhappa*.
Diet, غذا *ghizā* (f.), خوراک *khurāk* (f.), کهانا *khānā*, قوت *kūt*.
Difference, فرق *fark*, تفاوت *tafāwut*, بلگ *bilag*: see Discord.
Difficulty, دشواري *dushwārī*, اشکال *ishkāl*: see Labour, Trouble.
Diffidence, سنکوچ *sankōch*, دهڑکا *dhaṛkā*, شک *shakk*.
Digestion, هضم *hazm*, قوت هاضمه *kūwat-i-hāzima*.

Digit, انگل *angul*, (of the moon's diameter) کلا *kalā*. (f.)

Dignity, جاه *jāh* (f.), قدر *ḳadr* (f.), مرتبه *martaba*, شان *shān*. (f.)

Dilemma, دبدها *dubdhā* (f.), (dakh.) بهونجال *bhōnjāl*.

Diligence, سرگرمي *sar-garmī*, دهن *dhun* (f.), تن‌دهي *tan-dihī*.

Dimension, ماپ *māp*, مقدار *miḳdār*, اندازه *andāza*.

Diminution, گهتي *ghaṭī*, تخفيف *takhfīf* (f.), کمي *kam-ī*.

Din, شور *shōr*, غل *ghul*, (dakh.) غل غپاٹا *ghul ghapāṭā*.

Diploma, سند *sanad* (f.), منشور *manshūr*, دستاويز *dastāwēz*.

Direction, (way) راه *rāh* (f.), (label) پتا *patā*, (of a letter) سر نامه *sar-nāma*.

Dirt, (filth) ميل *mail* (f.), مل *mal*, (mud) کيچڑ *kīchaṛ*. (f.)

Disagreement, ناموافقت *nā-muwāfaḳat* (f.), (discord) نا خوشي *nā-khushī*, انبناٶ *anbanā'ō*, بگاڑ *bigāṛ*.

Disappointment, نا کامي *nā-kām-ī*, دهوکها *dhōkhā*, حرمان *ḥirmān*.

Disaster, مصيبت *muṣībat* (f.), بد بختي *bad-bakht-ī*, افت *āfat*. (f.)

Disbelief, بي‌اعتقادي *bē-i*tiḳādī*, بي‌اعتباري *bē-ī*tibārī*.

Disbursement, خرج *kharj*, خرچ *kharch*, اخراجات *ikhrājāt*.

Discernment, تميز *tamīz* (f.), زيرکي *zīrak-ī*, بيبيک *bibēk*.

Discharge, چهٹي *chhuṭṭī*, برطرفي *bar-ṭaraf-ī*, (of debt) ادا *adā*. (f.)

Disciple, سکه *sikh*, چيلا *chēlā*, شاگرد *shāgird*, تلميذ *talmīẕ*.

Discipline, تاديب *tādīb* (f.), تربيت *tarbiyat* (f.): see Punishment.

Discovery, دريافت *daryāft* (f.), انکشاف *inkishāf*: see Invention.

Discount, بٹا *baṭṭā*, چوٹا *chōṭā*,

Discourse, بات *bāt* (f.), بات چيت *bāt chīt* (f.), گفتگو *guftgū*. (f.)

Discretion, امتياز *imtīyāz*, عقل *ākl*, هوشياري *hōshyārī*.

Discus, چکر *chakr* or *chakkar*.

Discussion, مباحثه *mubāḥaṣa*, رد بدل *radd badal*. (f.)

Disdain, اهانت *ihānat* (f.), حقارت *ḥiḳārat*. (f.)

Disease, آزار *āzār*, روگ *rōg*, مرض *maraẓ*, دکه *dukh*.

Disgrace, رسوائي *ruswā'ī*, عار *ār*, (dismission) تغيري *taghīrī*.

Disguise, بهيس *bhēs*, بهيکه *bhēkh*, (sham) حيله *ḥīla*.

Disgust, نفرت *nafrat* (f.), گهن *ghin* (f.), کراهيت *karāhiyat*. (f.)

Dishonour, بي آبروئي *be-ābrū-ī*, بي حرمتي *bē-hurmatī.*
Disk (of the sun or moon), قرص *ḳurṣ:* see Discus.
Dislike, اعراض *iʿrāẓ*, چڑھ *chiṛh* (f.), گريز *gurēz.* (f.)
Dismission, رخصت *ruḵẖṣat* (f.), برطرفي *bar-ṭaraf-ī.*
Disorder, بيترتيبي *bē-tartīb-ī*, (illness) بيماري *bīmār-ī.*
Dispatch, شتابي *shitāb-ī:* see Messenger, Epistle.
Displeasure, آزردگي *āzurdagī*, ناخوشي *nā-ḵẖushī*, خفگي *ḵẖafagī.*
Disposition, انتظام *intiẓām*, (nature) خو *ḵẖō* (f.), مزاج *mizāj.*
Dispute, بحث *baḥṣ* (f.), (quarrel) جهگڑا *jhagṛā*, قضيه *ḳaẓiya.*
Disregard, بي پروائي *be-parwā'ī*, بي التفاتي *bē-iltifāt-ī.*
Disrespect, بی ادبي *be-adab-ī*, ترك ادب *tark-i-adab:* see Disregard.
Dissembler, ريا كار *riyā-kār*, مكار *makkār*, كپٹي *kapṭī.*
Distance, دوري *dūr-ī*, تفاوت *tafāwut*, مسافت *masāfat.* (f.)
Distemper, مرض *maraẓ*, آزار *āzār*, روگ *rōg*, بيماري *bīmārī.* (f.)
Distich, بيت *bait* (f.), دوها *dōhā*, دوهرا *dōhrā.*
Distraction, اضطراب *iẓṭirāb*, سراسيمگي *sarāsīma-gī.*
Distress, ايذا *īẕā* (f.), كشت *kashṭ*, بپت *bipat* (f.), آفت *āfat.* (f.)
District, ضلع *ẓilʿ*, چكلا *chaklā*, محل *maḥall*, پرگنه *pargana.*
Disturbance, هنگامه *hangāma*, هرج مرج *harj-marj.*
Diversion, (turning aside) انحراف *inḥirāf*, (sport) تماشا *tamāshā.*
Divination, علم غيب *ilm-i-ghaib*, رمل *ramal*, فالگوي *fāl-gō'ī.*
Division, تقسيم *taḳsīm* (f.), (share) قسمت *ḳismat:* see Difference.
Divorce, طلاق *ṭalāḳ* (f.), جورو وخصم كي جدائي *jōrū ō ḵẖaṣam kī judā-ī.*
Dizziness, دوران سر *daurān-i-sar*, گهمري *ghumrī.*
Doctrine, تعليم *taʿlīm* (f.), مذهب *maẕhab*, طريقه *ṭarīḳa.*
Doer, كرنيهارا *karnē-hārā*, كرتا *kartā*, فاعل *fāʿil.*
Doings, كام *kām*, كرتوت *kartūt*, كيا *kiyā*, افعال *afʿāl.*
Doll (child's), گڑيا *guṛiyā* (f.), پتلي *putlī*, كهلونا *khilaunā.*
Domestic (a servant), وابسته *wābasta*, خدمتگار *ḵẖidmatgār.*
Dominion, حكومت *ḥukūmat* (f.), مملكت *mamlukat* (f.), راج *rāj.*
Donation, Donative, بخشش *baḵẖshish* (f.), دان *dān.*
Doom, (sentence) حكم *ḥukm*, فتوىٰ *fatwā*, (fate) قضا *ḳaẓā.*

Dot, نقطہ *nuḳta*, بندا *bundā*, بندي *bindī*, سونا *sūnā*.

Double-dealer, دورنگا *do-rangā*, دغا باز *dag͟hā-bāz*.

Double-entendre, جنکا *janikā*, دو معنيدار بات *dō-ma'nī-dār bāt*.

Doubt, شک *shakk*, شبہہ *shubha*, گمان *gumān*, سنکا *sankā*. (f.)

Dovecot, کبوتر خانہ *kabūtar-k͟hāna*, دهابڑي *dhābṛī*.

Dough, گوندهن *gūndhan*, خمير *k͟hamīr*, لوئي *lū'ī* or *lō'ī*.

Down (hair, small feathers), روم *rōm*, نرم پر *narm par:* see Plain.

Drain, موري *mōrī*, نالي *nālī*, بدررو *badar-rau*. (f.)

Draught, (of liquor) گهونٹ *ghūnṭ*, (of a carriage) کهينچاؤ *khīnchā'o*, (plan) نقشہ *naḳsha*, (of a letter) مسودہ *musauwada*, (of soldiers) فوج کا ايک گروہ *fauj kā ēk gurōh*, (for money) هنڈي *hunḍī*.

Draughts (the game), مغل پٹهان *mughal paṭhān*, &c.

Drawer, (of a bill) هنڈي نويس *hunḍī-nawīs*, (of a chest) خانہ *k͟hāna*.

Drawing (delineation), نقاشي *naḳḳāshī*, نقش *naḳsh*.

Dream, خواب *k͟hwāb*, سپنا *sapnā*, (fancy) خيال *k͟hayāl*.

Dregs, ترچهٹ *tirchhaṭ* (f.), تلچهٹ *talchhaṭ* (f.), درد *durd*. (f.)

Drink, شرب *shurb*, شربت *sharbat*, شراب *sharāb*.

Drollery, مسخراپن *mask͟harā-pan*, ٹهٹهولي *ṭhaṭhōlī*, کهلي *khillī*.

Dross, ميل *mail* (f.), کيٹ *kīṭ*, زنگار *zangār*.

Drove, (of cattle) گلہ *galla*, (crowd) بهيڑ *bhīṛ* (f.), جماعت *jamā'āt*.

Drudgery, ٹهل *ṭahal* (f.), سخت محنت *sak͟ht miḥnat*. (f.)

Drunkard, شرابي *sharāb-ī*, ميخور *mai-k͟hōr*.

Dung, بيٹ *bīṭ* (f.), گوہ *gūh* (f.), (of the cow) گوبر *gōbar*, (of the horse or elephant) ليد *līd* (f.), (of birds) پيخال *pīk͟hāl:* see Manure.

Dungeon, بهکسي *bhaksī*, سياہ چاہ *siyāh chāh*, گڈنگي *giḍangī*.

Dunghill, مزبلہ *mazbala*, گهڑيا *guhaṛiyā*, گهور *ghūr*.

Dusk (twilight), دهرسانجه *dhur-sānjh* (f.), گودهولي *gōdhūlī*.

Dust, دهول *dhūl* (f.), دهور *dhūr* (f.), گرد *gard* (f.), غبار *g͟hubār*.

Duty, (obligation) فرض *farẓ*, (service) ٹهل *ṭahal* (f.): see Tax.

Dwelling (habitation), گهر *ghar*, مقام *muḳām*, مسکن *maskan*.

Earnest (money), بيعانہ *bai'āna*, دادني *dādnī*.

Earthquake, بهون چال *bhūn-chāl*, زلزله *zalzala.*

Ease, آرام *ārām*, كل *kal* (f.), چين *chain*, (facility) آساني *āsānī.*

Eaves, (of a roof), اولتي *ōltī*, اوري *ōrī*, پرچهتي *parchhatī.*

Ebb (of the tide), بهاٹها *bhāṭhā*, جزر *jazr*, گهٹتي *ghaṭtī.*

Ebony, آبنوس *ābnūs.*

Echo, گونج *gūnj* (f.), صدا *ṣadā.* (f.)

Economy, جزرسي *juz-rasī*: see Arrangement, System.

Ecstacy, وجد *wajd*, بيخودي *bē-khudī.*

Edge, (of a blade), دهار *dhār* (f.), باڑ *bāṛ* (f.): see Border.

Edging, جهالر *jhālar* (f.), مغزي *maghzī*, سنجاف *sanjāf.* (f.)

Edict, فرمان *farmān*, رقم *raḳam* (f.), ساسن *sāsan.*

Edition (of a book), چهاپا *chhāpā*, چهپائي *chhapā'ī.*

Editor, (compiler) موءلف *mu'allif*, (arranger) مرتب *murattib.*

Education, تربيت *tarbiyat* (f.), پرورش *parwarish.* (f.)

Eel, بام *bām* (f.), مارماهي *mār-māhī*, بام مچهلي *bām-machhlī.*

Effect, (impression) اثر *aṣar*, تاثير *tāṣīr* (f.), (result) حاصل *ḥāṣil.*

Effects, مال *māl*, اسباب *asbāb*, مال و متاع *māl ō matā*'.

Effigy, شكل *shakl* (f.), صورت *ṣūrat* (f.), مورت *mūrat.* (f.)

Effort, سعي *sa'ī*, كوشش *kōshish* (f.), محنت *miḥnat.* (f.)

Eft (newt), چهپكلي كي ايك قسم *chhipkalī kī ēk ḳism.*

Egg, انڈا *anḍā*, بيضه *baiẓa.*

Egotist, خود فروش *khud-farōsh*, خود نما *khud-numā.*

Egress, خروج *khurūj*, برامد *bar-āmad* (f.), روانگي *rawānagī.*

Election, برگزيدگي *barguzīdagī*, مقبوليت *maḳbūliyat.* (f.)

Elegance, لطف *luṭf*, لطافت *laṭafat* (f.), نزاكت *nazākat.* (f.)

Elegy, مرثيه *marṣiya*, سوز گداز كا قصيده *sōz-gudāz kā ḳaṣīda.*

Elevation, بلندي *bulund-ī*, بڑهتي *baṛhtī*, انچائي *unchā-ī.*

Elixir, اكسير *aksīr*: see Essence.

Elocution, زبان آوري *zabān-āwarī*, فصاحت *faṣāḥat.* (f.)

Eloquence, خوش تقريري *khush-taḳrīrī*, بلاغت *balāghāt*: see Elocution.

Embryo, جنين *janīn*, سانچا *sānchā*, گابها *gābhā.*

Emersion, طلوع *ṯulū* , اٹھاؤ *uṯhā'o*, برامد *bar-āmad.*

Eminence, انچان *unchān*, بزرگي *buzurgī*, فضل *fazl.*

Emissary, جاسوس *jāsūs*, بھيديا *bhēdiyā*, هركاره *harkāra.*

Emperor, شاهنشاه *shāhanshāh*, مهاراج *mahā-rāj.*

Empire, شاهنشاهي *shāhanshāh-ī*, سلطنت *salṯanat.* (f.)

Employ, Employment, شغل *shughl*, کام *kām*, عهده *ūhda.*

Emporium, اڑنگ *aṛang*, بازار *bāzār*, بندر *bandar.*

Empress, مهاراني *mahā-rānī*, بيگم شاهنشاه *bēgam-i-shāhanshāh.*

Emulation, غبطه *ghibṯa*, هسکا *hiskā*, رشك *rashk.*

Enamel, مينا *mīnā*, آب *āb*, جلا *jilā*, ميناکاري *mīnā-kārī.*

End, انت *ant*, سرا *sirā*, آخر *ākhir*, (object) غرض *gharaẓ.* (f.)

Engine, کل *kal* (f.), صنعت *ṣan'āt* (f.), هتهيار *hathyār.*

Enigma, پهيلي *pahēlī*, چستان *chistān*, معما *mu'āmmā.*

Enjoyment, تمتع *tamattu'*, مزه *maza*, عيش *āish*, خوشي *khushī.*

Enmity, عداوت *ādāwat* (f.), بير *bair*, دشمني *dushmanī.*

Entertainment, مهماني *mihmānī* : see Feast, Amusement.

Entrance, پيٹھ *paiṯh*, دخل *dakhl*, پيش آمد *pēsh-āmad.* (f.)

Entry, داخله *dākhila*, رسته *rasta* : see Door, Insertion.

Environs, اطراف *aṯrāf* (f.), پيرامن *pairāman*, آسپاس *ās-pās.*

Epistle, خط *khaṯṯ*, رقعه *ruḳ'ā*, نامه *nāma*, پاتي *pātī.*

Epitaph, کتابه *kitāba* : see Inscription.

Epithet, لقب *laḳab*, نعت *na't* (f.), صفت *ṣifat*, نام *nām.*

Epitome, اختصار *ikhtiṣār*, مختصر *mukhtaṣar.*

Epoch, تاريخ *tārīkh* (f.), سن *san*, سمبت *sambat*, سال *sāl.*

Equator, خط استوا *khaṯṯ-i-istiwā.*

Equipage, اسباب *asbāb*, سامان *sāmān*, سواري *sawārī*, رکاب *rikāb.* (f.)

Equity, انصاف *inṣāf*, عدل *ādl*, راستي *rāstī*, سچائي *sachā'ī.*

Era, تاريخ *tārīkh* (f.), ساکا *sākā*, سمبت *sambat.*

Ermine, قاقم *ḳāḳum*, سنجاب *sanjāb.*

Errand, سنديسا *sandēsā*, پيغام *paighām*, کام *kām.*

Errata (in a book), غلط نامه *ghalaṯ-nāma.*

Error, غلطي *ghalaṯī*, چوك *chūk* (f.), قصور *ḳuṣūr*, بهول *bhul.* (f.)

Eruption, خروج *khurūj*, ابهار *ubhār*, (of the skin) رکت پتي *rakt-pitti.*
Essay, سعي *sa'ī*, آزمايش *āzmā'ish* (f.), (treatise) رساله *risāla.*
Essence, ذات *zāt* (f.), هير *hīr*, (spirit) عرق *ārak*, (perfume) عطر *ātr.*
Estate, (condition) حال *hāl*, (possession) ملک *milk*: see Degree.
Esteem, تپاک *tapāk*, عزت *'izzat*, پيار *pyār*, قدر *kadr.* (f.)
Eternity, دوام *dawām*, ابد *abad*, هميشگي *hamēsha-gi.*
Ethics, اخلاق *akhlāk*, علم اخلاق *'ilm-i-akhlāk.*
Etiquette, آداب *ādāb*, تکلفات مجلس *takallufāt-i-majlis.*
Event, (incident) حادثه *hādisa*, سرگذشت *sar-guzasht.* (f.)
Evidence, گواهي *gawāhī*, دليل *dalīl* (f.), (witness) شاهد *shāhid.*
Evil, برائي *burā'ī*, زبوني *zabūn-ī*, (calamity) بلا *balā.* (f.)
Evildoer, بد کار *bad-kār*, گناه گار *gunāh-gār.*
Eulogy, تعريف *ta'rīf* (f.), مدح *madh* (f.), ثنا *sanā.* (f.)
Eunuch, خوجه *khōja*, خواجه سرا *khwāja-sarā*, هجڙا *hijṛā.*
Examination, آزمائش *āzmā'ish* (f.), امتحان *imtihān.*
Example, نمونه *namūna*, اداهرن *udāharan*: see Pattern.
Excellence, فوقيت *faukiyat* (f.), (as an address) حضرت *hazrat.* (f.)
Excess, افراط *ifrāt*, زيادتي *ziyādatī*: see Intemperance.
Exchange, ادلا بدلا *adlā badlā*, عوض *'iwaz*, (place) چوک *chauk.*
Excrement, گوه *gūh* (f.), غائط *ghā'it*: see Dung.
Excrescence, گره *girih* (f.), (fleshy) مسا *massā*, مسبرد *masbird.*
Excuse, عذر *uzr*, (pretence) بهانه *bahāna*, حجت *hujjat.* (f.)
Execution, کارگذاري *kār-guzār-ī*, (killing) قتل *katl.*
Executor, وصي *wasī* (m.). Executrix, وصيه *wasiya.* (f.)
Exercise, محنت *mihnat* (f.), (practice) عمل *āmal*, مشق *mashk.* (f.)
Exertion, کوشش *kōshish* (f.), سعي *sa'ī*, محنت *mihnat.* (f.)
Exhibition, اظهار *iz'hār*, دکهلائي *dikhlā'ī*, (show) تماشا *tamāshā.*
Exhortation, نصيحت *nasīhat* (f.), وعظ *wa'z*, ترغيب *targhīb.* (f.)
Exile, (banishment) جلا وطن *jilā-watan*, (banished) بيوطن *bē-watan.*
Existence, هستي *hastī*, وجود *wujūd*, (life) زندگي *zindagī.*
Expedient, تدبير *tadbīr* (f.), چاره *chāra*, اپائي *upā'ē.*
Expense, لاگت *lāgat* (f.), خرچ *kharch*: see Money, Cost.

Experience, Experiment, تجربه *tajriba*, آزمائش *āzmā'ịsh.* (f.)
Explanation, بيان *bayān*, تفصيل *tafṣīl* (f.), شرح *sharḥ.* (f.)
Express, (messenger) قاصد *ḳāṣid*, پيک *paik*: see Message.
Expression, تلفظ *talaffuẓ*, بات *bāt* (f.), (squeezing out) نچوڑ *nichōṛ.*
Extension, پهيلاؤ *phailā'ō*, کشادگي *kushādagī.*
Extract, هير *hīr*, خلاصه *khulāṣa*: see Essence, Selection.
Extreme, Extremity, سرا *sirā*, نهايت *nihāyat* (f.): see Distress.
Exuviæ (slough or skin), کينچلي *kēnchlī*, کينچل *kēnchul.* (f.)
Eyesore, خار انکهوں کا *khār ānkhōṅ kā.*
Fable, حکايت *ḥikāyat* (f.), نقل *naḳl* (f.), کهاني *kahānī.*
Fabrication, بناوٹ *banāwaṭ* (f.), ساخت *sākht.* (f.)
Facility, آساني *āsānī*, سهولت *sahūlat* (f.): see Readiness.
Fact, (deed) کام *kām*, فعل *fi'l*, (reality) حقيقت *ḥaḳīḳat.* (f.)
Factory, کوٹهي *kōṭhī*, کار خانه *kār-khāna.*
Factotum, هربابي *har-bāb-ī*, کلکلاں *kulkullān.*
Faculty, قوت *ḳūwat* (f.), (quality) گن *gun*, (skill) هنر *hunar.*
Fair, (market) ميلا *mēlā*, هاٹ *hāṭ* (f.), پينٹه *pēnṭh.* (f.)
Faith, (belief) ايمان *īmān*, عقيده *a̓ḳīda*, (religion) ملت *millat.* (f.)
Falsehood, Falsity, جهوٹه *jhūṭh*, دروغ *darōgh*, کذب *kiẕb.*
Fame, نام *nām*, اشتهار *ishtihār*, جس *jas*, شهرت *shuhrat.* (f.)
Familiarity, ارتباط *irtibāṭ*, صحبت *ṣuḥbat* (f.), الفت *ulfat.* (f.)
Family, گهربار *gharbār*, گهرانا *gharānā*, (race) خاندان *khāndān.*
Famine, قحط *ḳaḥṭ*, اکال *akāl*, دبهک *dubhuk.*
Fan, پنکها *pankhā*, پنکهي *pankhī*, (for grain) پرتي *partī*, سوپ *sūp.*
Fancy, خيال *khiyāl*, وهم *wahm*, (whim) لهر *lahar.* (f.)
Fare, (food) خوراک *khurāk* (f.), (hire) بهاڑا *bhāṛā*, کرايه *kirāya.*
Farewell, الوداع *al-widā'*, خدا حافظ *khudā ḥāfiẓ.*
Fashion, ڈول *ḍaul*, طور *ṭaur*, (form) شکل *shakl.* (f.)
Fast, فاقه *fāḳa*, روزه *rōza*, برت *barat*, اپاس *upās.*
Fat (of animals), چربي *charbī*, چکنائي *chiknā'ī.*
Fate, تقدير *taḳdīr* (f.), قسمت *ḳismat* (f.), (death) موت *maut.* (f.)
Fathom, چارهاته کي ناپ *chār hāth kī nāp*, بم *bam.* (f.)

Fatigue, تهكائي *thakā'ī*, ماندگي *māndagī*, سستي *sustī*.
Fault, قصور *ḳuṣūr*, عيب *ʿaib*, (crime) تقصير *taḳṣīr*. (f.)
Favour, مهرباني *mihrbānī*, توجه *tawajjuh* (f.): see Gift.
Feast, ضيافت *ẓiyāfat* (f.), دعوت *daʿwat* (f.): see Festival.
Feature, شكل *shakl* (f.), نقشه *naḳsha*, رخ *rukh*, چنه *chinh*.
Fee, اجر *ajr*, رسوم *rusūm*, محنتانه *miḥnatāna*, اجوره *ajūra*.
Feeling, لامسه *lāmisa*, (sense) حس *ḥiss*, (affection) پيار *pyār*.
Feint, بهانه *bahāna*, دهوكها *dhōkhā*, حيله *ḥīla*.
Felloe, چكر كا گهير يا حلقه *chakkar kā ghēr* or *ḥalḳa*.
Fellow, (equal) هم چشم *ham-chashm*: see Companion, Manikin.
Fellowship, صحبت *ṣuḥbat* (f.), انس *uns*, ميل *mēl*.
Felon, مجرم *mujrim*, تقصير وار *taḳṣīr-wār*: see Whitlow.
Felony, گناه كبيره *gunāh-i-kabīra*, جرم عظيم *jurm-i-ʿaẓīm*.
Fence, گهيرا *ghērā*, پناه *panāh* (f.), ٹٹري *ṭaṭrī*: see Defence.
Fermentation, جوش *jōsh*, ابال *ubāl*, (ferment) خمير *khamīr*.
Ferry, (passage) گذاره *guzāra*, معبر *maʿbar*: see Boat.
Festival, تيوهار *te'ōhār*, پرب *parab*, عيد *ʿīd*. (f.)
Festivity, شادي *shādī*, جشن *jashn*, عيش *ʿaish*, خوشي *khushī*.
Fetter, Fetters, بيڑي *bēṛī*, پيكڑها *paikaṛhā*, بيڑيان *bēṛiyān*.
Fiddle, سارنگي *sārangī*, كنگري *kingrī*, سارنده *sārinda*.
Fidelity, ايمانداري *īmān-dārī*, وفا *wafā* (f.), سچوٹي *sachauṭī*.
Fight, لڑائي *laṛā'ī*, جده *judh*, جنگ *jang*, رن *ran*: see Battle.
Figure, (for number) آنک *ānk*, رقم *raḳam*: see Form, Image.
File, (instrument) سوهن *sōhan* (f.), ريتي *rētī*: see Row.
Filings, چور *chūr*, براده *burāda*, (of iron) لوه چن *lōh-chun*.
Filth, ميل *mail* (f.), چرک *chirk*, آلائش *ālā'ish*. (f.)
Fin (of a fish) مچهلي كا پر يا بازو *machhlī kā par* or *bāzū*.
Finance, مال گذاري *māl-guzārī*, خراج *khirāj*, آمد *āmad*. (f.)
Firman, فرمان *farmān*, پروانه *parwāna*, حكم نامه *ḥukm-nāma*.
Fish-hook, بنسي *bansī*, كٹيا *kaṭiyā* (f.), كانٹا *kānṭā*.
Fissure, چاک *chāk*, تڑق *taṛaḳ*, شگاف *shigāf*, درز *darz*.
Fitness, لياقت *liyāḳat* (f.), سزاواري *sazāwārī*, شايستگي *shāyastagī*.

Flannel, لوئي *lō'ī*, دهوسا *dhōsā*.

Flask, (powder-horn) سينگڑا *sīngṛā*, باروت دان *bārūt-dān*: see Bottle.

Flattery, خوشامد *khushāmad* (f.), چاپلوسي *chāplūsī*.

Flavour, مزه *maza*, سواد *sawād*, لذت *lazzat* (f.), بوباس *bū-bās*. (f.)

Fleam, نشتر *nashtar*.

Flight, (of a bird) پرواز *parwāz* (f.), (running away) گريز *gurēz*. (f.)

Flock, (of animals) گله *galla*, جهنڈ *jhunḍ*, (of cotton) پہل *pahal*.

Flood, سيلاب *sailāb* (f.), باڑه *bāṛh* (f.), (tide) جوار *jawār* (f.): see Deluge.

Flower, پهول *phūl*, گل *gul*, (prime) بہار *bahār* (f.), جوبن *jōban*.

Flowers on cloth, بيل بوٹا *bēl-būṭā*.

A Fluid, پاني *pānī* (m.), عرق *ārak*, بہني كي چيز *bahnē kī chīz*.

Fold, (plait) ته *tah* (f.), چين *chīn* (f.), (of a door) پلا *pallā*.

Folk, لوگ *lōg*, آدمي *ādmī*, مردم *mardum*, اشخاص *ashkhāṣ*.

Folly, Foolishness, بيوقوفي *bēwukūfī*, حماقت *ḥimākat*. (f.)

Fondness, پيار *pyār*, سوق *shauk*, چاه *chāh*. (f.)

Food, كهانا *khānā*, خوراك *khurāk* (f.), غذا *ghizā* (f.), قوت *kūt*.

A Fool (buffoon), مسخره *maskhara*, بهانڈ *bhānḍ*.

Footman, نوكر *naukar*, هركاره *harkāra*, پياده *piyāda*.

Footpath, راه *rāh* (f.), پگڈنڈي *pag-ḍanḍī*, گلي *galī*.

Footstep, نقش پا *naksh-i-pā*, (step) قدم *kadam*.

Fop, بانكا *bānkā*, چهيلا *chhailā*, البيلا *albēlā*, چكنيا *chikaniyā*.

Force, زور *zōr*, بل *bal*, قوت *kūwat* (f.), جبر *jabr*.

Ford, پاياب *pāyāb*, تهاه *thāh*, (f.), گهاٹ *ghāṭ*.

Forefather, جد *jadd*, بزرگوار *buzurgwār*: see Ancestor.

Foreman, پيشكار *pēshkār*, پيشوا *pēshwā*, سردار *sardār*.

Forepart, اگواڑا *agwāṛā*, آگا *āgā*, اگلا حصه *aglā ḥiṣṣa*.

Forerunner, بيش رو *pēsh-rau*, پيش نما *pēsh-numā*.

Foresight, پيش بيني *pēsh-bīnī*, دور بيني *dūr-binī*: see Prudence.

Forfeit, Forfeiture, ڈانڈ *ḍānd*, جريمانه *jarīmāna*.

Forge, لوهار خانه *lōhār-khāna*, بهٹهي *bhaṭhī*.

Forgery, لباس *libās*, تغلب *taghallub*, جالسازي *jāl-sāzī*.

Fornication, چھنالا *chhinālā*, زنا *zinā* (f.), فسق *fisḳ*.

Fornicator, چھنلا *chhinalā*. Fornicatress, چھنال *chhināl*. (f.)

Fortitude, جرات *jur'at* (f.), جوانمردي *jawānmardī*: see Courage.

Fortune, (chance) قسمت *ḳismat* (f.), (portion) بھاگ *bhāg*, جہیز *jahēz*.

Foundation, (of a building) بنیاد *bunyād* (f.), آساس *āsās*. (f.)

Fraction, (bit) ٹکرا *ṭukrā*, ریزہ *rēza*, (in numbers) کسر *kasr*. (f.)

Fragrance, خوش بو *khush-bū* (f.), سگندھ *su-gandh*.

Frame, (plan) ڈھانچا *ḍhānchā*, (shape) ڈول *ḍaul*: see Shape.

Frankincense, لبان *lubān*, لوبان *lōbān*, بخور *bakhūr*.

Fraud, فریب *farēb*, دغا *daghā* (f.), چھل *chhal*, مکر *makr*.

Freckle, مگس *magas* (f.), لہسن *lahsan*, داغ *dāgh*.

Freedom, آزادگي *āzādagī*, خلاصي *khalāṣī*, نجات *najāt*. (f.)

Freehold, اپني خاص زمین *apnī khāṣṣ zamīn*, جاگیر *jāgīr*. (f.)

Freight, نول *naul*, بھرتي *bhartī*, (hire) بھاڑا *bhāṛā*.

Friday, جمعہ *jum'a*, آدینہ *ādīna*, سکروار *sukrwār*.

Friend, دوست *dōst*, محب *muhibb*, یار *yār*, متر *mitr*.

Friendship, دوستي *dōstī*, محبت *muhabbat* (f.), الفت *ulfat*. (f.)

Fright, ڈر *ḍar*, خوف *khauf*, دہشت *dahshat* (f.), سہم *sahm*.

Fringe, جھالر *jhālar* (f.), آنچل *ānchal*.

Fruit, پھل *phal*, میوہ *mēwa*, (profit) ثمرہ *ṣamara*, نفع *naf'*.

Fruition, کامیابي *kāmyābī*, تمتع *tamattu'*, حصول *huṣūl*.

Fulness, معموري *ma'mūrī*, پوراۓ *pūrā'ī*, سیري *sērī*, بھرتي *bhartī*.

Fun, تماشا *tamāshā*, کھیل *khēl*, بازي *bāzī*, شوخي *shōkhī*.

Fund, پونجي *pūnjī*, مایہ *māya*, سر مایہ *sar-māya*.

Funeral, تدفین *tadfīn* (f.), تجہیز *taj'hīz* (f.), جنازہ *janāza*.

Fur, پوستین *pōstīn*, سمور *samūr*, پشم *pashm* (f.), (scum) کاۓ *kā'ī*.

Furnace, بھٹھي *bhaṭhī*, بھاڑ *bhāṛ*, آتش دان *ātash-dān*.

Furniture, گھر کا اسباب *ghar kā asbāb*, سامان *sāmān*, ساج *sāj*.

Furrow, ہل سي بنا ھوا خط *hal sē banā hūā khaṭṭ*, ریگھاري *rēghārī*.

Fury, جذبہ *jazba*, جوش خروش *jōsh kharōsh*, غضب *ghazab*.

Gain, (earning) کماۓ *kamā'ī*, حاصل *hāṣil*, (profit) نفع *naf'*.

A Gallant, عشق باز *ishḳ-bāz*, رسیا *rasiyā*, عیاش *aiyāsh*.
Gallows, دار *dār*, سولي *sūlī*, پهانسي کاٹھ *phāṅsī-kāṭh*.
Game, (play) بازي *bāzī*, کهیل *khēl*, (prey) شکار *shikār*.
Gaming-house, جوي خانه *jū'ē-khāna*, پهڑ *phaṛ*. (f.)
Gang, غول *ghōl*, جتها *jathā*, طائفه *ṭā'ifa*, جوتهه *jūth*.
Gaol, بندي خانه *bandī-khāna*, قید خانه *ḳaid-khāna*.
Garb, پوشاك *pōshāk* (f.), لباس *libās*, (guise) بهیس *bhēs*.
Garland, پهول مالا *phūl-mālā* (f.), سهرا *sihrā*, هار *hār*.
Garner, انبارخانه *ambār-khāna*, گولا *gōlā*, غله خانه *ghalla-khāna*.
Gas, بخار *bukhār*, باپهه *bāph* (f.), بهاپهه *bhāph*. (f.)
Gauze, کپڑپهول *kapaṛ-phūl*, کپڑدهول *kapaṛdhūl*.
Gazette, اخبار نامه *akhbār-nāma*.
Gender, جنس *jins:* (fem.) تانیث *tānīs* (f.), (mas.) تذکیر *tazkīr*. (f.)
Generation, تولد *tawallud*, (race) نسل *nasl* (f.), پشت *pusht*. (f.)
Generosity, سخاوت *sakhawat* (f.), بخشش *bakhshish*. (f.)
Genitive case, حالت اضافت *ḥālat-i-izāfat*.
Gentleman, مرد آدمي *mard-i-ādmī*, خواجه *khwāja*, صاحب *ṣāḥib*.
Gentlewoman, اشرف زادي *ashraf-zādī*, بهلي بیبي *bhalī bībī*.
Geography, جغرافیه *jughrāfiya*.
Geomancy, رمل *ramal*, رمالي *rammāl-ī*.
Gesture, حرکت *ḥarakat* (f.), جنبش *jumbish* (f.), وضع *waz*. (f.)
Ghost, (spectre) بهوت *bhūt*, پریت *prēt*, (spirit) روح *rūḥ*. (f.)
Giant, مرد عظیم تن *mard-i azīm tan*, دیت *daiyat*.
Gift, انعام *in'ām*, بخشش *bakhshish* (f.), دان *dān*, صله *ṣila*.
Gilding, طلاکاري *ṭilā-kārī*, زرنگاري *zar-nigārī*, حل *ḥall*.
Gills, (of a fish) گلپهڑا *gal-phaṛā*, (dewlap, &c.) غبغب *ghabghab*.
Girth (of a horse), تنگ *tang*, پیٹي *pēṭī*, پشتنگ *pushtang*.
Gladness, خوشي *khushī*, شادي *shādī*, سرور *surūr*, آنند *ānand*.
Glass, (substance) کانچ *kānch*, شیشه *shīsha*, (vessel) مینا *mīnā*.
Globe, کره *kura*, گولا *gōlā*, (world) جهان *jahān*.
Gloom, Gloominess, دهملاي *dhumlā'ī*, (sadness) ملالت *malālat*. (f.)
Glory, (praise) حمد *ḥamd* (f.), (splendor) نور *nūr*, رونق *raunaḳ*. (f.)

Glossary, فرهنگ *farhang* (f.), لغات متروکہ *lughāt matrūka.*

Glue, سریش *sarēsh.*

Goodness, بهلائي *bhalā'ī,* نکوئي *nikō'ī,* خوبي *khūbī.*

Goods, (furniture) گهر کا اسباب *ghar kā asbāb,* (effects) مال *māl.*

Gossip, هرزہ گرد *harza-gard,* (sponsor) دهرم باپ یا ما *dharam-bap* or *-ma.*

Government, حکومت *ḥukūmat* (f.), راج *rāj,* (state) سرکار *sarkār.* (f.)

Grace, (divine) فضل *fazl,* (favour) فیض *faiz*: see Beauty.

Gracefulness, لطف *lutf* (f.), زیبائي *zēbā'ī,* سجاوٹ *sajāwaṭ.* (f.)

Grammar, صرف و نحو *ṣarf ō naḥō* (f.), قاعدہ *ḳā'ida.*

Grandee, عمدہ *ūmda,* امیر *amīr,* رکن *rukn,* اشرف *ashraf.*

Grandeur, بڑائي *baṛā'ī,* عظمت *āzamat* (f.), بزرگي *buzurgī.*

Grant, انعام *in'ām,* بخشش *bakhshish* (f.), عطا *āṭā.* (f.)

Gratitude, شکر *shukr,* شکرگذاري *shukr-guzārī.*

Grave, گور *gōr* (f.), قبر *ḳabr* (f.), مزار *mazār* (f.), مدفن *madfan.*

Gravitation, مرکز کي طرف میلان *markaz kī ṭaraf mailān.*

Grease, چربي *charbī,* چکنائي *chīknā'ī,* روغن *raughan.*

Greatness, بڑائي *baṛā'ī,* کلاني *kalānī,* بزرگي *buzurgī.*

Green (the colour) سبزہ *sabza,* (grassy plot) سبزہ زار *sabza-zār.*

Greyhound, تازي کتا *tāzī kuttā,* شکاري کتا *shikārī kuttā.*

Grief, غم *gham,* دکهہ *dukh,* الم *alam,* ماتم *mātam,* رنج *ranj.*

Grimace, کهیس *khīs* (f.), بندربهاؤ *bandar-bhā'ō.*

Gripe, (grasp) پکڑ *pakaṛ* (f.), قبضہ *ḳabza,* (squeeze) نچوڑ *nichōṛ.* (f.)

Grot, Grotto, کهف *kahf,* کهوہ *khōh,* تہ خانہ *tah-khāna.*

Grove, باغ *bāgh,* کنج *kunj,* درختوں کا جهنڈ *darakhtōn kā jhund.*

Groundwork, بنیاد *bunyād* (f.), اصل *aṣl* (f.), جڑ *jaṛ.* (f.)

Growth, (vegetation) روئیدگي *rō'īdugī,* (increase) بڑهتي *baṛhtī.*

Grudge, کینہ *kīna,* مدت کا کینہ *muddat kā kīna*: see Envy.

Guard, (watch) چوکیدار *chaukīdār,* (protection) حفاظت *ḥifāẓat.* (f.)

Guess, اٹکل *aṭkal* (f.), قیاس *ḳiyās,* انداز *andāz,* پندار *pindār.*

Guest, مهمان *mihmān,* وارد صادر *wārid ṣādir.*

Guidance, رهنمائي *rahnumā'ī,* هدایت *hidāyat.* (f.)

Guide, راه نما *rāh-numā*, آگوا *āgwā*, هادي *hādī*. (m.)

Guilt, گناه *gunāh*, دوکھ *dōkh*, قصور *ḳuṣūr*, خطا *khaṭā*. (f.)

Guitar, قيتار *ḳītār*, ستار *sitār*.

Gum, گوند *gōnd* (f.), صمغ *ṣamagh*.

Gutter, مهري *muhrī*, پرناله *parnāla*, نابدان *nābdān*.

Habit, (dress) لباس *libās*, (custom) عادت *ādat* (f.): see Mode.

Habitation, گهر *ghar*, مکان *makān*, مقام *muḳām*.

Haft, مٹھ *muṭh* (f.), قبضه *ḳabẓa*, دسته *dasta*.

Hag, (witch) ڈائين *ḍā'en* (f.), (fury) چڑيل *chuṛail*. (f.)

Halo, هاله *hāla*, منڈل *manḍal*, کنڈل *kunḍal*.

Halter, (for a horse) باگ ڈور *bāg-ḍōr* (f.), (noose) پهانسي *phānsī*.

Ham (of pork), سوأر کي نمک آلوده ران *sū'ar kī namak-ālūda rān*.

Hammer, (sledge) هتهوڑا *hathōṛā*, (small) هتهوڑي *hathauṛī*.

At hand, موجود *maujūd*, حاضر *ḥāẓir*.

From hand to hand, دست بدست *dast ba-dast*.

Handful, مٹهي *muṭhī*, لپ بهر *lap-bhar*, مشت *musht*.

Handle, دسته *dasta*, بينٹ *bēnṭ*, قبضه *ḳabẓa*, موٹھ *mūṭh*. (f.)

Handmaid, سهيلي *sahēlī*, اصيل *aṣīl* (f.), لونڈي *launḍī*.

Handwriting, خط *khaṭṭ*, دست خط *dast-khaṭṭ*.

Hap, (accident) اتفاق *ittifāḳ*, (luck) قسمت *ḳismat*. (f.)

Happiness, آرام *ārām*, آنند *ānand*, کامراني *kāmrānī*.

Hardware, لوکهر *lōkhar*, لوهي کي چيزين *lōhē kī chīzēn*.

Harm, نقصان *nuḳṣān*, ضرر *ẓarar*, زيان *ziyān*, رنج *ranj*.

Harmony, ميل *mēl*, اتحاد *ittiḥād*, سازگاري *sāzgārī*.

Harp, بربط *barbaṭ* (f.), چنگ *chang* (f.), بين *bīn*. (f.)

Harvest, (time) وقت درو *waḳt-i-dirau*, (grain) اناج *anāj*.

Haste, جلدي *jaldī*, شتابي *shitābī*, اتاولي *utā'ōlī*: see Rage.

Hate, Hatred, نفرت *nafrat* (f.), عداوت *ādāwat* (f.), گهن *ghin*. (f.)

Haughtiness, غرور *ghurūr*, گهمنڈ *ghamanḍ*, کبر *kibr*.

Health, تندرستي *tandurustī*, صحت *ṣiḥḥat* (f.), آرام *ārām*.

Heap, ڈهير *ḍhēr*, انبار *ambār*, توده *tōda*, راس *rās*.

By heart, نوک زبان *nōk-i-zabān*.

Hearth, چوکا *chaukā*, چولها *chūlhā*, (dakh.) چولا *chūlā*.

Heat, گرمي *garmī*, حرارت *ḥarārat* (f.), جلن *jalan*: see Summer.

Heathen, کافر *kāfir*, بت پرست *but-parast*, گبر *gabr*.

Height, اونچائي *ūnchā'ī*, چڑھائي *chaṛhā'ī*, بلندي *bulandī*.

Heir, وارث *wāris*, والي *wālī*, ولي عهد *walī-ahd*.

Help, مدد *madad* (f.), استعانت *isti'ānat* (f.): see Aid.

Hem, (border) مغزي *maghzī*, سنجاف *sanjāf* (f.), قور *ḳōr*. (f.)

Hemisphere, کري کا آدها *kurē kā ādhā*, ادهگولا *adh-gōlā*.

Hemistich مصراع *miṣrā'*, تک *tuk* (f.), چرن *charan*.

Heptagon, مسبع *musabba'*, سات کونا *sāt-kōnā*.

Herd, (flock) نار *nār*, گله *galla*, (crowd) غول *ghōl*, جهنڈ *jhunḍ*.

Heresy, بدعت *bid'at* (f.), الحاد *ilḥād*, کپته *kupath*.

Heritage, ميراث *mīrāṣ* (f.), ارث *irṣ*, بپوتي *bapauti*.

Hermaphrodite, خنثي *khunṣā*, هجڑا *hijṛā*.

Hero, بير *bīr*, پهلوان *pahlawān*, بهادر *bahādur*, شجاع *shujā'*.

Hexagon, مسدس *musaddas*, شش پهلو شکل *shash-pahlū shakl*.

Highlander, پهاڑيا *pahāṛiyā*, کوهستاني *kōhistānī*.

Highness, بلندي *bulandī*, (an address) حضرت *ḥaẓrat* (f.): see Height.

Highwater, بهرا جوار *bharā jawār*, مد کمال *madd-i-kamāl*.

Highway, شاه راه *shāh rāh* (f.), بڑا راسته *baṛā rāsta*.

Hilt, موٹه *mūṭh* (f.), قبضه *ḳabẓa*, دسته *dasta*.

Hinderance, اٹکاؤ *aṭkā'ō*, رکاؤ *rukā'ō*, حايل *ḥā'il*, آڑ *āṛ*. (f.)

Hint, اشاره *ishāra*, ايما *īmā* (f.), کنايه *kināya*.

Hire, طلب *ṭalab* (f.), کرايه *kirāya*, اجوره *ajūra*, بهاڑا *bhāṛā*.

Hireling, اجوره دار *ajūradār*, روزينه دار *rōzīna-dār*.

History, تواريخ *tawārīkh* (f.), تاريخ *tārīkh* (f.), روايت *rawāyat*. (f.)

Hive, چهتا *chhattā*, مکهيال *makhiyāl*, زنبور خانه *zambūr-khāna*.

Hock (of a horse) گهوڑي کي ايڑي *ghōṛē kī ēṛī*.

Hole, (pit) گڑها *gaṛhā*, (rent) چهيد *chhēd*, سوراخ *sūrākh*.

Hollow, نشيب گاه *nashēb gāh* (f.), جوف *jauf*, کهلار *khalār*.

Holyday, عيد *'īd* (f.), تيوهار *tē'ōhār*, پرب *parab*.

Home, گهر *ghar*, مکان *makān*, ديرا *dērā*, مسکن *maskan*, وطن *waṭan*.

Homicide, مردم کشي *mardum-kushī*: see Murderer.

Honesty, سچائي *sachā'ī*, راستي *rāstī*, کهرائي *kharā'ī*, صدق *ṣidḳ*.

Honey-comb, چهتا *chhattā* شان *shān*, شهد خانه *shahd-khāna*.

Honour, عزت *ʿizzat* (f.), پت *pat* (f.), (rank) مرتبه *martaba*.

Hoop, حلقه *ḥalḳa*, کنڈلي *kuṇḍlī*, چنبر *chambar*.

Horoscope, جنم پتري *janam-patrī*, زائچه *zā'īcha*.

Horror, هيبت *haibat* (f.), هول *haul*, وحشت *waḥshat*. (f.)

Horserace, گهڑدوڑ *ghuṛ-dauṛ*. (f.)

Horseshoe, نعل *naʿl*.

Horticulture, چمنبندي *chaman-bandī*, باغباني *bāgh-bānī*.

Hospital, بيمار خانه *bīmār-khāna*, دارالشفا *dāru-sh-shafā*.

Hospitality, مسافر پروري *musāfir-parwarī*, مهمانداري *mihmāndārī*.

Host, (entertainer) ميزبان *mēzbān*, مهماندار *mihmāndār*: see Army.

Hovel, جهونپڑا *jhōmpṛā*, چهپر *chhappar*, کٹي *kuṭī*.

Hound, شکاري کتا *shikārī kuttā*.

Hour-glass, شيشه ساعت *shīsha-e-sāʿat*, بالو کي گهڑي *bālū kī ghaṛī*.

Householder, گرهست *girhist*, خانه دار *khāna-dār*.

Hubbub, غل غپاره *ghul-ghapāra*, هڑبڑي *haṛbaṛī*.

Hue and cry, هانک پکار *hānk-pukār* (f.), غل *ghul*.

Humanity, آدميت *ādmiyat* (f.), بهلمنسات *bhalmansāt*. (f.)

Human kind, انسان *insān*, بني آدم *banī ādam*.

Humility, غريبي *gharībī*, ادهينتا *adhīntā*. (f.)

Humour, (juice) رس *ras*, تري *tarī*, (of the body) خلط *khilṭ*.

Hunger, بهوکه *bhūkh* (f.), جوع *jūʿ* (f.), گرسنگي *gursinagī*.

Hunt, Hunting, شکار *shikār*, صيد *ṣaid* (f.), کهديڑ *khadēṛ*.

Hurry, جلدي *jaldī*, شتابي *shitābī*, هڑبڑي *haṛbaṛī*.

Husbandry, کسنئي *kisna'ī*, کهيتي *khētī*, کشتکاري *kishtkārī*.

Husk, چهلکا *chhilkā*, بکلا *baklā*: see Chaff.

Hyperbole, مبالغه *mubālagha*, اغراق *ighrāḳ*.

Hypocrisy, ريا *riyā*, سالوس *sālūs*, مکر *makr*, کپٹ *kapaṭ*.

Jack, (engine) کل *kal* (f.), (for raising weights) دمکلا *damkalā*.

Jail, قيد خانه *ḳaid-khāna*, بنديخانه *bandīkhāna*.

Jalap, گل عباس كي جڙ *gul-i ăbbās kī jaṛ.*

Idea, خيال *khiyāl,* تصور *taṣauwur,* دهيان *dhyān.*

Idiom, طرز كلام *ṭarz-i-kalām* (f.), اصطلاح *iṣṭilāḥ.* (f.)

Idiot, جنمي مورکهہ *janamī mūrakh,* گيدي *gīdī,* پاگل *pāgal.*

Idleness (want of employment), بيكاري *bēkārī,* (laziness) سستي *sustī:* see Sloth.

Idol, بت *but,* صنم *ṣanam,* مورت *mūrat.* (f.)

Idolater, بت پرست *but-parast,* مشرك *mushrik,* گبر *gabr.*

Jealousy, ظن *ẓann,* بد گماني *bad-gumānī,* غيرت *ghairat.* (f.)

Jest, كهلي *khillī,* مزاخ *mazākh,* ٹهٹها *ṭhaṭhā.*

Jesus Christ, حضرت عيسي *ḥaẓrat-ĭsā.*

Jet, Jet d'eau, فواره *fawwāra,* آبخيزي *ābkhēzī,* سوت *sōt.*

Jew, يهود *yahūd,* يهودي *yahūdī.*

Jews-harp, مرچنگ *murchang,* مچنگ *muchang.*

Ignorance, جهالت *jahālat* (f.), ناداني *nādānī:* see Folly.

Ill, (evil) برائي *burāī,* (harm) آفت *āfat* (f.), بلا *balā.* (f.)

Image, پتلا *putlā,* مورت *mūrat* (f.): see Idol, Likeness.

Imagination, تصور *taṣauwur,* خيال *khiyāl,* دهيان *dhyān.*

Immodesty, بيحجابي *bē-ḥijābī,* بيحيائي *bē-ḥayāī.*

Impatience, بيصبري *bēṣabrī,* ناشكيبائي *nā-shikēbāī.*

Impertinence (disrespect), بي ادبي *bē-adabī,* گستاخي *gustākhī.*

Impiety, فسق *fisk,* نا خدا ترسي *nā-khudā-tarsī,* ادهرم *adharm.*

Import (meaning), معني *maĭnī,* مضمون *maẓmūn.*

Impostor, دغا باز *daghā-bāz,* ٹهگ *ṭhag,* مكار *makkār.*

Impression, (mark) نقش *naksh,* (print, edition) چهاپا *chhāpā.*

Imprisonment, قيد *kaid,* حبس *ḥabs,* بند *band.*

Improvement, بهتري *bihtarī,* ترقي *tarakkī,* اصلاح *iṣlāḥ.* (f.)

Inability, ناطاقتي *nā-ṭākatī,* بي مقدوري *bē-makdūrī.*

Incarnation, (of a divinity) اوتار *autār,* (of a wound) اندمال *indimāl.*

Incendiary, آتش افروز *ātash-afrōz,* (seditious) آتش انگيز *ātash-angēz.*

Incense, لوبان *lōbān,* بخور *bakhūr,* عود *ŭd.*

Inch, تسو *tassū,* انگل *ungal* or انگل *angul,* پور *pōr.* (f.)

Incision, كاٹ *kāṭ* (f.), برش *burrish* (f.), چیرا *chīrā.*

Inclination, میلان *mailān,* میل *mail,* (wish) رغبت *ra<u>gh</u>bat.*

Income, (rent) کرایہ *kirāya,* (revenue) آمد *āmad.* (f.)

Inconvenience, ناموافقت *nā-muwāfaḳat* (f.), تکلیف *taklīf.* (f.)

Increase, بڑھتي *baṛhtī,* افزوني *afzūnī,* ترقي *taraḳḳī.*

Incubus, کابوس *kābūs,* (dakh.) سینہ کونڈي *sīna-kōṅḍī.*

Indenture, عہد نامہ *ahd-nāma,* مچلکہ *machalka,* قبالہ *ḳabāla.*

Index, (pointer out) دال *dāll,* دلیل *dalīl,* (of a book) فہرست *fihrist.*

Indigo, (die) نیل *nīl,* (plant) نیل کا درخت *nīl kā dara<u>kh</u>t.*

Indisposition, (disinclination) نامرضي *nāmarẓī,* (illness) ماندگي *māndagī.*

Individual, فرد *fard,* ایک شخص *ēk sha<u>kh</u>ṣ,* واحد *wāḥid.*

Indolence, سستي *sustī,* کاهلي *kāhilī,* ڈھیلائي *ḍhīlā'ī.*

Industry, محنت *miḥnat* (f.), جد و جہد *jidd ō jahd.*

Infancy, بچپن *bachpan,* طفولیت *ṭufūliyat* (f.), طفلي *ṭiflī.*

Infection, سرایت *sirāyat* (f.), عفونت *ufūnat.* (f.)

Inference, نتیجہ *natīja,* حاصل *ḥāṣil,* اٹکل *aṭkal.* (f.)

Infidel, کافر *kāfir,* گبر *gabr,* بیدین *bēdīn,* مشرک *mushrik.*

Infidelity, کفر *kufr,* شرک *shirk,* بي ایماني *bē-īmānī.*

Inflammation, جلن *jalan,* سوزش *sōzish* (f.), التہاب *iltihāb.*

Influence, اثر *aṡar,* تاثیر *tāṡīr,* حکم *ḥukm,* بیاپ *byāp.*

Information, خبر *<u>kh</u>abar* (f.), اطلاع *iṭṭilā'* (f.), سدھ *sudh.* (f.)

Informer, نمام *nammām,* خفیہ نویس *<u>kh</u>ufya-nawīs.*

Infraction, فسخ *fas<u>kh</u>,* شکست *shikast* (f.), بھنگ *bhang.*

Ingot, ڈلا *ḍalā,* ٹھکا *ṭhakkā,* اینٹ *īnṭ.* (f.)

Ingratitude, ناشکري *nā-shukrī,* کفران نعمت *kufrān-i-ni'mat.*

Inhabitant, ساکن *sākin,* مقیم *muḳīm,* باشندہ *bāshanda.*

Inheritance, ارث *irṡ,* میراث *mīrāṡ,* بپوتي *bapautī.*

Injury, (hurt) آسیب *āsēb,* ایذا *īẕā* (f.): see Detriment, Injustice.

Injustice, بي انصافي *bē-inṣāfī,* (wrong) ظلم *ẓulm.*

Ink, سیاهي *siyāhī,* روشنائي *rōshnā'ī,* (red) سرخي *sur<u>kh</u>ī.*

Inkhorn, Inkstand, دوات *dawāt* (f.), قلم دان *ḳalam-dān.*

Innocence, بيگناهي *bēgunāhī*, عصمت *ismat* (f.), پاكي *pākī*.

Inquiry, پوچهہ پاچهہ *pūchh-pāchh* (f.), پرسش *pursish*. (f.)

Inscription, كتابه *kitāba*, لكهت *likhat* (f.), مرقوم *marḳūm*.

Insertion, ادخال *idkhāl*, اندراج *indirāj*, داخله *dākhila*.

Inspection, نگاه *nigāh* (f.), نظر *nazar* (f.), لحاظ *lihāz*.

Inspector, امين *amīn*, مهتمم *muhtamim*, داروغه *dārōgha*.

Inspiration, (drawing in the breath) دمكشي *damkashī*, (divine) وحي *wahī*. (f.)

Instalment, (to office) خلعت‌دهي *khil'at-dihī*, (portion) قسط *ḳist*. (f.)

Instance, (entreaty) درخواست *darkhwāst* (f.): see Affair, Example.

For instance, مثلا *masalan*, جيسا كه *jaisā ki*.

Instruction, تعليم *ta'līm*, (f.), سكهائي *sikhā'ī*: see Education.

Instrument, آله *āla*, جنتر *jantr*, هتهيار *hathyār*, باعث *bā'is*.

Musical Instrument, باجا *bājā*, ساز *sāz*.

Insult, چهيڑ *chhēṛ* (f.), طنز *tanz* (f.), شماتت *shamātat*. (f.)

Insurance (against loss), بيما *bīmā*.

Insurrection, بلوا *balwā*, هنگامه *hangāma*, فساد *fasād*.

Integer or Integral number, عدد صحيح *adad-i-sahīh*.

Intellect, Intelligence, عقل *aḳl* (f.), هوش *hōsh*, بدهہ *budh*. (f.)

Intelligence (news) خبر *khabar* (f.), اطلاع *ittilā'*, اگاهي *āgāhī*.

Intent, Intention, قصد *ḳasd*, اراده *irāda*, نيت *nīyat*. (f.)

Intercession, شفاعت *shafā'at* (f.), وساطت *wasātat*. (f.)

Intercourse, آمد شد *āmad-shud* (f.), علاقه *alāḳa*.

Interest, (for money) سود *sūd*, بياج *byāj*: see Concern, Benefit.

Interference, دخل *dakhl*, دست اندازي *dast-andāzī*.

Interjection (in grammar), حرف‌ندا *harf-i-nidā*, حرف *harf*.

Interim (in the), اس درميان ميں *is darmiyān meṅ*.

Interposition, Intervention, وساطت *wasātat* (f.), وسيله *wasīla*.

Interpretation, ترجمه *tarjuma*, تشريح *tashrīh*. (f.)

Interrogation, استفسار *istifsār*, استفهام *istifhām*.

Interruption, حركت *harakat* (f.), خلل *khalal*, هرج *harj*.

Interstice, فاصله *fāsila*, (between fingers or toes) گهائي *ghā'ī*.

Interval, درميان *darmiyān*, بيچ *bīch*, انتر *antar*.
Interview, ملاقات *mulāḳāt* (f.), بهينٹ *bhēnṭ*. (f.)
Intimation, اشاره *ishāra*, كنايه *kināya*, ايما *īmā*. (f.)
Intoxication, نشا *nashā*, مستي *mastī*, بيهوشي *bēhōshī*.
Introduction, ادخال *id<u>kh</u>āl*, (of a book) ديباجه *dībāja*.
Invective, گالي *gālī*, زبان درازي *zabān-darāzī*.
Invention, ايجاد *ījād*, اختراع *i<u>kh</u>tirāʿ*, ساخت *sā<u>kh</u>t*. (f.)
Inventor, موجد *mūjid*, واضع *wāziʿ*, باني *bānī*.
Inventory, سياها *siyāhā*, فرد *fard* (f.), تعليقه *taʿlīḳa*.
Investigation, تلاش *tālāsh* (f.), تفتيش *taftīsh*. (f.)
Invitation, دعوت *daʿwat* (f.), نيوتا *nyōtā*, طلب *ṭalab*. (f.)
Invoice, فهرست اجناس *fihrist-i-ajnās*, بيجك *bījak*.
Job, (work) ٹهل *ṭahal* (f.), ٹهيكا كام *ṭhīkā kām*, (stab) هول *hūl*. (f.)
Jointure, مهر *mahr*.
Joke, ٹهٹها *ṭhaṭhā*, كهلي *khillī*, مزاخ *mazā<u>kh</u>*.
Jolt, دهكا *dhakkā*, جهوك *jhōk* (f.), هچكولا *hachkōlā*.
Jot, Iota, ذره *zarra*, نقطه *nuḳṭa*, تل *til*.
Journal, روز نامه *rōz-nāma*, آوارجه *āwārja*, كهسرا *khasrā*.
Journey, سفر *safar*, مسافرت *musāfarat*. (f.)
Journeyman, كميرا *kamērā*, كارنده *kāranda*.
Joy, خوشي *<u>kh</u>ushī*, خرمي *<u>kh</u>urramī*, بلاس *bilās*, جي *jai*.
Irony, هجو مليح *hajō malīḥ* (f.), تسخر *tasa<u>kh</u><u>kh</u>ur*.
Itch, (disease) كهاج *khāj* (f.), كهجلي *khujlī*: see Desire.
Judgment, (decision) انصاف *inṣāf*, (sentence) حكم *ḥukm*: see Intellect.
Judgment (day), قيامت *ḳiyāmat* (f.), حشر *ḥashr*. (f.)
Juice, رس *ras*, عرق *ʿaraḳ*, شيره *shīra*, جوس *jūs*, پاني *pānī*. (m.)
Jump, كلانچ *kulānch* (f.), كود *kūd* (f.), جست *jast*. (f.)
Junction, جوڑ *jōṛ*, پيوند *paiwand*, وصل *waṣl*.
Juncture (time) وقت *waḳt*, حالت *ḥālat* (f.): see Junction.
Ivory, هاتهي دانت *hāthī-dānt*, عاج *ʿāj*, فيلدندان *fīl-dandān*.
Jurisdiction, حكم *ḥukm*, حكومت *ḥukūmat* (f.), قلمرو *ḳalam-rau*.

Jury, پنچایت *panchāyat* (f.), پنچ *panch.*

Justice, انصاف *inṣāf,* عدل *ādl,* نیاو *nyāw:* see Judge.

Kalendar, تقویم *taḳwīm* (f.), پترا *patrā.*

Kali, قلي *ḳalī,* سجي *sajjī.*

Keepsake, یادگاري *yādgārī,* یادبود *yād-būd,* نشاني *nishānī.*

Kennel, (for dogs) تازي خانه *tāzī-khāna:* see Gutter.

Kermes, قرمز *ḳirmiz.*

Kernel, مغز *maghz,* گودا *gūdā,* (of cocoa-nut) گري *garī.*

Kick, لات *lāt* (f.), ٹھوکر *ṭhōkar* (f.), لکد *lakad.* (f.)

Kiln, بھٹھي *bhaṭhī,* (especially for grain) بھاڑ *bhāṛ,* (potter's) آوا *āwā.*

Kin, ناتادار *nātā-dār,* سگا *sagā,* رشته دار *rishta-dār.*

Kind, (genus, race) جنس *jins,* ذات *ẕāt* (f.), نوع *nau*.

Kindness, مهرباني *mihrbānī,* توجه *tawajjuh.* (f.)

Kindred, بھاي بند *bhā'ī-band,* اقربا *aḳribā,* خویش *khwēsh.*

Kingdom, سلطنت *salṭanat* (f.), بادشاهت *bādshāhat.* (f.)

Kinsman, رشته دار *rishta-dār,* قرابتي *ḳarābatī.*

Kiss, چوما *chūmā,* بوسه *bōsa,* مچھي *machhī.*

Paper Kite, گڈي *guḍḍi,* پتنگ *patang,* تکل *tukkal.* (f.)

Knack, (habit) ڈھب *ḍhab,* سلیقه *salīḳa:* see Dexterity.

Knapsack, جھولا *jhōlā,* تھیلا *thailā,* جامه داني *jāma-dānī.*

Knave, دغاباز *daghā-bāz,* عیار *āiyār,* مکار *makkār.*

Kneading-trough, کٹھرا *kaṭhrā,* تغار *taghār,* کٹھوتي *kaṭhautī.*

Knight, بهادر *bahādur,* مرزا *mirzā,* (at chess) گھوڑا *ghōṛā.*

Knob, گانٹھ *gānṭh* (f.), (dakh.) گنڈي *gunḍī.*

Knocker (of a door), حلقه *ḥalḳa,* حلقه در *ḥalḳa-dar.*

Knot, گانٹھ *gānṭh* (f.), عقد *āḳd,* گره *girih* (f.), پیچ *pēch.*

Knowledge, علم *ilm,* بدھ *budh* (f.), دانست *dānist.* (f.)

Label, پتا *patā,* چٹھي *chiṭṭhī,* سرنامه *sar-nāma.*

Labour, محنت *miḥnat* (f.), دکھ *dukh,* (in birth) درد زه *dard-i-zih.*

Lace, (gold or silver) گوٹا *gōṭā,* کناري *kinārī,* (cord) ڈوري *ḍōrī.*

Lacker, (varnish) لک *luk,* روغن *raughan.*

Lady, بیبي *bībī,* خاتون *khātūn* (f.), خانم *khānam.* (f.)

Lamentation, ناله *nāla*, زاري *zārī*, نوحه *nauḥa*, گريه *giriya*.
Lampblack, كاجل *kājal*, دوده *dūda*, كجلا *kajlā*.
Lampoon, هجو *hajō* (f.), بهنڈوا *bhanḍauwā*.
Lancet, نشتر *nashtar*. (f.)
Landlord, زميندار *zamīndār*, (of an inn) ميزبان *mēzbān*.
Landmark, سوانه *siwāna*, مينڈ *mēnḍ* (f.), ڈانڈا *ḍānḍā*.
Landscape, كسو ملك يا سواد كي تصوير *kisū mulkyā sawād kī taṣwīr*. (f.)
Lane, گلي *galī*, راه *rāh* (f.), ناكا *nākā*.
Language, زبان *zabān* (f.), بولي *bōlī*, بهاكها *bhākhā*. (f.)
Lap, گود *gōd* (f.), گودي *gōdī*, زانو كي اوپر كي جگه *zānū kē ūpar kī jagah*.
Lappet, شمله *shamla*, پيرامن *pairāman*.
Lard, سوار كي پكي چربي *sū'ar kī pakki charbī*.
Lascar (from لشكري *lashkarī*, soldier), خلاصي *khalāṣī*.
Lash, (thong) كوڑا *kōṛā*, (stroke) ضرب چابك *ẓarb-i-chābuk*.
Lass, (young woman) دوشيزه *dōshīza* (f.), نايكا *nā'ēkā*. (f.)
Last (for a shoe), قالب كفش *ḳālib-i-kafsh*, كالبد *kālbud*.
Lathe, خراد *kharād* (f.), خراط *kharrāṭ*. (f.)
Latitude, چوڑائي *chauṛā'ī*, عرض *ărẓ* (f.), درجهٔ عرض *darja-e-ărẓ*.
Lattice, شبك *shabak*, جهنجهري *jhanjhṛī*, جال *jāl*, كهڑكي *khiṛkī*.
Lauḍanum, افيم كا عرق *afīm kā ăraḳ*.
Laughing-stock, مسخره *maskhara*, مضحك *muẓḥik*.
Laughter, Laugh, تضحيك *taẓḥīk* (f.), هنسي *hansī*.
Law, (rule) قاعده *ḳā'ida*, (statute) آئين *ā'īn*, قانون *ḳānūn*.
Lawn, مرغزار *marghzār*, ميدان *maidān*: see Muslin.
Lawsuit, دعوا *da'wā*, قضيه *ḳaẓiya*, مقدمه *muḳaddama*.
Laziness, سستي *sustī*, مجهولي *maj'hūlī*, ڈهيل *ḍhīl*. (f.)
Leader, پيشوا *pēshwā*, سردار *sardār*, سرگروه *sar-gurōh*.
Leaf, پتا *pattā*, پات *pāt*, برگ *barg*, (of a book) ورق *waraḳ*.
League, (alliance) ميل *mēl*, (three miles) فرسنگ *farsang*.
Leanness, دبلاپا *dublāpā*, لاغري *lāgharī*: see Poverty.
Leap, كود *kūd* (f.), جست *jast* (f.), پهاند *phānd*: see Jump.
Learning, علم *ĭlm*, بديا *bidyā* (f.), فضيلت *faẓīlat*. (f.)

Lease, كرايه *kirāya*, اجاره *ijāra*, (deed) پتّا *paṭṭā*.

Leather, چمڑا *chamṛā*, چرم *charm*, جلد *jild*. (f.)

Leave, اجازت *ijāzat* (f.), رضا *raẓā* (f.), (to depart) رخصت *rukh-ṣat*. (f.)

Leaven (ferment), خمير *khamīr*, مايه *māya*.

Leavings (offal), جهوٹها *jhūṭhā*, پس خورده *pas-khurda*.

Legacy, هبه *hiba*, وصيت *waṣīyat*. (f.)

Legerdemain, ڈيٹهه بندي *ḍīṭh-bandī*, شعبده بازي *sha*ʿ*bada-bāzī*.

Leisure, فرصت *furṣat* (f.), فراغت *farāghat* (f.), چهٹي *chhuṭṭī*. (f.)

Length, لمبا‌ئي *lambā'ī*, طول *ṭūl*, امتداد *imtidād*.

Lesson, سبق *sabaḳ*, درس *dars*, (precept) پند *pand*.

Letter, حرف *ḥarf*, (epistle) خط *khaṭṭ*, چٹهي *chiṭṭhī*.

Lexicographer, مؤلف لغت *mu'allif-i-lughat*.

Liberality, جود *jūd* (f.), عاليهمتي *ʿāli-himmatī*: see Generosity.

Liberty, (freedom) آزادي *āzādī*, رها‌ئي *rihā'ī*: see Leave.

Library, كتب خانه *kutub-khāna*, جميعت كتب *jamī'at-i-kutub*.

License, حكم *ḥukm*, فرمان *farmān*, پروانه *parwāna*: see Leave.

Licorice, سوس *sūs*, اصل السوس *aṣlu-s-sūs*, جيٹهي مدهه *jēṭhī-madh*.

Lie, جهوٹهه *jhūṭh*, دروغ *darōgh*, كذب *kiẕb*.

Lieutenant (deputy), قائم مقام *ḳā'im maḳām*, نائب *nā'ib*.

Life, جي *jī* (m.), جيو *jīw*, جان *jān*, (living) زندگي *zindagī*.

Lighter, (large boat) بهڑ *bhaṛ*.

Likelihood, احتمال *iḥtimāl*, صورت *ṣūrat* (f.), گمان *gumān*.

Likeness, شباهت *shabāhat* (f.), مماثلت *mumāsalat* (f.): see Form.

Limit, Limitation, حد *ḥadd* (f.), احاطه *iḥāṭa*, سوانا *siwānā*.

Line, (string) ڈور *ḍōr* (f.), طنب *ṭanab*, (streak) لكير *lakīr* (f.), (of a book) سطر *saṭar* (f.), (hemistich) مصراع *miṣrā*ʿ, (equinoctial) خط استوا *khaṭṭ-i-istiwā*: see Limit, Row, Lineage.

Lineage, نسل *nasl* (f.), خاندان *khāndān*, نسب *nasab*.

Lineament, خال *khāl*, خط *khaṭṭ*: see Feature.

Linen, كتان *kattān* or *katān*, كپڑا *kapṛā*.

Lining, استر *astar*, مرهن *marhan*. (f.)

Link, (of a chain) قلابه *ḳalāba*, كڑي *kaṛī*, (torch) مشعل *mash'al.*

Linseed, السي *alsī*, تخم كتان *tuḵẖm-i-katān*, اتسي *atasī.*

Liquefaction, پگهلاو *pighlā'o*, گلن *galan*, گداخت *gudāḵẖt.* (f.)

Liquid, Liquor, عرق *araḳ*, پاني *pānī* (m.), رس *ras*, شرب *shurb.*

List, (roll) فهرست *fihrist* (f.), فرد *fard* (f.), (bandage) پٹي *paṭṭī*, (border) كناره *kināra*, (palæstra) اكهاڑا *akhāṛā*: see Desire.

Litharge, مردار سنگ *murdār sang*, مرده سنگ *murda sang.*

Litter, (chair) پالكي *pālkī*, (straw) آخور *āḵẖōr* (f.), (brood) جهول *jhōl.*

A Little, كچهه *kuchh*, ذره *ẕarra*, قدر قليل *kadr-i-ḳalīl.*

Livelihood, روزي *rōzī*, رزق *rizḳ*, معيشت *ma'īshat.* (f.)

Load, بوجهه *bōjh*, بهار *bhār*, موٹهه *mōṭh* (f.), لاد *lād.* (f.)

Loaf, روٹ *rōṭ*, روٹي *rōṭī*, پانو روٹي *pānw rōṭī.*

Loan, قرض *ḳarẓ*, عاريت دهي *ariyat-dihī*, ادهار *udhār.*

Lock, (of a door) قفل *ḳufl*, تالا *tālā*, (of a gun) چانپ *chāmp* (f.), كل *kal* (f.), (of hair) زلف *zulf* (f.), كاكل *kākul* (f.), (for water) بند *band.*

Lodge (small house), چهوٹا گهر *chhōṭā ghar*, كوٹهري *kōṭhrī.*

Lodger, مقيم *muḳīm*, باشنده *bāshanda*, كرايه‌دار *kirāya-dār.*

Loftiness, (height) بلندي *bulandī*, (pride) غرور *g͟hurūr.*

Log, كنده *kunda*, تنه *tana*: see Block.

Logic, منطق *manṭiḳ* (f.), علم مناظره *ilm-i-munāẓara.*

Logician, منطقي *manṭiḳī*, نيايك *naiyāyik.*

Longitude, طول *ṭūl*, لنبان *lambān.*

Looby, ناتراشيده شخص *nā-tarāshīda shaḵẖṣ*, (dakh.) هيندرا *hēndrā.*

Loom, تانت *tānt* (f.): see Instrument.

Loop, پهلي *phalī*, تكمه *tukma*, حلقه *ḥalḳa*, پهانسي *phānsī.*

Looseness, كشادگي *kushādagī*, بيقيدي *bēḳaidī*: see Diarrhœa.

Lord, (master) مالك *mālik*, صاحب *ṣāḥib*, (nobleman) خان *ḵẖān*, بيگ *bēg*, مير *mīr*: see Husband, God.

Lordship, صاحبي *ṣāḥibī*, امارت *imārat* (f.), مالكيت *mālikīyat.* (f.)

Lore, علم *ilm*, بديا *bidyā* (f.), فضل *faẓl.*

Loss, نقصان *nuḳṣān*, خسارت *ḵẖisārat* (f.), (defeat, q. v.) هار *hār.* (f.)

Lot, نصيب *naṣīb*, قسمت *ḳismat* (f.), (share) حصه *ḥiṣṣa*.

Lottery, شرطي *sharṭī*, قرعه بازي *ḳur'ȧ-bāzī*, چٹھي کا کھيل *chiṭṭhī kā khēl*.

Lover, عاشق *ȧshiḳ*, طالب *ṭālib*, يار *yār*, سجن *sajjan*. (m. f.)

Lowland, زمين نشيب *zamīn-i-nashēb*, نيچان *nīchān*.

Lowness, نيچائي *nīchā'ī*, پستي *pustī*, (meanness) ذلت *ẕillat*. (f.)

Lucifer, (the planet Venus) زهره *zuhra* (f.), سکر *sukr*: see Devil.

Luck, (chance) اتفاق *ittifāḳ*, (fortune) نصيب *naṣīb*: see Lot.

Lucre, نفع *naf**, فائده *fā'ida*, سود *sūd*, لابه *lābh*.

Luggage, چيزبست *chīz-bast* (f.), سير کا اسباب *sair kā asbāb*.

Lumber, ناکاري چيز بست *nākārī chīz-bast*, اگڑبگڑ *agaṛbagaṛ*.

Lump, ڈلا *ḍalā*, ٹکڑا *ṭukṛā*, ٹک *ṭuk*, (of sugar, meat) ڈلي *ḍalī*.

Lunacy, ديوانگي *dīwānagī*, سڑ *siṛ* (f.), سودا *saudā*.

Lunch, Luncheon, کليوا *kalēwā*, ناشتا *nāshtā*, تفنن *tafannun*.

Lust, مستي *mastī*, شهوت *shahwat* (f.), هوا و هوس *hawā ō hawas*. (f.)

Lustre, نور *nūr*, چمک *chamak* (f.), جلا *jilā* (f.), جلوه *jalwa*.

Lute (instrument), بربط *barbaṭ* (f.), طنبور *ṭambūr*, بين *bīn*. (f.)

Luxury, عيش عشرت *ȧish ȧshrat* (f.), عياشي *ȧiyāshī*.

Lyre, بربط *barbaṭ* (f.): see Harp: (constellation) نسرالواقع *nasru-l-wāḳi**.

Mace, (club) سونٹا *sōnṭā*, عصا *ȧṣā*, گرز *gurz*: see under *Spices*.

Machine, کل *kal* (f.), جنتر *jantr*, آله *āla*, صنعت *ṣan'ȧt*. (f.)

Madam, بيبي *bībī*, بيبي صاحب *bībī ṣāḥib*, بيگم صاحبه *begām ṣāḥiba*.

Mademoiselle, لڑکي *laṛkī*, چهوکري *chhōkrī*, صبيه *ṣabīya*. (f.)

Madness, سڑ *siṛ* (f.), جنون *junūn*, ديوانگي *dīwānagī*.

Magazine, (store) خزانه *khizāna*, مخزن *makhzan*, (book) رساله *risāla*.

Magi (one of the), مجوس *majūs*, مغ *mugh*, گبر *gabr*.

Magic, حاضرات *ḥāẓirāt* (f.), جادو *jādū*, سحر *siḥr*, ٹوٹکا *ṭōṭkā*.

Magician, جادوگر *jādūgar*, نيرنگ ساز *nairang-sāz*, ساحر *sāḥir*.

Magistrate, فوجدار *faujdār*, حاکم *ḥākim*, عامل *ȧmil*.

Majesty, (royal title) جهان پناه *jahān-panāh*, حضرت *ḥaẓrat*: see Grandeur.

Maintenance, (protection) خبرگيري *<u>kh</u>abargīrī*, (food) پرورش *parwarish*. (f.)

Majority, (greater part) كثرت *kas̤rat* (f.), (full age) بلوغ *bulūg̲h*.

Make, (form) ڈول *ḍaul*, (structure) بناوٹ *banāwaṭ* (f.): see Fashion.

Maker, كرتا *kartā*, بنانيوالا *banānēwālā*: see Creator.

Malady, مرض *maraẓ*, بيماري *bīmārī*, روگ *rōg*, آزار *āzār*.

Malice, كينه *kīna*, بغض *bug̲hẓ*, عداوت *ădāwat* (f.), بدي *badī*.

Mallet, موگرا *mōgrā*, موگري *mūgrī*, ميخ چو *mē<u>kh</u>-chū*, كوبه *kōba*.

Mam, Mamma, ماما *māmā*, اما *ammā*, ما *mā*, ميا *maiyā*. (f.)

Manacle, هتهكڑي *hath-kaṛī*, (Manacles) هتهكڑياں *hath-kaṛiyāṅ*.

Management, سربراهي *sarbarāhī*, كارگذاري *kārguẕārī*: see Care.

Mane, يال *yāl* (f), ايال *ayāl* (f.), چونٹي *chōnṭī*.

Mange, خارش *<u>kh</u>ārish* (f.), جانوروں كي كهجلي *jānwarōṅ kī khujlī*.

Manger, كهرلي *khurlī*, كٹهرا *kaṭhrā*, تهان *thān*.

Manhood, جواني *jawāni*, شباب *shabāb*, مردي *mardī*.

Manikin, باؤنا *bā'ōnā*, مردك *mardak*, لڑكا *laṛkā*: see Dwarf.

Mankind, نوع انسان *nauʻi insān*, بني آدم *banī ādam*, بشر *bashar*.

Manna (in medicine), شيرخشت *shīr<u>kh</u>isht*, ترنجبين *taranjubīn*.

Manner, طرح *ṭaraḥ* (f.), ڈول *ḍaul*, ڈهب *ḍhab*, طور *ṭaur*.

Manners, (morals) اخلاق *a<u>kh</u>lāḳ*, (politeness) آداب *ādāb*.

Manufactory, كارخانه *kār<u>kh</u>āna*. Manufacture, كاريگري *kārīgarī*.

Manure, پانس *pāṅs*, كهات *khāt* (f.), كهاد *khād* (f.): see Dung.

Manuscript, (writing) دستخط *das<u>kh</u>aṭṭ*, (book) دست نوشته *dast-nawishta*.

Map, نقشه *naḳsha*, نقشه ملوك *naḳsha-i-mulūk*, پٹ *paṭ*.

A Marble (for playing with), انٹا *anṭā*, گولي *gōlī*.

March, (journey) كوچ *kūch*, سفر *safar*, (month) چيت *chait* (?).

Margin, حاشيه *ḥāshiya*, كناره *kināra*, لب *lab*.

Mark, (sign) نشان *nishān*, (stamp) داغ *dāg̲h*: see Coin, Butt.

Market, چوك *chauk*, بازار *bāzār*, هاٹ *hāṭ* (f.), پينٹه *pēnṭh*. (f.)

Marriage, بياه *byāh*, نكاح *nikāḥ*, شادي *shādī*, كدخدائي *kadkhudā'ī*.

Martingal, زيربند *zēr-band*, پيش بند *pēsh-band*.

Martyr, شهيد *shahīd*.

Mass, (lump) پنڈا *pinḍā*, ڈلا *ḍalā*, (multitude) جماؤ *jamā'ō*.

Massacre, قتل *ḳatl*, قتل عام *ḳatl-i-āmm*: see Carnage.

Master, (proprietor) مالک *mālik*, (lord) صاحب *ṣāḥib*, (teacher) استاد *ustād*.

Mastich, مصطكي *masṭakī*.

Mat, بوريا *bōriyā*, چٹائي *chaṭā'ī*, صف *ṣaff* (f.), پاٹي *pāṭī*.

Match, (contest) مقابله *muḳābala*, بازي *bāzī*, (an equal) نظير *naẓīr*.

Mate, (comrade) ساتهي *sāthī*, جفت *juft*: see Husband, Mate (of a ship).

Materials, اسباب *asbāb*, سامان *sāmān*, لوازمه *lawāzima*.

Mathematics, علم رياضي *ilm-i-riyāẓī*.

Matrice, Matrix, (mould) سانچا *sānchā*, (womb) رحم *riḥm*.

Matter, (substance) هيولا *hayūlā*, (pus) پيب *pīb* (f.): see Affair.

Maxim, (axiom) قاعده *ḳā'ida*, (adage) مقوله *maḳūla*.

Meadow, مرغزار *marghzār*, ترائي *tarā'ī*, چراگاه *charāgāh*.

Meal, (flour) آٹا *āṭā*, آرد *ārd*, (eating) کهانا *khānā*.

Meaning, معني *ma'nī*, اراده *irāda*, ارتهه *arth*, مقصد *maḳṣad*.

Measure, پيمائش *paimā'ish* (f.), ناپ *nāp* (f.), ماپ *māp*, (in verse) وزن *wazn*, ميزان *mīzān*, (in music) تال *tāl*, (portion) حصه *ḥiṣṣa*, (means) ڈول *ḍaul*, ترکيب *tarkīb* (f.), (a land measure) جريب *jarīb* (f.), کٹها *kaṭṭhā*, (for cloth) گز *gaz*.

Meat, (flesh) گوشت *gōsht*, مانس *māṅs*, (food) کهانا *khānā*: see Food.

Mechanics, علم جر ثقيل *ilm-i-jarr-i-ṡaḳīl*.

Medal, تغمه *taghma*, سکه *sikka*, مدرا *mudrā*. (f.)

Mediation, بيچ بچاؤ *bīch-bichā'ō*, وساطت *wasāṭat*. (f.)

Meditation, دهيان *dhyān*, (thought) فکر *fikr*, تامل *ta'ammul*.

Meed, صله *ṣila*, اجر *ajr*, جزا *jazā* (f.), تحفه *tuḥfa*.

Meeting, سبها *sabhā* (f.), جماؤ *jamā'ō*, جمعيت *jam'īyat*. (f.)

Melancholy, ماخوليا *mākhūliyā*, سودا *saudā*, ملال *malāl*.

Melody, نغمه *naghma*, سرود *sarōd*, آهنگ *āhang*.

Memoir, تواريخ *tawārīkh*, سرگذشت *sar-guẕasht* (f.), تذکره *taẕkira*.

Memorandum, ياد داشت *yād-dāsht* (f.), ياد آور *yād-āwar*.

Memorial, یادگار *yād-gār*, (petition) عرض داشت *ārẓ-dāsht.* (f.)

Memory (faculty of), حافظه *ḥāfiẓa*, حفظ *ḥifẓ*, (remembrance) یاد *yād.* (f.)

Mendicity, گدا'ي *gadā'ī*, فقيري *faḳīrī.*

Mending (repair), مرمت *marammat.* (f.)

Mensuration, پيمائِش *paimā'ish* (f.), (of land) جريب كشي *jarīb-kashī.*

Mention, ذكر *ẕikr*, چرچا *charchā*, مذكور *maẕkūr*, بت كهاؤ *bat-kahā'ō.*

Merchandise (goods), مال *māl*, جنس *jins* (f.), رقم *raḳam.* (f.)

Meridian, (noon) نصف النهار *niṣfu-n-nahār*, (line) خط نصف النهار *khaṭṭ-i-niṣfu-n-nahār.*

Merit, گن *gun*, قدر *ḳadr* (f.), جوهر *jauhar*, لياقت *liyāḳat.* (f.)

Mermaid, جلمانس *jalmānus* (m. *water-man*), بنت البحر *bintu-l-baḥr.* (f.)

Merryandrew, مسخره *maskhara*, بهانڈ *bhānḍ*, سوانگي *swāngī.* (m.)

Message, پيام *payām*, پيغام *paighām*, سنديسا *sandēsā.*

Messenger, پيغامبر *paighāmbar*, سنديسي *sandēsī*, هركاره *harkāra*, قاصد *ḳāṣid.*

Messiah, مسيح *masīḥ*, مسيحا *masīḥā*, حضرت عيسي *ḥaẓrat īsā.*

Metaphor, استعاره *isti'āra*, مجاز *majāz*, (simile) اپما *upamā.* (f.)

Metempsychosis, تناسخ *tanāsukh*, اوتار *autār*, آواگون *āwāgawan.*

Method, (order) اسلوب *uslūb*, (manner) طور *ṭaur*, ڈول *ḍaul*, سليقه *salīḳa.*

Metre, ميزان *mīzān* (f.), بحر *baḥr* (f.), نظم *naẓm* (f.), وزن *wazn.*

Metropolis, دارالسلطنت *dāru-s-salṭanat*, تختگاه *takhtgāh.* (f.)

Mettle, پهرت *phurt* (f.), همت *himmat* (f.), جانبازي *jānbāzī.*

Mice, چوهيان *chūhiyāṅ*, چوهي *chūhē.*

Mien, قيافه *ḳiyāfa*, چهره *chihra*, دهج *dhaj*, وضع *waẓ'.* (f.)

Might, قوت *ḳūwat* (f.), بل *bal*, زور *zōr*, مقدور *maḳdūr.*

Mildew, لينڈها *lēnḍhā*, چتي *chittī*, گيرؤي *gērū'ī*, هردا *hardā.*

Mile, ميل *mīl*, آدها كوس *ādhā kōs.*

Milestone, منار *manār*, مينار *mīnār*, ميل كا نشاندار پتهر *mīl kā nishān-dār patthar.*

Mill, چكي *chakkī*, چاك *chāk*, جانتا *jāntā*, آسيا *āsiyā*, (wind) پونچكي *pawan-chakkī*, (water) پنچكي *pan-chakkī.*

Minaret, منار *manār*, منارہ *manāra*, مينار *mīnār*.

Mine, کهان *khān* (f.), کان *kān* (f.), (under walls) سرنگ *surang*.

Mint (place of coining), ٹکسال *ṭaksāl* (f.), دارالضرب *dāru-ẓ-ẓarb*. (f.)

Miracle, خرق عادت *kharḳ-i-ʿādat*, کرامت *karāmat* (f.), معجزه *muʿjiza*.

Misbehaviour, بد سلوکي *bad-sulūkī*, کڈهنگي *kuḍhangī*.

Miscarriage, (failure) ناسربراهي *nā-sarbarāhī*, (abortion) اسقاط حمل *isḳāṭ-i-ḥaml*.

Miscellany, کچکول *kachkōl* (f.), جنگ *jung* (f.), مجموعه *majmūʿa*.

Mischief, بدي *badī*, برائي *burāʾī*, نقصان *nuḳṣān*, ضرر *ẓarar*.

Misery, خرابي *kharābī*, ذلت *ẓillat* (f.), پريشاني *parēshānī*.

Misfortune, بدبختي *bad-bakhtī*, بپت *bipat* (f.), بلا *balā*. (f.)

Miss, (young woman) کوري *kōrī*, بيٹي *bēṭī*, (lady) صاحبزادي *ṣāḥib-zādī*.

Miss, چوک *chūk* (f.), بهول *bhūl* (f.), (loss) قصور *ḳuṣūr*, نقص *naḳṣ*.

Mission, رسالت *risālat* (f.), پيغمبري *paighambarī*, ارسال *irsāl*.

Mistake, خطا *khaṭā* (f.), چوک *chūk* (f.), بهول *bhūl*. (f.)

Mistress, صاحبه *ṣāḥiba*, بيبي *bībī*, (sweetheart) پياري *pyārī*.

Misunderstanding, غلط فهمي *ghalaṭ-fahmī* : see Disagreement.

Mite, (particle) ذره *ẓarra*, ريزه *rēza*, (insect) گهن *ghun* : see Weevil.

Mixture, ملاو *milāʾō*, آميزش *āmēzish* (f.), (compound) مرکب *murakkab*.

Mob, بهيڑ *bhīṛ* (f.), هجوم *hujūm*, انبوه *ambōh*, مجموعه *majmūʿa*.

Mock, Mockery, مضحکه *maẓʾḥaka*, چڑاو *chiṛāʾō*, ٹهٹها *ṭhaṭṭhā*.

Mode, (custom) روش *rawish* (f.), آئين *āʾīn* (f.), (form) صورت *ṣūrat* (f.) : see Manner.

Model, نقشه *naḳsha*, نمونه *namūna*, ڈول *ḍaul*, قالب *ḳālib*.

Moderation, اعتدال *iʿtidāl*, قناعت *ḳanāʿat* (f.), پرهيز *parhēz*.

Modesty, لاج *lāj* (f.), شرم *sharm* (f.), حيا *ḥayā* (f.) : see Chastity.

Moistness, Moisture, رطوبت *ruṭūbat* (f.), طراوت *ṭarāwat* (f.), نمي *namī*.

Mole, (spot) تل *til*, خال *khāl*, (mound) پشته *pushta*, بانده *bāndh*.

Molestation, تکليف *taklīf* (f.), ايذا *īẓā* (f.), تصديع *taṣdīʿ* (f.), جنجال *janjāl*.

Monarchy, بادشاهي *bādshāhī*, سلطنت *saltanat* (f.), راج *rāj*.

Monastery, خانقاه *khānḳāh* (f.), دائره *dā'ira*.

Monday, دوشنبه *do shamba*, پير *pīr*, سوموار *sōmwār*.

Money, زر *zar*, پيسے *paisē* (plur.), روپي *rupai* (plur.), ٹكي *ṭakē*. (plur.)

Monk, درويش *darwēsh*, فقير *faḳīr*, قلندر *ḳalandar*, راهب *rāhib*.

Monument, يادگار *yād-gār*, (pillar, &c.) ستون *sutūn*, (tomb) روضه *rauẓa*.

Mood, (state) حالت *ḥālat* (f.), وضع *waẓ'* (f.), (in grammar) صيغه *ṣīgha*.

Moonlight, Moonshine, چاندني *chāndnī*, ماهتاب *māhtāb*.

Moor, (negro) زنگي *zangī* (m.), حبشي *ḥabshī* (m.): see Marsh, Bog.

Moral, (of a fable) نصيحت *naṣīḥat* (f.), خلاصه *khulāṣa*, نتيجه *natīja*.

Morality, Morals, اخلاق *akhlāḳ*, ادب *adab*, نيک سلوکي *nēk-sulūkī*.

Morsel, لقمه *luḳma*, نواله *nawāla*, كول *kawal*, ٹكرا *ṭukrā*, پاره *pāra*.

Mortality, فنا *fanā* (f.), چهي *chhai* (f.), (deaths) موتين *mautēṅ*.

Mortgagee, مرتهن *murtahin*, گرو يا بندهک گير *girau-* or *bandhak-gīr*.

Mortgager, راهن *rāhin*, گرودار *giraudār*, بندهک ديني والا *bandhak dēnē-wālā*.

Moss, كائي *kā'ī*, سوار *siwār* (Vallisneria spiralis), (dakh.) رون *rūṅ* (? Harris).

Mother (on vinegar, &c.), پهپهوندي جو سركي پر هوتي هي *phaphūndī jō sirkē par hōtī hai*.

Mother of pearl, صدف *ṣadaf* (f.), سيپي *sīpī*.

Motion, حركت *ḥarakat* (f.), جنبش *jumbish* (f.), هلاو *hilā'ō*: see Proposal.

Motive, باعث *bā'iṡ*, موجب *mūjib*, سبب *sabab*, واسطه *wāsiṭa*.

Motto, كتابت *kitābat* (f.), علامت *ālamat*. (f.)

Moveables, مال منقوله *māl-i-manḳūla*, چيز بست *chīz bast*. (f.)

Mountaineer, پهاڑيا *pahāṛiyā*, كوهي *kōhī*, پربتي *parbatī*, بهيل *bhīl*.

Mourning, (grief) غم *gham*, ماتم *mātam*, (dress) ماتمي لباس *mātamī libās*.

Mouse-trap, چوهي دان *chūhē-dān*, دبكر *dabkar*. (f.)

Mouth, منهه *muṅh*, (of a river, &c.) مهانا *muhānā*, (of a water-bag) دهانه *dahāna*.

Mouthful, لقمه *luḳma*, نواله *nawāla*, كول *kawal*.

Mucus, چتكا *chiṭkā*, لعاب *lu'āb*, رينٿ *rēnṭ*, بلغم *bal*g*h*am*.

Mud wall, كچي ديوار *kachchī dīwār*, متي كي ديوار *miṭṭī kī dīwār*.

Mullar (for grinding colours), بٿا *baṭṭā*, لوڙهيا *lōṛhiyā*, لوڙها *lōṛhā*.

Mulatto, مستيسا *mastīsā* (m. f.): see Mongrel.

Multiplication, (in arithmetic) ضرب *ẓarb* (f.), جوڙتي *jōṛtī*, (table) پهاڙا *pahāṛā*.

Multitude, (great number) كثرت *kas̤rat* (f.), غول *ghōl*: see Crowd.

Mummy, موميا *mōmiyā*, (a medicine) موميائي *mōmiyā'ī*.

Munificence, سخاوت *sakhāwat* (f.), جود *jūd* (f.), بخشش *bakhshish*. (f.)

Murder, خون *khūn*, هتيا *hatyā* (f.), بغض سي قتل *baghẓ sē ḳatl*.

Murderer, خوني *khūnī* (m. f.), خون ريز *khūn-rēz*, مردم كش *mardum-kush*.

Murrain, چار پايون كي وبا *chār-pāyōṅ kī wabā*, وبال حيوان *wabāl-i-ḥaiwān*.

Mushroom, دهرتي كا پهول *dhartī kā phūl*, سماروغ *samārūgh*, (dakh.) قدرتي *ḳudratī*.

Music, موسيقي *mūsīḳī*, نغمه *naghma*, الحان *alḥān*, راگ *rāg*.

Musk, مشك *mushk*, مسك *misk*.

Muslin, ململ *malmal* (f.), شبنم *shabnam*, آب روان *āb-i-rawān*.

Mustaches, موچهه *mūchh* (f.), موچهين *mūchhēṅ* (plur. f.), بروت *burūt*. (f.)

Muzzle, منهه *muṅh* (f.), مهڙا *muhṛā*, (bore of a gun) مهري *muhrī*, (for cattle) جاب *jāb*.

Myriad, (ten thousand) دس هزار *das hazār*, تومان *tōmān*.

Myrrh, (a gum-resin) مر *murr*, بول *bōl*.

Mystery, راز *rāz*, غيب *ghaib*, بهيد *bhēd*, (trade) كسب *kasb*.

Mythology, ديومالا *dē'ō-mālā*, ديوتاؤن كي كهاني *dēwtā'ōṅ kī kahānī*.

Nag, يابو *yābū*, ٹٹو *ṭaṭṭū*, گھوڑا *ghōṛā*.

Nail, (of iron, &c.) میخ *mēkh* (f.), کیل *kīl* (f.), (in measure) گره *girih.* (f.)

Nakedness, برهنگي *barahnagī*, عرياني *ūryānī*, ننگائي *nangā'ī*.

Name, نام *nām*, نانو *nāṅw*, اسم *ism*, (title) لقب *laḳab*: see Fame.

Namesake, هم نام *ham-nām*, سمي *samī*, سنامي *sanāmī* (?).

Nap, (short sleep) تهوڑي نيند *thōṛī nīnd* (f.), (of cloth) ريشه *rēsha*.

Napkin, دستمال *dastmāl*, رومال *rūmāl*, انگوچها *angūchhā*.

Narration, Narrative, نقل *naḳl* (f.), حکايت *ḥikāyat* (f.), قصه *ḳiṣṣa*.

Narrator, راوي *rāwī*, ناقل *nāḳil*, نقلي *naḳlī*, حاکي *ḥākī*.

Narrowness, تنگي *tangī*, سکرائي *sakrā'ī*, (meanness) تنگ دستي *tang-dastī*.

Nastiness, نجاست *najāsat* (f.), ميل *mail*, آلودگي *ālūdagī*, غلاظت *ghilāẓat*. (f.)

Native country, وطن *waṭan*, ديس *dēs*, زاد بوم *zād-būm*.

Nativity, تولد *tawallud*, جنم *janam*, (place) مولد *maulid*.

Nature, (constitution) طبيعت *ṭabī'at* (f.), مزاج *mizāj*: see Custom, World.

Navigation, ملاحي *mallāḥī*, ناخدائي *nākhudā'ī*, جهازي علم *jahāzī ilm*.

Nearness, نزديکي *nazdīkī*, قرب *ḳurb*, اتصال *ittiṣāl*: see Covetousness.

Necessaries (things needed), اسباب ضروري *asbāb-i-ẓarūrī*, لوازمه *lawāzima*.

Necessity, ضرورت *ẓarūrat* (f.), وجوب *wujūb*, (need) حاجت *ḥājat* (f.): see Force.

Necromancy, جادو *jādū*, جادوگري *jādūgarī*, ساحري *sāḥirī*, تسخير *taskhīr*. (f.)

Nectar, امرت *amrit*, شرابا طهورا *sharāban ṭahūrā*, آب کوثر *āb-i-kauṣar*.

Need, احتياج *iḥtiyāj* (f. m.), غرض *gharaẓ* (f.), تات پرج *tātparj*: see Necessity.

Needle, (for sewing) سوئي *sū'ī*, سوزن *sōzan* (f.), (packing) سوا *sū'ā*, (of the compass) قطب نما کي سوئي *ḳutb-numā kī sū'ī*, کانٹا *kānṭā*.

Eye of a needle, ناکا *nākā*, سوفار *sūfār*. (m. f.)

Negation, انکار *inkār*, نفي *nafī* (m.), سلب *salb*, رد *radd*.

Neglect, Negligence, غفلت *ghaflat* (f.), کاهلي *kāhilī*, سستي *sustī*.

Negotiation, معامله *mu'āmala*, کاروبار *kārōbār*.

Negro, حبشي *habshī*, زنگي *zangī*, سياه *siyāh*, سيدي *sīdī* or شيدي *shīdī* (?).

Neighbour, همسايه *hamsāya*, پروسي *parōsī*, همجوار *hamjawār*.

Neighbourhood, پروس *parōs*, جوار *jawār*, همسايه *hamsāya*.

Nest, گهونسلا *ghōṅslā*, کهوندها *khōndhā*, آشيانه *āshiyāna*, باسا *bāsā*.

Nestling, گيدا *gēdā*, آشياني *ashiyānī*, ليدا *lēdā*.

Net, جال *jāl*, ڈهابا *ḍhābā*, دام *dām*.

News, اخبار *akhbār*, (sing.) خبر *khabar* (f.), واقعات *wāḳi'āt*.

Nib, (point) نوک *nōk* (f.), اني *anī*, (beak) ٹهور *ṭhōr*. (f.)

Niche (recess in a wall), طاق *ṭāḳ*, طاقچه *ṭāḳcha*.

Nickname, بد لقب *bad laḳab*, عرفي نام *ūrfī nām*.

Niggard, بخيل *bakhīl*, ممسک *mumsik*, کنجوس *kanjūs*, سوم *sūm*.

Nitre, Saltpetre, شوره *shōra*, ابقر *abḳir* or *abḳar* (?).

Nobility, شرافت *sharāfat* (f.), نجابت *najābat* (f.), (nobles) شرفا *shurafā*.

Noble, Nobleman, امير *amīr*, منصبدار *manṣabdār*, عمده *ūmda*.

Nobody, کوئي نهين *kō'ī nahīṅ*, (figurat.) نا چيز *nā-chīz*.

Noise, شور *shōr*, بانگ *bāng* (f.), آواز *āwāz* (f.), غل *ghul*, غوغا *ghaughā*.

Nomenclature, نام مالا *nām-mālā*, فرهنگ *farhang* (f.), لغت *lughat*. (f.)

Nominative (in gram.), فاعل *fā'il*, حالت فاعليت *ḥālat-i-fā'iliyat*. (f.)

Nonce (purpose), اراده *irāda*, قصد *ḳaṣd*, مطلب *maṭlab*, غرض *gharaẓ*. (f.)

Nonentity, Nonexistence, عدم *ādam*, نيستي *nēstī*, نابودي *nā-būdī*.

Nonsense, بيمعني باتين *bē-ma'nī bātēṅ*, ياوه‌گوئي *yāwa-gō'ī*.

Nook, کونا *kōnā*, گوشه *gōsha*, (narrow place) کم چوڑي جگه *kam-chauṛī jagah*.

Noose, پهانسي *phāṅsī*, پهاندا *phāndā*, کمند *kamand*. (f.)

North-east, ايسان کون *īsān-kōn*, ايسان *īsān*.

North pole or star, قطب شمالي *ḳuṭb-i-shimālī*, دهرب *dhrub.*

North-west, بايب *bāyab.*

Nosegay, گلدسته *gul-dasta*, طره *ṭurra*, پهولون کا گچهه *phūloṅ kā guchchha.*

Notch (in a log of wood), كهندانا *khandānā.*

Note, (mark) نشان *nishān*, (letter) چٹهي *chiṭṭhī*: see Comment.

Nothing, کچهه نهين *kuchh nahīṅ*, هيچ *hēch*, (worthless) ناچيز *nā-chīz.*

Notice, (attention) غور *ghaur*, التفات *iltifāt* (f.), (information) اطلاع *iṭṭilā'* (f.), (notification) اعلام *i'lām*, خبر *khabar.* (f.)

Notion, دريافت *daryāft* (f.), پندار *pindār* (f.), راي *rā'ē* (f.), خيال *khayāl.*

Novel (tale), افسانه *afsāna*, قصه *ḳiṣṣa*, كهاني *kahānī*, داستان *dāstān.* (f.)

Novelty, تجدد *tajaddud*, نياپن *nayāpan*, نو طرزي *nau-ṭarzī.*

Nought, کچهه نهين *kuchh nahīṅ*, هيچ *hēch.*

Novice, نو آموز *nau-āmōz*, مبتدي *mubtadī*, اناڑي *anāṛī*, خام *khām*, کچا *kachchā.*

Noun, اسم *ism*, نام *nām.*

Nourishment, پرورش *parwarish* (f.), غذا *ghiẕā* (f.), خوراک *khōrāk.* (f.)

Nuisance, زيانكار چيز *ziyānkār chīz* (f.), وبال *wabāl*, چهاتي کا پتهر *chhātī kā patthar.*

Number, عدد *'adad*, آنک *āṅk*, (reckoning) گنتي *gintī*, شمار *shumār*: (in gram.) singular, واحد *wāḥid*; dual, تثنيه *tasṇiya*; plur. جمع *jam'.* (f.)

Numbness, ٹهٹهراهٹ *ṭhiṭhrāhaṭ* (f.), بيحسي *bē-ḥissī*, بيحركتي *bē-ḥarakatī.*

Numeration, حساب *ḥisāb*, گنتي *gintī*, تعداد *ti'dād* (f.), شمار *shumār.*

Nuptials, بياه *byāh*, شادي *shādī*, نکاح *nikāḥ.*

Nursery, دائيخانه *dā'ī-khāna*, (for plants) بهنور *bihnaur*, بيآڑ *bī'aṛ.* (f.)

Nursling, شيرخواره *shīr-khwāra*, دودهه پيا طفل *dūdh-piyā ṭifl.*

Nutriment, Nutriture, غذا *ghiẕā* (f.), پرورش *parwarish.* (f.)

Nymph, اپچهرا *apchharā* (f.), حور *ḥūr* (f.), حوري *ḥūrī.*

Oaf, اوت *ūt*, الو *ullū*, احمق *aḥmaḳ*: see Idiot, Dunce.

Oath, قسم *ḳasam* (f.), سوگند *saugand* (f.), سونہہ *sōṅh* (f.), (dakh.) سپت *sapat.* (f.)

Obedience, اطاعت *iṭā'at* (f.), تابعداري *tābi'dārī*, آدهينتا *ādhīntā.* (f.)

Obeisance, آداب *ādāb*, كورنش *kōrnish* (f.), سلام *salām*, ڈنڈوت *ḍanḍwat.* (f.)

Obelisk, مينار *mīnār*, لاٹ *lāṭ* (f.), كنداسا *kandāsā.*

Object, (purpose) مقصد *maḳṣad*, غرض *gharaẓ* (f.): see Affair, Meaning.

Objection, اعتراض *i'tirāẓ* (f.), پكڑ *pakaṛ* (f.), (argument) حجت *ḥujjat.* (f.)

Oblation, نياز *niyāz* (f.), نذر *nazr* (f.), قربان *ḳurbān*, بل *bal.*

Obligation, (contract) شرط *sharṭ* (f.), عهد *ahd*, (duty) فرض *farẓ*, وجوب *wujūb*, (favour) احسان *iḥsān*, نهورا *nihōrā.*

Oblivion, فراموشي *farāmōshī*, نسيان *nisyān*, بسراوٹ *bisrāwaṭ.*

Obloquy, طعن *ṭa'n*, طعن تشنيع *ta'n tashnī'* (f.), الزام *ilzām.*

Obsequies, تجهيز و تكفين *tajhīz ō takfīn* (f.), كريا كرم *kriyā-karm.*

Observance, (respect) اكرام *ikrām*, (attention) ملاحظه *mulāḥaẓa.*

Obstacle, مانع *māni'*, حائل *ḥā'il*, آڑ *āṛ* (f.), مزاحمت *muzāḥamat.* (f.)

Occasion, (cause) باعث *bā'iṣ*, (need) ضرورت *ẓarūrat* (f.), (time) فرصت *furṣat.* (f.)

Occupation, (business) كام *kām*, دهندها *dhandhā*: see Calling, Abode.

Occurrence, واقعه *wāḳi'a*, حادثه *ḥādiṣa*, سانحه *sāniḥa.*

Ode, غزل *ghazal* (f.), (long) قصيده *ḳaṣīda*, (Hindustani) ريخته *rēkhta.*

Odour, بو *bō* or *bū* (f.), گنده *gandh* (f.), مهك *mahak* (f.), سباس *subās.* (f.)

Offal, فضله *fuẓla*, آخور *ākhōr* (f.), پس خورده *pas-khurda.*

Offence, تقصير *taḳṣīr* (f.), گناه *gunāh*: see Injury, Displeasure.

Offender, گناهگار *gunāhgār*, تقصيروار *taḳṣīrwār*, عاصي *āṣī.*

Offering, قربان *ḳurbān*, بل *bal*, (present) نذر *nazr*, هديه *hadīya.*

Office, (service, duty) خدمت *khidmat* (f.), عهده *uhda*, (room) كچهري *kachahrī.*

Offset, پودها *paudhā*, کلغا *kalghā* (?).

Offspring, (child) فرزند *farzand* (m. f.), (children) اولاد *aulād* (f.): see Lineage.

Oil, تیل *tēl*, روغن *raughan*, (scented) پهلیل *phulēl*.

Oil-press, کولهو *kōlhū*, گهاني *ghānī*.

Omen, شگون *shugūn*, فال *fāl*. (f.)

Omission, چوك *chūk* (f.), بهول *bhūl* (f.), سهو *sahū* (f.), قصور *ḳuṣūr*.

Omnipotence, قدرت *ḳudrat* (f.), قادري *ḳādirī*, قدرت كلي *ḳudrat-i-kullī*.

Omniscience, همه داني *hama-dānī*, علم كل *ilm-i-kull*.

Openness, كشادگي *kushādagī*, (candour) سادگي *sādagī*, صفائي *ṣafā'ī*.

Operation, عمل *amal*, كار *kār*, (effect) اثر *aṣar*, تاثير *tāṣīr*. (f.)

Opinion, رائي *rā'ē* (f.), بوجه *būjh* (f.), خيال *khayāl*, ظن *ẓann*, فكر *fikr*.

Opium, افيون *afyūn* (f.), افيم *afīm* (f.), ترياق *tiryāḳ*.

Opportunity, فرصت *furṣat* (f.), قابو *ḳābū*, وقت *waḳt*, گون *gaun*. (f.)

Oppression, ظلم *ẓulm*, ستم *sitam*, جور *jaur*, تعدي *ta'addī*.

Oppressor, ظالم *ẓālim*, ستمگر *sitamgar*, مردم آزار *mardum-āzār*.

Optative (mood, in grammar), متمني *mutamannī*.

Option, اختيار *ikhtiyār*, چاه *chāh* (f.), مرضي *marẓī*, پسند *pasand*. (f.)

Opulence, دولت *daulat* (f.), توانگري *tawāngarī*, سمپت *sampat*. (f.)

Oration, كلام *kalām*, تقرير *taḳrīr* (f.), سخن *sukhun*, بات *bāt*. (f.)

Orb, كره *kura*, چرخ *charkh*, گردون *gardūn*, منڈل *manḍal*: see Globe.

Orbit, دائره *dā'ira*, (of the eye) حلقه چشم *ḥalḳa-e-chashm*.

Order, (command) حكم *ḥukm*, امر *amr*, (method) ترتيب *tartīb* (f.): see Class, Rank.

Ordinance, شرع *shar'*, قانون *ḳānūn*, (rite) رسم *rasm*: see Law.

Orifice, چهيد *chhēd*, سوراخ *sūrākh*, شگاف *shigāf*, منفذ *manfaẓ*.

Origin, اصل *aṣl* (f.), بنياد *bunyād* (f.), بيخ *bēkh* (f.): see Root, Family.

Ornament, زيور *zēwar*, زينت *zīnat* (f.), سنگار *singār*, آرائش *ārā'ish*. (f.)

Orphan, يتيم *yatīm*, مرها *murhā*.

Orthography, رسم خط *rasm-i-khaṭṭ*, املا *imlā*, اچهروٹي *achhrauṭī*.

Oscillation, ڈلاو *dulā'o*, جھلاو *jhulā'o*, تھرتھري *thartharī*.

Outcry, شور *shōr*, غوغا *ghaughā*, غل *ghul*, غل غپاره *ghul ghapāra*.

Outrage, ظلم *zulm*, ستم *sitam*, جفا *jafā* (f.), جور *jaur*. (f.)

Outside, باهر *bāhar*, باهرطرف *bāhar taraf*, اوپر *ūpar*, ظاهر *zāhir*.

Outworks, باهر کوٹا *bāhar kōṭā*, اڑتلا *aṛtalā*, مرحله *marhala*.

Owner, مالک *mālik*, حقدار *hakk-dār*, خاوند *khāwind*.

Oxymel, سکنجبين *sikanjabīn*. (f.)

Pace, (step) قدم *kadam*, (gait) رفتار *raftār* (f.), چلني کي وضع *chalnē kī waz*.

Pack, (bundle) گٹھا *gaṭṭhā*, بسته *basta*, موٹھ *mōṭh* (f.), (of cards) گنجيفه *ganjīfa*, (of hounds) لينڈھا *lēndhā*, جھنڈ *jhund*: see Crew.

Package, Parcel, گٹھري *gaṭhrī*, پوٹلي *pōṭlī*, بسته *basta*: see Pack.

Packcloth, بيٹھن *bēṭhan*, لفافه *lifāfa*.

Packet, (mail) خريطه *kharīṭa*, چٹھي کي تھيلي *chiṭṭhī kī thailī*: see Package.

Packhorse, پرتل کا گھوڑا *partal kā ghōṛā*, باربرداري کا ٹٹو *bārbardārī kā ṭaṭṭū*.

Packsaddle, گدي *gaddī*, پالان *pālān*, خوگير *khōgīr*.

Padlock, قفل *kufl*, کلف *kalaf* or *kulaf*, تالا *tālā*.

Pagan, بت پرست *but-parast*, گبر *gabr*, مشرک *mushrik*, کافر *kāfir*.

Page (of a book) صفحه *safha*, (servant) خواص *khawāṣṣ*, جلودار *jilaudār*.

Pagoda, بتکده *but-kada*, بتخانه *but-khāna*, شوالا *shiwālā*: see Idol.

Pain, دکھ *dukh*, درد *dard*, پير *pīr* (f.), رنج *ranj*: see Labour.

Pains (toil), محنت *mihnat* (f.), سعي *sa'ī*, (of labour) درد زه *dard-i-zih*.

Paint, رنگ *rang*, برن *barun*, روغن *raughan*.

A Pair, جوڑا *jōṛā*, جفت *juft*, جگ *jug*; (one of a pair) جوت *jōt*.

Palanquin, پالکي *pālkī*, نالکي *nālkī*.

Palisade, کٹھرا *kaṭharā*, کٹھگھرا *kaṭhgharā*, متکا *mutakkā* (?).

Pall (for the dead), چدر *chaddar* (f.), کفن *kafan*.

Pamphlet, چوپتي *chaupatī*, رساله *risāla*.

Pan (broad vessel) چوڑا برتن *chauṛā bartan*, (of a gun-lock) پیاله *piyāla*.

Pancake, مالپوا *mālpū'ā*, پوا *pū'ā*, کوکو *kūkū*.

Pane (of glass), پرکاله *parkāla*, شیشۂ چوگوشه *shīsha-e-chaugōsha*.

Pang, نهایت درد *nihāyat dard*, سیاست *siyāsat* (f.), (of death) نزع *naz**.

Panic, ناگهان ڈر *nāgahān ḍar*, هیبت *haibat* (f.), هول *haul*.

Paper, کاغذ *kāghaz*, قرطاس *ḳirṭās*.

Par (equality), مساوات *musāwāt* (f.), برابري *barābarī*; (at par) برابر *barābar*.

Parable, تمثيل *tamṣīl* (f.), مثل *maṣal* (f.), درشٹانت *drishṭānt*.

Paradise, فردوس *firdaus*, عدن *ādn*, بهشت *bihisht*. (f.)

Paragraph, فقره *fiḳra*, قطعة *ḳiṭ'ā*, پرکرن *prakaran*.

Parallel, Parallelism, برابري *barābarī*, تساوي *tasāwī*.

Paramour, آشنا *āshnā*, عاشق *āshiḳ*, یار *yār*, جار *jār*, دهگڑا *dhagṛā*.

Parasite, خوشامدي *khushāmadī*, مفت خور *muft-khōr*, طفيل *ṭufail*.

Parasol, چهوٹا چهاتا *chhōṭā chhātā*, چهتر *chhatr*, چتري *chatrī*.

Parcel, (bundle) بقچه *buḳcha*, گٹهري *gaṭhrī*, (part) حصه *ḥiṣṣa*.

Parchment, رق *raḳḳ*, میشي *mēshī* (?).

Pardon, معافي *mu'āfī*, عفو *āfū*, آمرزش *āmurzish*. (f.)

Parent, ما یا باپ *mā* (f.) or *bāp*, پدر یا مادر *pidar* or *mādar*.

Parents, ما باپ *mā bāp*, والدين *wālidain*, پترو *pitarau*.

Part, حصه *ḥiṣṣa*, بخرا *bakhrā*, بانٹ *bānṭ*, (duty) کام *kām*.

Parterre, سبزه زار *sabza-zār*, چمن *chaman*.

Partiality, طرفداري *ṭaraf-dārī*, پله کشي *palla-kashī*, پچه *pachh*.

Participle, (active) اسم فاعل *ism-i-fā'il*, (present) اسم حاليه *ism-i-ḥāliya*, (past or passive) اسم مفعول *ism-i-maf'ūl*, (past conjunctive) ماضي معطوف عليه *māẓī ma*ṭūf ālaihi*.

Particle, ٹک *ṭuk*, ذره *ẓarra*, کن *kan*, (in gram.) حرف *ḥarf*.

Partition, تقسيم *taḳsīm* (f.), تفريق *tafrīḳ* (f.), (fence) آڑ *āṛ*. (f.)

Partner, شريک *sharīk*, بخرادار *bakhrādār*, ساجهي *sājhī*: see Companion.

Partnership, شراکت *sharākat* (f.), ساجها *sājhā*, شرکت *shirkat.* (f.)

Party, (of men) غول *g͟hōl*, گروه *gurōh*, (in a suit) فريق *farīḳ*: see Assembly.

Pass, گلي *galī*, گهات *g͟hāṭ*, راه *rāh* (f.): see Passport.

Passage, گذاره *guẕāra*, رسته *rasta*, سڑک *saṛak* (f.): see Paragraph.

Passenger, مسافر *musāfir*, راهگير *rāhgīr*, بٹوهي *baṭōhī.* (m. f.)

Passport, پروانهٔ راهداري *parwāna-e-rāhdārī*, روانه *rawāna.*

Paste, ليي *lē'ī*, اهار *ahār*, ماڑني *māṛnī*, خمير *k͟hamīr*, ليت *lēt.*

Pasteboard, دفتين *daftīn* (f.), وصلي *waṣlī.*

Pastime, اوقات بسري *auḳāt-basarī*, کوتک *kautak*, بهلاو *bahlā'ō*: see Fun.

Pasturage, چري *charī*, علف *ȃlaf*, (or Pasture) چراگاه *charāgāh.* (f.)

Patent, سند *sanad* (f.), فرمان *farmān*, پروانه *parwāna.*

Path, Pathway, بات *bāṭ* (f.), رسته *rasta*, سڑک *saṛak* (f.), راه *rāh.* (f.)

Patriarch, گهراني کا سردار *gharānē kā sardār*, بزرگ *buzurg.*

Patrician, شريف *sharīf*, عمده *ȗmda*, عاليشان *ȃlīshān.*

Patrimony, ميراث *mīrāṡ* (f.), بپوتي *bapautī*, ارث *irṡ.*

Patriot, وطن دوست *waṭan-dōst*, حب الوطني *ḥabbu-l-waṭanī.*

Patriotism, حب الوطن *ḥabbu-l-waṭan*, ديسپالتا *dēspāltā.* (f.)

Patron, مربي *murabbī*, دستگير *dastgīr*, حامي *ḥāmī*, قدردان *ḳadrdān.*

Patronage, مربي گري *murabbī-garī*, حمايت *ḥimāyat* (f.), پرورش *parwarish.* (f.)

Pattern, نمونه *namūna*, بانگي *bāngī*, (leader) قدوه *ḳidwa*: see Leader.

Paucity, کمي *kamī*, گهٹتي *ghaṭṭī*, کمتي *kamtī*, قلت *ḳillat.* (f.)

Pavement, فرش *farsh*, کهرنجا *kharanjā*, پٹاو *paṭā'ō.*

Pay, (payment) ادا *adā* (f.), (wages) تنخواه *tank͟hwāh* (f.), طلب *ṭalab.* (f.)

Peace, صلح *ṣulḥ* (f.), آشتي *āshtī*, (ease) آرام *ārām*, (concord) ميل *mēl.*

Peak, (top of a hill) چونٹي *chōnṭī*, سکهر *sikhar*, (point) نوک *nōk.*

Peal, ٹهاکا *ṭhahākā*, گڑگڑاهٹ *gaṛgaṛahaṭ* (f.), دهمکا *dhamkā.*

Pearl, موتي *mōtī* (m.), در *dur*, گوهر *gauhar*, لولو *lūlū.*

Peasant, گنوار *gaṅwār*, کسان *kisān*, دهقاني *dihḳānī*.

Peasantry, رعايا *ri'āyā*, دهقاني لوگ *dihḳānī lōg*, رعيت *ra'iyat*. (f.)

Pebble, کنکر *kankar*, گول سنگريزه *gōl sangrēza*, روڙا *rōṛā*.

Pedestal of a column, پاۓ ستون *pā'ē sitūn*, بن ستون *bun-i-sitūn*.

Pedigree, نسب *nasab*, سلسله *silsila*, (table of) نسب نامه *nasab-nāma*.

Peel, پوست *pōst*, چهال *chhāl* (f.), چهلکا *chhilkā*, بکلا *baklā*.

Peer, هم سر *ham-sar*, (nobleman) امير *amīr*, صاحب *ṣāḥib*: see Nobleman.

Peg, ميخ *mēkh* (f.), کهونٹي *khūnṭī*, کهونٹا *khūnṭā*.

Pellet, غليله *ghulēla*, گولي *gōlī*, گردگان *girdgān*.

Pellicle, جهلي *jhillī*, چهالي *chhālī*.

Pen, قلم *ḳalam*, خامه *khāma*, (enclosure) احاطه *iḥāṭa*.

Penalty, سزا *sazā* (f.), تاوان *tāwān*, ڈانڈ *ḍānḍ*, جريمانه *jarīmāna*.

Pence (money), پيسے *paisē*, ٹکے *ṭakē*: see Penny.

Pencil, (of lead) سلائي *salā'ī*, (of hair) موقلم *mū-ḳalam*.

Pendant, آويزه *āwēza*, جهمکا *jhumkā*, لٹکن *laṭkan*.

Penitence, توبه *tauba*, ندامت *nadāmat* (f.), استغفار *istighfār*.

Penny, ايک قسم کا انگريزي پيسا *ēk ḳism kā angrēzī paisā*.

Pension, وظيفه *waẓīfa*, جاگير *jāgīr* (f.), بندهان *bandhān*.

Pentagon, مخمس *mukhammas*, شکل پنج گوشه *shakl-i-panj-gōsha*.

Penury, تنگدستي *tangdastī*, تهيدستي *tihīdastī*, مفلسي *muflisī*.

People, لوگ *lōg*, اشخاص *ashkhāṣ*, خلائق *khalā'iḳ*. (f.)

Perception, دريافت *daryāft* (f.), بوجه *būjh* (f.), بصارت *baṣārat*. (f.)

Perch (for birds), چکس *chakkas*, اڈا *aḍḍā*.

Perfection, تکميل *takmīl* (f.), کمال *kamāl*, (completion) اتمام *itmām*.

Perfume, خوش بو *khush-bō* (f.), عطر *ʿaṭr*, سباس *subās*. (f.)

Period, (circuit) دور *daur*, (time) زمانه *zamāna*: see Sentence.

Perjury, جهوٹهي قسم *jhūṭhī ḳasam*, سوگند کاذب *saugand-i-kāẕib*.

Permission, اجازت *ijāzat* (f.), اذن *iẕn*, رخصت *rukhṣat*. (f.)

A Permit, نکاسي کي چٹهي *nikāsī kī chiṭṭhī*, پروانه *parwāna*.

Person, شخص *shakhṣ*, آدمي *ādmī* (m.), (in gram.) صيغه *ṣīgha*: see Body, Form.

Perspicuity, سلاست *salāsat* (f.), صراحت *ṣarāḥat* (f.), صفائي *ṣafā'ī.*

Perturbation, گهبراهت *ghabrāhaṭ* (f.), تشويش *tashwīsh.* (f.)

Petal, پهول كي پتي *phūl kī pattī,* پكهڑي *pakhṛī.*

Petition, عرض *ārẓ* (f.), عرضي *ārẓī,* ارداس *ardās.* (f.)

Petitioner, عرض كرنيوالا *ārz-karnēwālā,* داد خواه *dād-khwāh.*

Phantasm, Phantom, نمود بيبود *namūd-i-bēbūd,* چهايا *chhāyā.*

Philology, علم صرف و نحو *ilm-i-ṣarf ō naḥō.*

Phrase, بات *bāt* (f.), اصطلاح *iṣṭilāḥ* (f.), عبارت *ibārat.* (f.)

Piece, (bit) ٹكڑا *ṭukṛā* ٹك *ṭuk,* پارچه *pārcha,* (patch) جوڑ *jōṛ.*

Piety, تقوى *taḳwā,* بهگتائي *bhagtā'ī,* (to parents) پدرومادرپرستي *pidar-ō-mādar-parastī.*

Pilgrimage, جاترا *jātrā* (f.), زيارت *ziyārat* (f.), (to Mecca) حج *ḥajj.*

Pill, گولي *gōlī,* حب *ḥabb,* دوا كي گولي *dawā kī gōlī.*

Pillory, چنبرگردن *chambar-i-gardan,* دوشاخه *do-shākha.*

Pimp, بهڑوا *bhaṛwā,* كٹنا *kuṭnā,* قلتبان *ḳultabān.*

Pimple, (on the face) مهاسا *muhāsā,* (on the skin) پهنسي *phunsī.*

Pin, سوئي *sū'ī,* كانٹا *kānṭā,* (peg) ميخ *mēkh:* see Peg, Straw.

Pincers, سنڈاسي *sanḍāsī,* سنگسي *sangsī,* موچنا *mūchnā.*

Pinion, گڈي *guḍḍī,* پر *par,* بازو *bāzū,* (quill) شهپر *shahpar.*

Pinnacle, كلس *kalas,* كنگوره *kangūra,* (peak) سكهر *sikhar.*

Pipe, (tube) نل *nal,* نلي *nalī,* (musical) بانسري *bānsrī:* see Cask.

Pitch, (resin from the pine) رال *rāl* (f.), قير *ḳīr:* see Degree.

Pitfall, ڈهك *ḍahak,* چورگڑها *chōr-gaṛhā.*

Pith, مغز *maghz,* سار *sār* (f.), هير *hīr,* گودا *gūdā.*

Pity, رحم *raḥm,* درد *dard,* ترس *tars,* ديا *dayā* (f.), غم *gham.*

Place, جگه *jagah* (f.), مكان *makān,* (office) عهده *uhda.*

Plainness, همواري *hamwārī,* (sincerity) سادگي *sādagī:* see Clearness.

Plaintiff, فريادي *faryādī,* داد خواه *dād-khwāh,* مدعي *mudda'ī.*

Plait, ته *tah* (f.), شكن *shikan,* چين *chīn* (f.), (plaits) چنت *chunat.* (f.)

Plan, (scheme) منصوبه *manṣūba,* تجويز *tajwīz* (f.): see Model.

Plane (joiner's tool), رنده *randa,* (tree) چنار *chanār.*

Plank, تخته *takhta*, لوح *lauḥ* (f.), پٹرا *paṭrā*, پٹري *paṭrī*.

Plantation, (place planted) نخلستان *nakhlistān*, (colony) بستي *bastī*.

Plaster, (cement) ريخته *rēkhta*, گچ *gach*, (salve) مرهم *marham*.

Play, كهيل *khēl*, بازي *bāzī*, كلول *kalōl* (f.), كوتك *kautuk*.

Plaything, كهلونا *khilaunā*, لعبت *la*bat* (f.), بازيچه *bāzīcha*.

Plea, (argument) حجت *ḥujjat* (f.), (suit) دعوا *da*wā*: see Excuse.

Pleading, مباحثه *mubāḥasa*, تكرار *takrār* (f.), حجت *ḥujjat*. (f.)

Pleasantness, لطافت *laṭāfat* (f.). Pleasantry, مزاخ *mazākh*.

Pleasure, خوشي *khushī*, عيش *aish*, حظ *ḥazz*, (assent) مرضي *marẓī*.

Pledge, گرو *girō*, بندهك *bandhak*, رهن *rihn*: see Bail.

Pleiades, ثريا *suraiyā*, پروين *parwīn*, كچپچيا *kachpachiyā*.

Plenty, افراط *ifrāṭ*, وفور *wafūr*, (enough) بهرپور *bhar-pūr*.

Pliers, جمٹا *chimṭā*, سنڈاسي *sanḍāsī*, چيونٹا *chē'ūnṭā* (?).

Plot, بندش *bandish* (f.), منصوبه *manṣūba*, (of ground) فضا *faẓā*. (f.)

Plug, ڈٹا *ḍaṭṭā*, ٹهينٹهي *ṭhēnṭhī*, ٹهيپي *ṭhēpī*.

Plume, (ornament) طره *ṭurra*, كلغي *kalghī*: see Feather.

Plummet, ساهول *sāhūl*, سهول *sahōl*, (plumb or lead) لٹكن *laṭkan*.

Plunge, ڈبكي *ḍubkī*, غوطه *ghōṭa*, بڑكي *buṛkī* (?).

Plural (number), جمع *jam** (f.), صيغهٔ جمع *sīgha-i-jam**.

Ply, ته *tah* (f.), چين *chīn* (f.), پرت *parat*, شكن *shikan*. (f.)

Pocket, جيب *jēb* (f.), كهيسا *khīsā*, خريطه *kharīṭa*, جهولي *jhōlī*.

Pod, چهيمي *chhēmī*, پهلي *phalī*, چهلكا *chhilkā*, پوست *pōst*.

Poem, غزل *ghazal* (f.), قصيده *kaṣīda*, مثنوي *masnawī*.

Poesy, Poetry, شعر *shi*r*, نظم *naẓm* (f.), كبت *kabit*.

Point, (end) نوك *nōk* (f.), اني *anī*, (stop) نقطهٔ وقف *nuḳṭa-e-waḳf*.

Poison, زهر *zahr*, بس *bis*, بكه *bikh*, هلاهل *halāhal*, سم *samm*.

Pole, لاٹه *lāṭh* (f.), چوب *chōb*, (of the earth) قطب *ḳuṭb*.

Polestar, قطب *ḳuṭb*, قطب شمالي *ḳuṭb-i-shimālī*: see Guide.

Police, شهركي ضبط و ربط *shahr kī ẓabṭ ō rabṭ*, كوتوالي *kōtwālī*.

Polish, چكناهٹ *chiknāhaṭ* (f.), صيقل *ṣaiḳal*, (of manners) خلق *khulḳ*.

Politics, علم سياست *ilm-i-siyāsat*, امور مملكت *umūr-i-mamlukat*.

Polygon, شكل كثير الزاويه *shakl-i-kasīru-z-zāwiya*.

Poppy, كوكنار *kōknār*, (head) پوست *pōst*, (seed) خشخش *khashkhash*.
Populace, عوام الناس *awāmmu-n-nās*, جمهور *jamhūr*, عام *āmm*.
Population, آبادي *ābādī*, بستي *bastī*, معموري *ma*mūrī*.
Portion, حصه *hiṣṣa*, بخرا *bakhrā*, (bride's) جهيز *jahēz*.
Portmanteau, خورجين *khurjīn*, جامداني *jāmadānī*.
Portrait, شبيه *shabīh* (f.), تصوير *taṣwīr*. (f.)
Position, جگه *jagah* (f.), محل *maḥall*, حالت *ḥālat* (f.), طرح *ṭaraḥ*. (f.)
Possession, تصرف *taṣarruf*, عمل *āmal*, قبضه *ḳabẓa*, ضبط *ẓabṭ*.
Possessor, مالك *mālik*, صاحب *ṣāḥib*, متصرف *mutaṣarrif*.
Post, (stump) كهنبها *khambhā*, چوب *chōb*, (business) عهده *ūhda*, كام *kām*, (for conveying letters) ڈاك *ḍāk*, (post office) ڈاك گهر *ḍāk-ghar*, (man) ڈاكيا *ḍākiyā*, قاصد *ḳāṣid*, ڈاك *ḍāk*.
Postage, ڈاك كا محصول *ḍāk kā maḥṣūl*, رسوم *rusūm*.
Posterity, ال *āl* (f.), اولاد *aulād* (f.), سنتت *santat*, نسل *nasl*.
Posture, وضع *waẓ** (f.), صورت *ṣūrat* (f.), نشست *nishast*. (f.)
Potash, كهار *khār*, سجي مٹي *sajjī miṭṭī*.
Potsherd, ٹهكرا *ṭhikrā*, سفال *sifāl*.
Poverty, افلاس *iflās*, مفلسي *muflisī*, تنگدستي *tangdastī*.
Pound, (weight) آدهسير *ādh-sēr*, رطل *raṭl*, (fold) بيڑها *bēṛhā*.
Powder, بكني *buknī*, (medicine) سفوف *safūf*, (gun) باروت *bārūt*. (f.)
Power, توانائي *tawānā'ī*, (authority) اختيار *ikhtiyār*: see Force.
Practice, (use) مشق *mashḳ* (f.), (custom) عادت *ādat* (f.), معمول *ma*mūl*.
Praise, تعريف *ta*rīf* (f.), سپاس *sipās* (f.), ثنا *ṣanā* (f.), مدح *madḥ*. (f.)
Prayer, (request) التماس *iltimās*, (to heaven) نماز *namāz*. (f.)
Precaution, عاقبت انديشي *āḳibat-andēshī*, تدارك *tadāruk*.
Precedent, نمونه *namūna*, دستورالعمل *dastūru-l āmal*.
Precinct, حد *ḥadd* (f.), سوانه *siwāna*.
Precipice, ڈهانگ *ḍhāng* (f.), سرنگ *sring*, كندلا *kandalā*.
Predecessor, پيشين *pēshīn*, سابق *sābiḳ*, مقدم *muḳaddam*.
Predestination, تقدير *taḳdīr* (f.), سرنوشت *sar-nawisht*. (f.)
Preface, ديباجه *dībāja*, (f.), ديباچه *dībācha*, مقدمه *muḳaddama*.

Preference, ترجيح *tarjīḥ* (f.), فوقيت *faukiyat* (f.), سرسائي *sarsā'ī*.
Preferment, بڑھتي *baṛhtī*, ترقي *ṭarakkī*, سرفرازي *sarfarāzī*.
Pregnancy, حمل *ḥaml*, گربھ *garbh*, آبستني *ābistanī*.
Prejudice, تعصب *ta'aṣṣub*, طرفداري *ṭarafdārī*: see Detriment.
Premises (houses, lands), اموال غير منقوله *amwāl-i ghair mankūla*.
Premium, (on bills, &c.) بيشي *bēshī*, چوٹا *chōṭā*: see Gift, Bounty.
Preparation, تياري *taiyārī*, بناوري *banāwarī*, تهيت *tahīyat*. (f.)
Prepuce, کھلڑي *khalṛī*, غلف *ghalf*, چھچڑا *chhichṛā*.
Prerogative, خاص حق *khāṣṣ ḥakk*.
Presage, فال *fāl* (f.), شگون *shugūn*, دلالت *dalālat*. (f.)
Prescience, غيبداني *ghaib-dānī*, پيشبيني *pēshbīnī*.
Prescription, (medical) نسخه *nuskha*, (custom) رسم *rasm*: see Custom.
Presence, حاضري *ḥāẓirī*, حضوري *ḥuẓūrī*, (view) ديدار *dīdār*.
Present, بخشش *bakhshish* (f.), (in gram.) حال *ḥāl*: see Gift.
Preservation, بچاو *bachā'ō*, حفاظت *ḥifāẓat* (f.), آسرا *āsra*.
Press, (for oil) کولھو *kōlhū*, (for bookbinding) شکنجه *shikanja*, (for printing) چھاپني کي کل *chhāpnē kī kal*: see Crowd.
Pressure, (weight) داب *dāb*, چاپ *chāp*, (urgency) تقاضا *takāẓā*.
Presumption, (arrogance) ڈھٹھائي *ḍhiṭhā'ī*, گستاخي *gustākhī*: see Guess.
Pretence, بهانه *bahāna*, ساخت *sākht*. (f.) Pretension, دعوا *da'wā*.
Preterimperfect, ماضي استمراري *māẓī istimrārī*.
Preterite, ماضي *māẓī*, گذشته *guzashta*.
Preterperfect, ماضي قريب *māẓī karīb*.
Preterpluperfect, ماضي بعيد *māẓī ba'īd*.
Prevarication, چکر مکر *chakar-makar*, حيله حواله *ḥīla-ḥawāla*.
Prey, لوٹ *lūṭ* (f.), غنيمت *ghanīmat* (f.), (game) صيد *ṣaid*. (f.)
Price, مول *mōl*, قيمت *kīmat* (f.), بها *bahā*, (reward) اجر *ajr*.
Prick, چھيد *chhēd*, بندھ *bindh*. Prickle, کانٹا *kānṭā*, خار *khār*.
Pride, خود بيني *khud-bīnī*, غرور *ghurūr*, اهنکار *ahankār*.
Primogeniture, اول پيدائش *awwal paidā'ish* (f.), بڑائي *baṛā'ī*.
Principal, (head man) سردار *sardār*, رئيس *ra'īs*, (sum) پونجي *pūnjī*.

Principle, اصل *aṣl* (f.), جڑ *jaṛ* (f.), (tenet) راي *rā'ē* (f.): see Canon.
Print, نقش *naḳsh*, نشان *nishān*, چهاپ *chhāp*.
Prison, قيد خانه *ḳaid-ḳhāna*, بندیخانه *bandī-ḳhāna*, زندان *zindān*.
Prisoner, قيدي *ḳaid-ī*, بندهوا *bandhū'ā*, اسير *asīr*.
Privilege, مخصوص فايده *maḳhṣūṣ fā'ida*, حق *ḥaḳḳ*.
Privity, (secrecy) بهيد *bhēd*, (collusion) سازش *sāzish*. (f.)
Prize, (reward) انعام *in'ām*, (winnings) بازي *bāzī*: see Plunder.
Probe (surgeon's), جراح كي سلائي *jarrāḥ kī salā'ī*, ميل *mīl*. (f.)
Problem, سوال *suwāl*, مسله *masla*.
Proboscis, هاتهي كي سونڈ *hāthī kī sūnḍ*, خرطوم *ḳhurṭūm*.
Procedure, حركت *ḥarakat* (f.), چال *chāl* (f.), معامله *mu'āmala*.
Proceeding, Process, كام *kām*, كرتوت *kartut* (f.): see Method, Affair.
Proclamation, منادي *manādī*, (by drum) ڈهنڈهورا *ḍhanḍhōrā*.
Procuress, كٹني *kuṭnī*, دلاله *dallāla*. (f.) Procurer, بهڑوا *bhaṛwā*.
Prodigal, زياده خرچ كرنيوالا *ziyāda ḳharch karnē-wālā*, اڑاؤ *uṛā'ū*.
Produce, Product, Production, حاصل *ḥāṣil*, پيدائش *paidā'ish*. (f.)
Profit, فايده *fā'ida*, نفع *naf'*, لابه *lābh*, منافع *manāfi'*.
Progeny, اولاد *aulād* (f.), نسل *nasl* (f.), بنس *bans*.
Progress, Progression, پيشرواني *pēshrawānī*, ترقي *taraḳḳī*.
Prohibition, ممانعت *mumāna'at* (f.), منع *man'*.
Project, منصوبه *manṣūba*, تجويز *tajwīz* (f.): see Invention.
Promise, قول *ḳaul*, بچن *bachan*, اقرار *iḳrār*, وعده *wa'da*.
Promotion, بڑهتي *baṛhtī*, ترقي *taraḳḳī*, سرفرازي *sarfarāzī*.
Prong, كانٹا *kānṭā*, شاخ *shāḳh*, سول *sūl*.
Pronoun, ضمير *ẓamīr*, (demonst.) اسم اشاره *ism-i-ishāra*, (interrog.) حرف استفهام *ḥarf-i-istifhām*, (relat.) اسم موصول *ism-i-mauṣūl*.
Pronunciation, تلفظ *talaffuẓ*, مخرج *maḳhraj*, اچار *uchchār*.
Proof, آزمائش *āzmā'ish* (f.), (confirmation) اثبات *iṡbāt*, دليل *dalīl*. (f.)
Prop, تهوني *thūnī*, ٹيكن *ṭēkan*, ٹيك *ṭēk* (f.), پشت *pusht* (f.).
Property, خاصيت *ḳhaṣṣiyat* (f.), (possession) ملك *milk* (f.), مال *māl*.
Proportion, اندازه *andāza*, مقدار *miḳdār*, سڈولي *suḍaulī*.

Proposal, درخواست *darkhwāst* (f.). Proposition, مسله *masla.*

Proprietor, مالك *mālik,* خاوند *khāwind,* صاحب *ṣāḥib.*

Prose, نثر *naṣr* (f.), كلام منثور *kalām-i-manṣūr.*

Prosecution, (suit) قضيه *ḳaẓiya,* مقدمه *muḳaddama.*

Prosody, علم عروض *ilm-i-ārūẓ,* ميزان *mīzān.* (f.)

Prospect, (view) نظر *naẓar* (f.), مد نظر *madd-i-naẓar* : see Hope.

Prosperity, كاميابي *kāmyābī,* بختاوري *bakhtāwarī,* سعادت *sa'ādat.* (f.)

Prostitute, بيسوا *bēswā* (f.), چهنال *chhināl* (f.), قحبه *ḳaḥba.* (f.)

Protection, حمايت *ḥimāyat* (f.), بچاو *bachā'ō,* پرورش *parwarish.* (f.)

Protector, حامي *ḥāmī,* نگاهبان *nigāh-bān,* حافظ *ḥafiẓ.*

Provender, چاره *chāra,* دانه *dāna,* ليهنا *lēhna,* گهاس *ghās.* (f.)

Proverb, مثل *maṣal* (f.), كهاوت *kahāwat* (f.), ضرب‌المثل *ẓarbu-l-maṣal.*

Providence, (of God) خداي *khudā'ī,* رزاقي *razzāḳī* : see Foresight.

Provision, (food) كهانا *khānā,* غذا *ghiẓā* (f.) : see Preparation.

Proximity, قرب *ḳurb,* نزديكي *nazdīkī,* سميپي *samīpī.*

Prudence, حذر *ḥaẓar,* احتياط *iḥtiyāṭ* (f.), پيش بيني *pēsh-bīnī.*

Psalm, استت *astut* (f.), پاك سرود *pāk sarōd,* زبور *zabūr.* (f.)

Puberty, بلوغت *bulūghat* (f.), جواني *jawānī,* شباب *shabāb.*

The Public, خلق *khalḳ* (f.), خلايق *khalā'iḳ* (f.): see People.

Publication, اظهار *iẓ'hār,* (of a book) چهاپكي ظاهر كرنا *chhāpkē ẓāhir karnā.*

Pulley, چرخي *charkhī,* پهركي *phirkī,* گهرني *ghirnī.*

Pulpit, منبر *mimbar,* سنگهاسن *singhāsan.*

Pump, پچكا *pichakkā,* پچوكا *pachūkā,* بنبا *bambā.*

Pun, جگت *jugut* (f.), زٹل *zaṭal.* (f.)

Punch, (the instrument), چهيني *chhēnī* or چهيوني *chhē'ōnī.*

Puncheon, (instrument) چهاپ *chhāp* (f.): see Punch, Cask.

Puncture, چهيد *chhēd,* سوراخ *sūrākh.*

Punishment, سزا *sazā* (f.), عذاب *āẓāb,* سياست *siyāsat.* (f.)

Puppet (doll), گوڑيا *gūṛiyā,* پتلي *putlī.*

Purchase, خريد *kharīd* (f.), بساه *bisāh.* (f.)

Purchaser, خريدار *kharīdār*, گاهك *gāhak*, مشتري *mushtarī*. (m.)
Pureness, Purity, پاكي *pākī*, صفائي *ṣafā'ī*, نرملتا *nirmaltā*. (f.)
Purport, معني *ma'nī*, مقصد *maḳṣad*, مراد *murād*. (f.)
Purpose, اراده *irāda*, قصد *ḳaṣd*, نيت *nīyat* (f.), غرض *gharaẓ*. (f.)
Purse, تهيلي *thailī*, كيسه *kīsa*, صره *ṣurra*, توڑا *tōṛā*.
Pursuit, تعقب *ta'āḳḳub*, پيروي *pairawī*, رگيد *ragēd*. (f.)
Putty, قلعي كشته *ḳala'ī-i kushta*, لبي *lē'ī*, سريش *sarēsh* (?).
Pyramid, منار *manār*, مينار *mīnār*, گاودم *gāw-dum*. (f.)
Quadrangle, شكل چوگوشه *shakl-i-chaugōsha*.
Quadruped, چارپايه *chārpāya*, ستور *sutūr*.
Quality, صفت *ṣifat* (f.), اوصاف *auṣāf*, (rank) مرتبه *martaba*.
Quantity, مقدار *miḳdār*, (heap) ڈهير *ḍhēr*, قدر *ḳadr* (f.): see Part.
Quarantine, چلا *chillā*, (after the death of a relative, &c.) چاليسي *chālīsī*.
Quarrel, جهگڑا *jhagṛā*, قضيه *ḳaẓiya*, بگاڑ *bigāṛ*.
Quarry, پتهركي كان *patthar kī kān*, سنگستان *sangistān*.
Quarter, چوتهائي *chauthā'ī*, (district) محله *maḥalla*: see Abode, Pardon.
Quean, قطامه *ḳuṭṭāma*, فاجره *fājira*, زن فاحشه *zan-i fāḥisha*.
Query, Question, سوال *suwāl* پرسش *pursish* (f.), استفهام *istifhām*.
Quest, كهوج *khōj*, تلاش *talāsh* (f.), جست وجو *just-ō-jū*. (f.)
Quickness, شتابي *shitābī*, جلدي *jaldī*, چالاكي *chālākī*, تيزي *tēzī*.
Quietness, Quietude, سكون *sukūn*, آرام *ārām*, قرار *ḳarār*.
Quill, پر كا قلم *par kā ḳalam*, شهپر *shahpar*, (porcupine) كانٹا *kānṭā*.
Quintessence, خلاصه *khulāṣa*, ست *sat*, سار *sār*. (f.)
Quire, (of paper) دسته *dasta*, بيٹها *bīṭhā*, (choir) طائفه *ṭā'ifa*.
Quota, حصه *ḥiṣṣa*, بخرا *bakhrā*, بهري *bihrī*, بهره *bahra*.
Quotation, اقتباس *iḳtibās*, استخراج *istikhrāj*, داخله *dākhila* (?).
Quotient, حاصل *ḥāṣil*, مبلغ *mablagh*.
Race, دوڑ *dauṛ* (f.), دوڑادوڑي *dauṛā-dauṛī*: see Breed, Family.
Rack, (engine of torture) شكنجه *shikanja*: see Anguish.
Radiance, شعاع *shu'ā'* (f.), پرتو *partau*, تجلي *tajallī*, جوت *jōt*. (f.)
Rafter, برگا *bargā*, كانڈي *kānḍī*, كورو *kōrō*.

Rag, جهڑا *chithṛā,* لتا *lattā,* دهجي *dhajjī,* گودڑ *gūdaṛ.*

Rail, Railing, کٹهرا *kaṭharā,* کٹهگهرا *kaṭhgharā.*

Raillery, ٹهٹها *ṭhaṭṭhā,* مزاخ *mazākh,* ٹهٹهولي *ṭhaṭhōlī.*

Ramrod, گز *gaz,* ٹهسني *ṭhasnī.*

Rank, (row) قطار *kaṭār* (f.), صف *ṣaff* (f.), (degree) درجه *darja.*

Ransom, فدا *fidā* (f.), فديه *fidya,* نعلبندي *na*ʽ*lbandī.*

Rap, دهول *dhaul* (f.), ٹهپر *ṭhappar,* تماچا *tamāchā.*

Rapture, وجد *wajd,* جذب *jazb,* حال *ḥāl,* وجدان *wajdān.*

Rascal, حرامزاده *ḥarām-zāda,* مردك *mardak:* see Base.

Rate, (price) قيمت *ḳīmat* (f.), بهاو *bhā'ō,* نرخ *nirkh:* see Tax.

Ratio, اندازه *andāza,* بهاو *bhā'ō,* نرخ *nirkh.*

Ray, كرن *kiran.* (f.) Rays of the sun, شعاع *shu'ā*ʽ. (f.)

Razor, استره *ustura,* چهرا *chhurā.*

Readiness, تياري *taiyārī,* آمادگي *āmādagī:* see Alacrity.

Ready money, نقد *naḳd,* روك *rōk,* روكڑ *rōkaṛ.* (f.)

Rear, پيچها *pīchhā,* پچهواڑا *pichhwāṛā,* پچهاڑي *pichhāṛī.*

Receipt, (reception) پانا *pānā,* (for money, &c.) رسيد *rasīd.* (f.)

Receptacle, گهر *ghar,* خانه *khāna,* جگهه *jagah.* (f.)

Reception, گرفتگي *giriftagī,* اخذ *akhz,* يافت *yāft.* (f.)

Recess, روانگي *rawānagī,* رحلت *riḥlat,* (respite) وقفه *waḳfa,* ناغه *nāgha.*

Recipe (medical prescription), نسخه *nuskha.*

Reckoning, گنتي *gintī,* حساب *ḥisāb,* شمار *shumār.*

Recollection, ياد *yād* (f.), ياداوري *yādāwarī,* سده *sudh.* (f.)

Recommendation, سفارش *sifārish* (f.), تقريب *taḳrīb.* (f.)

Record, دفتر *daftar,* تواريخ *tawārīkh.*

Recovery, بازيافت *bāz-yāft* (f.), (from illness) شفا *shifā.* (f.)

Recreation, بهلاو *bahlā'ō,* سير *sair* (f.): see Amusement.

Recruit, (soldier) نيا سپاهي *nayā sipāhī,* (supply) سربراهي *sarbarāhī.*

Redemption, چهٹكارا *chhuṭkārā,* استخلاص *istikhlāṣ.*

Redness, سرخي *surkhī,* لالي *lālī,* (pale) گرائي *gurā'ī.*

Redress, چاره سازي *chāra-sāzī,* حمايت *ḥimāyat* (f.), تدارك *tadāruk.*

Reel, (frame) اٹیرن *aṭēran*, (dance) ایک قسم کا ناچ *ēk ḳism kā nāch.*

Reference, رجوع *rujū**, لگاؤ *lagā'ō*, علاقہ *ālāḳa*, نسبت *nisbat.* (f.)

Reflection, (throwing back) انعکاس *in'ikās*, عکس *aks*: see Thought.

Reform, Reformation, اصلاح *iṣlāḥ* (f.), تصحیح *taṣḥīḥ.* (f.)

Refuge, پناہ *panāh* (f.), امن *amn*, آسرا *āsrā*, ملاذ *malāẕ.*

Refulgence, تجلي *tajallī*, جلوہ *jalwa*, نور *nūr*, جوت *jōt.* (f.)

Refusal, انکار *inkār*, نفي *nafī* (m.), ابا *ibā*, منع *man**.

Regard, ملاحظہ *mulāḥaẓa*, توجہ *tawajjuh* (f.), (look) نظر *naẓar.* (f.)

With Regard to, بنسبت *ba-nisbat*, حق میں *ḥaḳḳ mēn.*

Region, ملک *mulk*, سرزمین *sar-zamīn* (f.), اقلیم *iḳlīm.*

Register, (book) دفتر *daftar*, (officer), سررشتہ دار *sar-rishta-dār.*

Regret, افسوس *afsōs*, حسرت *ḥasrat* (f.), تاسف *ta'assuf*: see Grief.

Regulation, انتظام *intiẓām*, بندوبست *bandōbast*: see Law.

Rein (of a bridle), عنان *inān* (f.), باگ *bāg* (f.), راس *rās.* (f.)

Reiteration, تکرار *takrār* (f.), دوہراو *dōhrā'ō.*

Relation, (recital) تقریر *taḳrīr* (f.), (affinity) نسبت *nisbat.* (f.)

Relative, رشتہ دار *rishta-dār*, قرابتي *ḳarābatī*, خویش *khwēsh.*

Reliance, اعتماد *i***timād*, اعتبار *i***tibār*, آسرا *āsrā*, آس *ās.* (f.)

Relief, مدد *madad* (f.), پشتي *pushtī*, تخفیف *takhfīf.* (f.)

Religion, دین *dīn*, مذہب *maẕ'hab*, دہرم *dharam*: see Piety.

Relish, مزہ *maza*, لذت *lazzat* (f.), سواد *sawād*, خوشي *khushī.*

Remainder, باقي *bāḳī*, بچتي *bachtī*, تتمہ *tatimma*, مابقي *mābaḳī.*

Remark, قول *ḳaul*, بات *bāt* (f.), (note) شرح *sharḥ* (f.): see Regard.

Remedy, چارہ *chāra*, علاج *ilāj* (f.), اپاي *upā'e*, تدارک *tadāruk.*

Remembrance, یاد *yād* (f.), چیت *chēt*, سدھ *sudh.* (f.)

Remorse, پچھتاوا *pachhtāwā*, افسوس *afsōs*, تاسف *ta'assuf.*

Rencounter, مقابلہ *muḳābala*, براز ناگاہ *barāz-i nāgāh.*

Rennet (for curdling), پنیر مایہ *panīr-māya*, مایۂ شیر *māya-i-shīr.*

Renown, نام *nām*, ناموري *nām-warī*, شہرت *shuhrat.* (f.)

Rent, (split) چاک *chāk*, چیر *chīr*, (hire) کرایہ *kirāya*, خراج *khirāj.*

Repentance, پچھتاوا *pachhtāwā*, پشیماني *pashēmānī*: see Regret.

Repetition, تکرار *takrār* (f.), دوہراو *dōhrā'ō*, (rehearsal) بیان *bayān.*

Report, خبر *khabar* (f.), (rumour) شہرہ *shuhra*, (sound) آواز *āwāz*. (f.)
Repose, آرام *ārām*, آسائش *āsā'ish* (f.), چین *chain*, سکھ *sukh*.
Reprehension, Reprimand, ملامت *malāmat* (f.), تاڑنا *tāṛnā*.
Reproof, طعن *ta*ʿ*n*, گوشمالی *gōsh-mālī*, سرزنش *sar-zanish*. (f.)
Reputation, نیکنامی *nēk-nāmī*, آبرو *ābrū* (f.), نام *nām*.
Request, درخواست *darkhwāst* (f.), التماس *iltimās*: see Question.
Research, تلاش *talāsh* (f.), تفتیش *taftīsh* (f.), کھوج *khōj*.
Residence, گھر *ghar*, مقام *maḳām*, بودوباش *būd-ō-bāsh*. (f.)
Resin, Rosin, دھونا *dhūnā*, رال *rāl* (f.), دھوپ *dhūp*. (f.)
Resolution, Resolve, قصد مصمم *ḳaṣd-i-muṣammam*.
Resource, چارہ *chāra*, علاج *ʿilāj*, اپائے *upā'ē*, حکمت *ḥikmat*. (f.)
Respect, تعظیم *ta*ʿ*ẓīm* (f.), تکریم *takrīm* (f.), ادب *adab*: see Relation.
Respite, وقفہ *waḳfa*, قتل کا وقفہ *ḳatl kā waḳfa*, ناغہ *nāgha*.
Rest, سکون *sukūn*, (quiet) آرام *ārām*, قرار *ḳarār*: see Remainder.
Result, حاصل *ḥāṣil*, ثمرہ *s̤amara*: see Consequence.
Resurrection, بعث و نشر *ba*ʿ*s̤ ō nashr*: see Judgment (day of).
Retaliation, Revenge, انتقام *intiḳām*, عوض *ʿiwaẓ*, بدلا *badlā*.
Reticle, چھوٹا جال *chhōṭā jāl*, چھوٹی تھیلی *chhōṭī thailī*.
Retinue, جلو *jilau* (f.), سواری *sawārī*, تزک *tuzuk*, قور *ḳōr*. (f.)
Retirement, Retreat, خلوت *khalwat* (f.), خلوتگاہ *khalwatgāh*. (f.)
Revenue, آمد *āmad* (f.), مداخل *madākhil*, محصول *maḥṣūl*.
Reverence, تکریم *takrīm* (f.), احترام *iḥtirām*, (bow) تسلیم *taslīm*. (f.)
Reverse, (opposite side) پھیر *phēr*, عکس *ʿaks*: see Adversity.
Revolution, (going round) گردش *gardish* (f.), (change) انقلاب *inḳilāb*.
Reward, اجر *ajr*, جزا *jazā* (f.), ثواب *s̤awāb*, بخشش *bakhshish*. (f.)
Rhetoric, علم کلام یا بلاغت *ʿilm-i-kalām* or *-balāghat*.
Rhyme, قافیہ *ḳāfiya*, ردیف *radīf*, سجع *saj*ʿ, تک *tuk*. (f.)
Ribaldry, فحش *fuḥsh*, پھکڑ *phakkaṛ*, پوچ *pūch*.
Riband, Ribbon, ابریشم کا فیتہ *ābrēsham kā fīta*, قور *ḳōr*. (f.)
Riches, دولت *daulat* (f.), مال *māl*, مال متاع *māl matā*ʿ. (f.)
Rick, تودہ *tūda*, ٹال *ṭāl*, ٹالا *ṭālā*, ڈھیر *ḍhēr*, انبار *ambār*.

Riddle (enigma), پهيلي *pahēlī*, معما *mu'ammā*, چستان *chistān*.
Ridicule, هنسي *hansī*, مضحكه *maẓ'ḥaka*, ٹهٹهولي *ṭhaṭhōlī*.
Right, حق *ḥakk*, دعوا *da'wā*, (hand) دهينا *dahīnā*: see Property.
Ring (circle), حلقه *ḥalḳa*, كنڈلي *kunḍlī*: see under *Apparel, Dress*.
Ringleader, سر حلقه *sar-ḥalḳa*, سرگروه *sar-gurōh*: see Chief.
Ringlet (small ring), چهوٹي انگوٹهي *chhōṭī angūṭhī*: see Curl.
Riot, هلڑ *hullaṛ*, هنگامه *hangāma*, خر مستي *khar-mastī*.
Ripeness, پختگي *pukhtagī*, پكائي *pakā'ī*: see Perfection.
Risk, خطره *khaṭra*, جوكهم *jōkhim* (f.), چنتا *chintā*. (f.)
Rite, آئين دين *ā'īn-i dīn*, ريت *rīt* (f.), طريق *ṭarīḳ* (f.), رسم *rasm*.
Rivet, ميخ *mēkh* (f.), پچري *pachrī*, اندهيري *andhērī* (?): see Nail.
Road, رسته *rasta*, سڑك *saṛak* (f.), راه *rāh* (f.), باٹ *bāṭ*. (f.)
Roar, گرج *garj* (f.), گونج *gūnj* (f.), غرش *ghurrish*. (f.)
Robbery, چوري *chōrī*, دزدي *duzdī*, ڈكيتي *ḍakaitī*, راهزني *rāhzanī*.
Rocket, (used in battle) بان *bān*, (skyrocket) هوائي *hawā'ī*.
Rogue, حرام زاده *ḥarām-zāda*, ٹهگ *ṭhag*, لچا *luchchā*.
Room, (space, place) جگهه *jagah* (f.), مقام *maḳām*: see Chamber.
Roost, اڈا *aḍḍā*, چكس *chakkas*, بسيرا *basērā*.
Root, جڑ *jaṛ* (f.), مول *mūl*, بيخ *bēkh* (f.): see Origin.
Rope, رسي *rassī*, جيوڑي *jē'oṛī*, ڈوري *ḍōrī*, رسن *rasan*.
Rosary, (of beads) تسبيح *tasbīḥ* (f.), (rose bed) گلابستان *gulābistān*.
Round, (turn) گردش *gardish* (f.), دور *daur*: see Circle, Ring.
Row, صف *ṣaff* (f.), قطار *ḳaṭār* (f.), قور *ḳōr* (f.), پانت *pānt*. (f.)
Rubbish, كركٹ *kurkuṭ* (f.), خاشاك *khāshāk*, كوڑا *kūṛā*.
Ruffian, حرامي *ḥarāmī*, چنڈال *chanḍāl*, كٹر *kaṭar*, جلاد *jallād*.
Ruin, خرابي *kharābī*, پائمالي *pā'ēmālī*, تباهي *tabāhī*.
Rule, قانون *ḳānūn*, قاعده *ḳā'ida*, (sway) حكم *ḥukm*, عمل *'amal*.
Rumour, افواه *afwāh* (f.), شهرت *shuhrat* (f.), گپ *gap*. (f.)
Rupture, درار *darār*, ٹوٹ *ṭūṭ* (f.), (hernia) انڈ كوس *anḍ-kōs*.
Rust, زنگ *zang*, زنگار *zangār*, مورچه *mōrcha*, ميل *mail*. (f.)
Sabre, شمشير *shamshēr* (f.), تيغا *tēghā*, صمصام *ṣamṣām*. (f.)
Sack, (bag) گون *gōn* (f.), بورا *bōrā*, (plunder) تاخت تاراج *takht-tārāj*.

Sackcloth, ٹات *ṭāṭ*, میکھلي *mēkhlī*, ماتمي ٹات *mātamī ṭāṭ*.

Sacrifice, قربان *ḳurbān*, بل *bal*, ذبح *ẕabḥ* (f.), فدا *fidā*. (f.)

Saddle, زین *zīn*, کاٹھي *kāṭhī*, (pack) پالان *pālān*, (camel's) کجاوہ *ḳajāwa*.

Sadness, اداسي *udāsī*, غم *gham*, ملال *malāl*, دلگیري *dil-gīrī*.

Safety, سلامتي *salāmatī*, امن *amn*, بچاؤ *bachā'ō*, رچھا *rachchhā*. (f.)

Sage (person), دانا آدمي *dānā ādmī*, عالم *ālim*, فاضل *fāẓil*, من *muni*.

Sago, ساگودانہ *sāgū-dāna*. (From the pith of the Sagus Rumphii).

Saint, ولي *walī* (m.), سدھ *sidh*, پیر *pīr*, غوث *ghauṣ*.

Sake, واسطہ *wāsṭa*, سبب *sabab*, خاطر *khāṭir*, (f.), ھیت *hēt* or *hētu*.

For the sake, واسطي *wāsṭē*, سبب *sabab*, خاطر *khāṭir* (f.), لیي *liyē*.

Salad, (English) سلاتہ *salāta* (?).

Salary, سالیانہ *sāliyāna*, وظیفہ *waẓīfa*, تنخواہ *tankhwāh*. (f.)

Sale, بکاؤ *bikā'ō*, بکري *bikrī*, فروخت *farōkht* (f.): see Auction.

Salvation, نجات *najāt* (f.), مکت *mukt* (f.), رستگاري *rastagārī*.

Salutation, سلام *salām*, کورنش *kōrnish* (f.), بندگي *bandagī*.

Sample, نمونہ *namūna*, بانگي *bāngī*, مادري *mādarī*.

Sandal, الگا *algā*, کھرپا *kharpā*, (pair of sandals) نعلین *na'lain* (?).

Sandal wood, Sanders, چندن *chandan*, صندل *ṣandal*.

Sap, رس *ras*, عرق *araḳ*, پاني *pānī* (m.), دودھ *dūdh*.

Sarsaparilla (Smilax, sp.?), عشبہ *ushba*, مکوي *makō'ē*.

Sash (for dress), جال *jāl*, پٹکا *paṭkā*, سیلي *sēlī*, بدھي *baddhī*.

Satiety, اگھاي *aghā'ī*, بھرتي *bhartī*, سیري *sērī*, چھکاي *chhakā'ī*.

Satin, اطلس *aṭlas*, پیلام *pīlām*, تافتہ *tāfta*, ساٹن *sāṭin* (?).

Satire, ھجو *hajō* (f.), بھنڈوا *bhanḍauwā*, نندا *nindā*. (f.)

Satisfaction, (content) خاطرجمعي *khāṭir-jam'ī*: see Retaliation.

Saturday, سنیچار *sanīchar*, شنبہ *shamba*, ھفتہ *hafta*.

Sauce, چاشني *chāshnī*, چٹني *chaṭnī*, بنجن *binjan*.

Saucer, تشتري *tashtarī*, سکوري *sakōrī*, پرچ *pirich* (?).

Savour, بو *bō* or *bū* (f.), گندھ *gandh* (f.), مزہ *maza*, سواد *sawād*.

Saw, کرانت *karānt*, آرہ *āra*, آرا *ārā*, منشار *minshār*.

Saying, کہاوت *kahāwat* (f.), مثل *maṣal* (f.), بات *bāt*. (f.)

Scab, کهوتهي *khūṭhī*, کهسرا *khasrā*, چٿ *chaṭ* (f.), پپڙي *papṛī*.

Scabbard, نيام *niyām*, کاٿهي *kāṭhī*, غلاف *ghilāf*, ميان *miyān*.

Scaffold, مچان *machān*, دونجا *daunjā*, پايتهه *pāyaṭh*, پاڙ *pāṛ*. (f.)

Scale (of a balance), پلا *pallā*, پلڙا *palṛā*, (fish) چهلکا *chhilkā*.

Scalp, کهوپري کا چمڙا *khōprī kā chamṛā*.

Scammony, سقمونيا *saḳmūniyā*. (From Convolvulus scammonea.)

Scandal, عيب *āib*, داغ *dāgh*, کلنک *kalank*, بدنامي *badnāmī*.

Scapula, کاندهي کي هڏي *kāndhē kī haḍḍī*.

Scarceness, Scarcity, کمتي *kamtī*, کميابي *kamyābī*, تنگي *tangī*.

Scarf, اوڙهني *ōṛhnī*, ايکپٿه *ēk-paṭṭa*, دوپٿه *dō-paṭṭa*, اپرنا *uparnā*.

Scene, ديد *dīd*, مد نظر *madd-i-nazar*, (theatre) اکهاڙا *akhāṛā*.

Scent, بو *bō* or *bū* (f.), باس *bās*, گندهه *gandh* (f.), مهک *mahak*. (f.)

Sceptre, عصاي شاهي *āṣā-i-shāhī*, قبضهٔ سلطنت *ḳabẓa-i-salṭanat*.

Scheme, (plan) نقشه *naḳsha*, (contrivance) حکمت *ḥikmat* (f.): see Project.

School, مکتب *maktab*, مدرسه *madrasa*, دبستان *dabistān*.

Science, علم *īlm*, بديا *bidyā* (f.), حکمت *ḥikmat* (f.), فن *fann*.

Scissors, مقراض *miḳrāẓ*, قينچي *ḳainchī*, کترني *katarnī*.

Sconce, شمعدان *sham*dān*, ديوارگير *dīwār-gīr*, جهاڙ *jhāṛ*: see Head.

Scope, (space) جگهه *jagah* (f.), پهيلاو *phailā'ō*, (aim) مقصد *maḳṣud*.

Score, (notch) کهندانا *khandānā*, (line) خط *khaṭṭ*: see Account, Twenty.

Scorn, استهزا *istihzā*, اهانت *ihānat* (f.), حقارت *iḳārat*. (f.)

Scoundrel, قرمساق *ḳurramsāḳ*, شهدا *shuhdā*, بد ذات *bad-ẕāt*.

Scourge, کوڙا *kōṛā*, تازيانه *tāziyāna*: see Punishment, Affliction.

Scout, جاسوس *jāsūs*, بهيديا *bhēdiyā*, هرکاره *harkāra*.

Scrape, تنگي *tangī*, کشمکش *kashmakash* (f.), جهنجهٿ *jhanjhaṭ*.

Screen, Skreen, ٿٿي *ṭaṭṭī*, جهانپ *jhāmp*, قنات *ḳanāt*. (f.)

Screw, پيچ *pēch*, مڙوڙي *maṛōṛī*: see Nail.

Scrotum, فوطه *fōṭa*, پوته *pōta*.

Scrutiny, تلاش *talāsh* (f.), جستوجو *justōjū* (f.): see Examination.

Scuffle, کهيچاکهينچي *khaiñchā-khaiñchī*, دهول دهپا *dhaul-dhappā*.

Sculpture, نقاشي *naḳḳāshī*, (work of) کهودا هوا نقشه *khōdā hū'ā naḳsha*.

Scurf, بفا *bafā* (f.), پپڑي *papṛī*, رِسي *rūsī*, سبوسه *sabūsa*.

Seal (stamp), مهر *muhr* (f.), چهاپ *chhāp* (f.), خاتم *khātim*.

Sealing-wax, لاکه *lākh*, لاه *lāh*.

Seam, دوخت *dōkht* (f.), سيون *sīwan*, جوڑ *jōṛ*, درز *darz*.

Season, موسم *mausim*, رت *rit* or *rut* (f.), فصل *faṣl* (f.), ايام *aiyām*.

Seat, (chair) چوکي *chaukī*, (mansion) مکان *makān*, (place) مقام *maḳām*.

Secession, اعتزال *i*tizāl*, پهوٹ *phūṭ* (f.), انحراف *inḥirāf*.

Secrecy, اخفا *ikhfā*, پرده *parda*, رازداري *rāz-dārī*, خلوت *khalwat*. (f.)

Secret, راز *rāz*, سر *sirr*, بهيد *bhēd*, پيٹ کي بات *pēṭ kī bāt*.

Sect, ذات *ẕāt* (f.), فرقه *firḳa*, جماعت *jamā'ăt* (f.), مذهب *maẕ'hab*.

Section, قطعه *ḳiṭ'ă* (vulg. *ḳaṭ'ă*), کهنڈ *khanḍ*, جز *juz*, فصل *faṣl*. (f.)

Sedition, هنگامه *hangāma*, بلوا *balwā*, فساد *fasād*, دنگا *dangā*.

Seduction, اغوا *ighwā*, بهٹکاؤ *bhaṭkā'ō*, بدراهسازي *badrāhsāzī*.

Seed, بيج *bīj*, تخم *tukhm*, بهن *bihan*, (sperm) نطفه *nuṭfa*.

Segment, ٹکڑا *ṭukṛā*, (of a circle) دائرے کا ايک حصه *dā'irē kā ēk ḥiṣṣa*.

Selection, انتخاب *intikhāb*, چهانٹ *chhānṭ* (f.), باچه *bāchh*. (f.)

Self, اپ *āp*, خود *khud*, آپني *āp-nē*, ذات *ẕāt* (f.), نفس *nafs*.

Semicircle, نيمدائره *nīm-dā'ira*, ادهگهيرا *adh-ghērā*.

Senna, سنا *sanā*, سنامکي *sanā-makkī*.

Sense, Sensation, حس *ḥiss*, اوسان *ausān*, سده *sudh* (f.): see Meaning.

Sentence (decision), فتوي *fatwạ*, حکم *ḥukm*, قضا *ḳaẓā*. (f.)

Sentence (period in writing), جمله *jumla*, فقره *fiḳra*.

Sentiment, فکر *fikr*, رائے *rā'ē* (f.), ظن *ẓann*, بوجه *būjh*. (f.)

Sepulchre, گور *gōr* (f.), قبر *ḳabr* (f.), مزار *mazār*, تربت *turbat*. (f.)

Sergeant, (military) دفعدار *daf*dār*, (at law) وکيل *wakīl*.

Series, سرشته *sarishta*, سلسله *silsila*, دور *daur*.

Sermon, وعظ *wa*ẓ*, خطبه *khuṭba*, نصيحت *naṣīḥat*. (f.)

Service, نوکري *naukarī*, چاکري *chākarī*, خدمت *khidmat*. (f.)

Set, گنج *ganj*, جوڑ *jōṛ*, ميل *mēl*, طائفه *ṭā'ifa*.

Seton, ناته *nāth*, گل *gul*.

Settlement, بند و بست *band-ō-bast*, انفصال *infiṣāl*: see Abode.

Sex, لنگ *ling*, جنس *jins* (f.), ذات *ẕāt* (f.), جات *jāt*. (f.)

Shackles, زنجير *zanjīr* (f.), بيڑي *bēṛī*, قيد *ḳaid* (f.), بند *band*.

Shade, چهانو *chhāṅw* (f.), سايه *sāya*: see Darkness, Shelter.

Shadow, پرچهائين *parchhā'īṅ* (f.), عكس *ʿaks*: see Protection.

Shaft, (column) ستون *sitūn*, (pit) کهانکهر *khānkhar*: see Arrow.

Sham, بناوٹ *banāwaṭ* (f.), پيکهنا *pēkhnā*, جهوٹه *jhūṭh*.

Shambles, مسلخ *maslakh*, قصابخانه *ḳaṣṣāb-khāna*.

Shank, پهلي *phillī*, نرهڑ *narhaṛ*, (of a tool) ڈنڈي *ḍanḍī*.

Shape, شکل *shakl* (f.), صورت *ṣūrat* (f.), قطع *ḳaṭʿ*. (f.)

Share, بانٹ *bānṭ*, حصه *ḥiṣṣa*, (plough-) پهال *phāl*, توڑا *tōṛā*.

Shark, هانگر *hāngar*, نهنگ *nihang*, گراه *grāh*: see Artful.

Sheet, (cloth) چادر *chādar* (f.), (of paper) فرد *fard* (f.), تاو *ta'o*, تخته *takhta*.

Shell, سيپ *sīp* (f.), گهونگا *ghōngā*, کوڑي *kauṛī*: see Case, Husk.

Shelter, بچاو *bachā'ō*, پناه *panāh* (f.), آڑ *āṛ* (f.), سايه *sāya*.

Shift, ٹال *ṭāl* (f.), حيله حواله *ḥīla-ḥawāla*: see Contrivance, Shirt.

Shillishalli, آگا پيچها *āgā-pīchhā*, پس و پيش *pas-ō-pēsh*.

Shot, (shooting) پهينک *phēnk* (f.), ضرب *ẓarb* (f.), (bullet) گولي *gōlī*.

Shroud, کفن *kafan*, لفافه *lifāfa*: see Shelter.

Shutter, (of a window) جهلمل *jhilmil*, چلون *chilwan*, چک *chik* (f.), (of a door) کيواڑ *kēwāṛ*, (matted) ٹٹي *ṭaṭṭī*, جهانپ *jhāmp*.

Sickness, بيماري *bīmārī*, آزار *āzār*, مرض *maraẓ*, روگ *rōg*.

Side, پهلو *pahlū*, پانجر *pānjar*, طرف *ṭaraf* (f.), (party) فرقه *firḳa*: (on this side) اس طرف *is ṭaraf* (f.), (on all sides) چارون اور *chārōṅ ōr*.

Siege, محاصره *muḥāṣara*, گهيرا *ghērā*, گرداوري *girdāwarī*.

Sigh, آه *ah* (f.), هائي *hā'ē* (f.), سانس *sāṅs* (f.), دريغ *darēgh*.

Sign, علامت *ʿalāmat* (f.), نشان *nishān*, (hint) اشاره *ishāra*, ايما *īmā*. (f.)

Signal, اشارت *ishārat* (f.), جناو *janā'ō*, دليل *dalīl*. (f.)

Signature, دستخط *dast-khaṭṭ*, لکهاوٹ *likhāwaṭ* (f.): see Mark.

Signification, معني *maʿnī*, ارته *arth*, مضمون *maẓmūn*.

Silence, خاموشي *khāmōshī*, سکوت *sukūt* (f.), مون *maun*.

Silk, (thread) ابريشم *abrēsham*, (cloth) ريشمي كپڑا *rēshmī kapṛā*.

Silliness, بهولاپن *bhōlā-pan*, اناڑپن *anāṛ-pan*, نادانی *nādānī*.

Similarity, برابري *barābarī*, مساوات *musāwāt* (f.) : see Likeness.

Simile, مثل *maṣal* (f.), مثال *miṣāl* (f.), تشبيح *tashbīḥ*. (f.)

Simpleton, ضعيف العقل *ẓa'īfu-l-ākl*, مورکه *mūrakh*.

Simplicity, نرائي *nirā'ī*, سادگي *sādagī* : see Folly.

Sin, گناه *gunāh*, پاپ *pāp*, جرم *jurm*, معصيت *ma'ṣiyat*. (f.)

Singer, گويا *gawaiyā*, سرودي *sarōdī*, گائِن *ga'in*, کلاونت *kalāwant*.

Singing, گان *gān*, سرود *sarōd*, تغني *taghannī* : see Song.

A Sink, پنبهاؤ *panbahā'ō*, نالي *nālī*, پتال مهري *patāl muhrī*.

Sinner, گناهگار *gunāh-gār*, پاپي *pāpī*, بدکار *badkār*, عاصي *āṣī*.

Sir, صاحب *ṣāḥib*, ميان *miyāṅ*, بابو *bābū*, جي *jī*.

Sire, بابا *bābā*, پادشاهون کا ايک خطاب *pādshāhōṅ kā ēk khiṭāb*.

Sirius (the star in the great dog), شعري *shi'rā* or *shi'rī*.

Sirname, گهراني کا خطاب يا لقب *gharānē kā khiṭāb* or *lakab*.

Sirup, شيره *shīra*, رب *rub*, راب *rāb* (f.), ميٹها رس *mīṭhā ras*.

Site, Situation, جگه *jagah* (f.), ٹهکانا *ṭhikānā* : see Condition.

Sitting, نشست *nishast* (f.), بيٹهک *baiṭhak* (f.), جلوس *julūs*.

Size, مقدار *mikdār*, ڈيل *ḍīl*, قد *kadd* : see Bulk, Starch.

Skein, پهينٹي *phēnṭī*, آنٹي *ānṭī*, کلاوه *kalāwa*, لرچها *larchhā*.

Skeleton, ٹهٹهري *ṭhaṭhrī*, تڈا *tiḍḍā*.

Sketch, نقشه *naksha*, سانچا *sānchā*, کهرا *kharrā*.

Skewer, سيخچه *sīkhcha*, سيخ *sīkh*.

Skill, شعور *shu'ūr*, رسائي *rasā'ī*, هنر *hunar*, گن *gun*.

Skirt, کناره *kināra*, دامن *dāman*, ذيل *zail*.

Skylight, تابدان *tābdān*, روشندان *raushan-dān*, جهروکها *jharōkhā*.

Slander, تهمت *tuhmat* (f.), بندش *bandish* (f.), غيبت *ghībat*. (f.)

Slavery, غلامي *ghulāmī*, لونڈيپنا *launḍī-panā*.

Sleep, نيند *nīnd* (f.), خواب *khwāb*, اونگهائي *ūnghā'ī* : see Rest.

Sleeve, آستين *āstīn* (f.), خريطه *kharīṭa*, هتها *hatthā*.

Slight, (indignity) خفت *khiffat* (f.), (sleight) شعبده *shu'bada*.

Sliness, سيانپن *siyān-pan*, چترائي *chaturā'ī*, عيارگي *āiyargī*.

Slope, ڈھال *ḍhāl*, اتار *utār*, سرازيري *sarāzērī*.

Sloth, سستي *sustī*, کاهلي *kāhilī*, اسکت *askat* (f.), الس *alas*.

Slough, (of a snake) کينچلي *kēnchlī*, (of a sore) چهچڙا *chhichṛā*.

Slowness, آهستگي *āhistagī*, ڈھيل *ḍhīl* (f.), سستي *sustī*, مجهولي *majhūlī*.

Sluice, مهري *muhrī*, خوراب *khurāb*: see Drain.

Slumber, اونگهاي *ūnghā'ī*, کچي نيند *kachchī nīnd*: see Sleep.

A Slut, پهوهڑ *phūhaṛ* (f.), اناڑن *anāṛin* (f.), چڑيل *chuṛail*. (f.)

Smallness, چهوٹائي *chhōṭā'ī*, خوردي *khurdī*, کوچکي *kūchakī*.

Smell, سونگه *sūngh* (f.), (odour) گندھ *gandh* (f.), بو *bō* (f.), باس *bās*. (f.)

Smile, مسکراهٹ *muskurāhaṭ* (f.), تبسم *tabassum*.

Smut, (spot) کالک *kālak*, (obscenity), خرافات *khurāfāt* (f.): see Mildew.

Snare, دام *dām*, پهاندا *phāndā*, (dakh. also) سرک *sarak*.

Sneer, ناک چڑهي *nāk-chaṛhī*, استهزا *istihzā*, ٹهيسرا *ṭhēsrā*.

Snout, تهوتهني *thūthnī* (?), (elephant's) سونڈ *sūnḍ* (f.), (crocodile's) تومري *tūmrī*.

Snowdrop (Galanthus nivalis), گل چاندني *gul-i-chāndnī*. (?)

Snuff, (of a candle) گل *gul*, (the powder) ناس *nās* (f.), سونگهني *sūnghnī*.

Snuffbox, ناس‌دان *nās-dān*.

Soap, صابون *ṣābūn*, سکليکرم *suklīkarm*.

Sobriety, پرهيزگاري *parhēzgārī*, هوشياري *hōshyārī*: see Moderation.

Society, انس *uns*, صحبت *ṣuḥbat* (f.), مشارکت *mushārakat* (f.): see Company.

Soda, کهار *khār*, ايک قسم کي سجي مٹي *ēk ḳism kī sajjī miṭṭī*.

Softness, نرمي *narmī*, کوملتا *kōmaltā* (f.), ملايمت *mulāyamat*. (f.)

Solicitation, درخواست *darkhwāst* (f.), طلب *ṭalab* (f.), منت *minnat*. (f.)

Solitude, تنهاي *tanhā'ī*, اکلاي *iklā'ī*: see Desert, Retirement.

Solution, پگهلاو *pighlā'ō*, گلاو *galā'ō*, حل *ḥall*: see Explanation.

Somnolency, نندا‌س *nindās* (f.), خواب آلودگي *khwāb-ālūdagī*.

Song, گیت *gīt*, گان *gān*, سرود *sarōd*, نغمه *naghma*, راگ *rāg*.

Sorrow, افسوس *afsōs*, غم *gham*, کڑهن *kuṛhan* (f.): see Grief.

Sort, قسم *ḳism* (f.), بهانت *bhānt* (f.), طرح *ṭaraḥ* (f.), جنس *jins*. (f.)

Sound, آواز *āwāz* (f.), صدا *ṣadā* (f.), آهٹ *āhaṭ*, بانگ *bāng*. (f.)

Space, عرصه *ărsa*, فاصله *fāṣila*: see Room, Distance, Interval.

Span, بالشت *bālisht* (f.), بتا *bittā*, وجب *wajab*, بلاند *bilānd*. (f.)

Spasm, جکڑ *jakaṛ*, اینٹه *ainṭh* (f.), پیچش *pēchish* (f.): see Twist.

Spawn, مچهلیون اور مینڈکون کي انڈي *machhliyōn aur mēnḍakōn kē anḍē*.

Speaker, متکلم *mutakallim*, بولویا *bōlwaiyā*: see President.

Specimen, نمونه *namūna*, بانگي *bāngī*, مادري *mādarī*.

Speck, داغ *dāgh*, چٹکارا *chiṭkārā*, (in the eye) پهولي *phūlī*.

Spectacle, تماشا *tamāshā*, عجب نمائش *ăjab numā'ish*.

Spectacles, چشمه *chashma*, چشمک *chashmak*, عینک *ăinak*. (f.)

Spectre, سایه *sāya*, بهوت *bhūt*, شیطان *shaiṭān*.

Speech, زبان *zubān* (f.), بولي *bōlī*, نطق *nuṭḳ*, بهاکها *bhākhā*. (f.)

Speed, جلدي *jaldī*, هڑبڑي *haṛbaṛī*, شتابي *shitābī*.

Spell, منتر *mantar*, جادو *jādū*: see Turn, Time.

Spendthrift, اڑاؤ *uṛā'ū*, فضول خرچ *fazūl-kharch*.

Sperm, مني *manī*, دهات *dhāt* (f.), بیج *bīj*: see Seed.

Sphere, see Globe. Spheroid, بیضوي چیز *baizawī chīz*.

Spike, (of corn) بال *bāl* (f.), خوشه *khōsha*, (nail) میخ *mēkh*.

Spindle, تکلا *taklā*, تکوا *takū'ā*, چمرکه *chamrakh*.

Spinning, چرخ زني *charkh-zanī*, (-wheel) چرخا *charkhā*.

Spirits, (liquors) شراب *sharāb* (f.), تیز عرق *tēz ăraḳ*: see Mirth.

Splendour, جلوه *jalwa*, چمک *chamak* (f.), رونق *raunaḳ*. (f.)

Splinter, کرچ *kirch* (f.), سینک *sīnk* (f.), کهپاچ *khapāch*. (f.)

Spoke (of a wheel), چکر کا آڑا *chakkar kā āṛā*, بیني *bēnī*.

Sponge, موا بادل *mū'ā bādal* اسفنج *isfanj*.

Sport, (of the field) شکار *shikār*, (play) کهیل *khēl*, بازي *bāzī*.

Sportsman, شکاري *shikārī*, شکارباز *shikār-bāz*, اهیري *ahērī*.

Spot, (speck) داغ *dāgh*, (disgrace) کلنک *kalank*: see Place.

Spout, ٹونٹي *ṭōnṭī*, پينالا *painālā*, (pipe) پوٹ *pōṭ* (f.), نل *nal.*

Spread, پهيلاؤ *phailā'ō*, احاطه *iḥāṭa*, گهير *ghēr*: see Extension.

Sprig, Sprout, پهنگي *phungī*, شاخچه *shākhcha*, ڈالي *ḍālī.*

Sprightliness, چالاکي *chālākī*, اچپلي *achpalī*, بشاشت *bashāshat.* (f.)

Spur, کانٹا *kānṭā*, ايڑ *ēṛ* (f.), مهميز *mahmēz.* (f.)

Spy, جاسوس *jāsūs*, بهيديا *bhēdiyā*, نظرباز *naẓar-bāz*: see Scout.

A Square, شکل مربع *shakl-i murabbā*, چوکا *chaukā.*

Squib, (firework) پٹاخا *paṭākhā*, (lampoon) هجو *hajō.* (f.)

Squire, مرزا *mirzā*, صاحب زاده *ṣāḥib-zāda*, لالا *lālā.*

A Squirt, پچکاري *pichkārī*, دمکلا *damkalā*, پچکا *pichukkā.*

A Stab, هول *hūl* (f.), بهونک *bhōnk* (f.), کهونچا *khōnchā.*

Stability, قرار *ḳarār*, ٹهراؤ *ṭhahrā'ō*, استواري *ustuwārī.*

Stack, ٹال *ṭāl* (f.), اٹال *aṭāl* (f.), انبار *ambār*, توده *tūda.*

Staff, عصا *āṣā*, لاٹهي *lāṭhī*, چهڑي *chhaṛī*, چوب *chōb.* (f.)

Stage, منزل *manzil* (f.), (platform) مچان *machān*, (of a playhouse) تماشاگاه *tamāshā-gāh* (f.), اکهاڑا *akhāṛā*: see Station.

Stain, داغ *dāgh* ليک *līk* (f.), کلنک *kalank*, (on cloth) دهپا *dhappā.*

Staircase, پيڑي *paiṛī*, نردبان *nardbān*, پهرکي *pharkī.* (?)

Stake, (post) کهنبها *khambhā*, کهونٹا *khūnṭā*: see Peg, Wager.

Stalk, ڈالي *ḍālī*, ڈٹها *ḍaṭhā*, بونٹ *bōnṭ*, تنه *tana*, ڈانٹهي *ḍānṭhī.*

Stall, (for a beast) تهان *thān*, طويله *ṭawēla*, آرگڑا *ārgaṛā* (?): see Bench, Shelf.

Stallion, سانڈ *sānḍ*, بيج کا گهوڑا *bīj kā ghōṛā.*

Stammerer, Stutterer, هکلاها *haklāhā*, لکنتي *luknatī.*

Stamp, (instrument) چهاپا *chhāpā*, مهر *muhr* (f.): see Print.

Stanchion, ڈنڈا *ḍanḍā*, تهوني *thūnī*, ٹيکني *ṭēknī*, پشتي *pushtī.*

Stand, (stop) اٹکاؤ *aṭkā'ō*, (station) ٹهکانا *ṭhikānā*: see Cessation.

Stanza, قطعه *ḳiṭ'ā*, شعر *shi'r* بيت *bait* (f.), دوها *dōhā.*

Starch, نشاسته *nishāsta*, کلپ *kalap*, ماوا *māwā.* (f.)

A Start, چونک *chaunk* (f.), جهجهک *jhijhak* (f.), بهڑک *bhaṛak.* (f.)

State, حالت *ḥālat* (f.), وضع *waẓ'* (f.), عالم *ālam*: see Kingdom.

State, Stateliness, طمطراق *ṭamṭarāḳ*, دبدبه *dabdaba.*

Station, جگہہ *jagah* (f.), ٹھکانا *ṭhikānā:* see Place, Degree.

Statue, مورت *mūrat* (f.), بت *but,* پوتلا *pūtlā,* لعبت *la'bat.* (f.)

Stature, قد *ḳadd,* ڈیل *ḍīl,* قامت *ḳāmat* (f.), اندازہ *andāza.*

Statute, قانون *ḳānūn,* قاعدہ *ḳā'ida,* آئین *ā'īn,* ریت *rīt.* (f.)

Stay, ٹکاؤ *ṭikā'o,* بودوباش *būdōbāsh* (f.), رہائش *rahā'ish.* (f.)

Stead, جگہہ *jagah* (f.), موقع *mauḳa',* (instead) عوض *'iwaẓ.*

Steak, تکا *tikkā,* بوٹي *bōṭī.* Stealth, چوري *chōrī,* دزدي *duzdī.*

Steed, گھوڑا *ghōṛā,* بادپا *bādpā,* سمند *samand.*

Steeple, مینار *mīnār,* لاٹ *lāṭ* (f.), دھورھرا *dhaurahrā.* (?)

Stem, (stalk, twig) شاخ *shākh,* ڈانٹھي *ḍānṭhī:* see Lineage.

Step, قدم *ḳadam,* گام *gām,* ڈیگ *ḍēg,* (of stairs, &c.) سیڑھي *sīṛhī.*

Sterility, اوسرا'ي *ūsarā'ī,* کلرا'ي *kallarā'ī,* بانجھپن *bānjhpan.*

Stick, لکڑي *lakṛī,* لاٹھي *lāṭhī,* عصا *'asā,* چوب *chōb,* ڈنڈا *ḍanḍā.*

Stigma, داغ *dāgh,* چنھہ *chinh,* (disgrace) کلنک *kalank,* حرف *ḥarf.*

Stillness, سنساني *sunsānī,* سناھٹ *sunāhaṭ* (f.): see Silence.

Sting, ڈنک *ḍank,* ڈانک *ḍānk,* نیش *nēsh,* چبھک *chabhak.* (f.)

Stink, بدبو *bad-bū* (f.), درگندھ *durgandh* (f.), تعفن *ta'affun.*

Stipulation, شرط *sharṭ* (f.), قول قرار *ḳaul-ḳarār:* see Contract.

Stirrup, رکاب *rikāb* (f.). Stirrup-leather, رکاب دوال *rikāb-dō'āl.*

Stitch, ٹانکا *ṭānkā,* لپکي *lapkī,* (pain) ٹسک *ṭasak.* (f.)

Stock, تنہ *tana,* (gun-) کندہ *kunda,* (capital) مول *mūl:* see Cattle.

Stocks, (wooden) ہڑ *haṛ,* کاٹھ *kāṭh,* (funds) حصي کسي پونجي میں *ḥiṣṣē kisī pūnjī mēṅ.*

Stop, Stoppage, اٹکاؤ *aṭkā'o,* اٹک *aṭak* (f.), (in gram.) بسرام *bisrām.*

Store, (plenty) ڈھیر *ḍhēr,* (house) خزانہ *khazāna,* بھنڈار *bhanḍār.*

Story, (tale) قصہ *ḳiṣṣa,* کہاني *kahānī,* (floor) منزل *manzil.* (f.)

Stove, گلخن *gul-khan,* تنور *tanūr,* انگیٹھي *angēṭhī,* بھاڑ *bhāṛ.*

Stranger, غیرجانب *ghair-jānib,* پردیسي *par-dēsī:* see Guest.

Strap, (of leather) دوال *dō'āl,* (razor) چموٹي *chamōṭī:* see Belt.

Stratum, پرت *parat,* تہ *tah* (f.), طبق *ṭabaḳ,* طباق *ṭibāḳ.*

Straw (stalk of grain), نالي *nālī,* پوال *puwāl* (f.), تنکا *tinkā.*

Streak, لکیر *lakīr* (f.), لہر *lahar* (f.), خط *khaṭṭ:* see Line, Ray.

Stream (current), دهارا *dhārā* (f.), دهار *dhār* (f.): see Brook, River.

Street, كوچه *kūcha*, رسته *rasta*, گلي *galī*, سڑک *saṛak*. (f.)

Strength, زور *zōr*, بل *bal*, قوت *ḳūwat* (f.), مضبوطي *mazbūṭī*.

Stress, زور *zōr*, چوٹ *chōṭ* (f.), بوجه *bōjh*, بار *bār*.

Stretch, پهيلاؤ *phailā'ō*, پسار *pasār*, كساؤ *kasā'ō*: see Effort.

Strife, ٹنٹا *ṭanṭā*, جهگڑا *jhagṛā*, ٹوكاٹوكي *ṭōkā-ṭōkī*: see Dispute.

String, ڈوري *ḍōrī*, رسي *rassī*, سوتلي *sūtlī*, جيل *jēl*: see Row.

Strip (slip), دهجي *dhajjī*, كترن *katran*, ٹكڑا *ṭukṛā*, پٹي *paṭṭī*.

Stripe, (line) لكير *lakīr* (f.), (from a whip) مار *mār* (f.), كوڑا *kōṛā*.

Stroke, مار *mār* (f.), چوٹ *chōṭ* (f.), ٹهونک *ṭhōnk*: see Stripe.

Strophe, مطلع *maṭla'*, قطعه *ḳiṭ'a*: see Stanza.

Structure, تعمير *ta'mīr* (f.), (edifice) عمارت *'imārat* (f.): see Shape.

Stubble, باڈه *bāḍh* (f.), ٹهونٹهي *ṭhūnṭhī*, ناري *nārī*.

Stucco, چوني كا ليپ *chūnē kā lēp*.

Stud, (of horses) خيل *khail*, پاگا *pāgā*, (button) پهول *phūl*.

Study, مطالعه *muṭāla'a*, (room) مطالعه خانه *muṭāla'a-khāna*.

Stuff, ماده *mādda*, رخت *rakht*, قماش *ḳimāsh*: see Nonsense.

Stump, ٹونڈي *ṭūnḍī*, ٹونڈ *ṭūnḍ*, ٹهونٹه *ṭhūnṭh*: see Root.

Stupefaction, بيهوشي *bē-hōshī*, مورچها *mūrchhā*. (f.)

Stupidity, بيوقوفي *bē-wuḳūfī*, حماقت *ḥimāḳat* (f.), كندي *kundī*.

Style, (idiom) اصطلاح *iṣṭilāḥ* (f.), عبارت *'ibārat* (f.): see Title.

Subject, رعيت *ra'aiyat* (f.), پرجا *parjā* (f.), (matter) ماده *mādda*.

Sublimity, علويت *'ulwiyat* (f.), بلندي *bulandī*: see Height.

Submission, عذر خواهي *'uzr-khwāhī*, دباؤ *dabā'ō*: see Obedience.

Subpœna, طلب چٹهي *ṭalab-chiṭṭhī*, سفينه *safīna*.

Subscription, (signing) دستخط *dastkhaṭṭ*, (sum) چندا *chandā*.

Subsidy, رپي كي مددگاري *rupai kī madadgārī*: see Aid, Tribute.

Subsistence, (being) هستي *hastī*, وجود *wujūd*: see Livelihood.

Substance, (being) هستي *hastī*, (matter) ماده *mādda*: see Body, Goods.

Substantive, اسم *ism*, نام *nām*.

Substitute, قائم مقام *ḳā'im-maḳām*, عوضي *'iwazī*: see Agent.

Subtileness, Subtilty, (fineness) باريكي *bārīkī*: see Artifice.

Subtraction, هرن *haran*, وضع *waẓ'* (f.), گهٹائي *ghaṭā'ī*.

Subversion, انقلاب *inḳilāb*, زيرزبري *zērzabari*, پائيمالي *pā'ēmālī*.

Suburbs, دامن شهر *dāman-shahar*, شهر پورا *shahar-pūrā*.

Success, كاميابي *kāmyābī*, عهده براٴي *ŭhda-barā'ī*.

Succession, تسلسل *tasalsul*, لگاٴو *lagā'ō*: see Series, Lineage.

Successor, جانشين *jā-nishīn*, قائم مقام *ḳā'im-maḳām*.

Sucker (a shoot), كونپل *kōmpal*, كرل *karil*: see Sprig.

Suckling, شيرخوارا *shīr-khwārā*, دودھ كا بچه *dūdh kā bachcha*.

Sufficiency, كفايت *kifāyat* (f.), وفور *wufur*, وفا *wafā*. (f.)

Suffocation, جبس النفس *ḥabsu-n-nafas*, دمبستگي *dambastagī*.

Sugar, شكر *shakar* (f.), (coarse) چيني *chīnī*, كهانڈ *khānḍ*, (candy) مصري *miṣrī*, قند *ḳand*, (-cane) اوكھ *ūkh* (f.), گنا *gannā*, كتارا *katārā*.

Suggestion, اشاره *ishāra*, گوش گذاري *gōsh-guẓārī*, صلاح *ṣalāḥ*. (f.)

Suicide, خود كشي *khud-kushī*, (murderer) خود كش *khud-kush*.

Suit, جوڑا *jōṛā*, (retinue) حشمت *ḥashmat* (f.): see Lawsuit.

Suitor, (plaintiff) دادخواه *dād-khwāh*, (wooer) عاشق *ăshiḳ*.

Sum, مبلغ *mablagh*, كلي *kullī*, (summary) مجمل *mujmal*.

Summerhouse, بارهدري *bārah-darī*, بنگلا *banglā*.

Summit, پهننگ *phunang* (f.), چونٹي *chōnṭī*, قله *ḳulla*.

Summons, طلب *ṭalab* (f.), طلب چٹھي *ṭalab-chiṭṭhī*.

Sunbeam, كرن *kiran*, آفتاب كا پرتو *āftāb kā partau*.

Sunday, اتوار *itwār*, ربار *rabibār*, ايك شنبه *ēk shamba*.

Sunrise, طلوع آفتاب *ṭulū'ī āftāb*, سورج ادي *sūraj-udai*.

Sunset, غروب آفتاب *ghurūb-i-āftāb*, سورج است *sūraj-ast*.

Superficies, سطح *saṭḥ* (f.), وسعت *wus'ăt* (f.): see Outside.

Superfluity, ازدياد *izdiyād*, كثرت *kaṣrat* (f.), بهتات *bahutāt*. (f.)

Superintendence, نگهباني *nigahbānī*, سربراهي *sarbarāhī*.

Superiority, برتري *bartarī*, فوقيت *fauḳīyat* (f.), بڑاٴي *baṛā'ī*.

Superstition, دين باطل *dīn-i-bāṭil*, تعصب *ta'ăṣṣub*.

Supplement, تتمه *tatimma*.

Supplication, استدعا *istid'ā* (f.), دعا *du'ā* (f.), زاري *zārī*.

Supply, بهرتي *bhartī*, رسد *rasad* (f.), آمد *āmad* (f.), كهيپ *khēp*. (f.)

Support, (prop) استاده *istāda*, (sustenance) پرورش *parwarish*. (f.)

Supposition, اٹكل *aṭkal* (f.), قياس *ḳiyās*, اندازه *andāza*.

Suppression, دباؤ *dabā'ō*, چهپاؤ *chhipā'ō*.

Suppuration, پكاؤ *pakā'ō*, پيبياهٹ *pībiyāhaṭ* (f.), نضج *nuẓj*.

Supremacy, اوليت *awwalīyat* (f.), سرداري *sardārī*.

Surcingle, پيٹي *pēṭī*, بالا تنگ *bālā-tang*, كوتل كش *kōtal-kash*.

Surety, (bondsman) ضامن *ẓāmin*, (bail) ضامني *ẓāminī*.

Surf, Surge, موج بحر *mauj-i-baḥr*, هلكوره *hilkōra*, لهر *lahar*. (f.)

Surface, سطح *saṭḥ* (f.), رو *rū*, باهر *bāhar*, بساط *bisāṭ*. (f.)

Surfeit, اجيرن *ajīran*, اپهراي *aphrā'ī*, كچاي *kachā'ī*.

Surgery (practice of a surgeon), جراحي *jarrāḥī*.

Surplus, بيشي *bēshī*, بڑهتي *baṛhtī*, بچتي *bachtī*, فاضل *fāẓil*.

Surprise, تعجب *ta'ajjub*, ناگهاني *nāgahānī*, اچانك *achānak*.

Survey, نگاه *nigāh* (f.), نظر *naẓar* (f.): see Mensuration.

Surveyor, ناظر *nāẓir*, نگاهبان *nigāhbān*: see Land-surveyor.

Surviver, پسمانده *pasmānda*, پس زنده *pas-zinda*.

Suspense, خوف و رجا *khauf ō rajā* (f.), دبدها *dubdhā*. (f.)

Suspension, لٹكاؤ *laṭkā'ō*, (putting off) چند روز كي ليئي معزولي *chand rōz kē li'ē ma'zūlī*.

Sustenance, اهار *ahār*, خوراك *khurāk* (f.), جيكا *jīkā*: see Livelihood.

Suture, (seam) سيون *sīwan*, سلاي *silā'ī*, (of the skull) جوڑ *jōṛ*.

Swain, جوان *jawān*, چوپاني جوان *chaupānī jawān*, نايك *nāyak*.

Swamp, دلدل *daldal* (f.), دهسن *dhasan* (f.), چور زمين *chōr zamīn*.

Swarm, جهنڈ *jhunḍ*, منڈل *manḍal*, ازدحام *izdiḥām*.

Sway, حكومت *ḥukūmat* (f.), فرمانرواي *farmān-rawā'ī*.

Sweepings, جهاڑن *jhāṛan* (f.), بهارن *buhāran* (f.), كوڑا *kūṛā*.

Sweetheart, پيارا *pyārā* (m.), معشوقه *ma'shūḳa* (f.): see Beloved.

Swell, پهولن *phūlan*, سوجن *sūjan*, (wave) موج *mauj* (f.): see Increase.

Swiftness, تيزي *tēzī*, جلدي *jaldī*, چالاكي *chālākī*, شتابي *shitābī*.

Swindler, مردم فريب *mardum-farēb*, بٹيباز *baṭṭē-bāz*.

Swing, جهلاو *jhulā'ō*, (machine) جهولا *jhūlā*, هنڈولا *hinḍōlā*.

Swoop, جهپٹ *jhapaṭ*. (f.) Swop, ادلا بدلا *adlā-badlā*.

Sycophant, خوشامدي *khushāmadī*, چغل خور *chughul-khōr*.

Syllable هجي *hijē*, كلمه *kalima*. Syllabus, see Abstract.

Syllogism, قضيه *ḳaẓiya*, قياس *ḳiyās*, دليل *dalīl*. (f.)

Symbol, نشان *nishān*, علامت *ālāmat* (f.), مراد *murād*. (f.)

Symmetry, قرينه *ḳarīna*, سڈولي *suḍaulī*, انداز *andāz*.

Sympathy, همدردي *ham-dardī*, دلسوزي *dil-sōzī*, رقت *riḳḳat*. (f.)

Symphony, هماهنگي *ham-āhangī*, هماوازي *ham-āwāzī*.

Symptom, علامت *ālāmat* (f.), نشان *nishān*, اثر *aṣar*.

Syncope, see Fainting; (in gram.) لفظ كي ترخيم *lafẓ kī tarkhīm*.

Synopsis, مختصر *mukhtaṣar*, مجمل *mujmal*, اجمال *ijmāl*.

Syntax, نحو *naḥō*. (f.) Syringe, پچكاري *pichkārī*, حقنه *ḥuḳna*.

System, قانون *ḳānūn*, قاعده *ḳā'ida*, (plan) نقشه *naḳsha*.

Tablet, لوح *lauḥ* (f.), پاٹي *pāṭī*, تختي *takhtī*.

Tackle, Tackling, سرانجام *sar-anjām*, كيل كانٹا *kīl-kānṭā*.

Tactics, فن جنگ *fann-i-jang*, صف آراٴي *ṣaff-ārā'ī*.

Taffeta, تافته *tāfta*, درياٴي *daryā'ī*, چيولي *chē'ōlī*.

Tail, دم *dum* (f.), پونچهه *pūnchh* (f.), دنبال *dumbāl*.

Taint, (stain) داغ *dāgh*, (corruption) بو *bū* (f.), باس *bās*. (f.)

Tale, قصه *ḳiṣṣa*, كهاني *kahānī*, نقل *naḳl* (f.): see Calculation.

Talebearer, چغل خور *chughul-khōr*, غماز *ghammāz*.

Talent, (weight) وزن *wazn*, (coin) سكه *sikka*: see Faculty.

Talisman, طلسم *ṭilism*, (or plur.) طلسمات *ṭilismāt*.

Talk, بات *bāt* (f.), بات چيت *bāt-chīt* (f.), بولچال *bōlchāl*. (f.)

Talkativeness, زياده گوٴي *ziyāda-gō'ī*, بسيار گوٴي *bisyār-gō'ī*.

Tallow, چربي *charbī*, پيه *pīh* (f.): see Fat.

Talness, قد كي لمباٴي *ḳadd kī lambā'ī*, اونچاٴي *ūnchā'ī*.

Talon, ناخن *nākhun*, نه *nuh*, نكه *nakh*, پنجه *panja*.

Tambourin, خنجري *khanjarī*, طبله *ṭabla*, ڈپه *ḍaph*.

Tameness, هلاٴي *hilā'ī*, رامي *rāmī*, پوسواٴي *pōswā'ī*.

Tap, تهاپ *thāp* (f.), تهپكي *thapkī*, ٹهوك *ṭhōk*, ٹكورا *ṭakōrā*.

Tape, قور *ḳōr* (f.), پٹي *paṭṭī*, (coarse) نوار *niwār*. (f.)
Tapestry, ديوار گيري *dīwār-gīrī*, مشجر *mushajjar*.
Tar, قطران *ḳiṭrān*, رال *rāl*, (sailor) خلاصي *khalāṣī*.
Tardiness, آهستگي *āhistagī*, سستي *sustī*, ديري *dērī* : see Sloth.
Tare, (weed) گهاس *ghās*, (in weight) دهرا *dharā*, دهرات *dharāt*.
Tariff (Arab. تعريف), محصول كا نرخنامه *maḥṣūl kā nirkh-nāma*.
Tartness, ترشي *turshī*, كڑواۓ *kaṛwā'ī*, سختي *sakhtī*.
Task, وظيفه *waẓīfa*, كام *kām*, چكوتا *chukautā*, كوت *kūt*.
Tassel, جهبا *jhabbā*, پهندنا *phundnā*, لٹكن *laṭkan*.
Taste, مزه *maza*, لذت *lazzat* (f.), ذائقه *ẕā'iḳa* : see Discernment.
Tattler, بكي *bakkī*, گپي *gappī*, بڑبڑيا *baṛbaṛiyā*.
Tavern, شراب خانه *sharāb-khāna*, بهنگير خانه *bhangēr-khāna*.
Taunt, طعن *ṭa'n*, طعنه زني *ṭa'na-zanī*, مهنا *mihnā*, طنز *ṭanz*. (f.)
Tautology, تكرار *takrār* (f.), تكرر *takarrur*.
Tax, محصول *maḥṣūl*, حاصل *ḥāṣil*, خراج *khirāj*, خزانه *khazāna*.
Teacher, معلم *mu'allim*, استاد *ustād*, مدرس *mudarris*, گرو *gurū*.
Teacup, چا كي پيالي *chā kī piyālī*. Teapot, چادان *chā-dān*.
Te Deum, جي كا گيت *jai kā gīt*.
Telescope, دوربين *dūr-bīn*.
Teller, كهنيوالا *kahnēwālā*, گنيوالا *ginnēwālā* : see Accountant.
Telltale, چغل خور *chughul-khōr*, لترا *lutrā*, نيشزن *nēsh-zan*.
Temerity, بيتدبيري *bē-tadbīrī*, تهور *tahawwur*.
Temper, Temperament, مزاج *mizāj*, سرشت *sarisht*. (f.)
Temperance, Temperateness, اعتدال *i'tidāl*, پرهيز *parhēz*.
Temperature, اعتدال *i'tidāl*, حالت سردي و گرمي *ḥālat-i-sardī ō garmī*.
Temptation, ترغيب *targhīb* (f.), اغوا *ighwā*, امتحان *imtiḥān*.
Tenacity, لسلساهٹ *laslasāhaṭ* (f.), چپچپاهٹ *chipchipāhaṭ*. (f.)
Tendency, ميل *mail*, ميلان *mailān*, جهكاؤ *jhukā'ō*.
Tenderness, نرمي *narmī*, كوملتا *kōmaltā* (f.) : see Pity.
Tendril, سوت *sūt*, ريشه *rēsha*, (of a vine) بيل *bēl*, بيلي *bēlī*.
Tenour, (continuity) روش *rawish* (f.), (drift) فحوا *faḥwā* : see Meaning.

Tense, صيغه *ṣīgha*, زمانۂ فعل *zamāna-i-fi'l.* Past, ماضي *māẓī.* Present, حال *ḥāl.* Future, مستقبل *mustaḳbil.*

Tension, Tenseness, کساؤ *kasā'o*, کھچاؤ *khichā'o*, تان *tān.* (f.)

Tenter (hook), انکڑي *ankṛī*, انکسي *anksī.*

Term, (limit) حد *ḥadd* (f.), (word) بات *bāt* (f.): see Condition.

Termination, حد *ḥadd*, آخر *ā<u>kh</u>ir*, (of a word) حرف آخري *ḥarf-i-ā<u>kh</u>irī.*

Terrace, چبوتره *chabūtara* or چوتره *chautara*, بام *bām.*

Terrour, دهشت *dahshat* (f.), هول *haul*, ڈر *ḍar*, خوف *<u>kh</u>auf.*

Testament (last will), وصيت نامه *waṣīyat-nāma.*

Testicle, خايه *<u>kh</u>āya*, خصيه *<u>kh</u>uṣya*, انڈ *anḍ*, پيلڑا *pēlṛā.*

Testimony, شهادت *shahādat* (f.), گواهي *gawāhī*: see Evidence.

Tether, گرانون *garāṅwan*, پگها *paghā* or پگا *pagā.*

Tetter, داد *dād*, دنائي *dinā'ī*, سينهوا *sēṅhū'ā*, سيلي *sēlī.*

Text, متن *matn*, اصل *aṣl* (f.), مول *mūl*, روان *rawāṅ.*

Texture, بناوت *bināwaṭ* (f.), بناوت *bunāwaṭ*, قماش *ḳimāsh.*

Thanks, Thanksgiving, شکر *shukr*, شکر گذاري *shukr-guẕārī.*

Thaw, پالے کا پگهلاؤ *pālē kā pighlā'o*, گداخت *gudā<u>kh</u>t.* (f.)

Theft, چوري *chōrī*, دزدي *duzdī*, تسکري *taskarī*, سرقه *sariḳa.*

Theme, منشا *manshā*, مصدر *maṣdar*, مبحث *mab'ḥaṣ.*

Theorem, مسله *masla*, قياس *ḳiyās.* Theory, قياس *ḳiyās.*

Thermometer, گرمي سردي ناپني کا ايک آله *garmī sardī nāpnē kā ēk āla.*

Thicket, جهنڈ *jhunḍ*, جهاڑ جهوڑ *jhāṛ-jhūṛ* (f.), جنگل *jangal.*

Thickness, موٹائي *mōṭā'ī*, کثافت *kaṣāfat* (f.), گنجاني *gunjānī.*

Thimble, انگشتانه *angushtāna*, ٹوپ *ṭōp.*

Thinness, تنکي *tunukī*, پتلائي *patlā'ī*, رقت *riḳkat.* (f.)

Thong, تسمه *tasma*, سلو *sallū*: see Strap.

Thorax, پيٹي *pēṭī*, چهاتي کي بهيتري طرف *chhātī kī bhītrī ṭaraf.*

Thorn, (tree) کانٹے کا درخت *ḳāṅṭē kā dara<u>kh</u>t*, (spine) کانٹا *kāṅṭā.*

Thought, سوچنا *sōchnā*, خيال *<u>kh</u>iyāl*, انديشه *andēsha*, دهيان *dhyān.*

Thraldom, Thrall, غلامي *<u>gh</u>ulāmī*, عبوديت *'ubūdīyat.* (f.)

Thread, سوت *sūt*, تاگ *tāg*, رشته *rishta*, دهاگا *dhāgā.*

Threat, Threatening, دهمکا *dhamkā*, تهدید *tahdīd* (f.), زجر *zijr*.

Thrift, جزرسي *juzrasī*, کم خرچي *kam-kharchī*, وارا *wārā*.

Throe, بڑا درد *baṛā dard*, پير *pīr* (f.), درد زه *dard-i-zih*.

Throne, تخت *takht*, سنگهاسن *singhāsan*, مسند *masnad*. (f.)

Throng, بهيڙ *bhīṛ* (f.), انبوه *ambōh*, ازدحام *izdiḥām*, هجوم *hujūm*.

Thrust, کهونچا *khōnchā*, ٹهيل *ṭhēl* (f.), دهکا *dhakkā*, بهونک *bhōnk*. (f.)

Thump, Thumping, دهمکا *dhamkā*, دهمک *dhamak* (f.) : see Stroke.

Thursday, جمعرات *jum'a-rāt* (f.), پنجشنبه *panj-shamba*.

Ticket, چٹهي *chiṭṭhī*, ٹيپ *ṭīp* (f.), دستاويز *dastāwēz*. (f.)

Tide, (flood) جوار *jawār* (f.), مد *madd* (f.), (ebb) بهاٹها *bhāṭhā*, جزر *jazr*.

Tidings, اخبار *akhbār*, سنديسا *sandēsā*, سماچار *samāchār*.

Tier (row), ته *tah* (f.), پرت *parat*, طبقه *ṭabḳa*, قطار *ḳaṭār*.

Tightness, کسائي *kasā'ī*, تنگي *tangī*, چستي *chustī*, تناؤ *tanā'ō*.

Tillage, جتائي *jutā'ī*, هلواهي *halwāhī*, کسنئي *kisna'ī*.

Tiller, هلواها *halwāhā*, هل جوتا *hal-jōtā*, قلبه ران *ḳulba-rān*.

Timber, لکڑي *lakṛī*, گول کاٹه *gōl-kāṭh*, گولا *gōlā*, چوب *chōb*. (f.)

Timbrel, طبله *ṭabla*, مردنگ *mirdang*, پکهاوج *pakhāwaj*. (f.)

Timidity, خوف *khauf*, دهشت *dahshat* (f.), کم جراتي *kam-jur'atī*.

Tincture, (extract) عرق *'araḳ*, (colour) رنگ *rang*, (quality) گن *gun*.

Tinder, سوخته *sōkhta*, گل *gul*, شعله *shu'la*.

Tinsel, رونق بي نور و بها *raunaḳ-i-bē-nūr ō bahā*, جگجگا *jagjagā*.

Tint, رنگ *rang*. Tip, سر *sir*, نوک *nōk*, (blow) هلکي ضرب *halkī ẓarb*.

Tippler, چسکر *chusakkar*, پيوکڑ *pīwakkaṛ*, شرابي *sharābī*.

Tissue (brocade), زربفت *zar-baft*, بادلا *bādlā*, تمامي *tamāmī*.

Titbit, لقمه تر *luḳma-tar*, نعمت *ni'mat* (f.), چرب نواله *charb nawāla*.

Tithe, دسانس *dasāns*, عشر *'ushr*, دهيک *dahyak*.

Titillation, گدگدي *gudgudī*, سرسري *sursurī*.

Title, خطاب *khiṭāb*, لقب *laḳab* or (plur.) القاب *alḳāb*.

Titlepage, سرنامه *sar-nāma*, سرلوح *sar-i-lauḥ*.

Tittle, (dot, particle,) ذره *ẕarra*, تنکا *tinkā*, سرمو *sar-i-mū*.

Tittletattle, گپشپ *gapshap* (f.), بکجھک *bak-jhak.* (f.)

Toast (dried bread), سینکي هوي روٹي *sēnkī hū'ī roṭī.*

Tobacco, تنباکو *tambākū,* بھیلسا *bhēlsā,* گال *gāl.*

Toil, محنت *mihnat* (f.), دوڑ دھوپ *dauṛ-dhūp* (f.), ٹہل *ṭahal.* (f.)

Token, نشان *nishān,* پتا *patā,* (memorial) یادگاري *yādgārī.*

Tolerance, Toleration, برداشت *bardāsht* (f.), سہاؤ *sahā'ō.*

Toll, باج *bāj,* چنگي *chungī,* راهداري *rāhdārī,* کر *kar.*

Tomb, قبر *kabr* (f.), گور *gōr* (f.), مقبره *makbara :* see Grave.

Ton or Tun, قریب تیس من کا ایک وزن *karīb tīs man kā ēk wazn.*

Tone, آواز *āwāz* (f.), صدا *ṣadā* (f.), لہجہ *lahja,* لي *lai.* (f.)

Tongs, دست پناه *dast-panāh,* سنڈاسي *sanḍāsī.* (f.)

Tonsil, کوڑي *kauṛī,* گلٹي *gilṭī.* Tonsure, منڈن *munḍan.*

Tool, هتھیار *hathyār,* آلت *ālat* (f.); (tools) اوزار *auzār.*

Top, سر *sir,* پھننگ *phunang* (f.), سکھر *sikhar,* چونٹي *chōnṭī.*

Toper, پیوکر *pīwakkar,* ڈبوسو *ḍabūsū* (?) : see Tippler.

Topic, مضمون *mazmūn,* موضوع *mauzū',* مدعا *mudda'ā.*

Topography, جگھوں کا بیان *jaghōṅ kā bayān.*

Torch, مشعل *mash'al* (f.), فلیته *falīta,* ڈامر *ḍāmar.*

Torment, سیاست *siyāsat* (f.), اذیت *azīyat* (f.), ایذا *īzā.* (f.)

Torpor, بیحرکتي *bē-harakatī,* لاجنبشي *lā-jumbishī,* سني *sunī.*

Torrent, تیزدھارا *tēz dhārā,* سیل *sail* (f.), توڑ *tōṛ,* ندي *nadī.*

Torture, جان کني *jān-kanī,* عقوبت *'ukūbat* (f.), سولي *sūlī.*

Total, Totality, جمله *jumla,* جمع *jam'* (f.), موٹھ *mōṭh.* (f.)

Touchhole, رنجک کا سوراخ *ranjak kā sūrākh.*

Touchstone, کسوٹي *kasauṭī,* محک *mihakk* (f.), سنگ عیار *sang-i-'ayār.*

Tour, دور *daur,* سیر *sair* (f.), گردش *gardish* (f.), (turn) باري *bārī.*

Tow, جھاڑا هوا سان یا پاٹ *jhāṛā hū'ā sān* or *pāṭ.*

Town, شہر *shahr,* قصبه *kaṣba,* بلده *balda,* گانو *gāṅw.*

Townsman, هم شہري *ham-shahrī,* (of a town) شہري *shahrī.*

Toy, کھلونا *khilaunā,* بازیچه *bāzīcha,* کھیلني کي چیز *khēlnē kī chīz.*

Trace, Track, لیک *līk* (f.), نقشۂ پا *naksha-i-pā :* see Footpath.

Tract, (of country) جنب *jamb,* نواح *nawāh* (f.) : see Country, Treatise.

Trade, سوداگري *saudāgarī*, تجارت *tijārat* (f.), پيشه *pēsha*.

Tradition, روايت *riwāyat* (f.), تداول *tadāwul*, حديث *ḥadīs*.

Traffic, بيپار *baipār*, تجارت *tijārat* (f.), سوداگري *saudāgarī*.

Train, دم *dum* (f.), (skirt), دامن *dāman*: see Retinue, Series.

Traitor, دغاباز *dag͟hābāz*, نمك حرام *namak-ḥarām*, باغي *bāg͟hī*.

Trammel, چهاند *chhānd* (f.), لنبا جال *lambā jāl*, پيكڑها *paikaṛhā*.

Trance, سكته *sakta*, لوهار *lauhār*, (ecstacy) وجد *wajd*: see Swoon.

Tranquillity, آرام *ārām*, آسودگي *āsūdagī*, كل *kal* (f.), راحت *rāḥat*. (f.)

Transaction, كاروبار *kārōbār*, معامله *mu'āmala*, كرتوت *kartūt*. (f.)

Transfer, تحويل *taḥwīl* (f.), تسليم *taslīm*. (f.)

Transformation, تبديل صورت يا شكل *tabdīl-i-ṣūrat* or *-shakl*.

Transgression, تجاوز *tajāwuz*, توڑ *tōṛ*, تعدي *ta'āddī*: see Fault.

Transit, Transition, گذار *guzār*, عبور *ūbūr*, تبديل *tabdīl*. (f.)

Translation, (version) ترجمه *tarjuma*, (removal) انتقال *intiḳāl*.

Transmigration, نقل مكان *nakl-i-makān*: see Metempsychosis.

Transparency, شفافي *shaffāfī*, براقي *barrāḳī*: see Clearness.

Transportation, انتقال *intiḳāl*: see Banishment.

Trap, كل *kal* (f.), دبكر *dabkar* (f.), جانتي *jāntī*: see Snare.

Trappings, آرائشين *ārā'ishēṅ* (f. plur.), (dress) پوشاكين *pōshākēṅ*. (f. plur.)

Trash, اگڑ بگڑ *agaṛ bagaṛ*, (unripe fruit) كچا پهل *kachchā phal*.

Travail, see Throe. Travel, سفر *safar*, مسافرت *musāfarat*. (f.)

Treacle, گڑ *guṛ*, چوٹا *chōṭā*, راب *rāb* (f.), ترياق *tiryāḳ*.

Tread, قدم *ḳadam*, قدم زني *ḳadam-zanī*, چال *chāl*.

Treason, نمكحرامي *namak-ḥarāmī*, بغاوت *bag͟hāwat*. (f.)

Treasure, خزانه *k͟hazāna*, روكڑ *rōkaṛ* (f.), ذخيره *zak͟hīra*.

Treasury, خزانه *k͟hazāna*, خزينه *k͟hazīna*, گنجينه *ganjīna*.

A Treat, ضيافت *ziyāfat* (f.), دعوت *da'wat* (f.), جيونار *jē'ōnār*. (f.)

Treatise, رساله *risāla*, نسخه *nusk͟ha*, نامه *nāma*, كتاب *kitāb*. (f.)

Treatment, سلوك *sulūk*, ڈهنگ *ḍhang*, معالجه *mu'ālaja*.

Treaty, معامله *mu'āmala*, صلح *ṣulḥ* (f.), قول قرار *ḳaul-ḳarār*.

Tremour, كپكپي *kapkapī*, لرزش *larzish* (f.), رعشه *ra'sha*.

Trencher, كٹهوتي *kaṭhautī*, (trench-digger) كهائي گر *khā'ī-gar*.

Trepan (saw used in surgery), ماه *māh* (?), پرماه *parmāh* (?), پيچه *pēcha*. (?)

Trepidation, تهرتهري *thartharī*, لرزه *larza*, ڈول مال *ḍōl-māl*. (?)

Trespass, خطا *khaṭā* (f.), تقصير *taḳṣīr* (f.), گناه *gunāh*.

Tresses, زلف *zulf* (f.), كاكل *kākul* (f.), گيسو *gēsū*, ببري *babrī*.

Tret (an allowance), اوپرلپ *ūparlap*, سوختني *sōkhtanī*, پهاؤ *phā'ō*.

Trial, آزمائش *āzmā'ish* (f.), امتحان *imtiḥān*, (legal) تحقيق *taḥḳīḳ*. (f.)

Triangle, خط مثلث *khaṭṭ-i-muṡallaṡ*, سه گوشه *si-gōsha*.

Tribunal, عدالت *'adālat* (f.), محكمه *maḥkama*, مسند *masnad*. (f.)

Tribute, باج *bāj*, خراج *khirāj*, كر *kar*, پيشكش *pēshkash*.

Trice, لحظه *laḥẓa*, دم *dam*; in a trice, جهپ سي *jhap sē*.

Trick, حيله *ḥīla*, ٹال ٹول *ṭāl-ṭōl*, فريب *farēb*, فن *fann*, چهل *chhal*.

Trident, ترسول *tirsūl* or *trisūl*.

Trifle, ناچيز *nā-chīz*, تهوڑي بات *thōṛī bāt* (f.), هيچ *hēch*.

Trifler, مكهي مار *makkhī-mār*, ٹاپاٹوئيا *ṭāpāṭō'iyā*, هرزه كار *harza-kār*.

Trigger, بندوق كي كل *bandūḳ kī kal*.

Trill, لهرا *lahrā*, آواز كي تهرتهري *āwāz kī thartharī*.

Trimming, زرق برق *zarḳ-barḳ*, جهلاجهل *jhalājhal*. (f.)

Trinity, تثليث *taṡlīṡ* (f.), ثالث ثلاثه *ṡāliṡ-ṡalāṡa*.

Trinket, زيور *zēwar*, گهنا *gahnā*, پتا *pattā* : see Toy.

Trio, تين شخص ملكر گاني كا ايك راگ *tīn shakhṣ milkar gānē kā ēk rāg*.

Trip, (stumble) لچك *lachak* (f.), ٹهوكر *ṭhokar* (f.) : see Error, Journey.

Tripe, انتڑي *antṛī*, آنت *ānt* (f.), روده *rōda*, بٹ *baṭ*, اوجهڑي *ōjhaṛī*.

Triplet, مثلث *muṡallaṡ*, ترپد كبت *tripad-kabit*.

Trituration, رگراهٹ *ragrāhaṭ* (f.), پساؤ *pisā'ō*.

Triumph, جي *jai*, فتح *fatḥ* (f.), فيروزي *fīrōzī*, جي گيت *jai-gīt*.

Trollop, پهوهڑ *phūhaṛ* (f.), بودلي *bōdlī*, گيگلي *gēglī*.

Trope, مجاز *majāz*, عبارت *'ibārat* (f.), كنايه *kināya* : see Metaphor.

Trophy, فتح كا نشان *fatḥ kā nishān*, غنيمت *ghanīmat*. (f.)

Tropic, (of Cancer) خط سرطان *khaṭṭ-i-saraṭān*, (of Capricorn) خط جدي *khaṭṭ-i-jadī*.

Trot, دلكي *dulkī*, كوكرچال *kūkar-chāl*. (f.)
Trouble, دكھ *dukh*, تكليف *taklīf* (f.), تصديع *taṣdīʿ* (f.), ايذا *īẕā*. (f.)
Trowel, كرني *karnī*, تهاپي *thāpī*, سرميئي *surma'ī*. (?)
Truce, تهوڑي زماني كي ليي صلح *thōṛē zamānē kē liyē ṣulḥ*. (f.)
Truck, چهوٹي پهيي دار گاڑي *chhōṭē-pahiyē-dār gāṛī* : see Barter.
Trull, مال زادي *māl-zādī*, كسبي *kasbī*, بيسوا *bēswā*. (f.)
Trumpery, هرزه گوئي *harza-gō'ī*, اگڑ بگڑ *agaṛ bagaṛ* : see Trash.
Trumpeter, نفير بجانيوالا *nafīr-bajānēwālā*, قرناچي *ḳarnāchī*.
Truncheon, عصاي حكم *āṣā-i-ḥukm*, چوب *chōb* (f.) : see Club.
Trunk, (of a tree) تنه *tana*, جڑوٹ *jaṛwaṭ* : see Box, Proboscis.
Truss, (of straw, &c.) پولا *pūlā*, (bandage) پٹي *paṭṭī*, لنگوٹا *langōṭā*.
Trustee, امانت دار *amānat-dār*, امين *amīn*, ذمه دار *ẕimma-dār*.
Truth, سچ *sach*, راستي *rāstī*, صدق *ṣidḳ* : see Fidelity.
Tube, نلي *nalī*, چونگي *chōngī*, ني *nai* (f.), پهوكني *phūknī*.
Tuesday, منگل *mangal*, سه شنبه *si-shamba*.
Tuft, طره *ṭurra*, جهنڈ *jhunḍ*, گچھه *guchchha*, (of hair) چونڈا *chōnḍā*.
Tug, كهينچ *khainch* (f.), اينچ *ainch* (f.), كشش *kashish*. (f.)
Tuition, نگاهباني *nigāhbānī*, پرورش *parwarish* (f.) : see Instruction.
Tumbler, نٹ *naṭ*, كلاباز *kalā-bāz*, (pigeon) گهرني *ghirnī* : see Glass.
Tumult, بكهيڑا *bakhēṛā*, هنگامه *hangāma*, آشوب *āshōb*.
Tune, آواز *āwāz* (f.), سرود *sarōd*, سر *sur*, لي *lai* (f.), تان *tān*. (f.)
Tunic, چولي *chōlī*, كرته *kurta*, (membrane) كهلڑي *khalṛī*.
Tunnel, (funnel) چونگا *chōngā*, (shaft) راه *rāh* (f.) : see Chimney.
Turbulence, اضطراب *iẓṭirāb*, كهلبلي *khalbalī*, دنگابازي *dangābāzī*.
Turn, پهير *phēr*, گهماؤ *ghumā'ō*, (tour) باري *bārī* : see Change.
Turncoat, زمانه ساز *zamāna-sāz*.
Turning, گردش *gardish* (f.), پهراؤ *phirā'ō*, (of a river) بانك *bānk*.
Turpentine, گنده بروزه *ganda birōza*.
Turret, كنگوره *kangūra*, منار *manār*, برجي *burjī*, كلس *kalas*.
Tusk, بير *bīr* (f.), كهانگ *khāng*, ناب *nāb*.
Twang, ٹنكار *ṭankār* (f.), ٹنكور *ṭankōr* (f.), ٹن *ṭan*, هڑهڑي *haṛhaṛī*.
Tweezers, موچنا *mūchnā*, چمٹا *chimṭā*.

Twig, ليس *lais*, چهڑي *chhaṛī*, پلو *pallō*, ڈالي *ḍālī*.
Twine, سوتلي *sūtlī*, ريسمان *rēsmān*, (twist) پيچ *pēch*: see Twist.
Twinkle, Twinkling (of the eye), آنکھ کي جهپکي *ānkh kī jhapkī*.
Twist, (wrench) اينٹھ *ainṭh* (f.), مروڑ *marōṛ* (f.): see Bend, Thread.
Type, (mark) علامت *ʿalāmat* (f.), (emblem) تمثيل *tamṣīl*. (f.)
Types (printer's), چهاپي کي حروف *chhāpē kē ḥurūf*.
Typographer, چهاپيگر *chhāpēgar*. Typography, چهاپاگري *chhāpāgarī*.
Tyranny, ظلم *ẓulm*, جبر *jabr*, اندهير *andhēr*, قهر *ḳahr*.
Tyrant, ظالم *ẓālim*, ستمگر *sitamgar*, جفاکار *jafākār*.
Tyro, نوآموز *nau-āmōz*, مبتدي *mubtadī*. (m.)
Vacancy, Vacuity, خلو *khulū*, خلا *khalā*, جوف *jauf*: see Leisure.
Vacation, ناغه *nāgha*, انتر *antar*, تعطيل *taʿṭīl*. (f.)
Vagabond, Vagrant, اوباش *aubāsh*, آواره *āwāra*, لچا *luchchā*.
Valerian, جال لکڑي *jāl lakṛī*, بليلوٹن *billī-lōṭan*.
Valet, خدمتگار *khidmatgār*.
Valetudinarian, دائم‌المرض *dā'imu-l-maraẓ*, جنم روگي *janam-rōgī*.
Validity, استواري *ustuwārī*, استحکام *istiḥkām*, يقيني *yaḳīnī*.
Valley, Vale, نچان *nichān*, گهاٹي *ghāṭī*, وادي *wādī*, دره *dara*.
Valuation, تعين قيمت *taʿīn-i-ḳīmat* (f.), انکاؤ *ankā'ō*.
Value, قيمت *ḳīmat* (f.), مول *mōl*, بها *bahā*, قدر *ḳadr*. (f.)
Valve, کيواڑ *kēwāṛ*, کهڑکي *khiṛkī*, (lid) ڈهکني *ḍhaknī*.
Van, Vanguard, مهرا *muhrā*, هراول *harāwal*, اگاڑي *agāṛī*.
Vane (weathercock), بادنما *bādnumā*, پهرهرا *pharahrā*.
Vanity, جهوٹها فخر *jhūṭhā fakhr*, شيخي *shēkhī*: see Boast.
Variance, اختلاف *ikhtilāf*, عکس *ʿaks*, ضد *ẓidd* (f.), پهوٹ *phūṭ*. (f.)
Variation, تبديل *tabdīl* (f.), (of the compass) فرقت *furḳat*. (f. ?)
Variety, فرق *farḳ*, (mixture) طرح بطرح *ṭarḥ ba-ṭaraḥ*: see Sort.
Varnish, لک *luk*, روغن *raughan*, لاکه *lākh*.
Vase, برتن کي صورت کا ايک نقشه *bartan kī ṣūrat kā ēk naḳsha*.
Vassal, اسامي *asāmī*, تابعدار *tābiʿdār*. Vassalage, غلامي *ghulāmī*.
Vat, حوض *ḥauẓ*, چهبچه *chahbachcha*.
Udder, ليوا *lēwā*, تهن *than*, کهيري *khīrī*.

Vegetation, نباتات كي باليدگي *nabātāt kī bālīdagī*, نمو *namū*.
Vehemence, شدت *shiddat* (f.), سختي *sakhtī*, زور *zōr*, تندي *tundī*.
Vehicle, سواري *sawārī*, باربرداري *bārbardārī*, مركب *markab*.
Velocity, تيزي *tēzī*, جلدي *jaldī*, تندي *tundī*, تيزروي *tēzrawī*.
Velvet, مخمل *makhmal*.
Veneration, اكرام *ikrām*, تكريم *takrīm* (f.), پوجا *pūjā*. (f.)
Venom, زهر *zahr*, سم *samm*, بكهه *bikh*, بس *bis*.
Vent, چهيد *chhēd*, سوراخ *sūrākh*, نكاس *nikās*: see Breath, Sale.
Ventilator, بادكش *bādkash*. Ventilation, بادكشي *bādkashī*.
Venture, خطره *khatra*, جوكهم *jōkhim* (f.), (of goods) ٹانڈا *ṭāndā*.
Veracity, راستي *rāstī*, سچائي *sachā'ī*, صداقت *ṣadāḳat*. (f.)
Verb, فعل *fi'l*. Verdict, تجويز *tajwīz* (f.), انفصال *infiṣāl*.
Verdigrise, زنگار *zangār*, پترائي *pitrā'ī*, (dakh.) زنگال *zangāl*.
Verdure, سبزي *sabzī*, سرسبزي *sarsabzī*, هرائي *harā'ī*.
Verge, (border) لب *lab*, كناره *kināra*, (wand) چهڑي *chhaṛī*.
Vermicelli, كرماني گندم *kirmānī gandum*, سيوئين *sēwa'īn*. (f.)
Vermilion, شنگرف *shingarf*, اينگر *īngur*.
Verse (line), مصرع *miṣra'*, تك *tuk*, فرد *fard* (f.): see Poesy.
Versification, تنظيم *tanẓīm* (f.), قافيه بندي *ḳāfiya-bandī*.
Vertebra, ڈانڈ كي گره *ḍānḍ kī girih*, (of the neck) منكا *mankā*.
Vespers, نماز شام *namāz-i shām*, سانجها *sanjhā* (f.), عشا *'ishā*.
Vessel, (cask) پيپا *pīpā*, (bason) برتن *bartan*, (ship) جهاز *jahāz*: see Tube.
Vestige, نقشهٔ پا *naḳsha-i-pā*, نشان *nishān*, پتا *patā*.
Veteran, جنگ آزموده *jang-āzmūda*, پرانا سپاهي *purānā sipāhī*.
Vexation, تصديع *taṣdī'* (f.), ايذا *īẓā* (f.), دكهه *dukh*.
Ugliness, بدصورتي *bad-ṣūratī*, زشت روئي *zisht-ru'ī*.
Vibration, تهرتهري *thartharī*, پهڑك *phaṛak* (f.), جنبش *jumbish*. (f.)
Vice, بدي *badī*, برائي *burā'ī*, عيب *'aib*, شرارت *sharārat*. (f.)
Vicinity, جوار *jawār*, قرابت *ḳarābat* (f.), پروس *parōs*.
Vicissitude, نوبت *naubat* (f.), باري *bārī*, داؤ *dā'ō*: see Change.
Victim, قربان *ḳurbān*, بل *bal*, نچهاور *nichhāwar*. (f.)

Victor, ظافر *ẓāfir*, غالب *ghālib*, فتح مند *fatḥ-mand*, غازي *ghāzī*.
View, نگاه *nigāh* (f.), نظر *naẓar* (f.), درشٹ *drishṭ* (f.): see Prospect.
Vigilance, بيداري *bēdārī*, خبرداري *khabardārī*, هوشياري *hōshyārī*.
Vigour, زور *zōr*, قوت *ḳūwat* (f.), بل *bal*, طاقت *ṭāḳat*. (f.)
Villa, باغ *bāgh*, باٹکا *bāṭikā*, خانه باغ *khāna-bāgh*.
Villain, حرامزاده *ḥarāmzāda*, چنڈال *chanḍāl*, پاجي *pājī*. (m.)
Villany, حرامزادگي *ḥarāmzādagī*, دغابازي *daghābāzī*.
Vine, تاک *tāk*, انگور کا درخت *angūr kā darakht*.
Vinegar, سرکه *sirka*, خل *khall*. Vineyard, انگورستان *angūristān*.
Vintage, انگور کي فصل *angūr kī faṣl*.
Violation, فسخ *faskh*, شکستگي *shikastagī*, بگاڑ *bigāṛ*.
Violence, زور *zōr*, توڑ *tōṛ*, جبر *jabr*, غضب *ghaẓab*, ستم *sitam*.
Virginity, بکارت *bakārat* (f.), بکر *bikr* (f.), دوشيزگي *dōshīzagī*.
Virility, مردي *mardī*, رجوليت *rajūliyat* (f.), باه *bāh*. (f.)
Virtue, نيکي *nēkī*, نيکوئي *nēkō'ī*, (efficacy) گن *gun*: see Effect.
Virulence, شدت *shiddat* (f.), سختي *sakhtī*, تندي *tundī*.
Visage, رو *rū*, روئي *rū'ē*, ديدار *dīdār*, چهره *chihra*.
Visibility, Visibleness, ظهور *ẓuhūr*, نموداري *namūdārī*.
Vision, بينائي *bīnā'ī*, (phantom) خيال *khiyāl*: see Sight.
Visit, ملاقات *mulāḳāt* (f.), بهينٹ *bhēnṭ* (f.), مجرا *mujrā*.
Visitant, Visitor, مجرائي *mujrā'ī*, بهينٹويا *bhēnṭwaiyā*.
Vitality, روح پروري *rūḥ-parwarī*, جانداري *jāndārī*.
Vitriol, زاج *zāj*, (blue) توتيا *tūtiyā*.
Vivacity, زنده دلي *zinda-dilī*, دل شادي *dil-shādī*.
Vixen, لڑانکي *laṛānkī*. Vizard, Vizor, مکهه چهاپ *mukh-chhāp*.
Umbrella, چهاتا *chhātā*, چهتر *chhattar*, چهتري *chhatrī*.
Umpire, ثالث *ṣāliṣ*, درمياني *darmiyānī*, منصف *munṣif*.
Unanimity, اتفاق *ittifāḳ*, ايک دلي *ēk-dilī*, ايک مني *ēk-manī*.
Unbelief, بي اعتقادي *bē-i*tiḳādī*, کفر *kufr*, الحاد *ilḥād*.
Unbeliever, غير معتقد *ghair mu*taḳid*, کافر *kāfir*: see Infidel.
Uncertainty, غير مقرري *ghair muḳarrarī*, شک *shakk*.
Uncleanness, ناپاکي *nā-pākī*, ناصافي *nā-ṣāfī*: see Filth.

Unction, مالش *mālish* (f.), تيل ملائي *tēl-malā'ī*: see Ointment.

Underling, زيردست *zēr-dast*, تہلوا *ṭahlū'ā*, تلہڑو *taliḥṛū*.

Undertaker, (of funerals) كفن دوز *kafan-dōz*: see Contractor.

Underwood, جھاڑ *jhāṛ*, جھانکڑ *jhānkaṛ*, جھاڑي *jhāṛī*.

Underwriter, بيمي والا *bīmē-wālā*.

Undulation, لہر *lahar* (f.), هلورا *hilōrā*, هلكور *hilkōr*. (f.)

Uneasiness, بي آرامي *bē-ārāmī*, بيتابي *bētābī*, بيچيني *bēchainī*.

Unevenness, ناهمواري *nā-hamwārī*, نشيبفرازي *nashēbfarāzī*.

Unfavourableness, نامرادي *nā-murādī*. Unfitness, نارسائي *nā-rasā'ī*.

Ungracefulness, نازيبائش *nā-zēbā'ish*. (f.)

Ungratefulness, ناسپاسي *nā-sipāsī*.

Uniformity, ايكساني *ēk-sānī*, برابري *barābarī*, ميل *mēl*.

Union, يگانگي *yagānagī*, جوڑ *jōṛ*, پيوستگي *paiwastagī*.

Unit, يكائي *yakā'ī*, احد *aḥad*, اكا *ikkā*.

Unitarian, موحد *muwaḥḥid*, منكر تثليث *munkir-i-taṣlīṣ*.

Unity, احديت *aḥadīyat* (f.), يكتائي *yaktā'ī*, يگانگي *yagānagī*.

Universality, كليت *kullīyat* (f.), عموميت *ʿumūmiyat*. (f.)

Universe, عالم *ʿālam*, كائنات *kā'ināt* (f.), ترلوك *tri-lōk*.

Unkindness, نامهرباني *nā-mihrbānī*, بي مهري *bē-mihrī*.

Unlawfulness, نادرستي *nā-durustī*, بي انصافي *bē-inṣāfī*.

Unreasonableness, نامعقولي *nā-maʿḳūlī*.

Unruliness, بي ضبطي *bē-ẓabṭī*, بي لگامي *bē-lagāmī*, مگرائي *magrā'ī*.

Unseasonableness, بي وقتي *bē-waḳtī*, بي هنگامي *bē-hangāmī*.

Unsteadiness, بي قراري *bē-ḳarārī*, بي ثباتي *bē-ṡabātī*.

Unsuccessfulness, بي مقصدي *bē-maḳṣadī*, ناكاميابي *nā-kāmyābī*.

Untruth, ناراستي *nā-rāstī*, جھوٹھ *jhūṭh*: see Falsehood.

Unworthiness, بي قدري *be-ḳadrı*, نارسائي *nā-rasā'ī*.

Vocabulary, فرهنگ *farhang* (f.), لغت *lughat* (f.), نام مالا *nām-mālā*.

Vocative (case), ندا *nidā* (f.), سمبودهن *sambōdhan*.

Vociferation, شور پشتي *shōr-pushtī*, غوغا *ghaughā*: see Noise.

Vogue (fashion), رواج *riwāj* (f.), چال *chāl*, چلن *chalan*.

Void (empty space), خالي جگہ *khālī jagah*, خلا *khalā*, خلو *khulū*.

Volcano, جوالامکھي *jwālā-mukhī*, کوه آتش‌افشان *kōh-i-ātashafshān*.
Volley, شلخ *shalkh*, ڏيهڙ *ḍēhuṛ* (f.), (dakh.) ديوڑ *dēwaṛ*. (f.)
Volubility, (aptness to roll) لڑهائي *luṛhā'ī*: see Eloquence.
Volume, جلد *jild* (f.), دفتر *daftar*, (compass) پهيلاو *phailā'ō*.
Volunteer, نجيب *najīb*. Voluptuary, عياش *ʿaiyāsh*.
Vomit, مستفرغ *mustafrigh*, دواي قي آور *dawā-i-ḳai-āwar*.
Voracity, جوع البقري *jū'u-l-baḳarī*, جوع الكلبي *ju'u-l-kalbī*.
Vortex, چکر *chakr*, گرداب *girdāb*, بهنور *bhanwar*.
Votary, فدوي *fidwī*, بنده *banda*, غلام *ghulām*, داس *dās*.
Vote, قول *ḳaul*, بات *bāt* (f.), بولي *bōlī*: see Consent.
Voucher, گواه *gawāh*, دليل *dalīl* (f.), دستاويز *dastāwēz*. (f.)
Vow, نيت *nīyat* (f.), نذر *nazr* (f.), سنکلپ *sankalp*.
Voyage, درياي سفر *daryā'ī safar*, تري کا سفر *tarī kā safar*.
Upholstery, گهر کا اسباب *ghar kā asbāb*, سامان خانه *sāmān-i-khāna*.
Upland, اونچي زمين *ūnchī zamīn*. (f.)
Uproar, غل غپاره *ghul-ghapāra*, غوغا *ghaughā*, هنگامه *hangāma*.
Upshot (result, consequence), انجام *anjām*, نتيجه *natīja*.
Upside, اوپرکي طرف *ūpar kī ṭaraf*. Upstart, نودولت *nau-daulat*.
Urbanity, مروت *murūwat* (f.), بهلمنسائي *bhalmansā'ī*.
Urchin, see Hedge-hog; لونڈا *launḍā*, بچه *bachcha*.
Urethra, نائژه *nā'ịzha* or نائزه *nā'ịza*, موتني *mūtnī*.
Urgency, تقاضا *taḳāẓā*, سختي *sakhtī*, ضرورت *ẓarūrat*. (f.)
Urinal, قاروره *ḳārūra*, بول دان *baul-dān*, پيشاب دان *pēshāb-dān*.
Urn, چرس *charas*, دلو *dalw*, گلدان *guldān*, ستيواڑ *satīwāṛ*. (f.)
Usage, سلوك *sulūk*, ريت *rīt* (f.), چال *chāl* (f.), دستور *dastūr*.
Use, استعمال *istiʿmāl*, عمل *ʿamal*, کام *kām*: see Custom, Need.
Uselessness, نابکاري *nā-bakārī*, لاحاصلي *lā-ḥāṣilī*, اکاج *akāj*.
Usurer, بياج خور *byāj-khōr*, سود خور *sūd-khōr*, بياجي *byājī*.
Usurper, دست دراز *dast-darāz*, زبردست *zabar-dast*, غاصب *ghāṣib*.
Usury, بياج *byāj*, or (dakh.) بياز *byāz*, بيدستور سود *bēdastūr sūd*.
Utensil, برتن *bartan*, ظرف *ẓarf*, هتهيار *hathyār*: see Tool.
Utility, Usefulness, کام *kām*, فائده *fa'ịda*, نفع *nafʿ*, لابه *lābh*.

Utterance, اچار *uchchār*, تلفظ *talaffuẓ*, لب و لہجہ *lab-o-lahja.*

Uttermost, Utmost, نہایت *nihāyat* (f.), غایت *g͟hāyat* (f.), نپٹ *nipaṭ.*

Vulgar, عوام الناس *ăwāmmu-n-nās*, کنجڑے *kunjṛē*, ارزال *arzāl.*

Uvula, حلق کا کوا *ḥalḳ kā kawwā*, لہات *lahāt* (?), لولا *lōlā* (?).

Uxoriousness, زن مریدي *zan-murīdī*, جورو پرستي *jōrū-parastī.*

Wad, Wadding (of a gun), نوالہ *nawāla*, کسن *kasan* (?).

Wafer, ٹکلي *ṭiklī*, چپرا *chaprā*, ٹکیا *ṭikiyā*, چپٹا *chipṭā.*

Wager, شرط *sharṭ* (f.), هوڑ *hōṛ* (f.), داؤ *dā'ō*, برد باخت *burd-bāk͟ht.* (f.)

Wages, طلب *ṭalab*, محنتانہ *miḥnatāna*, مشاهرہ *mushāhara.*

Waggery, ظریفي *ẓarīfī*, ٹھٹھیبازي *ṭhaṭhēbāzī*, هنسي *hansī.*

Wail, Wailing, نالہ وزاري *nāla-ō-zārī*, نوحہ *nauḥa.*

Wainscoat, تختہ بندي *tak͟hta-bandī*, خاتم بندي *k͟hātim-bandī.*

Walk, سیر *sair* (f.), گشت *gasht*, (gait) چال *chāl*, (path) راہ *rāh.* (f.)

Wallet, جهولا *jhōlā*, زنبیل *zambīl* (f.), جهولي *jhōlī.*

Walnut, اخروٹ *ak͟hrōṭ*, چارمغز *chār-mag͟hz.*

Wand, چهڑي *chhaṛī*, عصا *ăṣā*, قمچي *ḳamchī*, پٹکن *paṭkan.*

Want, احتیاج *iḥtiyāj*, حاجت *ḥājat* (f.), تنگي *tangī*, گهاٹ *ghāṭ.*

Ward, (guarding) چوکي *chaukī*, (of a lock), جهڑ *jhaṛ:* see District.

Wardrobe, لباسدان *libāsdān*, توشہ خانہ *tōsha-k͟hāna.*

Ware, Wares, سودا *saudā*, جنس *jins* (f.), مال *māl*, چیز *chīz.* (f.)

Warfare, جنگاوري *jang-āwarī*, جنگبازي *jangbāzī.*

Warmth, گرمي *garmī*, حرارت *ḥarārat* (f.), (ardour) تپاک *tapāk.*

Warning, اطلاع *iṭṭilā`* (f.), خبر *k͟habar* (f.), آگاهي *āgāhī.*

Warp (the threads lengthwise in a loom), تاني *tānī*, تار *tār.*

Warrant, دستک *dastak* (f.), فرمان *farmān*, (voucher) سند *sanad.* (f.)

Wash, (cosmetic) ابٹن *ubṭan*, گلگونہ *gulgūna*, (washing) دهلائي *dhulā'ī.*

Waste, (land) ویرانہ *wīrāna*, خرابہ *k͟harāba :* see Ruin.

Waste-book, کهاتا *khātā*, جانکڑ کي بهي *jānkaṛ kī bahī*, کهسرا *khasrā.*

Watch, بیداري *bēdārī*, (guard, watching) چوکي *chaukī*, (guard, sentinel) پهرا *pahrā*, پاسبان *pāsbān*, (time piece) گهڑي *ghaṛī.*

Watchhouse, چوکي خانہ *chaukī-k͟hāna.*

Watchmaker, گهڑي بناني والا *gharī-banānē-wālā*.

Waterfall, آبشار *ābshār*, جهرنا *jharnā*, چادر *chādar*. (f.)

Wax, موم *mōm*, شمع *sham** (f.), (sealing) لاکه *lākh*, لاك *lāk*.

Way, (road) راه *rāh* (f.), رسته *rasta*, سڑك *saṛak* (f.): see Method.

Wayfarer, راهي *rāhī* (m.), بٹوهي *baṭōhī* (m.), راهگير *rāhgīr*.

Weakness, كمزوري *kamzōrī*, ناتواني *nātawānī*, ضعيفي *ẓa'īfī*.

Weal, رفاهيت *rafāhiyat* (f.), ترقي *taraḳḳī*, اقبالمندي *iḳbālmandī*.

Wealth, دولت *daulat* (f.), دهن *dhan*, مال *māl*, لچهمي *lachhmī*.

Weapon, هتهيار *hathyār*, حربه *ḥarba*, سلاح *silāḥ*. (f.)

Weariness, ماندگي *māndagī*, تهكاهٹ *thakāhaṭ* (f.), عاجزي *ājizī*.

Weather, موسم *mausim*, ايام *aiyām*, رت *rit* (f.), دن *din*.

Web, جالي *jālī*, بناوٹ *bināwaṭ* (f.), تهان *thān*, (film) جهلي *jhillī*.

Wedding, بياه *byāh*, شادي *shādī*, (feast) جشن *jashn*.

Wedge, پچڑ *pachchar* (f.), پهني *phanī*, ميخ *mēkh* (f.), ٹهيكا *ṭhēkā*.

Wedlock, حالت نكاحي *ḥālat-i-nikāḥī*.

Wednesday, بده *budh*, چارشنبه *chār-shamba*.

Weed, چكهرن *chikhuran*, گهاس *ghās*, (widow's weeds) رانڈسالا *rānḍsālā*.

Weight, (for weighing) باٹ *bāṭ*, بٹ كهرا *baṭ-kharā*, سنگ *sang*, وزن *wazn*, (heaviness) بهار *bhār*, (importance) قدر *ḳadr*. (f.)

Welcome, آؤبهگت *ā'ōbhagat* (f.), تواضع *tawāẓu** (f.): see Respect.

Welfare, بهلائي *bhalā'ī*, بهتري *bihtarī*, چهيم كشل *chhēm-kushal*. (f.)

Welkin, اكاس *akās*, هوا *hawā* (f.): see Sky.

Wellbeing, بهبودي *bihbūdī* خير *khair*: see Welfare, Prosperity.

Wellwisher, خيرخواه *khair-khwāh*, نيكخواه *nēk-khwāh*.

Wench, جوان رنڈي *jawān ranḍī*, چهوكري *chhōkrī*, لونڈي *launḍī*.

Wetness, نمناكي *namnākī*, گيلائي *gīlā'ī*, رطوبت داري *ruṭūbat-dārī*, تري *tarī*.

Whale, مگرمچه *magar machchh* (?), حوت *ḥūt* (f.?).

Wharf, گهاٹ *ghāṭ*. Wharfage, گهٹواري *ghaṭwārī*.

Wheel, چكر *chakr*, پهيا *pahiyā*, (potter's) چاك *chāk*: see Spinning.

Wheelwright, پهيا بناني والا *pahiyā-banānē-wālā*.

Whelp, پلا *pillā*, سگ بچه *sag-bachcha*, (tiger's) بگهيلا *baghēlā*.

Whetstone, سان *sān* (f.), سلي *silī*, پتهري *patthrī*, فسان *fisān*.

Whiff, سانس *sāṅs* (f.), دم *dam*, پهونک *phūnk* (f.), جهورک *jhūrak* (?).

While, (time) وقت *waḳt*, (length of time) مدت *muddat*. (f.)

Whim, Whimsey, خيال *khiyāl*, لهر *lahar* (f.), للک *lalak* (f.), موج *mauj*. (f.)

Whip, چابک *chābuk*, کوڙا *kōṛā*, قمچي *ḳamchī*, تازيانه *tāziyāna*.

Whirl, گردش *gardish* (f.), گهماؤ *ghumā'ō*, باد ريشه *bād-rēsha*.

Whiskers, موچهه *mūchh* (f.), بروت *burūt* (f.), گونچهه *gōṅchh* (?).

Whispering, پهسپهساهٹ *phasphasāhaṭ* (f.), کهسرپهسر *khusar-phusar*.

Whistle, (musical pipe) بانسري *bānsrī*, (whistling) سيٹي *sīṭī*.

Whit (point, jot, tittle), نقطه *nuḳṭa*, رتي *ratī*, تل *til*, تنکا *tinkā*.

Whiteness, سفيدي *sufaidī*, بياض *bayāẓ* (f.), اجلاي *ujlā'ī*.

Whitewash (a compos. of lime and water), کلي *kalī*.

Whiting, ايک قسم کي مچهلي *ēk ḳism kī machhlī*: see Chalk.

The Whole, کليه *kulliya*, جمع *jam'* (f.), جمله *jumla*: see Total.

Wick, بتي *battī*, باتي *bātī*, فليته *falīta*.

Wickedness, بدي *badī*, زبوني *zabūnī*, شرارت *sharārat*. (f.)

Wicket, کهڙکي *khiṛkī*, دريچه *darīcha*.

Widow, بيوا *bēwā* (f.), رانڈ *rānḍ*. (f.) Widower, رنڈوا *ranḍū'ā*.

Widowhood, رنڈاپا *ranḍāpā*, بيوگي *bēwagī*, بيواپن *bēwāpan*.

Width, چوڙاي *chauṛā'ī*, کشادگي *kushādagī*, (of cloth) پاٹ *pāṭ*, بر *bar*.

Wig, بال کي ٹوپي *bāl kī ṭōpī*, برکي *barkī* (?).

Wight, آدمي *ādmī* (m. f.), جن *jan*, شخص *shaḳhṣ*, کس *kas*.

Wild, Wilderness, بيابان *bayābān*, صحرا *ṣaḥrā*, جنگل *jangal*.

Wildgoosechase, بيفايده سعي *bēfā'ida sa'ī*, برباد محنت *barbād miḥnat*. (f.)

Wile, حيله *ḥīla*, مکر *makar*, فطرت *fiṭrat* (f.), بتا *buttā*.

Will, (choice) مرضي *marẓī*, چاه *chāh*, (last) وصيت نامه *waṣīyat nāma*.

Will-o'-the-wisp, چهلاوا *chhalāwā*, لکاري *lukārī* (?).

Wimble, برما *barmā*. Winch, چرخي کا دسته *charkhī kā dasta*.

Windegg, خاکي انڈا *khākī anḍā*. Windingsheet, کفن *kafan*.

Windfall, چوا *chō'ā*, پڑا پهل *paṛā phal*, (figur.) خدا داد *khudā-dād*.

Windlass, ارگباد *argbād* (?), منجنيق *manjanīḳ*.

Wink, جهپكي *jhapkī*: see Hint. Wipe, پونچهه *pōnchh*: see Stroke.

Wire, تار *tār*, رشته *rishta*. Wire chain, سيكري *sīkrī*, سئي *sa'ī*.

Wisdom, عقل *ặḳl* (f.), دانائي *dānā'ī*, بدهه *budh* (f.), گيان *gyān*.

Wise, طرح *ṭaraḥ* (f.): see Manner.

Wiseacre, كچا بزرگ *kachchā buzurg*, لال بجهكڑ *lāl-bujhakkaṛ*.

Wisp, پولا *pūlā*, آنٿي *ānṭī*, جونا *jūnā*, گوڑهي *gūṛhī* (?).

Wit, تيزفهمي *tēz-fahmī*, ذهن *ẕihn*: a Wit, زيرك آدمي *zīrak ādmī*.

Witch, ڈائين *ḍā'ēn* (f.), ڈنكني *ḍankanī*, جادوگرني *jādūgarnī*.

Witchcraft, جادو *jādū*, ٿونا *ṭōnā*, سحر *siḥr*, اوجهائي *ōjhā'ī* (?).

Witness, (testimony) شهادت *shahādat* (f.), (person) شاهد *shāhid*.

Witticism, نكته *nukta*, زيركي *zīrakī*, بزله *bazla*, جگت *jugat*. (f.)

Wo, غم *gham*, اندوه *andōh*, سوگ *sōg*, افسوس *afsōs*, ماتم *mātam*.

Womankind, رنڈي ذات *ranḍī-ẕāt* (f.), عالم نسا *ặlam-i-nisā*.

Womb, رحم *riḥm*, بچه دان *bachcha-dān*, كوكهه *kōkh* (f.), پيٿ *pēṭ*.

Wonder, تعجب *ta'ặjjub*, اچنبها *achambhā*, حيرت *ḥairat*. (f.)

Wood, (the substance) لكڑي *lakṛī*, كاٿهه *kāṭh*: see Forest, Timber.

Woof, پود *pūd*, بهرني *bharnī*, بانا *bānā*.

Wool, اون *ūn* (f.), پشم *pashm* (f.), روان *rō'ān*, صوف *ṣūf*.

Word, بات *bāt* (f.), بچن *bachan*, سخن *sukhan*: see Message, Promise.

Work, كام *kām*, كاج *kāj*, محنت *miḥnat* (f.): see Book, Workmanship.

Workmanship, كاريگري *kārīgarī*, صنعت *ṣan'ặt* (f.), مصنوع *maṣnū*ʿ.

Worship, پرستش *parastish* (f.), عبادت *ʿibādat* (f.), بهجن *bhajan*.

Worth, قيمت *ḳīmat* (f.), مول *mōl*, قدر *ḳadr* (f.), فضيلت *fazīlat*. (f.)

Wrangle, Wrangling, جهگڑا *jhagṛā*, جهنجهٿ *jhanjhaṭ*, رگڑا *ragṛā*.

Wrangler, جهگڑالو *jhagṛālū*, لڑانكا *laṛānkā*, حجتي *ḥujjatī*.

Wrapper, لفافه *lifāfa*, بيٿهن *bēṭhan*, دست بقچه *dast-buḳcha*.

Wrath, غضب *ghazab*, قهر *ḳahr*, جذبه *jaẕba*, كوپ *kōp*.

Wreath, (garland) سهرا *sihrā*, مور *maur*, (thing twisted) پيچ *pēch*.

Wreck, (of a ship) كهكهرا *khakhrā* (?), كشتي كي غارتي *kishtī kī ghāratī*: see Ruin.

Wrench, (instrument) پيچ ديني کا ايک هتهيار *pēch dēnē kā ēk hath-yār:* see Twist.

Wretch, کمبخت *kam-bakht*, نگوڑا *nigōṛā*, ناکس *nā-kas:* see Poor.

Wretchedness, کمبختي *kambakhtī*, پريشاني *parēshānī*, ذلت *zillat.* (f.)

Wrinkle, چين *chīn* (f.), شکن *shikan* (f.), جهري *jhurī*, سکوڑ *sikōṛ.* (f.)

Writing, Writ, تحرير *taḥrīr* (f.), لکهاوٹ *likhāwaṭ* (f.), تصنيف *taṣ-nīf.* (f.)

Wrong, ظلم *zulm*, ناحقي *nā-ḥakkī*, بدعت *bid'at* (f.).

Yard, (measure) گز *gaz*, ذراع *zirā*, (enclosure) صحن *ṣaḥn*, انگنا *angnā.*

Yarn, اون کا سوت *ūn kā sūt*, سوت *sūt.*

Yearning, بڑي چاه يا خواهش *baṛī chāh* or *khwāhish*, درد *dard.*

Yeast, مايه *māya*, خمير *khamīr*, تاڑي *tāṛī:* see Leaven.

Yell, چيخ *chīkh* (f.), چکر *chikkar* (?): see Roar.

Yeoman, ملکي لوگ *milkī lōg*, مالگذار *mālguzār*, کسان *kisān.*

Yoke, جوا *jū'ā*, جواٹه *jū'āṭh*, (pair) جوڑا *jōṛā*, جفت *juft.*

Yolk, (or Yelk) of an egg, انڈي کي زردي *anḍē kī zardī*, ماوا *māwā.* (f.)

Young (of any creature), بچه *bachcha*, طفل *tifl:* see Child.

Youth, جواني *jawānī*, شباب *shabāb*, جوبن *jōban:* see Young man.

Zeal, گرمي *garmī*, حميت *ḥamīyat* (f.), سرگرمي *sar-garmī.*

Zone, (girdle) کمربند *kamarband*, (frigid) منطقهٔ مبروده *minṭaka-e-mabrūda*, (temperate) منطقهٔ معتدله *minṭaka-e-mu'tadila*, (torrid) منطقهٔ محروقه *minṭaka-e-maḥrūka.*

Zoology, علم حيوانات *'ilm-i-ḥaiwānāt.*

VERBS OF FREQUENT USE.

To abandon, تجنا *tajnā*, ترک کرنا *tark-karnā*, چهوڑنا *chhōṛnā.*

To abase, پچهاڑنا *pachhāṛnā*, گرانا *girānā*, ذليل کرنا *zalīl karnā.*

To be abashed, لجانا *lajānā*, شرمانا *sharmānā*, سکچنا *sukuchnā.*

To abate, گهٹانا *ghaṭānā*, قيمت کم کرنا *ḳīmat kam karnā.*

To abdicate, تیاگنا *tyāgnā*, چھوڑنا *chhōṛnā:* see To abandon.

To abet, مدد کرنا *madad karnā*, همت یا ترغیب دینا *himmat* or *targhīb dēnā*.

To abhor, دور بھاگنا *dūr bhāgnā*, کراهیت یا نفرت رکھنا *karāhiyat* or *nafrat rakhnā*.

To abide, بسنا *basnā*, ٹھہرنا *ṭhaharnā*, رهنا *rahnā*.

To abjure, انحراف کرنا *inḥirāf karnā*, حدیث کرنا *ḥadīṣ karnā:* see To reject.

To be able, سکنا *saknā*, لائق هونا *lā'iḳ honā*, طاقت رکھنا *ṭāḳat rakhnā*.

To abolish, اٹھا دینا *uṭhā dēnā*, مٹانا *miṭānā*, موقوف کرنا *mauḳūf karnā*.

To abound, امڈنا *umaḍnā* or امنڈنا *umanḍnā*, معمور هونا *ma'mūr hōnā*.

To abrade, (act.) رگڑنا *ragaṛnā*, گھسانا *ghisānā*, (act. or neut.) گھسنا *ghisnā*.

To abridge, مختصر کرنا *mukhtaṣar karnā*, اختصار کرنا *ikhtiṣār karnā*.

To abscond, چھپا رهنا *chhipā rahnā*, بھاگنا *bhāgnā*, روپوش هونا *rūpōsh hōnā*.

To absolve, مبرا کرنا *mubarrā karnā*, معاف کرنا *mu'āf karnā*.

To absorb, سوکھنا *sōkhnā*, جذب کرنا *jaẕb karnā*, کھپانا *khapānā*.

To abstain (from), بر یا باز آنا *bar* or *bāz ānā*, پرهیز کرنا *parhēz karnā*.

To abstract, انتخاب کرنا *intikhāb karnā:* see To select, extract.

To abuse, (revile) گالي دینا *gālī dēnā*, (ill treat) بد سلوکي کرنا *bad-sulūkī karnā*.

To accept, لینا *lēnā*, قبول کرنا *ḳabūl karnā*, ماننا *mānnā*.

To accept (a bill of exchange, &c.), سکارنا *sakārnā*.

To accommodate, خبر گیري کرنا *khabar-gīrī karnā*, منانا *manānā*.

To accompany, همراه هونا *hamrāh hōnā*, رفاقت کرنا *rifāḳat karnā*.

To accomplish, پورا کرنا *pūrā karnā*, نباهنا *nibāhnā*, سارنا *sārnā*.

To account, (compute) شمار کرنا *shumār karnā*, (answer for) جوابدهي کرنا *jawāb-dihī karnā*.

To accuse, دوکھنا *dōkhnā*, دعوی کرنا *da'wā karnā*, ڈهانسنا *ḍhānsnā*.

To accustom, عادت یا محاوره یا ربط کرنا *'ādat* or *muḥāwara* or *rabṭ karnā*.

To ache, دکهنا *dukhnā*, پرانا *pirānā*, درد کرنا *dard karnā.*

To acknowledge, اقرار کرنا *iḳrār karnā*, ماننا *mānnā.*

To acquaint, اطلاع یا خبر کرنا *iṯṯilā'* or *khabar karnā:* see To inform.

To acquire, حاصل کرنا *ḥāṣil karnā*, پیدا کرنا *paidā karnā*, کمانا *kamānā.*

To acquit (of crime), بیگناہ ٹھہرانا *be-gunāh ṭhahrānā:* see To absolve.

To act, کرنا *karnā*, (a character) نقل کرنا *naḳl karnā.*

To actuate, حرکت دینا *ḥarakat dēna*, سرکانا *sarkāna.*

To adapt, موافق یا مناسب کرنا *muwāfiḳ* or *munāsib karnā.*

To add, لگانا *lagānā*, جوڑنا *joṛnā*, (up figures) گٹھری کرنا *gaṭhrī karnā.*

To address (a letter), چٹھي کا سرنامہ لکھنا *chiṭṭhī kā sarnāma likhnā.*

To adduce, لانا *lānā*, بتلانا *batlānā:* see To bring, relate.

To adjust, ترتیب دینا *tartīb dēnā*, چکانا *chukānā*, درست کرنا *durust karnā.*

To admit, آنے دینا *ānē dēnā;* (to allow) قبول کرنا *ḳabūl karnā.*

To admonish, سمجہانا *samjhānā*, نصیحت کرنا *naṣīḥat karnā.*

To adopt, متبنیٰ کو اختیار کرنا *mutabannā kō ikhtiyār karnā*, (use) عمل میں لانا *āmal mēṅ lānā.*

To adore, پوجنا *pūjnā*, بهجنا *bhajnā*, بهجن کرنا *bhajan karnā.*

To adorn, سنوارنا *saṅwārnā*, سدهارنا *sudhārnā*, بنانا *banānā.*

To advance (v. n.), بڑهنا *baṛhnā*, ترقي کرنا *taraḳḳī karnā.*

To advance (v. a.), بڑهانا *baṛhānā*, چلانا *chalānā:* see To propose.

To advance (money), پیشگي دینا *pēshgī dēnā.*

To advertise, اشتہار کرنا *ishtihār karnā*, ظاهر کرنا *ẓāhir karnā.*

To advise, نصیحت دینا *naṣīḥat dēnā*, خبر کرنا *khabar karnā.*

To afflict, ستانا *satānā*, تکلیف دینا *taklīf dēnā.*

To agitate, هلانا *hilānā*, جنبش دینا *jumbish dēnā*, (in the mind) فکر کرنا *fikr karnā.*

To agree, راضي یا متفق هونا *rāẓī* or *muttafiḳ hōnā*, ماننا *mānnā.*

To agree (to stipulate), شرط یا اقرار یا بچن کرنا *sharṭ* or *iḳrār* or *bachan karnā.*

To aim, شست باندهنا *shast bāndhnā*, تکنا *taknā:* see To guess.

To alight, اترنا *utarnā*, فرود هونا *farōd hōnā.*

To allow, ماننا *mānnā*, قبول کرنا *ḳabūl karnā*; (to permit), دینا *dēnā*; (to abate) گھٹانا *ghaṭānā*, تخفیف دینا *takhfīf dēnā*.

To allure, فریب دینا *farēb dēnā*, لبھانا *lubhānā*, پھسلانا *phuslānā*.

To alter, بدلنا *badalnā*, تبدیل کرنا *tabdīl karnā*, تغیر کرنا *taghīr karnā*.

To amass, فراهم کرنا *farāham karnā*, جمع کرنا *jam' karnā*.

To amaze, بھچکانا *bhachkānā*, حیران کرنا *ḥairān karnā*.

To amuse, بہلانا *bahlānā*, تفریح دینا *tafrīḥ dēnā*.

To animate, جلانا *jilānā*; (to encourage) ڈھارس دینا *ḍhāṛas dēnā*.

To annex, لگانا *lagānā*, جوڑنا *jōṛnā*, پیوند کرنا *paiwand karnā*.

To annoy, کھجانا *khijānā*, تصدیع دینا *taṣdī' dēnā*.

To anoint, طلا یا تدهین کرنا *ṭilā* or *tadhīn karnā*, ملنا *malnā*.

To answer, جواب یا اتر دینا *jawāb* or *uttar dēnā*, (to suit) ٹھیک آنا *ṭhīk ānā*.

To appear, سوجھنا *sūjhnā*, نظر آنا *naẓar ānā*, دکھلائی دینا *dikhlā'ī dēnā*.

To applaud, آفرین کرنا *āfrin karnā*, سراهنا *sarāhnā*, شاباشي دینا *shābāshī dēnā*.

To apply, (v. n.) لگنا *lagnā*; (to suit) ٹھیک آنا *ṭhīk ānā*; (v. a.) لگانا *lagānā*, جوڑنا *jōṛnā*; (to address to) درخواست کرنا *darkhwāst karnā*.

To appoint, ٹھہرانا *ṭhahrānā*, مقرر کرنا *muḳarrar karnā*.

To appraise, کوتنا *kūtnā*, آنکنا *ānknā*, مول ٹھہرانا *mōl ṭhahrānā*.

To approach, نزدیک یا پاس یا قریب آنا *nazdīk* or *pās* or *ḳarīb ānā*.

To approve, پسند کرنا *pasand karnā*, چاهنا *chāhnā*, قبولنا *ḳabūlnā*.

To argue, حجت کرنا *ḥujjat karnā*, بحث کرنا *baḥṣ karnā*, باد کرنا *bād karnā*.

To arise, اٹھنا *uṭhnā*, چڑھنا *chaṛhnā*.

To arrange, ترتیب دینا *tartīb dēnā*, سنوارنا *sanwārnā*.

To arrive, پہنچنا *pahunchnā*, آنا *ānā*, واقع هونا *wāḳi' hōnā*.

To ascend, چڑھنا *chaṛhnā*, بلند هونا *buland hōnā*, بلنگنا *bilangnā*.

To ascertain, تحقیق کرنا *taḥḳīḳ karnā*, ٹھہرانا *ṭhahrānā*.

To ascertain (a disease), تشخیص کرنا *tashkhīṣ karnā*.

To ask, پوچھنا *pūchhnā*, چاهنا *chāhnā*; (ask for) مانگنا *māngnā*.

To assault, حمله يا تاخت كرنا *ḥamla* or *tākht karnā.*

To assist, مدد كرنا *madad karnā,* سمبهالنا *sambhālnā:* see To help.

To assuage, تخفيف دينا *takhfīf dēnā,* ٹهنڈا كرنا *ṭhanḍā karnā.*

To assume, لينا *lēnā,* (grant, admit) فرض كرنا *farẓ karnā.*

To assure, اقرار كرنا *iḳrār karnā,* (to comfort) تسلي دينا *tasallī dēnā.*

To astonish, حيران كرنا *ḥairān karnā,* جهبكانا *jhabkānā.*

To attain, (v. n.) بهم پهنچنا *baham pahunchnā,* (v. a.) لابه كرنا *lābh karnā.*

To attempt, كوشش يا سعي يا قصد كرنا *kōshish* or *sa'ī* or *ḳaṣd karnā.*

To attend, (wait on) حاضر رهنا *ḥāẓir rahnā,* (observe) دهيان كرنا *dhyān karnā,* (as a physician) معالجه يا دوا كرنا *mu'ālaja* or *dawā karnā.*

To attest, شاهدي يا گواهي دينا *shāhidī* or *gawāhī dēnā,* (to sign) صحيح كرنا *ṣaḥīḥ karnā.*

To attract, كهينچنا *khainchnā,* جذب كرنا *jaẕb karnā:* see To allure.

To avail, كام آنا *kām ānā,* فائده كرنا *fā'ida karnā.*

To avert, دور يا دفع كرنا *dūr* or *daf' karnā,* ٹالنا *ṭālnā.*

To augment, بڑهانا *baṛhānā,* زياده كرنا *ziyāda karnā.*

To avoid, پرهيز يا احتراز كرنا *parhēz* or *iḥtirāz karnā,* بچنا *bachnā.*

To avouch, avow, كهنا *kahnā,* اقرار كرنا *iḳrār karnā,* ظاهر كرنا *ẓāhir karnā.*

To awake, (v. n.) جاگنا *jāgnā,* جگنا *jagnā,* (v. a.) جگانا *jagānā.*

To babble, بكنا *baknā,* اڑبڑ بكنا *aṛbaṛ baknā,* بڑبڑانا *baṛbaṛānā.*

To back, (mount a horse) سوار هونا *sawār hōnā,* (second) پشتي كرنا *pushtī karnā.*

To backbite, چغلي كهانا *chughlī khānā,* غيبت كرنا *ghībat karnā.*

To bait, (a hook) چاره ركهنا *chāra rakhnā,* (take food) ناشته كرنا *nāshta karnā.*

To bake, پكانا *pakānā,* (to make bread) پونا *pōnā.*

To balk, بالا دينا *bālā dēnā,* نااميد يا محروم كرنا *nā-ummēd* or *maḥrūm karnā.*

To bang, مارنا *mārnā,* پيٹنا *pīṭnā,* دهول لگانا *dhaul lagānā.*

To bar, بینڈا لگانا *bēṇḍā lagānā*, (obstruct) روکنا *rōknā*, سد کرنا *sadd karnā.*

To banish, جلاوطن کرنا *jilā-waṭan karnā*, دیس نکالا دینا *dēs-nikālā dēnā.*

To bargain, (promise) وعدہ کرنا *wa*da karnā*, (to buy) مول لینا *mōl lēnā.*

To bark, (as a dog) بھونکنا *bhaunknā*, (v. a. a tree, &c.) چھیلنا *chhīlnā.*

To bate, گھٹانا *ghaṭānā*, قیمت کو کم کرنا *ḳīmat kō kam karnā.*

To bathe, (v. n.) نہانا *nahānā*, (v. a.) غسل کرنا *g͟husl karnā*, نہلانا *nahlānā.*

To bawl, پکارنا *pukārnā*, چلانا *chillānā*, ھانک مارنا *hānk mārnā.*

To be, to become, ھونا *hōnā*, رھنا *rahnā*, بنا *bannā*, ھوجانا *hōjānā.*

To bear, (endure) سہنا *sahnā*, برداشت کرنا *bardāsht karnā*, (carry) لینا *lēnā.*

To beat, پیٹنا *pīṭnā*, مارنا *mārnā*, کوٹنا *kūṭnā*: see To conquer.

To beckon, اشارہ یا ایما کرنا *ishāra* or *īmā karnā.*

To become, (suit) موافق یا لائق ھونا *muwāfiḳ* or *lā'iḳ hōnā*: see To be.

To beget, جنمانا *janmānā*, پیدا کرنا *paidā karnā.*

To beg, بھیکھ مانگنا *bhīkh māngnā*, سوال کرنا *suwāl karnā*, چاھنا *chāhnā.*

To begin, (v. a.) شروع کرنا *shurū* karnā*, (v. n.) لگنا *lagnā*, نندھنا *nandhnā.*

To begird, کمر باندھنا *kamar bāndhnā*, لپیٹنا *lapēṭnā*, بند کرنا *band karnā.*

To beguile, بہکانا *bahkānā*, فریب دینا *farēb dēnā*, دم دینا *dam dēnā.*

To behave, چلن چلنا *chalan chalnā*, نباھنا *nibāhnā.*

To behead, گردن مارنا *gardan mārnā*, سر کاٹنا *sir kāṭnā.*

To behold, دیکھنا *dēkhnā*, بلوکنا *bilōknā*, نظر کرنا *nazar karnā.*

To behove, موافق یا مناسب ھونا *muwāfiḳ* or *munāsib hōnā.*

To believe, ماننا *mānnā*, باور کرنا *bāwar karnā*, جاننا *jānnā.*

To bellow, ڈکارنا *ḍakārnā*, چلانا *chillānā*, شور کرنا *shōr karnā.*

To belong, لگنا *lagnā*, متعلق ھونا *muta'ālliḳ hōnā.*

To bend (v. a.), ٹیڑھا یا خم کرنا *ṭēṛhā* or *k͟ham karnā*, نہڑانا *nihuṛānā.*

To benum (v. a.), ٹھٹھرانا *ṭhiṭhurānā* or *ṭhiṭhirānā*, سن کرنا *sun karnā.*

To bequeath, دے مرنا *dē marnā*, وصیت یا ھبہ کرنا *waṣīyat* or *hiba karnā.*

To beseech, گڑگڑانا *girgiṛānā,* بنتي يا عاجزي كرنا *bintī* or *ājizī karnā.*

To beset, گھيرنا *ghērnā,* محاصره كرنا *muḥāṣara karnā.*

To besiege, گھير لينا *ghēr lēnā,* محاصره كرنا *muḥāṣara karnā.*

To besmear, ليپنا *lēpnā,* چپڑنا *chupaṛnā,* طلا كرنا *ṭilā karnā.*

To bestow, بخش دينا *bakhsh dēnā,* عطا كرنا *ʿaṭā karnā,* دينا *dēnā.*

To betoken, دلالت كرنا *dalālat karnā,* بتلانا *batlānā.*

To betray, دغابازي سي سونپنا *daghā-bāzī sē sōmpnā,* (a secret) پھوڑنا *phōṛnā,* پردهدري كرنا *parda-darī karnā.*

To betroth, نسبت يا منگني كرنا *nisbat* or *mangnī karnā,* منسوب كرنا *mansūb karnā.*

To bid, كهنا *kahnā,* سنانا *sunānā:* see To command, invite.

To bid for (offer a price), مول كرنا *mōl karnā.*

To bilk, دغابازي كرنا *daghābāzī karnā,* فريب كرنا *farēb karnā.*

To bind, باندهنا *bāndhnā,* جكڑنا *jakaṛnā,* چهاندنا *chhāndnā.*

To bisect, برابر دو حصي كرنا *barābar dō ḥiṣṣē karnā.*

To bite, كاٹنا *kāṭnā,* دانت سي كاٹنا *dānt sē kāṭnā,* چبانا *chabānā.*

To blab, پرده دري كرنا *parda-darī karnā,* راز كو فاش كرنا *rāz kō fāsh karnā.*

To blame, دوكهنا *dōkhnā,* ملامت كرنا *malāmat karnā.*

To be blasted, مرجهانا *murjhānā,* كمهلانا *kumhlānā.*

To blaze, دهدهكنا *dhadhaknā,* (blaze forth) بهڑكنا *bhaṛaknā.*

To bleach, نكهارنا *nikhārnā,* اجلا يا صاف كرنا *ujlā* or *ṣāf karnā.*

To bleat, ممیانا *mimiyānā,* (dakh.) بهين بهين كرنا *bhēṅ bhēṅ karnā.*

To bleed, (lose blood) لوهو دينا *lōhū dēnā,* (let blood) فصد كهولنا *fasd khōlnā.*

To blemish, داغي كرنا *dāghī karnā,* عيب لگانا *ʿaib lagānā,* نقصان كرنا *nuḳṣān karnā.*

To blend, ملانا *milānā,* آميز يا مخلوط كرنا *āmēz* or *makhlūṭ karnā.*

To bless, دعا دينا *duʿā dēnā,* اسيس دينا *asīs denā,* مبارك كرنا *mubārak karnā.*

To blight, جهلس دينا *jhulas dēnā,* پژمرده كرنا *pazhmurda karnā.*

To bloom or blossom, كهلنا *khilnā,* پهولنا *phūlnā,* بكسنا *bikasnā.*

To blow, (v. n.) بهنا *bahnā*, چلنا *chalnā*, (v. a.) پهونكنا *phūnknā*.

To blunder, چوكنا *chūknā*, بهولنا *bhūlnā*, خطا كرنا *khaṭā karnā*.

To blush, خجلت اٹهانا *khijlat uṭhānā*, خجل هونا *khajil hōnā*.

To boast, brag, لاف زني كرنا *lāf-zanī karnā*, فخر كرنا *fakhr karnā*.

To bode, شگون دينا *shugūn dēnā*, دلالت كرنا *dalālat karnā*.

To boggle, ٹهٹهكنا *ṭhiṭhaknā*, جهجهكنا *jhajhaknā*.

To boil, (v. n.) كهولنا *khaulnā*, ابلنا *ubalnā*, (v. a.) ابالنا *ubālnā*, (cook by boiling) جوش دينا *jōsh dēnā*.

To book, درج كرنا *darj karnā*. To boot, فائده كرنا *fā'ida karnā*.

To bore, چهيدنا *chhēdnā*, بيدهنا *bēdhnā*, برمانا *barmānā*.

To be born, جننا *jannā*, جنمنا *janamnā*, پيدا هونا *paidā hōnā*.

To borrow, مانگ لينا *māng lēnā*, قرض لينا *ḳarẓ lēnā*.

To bounce (jump up), چونك پڑنا *chaunk paṛnā*, چوكڑي بهرنا *chaukaṛī bharnā*.

To bound (jump up), كودنا *kūdnā*, اچهلنا *uchhalnā*.

To bound (limit), حد باندهنا *ḥadd bāndhnā*, بند كرنا *band karnā*.

To bow, (v. n. to stoop) نهڑنا *nihuṛnā*, جهكنا *jhuknā*, (v.a.) see To bend.

To box (strike), گهوسا مارنا *ghūsā mārnā*, تماچه مارنا *tamācha mārnā*.

To brace, سميٹنا *samēṭnā*, كسنا *kasnā*, (a drum) چڑهانا *chaṛhānā*.

To braid, گوندهنا *gūndhnā*, بنا *bunnā*.

To brand, داغ دينا *dāgh dēnā*, گل لگانا *gul lagānā*, داغنا *dāghnā*.

To brandish, گهمانا *ghumānā*, چمكانا *chamkānā*, پهرانا *phirānā*.

To bray, (to pound) كوٹنا *kūṭnā*, (as an ass) رينكنا *rēnknā*.

To break, (v. a.) توڑنا *tōṛnā*, پهوڑنا *phōṛnā*, (v. n.) ٹوٹنا *ṭūṭnā*.

To break (become bankrupt), مفلس هو جانا *muflis hō jānā*.

To break (v. a. break in, tame), رام كرنا *rām karnā*, سادهنا *sādhnā*.

To break (v. a. dismiss), معزول كرنا *ma'zūl karnā*.

To breathe, (draw breath) دم لينا *dam lēnā*, (expel breath) دم چهوڑنا *dam chhōṛnā*.

To breed, (produce) جنانا *janānā*, پيدا كرنا *paidā karnā*, (nourish) پالنا *pālnā*.

To bring, لانا *lānā* (v. n.) or لے آنا *lē-ānā*, (v. a.) آننا *ānnā*.

To broil, بهوننا *bhūnnā*, کباب کرنا *kabāb karnā*, گرم کرنا *garm karnā*.

To brood, سیونا *sewnā*, (over) اندیشه کرنا *andēsha karnā*.

To browbeat, دبکانا *dabkānā*, آنکھ دکھلانا *ānkh dikhlānā*.

To bruise, کچلنا *kuchalnā*, پیسنا *pīsnā*, ڈالنا *ḍālnā*.

To brush, جهاڑنا *jhāṛnā*, برش سے صاف کرنا *barash sē ṣāf karnā*.

To bud (v. n.), کلیانا *kaliyānā*, کونپل پهوٹنا *kōnpal phūṭnā*.

To budge, هٹنا *haṭnā*, ٹلنا *ṭalnā*, سرکنا *saraknā*.

To build, تعمیر کرنا *ta*ʿ*mīr karnā*, بنا کرنا *binā karnā*.

To burden, بوجھ لادنا یا رکهنا *bōjh lādnā* or *rakhnā*, زیر بار کرنا *zēr bār karnā*.

To burn, (v. n.) جلنا *jalnā*, بلنا *balnā*, دهنا *dahnā*, (v. a.) جلانا *jalānā*.

To burnish, جهلکانا *jhalkānā*, چمکانا *chamkānā*, صیقل کرنا *ṣaiḳal karnā*.

To burst, (v. n.) پهوٹنا *phūṭnā*, پهٹنا *phaṭnā*, (v. a.) پهوڑنا *phōṛnā*.

To bury, گاڑنا *gāṛnā*, دفن کرنا *dafn karnā*: see To hide.

To buy, مول لینا *mōl lēnā*, خریدنا *kharīdnā*, کینا *kīnnā*.

To buzz, بهنبهنانا *bhimbhinānā*, (whisper) پهسپهسانا *phusphusānā*.

To cajole, پهسلانا *phuslānā*, دم یا فریب دینا *dam* or *farēb dēnā*.

To calculate, گننا *ginnā*, حساب کرنا *ḥisāb karnā*: see To guess.

To calk (a ship, &c.), کالا پتی کرنا *kālā-pattī karnā*, گابنا *gābnā*.

To call, بلانا *bulānā*, (send for) طلب کرنا *ṭalab karnā*, بلا بهیجنا *bulā bhējnā*, (name) نام رکهنا *nām rakhnā*, (cry out) پکارنا *pukārnā*.

To calve, (v. n.) بیانا *byānā*, بچهڑے کو جننا *bachhrē kō jannā*.

To calumniate, تهمت لگانا *tuhmat lagānā*: see To revile.

Can, سکنا *saknā*: see To be able.

To cancel, میٹنا *mēṭnā*, محو کرنا *maḥw karnā*, مٹانا *miṭānā*.

To cannonade, توپیں مارنا یا چلانا *tōpēṅ mārnā* or *chalānā*.

To canvass, (examine) چهاننا *chhānnā*, جانچنا *jānchnā*, بحثنا *baḥasnā*.

To caper, کودنا *kūdnā*, اچهلنا *uchhalnā*.

To captivate (to charm), موه لینا *mōh lēnā*, فریفته کرنا *farēfta karnā*.

To card (comb cotton, &c.), دهنکنا *dhunaknā*, دهننا *dhunnā*.

To care, فکر کرنا *fikr karnā*, (care for) خاطر میں لانا *khāṭir mēṅ lānā*.

To caress, پیار کرنا *pyār karnā*, نوازش کرنا *nawāzish karnā*.

To carry, ليجانا *lējānā*, ڈهونا *ḍhōnā*, اٹهانا *uṭhānā*.

To carve, کهودنا *khōdnā*, کنده کرنا *kanda karnā*, تراشنا *tarāshnā*.

To case, مڑهنا *maṛhnā*, منڈهنا *manḍhnā*, غلاف کرنا *ghilāf karnā*.

To cashier, برطرف کرنا *bar ṭaraf karnā*, معزول کرنا *ma*ʿ*zūl karnā*.

To cast, پهينکنا *phēnknā*, ڈالنا *ḍālnā*, جهونکنا *jhōnknā*, گرانا *girānā*.

To catch, پکڑنا *pakaṛnā*, پکڑ لينا *pakaṛ lēnā*, پهنسانا *phansānā*.

To cavil, نکته چيني يا حرف گيري کرنا *nukta-chīnī* or *ḥarf-gīrī karnā*.

To cause, کرانا *karānā*, کرنا *karnā*, نکالنا *nikālnā*, لانا *lānā*.

To cauterize, داغنا *dāghnā*, داغ يا گل دينا *dāgh* or *gul dēnā*.

To cease, (v. n.) باز رهنا *bāz rahnā*, دست بردار هونا *dast-bardār honā*.

To cease, (v. a.) چهوڑنا *chhōṛnā*, موقوف کرنا *mauḳūf karnā*.

To celebrate, سراهنا *sarāhnā*, تعريف کرنا *ta*ʿ*rīf karnā*.

To challenge, لڑائي مانگنا *laṛā'ī māngnā*, مقابله چاهنا *muḳābala chāhnā*.

To change (v. a.), تبديل کرنا *tabdīl karnā*, بدلانا *badlānā*.

To charge, (load) بهرنا *bharnā*, (impute) ٹههرانا *ṭhahrānā*, (attack) حمله کرنا *ḥamla karnā*, (enjoin) تاکيد کرنا *tākīd karnā*.

To charm, (bewitch) جادو کرنا *jādū karnā*, (enchant) موه لينا *mōh lēnā*.

To chastise, chasten, تنبيه يا تاديب کرنا *tambīh* or *tādīb karnā*.

To chat, بکنا *baknā*, گپ مارنا *gap mārnā*, گفتگو کرنا *guftgū karnā*.

To chatter, بڑبڑانا *baṛbaṛānā*, بکنا *baknā*, چرچرانا *chirchirānā*.

To cheapen, مول يا قيمت کرنا *mōl* or *ḳīmat karnā*, قيمت گهٹانا *ḳīmat ghaṭānā*.

To cheat, ٹهگنا *ṭhagnā*, چهلنا *chhalnā*, دغابازي کرنا *daghābāzī karnā*.

To check, اٹکانا *aṭkānā*, روکنا *rōknā*, دبانا *dabānā*, ڈانٹنا *ḍānṭnā*.

To cherish, پالنا *pālnā*, پرورش يا سيوا کرنا *parwarish* or *sēwā karnā*.

To chew, چابنا *chābnā*, چبانا *chabānā*, (the cud) جگالنا *jugālnā*.

To chide, ڈانٹنا *ḍānṭnā*, جهڑکنا *jhiṛaknā*, دوکهنا *dōkhnā*.

To chirp, چرگنا *churagnā*, چوں چوں کرنا *chūṅ chūṅ karnā*.

To choke, گلا گهونٹنا *galā ghōnṭnā*, گلا پهانسنا *galā phānsnā*: see To obstruct.

To choose, پسند کرنا *pasand karnā*, چننا *chunnā*, چاهنا *chāhnā*.

To chop, ايک چوٹ سي کاٹنا *ēk chōṭ sē kāṭnā*, پہاڑنا *phāṛnā:* see To exchange.

To churn, متہنا *mathnā*, مہنا *mahnā*, مسکہ نکالنا *maska nikālnā.*

To circulate, (v. n.) پہرنا *phirnā*, گہومنا *ghūmnā*, (v. a.) پہرانا *phirānā.*

To claim, دعوي يا تقاضا کرنا *dāʿwā* or *taķāẓā karnā.*

To clang, کہڑکنا *khaṛaknā*, (dakh.) چہنچہنانا *chhanchhanānā.*

To clap, (to place) لگانا *lagānā*, (strike hands) تالي بجانا *tālī bajānā.*

To clarify, صاف کرنا *ṣāf karnā*, ميل چہانٹنا *mail chhāṅṭnā.*

To class, ترتيب ميں رکہنا *tartīb mēṅ rakhnā.*

To clatter, کہڑکہڑانا *khaṛkhaṛānā:* see To chat, gabble.

To claw, نوچنا *nōchnā*, نکہيانا *nakhiyānā*, کہروچنا *kharōchnā.*

To cleave, (to split, v. a.) چيرنا *chīrnā*, پہاڑنا *phāṛnā:* see To cling.

To climb, چڑہنا *chaṛhnā*, بلنگنا *bilangnā.*

To cling, لپٹنا *lipaṭnā*, چمٹانا *chimṭānā*, لپٹا رہنا *lipṭā rahnā.*

To clip, کترنا *katarnā*, تراشنا *tarāshnā*, کاٹنا *kāṭnā.*

To close, (v. n.) مندنا *mundnā*, (v. a.) موندنا *mūndnā*, بند کرنا *band karnā.*

To clothe, کپڑا پہنانا *kapṛā pahnānā* or پہرانا *pahrānā.*

To cloy, چہکانا *chhakānā*, سيرکرنا *sēr karnā.*

To coagulate, (v. n.) جمنا *jamnā*, (v. a.) جمانا *jamānā.*

To coalesce, ملنا *milnā*, پيوستہ هونا *paiwasta hōnā.*

To coax, پہسلانا *phuslānā*, بہلانا *bhulānā*, دم دينا *dam dēnā.*

To cock, (set up) کہڑا کرنا *khaṛā karnā*, (a gun) گہوڑا چڑہانا *ghōṛā chaṛhānā.*

To collect, (v. a.) جمع يا ايکٹہا کرنا *jamʿ* or *ēkṭhā karnā*, جمانا *jamānā.*

To colour, (v. a.) رنگنا *rangnā*, رنگ بہرنا *rang bharnā:* see To blush.

To combine, (v. n.) ملنا *milnā*, جڑنا *juṛnā*, (v. a.) ملانا *milānā.*

To come, آنا *ānā*, (arrive) پہنچنا *pahunchnā*, (out) نکلنا *nikalnā.*

To comfort, تسلي دينا *tasallī dēnā*, خاطر جمعي دينا *khāṭir-jamʿī dēnā.*

To command, حکم کرنا *ḥukm karnā*, فرمانا *farmānā.*

To commence, (v.n.) شروع هونا *shurūʿ hōnā:* see To begin.

To commit, (entrust) حوالي کرنا *ḥawālē karnā:* see To imprison, do.

To compare, مقابله کرنا *muḳābala karnā*, ملانا *milānā*.

To complain, فریاد کرنا *faryād karnā*, (against) نالش کرنا *nālish karnā*.

To compose, بنانا *banānā*, (a book) تصنیف کرنا *taṣnīf karnā*.

To compound, ملانا *milānā*, مرکب کرنا *murakkab karnā*.

To comprehend, سمجهنا *samajhnā*, دریافت کرنا *daryāft karnā*.

To compute, گنا *ginnā*, شمار یا حساب کرنا *shumār* or *ḥisāb karnā*.

To conceal, چهپانا *chhipānā*, ڈهانپنا *ḍhāmpnā*.

To conceive, حامله هونا *ḥāmila hōnā*, (think) جاننا *jānnā*.

To conclude, (v. n.) چکنا *chuknā*, تمام هونا *tamām hōnā*, (v. a.) تمام کرنا *tamām karnā*.

To concur, متفق هونا *muttafiḳ hōnā*, (agree) ماننا *mānnā*.

To condemn, گنهگار ٹهہرانا *gunahgār ṭhahrānā*, فتوی دینا *fatwā dēnā*.

To conduct, راه نمائی کرنا *rāh-numā'ī karnā*, لیچلنا *le-chalnā*.

To confess, ماننا *mānnā*, قائل هونا *ḳā'il hōnā*, اقرار کرنا *iḳrār karnā*.

To confine (v. a.), بند یا قید کرنا *band* or *ḳaid karnā*.

To confirm, (prove) ثابت کرنا *ṡābit karnā*, (establish) مقرر کرنا *muḳarrar karnā*.

To confiscate, ضبط یا قرق کرنا *ẓabṭ* or *ḳurḳ karnā*.

To confound, (mix) ملانا *milānā*, (perplex) پریشان کرنا *parēshān karnā*.

To confuse, درهم برهم کرنا *darham barham karnā*: see To confound.

To congeal, be congealed, جمنا *jamnā*, منجمد هونا *munjamid hōnā*.

To congratulate, مبارك باد کهنا *mubārak-bād kahnā*.

To connect, conjoin, جوڑنا *jōṛnā*, ملانا *milānā*, لگانا *lagānā*.

To connive at, اغماض کرنا *ighmāẓ karnā*, مٹیانا *maṭiyānā*.

To conquer, جیتنا *jītnā*, فتح کرنا *fatḥ karnā*.

To consent, ماننا *mānnā*, راضي هونا *rāẓī hōnā*, قبول کرنا *ḳabūl karnā*.

To consider, سوچنا *sōchnā*, عقل دوڑانا *āḳl dauṛānā*.

To consign, حوالے کرنا *ḥawālē karnā*, سونپنا *sōmpnā*.

To console, تسلي یا تسکین دینا *tasallī* or *taskīn dēnā*.

To construct, بنانا *banānā*, بنا یا نقشه کرنا *binā* or *naḳsha karnā*.

To consult, مصلحت یا مشورت کرنا *maṣlaḥat* or *mashwarat karnā*.

To contain, رکهنا *rakhnā*, مشتمل هونا *mushtamil hōnā*: see To restrain.

To be contained, سمانا *samānā*, امانا *amānā*, انٹنا *anṭnā*.

To contemn, حقیر جاننا *ḥaḳīr jānnā*, اهانت کرنا *ihānat karnā*.

To continue, رهنا *rahnā*, بحال یا برپا رهنا *ba-ḥāl* or *bar-pā rahnā*.

To contract, (v.n.) سمٹنا *simaṭnā*, (bargain) شرط باندهنا *sharṭ bāndhnā*.

To contribute, (give) دینا *dēnā*, (bear a part) چندا دینا *chandā dēnā*.

To contrive, ایجاد کرنا *ījād karnā*, نکالنا *nikālnā*, تدبیر کرنا *tadbīr karnā*.

To cook, پکانا *pakānā*, راندهنا *rāndhnā*, رسوئی بنانا *rasō'ī banānā*.

To copy, نقل کرنا *naḳl karnā*, نقل نویسی کرنا *naḳl-nawīsī karnā*.

To correct, صحیح یا ٹهیک کرنا *ṣaḥīḥ* or *ṭhīk karnā* : see To punish.

To corrode, کاٹنا *kāṭnā*, کها لینا *khā lēnā*, کها جانا *khā jānā*.

To corrupt, (cause to rot) سڑانا *saṛānā*, (spoil) بگاڑنا *bigāṛnā*.

To cost, قیمت پڑنا یا لگنا *ḳīmat paṛnā* or *lagnā*, آنا *ānā*, بیٹهنا *baiṭhnā*.

To cover, ڈهانپنا *ḍhāmpnā*, چهانا *chhānā*, ڈهانکنا *ḍhānknā*.

To covet, لالچ کرنا *lālach karnā*, للچانا *lalchānā*.

To cough, (v. n.) کهانسنا *khānsnā*, کهونکهنا *khōnkhnā*.

To count, گننا *ginnā*, شمار کرنا *shumār karnā*, (sum up) جوڑنا *jōṛnā*.

To counterfeit, تقلید کرنا *taḳlīd karnā*, بهیس کرنا *bhēs karnā*.

To crack, (v. n.) تڑقنا *taṛaḳnā*, پهٹنا *phaṭnā*, (v.a.) تڑقانا *taṛḳānā*.

To crackle, چٹکنا *chaṭaknā*, چڑچڑانا *chaṛchaṛānā*.

To cram, ٹهاسنا *ṭhāsnā*, کهونچنا *khōnchnā*, دهوسنا *dhūsnā*.

To crave, مانگنا *māngnā*, چاهنا *chāhnā*, منت کرنا *minnat karnā*.

To creak, چڑچڑانا *chaṛchaṛānā*, مچمچانا *machmachānā*.

To create, پیدا کرنا *paidā karnā*, سرجنا *sirajnā*, کرنا *karnā*.

To creep, رینگنا *rīngnā*, (as a snake) سرسرانا *sarsarānā*.

To crop, کاٹنا *kāṭnā*, چهانٹنا *chhānṭnā*, تراشنا *tarāshnā*.

To cross, (pass over) پار کرنا *pār karnā*, (lay across) آڑا رکهنا *āṛā rakhnā*.

To crouch, دبکنا *dabaknā*, (to fawn) چاپلوسی کرنا *chāplūsī karnā*.

To crow, بانگ مارنا *bāng mārnā*. To crowd, بهڑنا *bhiṛnā*, جمنا *jamnā*.

To crush, کچلنا *kuchalnā*, (squeeze) نچوڑنا *nichōṛnā*.

To cry, (out) چلانا *chillānā*, پکارنا *pukārnā*, (weep) رونا *rōnā*.

To cull, چننا *chunnā*, انتخاب کرنا *intikhāb karnā*.

To cultivate, (till) جوتنا *jōtnā*, هل چلانا *hal chalānā* : see To people.

To curb, روکنا *rōknā*, تهامنا *thāmnā :* see To restrain.

To cure, علاج کرنا *ʿilāj karnā*, شفا دینا *shifā dēnā :* see To heal.

To curse, کوسنا *kōsnā*, سراپنا *sarāpnā*, لعنت کرنا *laʿnat karnā*.

To cut, کاٹنا *kāṭnā*, تراشنا *tarāshnā*, قطع کرنا *ḳaṭʿ karnā :* see To carve.

To dally, (delay) دیري کرنا *dērī karnā*, (trifle) ٹاپاٹوئي کرنا *ṭāpāṭō'ī karnā*.

To damage, خسارت کرنا *khisārat karnā*, بگاڑنا *bigāṛnā*.

To dance, ناچنا *nāchnā*, رقص کرنا *raḳṣ karnā*, (jump) کودنا *kūdnā*.

To dangle, لٹکنا *laṭaknā*, هلگنا *hilagnā*.

To dare, جرات کرنا *jur'at karnā*, (defy) دهمکانا *dhamkānā*.

To darn, رفو کرنا *rafū karnā*, بهر دینا *bhar dēnā*.

To dash, پٹکنا *paṭaknā*, دي مارنا *dē mārnā*, (sprinkle) چهڑکنا *chhiṛaknā*.

To daunt, ڈرانا *ḍarānā*, دهمکانا *dhamkānā*, دبکانا *dabkānā*.

To deal, بانٹ دینا *bānṭ dēnā*, حصه کر دینا *ḥiṣṣa kar dēnā*.

To debate, (think) تامل کرنا *ta'ammul karnā*, (dispute) تکرار کرنا *takrār karnā :* see To argue.

To decamp, کوچ کرنا *kūch karnā*, (move off) چلي جانا *chalē jānā*.

To deceive, دهوکها دینا *dhōkhā dēnā*, چهلنا *chhalnā*, ٹهگنا *ṭhagnā*.

To decide, ٹههرانا *ṭhahrānā*, انفصال کرنا *infiṣāl karnā*, چکانا *chukānā*.

To deck, سنوارنا *sanwārnā*, آراسته کرنا *ārāsta karnā*, سنگارنا *singārnā*.

To declare, کهنا *kahnā*, جتانا *jatānā*, اقرار کرنا *iḳrār karnā*.

To decline, (as the sun) ڈهلنا *ḍhalnā :* see To bow, refuse.

To decoy, فریب دینا *farēb dēnā*, پهنسانا *phansānā*.

To decrease, گهٹنا *ghaṭnā*, کم هونا *kam hōnā*.

To dedicate, نیاز یا وقف کرنا *niyāz* or *wakf karnā*, کي نام بنانا *kē nām banānā*.

To deduct, وضع کرنا *waẓʿ karnā*, نکال ڈالنا *nikāl ḍālnā*.

To deem, جاننا *jānnā*, تجویز کرنا *tajwīz karnā*, قیاس کرنا *ḳiyās karnā*.

To deface, مٹا دینا *miṭā dēnā*, محو کرنا *maḥw karnā*, بگاڑنا *bigāṛnā*.

To defame, بد نام کرنا *bad-nām karnā*, عیب لگانا *ʿaib lagānā*.

To defeat, شکست دینا *shikast dēnā*, هرانا *harānā*, (frustrate) کاٹنا *kāṭnā*.

To defend, حمایت یا دستگیري کرنا *ḥimāyat* or *dastgīrī karnā*.

To defile, میلا یا ناپاک کرنا *mailā* or *nā-pāk karnā.*

To deform, شکل بگاڑنا *shakl bigāṛnā,* بیڈول کرنا *bēḍaul karnā.*

To defy, لڑائي چاهنا *laṛā'ī chāhnā,* انگوٹها دکهانا *angūṭhā dikhānā.*

To deign, متوجه هونا *mutawajjih hōnā,* قبول کرنا *ḳabūl karnā.*

To delay, (v. n.) ديري کرنا *dērī karnā,* (v. a.) ٹالنا *ṭālnā.*

To deliver, (free) رها يا آزاد کرنا *rihā* or *āzād karnā:* see To give.

To demand, (claim) دعوا کرنا *daʿwā karnā:* see To ask.

To demolish, اجاڑنا *ujāṛnā,* گرانا *girānā:* see To destroy.

To deny, انکار کرنا *inkār karnā,* نمانّا *na-mānnā.*

To depart, چلي جانا *chalē-jānā,* سدهارنا *sidhārnā.*

To depend, لٹکنا *laṭaknā,* (upon) دامن پکڑنا *dāman pakaṛnā.*

To depopulate, اجاڑنا *ujāṛnā,* ويران کرنا *wīrān karnā.*

To deposite, سونپنا *sōmpnā,* امانت رکهنا *amānat rakhnā.*

To depress, دابنا *dābnā,* پست کرنا *past karnā,* دبانا *dabānā.*

To derive, (v. a.) نکالنا *nikālnā,* (v. n.) مشتق هونا *mushtaḳḳ hōnā.*

To descend, اترنا *utarnā,* نيچي جانا *nīchē jānā,* نازل هونا *nāzil hōnā.*

To describe, بکهاننا *bakhānnā,* تقرير کرنا *taḳrīr karnā.*

To desert, ترک کرنا *tark karnā,* چهوڑنا *chhōṛnā.*

To design, (intend) اراده کرنا *irāda karnā,* (plan) نقشه کرنا *naḳsha karnā.*

To desire, چاهنا *chāhnā,* خواهش کرنا *khwāhish karnā.*

To desist, باز رهنا *bāz rahnā,* ره جانا *rah jānā.*

To despair, despond, نااميد هونا *nā-ummēd hōnā,* نراس هونا *nirās hōnā.*

To despise, حقير جاننا *ḥaḳīr jānnā,* حقارت کرنا *ḥiḳārat karnā.*

To destroy, اجاڑ دينا *ujāṛ dēnā,* نيست يا هلاک کرنا *nēst* or *halāk karnā.*

To detain, باز رکهنا *bāz rakhnā,* روکنا *rōknā,* قيد کرنا *ḳaid karnā.*

To deter, ڈرانا *ḍarānā,* بيهمت کرنا *bē-himmat karnā.*

To determine, ٹههرانا *ṭhahrānā,* ٹهيک کرنا *ṭhīk karnā:* see To decide.

To dethrone, تخت سي اتارنا *takht sē utārnā.*

To devise (by will), وصيت کرنا *waṣīyat karnā:* see To invent.

To devote, نياز يا فدا يا قربان کرنا *niyāz* or *fidā* or *ḳurbān karnā.*

To devour, بهكهنا *bhakhnā*, كها جانا *khā jānā*, كها لينا *khā lēnā*.

To die (colour), رنگنا *rangnā*, رنگ چڑهانا *rang chaṛhānā*.

To die (expire), مرنا *marnā*, فوت يا هلاك هونا *faut* or *halāk hōnā*.

To differ, تفاوت هونا *tafāwut hōnā*, (quarrel) جهگڑنا *jhagaṛnā*.

To diffuse, پهيلانا *phailānā*, بستارنا *bistārnā*, بچهانا *bichhānā*.

To dig, كهودنا *khōdnā*, گوڑنا *gōṛnā*, (up) اكهاڑنا *ukhāṛnā*.

To digest, هضم كرنا *hazm karnā*, پچانا *pachānā*: see To arrange.

To dignify, سر فراز كرنا *sar-farāz karnā*, بڑهانا *baṛhānā*.

To diminish, (v. n.) گهٹنا *ghaṭnā*, (v. a.) گهٹانا *ghaṭānā*.

To dine, كهانا كهانا *khānā khānā*, چاشت كرنا *chāsht karnā*.

To dip, (v. n.) ڈوبنا *ḍūbnā*, (v. a.) ڈبانا *ḍubānā*, ڈبكي دينا *ḍubkī dēnā*.

To direct, (shew) دكهلانا *dikhlānā*, (command) فرمانا *farmānā*.

To disagree, ناموافق هونا *nā-muwāfiḳ honā*, (quarrel) بگڑنا *bigaṛnā*.

To disallow, انكار يا منع كرنا *inkār* or *man* *karnā*, بارنا *bārnā*: see To deny.

To disappear, چهپنا *chhipnā*, چنپت هونا *champat hōnā*.

To disappoint, نا مراد كرنا *nā murād karnā*, ڈهكانا *ḍahkānā*.

To disapprove, نا پسند كرنا *nā-pasand karnā*, رد كرنا *radd karnā*.

To disband, جواب دينا *jawāb dēnā*, چهوڑا دينا *chhōṛā dēnā*.

To disbelieve, نماننا *na-mānnā*, انكار كرنا *inkār karnā*.

To discern, امتياز كرنا *imtiyāz karnā*, ديكهنا *dēkhnā*.

To discharge, چهڑانا *chhuṛānā*, برطرف كرنا *bar-ṭaraf karnā*.

To disclose, كهولنا *khōlnā*, اظهار كرنا *iz̤'hār karnā*.

To discontinue, ناغه كرنا *nāgha karnā*, موقوف كرنا *mauḳūf karnā*.

To discover, پيدا كرنا *paidā karnā*, ظاهر كرنا *z̤āhir karnā*: see To show.

To disembark, (v. n.) اترنا *utarnā*, (v. a.) اتارنا *utārnā*.

To disengage, جدا كرنا *judā karnā*, كهولنا *khōlnā*.

To disfigure, بگاڑنا *bigāṛnā*, خراب كرنا *kharāb kārnā*.

To disgrace, حرمت توڑنا *ḥurmat tōṛnā*, معزول كرنا *ma*zūl karnā*.

To disgust, كڑهانا *kuṛhānā*, بيزار كرنا *bēzār karnā*.

To dishonour, آبرو اتارنا *ābrū utārnā*, بيحرمت كرنا *bēḥurmat karnā*.

To dislike, نچاهنا *na-chāhnā*, ناپسند كرنا *nā-pasand karnā*.

To dismiss, رخصت کرنا *rukhṣat karnā*, برطرف کرنا *bar-ṭaraf karnā*.

To dismount, (v. n.) اترنا *utarnā*, (v. a.) اتارنا *utārnā*.

To dispatch, روانه کرنا *rawāna karnā*: see To kill, waylay.

To dispel, دور کرنا *dūr karnā*, دفع کرنا *daf* karnā*.

To disperse, چھٹکانا *chhiṭkānā*, منتشر کرنا *muntashir karnā*.

To displease, ناخوش کرنا *nā-khush karnā*, آزرده کرنا *āzurda karnā*.

To dispose, آراسته کرنا *ārāsta karnā*: see To arrange, give.

To dispute, بحثنا *baḥaṣnā*, (quarrel) جھگڑنا *jhagaṛnā*.

To dissipate, اڑانا *uṛānā*, اسراف کرنا *isrāf karnā*, اڑا دینا *uṛā dēnā*.

To dissolve, (v. n.) گلنا *galnā*, گھلنا *ghulnā*, (v. a.) پگھلانا *pighlānā*.

To dissuade, باز رکھنا *bāz rakhnā*, منع کرنا *man* karnā*.

To distil, (v. n.) چونا *chūnā*, ٹپکنا *ṭapaknā*, (v. a.) چوانا *chō'ānā*, &c.

To distil (as spirits), مقطر کرنا *muḳaṭṭar karnā*.

To distinguish, فرق کرنا *farḳ karnā*, امتیاز کرنا *imtiyāz karnā*.

To distribute, بانٹنا *bānṭnā*, حصه کرنا *ḥiṣṣa karnā*.

To disturb, مضطرب کرنا *muẓṭarib karnā*, چھیڑنا *chhēṛnā*.

To dive, غوطه مارنا *ghōṭa mārnā*, ڈوبنا *ḍūbnā*.

To divert, (amuse) بهلانا *bahlānā*, (turn away) پھرانا *phirānā*.

To divide, تقسیم کرنا *taḳsīm karnā*: see To distribute.

To divulge, فاش کرنا *fāsh karnā*, بتلانا *batlānā*.

To do, کرنا *karnā*, بنانا *banānā*, بجا لانا *ba-jā lānā*.

To dodge, کنیانا *kaniyānā*, پیچھے لگنا *pīchhē lagnā*.

To doff, اتارنا *utārnā*, (to doff clothes, کپڑے اتارنا *kapṛē utārnā*).

To doubt, شک کرنا *shakk karnā*, یقین نجاننا *yaḳīn na-jānnā*.

To doze, اونگھنا *ūnghnā*, جھپکی میں ہونا *jhapkī meṅ hōnā*.

To drag, (v. a.) گھسیٹنا *ghasīṭnā*, (v. n.) گھسٹنا *ghasiṭnā*: see To draw.

To drain, چھاننا *chhānnā*, پانی نکال ڈالنا *pānī nikāl ḍālnā*.

To draw, کھینچنا *khīnchnā*, (a sword) کاڑھنا *kāṛhnā*, (out) نکالنا *nikālnā*, (on, as a garment) چڑھانا *chaṛhānā*.

To dread, ڈرنا *ḍarnā*, دهشت کھانا *dahshat khānā*.

To dream, خواب دیکھنا *khwāb dēkhnā*, (dakh.) بشاره دیکھنا *bashāra dēkhnā*.

To dress, پہننا *pahannā* or *pahinnā*, (food) پکانا *pakānā*.

To drink, پینا *pīnā*, گھونٹنا *ghūnṭnā*, نشا کھانا *nashā khānā*.

To drive, (v. n.) دوڑنا *dauṛnā*, (v. a.) چلانا *chalānā*, دوڑانا *dauṛānā*.

To droop, مرجھانا *murjhānā*, پژمردہ ہونا *pazhmurda hōnā*.

To drop, (distil, v. n.) چونا *chūnā*, (v. a.) ٹپکانا *ṭapkānā* : see To fall.

To drown, (v. a.) ڈبونا *ḍubōnā*, (v. n.) ڈوبنا *ḍūbnā*.

To drum, طبل بجانا *ṭabl bajānā*, طنبور ٹھونکنا *ṭambūr ṭhōnknā*.

To dry, (v. n.) سوکھنا *sūkhnā*, (v. a.) سکھانا *sukhānā*.

To dwell, بسنا *basnā*, رہنا *rahnā*, سکونت کرنا *sukūnat karnā*.

To earn, کمانا *kamānā*, پیدا یا حاصل کرنا *paidā* or *ḥāṣil karnā*.

To eat, کھانا *khānā*, تناول کرنا *tanāwul karnā*: see To corrode.

To educate, تربیت کرنا *tarbiyat karnā*, سکھانا *sikhānā*.

To efface, میٹنا *mēṭnā*, مٹانا *miṭānā*, چھیلنا *chhīlnā*.

To effect, کرنا *karnā*, عمل میں لانا *ʿamal mēṅ lānā*.

To eject, نکال دینا *nikāl dēnā*, دور کرنا *dūr karnā*.

To elapse, گذرنا *guẕarnā*, گذشتہ ہونا *guẕashta hōnā*.

To elect, چن لینا *chun lēnā*, پسند کرنا *pasand karnā*.

To elevate, اٹھانا *uthānā*, بلند کرنا *buland karnā*, بڑھانا *baṛhānā*.

To embark, جہاز پر چڑھنا یا چڑھانا *jahāz par chaṛhnā* or *chaṛhānā*.

To embellish, سنگارنا *singārnā*, بناؤ کرنا *banā'ō karnā*.

To embrace, بغل گیر ہونا *baghal-gīr hōnā*, گلے لگنا *galē lagnā*.

To embroider, کارچوبی کرنا *kār-chōbī karnā*.

To emigrate, جلا وطن ہونا *jilā-waṭan hōnā*, دیس چھوڑنا *dēs chhōṛnā*.

To employ, استعمال کرنا *istiʿmāl karnā*, کام میں لانا *kām mēṅ lānā*.

To enable, قوت یا تقویت دینا *kūwat* or *taḳwiyat dēnā*.

To encamp, خیمہ یا دیرا یا مقام کرنا *khaima* or *dērā* or *muḳām karnā*.

To enchant, افسون یا جادو یا ٹونا کرنا *afsūn* or *jādū* or *ṭōnā karnā*.

To encircle, گرد یا محاصرہ کرنا *gird* or *muḥāṣara karnā*, گھیرنا *ghērnā*.

To enclose, گھیرنا *ghērnā*, احاطہ کرنا *iḥāṭa karnā*, باندھنا *bāndhnā*.

To encourage, ہمت یا دلاسا دینا *himmat* or *dilāsā dēnā*.

To end, (v. n.) آخر یا تمام ہونا *ākhir* or *tamām hōnā*.

To endanger, خطرے میں ڈالنا *khatrē mēṅ ḍālnā*.

To endeavour, سعي يا جد و جهد كرنا *sa'ī* or *jidd-ō-jahd karnā.*

To endure, (v. n.) رهنا *rahnā,* (v. a.) برداشت كرنا *bardāsht karnā.*

To engage, (in service, &c.) ركهہ لينا *rakh lēnā* : see To employ, allure.

To engrave, كهودنا *khōdnā,* كنده يا نقش كرنا *kanda* or *naḳsh karnā.*

To enjoin, تاكيد كرنا *tākīd karnā,* حكم كرنا *ḥukm karnā.*

To enjoy, پانا *pānā,* اٹهانا *uṭhānā,* بهگتنا *bhugatnā.*

To enlarge, بڑهانا *baṛhānā,* كشاده كرنا *kushāda karnā.*

To enlighten, اجلا يا منور كرنا *ujlā* or *munauwar karnā:* see To teach.

To enrage, غصي يا غضبناك كرنا *ghuṣṣē* or *ghaẓab-nāk karnā.*

To enrol, دفتر ميں داخل كرنا *daftar mēṅ dākhil karnā.*

To ensnare, پهانسنا *phānsnā,* بجهانا *bajhānā,* بلبهانا *balbhānā.*

To entangle, پهسانا *phasānā,* پهاندنا *phāndnā,* الجهانا *uljhānā.*

To enter, (v. n.) پيٹهنا *paiṭhnā,* داخل هونا *dākhil hōnā.*

To entertain, مهماني يا ضيافت كرنا *mihmānī* or *ẓiyāfat karnā.*

To enthrone, تخت پر بيٹهالنا *takht par baiṭhālnā.*

To entice, پهسلانا *phuslānā,* لبهانا *lubhānā:* see To allure.

To entrap, پهاندنا *phāndnā,* پهنسانا *phansānā.*

To entreat, التجا كرنا *iltijā karnā,* (dakh.) ترسنا *tarasnā.*

To equip, ساز و سامان دينا *sāz ō sāmān dēnā,* سجانا *sajānā.*

To erect, اٹهانا *uṭhānā,* قائم كرنا *ḳā'im karnā:* see To build.

To err, چوكنا *chūknā,* گمراه هونا *gum-rāh hōnā,* بهولنا *bhūlnā.*

To escape, بچنا *bachnā,* نكل بهاگنا *nikal bhāgnā,* چهوٹنا *chhūṭnā.*

To espy, ديكهنا *dēkhnā,* تكنا *taknā,* ڈٹنا *ḍiṭnā.*

To establish, قائم كرنا *ḳā'im karnā,* ٹهہرانا *ṭhahrānā.*

To estimate, اٹكلنا *aṭkalnā,* كوتنا *kūtnā,* قيمت كرنا *ḳīmat karnā.*

To evacuate, خالي كرنا *khālī karnā,* نكالنا *nikālnā,* چهوڑنا *chhōṛnā.*

To evade, ٹالنا *ṭalna,* اڑانا *uṛana,* چهلنا *chhalnā.*

To exaggerate, مبالغه كرنا *mubālagha karnā,* بڑهانا *baṛhānā.*

To exalt, بلند كرنا *buland karnā,* بڑهانا *baṛhānā,* چڑهانا *chaṛhānā.*

To examine, آزمانا *āzmānā,* (as money) پركهنا *parakhnā.*

To excavate, كوڑنا *kōṛnā,* كهوكها كرنا *khōkhā karnā.*

To exceed, زياده هونا *zīyāda hōnā,* بڑهنا *baṛhnā:* see To excel.

To excel, سبقت لینا *sabḳat lēnā,* غالب هونا *ghālib hōnā.*

To exchange, بدلنا *badalnā,* ادلا بدلي کرنا *adlā-badlī karnā.*

To excite, چهيڑنا *chhēṛnā,* ترغيب دينا *targhīb dēnā.*

To exclaim, چلانا *chillanā,* پکار اٹهنا *pukār uṭhnā.*

To excuse, معاف کرنا *mu'āf karnā,* (make excuse) عذر کرنا *ūẕr karnā.*

To execute, کرنا *karnā,* انجام کرنا *anjām karnā:* see To kill.

To exhibit, دکهلانا *dikhlānā,* ظاهر کرنا *ẓāhir karnā.*

To exist, هونا *hōnā,* موجود هونا *maujūd hōnā,* اچهنا *achhnā.*

To expand, (v. n.) پهيلنا *phailnā,* (v. a.) پهيلانا *phailānā.*

To expect, انتظار کرنا *intiẓār karnā,* راه ديکهنا *rāh dēkhnā.*

To expel, نکال دينا *nikāl dēnā,* شهر بدر کرنا *shahr ba-dar karnā.*

To expend, خرچ کرنا *kharch karnā,* اٹهانا *uṭhānā,* اڑانا *uṛānā.*

To expire, دم چهوڑنا *dam chhōṛnā,* (to die) مرنا *marnā.*

To explain, سمجهانا *samjhānā,* بتلانا *batlānā,* ظاهر کرنا *ẓāhir karnā.*

To explore, کهوجنا *khōjnā,* چهان مارنا *chhān mārnā:* see To seek.

To express, (utter) اچارنا *uchchārnā,* (squeeze out) نچوڑنا *nichōṛnā.*

To expunge, مٹانا *miṭānā,* محو کرنا *maḥw karnā.*

To extend, پسارنا *pasārnā,* (v. n.) پهيلنا *phailnā:* see To spread.

To extinguish, بجهانا *bujhānā,* گل کرنا *gul karnā:* see To destroy.

To extirpate, اکهاڑنا *ukhāṛnā,* جڑ کهود اٹهانا *jaṛ khōd uṭhānā.*

To extort, بزور لينا *ba-zōr lēnā,* نچوڑ لينا *nichōṛ lēnā.*

To extract, استخراج کرنا *istikhrāj karnā,* کهينچ لينا *khainch lēnā.*

To extricate, چهڑانا *chhuṛānā,* خلاص کرنا *khalāṣ karnā.*

To face, سامني هونا *sāmnē hōnā,* (oppose) مقابله کرنا *muḳābala karnā.*

To fail, چوکنا *chūknā,* (become bankrupt) مفلس هونا *muflis hōnā.*

To faint, غش آنا *ghash ānā,* مورچها کهانا *mūrchhā khānā.*

To fall, گرنا *girnā,* پڑنا *paṛnā,* (decrease) گهٹنا *ghaṭnā.*

To famish, (v. n.) فاقون يا بهوکهون مرنا *fāḳōn* or *bhūkhōn marnā.*

To fasten, مستحکم کرنا *mustaḥkim karnā,* (tie) باندهنا *bāndhnā.*

To father, باپ کهلانا *bāp kahlānā,* لي پالنا *lē pālnā:* see To apply.

To fear, ڈرنا *ḍarnā,* بهي کهانا *bhai khānā,* سهمنا *sahmnā.*

To feed, کهلانا *khilānā,* خوراک دينا *khurāk dēnā:* see To graze.

To feel, (touch) چهونا *chhūnā,* لمس كرنا *lams karnā:* see To know.

To feign, بنانا *banānā,* بهانه كرنا *bahāna karnā.*

To fell, كاٹ ڈالنا *kāṭ ḍālnā,* كاٹ دينا *kāṭ dēnā:* see To cut.

To ferment, (v. n.) جوش كي ساتھ اٹھنا *jōsh ke sāth uṭhnā.*

To ferry over, پار اتارنا *pār utārnā,* پار كرنا *pār karnā.*

To fetch, لي آنا *lē-ānā,* ليكر آنا *lēkar ānā:* see To reach.

To fight, لڑنا *laṛnā,* جنگ كرنا *jang karnā:* see To quarrel.

To fill, بهرنا *bharnā,* بهر دينا *bhar dēnā,* پورا كرنا *pūrā karnā.*

To filter, نتهارنا *nithārnā,* چهاننا *chhānnā.*

To find, پانا *pānā,* كهوج نكالنا *khōj nikālnā,* نكالنا *nikālnā.*

To finger, ٹٹولنا *ṭaṭōlnā,* چهونا *chhūnā,* انگليانا *ungliyānā.*

To finish, تمام يا ختم كرنا *tamām* or *khatm karnā.*

To fire, (a gun, &c.) چهوڑنا *chhōṛnā,* داغنا *dāghnā:* see To kindle.

To fish, مچهلي كا شكار كرنا *machhlī kā shikār karnā:* see To seek.

To fit, (v. n.) ٹهيك آنا *ṭhīk ānā,* (v. a.) آراسته كرنا *ārāsta karnā.*

To fix, باندهنا *bāndhnā,* لگانا *lagānā,* مقرر كرنا *mukarrar karnā.*

To flame, شعله اٹهنا *shuʻla uṭhnā,* جهلكنا *jhalaknā.*

To flap, جهلنا *jhalnā,* (the wings) پهٹپهٹانا *phaṭphaṭānā.*

To flatter, چاپلوسي كرنا *chāplūsī karnā,* پهسلانا *phuslānā.*

To flee, بهاگنا *bhāgnā,* گريز كرنا *gurēz karnā,* فرار هونا *firār hōnā.*

To flinch, هٹنا *haṭnā,* ٹلنا *ṭalnā,* پهرنا *phirnā.*

To fling, پهينكنا *phēnknā,* چلانا *chalānā,* ڈالنا *ḍālnā.*

To float, بهنا *bahnā,* بهسنا *bhasnā,* تيرنا *tairnā.*

To flog, چابك مارنا *chābuk mārnā,* كوڑي مارنا *kōṛē mārnā.*

To flounder, تڑپنا *taṛapnā,* چهٹپٹانا *chhaṭpaṭānā.*

To flourish, (v. n.) تر و تازه هونا *tar ō tāza hōnā,* (v. a.) گهمانا *ghumānā.*

To flow, بهنا *bahnā,* روان يا جاري هونا *rawān* or *jārī hōnā.*

To flutter, تڑپهڑانا *taṛphaṛānā,* پهڑپهڑانا *phaṛphaṛānā.*

To fly, اڑنا *uṛnā,* پرواز كرنا *parwāz karnā:* see To flee.

To foal, بيانا *byānā,* جننا *jannā,* بچهيرا بيانا *bachhērā byānā.*

To fold, تهانا *tahānā,* لپيٹنا *lapēṭnā,* ته كرنا *tah karnā.*

To follow, پيچهي آنا يا جانا *pīchhē ānā* or *jānā*, پيروئي كرنا *pairau'ī karnā.*

To forbid, منع كرنا *man'* *karnā*, روكنا *rōknā*, بارنا *bārnā.*

To foretel, آگي سي جتانا *āgē sē jatānā*, آگم كهنا *āgam kahnā.*

To forge, پيٹكي گڑهنا *pīṭkē gaṛhnā*, لباس كرنا *libās karnā.*

To forget, بهولنا *bhūlnā*, فراموش كرنا *farāmōsh karnā.*

To forgive, معاف كرنا *mu'āf karnā*, چهوڑنا *chhōṛnā.*

To form, پيدا كرنا *paidā karnā*, بنانا *banānā*, كرنا *karnā.*

To forsake, چهوڑنا *chhōṛnā*, تياگنا *tyāgnā*, ترك كرنا *tark karnā.*

To forswear, (swear falsely) جهوٹهي قسم كهانا *jhūṭhī ḳasam khānā.*

To fortify, (make a fort) قلعه بندي كرنا *ḳal'ā-bandī karnā.*

To frame, بنانا *banānā*, ڈول و ڈهب باندهنا *ḍaul ō ḍhab bāndhnā.*

To free, آزاد يا خلاص كرنا *āzād* or *khalāṣ karnā*, چهوڑنا *chhōṛnā.*

To freeze, (v. n.) جمنا *jamnā*, ٹهنڈائي سي جمنا *ṭhanḍī sē jamnā.*

To frighten, ڈرانا *ḍarānā*, (scare) بهڑكانا *bhaṛkānā.*

To frisk, كدكنا *kudaknā*, پهدكنا *phudaknā.*

To front, سامني يا مقابل هونا *sāmnē* or *muḳābil hōnā.*

To frustrate, محروم كرنا *maḥrūm karnā:* see To disappoint.

To fry, بهوننا *bhūnnā*, بريان كرنا *biryān karnā*, تلنا *talnā.*

To fulfil, (complete) پورا كرنا *pūrā karnā*, (perform) ادا كرنا *adā karnā.*

To furl, لپيٹنا *lapēṭnā*, كهينچنا *khainchnā.*

To furnish, پهنچانا *pahunchānā*, آراسته كرنا *ārāsta karnā.*

To gabble, بك بك كرنا *bak bak karnā*, غين پين كرنا *ghēṅ pēṅ karnā.*

To gain, (earn) كمانا *kamāna*, (get) پانا *pānā*, حاصل كرنا *ḥāṣil karnā.*

To gall, (v. a.) گهسكي چمڑا چهيلنا *ghiskē chamṛā chhīlnā.*

To gallop, (v. n.) ڈپٹنا *ḍapaṭnā*, (v. a.) سرپٹ پهينكنا *sarpaṭ phēnknā.*

To gamble, جوا كهيلنا *jū'ā khēlnā*, قماربازي كرنا *ḳimār-bāzī karnā.*

To gape, (yawn) جمهائي لينا *jamhā'ī lēnā*, (with surprise) منه پسارنا *muṅh pasārnā.*

To garnish, سدهارنا *sudhārnā*, آراسته كرنا *ārāsta karnā.*

To gasp, سانس الٹي لينا *sāṅs ulṭī lēnā*, لكهلكهانا *lakhlakhānā.*

To gather, جمع کرنا *jam' karnā*, بٹورنا *baṭōrnā*, چنا *chunnā*.

To gaze, گھورنا *ghūrnā*, تک رهنا *tak rahnā*, دیکھ رهنا *dēkh rahnā*.

To gesticulate, بهاو بتانا *bhā'ō batānā*.

To get, پانا *pānā*, حاصل یا پیدا کرنا *ḥāṣil* or *paidā karnā*.

To gild, سونهلا یا حل کرنا *sōnahlā* or *ḥall karnā*.

To gingle, جهنجهنانا *jhanjhanānā*, ٹهنٹهنانا *ṭhanṭhanānā*.

To gird, لپیٹکی باندهنا *lapēṭkē bāndhnā*: see To tie, reproach.

To give, دینا *dēnā*, بخشنا *bakhshnā*, سونپنا *sōmpnā*.

To glad, gladden, خوش کرنا *khush karnā*, هلسانا *halsānā*.

To glitter, چمکنا *chamaknā*, جهلکنا *jhalaknā*.

To glow, دگدگانا *dagdagānā*, دهکنا *dahaknā*.

To gnash (the teeth), کچکچانا *kichkichānā*, پیسنا *pīsnā*.

To gnaw, چابنا *chābnā*, کاٹنا *kāṭnā*, چبانا *chabānā*.

To go, جانا *jānā*, چلنا *chalnā*, روانه هونا *rawāna hōnā*.

To govern, حکومت کرنا *ḥukūmat karnā*, (actuate) چلانا *chalānā*.

To graft, پیوند کرنا *paiwand karnā*, قلم لگانا *ḳalam lagānā*.

To grant, دینا *dēnā*, بخشنا *bakhshnā*, ماننا *mānnā*.

To grasp, پکڑنا *pakaṛnā*, گهنا *gahnā*, گرفت کرنا *girift karnā*.

To gratify, خوش کرنا *khush karnā*, (requite) جزا کرنا *jazā karnā*.

To graze, چرنا *charnā*, چگنا *chugnā*, (touch) چهو جانا *chhū jānā*.

To grin, دانت نکالنا *dānt nikālnā*, کهیس نکالنا *khīs nikālnā*.

To grind, پیسنا *pīsnā*, بوکنا *būknā*, (afflict) ستانا *satānā*.

To groan, کراهنا *karāhnā*, آه و زاري کرنا *āh ō zārī karnā*.

To grope, ٹٹولنا *ṭaṭōlnā*, ٹونا *ṭōnā*, ٹوا ٹوئي کرنا *ṭō'ā-ṭō'ī karnā*.

To grow, (vegetate) اگنا *ugnā*, (increase) بڑهنا *baṛhnā*.

To grub, کهود ڈالنا *khōd ḍālnā*, اکهاڑنا *ukhāṛnā*.

To grumble, بڑبڑانا *buṛbuṛānā*, ترانا *tarrānā*, کڑکڑانا *kuṛkuṛānā*.

To guess, اٹکلنا *aṭkalnā*, قیاس کرنا *ḳiyās karnā*.

To guide, رهنمائي کرنا *rahnumā'ī karnā*, چلانا *chalānā*.

To gush, جوش سي جاري هونا *jōsh sē jārī hōnā*.

To hail, (v. n.) اولي پڑنا *ōlē paṛnā*, (salute) سلام کرنا *salām karnā*.

To halt, (limp) لنگڑانا *langṛānā*, (stop) کهڑا رهنا *khaṛā rahnā*.

To hang, (v. n.) لٹکنا *laṭaknā*, (v. a.) لٹکانا *laṭkānā*: see To choke.

To happen, آن پڑنا *ān paṛnā*, آ جانا *ā jānā*, بیتنا *bītnā*.

To harrow, هینگا پهیرنا *hēngā phērnā*, (disturb) رنج دینا *ranj dēnā*.

To hasten, جلدي کرنا *jaldī karnā*, (v. a.) شتابتر چلانا *shitābtar chalānā*.

To hate (detest), نفرت کرنا *nafrat karnā*, مکروه جاننا *makrūh jānnā*.

To have, رکهنا *rakhnā*, پانا *pānā*, پکڑنا *pakaṛnā*, هونا *hōnā*.

To heal, (v. n.) التیام هونا *iltiyām hōnā*, (v. a.) چنگا کرنا *changā karnā*.

To heap, جمع کرنا *jam* karnā*, ڈهیر لگانا *ḍhēr lagānā*.

To hear, hearken, سننا *sunnā*, کان دهرنا *kān dharnā*.

To heat, گرم کرنا *garm karnā*, آگ کرنا *āg karnā*: see To enrage.

To heed, take heed, دهیان یا پاس رکهنا *dhyān* or *pās rakhnā*.

To help, مدد یا استعانت کرنا *madad* or *isti'ānat karnā*.

To hem, مغزي لگانا *maghzī lagānā*, لڑهیانا *luṛhiyānā*.

To hesitate, پس و پیش کرنا *pas ō pēsh karnā*, هچکچانا *hichkichānā*.

To hew, کلهاڑي سي کاٹنا *kulhāṛī sē kāṭnā*, تراشنا *tarāshnā*.

To hide, چهپانا *chhipānā*, لکانا *lukānā*, (v. n.) چهپنا *chhipnā*.

To hie, جلد جانا *jald jānā*, شتابتر جانا *shitābtar jānā*.

To hinder, روکنا *rōknā*, اٹکانا *aṭkānā*, منع کرنا *man* karnā*.

To hire, کرایه لینا *kirāya lēnā*, (to let) کرائي کرنا *kirā'ē karnā*.

To hit, (v. a.) مارنا *mārnā*, ضرب دینا *ẓarb dēnā*, (v. n.) لگنا *lagnā*.

To hold, رکهنا *rakhnā*, پکڑنا *pakaṛnā*, گهنا *gahnā*: see To think.

To honour (shew respect), ادب یا عزت کرنا *adab* or *'izzat karnā*.

To hop, ایک پانو سي کودنا *ēk pāṅw sē kūdnā*, لنگڑانا *langṛānā*.

To hunt, شکار کرنا *shikār karnā*, کهدیڑنا *khadēṛnā*.

To go a hunting, شکار کهیلنا *shikār khēlnā*.

To hurry, جلدي کرنا *jaldi karnā*, هلبلانا *halbalānā*: see To hasten.

To hurt, (pain) دکهانا *dukhānā*, (injure) نقصان کرنا *nuksān karnā*.

To jabber, بکنا *baknā*, (dakh.) وٹوٹانا *waṭwaṭānā*.

To jeer, طعن تشنیع کرنا *ta'n tashnī* karnā*, چڑانا *chiṛānā*.

To jest, ٹهٹها مارنا یا کرنا *ṭhaṭhā mārnā* or *karnā*.

To illumine, روشن یا اجالا کرنا *rōshan* or *ujālā karnā*.

To illustrate, (explain) تشریح کرنا *tashrīḥ karnā*: see To illumine.
To imagine, تصور کرنا *taṣauwur karnā*, سوچنا *sōchnā*.
To imitate, (follow, ape) تتبع کرنا *tatabbuʿ karnā*: see To copy.
To immerse, ڈبونا *ḍubōnā*, بوڑنا *bōṛnā*, غرق کرنا *gharḳ karnā*.
To impart, (inform) کہنا *kahnā*, بتلانا *batlānā*: see To grant.
To impel, چلانا *chalānā*, دوڑانا *dauṛānā*.
To imply, دلالت کرنا *dalālat karnā*, معنی رکھنا *maʿnī rakhnā*.
To import (as merchandise), سوداگری مال لانا *saudāgarī māl lānā*.
To importune, تقاضا کرنا *taḳāẓā karnā*, پیچھے لینا *pīchhē lēnā*.
To imprison, قید یا محبوس یا بند کرنا *ḳaid* or *maḥbūs* or *band karnā*.
To improve, (v. n.) بہتر ہونا *bihtar hōnā*, (v. a.) سدھارنا *sudhārnā*.
To impute, لگانا *lagānā*, ٹھہرانا *ṭhahrānā*, باندھنا *bāndhna*.
To incite, ترغیب دینا *targhīb dēnā*, اٹھانا *uṭhānā*, چھیڑنا *chhēṛnā*.
To include, داخل کرنا *dākhil karnā*, (surround) گھیرنا *ghērnā*.
To increase, (v. n.) بڑھنا *baṛhnā*, (v. a.) بڑھانا *baṛhānā*.
To indicate, دلالت کرنا *dalālat karnā*, بتلانا *batlānā*.
To induce, ترغیب یا تحریص دینا *targhīb* or *taḥrīṣ dēnā*, لانا *lana*.
To inflame, جلانا *jalānā*, آگ لگانا *āg lagānā*, پھونکنا *phūnknā*.
To inflate, پھلانا *phulānā*, نفخ کرنا *nafkh karnā*, پھونکنا *phūnknā*.
To inform, جتانا *jatānā*, سمجھانا *samjhānā*, آگاہ کرنا *āgāh karnā*.
To ingraft, پیوند لگانا *paiwand lagānā*, (fix) بیٹھالنا *baiṭhālnā*.
To inhabit, بسنا *basnā*, رهنا *rahnā*, سکونت کرنا *sukūnat karnā*.
To inherit, وارث ہونا *wāriṡ hōnā*, ارث لینا *irṡ lēnā*.
To inject, ڈالنا *ḍālnā*, (with a syringe) پچکاری مارنا *pichkārī mārnā*.
To inquire, پوچھنا *pūchhnā*, پرسش کرنا *pursish karnā*.
To instigate, ورغلانا *warghalānnā*, اکسانا *uksānā*: see To incite.
To instruct, سکھلانا *sikhlānā*, تعلیم کرنا *taʿlīm karnā*.
To intend, ارادہ یا قصد کرنا *irāda* or *ḳaṣd karnā*, چاهنا *chāhnā*.
To interfere, دخل کرنا *dakhl karnā*, هاتھ لگانا *hāth lagānā*.
To interpret, ترجمہ کرنا *tarjuma karnā*: see To explain.
To interrupt (hinder, stop), روکنا *rōknā*, بات کاٹنا *bāt kāṭnā*.
To intimate, اشارہ کرنا *ishāra karnā*, خبر دینا *khabar dēnā*.

To introduce, (to a person) ملاقات کرانا *mulāḳāt karānā:* see To include.

To intrude, دخل کرنا *daḵẖl karnā,* گهس پڑنا *ghus paṛnā.*

To intrust, سونپنا *sōmpnā,* سپرد یا ذمہ کرنا *sipurd* or *ẕimma karnā.*

To invade, چڑهائی کرنا *chaṛhā'ī karnā,* چڑه آنا *chaṛh ānā.*

To inveigle, ابهارنا *ubhārnā,* بلبهانا *balbhānā,* للچانا *lalchānā.*

To invent, ایجاد کرنا *ījād karnā,* نکالنا *nikālnā:* see To feign.

To investigate, تفتیش یا تحقیق کرنا *taftīsh* or *taḥḳīḳ karnā.*

To invite, نیوتنا *nyōtnā,* دعوت کرنا *da'wat karnā.*

To involve, (wrap) لپیٹکی باندهنا *lapēṭkē bāndhnā:* see To entangle.

To join, (v. n.) جتنا *juṭnā,* جڑنا *juṛnā,* (v. a.) جوڑنا *jōṛnā.*

To jostle, دهکا دینا *dhakkā dēnā,* دهکیلنا *dhakēlnā.*

To irrigate, سینچنا *sīnchnā,* تر کرنا *tar karnā.*

To irritate, کهجانا *khijānā,* چهیڑنا *chhēṛnā,* ستانا *satānā.*

To issue, (v. n.) نکلنا *nikalnā,* (v. a.) نکالنا *nikālnā.*

To judge, انصاف یا فیصل یا نیاؤ کرنا *inṣāf* or *faisal* or *nyāw karnā.*

To jumble, مخلوط کرنا *maḵẖlūṭ karnā,* (dakh.) کلانا *kalānā.*

To jump, کودنا *kūdnā,* (over) پهاندنا *phāndnā.*

To keep, رکهنا *rakhnā,* (preserve) بچانا *bachānā:* see To protect.

To kick, لتیانا *latiyānā,* لات یا ٹهوکر مارنا *lāt* or *ṭhōkar mārnā.*

To kill, مارڈالنا *mār-ḍālnā,* قتل یا خون کرنا *ḳatl* or *ḵẖūn karnā.*

To kindle, (v. a.) سلگانا *sulgānā,* (v. n.) سلگنا *sulagnā.*

To kiss, چومنا *chūmnā,* بوسہ دینا یا لینا *bōsa dēnā* or *lēnā.*

To knead, گوندنا *gūndnā,* ساننا *sānnā,* ماںڈنا *māndnā.*

To kneel, دو زانو بیٹهنا *dō-zānū baiṭhnā.*

To knit, بننا *binnā,* بغیر تانت کی بننا *baghair tānt kē binnā.*

To knock, ٹهونکنا *ṭhōnknā,* (at a door) کهٹکهٹانا *khaṭkhaṭānā.*

To know, جاننا *jānnā,* (recognise) پہچاننا *pahchānnā.*

To labour, محنت کرنا *miḥnat karnā,* دکه بهرنا *dukh bharnā.*

To lack, محتاج هونا *muḥtāj hōnā,* درکار هونا *darkār hōnā.*

To lament, نالہ کرنا *nāla karnā,* رونا *rōnā,* نوحہ کرنا *nauḥa karnā.*

To land, (v. n.) اترنا *utarnā,* (v. a.) اتارنا *utārnā.*

To lapse, (pass) گذرنا *guzarnā*, (err) چوکنا *chūknā:* see To fall.

To last, ٹکنا *ṭiknā*, ٹهہرنا *ṭhaharnā*, رهنا *rahnā.*

To laugh, هنسنا *hansnā*, (deride) ٹهٹها کرنا *ṭhaṭhā karnā.*

To lay, رکهنا *rakhnā*, دهرنا *dharnā*, (eggs) انڈا دینا *anḍā dēnā.*

To lead, لي چلنا *lē chalnā*, پیشوا هونا *pēshwā hōnā.*

To lean, مائل هونا *mā'il hōnā*, (on) تکیه لگانا *takiya lagānā.*

To leap, کودنا *kūdnā*, (over) پهاندنا *phāndnā*, ٹپنا *ṭapnā.*

To learn, سیکهنا *sīkhnā*, علم حاصل کرنا *ʿilm ḥāṣil karnā.*

To leave, چهوڑنا *chhōṛnā*, ترک کرنا *tark karnā*, (by will) هبه کرنا *hiba karnā.*

To lend, عاریتاً دینا *ʿāriyatan dēnā*, قرض دینا *ḳarẓ dēnā.*

To lengthen, بڑهانا *baṛhānā*, لمبانا *lambānā:* see To delay.

To lessen, (v. n.) گهٹنا *ghaṭnā*, (v. a.) گهٹانا *ghaṭānā.*

To let, (permit) دینا *dēnā*, (let go) چهوڑ دینا *chhōṛ dēnā:* see To hire.

To lick, چاٹنا *chāṭnā*, لیسنا *lēsnā*, (to beat) مارنا *mārnā.*

To lie, (rest) لیٹنا *lēṭnā*, پڑنا *paṛnā*, رهنا *rahnā:* see To lean on.

To lie (speak falsely), جهوٹه بولنا یا کهنا *jhūṭh bōlnā* or *kahnā.*

To lift, اٹهانا *uṭhānā*, اٹها لینا *uṭhā lēnā*, بڑهانا *baṛhānā.*

To light, (kindle) جلانا *jalānā*, (make bright) روشن کرنا *roshan karnā.*

To lighten (v. n. to flash), چمکنا *chamaknā*, لهکنا *lahaknā.*

To lighten (make light), هلکا کرنا *halkā karnā:* see To descend.

To like, پسند یا قبول کرنا *pasand* or *ḳabūl karnā*, چاهنا *chāhnā.*

To liken, مقابله یا برابري کرنا *muḳābala* or *barābarī karnā.*

To listen, سننا *sunnā*, کان لگانا یا دهرنا *kān lagānā* or *dharnā.*

To live, (exist) جینا *jīnā*, (dwell) رهنا *rahnā*, بسنا *basnā.*

To load, لادنا *lādnā*, بوجهنا *bōjhnā*, بهرنا *bharnā.*

To lock, قفل لگانا *ḳufl lagānā*, تالا دینا *tālā dēnā:* see To fasten.

To lodge, (v. a. to place) بسانا *basānā*, بیٹهالنا *baiṭhālnā:* see To dwell.

To long, ترسنا *tarasnā*, للچانا *lalchānā*, مشتاق هونا *mushtāḳ hōnā.*

To look, (v. n. to seem) سوجهنا *sūjhnā*, (v. a. to behold) نظر کرنا *naẓar karnā*, دیکهنا *dēkhnā*, تکنا *taknā*, (for) ڈهونڈهنا *ḍhūnḍhnā*, (to expect) انتظار کرنا *intiẓār karnā.*

To loose, loosen, کھولنا *khōlnā*, چھوڑ دینا *chhōṛ dēnā*.

To lop, چھانٹنا *chhāṅṭnā*, کاٹنا *kāṭnā*, تراشنا *tarāshnā*.

To lose, کھونا *khōnā*, (at play) هارنا *hārnā*, (err) چوکنا *chūknā*.

To love, چاهنا *chāhnā*, پیار کرنا *pyār karnā*, عشق رکھنا *ʻishḳ rakhnā*.

To lounge a horse, گھوڑے کو چکر دینا *ghōṛē kō chakkar dēnā*.

To lower, نیچا کرنا *nīchā karnā*, (the clouds) گھرنا *ghirnā*: see To depress.

To lug, (drag) گھسیٹنا *ghasīṭnā*, (by the ears) کان پکڑکے لانا *kān pakarkē lānā*.

To lull, سلانا *sulānā*, نیند لانا *nīnd lānā*.

To lurk, گھات میں بیٹھنا *ghāt mēṅ baiṭhnā*, دبکنا *dabaknā*.

To maintain, (defend) سمبھالنا *sambhālnā*, (rear) پالنا *pālnā*: see To defend.

To make, بنانا *banānā*, پیدا کرنا *paidā karnā*: see To do, cause, get, reach.

To mar, بگاڑنا *bigāṛnā*, خلل یا خراب کرنا *khalal* or *kharāb karnā*.

To mark, نشان کرنا *nishān karnā*, (brand) داغ دینا *dāgh dēnā*.

To marry, بیاه کرنا *byāh karnā*, بیاهنا *byāhnā*, بیاه لانا *byāh lānā*.

To measure, ماپنا *māpnā*, ناپنا *nāpnā*, پیمائش کرنا *paimā'ish karnā*.

To meditate, دهیان کرنا *dhyān karnā*, (think) سوچنا *sōchnā*.

To meet, ملنا *milnā*, ملاقات کرنا *mulāḳāt karnā*, دوچار هونا *du-chār hōnā*.

To melt, (v. n.) گلنا *galnā*, پگھلنا *pighalnā*, (v. a.) پگھلانا *pighlānā*.

To menace, دهرانا *dhirānā*, دهمکانا *dhamkānā*, ڈانٹنا *ḍāṅṭnā*.

To mend, مرمت کرنا *marammat karnā*, سدهارنا *sudhārnā*, سارنا *sārnā*.

To mention, ذکر کرنا *ẕikr karnā*, کہنا *kahnā*, گوش گذار کرنا *gōsh-guẕār karnā*.

To milk, دوهنا *dōhnā*, دوده نکالنا *dūdh nikālnā*.

To mince, (hack) چھینچنا *chhēnchnā*, (mince meat) قیمه کرنا *ḳīma karnā*.

To mind, (regard, notice) لحاظ کرنا *liḥāẓ karnā*, (remind) یاد دلانا *yād dilānā*.

To mingle, ملانا *milānā*, مخلوط یا آمیز کرنا *makhlūṭ* or *āmēz karnā*.

To mislead, بهٹکانا *bhaṭkānā*, بہکانا *bahkānā*, گمراہ کرنا *gumrāh karnā*.

To miss, (not to find) نپانا *na-pānā*, (mistake) خطا کرنا *khaṭā karnā*.

To mistake, (v. n.) چوکنا *chūknā*, بہولنا *bhūlnā*: see To miss.

To mitigate, نرم یا ملائم یا ٹہنڈا کرنا *narm* or *mulā'im* or *ṭhanḍā karnā*.

To mix, (v. n.) ملنا *milnā*, (v. a.) ملانا *milānā*, مخلوط کرنا *makhlūṭ karnā*.

To moan, کڑہنا *kuṛhnā*, نالہ یا افسوس کرنا *nāla* or *afsōs karnā*: see To lament.

To mock, (make faces at) منہ بنانا *munh banānā*, (gibe) چڑانا *chiṛānā*, برانا *birānā*.

To molest, ستانا *satānā*, کہجانا *khijānā*, تکلیف دینا *taklīf dēnā*.

To mortgage, زمین و غیرہ گرو رکہنا *zamīn ō ghaira girau rakhna*.

To move, (stir, v. n.) ہلنا *hilnā*, سرکنا *saraknā*, (go) چلنا *chalnā*, (v. a.) ہلانا *hilānā*, چلانا *chalānā*, سرکانا *sarkānā*: see To excite, propose.

To mount, (v. n.) چڑہنا *chaṛhnā*, (a horse), سوار ہونا *sawār hōnā*, (v. a.) چڑہانا *chaṛhānā*.

To mourn, کڑہنا *kuṛhnā*, آہ و نالہ یا ماتم یا غم کرنا *āh ō nāla* or *mātam* or *ghum karnā*.

To mow (cut with a scythe), داس سے کاٹنا *dās sē kāṭnā*.

To multiply, (as in arithmetic) ضرب یا جوڑتی کرنا *zarb* or *jōṛtī karnā*: see To increase.

To mumble, mutter, زیر لب کہنا *zēr lab kahnā*, بڑبڑانا *baṛbaṛānā*.

To murder, خون کرنا *khūn karnā*, بغض سے قتل کرنا *bughz sē ḳatl karnā*.

To murmur, کڑکڑانا *kuṛkuṛānā*, (mutter) بڑبڑانا *baṛbaṛānā*.

To muse, سوچنا *sōchnā*, فکر اندیشہ یا خوض کرنا *fikr, andēsha* or *khauz karna*.

Must, لازم ہے *lāzim hai*, چاہیے *chāhiyē*, ہوگا *hōgā*, ضرور ہے *zarūr hai*.

To name, نام رکہنا *nām rakhnā*, (mention) نامزد کرنا *nāmzad karnā*.

To nauseate, feel nausea, جی متلانا *jī matlānā*, ہلیانا *haliyānā*: see To abhor.

To need, چاہنا *chāhnā*, محتاج یا درکار ہونا *muḥtāj* or *darkār hōnā*.

To neglect (act carelessly), غفلت کرنا *ghaflat karnā*, بهول جانا *bhūl jānā.*

To negotiate, معامله کرنا *mu'āmala karnā*, (a bill) هنڈي چلانا *hunḍī chalānā.*

To neigh (as a horse), هنهنانا *hinhinānā.*

To nibble, کهٹکنا *khuṭaknā*, ٹونگنا *ṭūngnā*, کترنا *kutarnā.*

To nip, نوچنا *nōchnā*, چٹکي لينا *chuṭkī lēnā.*

To nod, جهکنا *jhuknā*, سر جهکانا *sar jhukānā*, (from sleep) اونگهنا *ūnghnā.*

To nominate, نام بتلانا يا دينا *nām batlānā* or *dēnā*: see To appoint.

To note, (observe) غور کرنا *ghaur karnā*, (set down) لکه لينا *likh lēnā.*

To notify, (declare) اعلام کرنا *i*'*lām karnā*, (tell) جتانا *jatānā*: see To inform.

To nourish, پالنا *pālnā*, پوسنا *pōsnā*, پرورش کرنا *parwarish karnā.*

To number, گننا *ginnā*, شمار يا حساب کرنا *shumār* or *ḥisāb karnā.*

To nurse, (the sick) بيمارداري کرنا *bīmārdārī karnā*, (a child) دوده پلانا *dūdh pilānā*, داٸي گري کرنا *dā'ī-garī karnā.*

To obey, ماننا *mānnā*, فرمانبرداري يا تابعداري کرنا *farmān-bardārī* or *tābi*'*dārī karnā.*

To object (urge against), اعتراض کرنا *i*'*tirāẓ karnā*, پکڑنا *pakaṛnā.*

To oblige, (bind) بند يا وابسته کرنا *band* or *wābasta karnā*, (bind by gratitude) مرهون منت کرنا *marhūn-i-minnat karnā*: see To gratify.

To observe, (watch) نگاه کرنا *nigāh karnā*, (look to) نجهانا *nijhānā.*

To obstruct, روکنا *rōknā*, آڑنا *āṛnā*, مزاحم هونا *muzāḥim hōnā.*

To obtain, حاصل کرنا *ḥāṣil karnā*, پانا *pānā*, (be current) رايج هونا *rā'ij hōnā.*

To obtrude, داخل کرنا *dākhil karnā*, گهسانا *ghusānā.*

To obviate, بچانا *bachānā*, ٹالنا *ṭālnā*, رفع کرنا *raf*' *karnā.*

To occur, هونا *hōnā*, واقع هونا *wāḳi*' *hōnā*, سرزد هونا *sar-zad hōnā*: see To meet.

To offer, (present) سامهني ركهنا *sāmhnē rakhnā*, (sacrifice) قربان كرنا *ḳurbān karnā*.

To ogle, كنكهيون ديكهنا *kankhiyōṅ dēkhnā*, جهانولي لينا *jhāṅwlī lēnā*.

To omit, چهوڑنا *chhōṛnā*, بهول جانا *bhūl jānā*, فرو گذاشت كرنا *farō guẕāsht karnā*.

To ooze, نكلنا *nikalnā*, چونا *chūnā*, رسنا *risnā*, چهنا *chhannā*.

To open, (v. n. be opened) كهلنا *khulnā*, (v. a.) كهولنا *khōlnā*.

To operate, كام كرنا *kām karnā*, (upon) اثر كرنا *aṡar karnā*.

To oppose, مخالفت كرنا *mu<u>kh</u>ālafat karnā*, روكنا *rōknā*.

To ordain, ٹهہرانا *ṭhahrānā*, مقرر كرنا *muḳarrar karnā*: see To fix.

To order, (command) حكم كرنا *ḥukm karnā*, (regulate) ترتيب دينا *tartīb dēnā*.

To organize, تركيب كرنا *tarkīb karnā*.

To ossify, (v. n.) هڈي هوجانا *haḍḍī hōjānā*, (v. a.) هڈي كر ڈالنا *haḍḍī kar ḍālnā*.

To overawe, ڈرانا *ḍarānā*, دهشت دينا *dahshat dēnā*.

To overcome, فتح كرنا *fatḥ karnā*, شكست كرنا *shikast karnā*.

To overflow, (v. n.) چهلكنا *chhalaknā*, بہہ پڑنا *bah paṛnā*.

To overlook, (inspect) ديكهنا *dēkhnā*, (excuse) درگذر كرنا *darguẕar karnā*.

To overset, (v. a.) الٹ دينا *ulaṭ dēnā*, (v. n.) الٹ جانا *ulaṭ jānā*.

To overtake, برابر آنا *barābar ānā*, پكڑ لينا *pakaṛ lēnā*.

To overthrow, (overturn) الٹ دينا *ulaṭ dēnā*: see To overcome.

To overwhelm, (crush down) دبا دينا *dabā dēnā*, (immerse) غرق كرنا *<u>gh</u>arḳ karnā*.

Ought, چاهيي *chāhiyē*, ضرور يا لازم هي *ẓarūr* or *lāzim hai*.

To oust, نكالنا *nikālnā*, اٹها دينا *uṭhā dēnā*.

To outroot, اكهاڑ ڈالنا *ukhāṛ ḍālnā*, اكهاڑنا *ukhāṛnā*.

To outstrip, سبقت كرنا *sabḳat karnā*, آگي دهر لينا *āgē dhar lēnā*, پيچهي ڈالنا *pīchhē ḍālnā*.

To owe, دهارنا *dhārnā*, قرضدار هونا *ḳarẓ-dār hōnā*.

To own, (possess) مالك هونا *mālik hōnā*, ركهنا *rakhnā*: see To confess.

To pacify, ٹھنڈھا کرنا *ṭhanḍhā karnā*, تسکین دینا *taskīn dēnā.*

To pack, گٹھري باندھنا *gaṭhrī bāndhnā*, لپيٹنا *lapēṭnā.*

To paint, منقش كرنا *munaḳḳash karnā*, چيتنا *chītnā.*

To palpitate, كانپنا *kāmpnā*, پھڑكنا *phaṛaknā*, دھڑكنا *dhaṛaknā.*

To pant, هنپهنا *hamphnā*, هپهپهانا *haphhaphānā.*

To parch, بهوننا *bhūnnā*, بريان كرنا *biryān karnā.*

To pardon, معاف يا درگذر كرنا *mu'āf* or *darguẕar karnā.*

To pare, چهيلنا *chhīlnā*, كترنا *katarnā*, تراشنا *tarāshnā.*

To participate, بانٹنا *bānṭnā*, حصه دار هونا *ḥiṣṣa-dār hōnā.*

To pass, (v. n.) گذرنا *guẕarnā*, بهنا *bahnā*, (v. a.) گذارنا *guẕārnā.*

To pat (strike lightly), تهاپنا *thāpnā*, تماچا مارنا *tamāchā mārnā.*

To patch, جوڑنا *jōṛnā*, پيوند لگانا *paiwand lagānā*, ٹانكنا *ṭānknā.*

To pawn, گرو ركهنا *girō rakhnā*, بندهك ركهنا *bandhak rakhnā.*

To pay, ادا كرنا *adā karnā*, بهر دينا *bhar dēnā*: see To beat.

To peck, ٹونگنا *ṭūngnā*, ٹهونگانا *ṭhōngānā*, منقار مارنا *minḳār mārnā.*

To peel, (v. a.) چهيلنا *chhīlnā*, چهلكا اتارنا *chhilkā utārnā.*

To peep, پهلي نمود هونا *pahlī namūd hōnā*, (v. a.) جهانكنا *jhānknā.*

To penetrate, چونكنا *chōnknā*, چهيدنا *chhēdnā*, (affect) اثر كرنا *aṡar karnā.*

To people, بسانا *basānā*, آباد يا معمور كرنا *ābād* or *ma'mūr karnā.*

To perambulate, پهرنا *phirnā*, سير كرنا *sair karnā.*

To perceive, دريافت كرنا *daryāft karnā*, ديكه پانا *dēkh pānā.*

To perfect, (finish) تمام كرنا *tamām karnā*, نبيڑنا *nibēṛnā.*

To perform, كرنا *karnā*, نباهنا *nibāhnā*, بجالانا *bajā lānā.*

To perish, مرنا *marnā*, هلاك هونا *halāk hōnā*, جاتا رهنا *jātā rahnā.*

To permit, دينا *dēnā*, اجازت دينا *ijāzat dēnā*, روا ركهنا *rawā rakhnā.*

To perplex, حيران كرنا *ḥairān karnā*, پيچ ميں ڈالنا *pēch mēṅ ḍālnā.*

To persevere, persist, قايم رهنا *ḳā'im rahnā.*

To perspire, پسيجنا *pasījnā*, پسينا نكلنا *pasīnā nikalnā.*

To persuade, منانا *manānā*, مايل كرنا *mā'il karnā*, صلاح دينا *ṣalāḥ dēnā.*

To pervade, پيٹهنا *paiṭhnā*, پهيلنا *phailnā*, در آنا *dar ānā.*

To pervert, الٹانا *ulṭānā*, بگاڑنا *bigāṛnā*, خراب كرنا *kharāb karnā.*

To peruse, مطالعه كرنا *muṭāla'a karnā*, پڑھنا *paṛhnā*.

To pester, ستانا *satānā*, كهجانا *khijānā*, تكليف دينا *taklīf dēnā*.

To petition, عرض معروض كرنا *ārẓ ma'rūẓ karnā*: see To request.

To petrify, (v. n.) پتهرانا *pathrānā*, پتهر هوجانا *patthar hō-jānā*, (v. a.) پتهر كرنا *patthar karnā*, پتهرسا سخت كرنا *patthar-sā sakht karnā*.

To pick, چنا *chunnā*, چن لينا *chun lēnā*, چگنا *chugnā*: see To choose.

To pierce, چونكنا *chōnknā*, سالنا *sālnā*: see To bore.

To pilfer, موسنا *mūsnā*, چرانا *churānā*.

To pinch, نوچنا *nōchnā*, چتكي لينا *chuṭkī lēnā*, (press) دابنا *dābnā*.

To pine, جهورنا *jhūrnā*, افسرده هونا *afsurda hōnā*, مر رهنا *mar rahnā*.

To place, ركهنا *rakhnā*, بيٹهالنا *baiṭhālnā*, ٹهہرانا *ṭhahrānā*.

To plan, (scheme) تجويز كرنا *tajwīz karnā*, (design) نقشه باندهنا *nakṣha bāndhnā*.

To plant, (set) لگانا *lagānā*, رونپنا *rōmpnā*, (settle) بيٹهالنا *baiṭhālnā*.

To play, كهيلنا *khēlnā*, (to toy) راو چاو كرنا *rā'ō chā'ō karnā*, (music) بجانا *bajānā*.

To plead, حجت كرنا *ḥujjat karnā*, دليل لانا *dalīl lānā*: see To argue.

To please, خوش كرنا *khush karnā*, رجهانا *rijhānā*, (v. n.) رچنا *ruchnā*.

To pluck, چهين لينا *chhīn lēnā*, (as a fowl) پر اكهاڑنا *par ukhāṛnā*.

To plunge, (in water) غوطه مارنا *ghōṭa mārnā*, ڈوبنا *ḍūbnā*, (v. a.) ڈبانا *ḍubānā*.

To polish, صيقل يا صاف يا چكنا كرنا *ṣaiḳal* or *ṣāf* or *chiknā karnā*.

To pollute, ناپاك كرنا *nāpāk karnā*, بگاڑنا *bigāṛnā*.

To possess, ركهنا *rakhnā*, تصرف كرنا *taṣarruf karnā*, دهرنا *dharnā*.

To postpone, ٹالنا *ṭālnā*, تاخير كرنا *tākhīr karnā*.

To pound, كوٹنا *kuṭna*, ٹهونكنا *ṭhonkna*, چورنا *churnā*: see To confine.

To pour, ڈهالنا *ḍhālnā*, انڈيلنا *unḍēlnā*, (flow) بهنا *bahnā*.

To practise, كرنا *karnā*, كيا كرنا *kiyā karnā*, مشق كرنا *mashḳ karnā*.

To praise, سراهنا *sarāhnā*, تعريف كرنا *ta'rīf karnā*: see To applaud.

To prance, لنبيان كرنا *lambiyāṅ karnā*, شلنگ مارنا *shalang mārnā*.

To prate, prattle, گپشپ يا بكبك كرنا *gapshap* or *bakbak karnā*.

To pray, (entreat) مانگنا *māngnā*, (to heaven) نماز کرنا *namāz karnā*.

To preach, وعظ کرنا *wa*z karnā*, خطبه پڑھنا *khuṭba paṛhnā*.

To precede, اگي جانا *āgē jānā*, مقدم هونا *mukaddam hōnā*.

To precipitate, گرا دينا *girā dēnā*, دهکيل دينا *dhakēl dēnā*: see To hurry.

To preclude, باز رکهنا *bāz rakhnā*, کاٹنا *kāṭnā*, روکنا *rōknā*.

To predict, اگي سي کهنا يا بتلانا *āgē sē kahnā* or *batlānā*.

To prefer, ترجيح دينا *tarjīḥ dēnā*, احسن جاننا *aḥsan jānnā*: see To advance.

To premise, تمهيد کرنا *tamhīd karnā*, اگي سي جتانا *āgē sē jatānā*.

To prepare, تيار کرنا *taiyār karnā*, بنانا *banānā*, قابل کرنا *ḳābil karnā*.

To prescribe (medically), نسخه يا دوا بتلانا *nuskha* or *dawā batlānā*.

To preserve, بچانا *bachānā*, (as fruits, &c.) مربه کرنا *murabba karnā*.

To press, (squeeze) چاپنا *chāpnā*, (out) نچوڑنا *nichōṛnā*, (down) دبانا *dabānā*, (to distress) تنگ کرنا *tang karnā*, (urge) تاکيد کرنا *tākīd karnā*.

To presume, خيال کرنا *khiyāl karnā*, (be bold) گستاخي کرنا *gustākhī karnā*.

To pretend, بات بنانا *bāt banānā*, بهانه کرنا *bahāna karnā*.

To prevail, (be current) جاري هونا *jārī hōnā*: see To extend, conquer.

To prevent, روکنا *rōknā*, اٹکانا *aṭkānā*, آڑنا *āṛnā*: see To hinder.

To prick, (v.n.) چبهنا *chubhnā*, (v.a.) چبهونا *chubhōnā*, چونکنا *chōnknā*.

To prime, رنجک پلانا *ranjak pilānā*, (in painting) زمين بنانا *zamīn banānā*.

To print, چهاپنا *chhāpnā*, نقش يا چهاپا کرنا *naḳsh* or *chhāpā karnā*.

To proceed, (on) اگي جانا *āgē jānā*, چلنا *chalnā*, (from) نکلنا *nikalnā*.

To proclaim, ظاهر کرنا *ẓāhir karnā*, ڈهنڈهورا پهيرنا *ḍhanḍhōrā phērnā*.

To procrastinate, ٹالنا *ṭālnā*, آج کل يا ديري کرنا *āj-kal* or *dērī karnā*.

To procure, پيدا کرنا *paidā karnā*, بهم پهنچانا *baham pahunchānā*.

To produce, (bring forth) جننا *jannā*, (make grow) اپجانا *upjānā*.

To profess, اقرار کرنا *iḳrār karnā*, کهنا *kahnā*, جتانا *jatānā*.

To prohibit, منع کرنا *man* karnā*, باز رکهنا *bāz rakhnā*, روکنا *rōknā*.

To prolong, طویل کرنا *ṭawīl karnā*, بڑھانا *baṛhānā*, پھیلانا *phailānā*.

To promise, اقرار کرنا *iḳrār karnā*, بچن دینا *bachan dēnā*.

To promote, بڑھانا *baṛhānā*, ترقی کرنا *taraḳḳī karnā*.

To prompt, کہہ دینا *kah dēnā*, بتلانا *batlānā*, جتانا *jatānā*.

To pronounce, اچارنا *uchchārnā*, تلفظ کرنا *talaffuẓ karnā*.

To prop, ٹیکنا *ṭēknā*, تھامنا *thāmnā*, آڑنا *āṛnā*: see To support.

To propose, اظہار کرنا *iẓhār karnā*, عرض کرنا *ʿarẓ karnā*: see To intend.

To prosper, کامیاب یا بہرہ‌مند ہونا *kām-yāb* or *bahra-mand hōnā*.

To protect, رکھنا *rakhnā*, بچانا *bachānā*, حمایت کرنا *ḥimāyat karnā*.

To prove, (try) آزمانا *āzmānā*, (evince) ثابت کرنا *ṣābit karnā*.

To provide, مہیا کرنا *muhaiyā karnā*, دینا *dēnā*; بدنا *badnā*.

To pry into, بھید لینا *bhēd lēnā*, جھانکنا *jhānknā*.

To publish, مشہور کرنا *mashhūr karnā*, (a work) چھاپنا *chhāpnā*.

To pull, زور سے کھینچنا *zōr sē khīnchnā*, تاننا *tānnā*.

To punish, سزا دینا *sazā dēnā*, ڈانڈنا *ḍānḍnā*.

To purchase, خرید کرنا *kharīd karnā*, مول لینا *mōl lēnā*.

To pursue, پیچھا کرنا یا لینا *pīchhā-karnā* or *-lēnā*: see To hunt.

To push, ڈھکیلنا *ḍhakēlnā*, ٹھیلنا *ṭhēlnā*, پیلنا *pēlnā*.

To put, رکھنا *rakhnā*, دھرنا *dharnā*, ڈالنا *ḍālnā*.

To put off, (as dress) اتارنا *utārnā*, (defer) ٹالنا *ṭālnā*.

To put on (as dress), پہننا *pahannā* or *pahinnā*, اوڑھنا *ōṛhnā*.

To put out (extinguish), بجھانا *bujhānā*, گل کرنا *gul karnā*.

To put up with, سہنا *sahnā*, برداشت کرنا *bardāsht karnā*.

To putrefy, (v. n.) سڑنا *saṛnā*, گلنا *galnā*, (v. a.) سڑانا *saṛānā*.

To quake, کانپنا *kāmpnā*, لرزنا *laraznā*, کپنا *kapnā*.

To quarrel, جھگڑنا *jhagaṛnā*, لڑنا *laṛnā*, قضیہ کرنا *ḳaẓiya karnā*.

To quaver, لہکنا *lahakna*, آواز مروڑنا *āwāz marōṛnā*.

To quell, دبانا *dabānā*, توڑنا *tōṛnā*, رفع کرنا *rafʿ karnā*.

To quench, بجھانا *bujhānā*, ٹھنڈا کرنا *ṭhanḍā karnā*.

To question, سوال کرنا *suwāl karnā*: see To debate, To doubt.

To quit, چھوڑنا *chhōṛnā*, تجنا *tajnā*, ترک کرنا *tark karnā*.

To quiver, کپنا *kapnā*, لرزنا *laraznā*: see To quaver, quake.

To quote, اقتباس كرنا *iḳtibās karnā,* درج كرنا *darj karnā,* سند لانا *sanad lānā.*

Quoth (said), كها *kahā,* كتها *kuthā.*

To rain, (v. n.) برسنا *barasnā,* باني پڑنا *pānī paṛnā,* (v. a.) برسانا *barsānā.*

To raise, اٹھانا *uṭhānā,* برپا كرنا *bar-pā karnā,* چڑھانا *chaṛhānā.*

To ram down or in, ٹھاسنا *ṭhāsnā,* كسنا *kasnā,* ٹھيسنا *ṭhēsnā.*

To ramble, پهرنا *phirnā,* ڈولنا *ḍōlnā,* سير كرنا *sair karnā.*

To range, (place in order) بترتيب ركهنا *batartīb rakhnā:* see To ramble.

To ransack, چهان مارنا *chhān mārnā,* (pillage) لوٹنا *lūṭnā.*

To rattle, كهڑكهڑانا *khaṛkhaṛānā,* جهنكارنا *jhankārnā.*

To raze, مسمار كرنا *mismār karnā,* اجاڑنا *ujāṛnā,* ڈهانا *ḍhānā.*

To reach, هاتهسي پانا *hāth sē pānā,* لگنا *lagnā,* پهنچنا *pahunchnā.*

To read, پڑهنا *paṛhnā,* بانچنا *bānchnā,* مطالعه كرنا *muṭāla'ā karnā.*

To reap, فصل كاٹنا *faṣl kāṭnā,* درو كرنا *dirau karnā.*

To rebuke, ملامت كرنا *malāmat karnā,* ڈانٹنا *ḍānṭnā.*

To recede, پهر جانا *phir jānā,* دب جانا *dab jānā,* هٹنا *haṭnā.*

To receive, لينا *lēnā,* پانا *pānā,* قبول كرنا *ḳabūl karnā.*

To recite, بيان كرنا *bayān karnā,* تكرار كرنا *takrār karnā.*

To reckon, گننا *ginnā* شمار كرنا *shumār karnā:* see To deem.

To recognise, پهچاننا *pahchānnā:* see To allow.

To recollect, ياد كرنا *yād karnā,* هوش پكڑنا *hōsh pakaṛnā.*

To recommend, تقريب يا سفارش كرنا *taḳrīb* or *sifārish karnā.*

To reconcile, منانا *manānā,* صلح كرنا *ṣulḥ karṇā,* ملانا *milānā.*

To record, دفتر مين داخل كرنا *daftar mēn dāḵẖil karnā,* لكهنا *likhnā.*

To recover, پهر پانا *phir pānā,* (from sickness) شفا پانا *shifā pānā.*

To rectify, اصلاح دينا *iṣlāḥ dēnā,* سدهارنا *sudhārnā.*

To recur, پهر آنا *phir ānā,* (to the mind) ياد آنا *yād ānā.*

To reduce, گهٹانا *ghaṭānā,* كم كرنا *kam karnā:* see To subdue.

To reflect, بچارنا *bichārnā,* (throw back) عكس دينا *ăks dēnā.*

To reform, اصلاح كرنا *iṣlaḥ karnā,* سدهارنا *sudhārnā.*

To refuse, انکار یا منع کرنا *inkār* or *man*ʿ *karnā:* see To abstain.

To refute, باطل یا رد کرنا *bāṭil* or *radd karnā*, جھٹالنا *jhuṭālnā*.

To regard, التفات کرنا *iltifāt kārnā*, ماننا *mānnā:* see To behold.

To register, دفتر میں داخل کرنا *daftar mēṅ dā<u>kh</u>il karnā*.

To regret, پچھتانا *pachhtānā*, افسوس کرنا *afsōs karnā*.

To reject, پھیرنا *phērnā*, رد یا متروک کرنا *radd* or *matrūk karnā*.

To rejoice, ریجھنا *rījhnā*, خوش ہونا *<u>kh</u>ush hōnā:* see To glad.

To relapse, پھر پچھڑنا *phir pachhaṛnā*, پھر بیمار پڑنا *phir bīmār paṛnā*.

To relate, (tell) کہنا *kahnā*, (relate to) علاقہ رکھنا *ʿalāḳa rakhnā*.

To release, چھڑانا *chhuṛānā*, رہائي دینا *rihā'ī dēnā*.

To relieve, (ease) آرام دینا *ārām dēnā*, (help) تھامنا *thāmnā:* see To help.

To relinquish, چھوڑنا *chhōṛnā*, تیاگنا *tyāgnā:* see To leave.

To rely, بھروسا رکھنا *bharōsā rakhnā*, تکیہ کرنا *takiya karnā*.

To remain, رهنا *rahnā*, ٹکنا *ṭiknā*, ٹھہرنا *ṭhaharnā*, ابرنا *ubarnā*.

To remember, یاد کرنا *yād karnā*, خاطر میں رکھنا *<u>kh</u>aṭir mēṅ rakhnā*.

To remind, یاد دلانا *yād dilānā*, چتانا *chitānā*.

To remove, دور کرنا *dūr karnā*, سرکانا *sarkānā*, تغیر کرنا *ta<u>gh</u>īr karnā*.

To rend, پھاڑنا *phāṛnā*, چیرنا *chīrnā*, مسکانا *maskānā*, پھوڑنا *phōṛna*.

To render, (give back) پھرا دینا *phirā dēnā:* see To give, make, translate.

To renew, renovate, نیا کرنا *nayā karnā*, پھر لانا *phir lānā*.

To rent, کرایہ کرنا *kirāya karnā*, (take at rent) کرایہ لینا *kirāya lēnā*.

To repair, مرمت کرنا *marammat karnā*, درست کرنا *durust karnā*.

To repeal, منسوخ یا موقوف کرنا *mansū<u>kh</u>* or *mauḳūf karnā*.

To repeat, مکرر یا دوبارہ کرنا *mukarrar* or *dō-būra karnā:* see To tell.

To repent, پچھتانا *pachhtānā*, پشیمان ہونا *pashēmān hōnā*.

To reply, اتر یا جواب دینا *uttar* or *jawāb dēnā*, کہنا *kahnā*.

To repose, (v. n.) سونا *sōnā*, آرام کرنا *ārām karnā*, (v. a.) آرام دینا *ārām dēnā*.

To represent, عرض کرنا *ʿarẓ karnā*, (personate) نقل کرنا *naḳl karnā*.

To reproach, طعن یا ملامت کرنا *taʿn* or *malāmat karnā*.

To request, چاهنا *chāhnā*, درخواست کرنا *darkhwāst karnā*.
To require, مانگنا *māngnā*, طلب کرنا *ṭalab karnā:* see To need.
To reside, رهنا *rahnā*, بسنا *basnā*, گهر کرنا *ghar karnā*.
To resign, سونپنا *sōmpnā*, تسليم کرنا *taslīm karnā :* see To leave.
To resound, گونجنا *gūnjnā*, گونج رهنا *gūnj rahnā:* see To praise.
To respect, عزت يا تعظيم کرنا *ʿizzat* or *taʿẓīm karnā:* see To relate to.
To rest, آرام کرنا *ārām karnā*, دم لينا *dam lēnā :* see To sleep, lean on.
To restore, پهر لانا *phir lānā*, پهير دينا *phēr dēnā :* see To cure.
To restrain, روکنا *rōknā*, اٹکانا *aṭkānā*, باز رکهنا *bāz rakhnā*.
To retail, تهوڑا تهوڑا کرکي بيچنا *thōṛā thōṛā karkē bēchnā*.
To retain, رکهنا *rakhnā*, ٹکانا *ṭikānā:* see To keep, hire.
To retreat, پسپا هونا *paspā hōnā*, هٹنا *haṭnā*.
To return, (v. n.) پهر آنا يا جانا *phir ānā* or *jānā*, (v. a.) پلٹانا *palṭānā*.
To reveal, کهولنا *khōlnā*, (divulge) فاش کرنا *fāsh karnā*, کهنا *kahnā*.
To revenge, انتقام يا عوض يا بدلا لينا *intiḳām* or *ʿiwaẓ* or *badlā lēnā*.
To review, revise, نظر ثاني کرنا *naẓar-i-s̤ānī karnā*.
To revile, گليانا *galiyānā*, گالي دينا *gālī dēnā :* see To reproach.
To revoke, اٹها دينا *uṭhā dēnā*, ميٹ دينا *mēṭ dēnā :* see To repeal.
To rid, چهڑانا *chhuṛānā*, صاف کرنا *ṣāf karnā :* see To free.
To ride, سوار هونا *sawār hōnā*, گهوڑي پر چڑهنا *ghōṛē par chaṛhnā*.
To rinse, گهنگهولنا *ghanghōlnā*, کهنگهالنا *khanghālnā* (?).
To rip, پهاڑنا *phāṛnā*, ادهيڑنا *udhēṛnā*, چاک کرنا *chāk karnā*.
To ripe, ripen, (v. n.) پکنا *paknā*, (v. a.) پکانا *pakānā*.
To rise, اٹهنا *uṭhnā*, بڑهنا *baṛhnā*, چڑهنا *chaṛhnā*, (the sun or moon) ادي هونا *udai hōnā*, طلوع هونا *ṭulūʿ hōnā*, (the moon) اگنا *ugnā*.
To roast, کباب کرنا *kabāb karnā*, بريان کرنا *biryān karnā*.
To rob, چرانا *churānā*, راه مارنا *rāh mārnā*, لوٹنا *lūṭnā*.
To roll, (v. n.) پهرنا *phirnā*, لڑهنا *luṛhnā*, (v. a.) پهرانا *phirānā*, لڑهانا *luṛhānā*, گهمانا *ghumānā*, (roll up) لپيٹنا *lapēṭnā*.
To roof, پاٹنا *pāṭnā*, چهانا *chhānā*, چهپر دينا *chhappar dēnā*.
To rot, (v. n.) سڑنا *saṛnā*, گلنا *galnā*, (v. a.) سڑانا *saṛānā*.
To rouse, (v. n.) جاگنا *jāgnā*, اٹهنا *uṭhnā*, (v. a.) جگانا *jagānā*.

To row, کهيونا *khĕ'ōna*, ڈانڈ مارنا *ḍānḍ mārnā*.

To rub, (v. n. chafe) گهسنا *ghisnā*, (v. a.) رگڑنا *ragaṛnā*, ملنا *malnā*.

To rue, پچهتانا *pachhtānā*, رونا *rōnā*, ندامت کرنا *nadāmat karnā*.

To ruin, تباه يا ستياناس کرنا *tabāh* or *satyānās karnā*, توڑنا *tōṛnā*.

To rule, حکومت کرنا *ḥukūmat karnā*, (lines) مسطر کرنا *misṭar karnā*.

To ruminate, پگڑانا *paguṛānā*, جگالي کرنا *jugālī karnā*: see To muse.

To run, دوڑنا *dauṛnā*, دهانا *dhānā*: see To flee, dissolve.

To rush, دوڑنا *dauṛnā*, ريلنا *rēlnā*, (upon) جهپٹنا *jhapaṭnā*.

To sacrifice, چڑهانا *chaṛhānā*, قربان يا ذبح کرنا *ḳurbān* or *ẕabḥ karnā*.

To saddle, زين باندهنا *zīn bāndhnā*, چارجامه دينا *chār-jāma dēnā*.

To salivate, منهه لانا *muṅh lānā*, تهکانا *thukānā*.

To sally, خروج کرنا *khurūj karnā*, نکل پڑنا *nikal paṛnā*.

To salute, سلام يا کورنش کرنا *salām* or *kōrnish karnā*.

To sap, سرنگ کرنا *surang karnā*, سيندهه مارنا *sēndh mārnā*: see To ruin.

To sate, satiate, بهرنا *bharnā*, چهکانا *chhakānā*, (v. n.) اگهانا *aghānā*.

To satisfy, خوش يا راضي کرنا *khush* or *rāẓī karnā*, منانا *manānā*.

To save, بچانا *bachānā*, سلامت رکهنا *salāmat rakhnā*, رکهنا *rakhnā*.

To say, کهنا *kahnā*, بولنا *bōlnā*, بات کرنا *bāt karnā*, بتيانا *batiyānā*.

To scald, گرم پاني و غيره سي جلانا *garm pānī ō ghaira sē jalānā*.

To scan, (measure) تقطيع کرنا *taḳṭī* karnā*: see To examine.

To scare, ڈرانا *ḍarānā*, بهڑکانا *bhaṛkānā*, بچکانا *bichkānā*.

To scarify پچهنا دينا *pachhnā dēnā*, کهونچيانا *khōnchiyānā* (?).

To scatter, چهترانا *chhitrānā*, چهٹکانا *chhiṭkānā*, بتهرانا *bithrānā*.

To scoff, ٹهٹها يا طعن کرنا *ṭhaṭhā* or *ṭa'n karnā*, گليانا *galiyānā*.

To scold, جهڑکنا *jhiṛaknā*, دهمکانا *dhamkānā*, گالي دينا *gālī dēnā*.

To scorch, (v. n.) بهلسنا *bhulasnā*, (v. a.) جهلسانا *jhulsānā*.

To scour, مانجنا *mānjnā*, صاف کرنا *ṣāf karnā*, (purge v. n.) پيٹ چلنا *pēṭ chalnā*.

To scowl, بهون ٹيڑهي کرنا *bhauṅ ṭēṛhī karnā*, ناک چڑهانا *nāk chaṛhānā*.

To scrape, چهيلنا *chhīlnā*, کهرچنا *khurachnā*, چهولنا *chhōlnā*.

To scratch, کهرچنا *khurachnā*, کهجلانا *khujlānā*, نوچنا *nōchnā*.

To scream, چچيانا *chichiyānā*, چلانا *chillānā*, چلا اٹهنا *chillā uṭhnā*.

To sculk, چهپ رهنا *chhip rahnā*, دبکٹ رهنا *dabak rahnā*.

To seal, مهر کرنا *muhr karnā*, مهر کرکي بند کرنا *muhr karkē band karnā*.

To seclude, کناري رکهنا *kinārē rakhnā*, نکالنا *nikālnā*.

To seduce, پهسلانا *phuslānā*, ورغلاننا *warghalānnā*, بهٹکانا *bhaṭkānā*.

To see, ديکهنا *dēkhnā*, نظر کرنا *nazar karnā*, نهارنا *nihārnā*.

To seek, ڈهونڈهنا *ḍhūnḍhnā*, تلاش کرنا *talāsh karnā*, کهوجنا *khōjnā*.

To seem, سوجهنا *sūjhnā*, معلوم هونا *ma*ʻ*lūm hōnā*, نظر آنا *nazar ānā*.

To seeth, سجهانا *sijhānā*, اساننا *usānnā*, (v. n.) سيجنا *sījnā*.

To seize, پکڑنا *pakaṛnā*, قبض کرنا *ḳabẓ karnā :* see To confiscate.

To select, چننا *chunnā*, چن چهان لينا *chun chhān lēnā :* see To cull.

To sell, بيچنا *bēchnā*, فروخت کرنا *farokht karnā*, مول دينا *mōl dēnā*.

To send, بهيجنا *bhējnā*, ارسال کرنا *irsāl karnā*, چلانا *chalānā*.

To separate, توڑنا *tōṛnā*, بچهوڑنا *bichhōṛnā*, جدا کرنا *judā karnā*.

To serve, نوکري يا خدمت کرنا *naukarī* or *khidmat karnā:* see To help.

To set, (place) رکهنا *rakhnā*, دهرنا *dharnā*, (plant) بٹهلانا *biṭhlānā*, (as the sun) غروب يا است هونا *ghurūb* or *ast hōnā*, (set up) اٹهانا *uṭhānā*, see To raise, (set on) هلکارنا *hulkārnā*, see To excite, (set on fire) آگ لگانا *āg lagānā*, پهونکٹ دينا *phūnk dēnā*.

To settle, (v. n.) بيٹهنا *baiṭhnā*, (v. a.) بيٹهالنا *baiṭhālnā*, ٹهاننا *ṭhānnā*, (an account) چکانا *chukānā :* see To fix.

To sever, چيرنا *chīrnā*, پهاڑ دينا *phāṛ dēnā*, جدا کرنا *judā karnā*.

To sew, سينا *sīnā*, دوخت کرنا *dōkhht karnā*, سلانا *silānā*.

To shake, (v. n.) هلنا *hilnā*, ڈلنا *ḍulnā*, (v. a.) هلانا *hilānā :* see To quake.

To shape, بنانا *banānā*, گڑهنا *gaṛhnā*, شکل باندهنا *shakl bāndhnā*.

To sharpen, تيز کرنا *tēz karnā*, چوکهانا *chōkhānā*, باڑ دينا *bāṛ dēnā*.

To shave, مونڈنا *mūnḍnā*, حجامت کرنا *ḥajāmat karnā*.

To shear, کترنا *katarnā*, مقراض کرنا *miḳrāẓ karnā*, کاٹنا *kāṭnā*.

To shed, (v. n.) جهڑنا *jhaṛnā*, گرنا *girnā*, (v. a.) ڈالنا *ḍālnā*, گرانا *girānā*.

To shine, چمکنا *chamaknā*, جهلکنا *jhalaknā*, لوکنا *lauknā*.

To shiver, کانپنا *kāmpnā*, (to shatter) چورچور کرنا *chūr-chūr karnā*.

To shoot, (let go) چهوڑنا *chhōṛnā*, (bud) کليانا *kaliyānā :* see To hasten.

To shorten, کوتاہ کرنا *kōtāh karnā*, گھٹانا *ghaṭānā :* see To abridge.

To shove, دھکیلنا *dhakēlnā*, ٹھیلنا *ṭhēlnā*, ریلنا *rēlnā*, پیلنا *pēlnā*.

To shout, ٹیرنا *ṭērnā*, (huzza) جي جي کار کرنا *jai-jai-kār karnā :* see To cry.

To show, دکھلانا *dikhlānā*, بتانا *batānā*, ظاہر کرنا *ẓāhir karnā*.

To shrink, shrivel, سکڑنا *sukaṛnā*, سمیٹنا *samēṭnā*.

To shrug up the shoulders, کاندھا ہلانا *kāndhā hilānā*.

To shudder, تھرتھرانا *thartharānā*, ہڑہڑانا *haṛhaṛānā :* see To quake.

To shuffle, ٹالنا *ṭālnā*, ٹالمٹول کرنا *ṭālmaṭōl karnā :* see To mix.

To shun, ٹالنا *ṭālnā*, روگردان ہونا *rūgardān hōnā*, باز رہنا *bāz rahnā*.

To shut, بند کرنا *band karnā*, لگانا *lagānā*, موچنا *mūchnā*.

To sift, چالنا *chālnā*, جھاڑنا *jhāṛnā*, چھاننا *chhānnā*.

To sign (ratify by writing), دستخط یا صحیح کرنا *dast-khaṭṭ* or *ṣaḥīḥ karnā*.

To signify, بجھانا *bujhānā*, جتانا *jatānā*, معني رکھنا *ma*ʿ*nī rakhnā*.

To sing, گانا *gānā*, الاپنا *alāpnā* or *ālāpnā*, گان کرنا *gān karnā*.

To sink, ڈوبنا *ḍūbnā*, دھسکنا *dhasaknā*, گھٹنا *ghaṭnā*.

To sit, بیٹھنا *baiṭhnā*, نشست کرنا *nishast karnā :* see To fit.

To skim, (v. a.) کاچھنا *kāchhnā*, پسانا *pasānā*, (v. n.) چھو جانا *chhū jānā*.

To skin, کھال کھینچنا *khāl khīnchnā*, (a wound) گھاؤ بھرنا *ghā'ō bharnā*.

To slake, بجھانا *bujhānā*, سرد کرنا *sard karnā :* see To quench.

To slap, دھولیانا *dhauliyānā*, طمانچہ مارنا *ṭamāncha mārnā*.

To slash, کاٹنا *kāṭnā*, چیرنا *chīrnā*, کٹاکٹ کرنا *kaṭākaṭ karnā*.

To slaughter, slay, قتل کرنا *ḳatl karnā*, مار ڈالنا *mār-ḍālnā*.

To sleep, سونا *sōnā*, نیند لینا *nīnd lēnā*, سوتنا *sūtnā*.

To slight, غفلت کرنا *ghaflat karnā*, ہلکا جاننا *halkā jānnā*.

To slip, کھسلنا *khisalnā*, رپٹنا *rapaṭnā*, بچھلنا *bichhalnā*.

To slit, لنبا لنبي کاٹنا *lambā lambī kāṭnā*, چیرنا *chīrnā*, پھاڑنا *phāṛnā*.

To slop, پاني ڈالکي بھگونا *pānī ḍālkē bhigōnā*.

To smart, چرپرانا *charparānā*, پڑپڑانا *paṛpaṛānā*, دکھنا *dukhnā*.

To smell, سونگھنا *sūnghnā*, بو لینا *bō lēnā*, (v. n.) بوانا *bō'ānā*.

To smile, مسکرانا *muskurānā,* تبسم کرنا *tabassum karnā.*

To smite, (strike) مارنا *mārnā,* (kill) مار ڈالنا *mār-ḍālnā.*

To smoke, (emit smoke) دهونوارانا *dhūṅwārānā,* (tobacco) پينا *pīnā.*

To smuggle, گهاٹ مارنا *ghāṭ mārnā,* چوکي مارنا *chaukī mārnā.*

To snarl (a dog), گرجنا *gurajnā,* گهرکنا *ghuraknā,* گهرانا *ghurrānā.* (?)

To snatch, چهين لينا *chhīn lēnā,* جهپٹ لينا *jhapaṭ lēnā.*

To sneak, (creep slily) دبک جانا يا آنا *dabak jānā* or *ānā: see* To beseech.

To sneeze, چهينکنا *chhīnknā,* عطسه کرنا *ʿaṭsa karnā.*

To snub, ڈانٹنا *ḍānṭnā,* سانسنا *sānsnā,* کاٹنا *kāṭnā.*

To snuff, (a candle) گل لينا *gul lēnā,* (inhale) کهينچنا *khīnchnā.*

To soak, (v. n.) سيراب هونا *sērāb hōnā,* (v. a.) بهگونا *bhigōnā.*

To soar, اڑنا *uṛnā,* بلند پروازي کرنا *buland parwāzī karnā: see* To mount.

To sob, سسکنا *sisaknā,* ٹهنکنا *ṭhunuknā,* بسورنا *bisūrnā.*

To solicit, چاهنا *chāhnā,* منت يا استدعا کرنا *minnat* or *istidʿā karnā.*

To solve, حل کرنا *ḥall karnā,* صاف کرنا *ṣāf karnā: see* To explain.

To sooth, خوشامد کرنا *khushāmad karnā,* منانا *manānā,* چمکارنا *chumkārnā.*

To sow, بونا *bōnā,* بيج ڈالنا *bīj ḍālnā,* تخم ريزي کرنا *tukhm-rēzī karnā.*

To spare, (v. n.) جزرس هونا *juz-ras hōnā: see* To save, forgive.

To sparkle, چنگي چهوٹنا يا جهڑنا *chingī chhūṭna* or *jhaṛnā.*

To speak, بولنا *bōlnā,* کهنا *kahnā: see* To pronounce, praise.

To specify, ٹههرانا *ṭhahrānā,* تفصيلوار کهنا *tafṣīl-wār kahnā.*

To spell, املا يا هجي يا تهجي کرنا *imlā* or *hajē* or *tahajjī karnā.*

To spend, خرچ کرنا *kharch karnā,* اڑانا *uṛānā,* اٹهانا *uṭhānā.*

To spike, ميخ مارنا *mēkh mārnā,* ميخ سي بند کرنا *mēkh sē band karnā.*

To spill, ڈهالنا *ḍhālnā,* چهلکانا *chhalkānā,* بهانا *bāhānā.*

To spin, کاتنا *kātnā,* (out, protract) بڑهانا *baṛhānā.*

To spit (eject), تهوکنا *thūknā,* تهوک پهينکنا *thūk phēnknā.*

To spit (meat), سيخ لگانا *sīkh lagānā,* گوتهنا *gūthnā.*

To split, (v. a.) چيرنا *chīrnā,* پهاڑنا *phāṛnā,* (v. n.) پهٹنا *phaṭnā.*

To spoil, (v. n.) خراب هونا *kharāb hōnā*, (v. a.) بگاڑنا *bigāṛnā*, خراب کرنا *kharāb karnā*, (to plunder) لوٹنا *lūṭnā*.

To sport, کهيلنا *khēlnā*, الول کلول کرنا *alōl-kalōl karnā*.

To spout, چهوٹنا *chhūṭnā*, اچهلنا *uchhalnā*, (v. a.) چهوڑنا *chhōṛnā*.

To spread, (v. a.) بچهانا *bichhānā*, پسارنا *pasārnā*, (v. n.) پهيلنا *phailnā*.

To spring, اٹهنا *uṭhnā*, اگنا *ugnā*, (a mine) اڑانا *uṛānā*: see To leap.

To sprinkle, چهڑکنا *chhiṛaknā*, چهيٹنا *chhīṭnā*, بهگونا *bhigōnā*.

To spur, ايڑ يا کانٹا مارنا *ēṛ* or *kānṭā mārnā*, چلانا *chalānā*: see To incite.

To spurn, لات مارنا *lāt mārnā*, (reject) ٹالنا *ṭālnā*: see To despise.

To spy, جهانکنا *jhānknā*, تاکنا *tāknā*, نجهانا *nijhānā*: see To seek.

To squander, اڑانا *uṛānā*, گنوانا *gaṅwānā*, اسراف کرنا *isrāf karnā*.

To squeeze, (press down) دبانا *dabānā*, (crush) نچوڑنا *nichōṛnā*.

To squint, ترچها ديکهنا *tirchhā dēkhnā*, ٹيڑهي نگاه کرنا *ṭēṛhī nigāh karnā*.

To squirt, پچکاري مارنا يا چهوڑنا *pichkārī-mārnā* or *-chhōṛnā*.

To stab, بهونکنا *bhōnknā*, هولنا *hūlnā*, چونکنا *chōnknā*, کونچنا *kōnchnā*.

To stagger, ڈگمگانا *ḍagmagānā*, (be staggered) هچکچانا *hichkichānā*.

To stain, داغي کرنا *dāghī karnā*, دهپا ڈالنا *dhappā ḍālnā*.

To stammer, هکلانا *haklānā*, لڑبڑانا *laṛbaṛānā*.

To stamp, (with the foot) پاؤں سي پيٹنا *pā'ōṅ sē pīṭnā*: see To print.

To stand, کهڑا هونا يا رهنا *khaṛā hōnā* or *rahnā*: see To stay.

To starch, اهارنا *ahārnā*, کلپ دينا يا لگانا *kalap dēnā* or *lagānā*.

To stare, گهورنا *ghūrnā*, تاکنا *tāknā*, تک لگانا يا رهنا *tak lagānā* or *rahnā*.

To start, (up) چونک اٹهنا يا پڑنا *chaunk uṭhnā* or *paṛnā*: see To propose.

To startle, (v. n.) چمکنا *chamaknā*, (v. a.) چمکانا *chamkānā*: see To scare.

To starve, (v. n.) بهوکهون مرنا *bhūkhōṅ marnā*.

To state, (settle) مقرر کرنا *muḳarrar karnā*, (tell) اظهار کرنا *iẓ'hār karnā*.

To stay, رهنا *rahnā*, ٹکنا *ṭiknā*, بسنا *basnā*: see To prop, stop.

To steal, چرانا *churānā*, چرا ليجانا *churā lējānā*, موسنا *mūsnā*.

To steep, بگهونا *bhigōnā*, ڈال ڈبو رکهنا *ḍāl-ḍubō rakhnā*.

To steer, چلانا *chalānā*, ليجانا *lē-jānā*: see To direct, guide.

To step, قدم رکھنا يا اٹھانا *ḳadam rakhnā* or *uṭhānā*, چلنا *chalnā*.

To stew, دم پخت کرنا *dam-puḵẖt karnā*, سجھانا *sijhānā*: see To seeth.

To stick, (v. n.) چپٹنا *chipaṭnā*, چمٹنا *chimaṭnā*, (in mud) پهسنا *phasnā* or پهنسنا *phansnā*, (v. a.) چپٹانا *chipṭānā*: see To stab.

To stimulate, چلانا *chalānā*, دوڑانا *dauṛānā*, چهيڑنا *chhēṛnā*.

To sting, نيش مارنا *nēsh mārnā*, بندهنا *bindhnā*, ڈنکيانا *ḍankiyānā*.

To stink, بدبو يا درگندھ کرنا *bad-bō* or *durgandh karnā*, بوانا *bō'ānā*.

To stir, (v. n.) سرکنا *saraknā*, هلنا *hilnā*, (v. a.) سرکانا *sarkānā*.

To stitch, سينا *sīnā*, ترپنا *turapnā*, ٹانکنا *ṭānknā*.

To stone, پتھر مارنا *patthār mārnā*, سنگسار کرنا *sangsār karnā*.

To stoop, جهکنا *jhuknā*, نهرنا *nihurnā*, (submit) ماننا *mānnā*.

To stop, (v. n.) اٹکنا *aṭaknā* ٹکنا *ṭiknā*, (v. a.) اٹکانا *aṭkānā*.

To storm, تاخت کرنا *tāḵẖt karnā*, دوڑ مارنا *dauṛ mārnā*.

To straddle, ٹانگ چهتراکي چلنا *ṭāng chhitrākē chalnā*.

To straggle, جهاں تهاں پهرنا *jahāṅ tahāṅ phirnā*: see To ramble.

To strain, (filter) چهاننا *chhānnā*, (sprain) کچکانا *kachkānā*.

To strangle, تسمه کهينچنا *tasma khainchnā*, گلا گهونٹنا *galā ghōnṭnā*.

To stray, بهٹکنا *bhaṭaknā*, بهکنا *bahaknā*, بهولنا *bhūlnā*.

To strengthen, قوي يا مضبوط کرنا *ḳawī* or *maẓbūṭ karnā*.

To stretch, تاننا *tānnā*, پسارنا *pasārnā*, پهيلانا *phailānā*.

To strew, چهينٹنا *chhīnṭnā*, برسانا *barsānā*, بچهانا *bichhānā*.

To strike, مارنا *mārnā*, مار دينا *mār dēnā*, ٹهونکنا *ṭhōnknā*.

To string, ڈوري لگانا *ḍōrī lagānā*, (as pearls) پرونا *parōnā*.

To strip, (off dress) اتارنا *utārnā*, (make naked) ننگا کرنا *nangā karnā*.

To strive, جد و جهد کرنا *jidd ō jahd karnā*, زور مارنا *zōr mārnā*.

To stroke, سهلانا *sahlānā*, هاتھ پهيرنا *hāth phērnā*.

To struggle, هاتھ پير مارنا *hāth pair mārnā*, کشتي کرنا *kushtī karnā*: see To strive.

To strut, اينٹهنا *ainṭhnā*, اترانا *itrānā*, اکڑنا *akaṛnā*.

To study, مطالعه کرنا *muṭāla'ā karnā*, فکر کرنا *fikr karnā*.

To stuff, ٹهاسنا *ṭhāsnā*, بهرنا *bharnā*, (the belly) اپهرانا *aphrānā*.

To stumble, ٹهوکر کهانا *ṭhōkar khānā*, ٹهیس کهانا *ṭhēs khānā*.

To stun, ضرب یا آواز سي اچیت کرنا *ẓarb* or *āwāz sē achēt karnā*.

To stutter, هکلانا *haklānā*, لڑبڑانا *laṛbaṛānā*.

To style, نامزد کرنا *nāmzad karnā*, خطاب دینا *khiṭāb dēnā*.

To subdue, مغلوب یا تابع کرنا *maghlūb* or *tābiʻ karnā*, مارنا *mārnā*.

To submit, (v. n.) تسلیم هونا *taslīm hōnā*, (v. a.) رکهنا *rakhnā*.

To subscribe, دستخط یا صحیح کرنا *dastkhaṭṭ* or *ṣaḥīḥ karnā*.

To subsist, هونا *hōnā*, جینا *jīnā*, گذران کرنا *guẕrān karnā*.

To substitute, عوض یا بدلي رکهنا *ʻiwaẓ* or *badlī rakhnā*.

To substract, subtract, حصه لینا *ḥiṣṣa lēnā*, وضع کرنا *waẓʻ karnā*.

To subvert, ته و بالا یا زیر زبر کرنا *tah-ō-bālā* or *zēr-zabar karnā*.

To succeed, پیچهي آنا یا جانا *pīchhē ānā* or *jānā*: see To prosper.

To suck, چوسنا *chūsnā*, (as a child) دوده پینا *dūdh pīnā*.

To suckle, دوده دینا یا پلانا *dūdh dēnā* or *pilānā*.

To sue, عدالت مین کهینچنا *ʻadālat mēṅ khainchnā*: see To entreat.

To suffer, سهنا *sahnā*, تحمل یا صبر کرنا *taḥammul* or *ṣabr karnā*.

To suffocate, سانس یا دم روکنا *sāṅs* or *dam rōknā*: see To strangle.

To suggest, اشاري سي کهنا *ishārē sē kahnā*, چتانا *chitānā*.

To suit, ٹهیک آنا *ṭhīk ānā*, موافق هونا *muwāfiḳ hōnā*, پهبنا *phabnā*.

To sully, میلا کرنا *mailā karnā*, داغ ڈالنا *dāgh ḍālnā*.

To sum, جوڑنا *jōṛnā*, جمع کرنا *jamʻ karnā*, مجمل کرنا *mujmal karnā*.

To summon, طلب کرنا *ṭalab karnā*, بلوا بهیجنا *bulwā bhējnā*.

To sup, رات کا کهانا کهانا *rāt kā khānā khānā*.

To superintend, نظاره یا سربراهي کرنا *naẓāra* or *sarbarāhī karnā*.

To superscribe, اوپر یا سرخط لکهنا *ūpar* or *sar-khaṭṭ likhnā*.

To supersede, باطل یا رد یا کناره کرنا *bāṭil* or *radd* or *kināra karnā*.

To supervene, ناگهان انا یا آن پڑنا *nāgahān ānā* or *ān-paṛnā*.

To supplicate, استدعا یا التماس کرنا *istidʻā* or *iltimās karnā*.

To supply, بهرنا *bharnā*, بهرتي کرنا *bhartī karnā*, دینا *dēnā*.

To support, برداشت کرنا *bardāsht karnā*, اٹهانا *uṭhānā*, نباهنا *nibāhnā*.

To suppose, (admit) فرض کرنا *farẓ karnā*: see To guess, think, know.

To suppress, روک رکهنا *rōk rakhnā*, اٹکانا *aṭkānā*, دبانا *dabānā*.

To suppurate, پکنا *paknā*, پیبیانا *pībiyānā*, پیب لانا *pīb lānā*.

To surfeit, (v. a.) اپھرانا *aphrānā*, سیر کرنا *sēr karnā*, (v. n.) اگھانا *aghānā*.

To surpass, بڑھ چلنا *baṛh chalnā*, پیچھے ڈالنا *pīchhē ḍālnā*: see To outstrip.

To surprise, ایکا ایک لینا *ēk-ā-ēk lēnā*, اچانک آپڑنا *achānak ā-paṛnā*.

To surrender, تسلیم کرنا *taslīm karnā*: see To consign, resign.

To surround, گھیرنا *ghērnā*, گرد یا احاطہ کرنا *gird* or *iḥāṭa karnā*.

To survey, نظر کرنا *naẓar karnā*, (land) جریب کشی کرنا *jarīb-kashī karnā*.

To suspect, شک کرنا *shakk karnā*, شبہہ رکھنا *shubha rakhnā*.

To suspend, لٹکانا *laṭkānā*, (to stop) موقوف کرنا *mauḳūf karnā*.

To sustain, سمبھالنا *sambhālnā*, تھانبھنا *thāmbhnā*: see To support.

To swagger, شیخي یا لافزني کرنا *shaikhī* or *lāf-zanī karnā*: see To strut.

To swallow, نگلنا *nigalnā*, لیلنا *līlnā*, گھونٹنا *ghūnṭnā*, سرکنا *suruknā*.

To swarm (as flies, &c.), بھنکنا *bhinaknā*.

To sway, (incline) متوجہ کرنا *mutawajjih karnā*: see To rule.

To swear, قسم کھانا *ḳasam khānā*, (make) قسم دلانا *ḳasam dilānā*.

To sweat, (v. n.) پسیجنا *pasījnā*, (to toil) محنت کرنا *miḥnat karnā*.

To sweep, جھاڑنا *jhāṛnā*, بہارنا *buhārnā*, جھاڑ ڈالنا *jhāṛ ḍālnā*.

To sweeten, مٹھانا *miṭhānā*, شیرین یا میٹھا کرنا *shīrīn* or *mīṭhā karnā*.

To swell, پھولنا *phūlnā*, سوجنا *sūjnā*, (look big) بڑائي کرنا *baṛā'ī karnā*.

To swim, پیرنا *pairnā*, ترنا *tirnā*, (float) بھسنا *bhasnā*, بہنا *bahnā*.

To swing, (v. n.) جھولنا *jhūlnā*, ڈولنا *ḍōlnā*, (v. a.) جھلانا *jhulānā*.

To swoon, مورچھا آنا یا کھانا *mūrchhā ānā* or *khānā*.

To swoop, جھپٹ لینا یا مارنا *jhapaṭ lēnā* or *mārnā*.

To swop or swap, ادلا بدلا کرنا *adlā badlā karnā*.

To tack, ٹانکنا *ṭānknā*, جوڑنا *jōṛnā*, جہاز پھرانا *jahāz phirānā*.

To taint, (stain) داغي کرنا *dāghī karnā*: see To corrupt, spoil.

To take, لینا *lēnā*, پکڑنا *pakaṛnā*, (away) لیجانا *lējānā*: see To think.

To talk, بولنا *bōlnā*, بتیانا *batiyānā*: see To prate, chatter.

To tally, ملنا *milnā*, ٹھیک یا برابر ہونا *ṭhīk* or *barābar hōnā*.

To tan, دباغت کرنا *dibāghat karnā*, (in the sun) جهنوانا *jhanwānā*.

To tantalize, ترسانا *tarsānā*, ڈهکانا *ḍahkānā*, للچانا *lalchānā*.

To tap, ٹهکٹهکانا *ṭhakṭhakānā*, تهاپنا *thāpnā* : see To pierce.

To tarry, ٹهہرنا *ṭhaharnā*, ٹکنا *ṭiknā*, بلمبنا *bilambnā*.

To taste, چکهنا *chakhnā*, مزہ لینا *maza lēnā* : see To enjoy, feel.

To taunt, طعن کرنا *ta*n karnā*, چڑهانا *chiṛhānā* : see To revile.

To tax, خراج لگانا *khirāj lagānā*, (accuse) الزام دینا *ilzām dēnā*.

To teach, سکهانا *sikhānā* or سکهلانا *sikhlānā* : see To instruct.

To tear, پهاڑنا *phāṛnā*, چیرنا *chīrnā*, (v. n.) مسکنا *masaknā*, &c.

To tease, ستانا *satānā*, تصدیع دینا *taṣdī* dēnā* : see To vex.

To tell, کہنا *kahnā*, سنانا *sunānā* : see To count, betray.

To temper, معتدل کرنا *mu*tadil karnā* : see To mix.

To tempt, ورغلانا *warghalānnā*, للچانا *lalchānā* : see To excite.

To tend, (incline) مائل هونا *mā'il hōnā* : see To attend, aim.

To tender, تواضع یا نذر کرنا *tawāẓu** or *nazr karnā* : see To offer.

To terminate, (v. n.) آخر هونا *ākhir hōnā*, (v. a.) تمام کرنا *tamām karnā*.

To terrify, ڈرانا *ḍarānā*, دهشت دینا *dahshat dēnā* : see To frighten.

To testify, گواهي دینا *gawāhī dēnā*, دلالت کرنا *dalālat karnā* : see To prove.

To thank, return thanks, شکر کرنا *shukr karnā*, دهن ماننا *dhan mānnā*.

To thaw, (v. n.) پگهلنا *pighalnā*, ٹگهلنا *ṭighalnā*, (v. a.) پگهلانا *pighlānā*.

To thieve, چوري یا دزدي کرنا *chōrī* or *duzdī karnā*.

To think, سوچنا *sōchnā*, بوجهنا *būjhnā*, فکر کرنا *fikr karnā*.

To thirst, پیاسا هونا *pyāsā hōnā*, پیاس لگنا *pyās lagnā*.

To thrash or thresh, گاهنا *gāhnā*, ملنا *malnā*, پیٹنا *pīṭnā*.

To thread, پرونا *pirōna*, لڑیانا *laṛiyānā*, گونتهنا *gūthnā*, تاگنا *tāgnā*.

To threat, threaten, دهمکانا *dhamkānā*, جهڑکنا *jhiṛaknā*.

To thrive, بڑهنا *baṛhnā*, پنپنا *panapnā*, ترقي کرنا *tarakkī karnā*.

To throb, ٹیسنا *ṭīsnā*, ٹیس مارنا *ṭis mārnā*, دهمکنا *dhamaknā*.

To throng, بهیڑ یا هجوم کرنا *bhīṛ* or *hujūm karnā*, بهر آنا *bhar ānā*.

To throw, پهینکنا *phēnknā*, ڈالنا *ḍālnā*, (down) پچهاڑنا *pachhāṛnā*.

To thrust, (shove) دهكا دينا *dhakkā dēnā:* see To stab, shove, stuff.

To thump, ٹهونكنا *ṭhōnknā*, پيٹنا *pīṭnā*, (v. n.) دهمكنا *dhamaknā*.

To thunder, گرجنا *garajnā*, كڑكنا *kaṛaknā*, (in menace) دهمكانا *dhamkānā*.

To thwart, (oppose) ضد يا مخالفت كرنا *zidd* or *mukhālafat karnā*.

To ticket, بيجك دينا *bījak dēnā*, نشان سي جتانا *nishān sē jatānā*.

To tickle, گدگدانا *gudgudānā*, سہلانا *sahlānā*, هنسانا *hansānā*.

To tie, باندهنا *bāndhnā*, جكڑنا *jakaṛnā*, گانٹهنا *gānṭhnā*.

To tighten, كسنا *kasnā*, جكڑنا *jakaṛnā*, كهينچنا *khainchnā*.

To till, جوتنا *jōtnā*, چاس پهيرنا *chās phērnā*.

To tincture, tinge, آلوده كرنا *ālūda karnā*, رنگ دينا *rang dēnā*.

To tingle, تنتنانا *tantanānā*, چمچمانا *chamchamānā*.

To tinkle, جهنجهنانا *jhanjhanānā*, ٹهنٹهنانا *ṭhanṭhanānā*.

To tire, (v. n.) تهكنا *thaknā*, (v. a.) مانده كرنا *mānda karnā*, تهكانا *thakānā*.

To titter, منهه دابكي هنسنا *muṅh dābkē haṅsnā*.

To toast, سينكنا *sēnknā*, بهوننا *bhūnnā*, بريان كرنا *biryān karnā*.

To toil, محنت كرنا *miḥnat karnā*, دكهه بهرنا *dukh bharnā*.

To torment, كلپانا *kalpānā*, كڑهانا *kuṛhānā*, دكهانا *dukhānā*.

To toss, پهينكنا *phēnknā*, اچهالنا *uchhālnā*, جهونكنا *jhōnknā*.

To totter, ڈگمگانا *ḍagmagānā*, ڈولنا *ḍōlnā*, لرزنا *laraznā*.

To touch, (feel) چهونا *chhūnā*, مس كرنا *mass karnā*, (come in contact) لگنا *lagnā*, ملنا *milnā*, (handle) چهيڑنا *chhēṛnā*.

To tow, رسي لگاكي كهينچنا *rassī lagākē khainchnā*.

To toy, كهيلنا *khēlnā*, راؤچاؤ كرنا *rā'ō-chā'ō karnā*.

To trace, track, نقشهٔ پا كي پيروي كرنا *naḳsha-i-pā kī pairawī karnā*.

To trade, سوداگري يا بنج بيپار كرنا *saudāgarī* or *banij-baipār karnā*.

To traduce, تهمت لگانا *tuhmat lagānā*, بدنام كرنا *badnām karnā*.

To trail, گهسيٹنا *ghasīṭnā*, گهسيانا *ghisiyānā:* see To draw.

To train, تربيت يا هموار كرنا *tarbiyat* or *hamwār karnā:* see To teach.

To trample, پاؤں سي ملنا *pā'oṅ sē malnā*, كچلنا *kuchalnā*.

To transact, چلانا *chalānā*, معامله كرنا *mu'āmala karnā*.

To transfer, (make over) سونپنا *sōmpnā*, تسليم كرنا *taslīm karnā*.

To transgress, عدول يا تجاوز يا خطا كرنا *ŭdūl* or *tajāwuz* or *khaṭā karnā*.

To translate, نقل كرنا *naḳl karnā*, (interpret) ترجمه كرنا *tarjuma karnā*.

To transmit, روانه كرنا *rawāna karnā*, بهيجنا *bhējnā*.

To transport, ديس سي نكالنا *dēs sē nikālnā ;* see To banish : (put into ecstacy) وجد مين ركهنا *wajd mēṅ rakhnā*.

To travail, be in travail, درد كهانا *dard khānā*.

To travel, سفر كرنا *safar karnā*, پهرنا *phirnā*, چلنا *chalnā*.

To traverse, (lay athwart) آڑا لگانا *āṛā lagānā*, (pass) پهرنا *phirnā*.

To tread, قدم يا پانو ركهنا *ḳadam* or *pāṅw rakhnā*, (thrash) داؤنا *dā'ōnā*.

To treat, سلوك كرنا *sulūk karnā*, (of) ذكر كرنا *ẕikr karnā :* see To feed.

To tremble, كانپنا *kāmpnā*, دلدلانا *daldalānā*, لرزنا *laraznā*.

To trick, ٹهگنا *ṭhagnā*, چهلنا *chhalnā :* see To cheat, adorn.

To trickle, جهرجهرانا *jhirjhirānā*, بنديانا *bundiyānā*.

To trifle, مكهي مارنا *makkhī mārnā*, ٹاپا ٹوئي كرنا *ṭāpā-ṭō'ī karnā*.

To trim, چهانٹنا *chhāṅṭnā*, آراسته كرنا *ārāsta karnā :* see To shave.

To trip, (stumble) ٹهوكر كهانا *ṭhōkar khānā*, (up) لنگي مارنا *langī mārnā* (?).

To triumph, شاديانه بجانا *shādiyāna bajānā :* see To conquer.

To trot, دلكي جانا يا چلنا *dulkī jānā* or *chalnā*, كهودرانا *khūdrānā*.

To trouble, ستانا *satānā*, تكليف دينا *taklīf dēnā*, چهيڑنا *chhēṛnā*.

To trundle (v. n.) ڈگرنا *ḍagarnā*, (v. a.) ڈگرانا *ḍagrānā*, لڑهانا *luṛhānā*.

To trust, باور كرنا *bāwar karnā*, اعتبار ركهنا *iʿtibār rakhnā*, (sell on credit) قرض پر بيچنا *ḳarẓ par bēchnā :* see To consign.

To try, آزمائش كرنا *āzmā'ish karnā :* see To attempt, examine.

To tug, (pull along) كهينچنا *khainchnā*, (strive) زور مارنا *zōr mārnā*.

To tumble, (act as a tumbler) كلا بازي كرنا *kalā-bāzī karnā :* see To fall.

To tune, ملانا *milānā*, همساز كرنا *ham-sāz karnā*, (the voice) الاپنا *alāpnā*.

To turn, (v. n.) پهرنا *phirnā*, گهومنا *ghūmnā*, (v. a.) پهرانا *phirānā*.

To tweak, (pinch) نوچنا *nōchnā*, (twist) مروڑنا *marōṛnā*, ميسنا *mīsnā*.

To twine, بونڈيانا *baunḍiyānā*, (to plait) گوندهنا *gūndhnā :* see To fold.

To twinkle, ٹمٹمانا *ṭimṭimānā*, (move the eye) مٹكانا *maṭkānā*.

To twirl, (v. n.) گھومنا *ghūmnā*, (v. a.) جلدي پهرانا *jaldī phirānā.*

To twist, (v. n.) اينٹهنا *ainṭhnā*, بل کهانا *bal khānā*, (v. a.) بل دينا *bal dēnā*, مروڑنا *marōṛnā*, موڑنا *mōṛnā.*

To twit, طعنه مارنا *ṭaʿna mārnā*, ملامت كرنا *malāmat karnā.*

To twitch, نجهوٹنا *nijhōṭnā*, کهسوٹنا *khasōṭnā* : see To snatch.

To tyrannise, ظلم يا جبر يا زور كرنا *ẓulm* or *jabr* or *zōr karnā.*

To value, مول ٹهہرانا *mōl ṭhahrānā*, آنکنا *ānknā*, عزيز جاننا *ʿazīz jānnā.*

To vanish, جاتا رهنا *jātā rahnā*, چمپت يا غائب هونا *champat* or *g͟hāʾib hōnā.*

To vanquish, جيتنا *jītnā*, توڑنا *tōṛnā*, شكست كرنا *shikast karnā.*

To varnish, لک چڑهانا *luk chaṛhānā*, چپڑنا *chupaṛnā* : see To cover.

To vary, رنگارنگ كرنا *rangārang karnā*, پهيرنا *phērnā* : see To change.

To vault, (leap) كودنا *kūdnā*, see To leap, (arch) قبه بنانا *ḳubba banānā.*

To vaunt, لاف گزاف مارنا *lāf-guzāf mārnā*, لاف زني كرنا *lāf-zanī karnā.*

To veer, پهرنا *phirnā*, گهومنا *ghūmnā*, بدلنا *badalnā.*

To vegetate, نبات كي سي اگنا *nabāt kī sī ugnā*, جمنا *jamnā.*

To veil, برقع ڈالنا *burḳaʿ ḍālnā*, گهونگهٹ كرنا *ghūnghaṭ karnā.*

To ventilate, هوا سي ٹهنڈها كرنا *hawā sē ṭhanḍhā karnā.*

To venture, جوكهم اٹهانا *jōkhim uṭhānā* : see To dare.

To verify, ثابت يا اثبات كرنا *s̤ābit* or *is̤bāt karnā.*

To versify, نظم كرنا *naẓm karnā*, نظم مين لكهنا *naẓm mēṅ likhnā.*

To vex, دق كرنا *diḳḳ karnā*, چهيڑنا *chheṛnā*, ستانا *satānā.*

To vibrate, (v.n.) تهرتهرانا *tharthārānā*, ترمرانا *tirmirānā* : see To shake.

To vilify, بدنام يا مذمت كرنا *bad-nām* or *mazammat karnā.*

To vindicate (justify), بيگناه يا ثابت كرنا *bēgunāh* or *s̤ābit karnā.*

To violate, حرمت لينا *ḥurmat lēnā*, (infringe) فسخ كرنا *fask͟h karnā.*

To vitiate, بگاڑنا *bigāṛnā*, خراب كرنا *k͟harāb karnā*, نسانا *nasānā.*

To vivify, جلانا *jilānā*, زنده كرنا *zinda karnā.*

To unbind, كهولنا *khōlnā*, بندهن كهولنا *bandhan khōlnā.*

To unbolt, هڑكا يا بلي كهول دينا *huṛkā* or *billī khōl dēnā.*

To unbosom, راز كهولنا *rāz khōlnā*, فاش كرنا *fāsh karnā.*

To unbuckle, بكسوا كهولنا *baksūʾā khōlnā.*

To unbutton, گهنڈي کهولنا *ghunḍī khōlnā.*

To uncase, غلاف يا کهول سي نکالنا *ghilāf* or *khōl sē nikālnā.*

To undeceive, سمجهانا *samjhānā,* هوشيار کرنا *hōshyār karnā :* see To advise.

To undergo, اٹهانا *uṭhānā,* بهرنا *bharnā,* کهينچنا *khainchnā.*

To underline, نيچي خط يا لکير کهينچنا *nīchē khaṭṭ* or *lakīr khainchnā.*

To undermine, سرنگ دوڑانا *surang dauṛānā,* کني کاٹنا *kannī kāṭnā.*

To underrate, قيمت گهٹانا *ḳīmat ghaṭānā,* حقير جاننا *ḥaḳīr jānnā.*

To understand, سمجهنا *samajhnā,* بوجهنا *būjhnā,* جاننا *jānnā.*

To undertake, کرنا *karnā,* هاته لگانا *hāth lagānā :* see To accept.

To undervalue, کم قدر يا حقير جاننا *kam-ḳadr* or *ḥaḳīr jānnā.*

To underwrite, نيچي لکهنا يا صحيح کرنا *nīchē likhnā* or *ṣaḥīḥ karnā.*

To undo, (ruin) خراب کرنا *kharāb karnā,* (open) کهول ڈالنا *khōl ḍālnā.*

To undress, کپڑا اتارنا *kapṛa utārnā.* To undulate, لهرانا *lahrānā.*

To unfasten, کهولنا *khōlnā,* چهوڑنا *chhōṛnā.* To unfix, کهولنا *khōlnā.*

To unfold, کهولنا *khōlnā,* ادهيڑنا *udhēṛnā :* see To discover, explain.

To unfurl, کهولنا *khōlnā,* ادهيڑنا *udhēṛnā,* (spread) پسارنا *pasārnā.*

To ungird, کمربند يا تنگ کهولنا *kamarband* or *tang khōlnā.*

To unharness, ساز اتارنا *sāz utārnā,* کهول دينا *khōl dēnā.*

To unhinge, چول يا قبضه اکهاڑنا *chūl* or *ḳabza ukhāṛnā.*

To unhorse, گهوڑي سي گرانا *ghōṛē sē girānā.*

To unhusk, چهلکا اتارنا *chhilkā utārnā,* بهوسي نکالنا *bhūsī nikālnā.*

To unite, ملنا *milnā,* متفق هونا *muttafiḳ hōnā,* (v. a.) ملانا *milānā.*

To unlace, ڈوري کهولنا *ḍōrī khōlnā,* بندهن کهولنا *bandhan khōlnā.*

To unlade, unload, بوجه اتارنا *bōjh utārnā,* ابهاڑنا *ubhāṛnā.*

To unlatch, بلي کهولنا *billī khōlnā.* To unlock, قفل کهولنا *ḳufl khōlnā.*

To unloose, کهول دينا *khōl dēnā,* بند سي خلاص کرنا *band sē khalāṣ karnā.*

To unmask, برقع اتارنا *burḳaʿ utārnā,* ظاهر کرنا *ẓāhir karnā.*

To unpack, گٹها يا بسته يا موٹه کهولنا *gaṭṭhā* or *basta* or *mōṭh khōlnā.*

To unravel, (v.n.) سلجهنا *sulajhnā,* (v.a.) سلجهانا *suljhānā :* see To open.

To unriddle, حل کرنا *ḥall karnā,* کهولنا *khōlnā.*

To unrol, ادهيڑنا *udhēṛnā.* To unroot, جڑ اکهاڑنا *jaṛ ukhāṛnā.*

To unscrew, پیچ کھولنا *pēch khōlnā.* To unseal, مہر توڑنا *muhr tōṛnā.*

To unsheath, علم کرنا *ālam karnā,* نیام سے نکالنا *niyām sē nikālnā.*

To untie, کھولنا *khōlnā.* To untwist, پیچ کھولنا *pēch khōlnā.*

To unveil: see To unmask. To unyoke, جوا اتار دینا *jū'a utār dēnā.*

To vouch, گواہي دینا *gawāhī dēnā,* ثابت کرنا *s̤ābit karnā.*

To vouchsafe, مہرباني کرنا *mihrbānī karnā,* فرمانا *farmānā.*

To upbraid, سرزنش یا ملامت کرنا *sarzanish* or *malāmat karnā.*

To uphold, (support) تھانبھنا *thāmbhnā:* see To support, raise.

To urge, تقاضا یا تاکید کرنا *taķāẓā* or *tākīd karnā,* اڑانا *uṛānā.*

To use, برتنا *bartnā,* کام مین لانا *kām mēn lānā:* see To treat.

To usurp, چھین لینا *chhīn lēnā,* ناحق لینا *nā-ḥaķķ lēnā.*

To utter, کہنا *kahnā,* اچارنا *uchchārnā,* ذکر کرنا *z̤ikr karnā.*

To waddle, بطک یا ڈگمگي چال چلنا *baṭak-* or *ḍagmagī-chāl chalnā.*

To wage, شرط رکھنا *sharṭ rakhnā,* (war) جنگ کرنا *jang karnā.*

To wail, بلبلانا *bilbilānā,* ناله و زاري کرنا *nāla ō zārī karnā.*

To wait, انتظاري کرنا *intiz̤ārī karnā:* see To expect, attend.

To wake, (v. n.) جگنا *jagnā,* جاگنا *jāgnā,* (v. a.) جگانا *jagānā.*

To walk, چلنا *chalnā,* (go about) پھرنا *phirnā,* سیر کرنا *sair karnā.*

To wallow, چہلي مین لوٹنا *chahlē mēn loṭnā,* لوٹ پوٹ کرنا *lōṭ-pōṭ karnā.*

To wander, رمنا *ramnā,* پھرنا *phirnā,* (stray) بھٹکنا *bhaṭaknā.*

To wane, گھٹنا *ghaṭnā,* کم ہونا *kam hōnā,* زوال مین ہونا *zawāl mēn hōnā.*

To want, (be wanting) خالي ہونا *khālī hōnā,* (need) چاہنا *chāhnā:* see To wish.

To war, لڑنا *laṛnā.* To warble, لہکانا *lahkānā,* گانا *gānā.*

To ward off, کاٹ دینا *kāṭ dēnā,* بچانا *bachānā:* see To protect.

To warn, چتانا *chitānā,* آگاهي دینا *āgāhī dēnā,* جتانا *jatānā.*

To warp, (v. n.) کج خم ہونا *kaj kham hōnā,* (v. a.) مروڑ دینا *marōṛ dēnā.*

To warrant, جائز رکھنا *jā'iz rakhnā,* اختیار دینا *ikhtiyār dēnā.*

Was, تھا *thā,* ہوا *hū'ā,* رہا *rahā,* گیا *gayā.*

To wash, دھونا *dhōnā,* شست و شو کرنا *shust ō shū karnā:* see To bathe.

To waste, (v. n.) گهٹنا *ghaṭnā*, گلنا *galnā*, (v. a.) اڑانا *uṛānā*.

To watch, چوکي دينا *chaukī dēnā*, (not sleep) بيدار رهنا *bēdār rahnā*.

To water, پنيانا *paniyānā*, پاني دينا *pānī dēnā*, سيچنا *sīchnā*.

To waver, بيقرار يا متردد هونا *bēḳarār* or *mutaraddid hōnā*.

To wax, (v. a.) مومي کرنا *mōmī karnā*, (become) هونا *hōnā*: see To grow.

To waylay, راه مارنا *rāh mārnā*, گهات کرنا *ghāt karnā*.

To wean, دوده چهڑانا *dūdh chhuṛānā*, خو چهڑانا *khō chhuṛānā*.

To wear, (rub, v. n.) گهسنا *ghisnā*, (v. a.) گهسانا *ghisānā*, (dress) پهننا *pahannā*, (hold out) رهنا *rahnā*, ٹکنا *ṭiknā*.

To weary, تهکانا *thakānā*, مانده کرنا *mānda karnā*.

To weave, بننا *binnā* or *bunnā*, جالي کاڑهنا *jālī kāṛhnā*.

To wed, بياهنا *byāhnā*. To ween, جاننا *jānnā*: see To think.

To weep, رونا *rōnā*. To weigh, تولنا *tōlnā*: see To consider.

To welter, لوٹنا *lōṭnā*. To wend, جانا *jānā*, پهرنا *phirnā*.

Went, گيا *gayā*, (out) نکلا *niklā*. Were, تهي *thē*, هوي *hūē*.

To wet, (v. n.) بهيگنا *bhīgnā*, (v. a.) بهگونا *bhigōna*, نم کرنا *nam karnā*.

To wheedle, پهسلانا *phuslānā*. To wheeze, سنسنانا *sansanānā*.

To whet, سانا *sānnā*, تيز يا چوکه کرنا *tēz* or *chōkh karnā*.

To whine, جهيکهنا *jhīkhnā*. To whinny, هينچنا *hīnchnā* (?).

To whip, چابک يا کوڑا لگانا *chābuk* or *kōṛā lagānā*.

To whirl, (v. n.) پهرنا *phirnā*, گهومنا *ghūmnā*, (v. a.) گهمانا *ghumānā*.

To whisk, سيهٹنا *sēhathnā*. To whisper, پهسپهسانا *phusphusānā*.

To whistle, سيٹي بجانا *sīṭī bajānā*. To whiten, سفيد کرنا *sufēd karnā*.

To whitewash, کلي پهيرنا *kalī phērnā*, چههانا *chhuhānā*.

To whiz, پنپنانا *pinpinānā*. To whoop, کلکار مارنا *kilkār mārnā*.

To will, چاهنا *chāhnā*, اراده کرنا *irāda karnā*: see To command.

To win, جيتنا *jītnā*, جيت لينا *jīt lēnā*, بازي ليجانا *bāzī lējānā*.

To wince (from pain), درد سي چهٹپٹانا *dard sē chhaṭpaṭānā*.

To wind, (v. n.) گهومنا *ghūmnā*, پهرنا *phirnā*: see To twist, fold.

To wink, مٹکنا *maṭaknā*, (v. a.) مٹکانا *maṭkānā*: see To connive.

To winnow, اسانا *usānā*, پهٹکنا *phaṭaknā*, جهاڑنا *jhāṛnā*.

To wipe, پونچهنا *pōnchhnā*, صاف کرنا *ṣāf karnā*.

To wis, بوجهنا *būjhnā*. To wish, چاهنا *chāhnā*: see To desire.

To wit (adv.), يعني *ya'nē*, جانو *jānō*.

To withdraw, (v. n.) هٹنا *haṭnā*, باز رهنا *bāz rahnā*: see To take away.

To wither, کمهلانا *kumhlānā*, مرجهانا *murjhānā*, جهرنا *jhurnā*.

To withhold, باز يا پهير رکهنا *bāz* or *phēr rakhnā*, چهينکنا *chhēnknā*.

To withstand, آڑنا *āṛnā*, روکنا *rōknā*, تهامبهنا *thāmbhnā*, ٹالنا *ṭālnā*.

To witness, گواهي دينا *gawāhī dēnā*, شاهد هونا *shāhid hōnā*.

To wonder, تعجب کرنا *ta'ājjub karnā*. To be wont, کرنا *karnā*.

To woo, عشق کرنا *'ishḳ karnā*, مانگني کرنا *māngnī karnā*.

To work, کام کرنا *kām karnā*, (ferment) گجانا *gajānā*: see To embroider.

To worry, بهنبهوڑنا *bhambhōṛnā*, پهاڑ کهانا *phāṛ khānā*.

To worship, پوجنا *pūjnā*, بهجنا *bhajnā*, پرستش کرنا *parastish karnā*.

To worst, (foil) هٹانا *haṭānā*, هرانا *harānā*, بهگانا *bhagānā*.

To wound, چٹيانا *chuṭiyānā*, زخمي کرنا *zakhmī karnā*.

To wrangle, جهگڑنا *jhagaṛnā*, بحثنا *baḥaṣnā*, تکرار کرنا *takrār karnā*.

To wrap, لپيٹنا *lapēṭnā*. To wreak (revenge), انتقام لينا *intiḳām lēnā*.

To wrench, wrest, مروڑکي کهينچ لينا *marōṛkē khainch lēnā*.

To wrestle, کشتي کرنا *kushtī karnā*. To wriggle, تڑپنا *taṛapnā*.

To wring, نچوڑنا *nichōṛnā*, مروڑنا *marōṛnā*, پيچ دينا *pēch dēnā*.

To write, لکهنا *likhnā*, تحرير يا قلمبند کرنا *taḥrīr* or *ḳalamband karnā*.

To writhe, اکڑنا *akaṛnā*, اينٹهنا *ainṭhnā*, تڑپنا *taṛapnā*: see To twist.

To yawn, جمهانا *jamhānā*, جمهائي لينا *jamhā'ī lēnā*.

To yearn, شفقت رکهنا *shafaḳat rakhnā*, مروڑنا *marōṛnā*.

To yell, چلانا *chillānā*. To yelp, بهونکنا *bhaunknā*.

To yield, نکالنا *nikālnā*, پيدا کرنا *paidā karnā*: see To give, resign.

To yoke, جوتنا *jōtnā*, نادهنا *nādhnā*, جتانا *jutānā*.

ADJECTIVES, ADVERBS, &c., OF FREQUENT USE.

Aback, پچهلي طرف *pichhli taraf*, پيچهي *pīchhē*.

Abashed, لجت *lajjit*, پشيمان *pashēmān*, شرمنده *sharmanda*.

Abject, ذليل *zalīl*, پتت *patit*, خوار *khwār*, خراب *kharāb*.

Able, قابل *kābil*, سامرتهي *sāmarthī*, لائق *lā'ik*: see Capable.

Aboard (a ship), جهاز مين *jahāz mēn*, جهاز پر *jahāz par*.

Abominable, مكروه *makrūh*, گهنونا *ghinaunā*, كريه *karīh*.

Abortive, برتها *birthā*, ضائع *zā'i**, لاحاصل *lā-hāsil*.

Above, اوپر *ūpar*, پر *par*, زبر *zabar*.

About, آس پاس *ās-pās*, گرد پيش *gird-pēsh*, پاس *pās*.

Above-cited, above-mentioned, مذكور *mazkūr*, مسطور *mastūr*.

Abreast, برابر *barābar*, هم كنار *ham-kinār*, لگي لگي *lagē-lagē*.

Abridged, مختصر *mukhtasar*, سنچهيپ *sanchhēp*.

Abroad, باهر *bāhar*, پرديس *par-dēs*, غير ملك مين *ghair mulk mēn*.

Abrupt, بيهڑ *bēhar*, نشيب فراز *nishēb-farāz*, (sudden) اچانك *achānak*.

Absent, جدا *judā*, غير حاضر *ghair-hāzir*, (in mind) غافل *ghāfil*.

Absolved, معاف *mu'āf*, مكت *mukt*.

Absolute, (supreme) مختار *mukhtār*, (sole, complete) مطلق *mutlak*.

Abstemious, Abstinent, پرهيزگار *parhēzgār*, نيمي *nēmī*.

Abstruse, دقيق *dakīk*, مغلق *mughlak*, غامض *ghāmiz*, گوڑھ *gūrh*.

Absurd, باطل *bātil*, انرتھ *anarth*, نامعقول *nā-ma*kūl*, هرزه *harza*.

Abundant, بهتيرا *bahutērā*, اكثر *aksar*, فراوان *firāwān*, زياده *ziyāda*.

Acceptable, مقبول *makbūl*, مطبوع *matbu**, بروقت *bar-wakt*.

Accidental, اتفاقي *ittifakī*, ناگهاني *nāgahānī*.

According (to), موافق *muwāfik*, مطابق *mutabik*.

Accurate, ٹهيك *thīk*, صحيح *sahīh*, (person) چوكس *chaukas*.

Acid, كهٹا *khattā*, امل *aml*, ترش *tursh*.

Acquainted, واقف *wākif*, آگاه *āgāh*, (intimate) محرم *mahram*.

Across, آڑا *ārā*: (adv.) پار *pār*, وارپار *wār-pār*.

Active, چالاک *chālāk*, منچلا *man-chalā*, چرپهرا *charpharā*, چست *chust*.

Actual, سچا *sachchā*, حقيقي *ḥaḳīḳī*. Actually, في الحقيقت *fi-l-ḥaḳīḳat*.

Admirable, عجيب *ʿajīb*, نادر *nādir*, (interj.) کيا خوب *kyā khūb*.

Affable, ملنسار *milansār*, حليم *ḥalīm*, با مروت *bā-murūwat*.

Affectionate, شفيق *shafīḳ*, دياسيل *dayā-sīl*, چهوهي *chhōhī*.

Aforesaid, مذکور *maẕkūr*, مسطور *masṭūr*.

Afraid, ڈرا هوا *ḍarā hū'ā*, دهشتزده *dahshat-zada*.

After, پيچهي *pīchhē*, بعد *baʿd*.

Afterwards, بعد *baʿd*, بعد اسکي *baʿd is-kē*, تد *tad*.

Again, پهر *phir*, پهير *phēr*, علاوه *ʿalāwa*, دوباره *dō-bāra*.

Against, خلاف *khilāf*, (over against) سنمکه *sanmukh*.

Aged, بڈّها *buḍḍhā*, پرانا *purānā*, قديم *ḳadīm*: see Old.

Ago, آگي *āgē*, پيشتر *pēshtar*, سابق *sābiḳ*.

Agreeable, دل پسند *dil-pasand*. Agreeably (to), موافق *muwāfiḳ*.

Alert, خبردار *khabardār*, هوشيار *hoshyār*. Alien, پرديسي *pardēsī*.

Alike, برابر *barābar*, ايکسان *ēk-sāṅ*, سمان *samān*, شبيه *shabīh*.

Alive, جيتا *jītā*, زنده *zinda*, جاندار *jān-dār*.

All, سب *sab*, تمام *tamām*, سارا *sārā*, سکل *sakal*, بهر *bhar*.

Almost, عنقريب *ʿanḳarīb*, قريب *ḳarīb*, نزديکتر *nazdīktar*.

Alone, اکيلا *akēlā*, تنها *tanhā*, اکلا *iklā*, صرف *ṣirf*.

Although, اگرچه *agarchi*, هرچندکه *har-chand-ki*.

Altogether, مطلق *muṭlaḳ*, محض *maḥẓ*, نرا *nirā*.

Always, سدا *sadā*, هميشه *hamēsha*, هروقت *har waḳt*.

Ambiguous, مشکوک *mashkūk*, پيچدار *pēchdār*, مبهم *mubham*.

Ancient, قديم *ḳadīm*, پراچين *parāchīn*, پراتم *purātam*.

Anew, Afresh, پهر *phir*, سرنو *sar-i-nau*, نيي سرسي *nayē sir sē*.

Angry, غصي *ghuṣṣē* (in anger), خفه *khafa*, کرودهي *krōdhī*.

Angular, کونيدار *kōnēdār*, گوشيدار *gōshēdār*.

Animated, دلير *dilēr*, دل گرم *dil-garm*; (as language) نمکين *namkīn*.

Annual, ساليانه *sāliyānā*, برسوان *baras-wāṅ*, هرساله *har-sāla*.

Another, دوسرا *dūsrā*, ايک اور *ēk aur*, اور ايک *aur ēk*.

Anterior, پيش رو *pēsh-rau*, قبل *ḳabl*. Antique: see Ancient.

Anxious, فکرمند *fikr-mand*, متردد *mutaraddid.*

Any, کوئي *kō'ī*, کچهه *kuchh*, کوؤ *kō'ū.*

Apiece, هر ایک کو *har ēk kō.*

Apt, لائق *lā'ik*, تیار *taiyār*, قابل *ḳābil*, چالاک *chālāk.*

Aquatic, پنیها *panīhā*, آبي *ābī*, جلچر *jalchar*, دریائي *daryā'ī.*

Around, آس پاس *ās-pās*, گرد *gird*, پیرامن *pairāman.*

Arrogant, مغرور *maghrūr*, گستاخ *gustākh*, متکبر *mutakabbir.*

Artful, عیار *aiyār*, فن فریبي *fann-farēbī*, چهلي *chhalī*, چالاک *chālāk.*

Artificial, ساخته *sākhta*, بنایا هوا *banāyā hū'ā.*

Artless, اناڑي *anāṛī*, بهولا *bhōlā*, بیساخته *be-sākhta*, ساده *sāda.*

As, جیسا *jaisā ;* (conj.) کیونکه *kyūṅki :* as much, as many, جتنا *jitnā.*

Ashamed, شرمنده *sharmanda*, لجت *lajjit*, خجل *khajil.*

Aside, (apart), الگ *alag*, جدا *judā*, کناري *kinārē.*

Aslant, ترچهائي سي *tirchhā'ī sē*, ایک طرف *ēk ṭaraf.*

Asleep, سوتا هوا *sōtā hū'ā*, آرام مین *ārām mēṅ.*

Astonished, گهابرا *ghābrā*, مدهوش *madhūsh*, چکت *chakit*, حیران *ḥairān.*

Astray, بهتکا *bhaṭkā*, گمراه *gumrāh*, بهولا *bhulā*, بي راه *bē-rāh.*

Asunder, جدا *judā*, الگ *alag :* see Separate.

At all, مطلق *muṭlaḳ*, مطلقا *muṭlaḳā.*

At all times, هر وقت *har waḳt:* see Always.

At length, At last, آخر *ākhir*, پس *pas.*

Atrocious, نهایت شریر *nihāyat sharīr*, بهت معیوب *bahut ma'yūb.*

Attentive, چوکس *chaukas*, هوشیار *hōshyār*, متوجه *mutawajjih.*

Averse, مخالف *mukhālif*, ناراض *nā-rāẓ.*

Austere, سخت *sakht*, درشت *durusht*, تند *tund*, کڑا *kaṛā.*

Auxiliary, مددگار *madadgār*, کمکي *kumakī.*

Awake, جاگتا *jāgtā*, بیدار *bēdār*, هوشیار *hōshyār.*

Aware, واقف *wāḳif*, خبردار *khabardār*, آگاه *āgāh.*

Away (absent), غیر حاضر *ghair ḥāẓir*, تفاوت پر *tafāwut par*, جدا *judā.*

Awhile, چند مدت *chand muddat*, تهوڑا عرصه *thōṛā arṣa.*

Azure, آسماني *āsmānī*, ازرق *azraḳ*, نیل گون *nīl-gūn.*

Back, (adv.) پهیر *phēr*, باز *bāz*, واپس *wāpas.*

Backward (loath), رو گردان *rū-gardān*, كشيده *kashīda*, سست *sust*.
Bad, برا *burā*, بد *bad*, زبون *zabūn*, خراب *kharāb*, شرير *sharīr*.
Bald, چندلا *chandlā*, گنجا *ganjā*, (unadorned) نازيبا *nā-zēbā*.
Baneful, زهر دار *zahr-dār*, مضر *muẓirr*.
Bankrupt, ديواليا *dēwāliyā*, مفلس *muflis*, نادار *nā-dār*.
Barbarian, (adj.) جنگلي *janglī*, وحشي *waḥshī*, بيرحم *bē-raḥm*.
Bare, (naked) ننگا *nangā*, (plain) ساده *sāda*, (void) خالي *khālī*.
Barren, (land) اوسر *ūsar*, كلر *kallar*, (animal) بانجهه *bānjh*.
Base (adj.), پاجي *pājī*, كمينه *kamīna*, نيچ *nīch*, دون *dūn*.
Base-born, حرام زاده *ḥarām-zāda*, برن سنكر *barn-sankar*.
Bashful, شرميلا *sharmīlā*, لجيلا *lajīlā*, سنكوچي *sankōchī*.
Bay-coloured (a horse), كميت *kumait*, سمند *samand*.
Beastly, حيوان سا *ḥaiwān-sā*, نا پاك *nā-pāk*, گنده *ganda*.
Beautiful, خوبصورت *khūbṣūrat*, سندر *sundar*, سروپ *surūp*.
Because, زيرا كه *zīrā ki*, لهذا *lihaẕā*, كيونكه *kyūṅki*.
Becoming, لائق *lā'iḳ*, شايسته *shāyasta*, خوش نما *khush-numā*.
Before, آگي *āgē*, سامني *sāmnē*, پيش *pēsh*.
Behind, پيچهي *pīchhē*, عقب مين *aḳab mēṅ*, بعد *ba'd*.
Beloved, پيارا *pyārā* (m.), پياري *pyārī* (f.), محبوب *maḥbūb*, عزيز *azīz*.
Beneath, نيچي *nīchē*, (unworthy) نا لائق *nā-lā'iḳ*.
Beneficent, ديال *dayāl*, فياض *faiyaẓ*, داتا *dātā*.
Beneficial, مفيد *mufīd*, سودمند *sūdmand*, بهلا *bhalā*.
Beside, Besides, سوا *siwā*, علاوه *alāwa*, كناري *kinārē*, نزديك *nazdīk*.
Best, اتم *uttam*, سب سي بهلا *sab sē bhalā*, اولاتر *aulātar*.
Between, Betwixt, بيچ *bīch*, درميان *darmiyān*.
Beyond, پري *parē*, پار *pār*, آگي *āgē*.
Biennial, دوساله *dō-sāla*, دو سال تك رهني كا *dō sāl tak rahnē kā*.
Big, بڑا *baṛā*, موٹا *mōṭā*, كلان *kalān*, (pregnant) حامله *ḥāmila*.
Bigot, bigotted, متعصب *muta'aṣṣib*, هٹهي *haṭhī*.
Bilious, صفرائي *ṣafrā'ī*, صفراوي *ṣafrāwī*, زردابي *zardābī*.
Bitter, كڑوا *kaṛwā*, تيتا *tītā*, تلخ *talkh*: see Cruel, Sharp.
Black, كالا *kālā*, سياه *siyāh*, (complexion) كلوٹا *kalūṭā*, كاليا *kāliyā*.

Blamable, ملزم *mulzim*, قصوروار *ḳusūrwār*. Blameless: see Innocent.

Blank, (white) سفيد *sufed*, (unwritten) ساده *sāda*, بيلكها *bē-likhā*.

Bleak, (cold) سرد *sard*, ٹهنڈها *ṭhanḍhā*, (pale) زرد *zard*, پيلا *pīlā*.

Blear-eyed, چپڑا *chipṛā* (m.), ڈهلكا *ḍhalkā* (m.).

Blessed, مبارك *mubārak*, خوش حال *khush-ḥāl*, بهشتي *bihishtī*.

Blind, اندها *andhā*, كور *kōr*, نا بينا *nā-bīnā*, (of one eye) كانا *kānā*.

Blinkard, چندهلا *chundhlā*, دهندهلا *dhundhlā*.

Bloody, لوهو لهان *lōhū-luhān*, خون آلوده *khūn-ālūda*, خوني *khūnī*.

Blue, نيلا *nīlā*, ليلا *līlā*, نيلگون *nīl-gūn*, كبودي *kabūdī*: see Azure.

Blunt, (dull) كند *kund*, بهوتا *bhōtā*, (unpolite) بي امتياز *bē imtiyāz*.

Boisterous زور شور كرنيوالا *zōr-shōr-karnēwālā*, شديد *shadīd*, تند *tund*.

Bold, دلير *dilēr*, دلاور *dilāwar*, بهادر *bahādur*, منچلا *manchalā*.

Born, جنا *janā*, پيدا *paidā*, (in compos.) زاده *zāda*, زا *zā*.

Both, دونو *dōnū* or دونوں *dōnōṅ*, هر دو *har dō*.

Bounteous, bountiful, داتا *dātā*, كريم *karīm*, فياض *faiyāẓ*.

Brackish, كهارا *khārā*, شور *shōr*, لونا *lōnā*, نمكين *namkīn*.

Brave, بهادر *bahādur*, ساونت *sāwant*, مردانه *mardāna*: see Bold.

Brawny, هرمشٹا *hurmushṭā*, كنگرا *kungrā*, چهكيٹه *chahkaiṭh*.

Brazen, پيتلا *pītlā*, برنجي *birinjī*: see Impudent.

Brief, كوتاه *kōtāh*, مختصر *mukhtaṣar*, مجمل *mujmal*.

Briefly, اختصارسي *ikhtiṣār sē*, (in short) غرض *gharaẓ*, الغرض *algharaẓ*.

Bright, روشن *rōshan*, اجلا *ujlā*, صاف *ṣāf*: see Illustrious.

Brilliant, رونق دار *raunaḳ-dār*, تابناك *tābnāk*, چمكيلا *chamkīlā*.

Brimful, لبالب *lab-ā-lab*, بهرپور *bhar-pūr*.

Brisk, جلد *jald*, شوخ *shōkh*, چالاك *chālāk*, چست *chust*, تيز *tēz*.

Brittle, نازك *nāzuk*, باريك *bārīk*, پتلا *patlā*, تنك *tunak*.

Broad, چوڑا *chauṛā*, عريض *ārīẓ*, (vulgar) كمينه *kamīna*.

Brown, گندم رنگ *gandum-rang*, گندم گون *gandum-gūn*.

Brutal, حيواني *ḥaiwānī*, (savage) وحشي *waḥshī*: see Cruel.

Bulky, موٹا *mōṭā*, جسيم *jasīm*, بڑا *baṛā*, بهاري *bhārī*.

Busy, مشغول *mashghūl*, سرگرم *sar-garm*, مصروف *maṣrūf*.

But, (except) سوا *siwā*, جز *juz*, (conj.) مگر *magar*, ليكن *lēkin*.

By, سي *sē*, كي سبب *kē sabab*, به *ba* : see Near.

Calamitous, آفت زده *āfat-zada*, پريشان *parēshān* : see Wretched.

Callous, سخت *sakht*, گٹھيلا *gaṭhīlā*, کٹھور *kaṭhōr*, بي درد *bē-dard*.

Calm, دھيما *dhīmā*, معتدل *muʿtadil*, بند *band*, رکا *ruka*.

Cancelled, مٹايا گيا *miṭāyā gayā*, محو کيا گيا *maḥv kiyā gayā*.

Candid, صاف *ṣāf*, راست باز *rāst-bāz*, بي لگاؤ *bē-lagā'ō*.

Capable, قابل *ḳābil*, لائق *lā'iḳ*, پاتر *pātr*, جوگا *jōgā*.

Capacious, کشاده *kushāda*, فراخ *farākh*, چوڑا *chauṛā*.

Capital, (as a crime) جيمار *jīmār*, (principal) بڑا *baṛā*, عظيم *ʿaẓīm*.

Capricious, تلون طبع *talauwun-ṭabʿ*, اوچھا *ōchhā*.

Cardinal, اعظم *aʿẓam*, اکبر *akbar*, اول *awwal*.

Careful (cautious), خبردار *khabar-dār*, هوشيار *hōshyār*.

Careless, غافل *ghāfil*, بيفکر *be-fikr*, اسوچي *asōchī*.

Carnal, نفساني *nafsānī*, شهوت پرست *shahwat-parast*, کامي *kāmī*.

Carnivorous, گوشت خور *gōsht-khōr*, ماس ادهاري *mās-adhārī*.

Casual, اتفاقي *ittifāḳī*, عارضي *ʿāriẓī*, ناگهاني *nāgahānī*.

Cautious, هوشيار *hōshyār*, خبردار *khabardār*, چوکس *chaukas*.

Celestial, بهشتي *bihishtī*, جنتي *jannatī*, آسماني *āsmānī*.

Censorious, عيب جو *ʿaib-jō*, حرف گير *ḥarf-gīr*, نندک *nindak*.

Central, Centric, درمياني *darmiyānī*, بيچون بيچ *bīchōṅ bīch*.

Certain, يقين *yaḳīn*, بيشک *bē-shakk*, مقرر *muḳarrar*.

Certain, (some) بعضي *baʿẓē*, کوئي *kō'ī*, (person) فلان *fulān*, فلانه *fulāna*.

Certainly, البته *albatta*, يقيناً *yaḳīnan*, مقرر *muḳarrar*.

Charitable, مخير *mukhaiyir*, داتا *dātā*, سخي *sakhī*, فياض *faiyāẓ*.

Charming, موهنا *mōhnā*, سهاونا *suhāwanā*, دل چسپ *dil-chasp*.

Chary, هوشيار *hōshyār*, خبردار *khabardār*, (frugal) کفايتي *kifāyatī*.

Chaste, پاک *pāk*, پبتر *pabitr*, سده *sudh*, عفيفه *ʿafīfa* (f.).

Cheap, سستا *sastā*, مندا *mandā*, ارزان *arzān*, کم بها *kam-bahā*.

Cheerful, خنده رو *khanda-rū*, هنسمکه *haṅs-mukh*, خوش *khush*.

Cheerless, اداس *udās*, سونا *sūnā*, (dreary) لق و دق *laḳḳ ō daḳḳ*.

Chief (principal), اول *awwal* مقدم *muḳaddam*, بڑا *baṛā*.

Chiefly, غالباً *ghāliban*, اکثر *akṣar*, خصوصاً *khuṣūṣan*.

Childless, بي اولاد *bē-aulād*, لاولد *lā-walad*, نپوتا *nipūtā*.

Chill, Chilly, ٹھنڈا *ṭhanḍā*, سرد *sard*, ٹھنڈاسا *ṭhanḍā-sā*.

Choice, (select) خاصه *khāṣṣa*, (careful) معقول *ma*ʻ*ḳūl*, كفايتي *kifāyatī*.

Christian, عيسوي *ʻīsawī*, نصراني *naṣrānī*.

Chronic, Chronical, مزمن *muzmin*, دائمي *dā'imī*, ديرپا *dēr-pā*.

Chubby, گلپھولا *galphūlā*. Churlish, بي تميز *bē-tamīz*, دبنگ *dabang*.

Circular, مدور *mudauwar*, گول *gōl*, حلقه دار *ḥalḳa-dār*.

Circumjacent, متصل *muttaṣil*, قريب *ḳarīb*, آسپاس *āspās*, نزديك *nazdīk*.

Circumspect, چوكس *chaukas*, هوسيار *hōshyār*, چوكنا *chaukannā*.

Civil, (sociable) ملنسار *milansār*, (political) ملكي *mulkī*, (not military) مالي *mālī*.

Clammy, لسدار *las-dār*, لسلسا *laslasā*, چپچپا *chipchipā*.

Clandestine, پوشيده *pōshīda*, چهپا *chhipā*, گپت *gupt*.

Clean, صاف *ṣāf*, پاكيزه *pākīza*, اجلا *ujlā*, نرمل *nirmal*, پاك *pāk*.

Clear, (bright) شفاف *shaffāf*, صاف *ṣāf*, (not cloudy) پهرچها *pharchhā*, (evident) آشكارا *āshkārā*, ظاهر *ẓāhir*, (free) خالي *khālī*.

Clearly, صاف *ṣāf*, صريحاً *ṣarīḥan*: see Evidently.

Clever, چتر *chatur*, چالاك *chālāk*, هوشيار *hōshyār*, كامل *kāmil*.

Close, بند *band*, مندا *mundā*, گهنا *ghanā*, بهڑا *bhiṛā*.

Cloudless, كهلا هوا *khulā hū'ā*, بي ابر *bē abr*. Cloudy, گهنگهور *ghanghōr*.

Clumsy, اناڑي *anāṛī*, بي سليقه *bē salīḳa*, بدڈول *bad-ḍaul*.

Coarse, موٹا *mōṭā*, گنده *gunda*, (rude) درشت *durusht*.

Coeval, هم عمر *ham-ʻumr*, هم سن *ham-sinn*, هم جولي *ham-jōlī*.

Cold, ٹھنڈا *ṭhanḍā*, سرد *sard*, خنك *khunuk*, سيتل *sītal*.

Comical, Comic, ٹھٹھيباز *ṭhaṭhēbāz*, هنسوڑ *hansōṛ*.

Commercial, سوداگرانه *saudāgarāna*, تجارتي *tijāratī*.

Common, مشترك *mushtarak*, (inferior) كمينه *kamīna*.

Commonly, اكثر *akṡar*, بيشتر *bēshtar*.

Compact, ٹھوس *ṭhōs*, پركار *pur-kār*, غفس *ghafs*.

Compassionate, شفيق *shafīḳ*, ديال *dayāl*, نرم دل *narm-dil*.

Competent, لائق *lā'iḳ*, كافي *kāfī*, قابل *ḳābil*, بس *bas*.

Complete, پورا *pūrā*, تمام *tamām*, (ready) تيار *taiyār*.

Compound, compounded, مركب *murakkab*, سنجكت *sanjukt*.

Conceited, خود بين *khud-bīn*, دماغي *dimāghī*, اكڑباز *akaṛbāz*.

Concise, مختصر *mukhtaṣar*, سنچهيپ *sanchhēp*, كوتاه *kōtāh*.

Confessed, (declared) مشهور *mash'hūr*. Confessedly, اعتراف سي *i*ʻ*tirāf sē*.

Confident, منچلا *man-chalā*, ڈهيٹه *ḍhīṭh*, معتقد *muʻtaḳid*.

Conscious, واقف *wāḳif*, آگاه *āgāh*, خود خبر *khud-khabar*.

Consequently, لهذا *lihāẕā*, اسواسطي *us-wāṣtē*, ضرورتاً *ẓarūratan*.

Consistent, مناسب *munāsib*, لائق *lā'iḳ*.

Conspicuous, ظاهر *ẓāhir*, علانيه *ʻālāniya*, مشهور *mashhūr*, كهلا *khulā*.

Constant, ثابت *ṡābit*, اٹل *aṭal*, مستحكم *mustaḥkim*, قراري *ḳarārī*.

Constantly, نت اٹه *nit-uṭh*, هر آن *har ān*, علي الدوام *ʻāla-d-dawām*.

Contagious, ساري *sārī*.

Contemptible, حقير *ḥaḳīr*, ذليل *ẕalīl*, خوار *khwār*, سبك *subuk*.

Content, contented, راضي *rāẓī*, خوش *khush*, سنتوكهي *santōkhī*.

Contiguous, متصل *muttaṣil*, ملا هوا *milā hū'ā*, پيوسته *paiwasta*.

Continual, دائم *dā'im*, (continually) هميشه *hamēsha*.

Contrary, مخالف *mukhālif*, الٹا *ulṭā*, ضد *ẓidd*, خلاف *khilāf*.

Convenient, لائق *lā'iḳ*, مناسب *munāsib*, ٹهيك *ṭhīk*.

Convex, گنبذ دار *gumbaẕ-dār*, قبه دار *ḳubba-dār*.

Cool, ٹهنڈا *ṭhanḍā*, سيتل *sītal*, سرد *sard*.

Copious, بهت *bahut*, زياده *ziyāda*, كثير *kaṡīr*, بستار *bistār*.

Cordial, مقوي *muḳauwī*, (sincere) سچا *sachchā*, صادق *ṣādiḳ*, بيريا *bē-riyā*.

Corporeal, جسماني *jismānī*, سريري *sarīrī*.

Corpulent, جسيم *jasīm*, موٹا *mōṭā*, دلدار *daldār*, تناور *tanāwar*.

Correct, صحيح *ṣaḥīḥ*, ٹهيك *ṭhīk*, درست *durust*, تحقيق *taḥḳīḳ*.

Corrupt, فاسد *fāsid*, سڑا *saṛā*, ابسا *ubsā*, بگڑا *bigṛā*, خراب *kharāb*.

Costly, قيمتي *ḳīmatī*, بيش قيمت *bēsh-ḳīmat*.

Covetous, لالچي *lālchī*, حريص *ḥarīṣ*, لوبهي *lōbhī*.

Counterfeit, لباسي *libāsī*, جهوٹها *jhūṭhā*, كهوٹا *khōṭā*.

Country (adj.), دهقاني *dihḳānī*, گانوي *gānwī*, گنوار *ganwār*.

Courageous, دلير *dilēr*, بهادر *bahādur*: see Brave.

Courteous, مؤدب *mu'addab*, خوش اخلاق *khush-akhlāḳ*, نيک نهاد *nēk-nihād.*

Coward, Cowardly, ڈرپوکنا *ḍar-pōknā*, بزدل *buz-dil.*

Coy, شرميلا *sharmīlā*, پرحجاب *pur-ḥijāb*: see Bashful.

Crafty, عيار *ʿaiyār*, فطرتي *fiṭratī*, سيانا *syānā*, فيلسوف *failsūf.*

Creditable, معتبر *muʿtabar*, نامور *nāmwar*, رودار *rū-dār.*

Crimson, قرمزي *ḳirmizī*, ارغواني *arghawānī*, سوها *sūhā.*

Cripple, لنگڑا *langṛā*, لولا *lūlā*, پنگو *pangū.*

Crooked, ٹيڑھا *ṭēṛhā*, خم *kham*, ترچها *tirchhā*, کج *kaj.*

Cross, آڑا *āṛā*, ترچها *tirchhā*, (peevish) چڑچڑا *chiṛchiṛā.*

Crude, کچا *kachchā*, خام *khām*, ناپخته *nā-pukhta.*

Cruel, بي رحم *bē-raḥm*, کٹهور *kaṭhōr*, سنگ دل *sang-dil.*

Cumbersome, بهاري *bhārī*, رنجاور *ranjāwar.*

Cunning, سيانا *syānā*, عيار *ʿaiyār*, پکا *pakkā*, چتر *chatur.*

Curious, رازجو *rāz-jō*, (rare) انوٹها *anūṭhā*, (nice) باريک بين *bārīk-bīn.*

Current, (customary) رائج *rā'ij*, (flowing) جاري *jārī*, روان *rawān.*

Customary, مروج *murauwaj*, رسمي *rasmī*, دستوري *dastūrī*, رائج *rā'ij.*

Daily, روز بروز *rōz ba-rōz*, هرروز *har rōz*, روز روز *rōz rōz.*

Dainty, (squeamish) خوش خوراک *khush-khurāk*: see Delicious.

Damp, گيلا *gīlā*, تر *tar*, مرطوب *marṭūb*, نم *nam.*

Dangerous, خطرناک *khaṭar-nāk*, پرآفت *pur-āfat*, پربيم *pur-bīm.*

Dark, اندهيرا *andhērā*, تاريک *tārīk*: see Blind, Abstruse.

Darling, لاڑلا *lāṛlā*, پيارا *pyārā*, عزيز *ʿazīz*, محبوب *maḥbūb.*

Dauntless, نڈر *niḍar*, بيباک *bēbāk*, بيڈر *bēḍar.*

Dead, موا *mū'ā*, مرده *murda*, مرا *marā*, (insensible) سن *sun.*

Deadly, قاتل *ḳātil*, مهلک *muhlik*, هلاکو *halākū*, هلاهل *hălāhal.*

Deaf, بهرا *bahrā*, صم *ṣumm*, کر *kar.*

Dear, (costly) مهنگا *mahangā*, گران *girān*: see Beloved.

Deceitful, دغاباز *daghā-bāz*, چهلي *chhalī*, مکار *makkār.*

Decent, شايسته *shāyasta*, لائق *lā'iḳ*, اچت *uchit*, آراسته *ārāsta.*

Decisive, قاطع *ḳāṭiʿ*, صاف *ṣāf*, پورا *pūrā*, يقين *yaḳīn.*

Declinable (in gram.), متصرف *mutaṣarrif*, منصرف *munṣarif.*

Deep, گهرا *gahrā*, گنبهير *gambhīr*, (coloured) گهوررنگ *ghōr-rang*.

Defective, كهوٹا *khōṭā*, ناقص *nāḳiṣ*, نا تمام *nā-tamām*.

Deficient, كم *kam*, قاصر *ḳāṣir*, ناقص *nāḳiṣ*.

Definite, محدود *maḥdūd*. Definitive, متعين *muta'ăiyin*.

Deformed, بد شكل *bad-shakl*: see Ugly, Humpbacked.

Dejected, اداس *udās*, آزرده *āzurda*, غمگين *gham-gīn*.

Delicate, (exquisite) نفيس *nafīs*, (fine) نازك *nāzuk*: see Dainty.

Delicious, لذيذ *lazīz*, مزه دار *maza-dār*, خوش *khush*.

Delightful, دلچسپ *dil-chasp*, خوش آيند *khush-āyand*.

Delirious, بي هوش *bē-hōsh*, بيخود *be-khud*, ديوانه *dīwāna*.

Dense, كثيف *kaṣīf*, سنگين *sangīn*, بهارى *bhārī*, گاڑها *gāṛhā*.

Desirous, مشتاق *mushtāḳ*, راغب *rāghib*, شوقين *shauḳīn*.

Desolate, ويران *wīrān*, اجاڑ *ujāṛ*, بيچراغ *bē-chirāgh*, خالي *khālī*.

Desperate, (hopeless) نا اميد *nā-ummēd*: see Hopeless, Mad, Rash.

Despicable, ذليل *zalīl*, حقير *ḥaḳīr*, پاجي *pājī*, كمينه *kamīna*.

Destitute, لاچار *lā-chār*, درمانده *darmānda*, خالي *khālī*.

Detestable, مكروه *makrūh*, كريه *karīh*, گهنانا *ghinānā*.

Devilish, شيطاني *shaiṭan-ī*, آسري *āsur-ī*, زبون *zabūn*.

Devious, بيراه *bē-rāh*, بدراه *bad-rāh*, گمراه *gumrāh*, كجرو *kaj-rau*.

Devoted, جان نثار *jān-niṣār*, فدوي *fidwī*, معين *mu'ăiyan*.

Devout, متعبد *muta'ăbbid*, نمازي *namāz-ī*, عارف *ărif*.

Dexterous, چالاك دست *chālāk-dast*, دست كار *dast-kār*, چست *chust*.

Different, مختلف *mukhtalif*, نيارا *nyārā*, اور *aur*, الگ *alag*.

Difficult, مشكل *mushkil*, دشوار *dushwār*, كٹهن *kaṭhin*.

Diffident, شكي *shakkī*, وهمي *wahmī*, بيهمت *bē-himmat*.

Diffuse, منتشر *muntashir*, طويل *ṭawīl*, چهٹكا هوا *chhiṭkā hū'ā*.

Diligent, سر گرم *sar-garm*, مشغول *mashghūl*, چوكس *chaukas*.

Dim, اندهلا *andhlā*, چوندهلا *chōndhlā*, دهوندهرا *dhūndhrā*.

Diminutive, كوچك *kūchak*, ننها *nannhā*, چهوٹا *chhōṭā*.

Dire, ڈراونا *ḍarāwnā*, هيبت ناك *haibat-nāk*, مهيب *muhīb*.

Direct, سيدها *sīdhā*, مستوي *mustavī*, (open) صاف *ṣāf*.

Directly, ترت *turt*, في الحال *fi-l-ḥāl*, ابهي *abhī*: see Direct.

Dirty, (filthy) میلا *mailā*, نجس *najis*, غلیظ *g͟halīz̤*: see Base.

Disaffected, بد گمان *bad-gumān*, بد خواه *bad-k͟hwāh*.

Disagreeable, نا پسند *nā-pasand*, نا خوش *nā-k͟hush*.

Discontented, نا راض *nā-rāẓ*, نا خوش *nā-k͟hush*, شاكي *shākī*.

Discordant, نا موافق *nā-muwāfiḳ*, (in music) بیتال *bē-tāl*.

Discreet, با تمیز *bā-tamīz*, هوشیار *hōshyār*, ببیکي *bibēk-ī*.

Dishonest, نا راست *nā-rāst*, بي ایمان *be-īmān*, فریبي *farēbī*.

Disloyal, نمک حرام *namak-ḥarām*, بیوفا *bē-wafā*.

Dismal, هولناک *haul-nāk*, بهیانک *bhayānak*, اداس *udās*.

Disobedient, نا فرمان *nā-farmān*, سرکش *sar-kash*.

Displeased, نا خوش *nā-k͟hush*, بیزار *bēzār*, آزرده *āzurda*.

Disputatious, حجتي *ḥujjat-ī*, بحاث *baḥḥāṣ*, جهگڑالو *jhagṛālū*.

Disrespectful, بي ادب *bē-adab*, شوخ *shōk͟h*, بیلحاظ *bē-liḥāẓ*.

Dissatisfied, ناراض *nā-rāẓ*, نا خوش *nā-k͟hush*, بیزار *bēzār*.

Dissimilar, نا موافق *nā-muwāfiḳ*, مختلف *muk͟htalif*.

Dissolute, اوباش *aubāsh*, بي قید *bē-ḳaid*, آواره *āwāra*, رند *rind*.

Distant, دور *dūr*, بعید *ba'īd*: see Bashful, Shy.

Distinct, جدا *judā*, متفرق *mutafarriḳ*, (clear) صاف *ṣāf*.

Distracted, مضطرب *maẓṭarib*, گهابرا *ghābrā*, آشفته *āshufta*.

Ditto, ایضاً *aiẓan*, مذکور *maẕkūr*.

Divers, چند *chand*, کئي کئي *ka'ī ka'ī*, بهت بهت *bahut bahut*.

Divine, رباني *rabbānī*, الهي *ilāhī*, رحماني *raḥmānī*.

Diuretic, ادرار آور *idrār-āwar*, مدر *mudirr*.

Dizzy, سرگردان *sar-gardān*, مدهوش *madhūsh*.

Docile, تربیت پذیر *tarbiyat-paẕīr*, تیز ذهن *tēz-ẕihn*.

Domestic, خانگي *k͟hāngī*, گهریلا *ghar-ēlā*.

Done, کیا *kiya*, کیا هوا *kiyā hū'ā*, چکا *chukā*: see Good, Well.

Double, دونا *dūnā*, دوهرا *dōhrā*, دو چند *dō-chand*.

Doubtful, مشکوک *mashkūk*, مشتبه *mushtabih*.

Doubtless, بي شک *bē-shakk*, یقیناً *yaḳīnan*: see Certainly.

Down (prepos. or adv.), نیچے *nīchē*, تلي *talē*, هیٹه *hēṭh*.

Downcast, سرنگون *sar-nigūn*: see Bashful.

Dreadful, هولناك *haul-nāk*, بهيانك *bhayānak*, خوفناك *khaufnāk*.

Drowsy, نينداسا *nindāsā*, خواب آلوده *khwāb-ālūda*.

Drunk, متوالا *matwālā*, مست *mast*, كيفي *kaif-ī*.

Dry, (arid) خشك *khushk*, سوكها *sūkhā*: see Thirsty.

Dull, (blunt) كند *kund*, بهوتا *bhōtā*, (stupid) احمق *aḥmaḳ*.

Duly, جيسا چاهيي *jaisā chāhiyē*, تهيك *ṭhīk*.

Dumb, گونگا *gūngā*, لال *lāl*, گنگا *gungā*, بكم *bukm*.

Dunce, احمق *aḥmaḳ*, بهكوا *bhakwā*, بليد *balīd*, الو *ullū*.

Durable, پائيدار *pā'ē-dār*, قائم *ḳā'im*, ديرپا *dēr-pā*, باقي *bāḳī*.

During (postpos.), هوتي *hōtē*, مين *mēn*, رهتي *rahtē*, درميان *darmiyān*.

Duteous, Dutiful, مطيع *muṭīʿ*, (child) رشيد *rashīd*: see Obedient.

Dwarf, Dwarfish, باونا *bā'ōnā*, ناٹا *nāṭā*, ٹهمكا *ṭhumkā*.

Each, هر ايك *har ēk*, ايك ايك *ēk ēk*, كوئي دو مين سي *kō'ī dō mēn sē*.

Eager, سرگرم *sar-garm*, شوقين *shauḳīn*, آرزومند *ārzūmand*.

Early, (in the morning) سويري *sawērē*, (as fruit, &c.) اگمنا *agmanā*.

Earnest, بجد *ba-jidd*, ساعي *sā'ī*, مقيد *muḳaiyad*.

Earthen, گلي *gil-ī*, مٹي كا *miṭṭī kā*, (as ware) سفالي *sifāl-ī*.

Earthly, ارضي *arẓ-ī*, (worldly) دنياوي *dunyā-wī*.

Eastern, پوربي *pūrbī*, شرقي *sharḳī*, مشرقي *mashriḳī*.

Easy, آسان *āsān*, سهل *sahl*, (at ease) آسوده حال *āsūda-ḥāl*.

Economical, كفايتي *kifāyatī*, جزرس *juz-ras*.

Effectual, Efficacious, كارگر *kār-gar*, مؤثر *mu'assir*.

Effeminate, زن صفت *zan-ṣifat*, نا مرد *nā-mard*, رنڈيسا *ranḍī-sā*.

Egregious, بڑا *baṛā*, سخت *sakht*, عجب *ʿajab*, مشهور *mash'hūr*.

Eightfold, آٹهگنا *āṭh-gunā*.

Either, دونون كا ايك *dōnōn kā ēk*, كوئي *kō'ī*, (conj.) خواه *khwāh*.

Elastic, چمٹها *chimṭhā*, چمڑا *chimṛā*, دم دار *dam-dār*.

Elder, بڑا *baṛā*, جيٹها *jēṭhā*, كلان *kalān*, بزرگ *buzurg*.

Elegant, لطيف *laṭīf*, نازك *nāzuk*, ستهرا *suthrā*, خوب *khūb*.

Eloquent, فصيح *faṣīḥ*, خوش گو *khush-gō*, شيرين زبان *shīrīn-zabān*.

Else, (other) اور *aur*, دوسرا *dūsrā*, (conj.) الا *illā*.

Eminent, بلند *buland*, اعلي *aʿlā*, نامور *nām-war*, بزرگ *buzurg*.

Empty, خالي *khālī*, چهوچها *chhūchhā*, سونا *sūnā*, تهي *tihī*.
Endless, بي نهايت *bē-nihāyat*, بي حد *bē-ḥadd*, مدام *mudām*.
English, انگريزي *angrēzī*, انگلشتاني *inglishtānī*.
Enormous, عظيم *āẓīm*, سخت *sakht*, شديد *shadīd*.
Enough, بس *bas*, کافي *kāfī*, بهت *bahut*: see Sufficiency.
Entire, تمام *tamām*, کامل *kāmil*, پورا *pūrā*, صحيح *ṣaḥīḥ*.
Entirely, سراسر *sar-ā-sar*, بلکل *bilkull*, ايک قلم *ēk-ḳalam*.
Envious, حاسد *ḥāsid*, ڈاهي *ḍāhī*, بدچشم *bad-chashm*.
Equal, برابر *barābar*, ايک سان *ēk-sāṅ*, همسر *ham-sar*.
Equitable, راست *rāst*, منصف *munṣif*, حق *ḥaḳḳ*, ٹهيک *ṭhīk*.
Equivocal, مبهم *mub'ham*, دومعني دار *dō-ma'nī-dār*.
Erect, استاده *istāda*, مستقيم *mustaḳīm*, کهڑا *khaṛā*.
Ere long, تهوڑي زماني مين *thōṛē zamāne meṅ*.
Ere now, قبل ازين *ḳabl az-īn*, آگي اسکي *āgē is-kē*.
Erroneous, غلط *ghalaṭ*. Erroneously, غلطاً *ghalaṭan*, سهواً *sahwan*.
Esculent, خوردني *khurdanī*, کهاني کي قابل *khānē kē ḳābil*.
Especial, خاص *khāṣṣ*. Especially, خصوص *khuṣūṣ*, خصوصاً *khuṣuṣan*.
Et cætera, وغيره *wa ghaira*, غيرذالک *ghair ẓālik*.
Eternal, ابدي *abadī*, لايزال *lā-yazāl*, دائم *dā'im*.
Even, (level) هموار *hamwār*, چورس *chauras*: see Equal, Straight.
Even (adv. or conj.), سچ *such*, واقعي *wāḳi'ī*, بهي *bhī*.
Ever, (at some time) کبهي *kabhī*, کدهي *kadhī*: see Always.
Every, هر *har*, هر ايک *har ēk*, سب کوئي *sab kō'ī*.
Every where, هر کهين *har kahīṅ*, هرجگهه *har jagah*.
Evident, عيان *āyān*, ظاهر *ẓāhir*, کهلا *khulā*, آشکارا *āshkārā*.
Evidently, صريحاً *ṣarīḥan*, ظاهراً *ẓāhiran*, صاف *ṣāf*.
Evil, برا *burā*, بد *bad*, زبون *zabūn*, خوار *khwār*.
Exact, ٹهيک *ṭhīk*, درست *durust*, برابر *barābar*: see Nice.
Exactly, بعينه *ba-āini-hi*, هوبهو *hū-ba-hū*, ٹهيک *ṭhīk*.
Exalted, سرفراز *sar-farāz*, سربلند *sar-buland*.
Exceeding, نپٹ *nipaṭ*, زياده *ziyāda*, بهت *bahut*.
Excellent, بهتر *bihtar*, فائق *fā'iḳ*, اتم *uttam*, غالب *ghālib*.

Except, سوا *siwā*, بجز *ba-juz*, بغير *ba-ghair*, سوائي *siwā'ē*.
Excessive, زياده *ziyāda*, ادهك *adhik*, نهايت *nihāyat*.
Expeditious, جلد باز *jald-bāz*, تيزرو *tēz-rau*, چالاك *chālāk*.
Experienced, تجربه كار *tajriba-kār*, واقف كار *wāḳif-kār*.
Expert, ماهر *māhir*, پهرتيلا *phurtīlā*, پكا *pakkā*.
Express, صاف *ṣāf*, ظاهر *ẓāhir*. Expressly, قصداً *ḳaṣdan*.
Exquisite, نفيس *nafīs*, بهتر *bihtar*, نادر *nādir*.
Extempore, في البديهه *fi-l-badīha*, بي تأمل *bē-ta'ammul*.
Extensive, وسيع *wasī'*, كشاده *kushāda*, بڑا *baṛā*.
Exterior, External, صوري *ṣūrī*, ظاهري *ẓāhirī*, بيروني *bērūnī*.
Extra, ما سوا *mā siwā*, علاوه *ālāwa*, زياده *ziyāda*.
Extraordinary, انوٹها *anūṭhā*, عجب *ājab*, نادر *nādir*.
Extravagant, فضول خرچ *fazūl-kharch*, بيدستور *be-dastūr*.
Face to face, آمني سامني *āmnē sāmnē*, روبرو *rū-ba-rū*.
Facetious, خوش طبع *khush-ṭab'*, هنسوڑ *hansōṛ*, ٹهٹهول *ṭhaṭhōl*.
Facing, روبرو *rū-ba-rū*, مقابل *muḳābil*, سامني *sāmnē*.
Fair, (in complexion) گورا *gōrā*, (honest) راست *rāst* : see Beautiful.
Faithful, ايمان دار *īmān-dār*, وفادار *wafā-dār*, سچا *sachchā*.
Faithless, بيوفا *bē-wafā*, نمك حرام *namak-ḥarām*.
False, جهوٹها *jhūṭhā*, باطل *bāṭil*, (forged) تقليدي *taḳlīdī*.
Famous, نامي *nāmī*, نامدار *nāmdār*, مشهور *mash'hūr*.
Far, دور *dūr*, بعيد *ba'īd*, (much) بهت *bahut*, زياده *ziyāda*.
Farther, دورتر *dūrtar*, (besides, moreover) علاوه *ālāwa*.
Fast, (firm) مضبوط *mazbūṭ*, پوڑها *pauṛhā* or *pōṛhā* : see Swift.
Fat, موٹا *mōṭā*, فربه *farbih*, جسيم *jasīm*.
Fatal, مهلك *muhlik*, قاتل *ḳātil*, (fated) بدا *badā*.
Faultless, بي تقصير *bē-taḳṣīr*, لاجرم *lā-jurm*, بي عيب *bē-āib*.
Faulty, دوسي *dōsī*, تقصيروار *taḳṣīr-wār* : see Bad, Defective.
Favourable, مهربان *mihrbān*, (suitable) موافق *muwāfiḳ*.
Fearful, (afraid) دهشت ناك *dahshat-nāk*, (awful) مهيب *muhīb*.
Fearless, بي باك *bē-bāk*, نڈر *ni-ḍar* : see Bold.
Feeble, نا توان *nā-tawān*, ضعيف *za'īf*, كم زور *kam-zōr*.

Fell, سنگدل *sangdil*, خونخوار *khūnkhwār*, کٹر *kaṭar*.

Female, Feminine, مادہ *māda*: see Effeminate, Soft.

Ferocious, وحشي *waḥshī*, بي رحم *bē-raḥm*: see Cruel.

Fertile, زرخيز *zar-khēz*, سنسگر *sansgar*, جيد *jaiyid*.

Fetid, گندہ *ganda*, متعفن *muta'affin*, بساهندا *bisāhindā*.

Feverish, تپ گرفتہ *tap-girifta*, گرم *garm*, تپ مائل *tap-mā'il*.

Few, تھوڑا *thōṛā*, تھوڑي *thōṛē*, چند *chand*, کچھ *kuchh*.

Fickle, اوچھا *ōchhā*, تلون مزاج *talauwun-mizāj*, چانچل *chanchal*.

Fictitious, ساختہ *sākhta*, جھوٹھا *jhūṭhā*, تغلبي *taghallubī*.

Fierce, تند *tund*, شديد *shadīd*, درشت *durusht*, قوي *ḳawī*.

Fiery, آتشي *ātashī*, ناري *nārī*, (passionate) تيز *tēz*, تند *tund*.

Figurative, مجازي *majāzī*, تمثيلي *tamṡīlī*.

Filthy, ميلا *mailā*, نجس *najis*, ناپاک *nā-pāk*, غليظ *ghalīẓ*.

Final, آخري *ākhirī*, اخر *ākhir*, پچھلا *pichhlā*, کامل *kāmil*.

Fine, (not coarse) باريک *bārīk*, (showy) جلادار *jilādār*: see Elegant.

Finite, محدود *maḥdūd*, اندازہ و پاياندار *andāza ō pāyān-dār*.

Firm, مضبوط *maẓbūṭ*, سخت *sakht*, کڑا *kaṛā*, ثبوت *ṡubūt*.

First, پہلا *pahlā*, اگلا *aglā*, اول *awwal*: see Chief.

Fit, ٹھيک *ṭhīk*, لائق *lā'iḳ*, درست *durust*, مناسب *munāsib*.

Fixed, قائم *ḳā'im*, مستحکم *mustaḥkim*, ساکن *sākin*.

Flabby, Flaccid, پلپلا *pilpilā*, نرم *narm*, ڈھيلا *ḍhīlā*.

Flagrant, (burning) سوزان *sōzān*, (enormous) شديد *shadīd*.

Flat, برابر *barābar*, هموار *hamwār*, (insipid) پھيکا *phīkā*.

Flexible, چمڑا *chimṛā*, لچيلا *lachīlā*, نرم *narm*: see Soft.

Flimsy, پتلا *patlā*, پتيل *patīl*, کم زور *kam-zōr*, پاجي *pājī*.

Fond, شائق *shā'iḳ*, عاشق *āshiḳ*, مائل *mā'il*: see Fool.

Fool, Foolish, احمق *aḥmaḳ*, بيوقوف *bē wuḳūf*, مورکھ *mūrakh*.

Forasmuch, چونکہ *chūnki*, جبکہ *jabki*, زيراکہ *zīrāki*.

By Force, Forcibly, جبرا *jabran*, زور سي *zōr sē*, بزور *ba-zōr*.

Fore, اگلا *aglā*, پيش *pēsh*, پيشين *pēshīn*, پہلا *pahlā*.

Foreign, Foreigner, پرديسي *pardēsī*, اجنبي *ajnabī*, بديسي *bidēsī*.

Former, اگلا *aglā*, پہلا *pahlā*, پيشين *pēshīn*, سابق *sābiḳ*.

Formerly, آگي *āgē*, پيشتر *pēshtar*, سابق مين *sābiḳ mēn̄*.
Formidable, مهيب *muhīb*, هيبت ناك *haibat-nāk*.
Forth, (forwards) آگي *āgē*, (abroad) باهر *bāhar*.
Fortunate, نيك بخت *nēk-ba<u>kh</u>t*, بهاگونت *bhāgwant*.
Forward, (early) آگمنا *āgmanā*, (bold) شوخ *shō<u>kh</u>*: see Before.
Foul, ميلا *mailā*, ناصاف *nā-ṣāf*, نجس *najis*, آلوده *ālūda*.
Fragrant, خوش بودار *<u>kh</u>ush-bū-dār*, معطر *mu'aṭṭar*.
Frail, (weak) ضعيف *ẓa'īf*, (not durable) كم پا *kam-pā*, فاني *fānī*.
Free, آزاد *āzād*, مختار *mu<u>kh</u>tār*, وارسته *wārasta*.
French, فراسيس *farāsīs*, فراسيسي *farāsīsī*, فرانس كا *frāns kā*.
Frequent, اكثر *akṣar*, پيهم *paiham*, بهت *bahut*.
Frequently, اكثريه *akṣarīya*, باربار *bār-bār*, بيشتر *bēshtar*.
Fresh, (new) نيا *nayā*, تازه *tāza*, (not salt) الونا *alōnā*: see Cool.
Fretful, چڑچڑا *chiṛchiṛā*, خفا *<u>kh</u>afā*, ناخوش *nā-<u>kh</u>ush*.
Frightful, هولناك *haulnāk*, ڈراونا *ḍarāwnā*, مهيب *muhīb*.
Frivolous, هلكا *halkā*, ناچيز *nā-chīz*, سبك *subuk*.
Frosty, برف دار *barf-dār*, پالي كا سا *pālē kā sā*.
Fruitful, ميوه دار *mēwa-dār*, بارور *bārwar*: see Fertile.
Fruitless, اپهل *aphal*, بيبر *bē-bar*, (profitless) عبث *ābaṣ*.
Full, (complete) پورا *pūrā*, (replete) بهرا *bharā*, پر *pur*, سير *sēr*.
Fulsome, گهنونا *ghinaunā*, ناگوار *nā-gawār*, ناپسند *nā-pasand*.
Furious, تند *tund*, شديد *shadīd*, غضبناك *<u>gh</u>aẓab-nāk*.
Further, دورتر *dūrtar*, (furthermore) تس پر *tis par*.
Fusty, پهپهند *phaphund*, باسي *bāsī*, بساهندا *bisāhindā*.
Future, مستقبل *mustaḳbil*, آئنده *ā'inda*, آگمي *āgamī*.
Gamesome, چلبلا *chulbulā*, كهلاڑي *khilāṛī*, رسيا *rasiyā*.
Gaudy, بهڑكيلا *bhaṛkīlā*, چٹكيلا *chaṭkīlā*, رنگيلا *rangīlā*.
Gay, خوش *<u>kh</u>ush*, شادمان *shādmān*: see Gaudy.
General, عام *ām*, مروج *murauwaj*, اكثر *akṣar*.
Generally, اكثريه *akṣarīya*, اكثر *akṣar*, عموماً *umūman*.
Generous, سخي *sa<u>kh</u>ī*, داتا *dātā*, كريم *karīm*.
Gentle, (tame) هلا *hilā*, (well-bred) اصيل *aṣīl*.

Gently, آهستي *āhistē*, دهيمي *dhīmē*, نرم نرم *narm narm*.

Genuine, اصيل *aṣīl*, (pure) خالص *khāliṣ*, چوکها *chōkhā*.

Giddy, گهرني دار *ghurnī-dār*, (volatile) چنچل *chanchal*.

Glad, خوش *khush*, شاد *shād*, مسرور *masrūr*, خرم *khurram*.

Gladly, خوشي سي *khushī sē*, آنند سي *ānand sē*.

Globular, Globous, گول *gōl*, گولاسا *gōlā-sā*, کروي *kurawī*.

Glorious, جليل *jalīl*, جليل القدر *jalīlu-l-ḳadr*, مجيد *majīd*.

Glutinous, چپچپا *chipchipā*, لسلسا *laslasā*, لسدار *las-dār*.

Glutton, Gluttonous, پيٹو *pēṭū*, پيٹارتهو *pēṭārthū*, اکال *akkāl*.

Golden, سونهلا *sōnahlā*, زرين *zarrīn*, طلائي *ṭilā'ī*.

Good, اچها *achchhā*, بهلا *bhalā*, خوب *khūb*, نيک *nēk*.

Graceful, سجيلا *sajīlā*, جميل *jamīl*, طرحدار *ṭaraḥ-dār*.

Gradually, بتدريج *ba-tadrij*, رفته رفته *rafta rafta*.

Grammatical, با قاعده *bā-ḳā'ida*, مربوط *marbūṭ*.

Grand, بڑا *baṛā*, عظيم *ăẓīm*, کبير *kabīr*, بزرگ *buzurg*.

Grateful, شکرگذار *shukr-guẓār*, حق شناس *ḥaḳḳ-shinās*.

Gratis, Gratuitously, مفت *muft*, بيزر خريد *bē-zar kharīd*.

Grave, دهيرا *dhīrā*, سنجيده *sanjīda*, گنبهيرا *gambhīrā*.

Greasy, چربيدار *charbī-dār*, چکنا *chiknā*, چکٹ *chikkaṭ*.

Great, بڑا *baṛā*, عظيم *ăẓīm*, بزرگ *buzurg*, کبير *kabīr*.

Grecian, يوناني *yūnān-ī*.

Greedy, حريص *ḥarīṣ*, لالچي *lālchī*, (ravenous) مربهکها *mar-bhukkhā*.

Green, هرا *harā*, سبز *sabz*, (fresh) تازه *tāza*, (raw) کچا *kachchā*.

Grey, خاکستري *khākistarī*, کبرا *kabrā*, اشهب *ash'hab*.

Grievous, شديد *shadīd*, سخت *sakht*, دردانگيز *dard-angēz*.

Gritty, کرکرا *kirkirā*, (as bread) کسکسا *kaskasā*.

Gross, موٹا *mōṭā*, جسيم *jasīm*, بهاري *bhārī*: see Stupid.

Guiltless, بيگناه *bē-gunāh*, نردوکه *nirdōkh*, بري *barī*.

Guilty, گنهگار *gunahgār*, تقصيروار *taḳṣīrwār*.

Hairy, (full of hair) موئيدار *mū'ēdār*, (made of hair) پشمي *pashmī*.

Half, آدها *ādhā*, نصف *niṣf*, نيم *nīm*.

Half and half, in halves, نصفا نصفي *niṣfā niṣfī*.

Handsome, حسين *ḥasīn*, ستهرا *suthrā*: see Good, Beautiful.

Happy, (lucky) كامران *kāmrān*, (at ease) خوش‌حال *khush-ḥāl*.

Hard, سخت *sakht*, كڑا *kaṛā*: see Firm, Difficult.

Hardly, (with difficulty) دقت سي *diḳḳat sē*: see Scarcely.

Hark! سنو سنو *sunō sunō*, ديكهو ديكهو *dēkhō dēkhō*.

Harsh, درشت *durusht*, سخت *sakht*, (sour) ترش *tursh*.

Hasty, (quick) جلد *jald*, پهرتيلا *phurtīlā*, (rash) تند *tund*.

Haughty, مغرور *maghrūr*, گهمنڈي *ghamanḍī*: see Proud.

He, (pron.) وه *wuh*, يہ *yih*, (male) نر *nar*.

Healthy, Healthful, تندرست *tan-durust*, بهلا چنگا *bhalā changā*.

Hearty, (sincere) بيريا *bē-riyā*, صاف *ṣāf*: see Healthy, Strong.

Heavenly, آسماني *āsmānī*, سماوي *samāwī*, فلكي *falakī*.

Heavy, بهاري *bhārī*, گران *girān*: see Grievous, Stupid, Sad.

Hebrew, عبراني *ʿibrānī*, يهودي *yahūdī*.

Heedless, بيپروا *bē-parwā*, غافل *ghāfil*, اچيت *achēt*.

Helpless, لاچار *lā-chār*, بيچاره *bē-chāra*, بيبس *bē-bas*.

Hence, (adv.) يہان سي *yahaṅ sē*, (conj.) اسليي *is-liyē*.

Hence! (interj.), دور هو *dūr hō!* دفع هو *dafʿ hō!*

Henceforth, Henceforward, اب سي *ab sē*, آگي *āgē*, آئنده *ā'inda*.

Her, اس يا اس كا كي كي *us-* or *is-kā*, *-kē*, *-kī*, اس كو *us-kō*.

Hereafter, بعد اسكي *baʿd iskē*, آگي *āgē*, آئنده *ā'inda*.

Hereditary, موروثي *maurūṣī*, آبائي *ābā'ī*, پيترك *paitrik*.

Hideous, مهيب *muhīb*, هولناك *haulnāk*, كريه *karīh*.

High, بلند *buland*, اونچا *ūnchā*, (proud) متكبر *mutakabbir*.

High-born, اميرزاده *amīr-zāda*, عالي خاندان *ʿālī-khāndān*.

Highly, نهايت *nihāyat*, نپٹ *nipaṭ*, زياده *ziyāda*.

High-mettled (as a horse), جانباز *jān-bāz*, تيز *tēz*.

High-seasoned, چڑپڑا *chirpiṛā*, مصالح دار *maṣāliḥ-dār*.

Hind, Hinder, Hindermost, پچهلا *pichhlā*, آخر *ākhir*.

Hitherto, ابتك *ab-tak*, يهان تك *yahāṅ tak*, هنوز *hanōz*.

Hollow, چهوچها *chhūchhā*, مجوف *mujauwaf*, كهوكهلا *khōkhlā*.

Holy, مقدس *muḳaddas*, طاهر *ṭāhir*, پاك *pāk*.

Honest, کهرا *kharā*, راست‌باز *rāst-bāz*, سادهہ *sādh*.
Honourable, معزز *mu'azzaz*, نامور *nāmwar*: see Honest.
Hopeless, ناامید *nā-ummēd*, نراس *nirās*, مایوس *māyūs*.
Horrid, Horrible, مهیب *muhīb*, هولناک *haulnāk*: see Dreadful.
Hot, گرم *garm*, تتا *tattā*, تیز *tēz*: see Eager, Furious.
How long? کب تک *kab tak?* How oft? کي بير *kui bēr?*
How many? کتني *kitnē* (m.)? How much? کتنا *kitnā* (m.)?
However, (conj.), لیکن *lēkin*, مگر *magar*, پر *par*.
Human, انساني *insānī*, بشري *basharī*.
Humane, نرم‌دل *narm-dil*, حلیم *halīm*, سلیم *salīm*.
Humble, فروتن *farōtan*, غریب *gharīb*, عاجز *ājiz*.
Humid, نمناک *namnāk*, مرطوب *marṭūb*, تر *tar*.
Humpbacked, کبڑا *kubṛā*, کوزپشت *kūz-pusht*.
Hungry, بهوکها *bhūkhā*, گرسنه *gursina*.
Hurtful, زیانکار *ziyānkār*, مضر *muzirr*, مخل *mukhill*.
Hypocritical, Hypocrite, کپٹي *kapaṭī*, ریاکار *riyākār*.
Ideal, خیالي *khiyālī*, وهمي *wahmī*, فرضي *farzī*.
Idle, (unemployed) بیکار *bē-kār*, (lazy) سست *sust*.
Jealous, بدظن *bad-zann*, (emulous) غیرت‌کش *ghairat-kash*.
Ignorant, نادان *nā-dān*, بیخبر *bē-khabar*: see Fool.
Ill, (bad) برا *burā*, بد *bad*, (sick) بیمار *bīmar*: see Evil.
Ill-behaved, کچالي *kuchālī*, بداطوار *bad-aṭwār*: see Rude.
Illiterate, ناخوانده *nā-khwānda*, بیتعلیم *bē-ta'līm*, انسکه *ansikh*.
Ill-natured, بدباطن *bad-bāṭin*, بدنهاد *bad-nihād*.
Illustrious, نامي *nāmī*, مشهور *mashhūr*, ممتاز *mumtāz*.
Immediately, بمجرد *ba-mujarrad*, ترت *turt*, تبهي *tabhī*.
Immense, بیحد *bē-hadd*, بیقیاس *bē-kiyās*: see Infinite.
Immoderate, بي‌اندازه *bē-andāza*, زیاده *ziyāda*, بیحد *bē-hadd*.
Immodest, بیشرم *bē-sharm*, بیحیا *bē-hayā*.
Immoral, بدمعاش *bad-ma'āsh*, معیوب *ma'yūb*: see Bad.
Immortal, امر *amar*, بیمرگ *bē-marg*, لایزال *lā yazāl*.
Immovable, اچل *achal*, اٹل *aṭal*, غیرمتحرک *ghair mutaharrik*.

Impartial, بيغرض *bē-gharaẓ,* منصف *munṣif,* عادل *ʿādil.*

Impatient, بيصبر *bē-ṣabr,* ناشكيب *nā-shikēb,* گرم *garm.*

Imperfect, ناتمام *nā-tamām,* ناقص *nāḳis,* قاصر *ḳāṣir.*

Impious, بيدين *bē-dīn,* فاسق *fāsiḳ,* ادهرمي *adharmī.*

Important, اهم *ahamm,* بهاري *bhārī,* بڑا *baṛā.*

Impossible, غيرممكن *ghair mumkin,* انهونا *anhōnā.*

Impotent, (unable to propagate) نامرد *nā-mard:* see Weak.

Improbable, غيرمحتمل *ghair muḥtamil,* خلاف قياس *khilāf-i ḳiyās.*

Improper, بيجا *bē-jā,* نامعقول *nā-maʿḳūl,* ناهموار *nā-hamwār.*

Improvident, Imprudent, كوته انديش *kotah-andēsh,* بيتدبير *bē-tadbīr.*

Impudent, بيشرم *bē-sharm,* (bold) ڈهيٹه *ḍhīṭh.*

Impure, ناصاف *nā-ṣāf,* نجس *najis,* ناپاك *nā-pāk.*

In, مين *mēṅ,* بيچ *bīch,* بهيتر *bhītar,* (dakh. also) مني *manē.*

Inaccurate, غيرصحيح *ghair ṣaḥīḥ,* نادرست *nā-durust.*

Inactive, سست *sust,* ڈهيلا *ḍhīlā,* آرامي *ārāmī.*

Inadvertently, غفلت سي *ghaflat sē,* بهولكر *bhūlkar.*

Inanimate, Inanimated, بيجان *bē-jān,* بينمك *bē-namak.*

Inattentive, غافل *ghāfil,* بي التفات *bē-iltifāt,* بيپروا *bē-parwā.*

Incapable, قاصر *ḳāṣir,* غيرقابل *ghair ḳābil,* نارسا *nā-rasā.*

Incentive, ترغيب ده *targhīb-dih,* محرك *muḥarrik.*

Incessant, متواتر *mutawātir,* لگاتار *lagātār,* پيهم *paiham.*

Inclined, مائل *mā'il,* (desirous) راغب *rāghib,* شائق *shā'iḳ.*

Including, Inclusive, مشتمل *mushtamil,* شامل *shāmil.*

Incomparable, بينظير *bē-naẓīr,* لاثاني *lā-ṡānī.*

Incomplete, ناتمام *nā-tamām,* ناقص *nāḳiṣ.*

Inconstant, بيثبات *bē-ṡabāt,* بيقرار *bē-ḳarār.*

Incorrect, ناصحيح *nā-ṣaḥīḥ,* اسده *asudh,* غلط *ghalaṭ.*

Indebted, قرضدار *ḳarẓ-dār,* (obliged) ممنون *mamnūn.*

Indecent, Indecorous, بي ادب *bē-adab,* بيشرم *bē-sharm.*

Indeclinable (in gram.), غيرمتحرك *ghair mutaḥarrik.*

Indeed, واقعي *wāḳiʿī,* سچ *sach,* البته *albatta.*

Indefinite, غيرمقرر *ghair muḳarrar,* (noun) نكره *nakira.*

Independent, مستقل *mustaḳill,* سرخود *sar-khud.*

Indiscreet, بيلحاظ *bē-liḥāẓ,* بي امتياز *bē-imtiyāz.*

Indisposed, (disinclined) ناساز *nā-sāz,* (sick) كسلمند *kasalmand.*

Industrious, محنتي *miḥnat-ī,* كامكاجي *kāmkājī,* ساعي *sā'ī.*

Inestimable, بيبها *bē-bahā,* بي قيمت *bē-ḳīmat.*

Infamous, بد نام *bad-nām,* رسوا *ruswā,* اپجسي *apajasī.*

Inferior, نيچا *nīchā,* چهوٹا *chhōṭā,* فروتر *farōtar,* ادنا *adnā.*

Infinite, بيحد *bē-ḥadd,* بيپايان *bē-pāyān,* بي انتها *bē-intihā.*

Infirm, ضعيف *ẓa'īf,* دبلا *dublā,* ناتوان *nā-tawān,* روگي *rōgī.*

Ingenious, ذكي *ẕakī,* ذهين *ẕahīn,* چترا *chaturā.*

Initial, پهلا *pahlā,* مقدم *muḳaddam,* اول *awwal.*

Inlaid, منبت *munabbat,* جڑاؤ *jaṛā'ū.*

Innocent, پاك *pāk,* بيگناه *bē-gunāh,* (harmless) غريب *gharīb.*

Innumerable, بيشمار *bē-shumār,* انگنت *anginat.*

Insane, ديوانه *dīwāna,* باؤلا *bā'ōlā,* مجنون *majnūn.*

Insatiable, ناسير هوني كا *nā-sēr-hōnē kā,* مربهوكها *marbhūkhā* : see Greedy.

Insensible, بيحس *bē-ḥiss,* بيهوش *bē-hōsh* : see Gradually.

Inside, بهيتر *bhītar,* اندرون *andarūn,* اندر *andar.*

Insipid, بيمزه *bē-maza,* پهيكا *phīkā,* بينمك *bē-namak.*

Insolent, مگرا *magrā,* سركش *sar-kash,* گستاخ *gustākh.*

Instantly, ابهي *abhī,* اسي دم *isī dam,* في الفور *fi-l-faur.*

Instead, عوض *'iwaẓ,* بدل *badal,* بجائي *ba-jā'ē.*

Intelligent, عاقل *'āḳil,* فهيم *fahīm,* هوشيار *hōshyār.*

Intemperate, بد پرهيز *bad-parhēz,* شرابي *sharābī.*

Intentionally, قصداً *ḳaṣdan,* عمداً *'amdan,* جان بوجهكي *jān būjhkē.*

Interior, Internal, بهيتري *bhītrī,* دروني *darūnī.*

Intimate, همدم *ham-dam,* محرم *maḥram,* مونس *mūnis.*

Intransitive verb, فعل لازمي *fi'l-i-lāzimī,* اكرمك *akarmak.*

Intrepid, بيباك *bē-bāk,* نڈر *niḍar,* جانباز *jān-bāz.*

Intricate, پيچدار *pēch-dār,* پيچ در پيچ *pēch dar pēch.*

Intuitive knowledge, علم لدني *'ilm-i-ladunnī.*

Invalid, (null) باطل *bāṭil,* (sick) دائم المرض *dā'imu-l-maraẓ.*

Invaluable, بيبها *bē-bahā*, امول *amōl*, عزيز *āzīz*.
Inverse, Inverted, الٹا *ulṭā*, اوندها *aundhā*, مقلوب *maḳlūb*.
Invincible, اجيت *ajīt*, اٹل *aṭal*, غير مغلوب *ghair maghlūb*.
Invisible, انديكها *andēkhā*, غائب *ghā'ib*, ناپديد *nā-padīd*.
Involuntary, اضطراري *iẓṭirārī*, بي اختيار *bē-ikhtiyār*.
Jocular, Jocose, ٹهٹهول *ṭhaṭhōl*, هنسوڑ *hansōṛ*, ظريف *ẓarīf*.
Jolly, Jovial, خوش *khush*, زنده دل *zinda-dil*, بهوگي *bhōgī*.
Joyful, خوش *khush*, خرم *khurram*, شادمان *shādmān*.
Irregular, بي قاعده *bē-ḳā'ida*, خلاف قياس *khilāf-i-ḳiyās*.
Irremediable, لادوا *lā-dawā*, بي علاج *bē-ilāj*.
It, وه *wuh*, يهه *yih* or *yah*. Its, اسكا *us-kā*, اسكا *is-kā*.
Judicious, هوشيار *hōshyār*, عقلمند *āḳlmand*, پربين *parbīn*.
Jugular, گلي كا *galē kā*; vein, حبل الوريد *ḥablu-l-warīd*.
Juicy, رسيلا *rasīlā*, رسدار *rasdār*, شاداب *shādāb*.
Junior, چهوٹا *chhōṭā*, كوچك *kūchak*, صغير *ṣaghīr*.
Just, عادل *ādil*, راست *rāst*, سچا *sachchā*, ٹهيك *ṭhīk*.
Just now, ابهي *ab-hī*, الحال *alḥāl*, اب *ab*.
Keen, (eager) شائق *shā'iḳ*, (sharp) تيز *tēz*, (severe) تند *tund*.
Kind, مهربان *mihrbān*, دياونت *dayāwant*, شفيق *shafīḳ*.
Knotty, Knotted, گٹهيلا *gaṭhīlā*, (abstruse) مغلق *mughlaḳ*.
Knowing, واقف *wāḳif*, دانا *dānā*, گياني *gyānī*, ماهر *māhir*.
Laborious, محنتي *miḥnatī*: see Industrious, Difficult.
Lame, لنگڑا *langṛā*, لنگ *lang*, لنج *lunj*, (of the hands) لولا *lūlā*.
Languid, ضعيف *ẓa'īf*, مانده *mānda*, كاهل *kāhil*, سست *sust*.
Large, بڑا *baṛā*, موٹا *mōṭā*, فراخ *farākh*, بهاري *bhārī*.
Lascivious, مست *mast*, شهوتي *shahwatī*, چلهارا *chulhārā*.
Last, پچهلا *pichhlā*, آخر *ākhir*, اخير *akhīr*.
At last, آخر *ākhir*, ندان *nidān*, عاقبت *āḳibat*.
Late, (after time) دير *dēr*, (deceased) مرحوم *marḥūm*, (past) اگلا *aglā*.
Lately, تهوڑي دنون سي *thōṛē dinōn sē*, درين ولا *darīn wilā*.
Laudable, ممدوح *mamdūḥ*, تعريف كي قابل *ta'rif kē ḳābil*.
Lawful, شرعي *shar'ī*, (allowable) جائز *jā'iz*, حلال *ḥalāl*.

Lazy, سست *sust*, کاهل *kāhil*, نکهٹو *nikhaṭṭū*.

Lean, دبلا *dublā*, لاغر *lāghar*, حقیر *ḥaḳīr* : see Poor.

Learned, عالم *ālim*, فاضل *fāẓil*, کامل *kāmil*, پنڈت *panḍit*.

Least, سب سي چهوٹا *sab sē chhōṭā*, کمترین *kamtarīn*.

Left, (opposite to right) بایاں *bāyāṅ*, (remaining) باقي *bāḳī*.

Lenient, Lenitive, ملین *mulaiyin*, مسکن *musakkin*.

Leper, Leprous, کوڑهي *kōṛhī*, پیسي *pēsī*, جذامي *jaẕāmī*.

Less, کم *kam*, چهوٹا *chhōṭā*, کمتر *kamtar*, کهتر *kihtar*.

Lest, (that not) مبادا *mabādā*, (for fear that) ایسا نهو *aisā nahō*.

Level, برابر *barābar*, هموار *hamwār*, مسطح *musaṭṭaḥ*.

Liar, جهوٹها *jhūṭhā*, کاذب *kāẕib*, دروغ گو *darōgh-gō*.

Liberal, (munificent) سخي *sakhī*, داتا *dātā* : see Generous, Free.

Libertine, بیقید *bē-ḳaid*, لچا *luchchā*, رند *rind*, آواره *āwāra*.

Licentious, بیقید *bē-ḳaid*, سرکش *sarkash*, بدکار *badkār*.

Lifeless, بیجان *bē-jān*, (inactive) سست *sust*, مجهول *maj'hūl*.

Light, (bright) اجلا *ujlā*, روشن *rōshan*, (not heavy) هلکا *halkā*.

Like, (equal) موافق *muwāfiḳ*, (similar) سا *sā*, ایکساں *ēksāṅ*.

Likely, (probable) هونهار *hōnhār*, (probably) هووي *hōwē*, غالبا *ghāliban*.

Likewise, (adv.) بهي *bhī*, نیز *nīz*, اوپر اسکي *ūpar-iskē*.

Liquid (fluid), پتلا *patlā*, سیال *saiyāl*, مذاب *muẕāb*.

Little, تهوڑا *thōṛā*, (small) چهوٹا *chhōṭā*, خورد *khurd*.

Live, Living, جیتا *jītā*, زنده *zinda*, (burning) گرم *garm*.

Lively, زنده دل *zinda-dil*, شوخ *shōkh*, خوش طبع *khush-ṭab**: see Cheerful.

Lo! دیکهو *dēkhō*, لو *lō*, دیکه *dēkh*.

Loath, ناراض *nā-rāẓ*, کشیده *kashīda*, روگرداں *rūgardān*.

Lofty, (high) بلند *buland*, (proud) مغرور *maghrūr* : see Conceited.

Lone, Lonely, اکلا *iklā*, تنها *tanhā*, اکیلا *akēlā* : see Solitary.

Long, لمبا *lambā*, دراز *darāz*, (time, dilatory) درنگ *dirang*.

Loose, کهلا *khulā*, چهوٹا *chhūṭā*, ڈهیلا *ḍhīlā*, بیقید *bē-ḳaid*.

Lost, گم *gum*, خراب *kharāb*, گیا *gayā*, غایب *ghā'ib*.

Loud, شوري *shōrī*, بلند آواز *buland āwāz*, اونچا *ūnchā*.

Loudly, with a loud voice, پکارکي *pukārkē*, شورسي *shōr sē*.

Lovely, پیارا *pyārā*, نازنین *nāznīn*, دلبر *dilbar*.

Lovesick, فریفته *farēfta*, مفتون *maftūn*, مجنون *majnūn*.

Lousy, چلڑاها *chilṛāhā*, جوین بهرا *jū'eṅ-bharā*: see Base.

Low, نیچا *nīchā*, پست *past*, (weak) ضعیف *za'īf*: see Base.

Low, (adv. not loud) آهستي *āhistē*, دهیمي *dhīmē*: see Down.

Lowly, فروتن *farōtan*, حلیم *ḥalīm*, غریب *gharīb*: see Humble.

Loyal, نمک‌حلال *namak-ḥalāl*, مستقیم *mustaḳīm*: see Faithful.

Lucid, صاف *ṣāf*, براق *barrāḳ*, روشن *rōshan*, شفاف *shaffāf*.

Lucky, خوش نصیب *khush-naṣīb*, بختاور *bakhtāwar*: see Fortunate.

Ludicrous, مسخري *maskharī*, طناز *ṭannāz*, خنده‌انگیز *khanda-angēz*.

Lukewarm, شیرگرم *shīr-garm*, (dakh.) کمکما *kumkumā*.

Lunar, مهتابي *mahtābī*, قمري *ḳamarī*, (day) تته *tith*. (f.)

Luscious, میٹها *mīṭhā*, رسیلا *rasīlā*, لذیذ *laẕīẕ*: see Delicious.

Lusty, (stout) تناور *tanāwar*, قوي *ḳawī*, زوراور *zōrāwar*: see Corpulent.

Luxuriant, کثیر *kaṡīr*, وافر *wāfir*, زیاده *ziyāda*.

Luxurious, عیاش *āiyāsh*, خوش‌معاش *khush-ma'āsh*, پیٹو *pēṭū*, نفساني *nafsānī*.

Mad, دیوانه *dīwāna*, باؤلا *bā'ōlā*, (enraged) غضبناک *ghaẓabnāk*.

Made, بنایا هوا *banāyā hū'ā*, ساخته *sākhta*, کروایا *karwāyā*.

Magnificent, عظیم‌الشان *āẓīmu-sh-shān*: see Grand.

Main, (chief, principal) اول *awwal*, مقدم *muḳaddam*: see Important.

Major, بڑا *baṛā*, بزرگ *buzurg*, اول *awwal*, سردار *sardār*.

Male, نر *nar*, نروکه *narūkh*, نرینه *narīna*, مردانه *mardāna*.

Malicious, Malevolent, کینه‌کش *kīna-kash*, بدخواه *bad-khwāh*.

Manifest, واضح *wāẓiḥ*, ظاهر *ẓāhir*, کهلا *khulā*, آشکارا *āshkārā*.

Manlike, Manly, مردانه *mardāna*, جوانمرد *jawānmard*.

Many, بهت *bahut*, بهتیري *bahutērē* (m. plur.), بسیار *bisyār*.

Marine, Maritime, بحري *baḥrī*, دریائي *daryā'ī*.

Marvellous, عجیب *ājīb*, اچمبها *achambhā*, عجوبه *ājūba*.

Masculine, (in gender) مذکر *muẕakkar*, پلنگ *puling*: see Manly.

Material, (of matter) جسماني *jismānī*: see Important.

Maternal, Motherly, مادري *mādarī*: see under Grandfather, &c.

May be, شايد *shāyad*, هووي *hōwē*, هوگا *hōgā*, هو *hō*.

Mean, كمينه *kamīna*, پاجي *pājī*, (middle) ميانه *miyāna*.

Meek, بهولا *bhōlā*, حليم *ḥalīm*, سليم *salīm*, غريب *gharīb*.

Meet, مناسب *munāsib*, درست *durust*: see Fit.

Mellow, پكا *pakkā*, نرم *narm*, رسيده *rasīda*, خوش *khush*.

Mercantile, تجارتي *tijāratī*, سوداگري *saudāgarī*, مهاجني *mahājanī*.

Merciful, رحيم *raḥīm*, موم دل *mōm-dil*, دياونت *dayāwant*.

Merciless, بيرحم *bē-raḥm*, بيدرد *bē-dard*, سنگدل *sang-dil*.

Mere, (pure) نرا *nirā*, نرالا *nirālā*, (merely) صرف *ṣirf*, محض *maḥẓ*.

Merry, شادمان *shādmān*, هنسوڑ *hansōr*, مگن *magan*, خوش *khush*.

Metaphorical, مستعار *musta'ār*, مجازي *majāzī*, (adv.) مجازا *majāzan*.

Methinks, مجهي سوجهتا هي *mujhē sūjhtā hai*, مجه كو لگتا هي *mujh kō lagtā hai*.

Mid, Midst, ادهبيچ *adh-bīch*, بيچون بيچ *bīchōn bīch*.

Middle, Middling, ميانه *miyāna*, وسطي *wasaṭī*, مجهولا *majhōlā*.

Midway, اثناي راه *asnā'ē rah*, آدهي راه مين *ādhī rāh mēn*.

Mighty, بلونت *balwant*, قوي *ḳawī*, سامرتهي *sāmarthī*, (dakh.) مكهنڈ *mukhanḍ*.

Milch (giving milk), دودهار *dūdhār*, ددهيل *dudhail*.

Mild, ملائم *mulā'im*, نرم *narm*, حليم *ḥalīm*, كومل *kōmal*.

Military, لشكري *lashkarī*, جنگي *jangī*, عسكري *ʿaskarī*.

Million, دس لاكه *das lākh*, نجت *nijut*: ten millions, كروڑ *karōṛ*.

Mine, ميرا ميري يا ميري *mērā*, *mērē* or *mērī*, اپنا اپني اپني *apnā*, *apnē*, *apnī*.

Minor, خوردسال *khurd-sāl*, (شخص) نابالغ *nā-bāligh* (*shakhṣ*).

Minute (very small), نهايت چهوٹا *nihāyat chhōṭā*, مهين *mihīn*.

Miraculous, عجيب *ʿajīb*, عجوبه *ʿujūba*, كرامتي *karāmtī*, ادبهت *adbhut*.

Miser, بخيل *bakhīl*, ممسك *mumsik*, شوم *shūm*, كنجوس *kanjūs*.

Miserable, ذليل *ẕalīl*, خسته‌حال *khasta-ḥāl*, مفلس *muflis*.

Modern, متاخر *muta'akhkhir*, جديد *jadīd*, حالي *ḥālī*: see New.

Modest, (bashful) لجيلا *lajīlā*, حليم *ḥalīm*, (chaste) محجوب *maḥjūb*.

Moist, تر *tar*, نم *nam*, نمناك *namnāk*, گيلا *gīlā*, اودا *ōdā*.

Mongrel, دوغله *dōghla*, دونسله *dō-nasla*.

Moral, (of manners) اخلاق كا *akhlāḳ kā*, (virtuous) خليق *khalīḳ*.

More, اور *aur*, زياده *ziyāda*, ادهك *adhik*, بيش *bēsh*.

Moreover, تسپر *tis-par*, اوپر اسكي *ūpar iskē*, علاوه *ʿalāwa*.

Morose, درشت *durusht*, ترش رو *tursh-rū*, كڑا *kaṛā*.

Mortal, فاني *fānī*, موتي *mautī*, (deadly) مهلك *muhlik*, قاتل *ḳātil*.

Most, اكثر *akṣar*, بهت *bahut*, زياده *ziyāda*, بيشتر *bēshtar*.

Mostly, for the most part, اكثر *akṣar*, بيشتر *bēshtar*, غالباً *ghāliban*, اكثريه *akṣarīya*.

Motherly, مادري *mādarī*, ماسا *mā-sā*, مادرانه *mādarāna*.

Much, بهت *bahut*, بسيار *bisyār*, (adv.) نهايت *nihāyat*.

Muddy, (foul) ميلا *mailā*, گدلا *gadlā*, (stupid) گاودي *gāwdī*.

Murky, تاريك *tārīk*, اندهيرا *andhērā*, گهنگهور *ghanghōr*.

Musty, سڑا *saṛā*, بوسيده *bōsīda*, گمسا *gumsā*.

Mute, (dumb) گنگا *gungā*, لال *lāl*, (letter) حرف مخفي *ḥarf-i-makhfī*.

Mutual, Mutually, دوطرفي *dō-ṭarfī*, جانبين *jānibain*.

Myself, مين خود *main khud*, آپ *āp*, مين آپ *main āp*.

Mysterious, مخفي *makhfī*, پوشيده *pōshīda*.

Naked, ننگا *nangā*, برهنه *barahna*, عريان *ʿuryān*: see Bare.

Namely, يعني *yaʿnē*, خصوصاً *khuṣūṣan*, مثلاً *maṣalan*.

Narrow, تنگ *tang*, چست *chust*, سكڑا *sakṛā*, سكيت *sakēt*.

Nasty, ميلا *mailā*, پليد *palīd*, نجس *najis*, آلوده *ālūda*.

Native, كسي ملك كا اصل باشنده *kisī mulk kā aṣl bāshanda*.

Natural, طبيعي *ṭabīʿī*, ذاتي *ẕātī*, خلقي *khilkī*, (unaffected) بيساخته *bē-sākhta*, (illegitimate) حرامزاده *ḥarām-zāda*.

Naval, بحري *baḥrī*, جهازي *jahāzī*.

Naught, Naughty, بد *bad*, برا *burā*, خراب *kharāb*, شرير *sharīr*.

Nauseous, گهنونا *ghinaunā*, مكروه *makrūh*, كريه *karīh*.

Near, Nearly, (postpos.) پاس *pās*, نزديك *nazdīk*, (adj.) قريب *ḳarīb*, متصل *muttaṣil*, لگا *lagā*.

Neat, صاف *ṣāf*, پاک *pāk*, ستهرا *suthrā*, پاکیزه *pākīza*.

Necessarily, ضرورتاً *ẓarūratan*, لا بد *lā budd*, لا جرم *lā jaram*.

Necessary, Needful, ضرور *ẓarūr*, لازم *lāzim*, واجب *wājib*.

Needy, Necessitous, محتاج *muḥtāj*, کنگال *kangāl*, مفلس *muflis*.

Negative, منفي *manfī*, (sentence) سالبه *sāliba*.

Neglectful, Negligent, غافل *g͟hāfil*, بیخبر *bē-k͟habar*, سست *sust*.

Nether, Nethermost, ترلا *tarlā*, زیرین *zērīn*, اسفل *asfal*.

Never, هرگز نهين *hargiz nahīṅ*, کبهو نهين *kabhū nahīṅ*, زنهار *zinhār!*

Nevertheless, تس پر بهي *tis par bhī*, تو بهي *tau bhī*, تا هم *tā ham*.

Neuter, (in gram.) نپنسک *napunsak*, (a verb) لازمي *lāzimī*.

Neuter, Neutral, نه ادهر نه ادهر *na idhar na udhar*, الگ *alag*.

New, نیا *nayā*, نو *nau*, (fresh) تازه *tāza*, (modern) جدید *jadīd*.

Next, (postpos.) پاس *pās*, قریب *ḳarīb*, (second) دوسرا *dūsrā*, ثاني *ṣānī*.

Nice, ٹهیک *ṭhīk*, صحیح *ṣaḥīḥ*, مرزامزاج *mirzā-mizāj*: see Dainty.

Nigh, (postpos.) پاس *pās*, نزدیک *nazdīk*, (adj.) قریب *ḳarīb*.

Nightly, شبینه *shabīna*, رات کا *rāt kā*, (every night) هر رات *har rāt*.

Nimble, چالاک *chālāk*, جلد *jald*, چست *chust*, تیز *tēz*.

Noble, شریف *sharīf*, نجیب *najīb*, عمده *ūmda*: see Brave.

Nocturnal, شبینه *shabīna*, لیلي *lailī*, شبي *shabī*.

Noisy, پرشور *pur-shōr*, شور پشت *shor-pusht*, غوغائي *g͟haug͟hā'ī*.

Nolens volens, خواه مخواه *k͟hwāh ma-k͟hwāh*, چار ناچار *chār nā-chār*.

None, (no one) کوئي نهين *kō'ī nahīṅ*, (nothing) کچه نهين *kuchh nahīṅ*.

Northerly, Northern, شمالي *shimālī*, شمال رو *shimāl-rū*, اتراها *uttrāhā*.

Notorious, (well known) مشهور *mash'hūr*, معروف *ma*ʻ*rūf*: see Infamous.

Notwithstanding, باوجودي که *bā-wujūdē ki*, هر چند که *har chand ki*.

Novel, نیا *nayā*, جدید *jadīd*, اچمبها *achambhā*, بدیع *badī*ʻ.

Now, اب *ab*, بالفعل *bi-l-fi*ʻ*l*, الحال *alḥāl*, اکنون *aknūn*.

Nowadays, آج کل *āj kal*, ان دنون *in dinōṅ*.

Nowhere, کهين نهين *kahīṅ nahīṅ*.

Nowise, کسي طرح سي نهين *kisī ṭaraḥ sē nahīṅ*.

Noxious, مفسد *mufsid*, مضر *muẓirr*, فاسد *fāsid*: see Hurtful.

Nugatory, لا حاصل *lā-ḥāṣil*, نکما *nikammā*, هیچ *hēch*.

Null, باطل *bāṭil,* ردي *raddī,* منسوخ *mansūkh,* لاحاصل *lā-ḥāṣil.*
Numberless, بيشمار *bē-shumār,* انگنت *anginat,* بيحساب *bē-ḥisāb.*
Numerous, بہت *bahut,* کثير *kaṣīr,* وافر *wāfir.*
Nuptial, نکاحي *nikāḥī,* شاديانه *shādiyāna,* عروسي *ʿurūsī.*
Obdurate, سخت *sakht,* ناترس *nā-tars,* مگرا *magrā,* ڈھيٹھ *ḍhīṭh.*
Obedient, مطيع *muṭīʿ,* فرمانبردار *farmānbardār,* رام *rām.*
Objective (case), مفعول *mafʿūl,* مفعولي *mafʿūlī.*
Obliging, عميم‌الاحسان *ʿāmīmu-l-iḥsān,* خليق *khalīḳ.*
Oblique, کج *kaj,* ٹيڑھا *ṭēṛhā,* ترچھا *tirchhā,* کوناکوني *kōnākōnī.*
Oblong, کتابي *kitābī,* مربع‌مستطيل *murabbaʿ-i-mustaṭīl.*
Obscene, فاحش *fāḥish,* پوچ *pūch,* پھوھڑ *phūhaṛ,* ناپاک *nā-pāk.*
Obscure, تاريک *tārīk,* اندھيرا *andhērā,* (abstruse) مغلق *mughlaḳ.*
Obsequious, ادھين *adhīn,* تابعدار *tābiʿdār,* خايه‌بردار *khāya-bardār.*
Obsolete, متروک *matrūk,* منسوخ *mansūkh,* بيرواج *bē-rawāj.*
Obstinate, مگرا *magrā,* مچلا *machlā,* ہٹھي *haṭhī.*
Occasional, اتفاقي *ittifāḳī,* عارضي *ʿāriẓī,* داؤگھاتي *dāʼō-ghātī.*
Occult, پوشيده *pōshīda,* چھپا *chhipā,* مخفي *makhfī,* گپت *gupt.*
Octagon, Octangular, مثمن *muṣamman,* ہشت پہلو *hasht-pahlū.*
Odd, (unpaired) پھٹ *phuṭ,* طاق *ṭāḳ,* (in number) فرد *fard:* see Strange.
Odious, مکروه *makrūh,* گھنونا *ghinaunā,* کريه *karīh.*
Odoriferous, خوشبودار *khush-bō-dār,* معطر *muʿaṭṭar,* سباس *subās.*
Off, (distant) دور *dūr* (f.), سي *sē;* (be off!) دور ہو *dūr hō!* دت *dut!*
Offensive, (unpleasant) ناپسند *nā-pasand,* کريه *karīh:* see Hurtful.
Oft, Often, اکثر *akṣar,* بارہا *bārhā,* باربار *bār bār,* دفعتاً *dafʿatan.*
Oily, روغندار *raughan-dār,* روغني *raughanī,* چکنا *chiknā.*
Old, پرانا *purānā,* قديم *ḳadīm,* (as a man) بوڑھا *būṛhā.*
Omnipotent, قادرمطلق *ḳādir-i-muṭlaḳ,* ضابط الکل *ẓābiṭu-l-kull.*
Omnipresent, حاضر و ناظر *ḥāẓir ō nāẓir,* دانا و بينا *dānā ō bīnā.*
Omniscient, عالم‌الغيب *ʿālimu-l-ghaib,* همه‌دان *hama-dān.*
Once, ايک بار *ēk bār,* ايک دفعه *ēk dafʿa,* (formerly) آگي *āgē.*
At once, all at once, ايک بارگي *ēk bārgī,* ايک لخت *ēk lakht.*
Oneeyed, کانا *kānā,* ايک چشم *ēk chashm.*

Only, (adv.) صرف *ṣirf*, محض *maḥẓ*, (adj.) اكلوتا *iklautā:* see Single.

Onward, آگي *āgē*, بڑهكي *baṛhkē*, ادهر *udhar*, بتدريج *ba-tadrīj*.

Opaque, كثيف *kaṣīf*, غير شفاف *ghair shaffāf*.

Open, كهلا *khulā*, كشاده *kushāda*, واز *wāz*, (evident) ظاهر *ẓāhir*.

Openly, ظاهراً *ẓāhiran*, برملا *barmalā*, كهلا كهلا *khulā khulā*.

Opiniative, خود راٴي *khud-rā'ē*, خودپسند *khud-pasand*, مگرا *magrā*.

Opportune, Opportunely, بروقت *bar-waḳt*, برموقع *bar-mauḳa'*.

Opposite, مقابل *muḳābīl*, مخالف *mukhālif*, سامهني *sāmhnē*.

Ordinary, رسمي *rasmī*, چلني *chalanī*, (middling) مدهم *maddham*.

Organic (constitutional), خلقي *khilḳī*, ذاتي *ẕātī*, اصلي *aṣlī*.

Oriental, شرقي *sharḳī*, مشرقي *mashraḳī*, پوربي *pūrbī*.

Original, اصلي *aṣlī*, پهلا *pahlā*, (as writing) منقول عنه *manḳūl ánhu*.

Other, اور *aur*, دوسرا *dūsrā*, ديگر *dīgar*, غير *ghair*, پر *par*.

Otherwise, اور طرح *aur ṭarah*, ورنه *war na*, كچهه اور *kuchh aur*.

Oval, بيضه شكل *baiẓa-shakl*, بيضوي *baiẓawī*.

Over, اوپر *ūpar*, پر *par*, بالا *bālā*, (across) آڙي *āṛē*, پار *pār*.

Overboard, جهاز سي باهر *jahāz sē bāhar*.

Overcast (clouded), گهنگهور *ghanghōr*, اندهيرا *andhērā*.

Overhead, سر پر *sir par*, اوپر *ūpar*, بالا *bālā*.

Out, باهر *bāhar* or *bāhir*, بيرون *bērūn*, خارج *khārij*, سي *sē*.

Outcast, مردود *mardūd*, آواره *āwāra*, خارج *khārij*.

Outlandish, اجنبي *ajnabī*, بديسي *bidēsī*, (queer) بيرواج *bē-rawāj*.

Outright, صاف *ṣāf*, پورا *pūrā*, هي *hī*, بلا توقف *bilā tawaḳḳuf*.

Outward, باهر كو *bāhar kō*, باهري *bāharī*, بيروني *bērūnī*.

Outwardly, ظاهراً *ẓāhiran*, ظاهر اسباب *ẓāhir asbāb*.

Own, اپنا *apnā*, نج كا *nij kā*, خود كا *khud kā*, خاص *khāṣṣ*.

Pale, Pallid, زرد *zard*, پيلا *pīlā*, سيٹها *sīṭhā*, پهيكا *phīka*.

Parallel, برابر *barābar*, مساوي *musāwī*, محاذي *muḥāẕī*.

Partial, خاص *khāṣṣ*, (biassed) متعصب *mata'áṣṣib*.

Particular, خاص *khāṣṣ*, مخصوص *makhṣūṣ:* see Intimate.

Particularly, خصوصاً *khuṣūṣan*, الگ الگ *alag alag*, مفصلاً *mufaṣṣalan*.

Passionate, غصه‌ور *ghuṣṣa-war*, تندخو *tund-khō*.

Past, گذشته *guzashta*, گیا *gayā*, گذرا *guzrā*, (in gram.) ماضي *māẓī*.
Pat (fit, exact, fitly), ٹھیک *ṭhīk*, لائق *lā'iḳ*, تیار *taiyār*.
Paternal, پدري *pidarī*, پدرانه *pidarāna*, ابوي *abwī*.
Patient, صابر *ṣābir*, شکیبا *shikēbā*, (one sick) مریض *marīẓ*.
Peace! چپ *chup!* خاموش *khāmōsh!*
Peculiar, خاص *khāṣṣ*, مخصوص *makhṣūṣ*, نج کا *nij kā*.
Peevish, چڑچڑا *chiṛchiṛā*, زودرنج *zūd-ranj*.
Penitent, مستغفر *mustaghfir*, نادم *nādim*, پشیمان *pashēmān*.
Penultimate, ما قبل آخر *mā ḳabl ākhir*.
Peremptory, (decisive) قاطع *ḳāṭiʻ*, (absolute) لارد *lā-radd*.
Perfect, کامل *kāmil*, پورا *pūrā*, (faultless) بي‌عیب *bē-ʻaib*.
Perfectly, بالکل *bi-l-kull*, تمام و کمال *tamām ō kamāl*.
Perfidious, نمک‌حرام *namak-ḥarām*, بیوفا *bē-wafā*.
Perhaps, شاید *shāyad*, هوگا *hōgā*, اتفاقاً *ittifāḳan*.
Pernicious, مضر *muẓirr*, مفسد *mufsid*, زبون *zabūn*.
Perpetual, دائمي *dā'imī*, باقي *bāḳī*, استمراري *istimrārī*, قائم *ḳā'im*.
Perpetually, همیشه *hamēsha*, سدا *sadā*, علي الدوام *ʻala-d-dawām*.
Persian, فارسي *fārsī*.
Pert, شوخ *shōkh*, چنچل *chanchal*, ڈھیٹھ *ḍhīṭh*, مچلا *machlā*.
Pertinent, لائق *lā'iḳ*, شایسته *shāyasta*, مناسب *munāsib*.
Perverse, ضدي *ẓiddī*, هٹھیلا *haṭhīlā*, مچلا *machlā*.
Petty, چھوٹا *chhōṭā*, خورد *khurd*, کم مایه *kam-māya*, نیچ *nīch*.
Piebald, ابلق *ablaḳ*, کبرا *kabrā*, چتکبرا *chitkabrā*.
Pious, متقي *muttaḳī*, صالح *ṣāliḥ*, بھگت *bhagat*, دھرمي *dharmī*.
Pish! اف *uf*, پھش *phish*, چھي *chhī*.
Piteous, Pitiable, Pitiful, درد انگیز *dard-angēz*.
Plain, برابر *barābar*, هموار *hamwār*, (simple) ساده *sāda*: see Clear.
Plain, Plainly (adv.), ظاهراً *ẓāhiran*, صاف *ṣāf*, راستي سي *rāstī sē*.
Playful, الولا *alōlā*, چنچل *chanchal*, اچپل *achpal*, شوخ *shōkh*.
Pleasant, خوش *khush*, اچھا *achchhā*, لذیذ *laẕīẕ*: see Cheerful.
Plenteous, Plentiful, بهت *bahut*, کثیر *kaṡīr*, مالامال *mālāmāl*.
Plump, موٹا *mōṭā*, موٹلا *mōṭlā*, تر و تازه *tar ō tāza*.

Pointed, نوكدار *nōk-dār*, نوكيلا *nōkīlā*, هجوآميز *hajō-āmēz*.

Poisonous, زهردار *zahr-dār*, زهري *zahrī*, سمي *sammī*.

Polite, خليق *khalīk*, خوش اخلاق *khush-akhlāk*.

Politic, Political, ملكي *mulkī*, تدبيري *tadbīrī*: see Cunning.

Poor, (weak) ضعيف *za'īf*, (lean) كنگال *kangāl*, (needy) مفلس *muflis*.

Popular, هر دل عزيز *har dil ăzīz*, (usual) مروج *murauwaj*.

Populous, آباد *ābād*, معمور *ma'mūr*, لوگ سي بهرپور *lōg sē bhar-pūr*.

Positive (certain), يقيني *yakīnī*, لارد *lā-radd*, بيشك *bē-shakk*.

Positively, يقيناً *yakīnan*, بالضرورت *bi-z-zarūrat*: see Certainly.

Possible, ممكن *mumkin*, هونهار *hōnhār*, شدني *shudanī*.

Potbellied, توندیلا *tōndailā*, سبوشکم *sabū-shikam*.

Potent, زوراور *zōrāwar*, طاقتمند *ṭākatmand*, قوي *kuwī*.

Powerful, بلونت *balwant*, شهزور *shah-zōr*, زبردست *zabardast*.

Precious, قيمتي *kīmatī*, بيش بها *bēsh-bahā*, عزيز *ăzīz*.

Precise, (exact) ٹهيک *ṭhīk*, دقيق *dakīk*, (formal) قانوني *kānūnī*.

Pre-eminent, فائق *fā'ik*, افضل *afzal*, ممتاز *mumtāz*.

Pregnant, حامله *hāmila*, پيٹ سي *pēṭ sē*, بهرا *bharā*.

Present, حاضر *hāzir*, روبرو *rūbarū*, موجود *maujūd*, سامني *sāmnē*.

Presently, ابهي *ab-hī*, اب *ab*, في الفور *fi-l-faur*.

Presumptuous, شوخ *shōkh*, گستاخ *gustākh*: see Bold, Arrogant.

Pretty, ستهرا *suthrā*, see Beautiful, (in some degree) كچه *kuchh*.

Prevailing, Prevalent, (common) مروج *murauwaj*: see Victorious.

Previous, Previously, قبل *kabl*, آگي *āgē*, پهلي *pahlē*, پيشين *pēshīn*.

Primitive, Primeval, اصلي *aṣlī*, پهلا *pahlā*, آدو *ādau*: see Ancient.

Principal, اول *awwal*, بڑا *baṛā*, پهلا *pahlā*, (essential) اصلي *aṣlī*.

Principally, پهلي *pahlē*, خصوصاً *khuṣūṣan*, غالباً *ghāliban*.

Private, چهپا *chhipā*, نهفته *nihufta*, (own) خاص *khāṣṣ*, نج *nij*.

Probable, هونهار *hōnhār*, محتمل *muhtamil*, غالب *ghālib*.

Probably, شايد *shāyad*, هوي *hō'ē*, غالباً *ghāliban*, چاهيي *chāhiyē*.

Profitable, فايده‌مند *fā'ida-mand*, مفيد *mufīd*, سودمند *sūdmand*.

Profligate, فاسق *fāsik*, فاجر *fājir*, رند *rind*, بدكار *badkār*.

Prolix, طويل *ṭawīl*, طول كلام *ṭūl-kalām*, بستاري *bistārī*.

Prompt, تیار *taiyār*, حاضر *ḥāẓir*, چالاک *chālāk*, چوکس *chaukas*.
Proper, نج *nij*, خاص *khāṣṣ*, (fit) مناسب *munāsib*, ٹھیک *ṭhīk*.
Properly, جیسا چاهیے *jaisā chāhiyē*, کما ینبغي *kamā yambaghī*.
Proud, مغرور *maghrūr*, متکبر *mutakabbir*, مگرا *magrā*.
Prudent, هوشیار *hōshyār*, زیرک *zīrak*, چوکس *chaukas*.
Pshaw ! پهش *phish*, اف *uf*, چهي *chhī*.
Public, (common) عام *ʿāmm*, شامل *shāmil*, (manifest, q. v.) ظاهر *ẓāhir*.
Pugnacious, لڑاکا *laṛākā*, جنگي *jangī*, جهگڑالو *jhagṛālū*.
Punctual, ٹھیک *ṭhīk*, سچا *sachchā*, وعده وفا *waʿda-wafā*.
Pungent, حاد *ḥādd*, تیز *tēz*, تند *tund*, پڑپڑا *paṛpaṛā*.
Pure, خالص *khāliṣ*, صاف *ṣāf*, نرمل *nirmal*: see Genuine.
Purple, ارغواني *arghawānī*, لال نیلامیز *lāl-nīlāmēz*.
Putrid, سڑا *saṛā*, گلا *galā*, گنده *ganda*, بوسیده *bōsīda*.
Quadrangular, مربع *murabbaʿ*, چوگوشه *chau-gōsha*.
Quadrilateral, چوپهلو *chau-pahlū*.
Quadriliteral, چوحرفي *chau-ḥarfī*.
Quadruple, چوگنا *chaugunā*, چارچند *chār-chand*.
Quarrelsome, جهگڑالو *jhagṛālū*, قضیه جو *ḳaẓiya-jō*.
Queer, عجب *ʿajab*, عجیب *ʿajīb*, تماشیدار *tamāshēdār*.
Quick, جلدباز *jald-bāz*, چالاک *chālāk*, تیز *tēz*: see Alive.
Quickly, جلدي *jaldī*, ترنت *turant*, جهٹپٹ *jhaṭpaṭ*.
Quiet, Quiescent, ساکن *sākin*, (silent) چپ *chup*: see Still.
Quietly, دهیمي *dhīmē*, آهستي *āhistē*, آهسته *āhista*.
Quintuple, پنچگنا *panchgunā*, پانچتها *pānchtahā*.
Quite, بالکل *bi-l-kull*, خوب *khūb*, پورا *pūrā*, بعینه *bi-ʿainih*.
Radical, اصلي *aṣlī*, ذاتي *ẕātī*, بنیادي *bunyādī*.
Random, بیقصد *bē-ḳaṣd*. At Random, اٹکل پچو *aṭkal pachchū*.
Rapid, تیز *tēz*, تیزرو *tēz-rau*, جلد *jald*, تند *tund*.
Rare, نادر *nādir*, کمیاب *kam-yāb*, عجیب *ʿajīb*, برلا *birlā*.
Rash, اتاولا *utāʾōlā*, بیلحاظ *bē-liḥāẓ*, جلد *jald*, تیز *tēz*.
Rather, اول *awwal*, پهلي *pahlē*, پیشتر *pēshtar*, قبل *ḳabl*.
Rational, معقول *maʿḳūl*, عقلي *ʿaḳlī*, ناطق *nāṭiḳ*.

Raw, کچا *kachchā,* ناپخته *nā-pukhta,* (as skin) بیجلد *bē-jild.*

Ready, تیار *taiyār,* آماده *āmāda,* مستعد *musta'idd.*

Real, حقیقي *ḥaḳīḳī,* یقیني *yaḳīnī,* سچا *sachchā,* اصلي *aṣlī.*

Really, سچ *sach,* حقیقتاً *ḥaḳīḳatan,* في الواقع *fi-l-wāḳi'.*

Reasonable, عقلي *'aḳlī,* درست *durust,* ٹھیک *ṭhīk:* see Rational.

Rebel, Rebellious, باغي *bāghī,* سرکش *sarkash,* تاغي *tāghī.*

Recent, نیا *nayā,* نو *nau,* جدید *jadīd,* تازه *tāza,* تٹکا *taṭkā.*

Reciprocal, دوطرفي *dō-ṭarfī,* جانبین *jānibain.*

Reciprocally, آپس میں *āpas mēn,* جانبین سي *jānibain sē.*

Recumbent, متکي *muttakī,* تکیه‌زده *takiya-zada.*

Red, لال *lāl,* سرخ *surkh,* راتا *rātā,* احمر *aḥmar.*

Redundant, زیاده *ziyāda,* بہت *bahut,* ادهک *adhik.*

Regular, با قاعده *bā-ḳā'ida,* قیاسي *ḳiyāsī,* ٹھیک *ṭhīk.*

Relative to, متعلق *muta'allik,* بنسبت *ba-nisbat.*

Relaxed, ڈهیلا *ḍhīlā,* سست *sust,* کاهل *kāhil.*

Remediless, لاعلاج *lā-'ilāj,* لاچار *lā-chār,* ناچار *nā-chār.*

Remiss, ڈهیلا *ḍhīlā,* سست *sust,* مجهول *maj'hul,* غافل *ghāfil.*

Remote, دور *dūr,* دوردست *dūr-dast,* بعید *ba'īd.*

Renowned, نامور *nām-war,* نیک نام *nēk-nām,* مشهور *mash'hūr.*

Repeatedly, باربار *bār-bār,* دفعتاً *daf'atan,* پهرپهرکي *phir-phirkē.*

Reprobate, گیاگذرا *gayā-guzrā,* خراب *kharāb,* رند *rind.*

Resolute, مستقل *mustaḳill,* مضبوط *mazbūt,* استوار *ustuwār.*

Restiff, Restive, Resty, مچلا *machlā,* چلبدهرا *chalbidhrā.*

Restless, بي آرام *bē-ārām,* بیقرار *bē-ḳarār,* بیکل *bē-kal.*

Reverend, بزرگ *buzurg,* مکرم *mukarram,* حضرت *ḥazrat.*

Rich, دولتمند *daulatmand,* زردار *zar-dār:* see Fruitful, Sweet.

Right, درست *durust,* ٹھیک *ṭhīk,* راست *rāst,* (hand) دهنا *dahnā.*

Righteous, نیک *nēk,* بهلا *bhalā,* راستباز *rāst-bāz,* صادق *ṣādiḳ.*

Riotous, Rioter, دنگیباز *dangēbāz,* فتنه انگیز *fitna-angēz.*

Ripe, پکا *pakkā,* پخته *pukhta,* رسیده *rasīda,* پورا *pūrā.*

Rotten, سڑا *saṛā,* گلا *galā,* بوسیده *bōsīda,* گنده *ganda.*

Rough, کهرکهرا *kharkharā,* (rugged) اڑبڑ *aṛbaṛ:* see Harsh.

Round, گول *gōl*, چکریلا *chakrēlā*, مدور *mudauwar*.

Royal, شاهي *shāhī*, پادشاهي *pādshāhī*, شاهانه *shāhāna*.

Rude, بي ادب *bē-adab*, گستاخ *gustākh*: see Ignorant, Clumsy.

Rural, Rustic, ديهي *dīhī*, گانوي *gāṅwī*: see Peasant.

Russet, گندم رنگ *gandum-rang*, فندقي *finduḳī*.

Rusty, زنگ آلوده *zang-ālūda*, مرچاها *murchāhā*.

Ruthless, بيرحم *bē raḥm*, سنگدل *sang-dil*, بيدرد *bē-dard*.

Sacred, مقدس *muḳaddas*, پاک *pāk*, مجيد *majīd*, پبتر *pabitr*.

Sad, اداس *udās*, غمگين *gham-gīn*, ملول *malūl*, محزون *maḥzūn*.

Safe, مامون *māmūn*, محفوظ *maḥfūẓ*, سلامت *salāmat*.

Sallow, سانولا *sāṅwlā*, پهيکا *phīkā*, پيلا *pīlā*, ملين *malīn*.

Same, وهي *wuh-ī*, يهي *yih-ī*, ايکهي *ēk-hī*, همان *hamān*, برابر *barābar*.

Sandy, ريتلا *rētlā*, ريتيلا *rētīlā*, ريگي *rēgī*, بلوا *balū'ā*, کرکرا *kirkirā*.

Sanguine, پرخون *pur-khūn*, خوندار *khūn-dār*: see Confident.

Savage, (wild) جنگلي *janglī*, وحشي *waḥshī*: see Cruel.

Saucy, گستاخ *gustākh*, ڈهيٹه *ḍhīṭh*, بي ادب *bē-adab*, شوخ *shōkh*.

Save, Saving, سوا *siwā*, چهوڑکي *chhōṛkē*: see Except.

Savoury, مزه دار *maza-dār*, لذيذ *laẕīẕ*, خوشگوار *khushguwār*.

Scabby, خارشتي *khārishtī*, کهسراپر *khasrā-pur*: see Mean.

Scandalous, معيوب *ma'yūb*, مذموم *maẕmūm*, زبون *zabūn*.

Scant, Scanty, Scarce, کم *kam*, قليل *ḳalīl*, تهوڑا *thōṛā*: see Rare.

Scarce, Scarcely, کم *kam*, کمتر *kamtar*, دقت سي *diḳḳat sē*.

Scarlet, سلطاني سرخ *sulṭānī surkh*, قرمزي رنگ *ḳirmizī rang*.

Seasonable, بروقت *bar-waḳt*, با موقع *bā mauḳa'*, برمحل *bar-maḥall*.

Second, دوسرا *dūsrā*, ثاني *sānī*, دويم *dōyam*, (inferior) کم *kam*.

Second-hand, مستعمل *musta'mal*, اتارا *utārā*, استعمالي *isti'mālī*.

Secondly, دوسري *dūsrē*, ثانياً *sāniyan*.

Secret, پوشيده *pōshīda*, مخفي *makhfī*, چهپا *chhipā*, غايب *ghā'ib*.

Secretly, خفيتاً *khufyatan*, خفيه *khufya*, چهپاکي *chhipākē*.

Secure, مامون *māmūn*, محفوظ *maḥfūẓ*, بي خطره *bē-khatra*.

Sedate, آهسته *āhista*, دهيما *dhīmā*, دهيرا *dhīrā*, قرار *ḳarār*.

Seemly, شايسته *shāyasta*, دکهاؤ *dikhā'ū*, آراسته *ārāsta*.

Seldom, كم *kam,* شاذ *shāzz,* تهوڑا *thōṛā,* كبهي كبهي *kabhī kabhī.*

Selfish, غرضمند *gharazmand,* خود غرض *khud-gharaz.*

Senior, بڑا *baṛā,* كبير *kabīr,* كلان *kalān,* قديم *ḳadīm.*

Senseless, بيحس *bē-ḥiss,* سن *sun,* بيجان *bē-jān:* see Stupid.

Sensible, قابل حس *ḳābil-i-ḥiss,* محسوس *maḥsūs:* see Intelligent.

Sensual, نفساني *nafsānī,* شهوتي *shahwatī,* رسيا *rasiyā.*

Separate, جدا *judā,* الگ *alag,* تفاوت *tafāwut,* نيارا *nyārā.*

Separately, جدا جدا *judā judā,* الگ الگ *alag alag,* ايک ايک *ēk ēk.*

Septuple, ستپرتا *sat-partā,* ستگنا *sat-gunā,* هفت تها *haft-tahā.*

Several, متفرق *mutafarriḳ,* (many) بهت *bahut,* بعضي *ba*ẓē.*

Severe, تند *tund,* تيز *tēz,* سخت *sakht,* درشت *durusht.*

Shabby, پجوڑا *pajōṛā,* گدڑپوش *gudaṛ-pōsh* (?): see Mean.

Shallow, اتهلا *uthlā,* كم عمق *kam-ŭmuḳ,* (silly) اوچها *ōchhā.*

Sham, جهوٹها *jhūṭhā,* عملي *ămalī,* سوانگي *swāngī,* نقلي *naḳlī.*

Shameful, شرماور *sharm-āwar,* لجاؤ *lajā'ū:* see Bad, Vitious.

Shameless, بيشرم *bē-sharm,* بيحيا *bē-ḥayā,* گستاخ *gustākh.*

Sharp, تيز *tēz,* بران *burrān,* چوكها *chōkhā:* see Acid, Pointed.

Shocking, نفرت انگيز *nafrat-angēz,* وحشت انگيز *waḥshat-angēz.*

Short, چهوٹا *chhōṭā,* كوتاه *kōtāh,* تهوڑا *thōṛā,* كم *kam.*

Shortly, جلد *jald,* عن قريب *ăn-ḳarīb,* كوي دم ميں *kō'ī dam mēṅ.*

Showy, نمائيشي *numā'ishī,* نمودار *namūdār,* بهڑكيلا *bhaṛkīlā.*

Shrewd, تيزهوش *tēz-hōsh,* پكا *pakkā,* سيانا *siyānā.*

Shrill, تيز *tēz,* مهين *mihīn,* باريک *bārīk.*

Shy, بهڑكيل *bhaṛkēl,* وحشي *waḥshī,* محجوب *maḥjūb.*

Sick, بيمار *bīmār,* آزاري *āzārī,* روگي *rōgī:* see Displeased.

Signal, عجيب *ăjīb,* اچنبها *achambhā,* مشهور *mash'hūr.*

Silence! (interj.), چپ *chup,* خاموش *khāmōsh.*

Silent, خاموش *khāmōsh,* چپ چاپ *chup-chāp,* ساكت *sākit.*

Silken, Silky, ريشمي *rēshmī,* پاٹي *pāṭī,* حريري *ḥarīrī.*

Silly, بهولا *bhōlā,* نادان *nā-dān,* ساده *sāda,* كچا *kachchā.*

Similar, برابر *barābar,* ايک سان *ēk-sān,* متساوي *mutasāwī.*

Simple, (plain) ساده *sāda,* (single) مفرد *mufrad:* see Silly, Mere.

Since, (conj.) اسواسطيكه *is-wāsṭēki,* جبكه *jab-ki,* (adv.) آگي *āgē.*
Sincere, راست *rāst,* صادق *ṣādiḳ,* راستباز *rāst-bāz,* سچا *sachchā.*
Sinful, گناهگار *gunāh-gār,* پاپي *pāp-ī,* عاصي *āṣī,* ناپاك *nā-pāk.*
Single, اكيلا *akēlā,* تنها *tanhā,* (not married) مجرد *mujarrad.*
Singular, (uncommon) عجيب *ajīb,* (in gram.) واحد *wāḥid:* see Rare.
Sirrah! ابي *abē,* اري *arē,* بي *bē,* ري *rē,* (fem.) اري *arī,* ري *rī.*
Situate, واقع *wāḳiʿ,* موضوع *mauẓūʿ,* ركها *rakhā,* پڑا *paṛā.*
Skilful, ماهر *māhir,* واقف *wāḳif,* قابل *ḳābil,* گني *gunī.*
Slack, ڈهيلا *ḍhīlā,* سست *sust,* (as a knot) پهسكا *phuskā:* see Loose.
Slant, Slanting, ترچها *tirchhā,* ٹيڑها *ṭēṛhā,* ڈهالو *ḍhālū.*
Sleek, چكنا *chiknā,* صاف *ṣāf:* see Smooth.
Sleepy, نينداسا *nindāsā,* خوابناك *khwāb-nāk,* اونگهاسا *ūnghāsā.*
Slender, پتلا *patlā,* چهين *chhīn,* باريك *bārīk,* نازك *nāzuk.*
Slight, پتلا *patlā,* كاغذي *kāghazī,* تنك *tunuk,* چهوٹا *chhōṭā.*
Slim, پتلا *patlā,* باريك *bārīk,* دبلا *dublā,* نازك *nāzuk.*
Slippery, چكنا *chiknā,* پهسلها *phislahā,* (uncertain) ناقرار *nā-ḳarār.*
Slope, Sloping, ڈهالو *ḍhālū,* اتارو *utārū,* سرازير *sarāzēr.*
Sloppy, پنكيلا *pankīlā,* كچيلا *kuchailā,* جل تهل *jal-thal:* see Dirty.
Slothful, سست *sust,* كاهل *kāhil,* آرام طلب *ārām-ṭalab.*
Slovenly, بيسليقه *bē-salīḳa,* غليظ *ghalīẓ,* چركين *chirkīn.*
Slow, آهسته *āhista,* سست *sust,* ڈهيلا *ḍhīlā,* دهيما *dhīmā.*
Slowly, آهسته *āhista,* هولي هولي *haulē-haulē,* ديري سي *dērī sē.*
Sluggard, Sluggish, اسكتي *askatī,* آرام طلب *ārām-ṭalab.*
Sly, سيانا *siyānā,* چتر *chatur,* فيلسوف *failsūf,* غدار *ghaddār.*
Small, چهوٹا *chhōṭā,* ننها *nannhā,* كوچك *kūchak,* خورد *khurd.*
Smart, (active) شتابكار *shitāb-kār,* پهرتيلا *phurtīlā:* see Keen.
Smoky, دهواندهار *dhū'āṅ-dhār,* دود آلوده *dūd-ālūda.*
Smooth, برابر *barābar,* هموار *hamwār,* چورس *chauras,* صاف *ṣāf.*
Smutty, (obscene) غليظ *ghalīẓ,* خرافاتي *khurāfātī:* see Dirty.
Snappish, كٹها *kaṭahā,* چڑچڑا *chiṛchiṛā,* هركيا *harkiyā.*
Snug, (private) پوشيده *pōshīda,* (neat) ستهرا *suthrā:* see Fit.
So, ايسا *aisā,* ويسا *waisā,* سو *sō,* اسطرح *is-ṭaraḥ,* يونهي *yūṅhī.*

Sober, هوشيار *hōshyār*, پرهيزگار *parhēzgār*, (grave) سنجيده *sanjīda*.
Sociable, ملنسار *milansār*, ملاپي *milāpī*, آشنا پرست *āshnā-parast*.
Soft, نرم *narm*, ملائم *mulā'im*, پلپلا *pilpilā*, كومل *kōmal*: see Easy.
Solar, Solary, شمسي *shamsī*, آفتابي *āftābī*.
Sole, اكلا *iklā*, اكيلا *akēlā*, تنها *tanhā*, مجرد *mujarrad*.
Solemn, (grave) سنجيده *sanjīda*, بهاري *bhārī*, (awful) عبرتي *ʿibratī*.
Solid, منجمد *munjamid*, ٹانٹها *ṭānṭhā*, ٹهوس *ṭhōs*, سخت *sakht*.
Solitary, تنها *tanhā*, اكلا *iklā*, نرالا *nirālā*: see Sole, Hermit.
Some, كچهه *kuchh*, كوئي *kō'ī*, كوئي ايك *kō'ī ēk*, چند *chand*: see Few.
Sonorous, پرآواز *pur-āwāz*, بلند آواز *buland-āwāz*.
Soon, جلدي *jaldī*, شتاب *shitāb*, بيگ *bēg*, حالي *ḥālī*, ابهي *abhī*.
Sore, پردرد *pur-dard*, دكهاؤ *dukhā'ū*. Sorely, شدت سي *shiddat sē*.
Sorrowful, دلگير *dilgīr*, غمگين *ghamgīn*, ملول *malūl*: see Sad.
Sorry, پشيمان *pashēmān*, (worthless) ناكاره *nā-kāra*: see Vile.
Sound, صحيح *ṣaḥīḥ*, سلامت *salāmat*, بهلا چنگا *bhalā changā*: see Firm.
Sour, ترش *tursh*, كهٹا *khaṭṭā*, چوك *chūk*, حامض *ḥāmiẓ*.
South, Southerly, Southern, دكهني *dakhnī*, جنوبي *janūbī*.
Spacious, واسع *wāsiʿ*, كشاده *kushāda*, پهيلا *phailā*, فراخ *farākh*.
Spare, قليل *ḳalīl*, تهوڑا *thōṛā*; (to spare) زياده *ziyāda*: see More.
Sparing, كفايتي *kifāyatī*, كم خرچ *kam-kharch*: see Economical.
Special, خاص *khāṣṣ*, مخصوص *makhṣūṣ*: see Great.
Specious, ظاهرنما *ẓāhir-numā*, صورت حرام *ṣūrat-ḥarām*.
Speechless, بيزبان *bē-zubān*, زبان بسته *zubān-basta*, انبول *anbōl*.
Speedily, جلدي سي *jaldī sē*, دوڑادوڑي سي *dauṛā-dauṛī sē*.
Spick and span new, ٹٹكا *ṭaṭkā*, تهدرز *tah-darz*, كورا *kōrā*.
Spirited, جاندار *jān-dār*, زنده دل *zinda-dil*, دلير *dilēr*.
Spirituous, Spiritous, تيز *tēz*, تند *tund*, چوكها *chokhā*.
Spiteful, كينه ور *kīna-war*, لاگي *lāgī*, كپٹي *kapaṭī*.
Splendid, چٹكيلا *chaṭkīlā*, بهڑكيلا *bhaṛkīlā*, رنگيلا *rangīlā*.
Spoken, بولا هوا *bōlā-hū'ā*, كها هوا *kahā-hū'ā*, گفته *gufta*.
Spontaneous, اختياري *ikhtiyārī*. Spontaneously, آپ سي *āp-sē*.
Sportive, خوش *khush*, خوش طبع *khush-ṭabʿ*, اچپل *achpal*.

Sprightly, چست *chust*, چابک *chābuk*, شوخ *shōkh*, هنسور *hańsōr*.
Spurious, جهوٹها *jhūṭhā*, جال *jāl*, لباسي *libāsī*, ساخته *sākhta*.
Square, مربع *murabba'*, چوکونا *chau-kōnā*, چوگوشه *chau-gōsha*.
Stable, برقرار *bar-ķarār*, قائم *ķā'im*, پائدار *pā'ēdār* : see Firm.
Stagnant, بند *band*, ناروان *nā-rawān*, ساکن *sākin*, تهر *thir*.
Standing, کهڑا *khaṛā*, قائم *ķā'im*, برپا *bar-pā* : see Stagnant.
Stark, (adj.) سخت *sakht*, لچ *luch*, (adv.) مطلق *muṭlaķ*, محض *maḥẓ*.
Stately, بڑا *baṛā*, عمده *'umda*, عاليشان *'ālī-shān*.
Stationary, ساکن *sākin*, استهر *asthir*, قائم *ķā'im* : see Standing.
Steadfast, قائم *ķā'im*, مستحکم *mustaḥkam*, اتل *atal*.
Steady, مضبوط *mazbūt*, استوار *ustuwār*, ثابت قدم *ṣābit-ķadam*.
Steep, کهڑا *khaṛā*, تهاڑه *ṭhāṛh*, اونچا *ūnchā*, اوگهٹ *aughaṭ*.
Sterling, سکه *sikka*, خالص *khāliṣ*, نرالا *nirālā*, چوکها *chōkhā*.
Stern, روکهي صورت *rūkhī-ṣūrat*, کڑوا *kaṛwā*, تلخ رو *talkh-rū*.
Sticky, (viscous, adhesive) چپچپا *chipchipā*, لسلسا *laslasā*.
Stiff, اکڑا *akṛā*, کڑا *kaṛā*, بجر *bajr*, (stubborn) مگرا *magrā*.
Still, تهر *thir*, کهڑا *khaṛā*, (silent) سنسان *sunsān*, چپ *chup*.
Stillborn, موا جنا *mū'ā janā*. Stingy, تنگچشم *tang-chashm*.
Stomachic, هاضم *hāẓim*, پاچک *pāchak*, مشتهي *mushtahī* (?).
Stormy, طوفاني *ṭūfānī*, اندهياها *andhiyāhā*, غضبناک *ghaẓabnāk*.
Stout, مضبوط *mazbūṭ*, قوي *ķawī*, چودنت *chau-dant*.
Straight, سيدها *sīdhā*, راست *rāst*. Straightways, ترنت *turant*.
Strait, سکرا *sakrā*, تنگ *tang*, ناپهن *nā-pahan*, چست *chust*.
Strange, (foreign) بيگانه *bēgāna*, (unusual) عجيب *'ajīb*.
Streaked, Streaky, دهاري *dhārī*, لهريا *lahriyā*, خطدار *khaṭṭ-dār*.
Strenuous, بجد *ba-jidd*, سرگرم *sar-garm*, مضبوط *mazbūṭ*.
Strict, سخت *sakht*, تنگ *tang*, (exact) دقيق *daķīķ*, ٹهيک *ṭhīk*.
Stringy, ريشه دار *rēsha-dār*, (viscous) لجلجا *lijlijā*.
Strong, قوي *ķawī*, زوراور *zōrāwar*, بلي *balī*, مضبوط *mazbuṭ*.
Stubborn, هٹهيلا *haṭhīlā*, مگرا *magrā*, اڑيل *aṛyal*, ضدي *ẓiddī*.
Studious, علم دوست *'ilm-dōst*, مطالعه دوست *muṭāla'ā-dōst*.
Stupendous, عجيب *'ajīb*, نادر *nādir*, ادبهت *adbhut*, عظيم *'aẓīm*.

Stupid, احمق *aḥmaḳ*, بيهوش *bē-hōsh*, بيوقوف *bē-wuḳūf*.
Sturdy, مستنڈہ *mustanḍa*, چودنت *chaudant*, بلونت *balwant*.
Subaltern, نيچا *nīchā*, تابع *tābiʿ*, کہتر *kihtar*: see Inferior.
Subject, تابعدار *tābiʿdār*, مغلوب *maghlūb*, متحمل *mutaḥammil*.
Sublime, معلي *muʿallā*, عالي *ʿālī*, عمده *ʿumda*, بلند *buland*.
Submissive, حلقه بگوش *ḥalḳa ba-gōsh*, دبيل *dabēl*: see Humble.
Subsequent, پچهلا *pichhlā*. Subsequently, پيچهي *pīchhē*.
Substantial, اصلي *aṣlī*, جوهري *jauharī*, جسماني *jismānī*: see Real.
Subterranean, زيرزمين *zēr-i-zamīn*, تحت الارض *taḥtu-l-arẓ*.
Subtile, Subtle, دقيق *daḳīḳ*, (witty) لطيف *laṭīf*, چترا *chaturā*: see Fine, Thin.
Successful, کامياب يا بيداربخت (هونا) *kām-yāb* or *bēdār-bakht* (*hōnā*).
Successive, متواتر *mutawātir*, متوالي *mutawālī*, لگاتار *lagātār*.
Successively, پي در پي *pai dar pai*, تابڑتوڑ *tābaṛtōṛ*, پيهم *paiham*.
Succulent, رسدار *ras-dār*, شاداب *shādāb*, رس بهرا *ras-bharā*.
Such, ويسا *waisā*, ايسا *aisā*, جيسا *jaisā*, اس طرح کا *is ṭarḥ kā*.
Sudden, ناگاهي *nāgāhī*. Suddenly, اچانک *achānak*, ناگهان *nāgahān*.
Sufficient, بس *bas*, کافي *kāfī*. Sufficiently, جيسا چاهيي *jaisā chāhiyē*.
Suitable, سزاوار *sazāwār*, موافق *muwāfiḳ*, سميل *sumēl*.
Sullen, مکدر *mukaddar*, برهم *barham*, ناخوش *nā-khush*.
Sultry, کهمس *khamas*, کهمسا *khamsā* (?), اکهمج *ukhmaj* (?).
Sundry, دوتين *dō tīn*, کئي ايک *kaʾī ēk*, بعضي *baʿẓē*, چند *chand*.
Superb, عظيم *ʿaẓīm*, کبير *kabīr*, عاليشان *ʿālīshān*, عمده *ʿumda*.
Superficial, اپرلا *uparlā*, اپرونچا *upraunchā*: see Shallow.
Superfine, بهت مهين *bahut mihīn*, باريک سي باريک *bārīk sē bārīk*.
Superfluous, زائد *zāʾid*, زائد الاحتياج *zāʾidu-l-iḥtiyāj*.
Superior, برتر *bartar*, اولا *aulā*, فائق *fāʾiḳ*, بڑا *baṛā*, اعلي *ʿālā*.
Superlative, افضل *afẓal*, سب سي بهلا يا بڑا *sab sē bhalā* or *baṛā*.
Supernatural, فوق العادت *fauḳu-l-ʿādat*.
Superstitious, متعصب *mutaʿaṣṣib*, وهمي *wahmī*.
Supine, اتان *utān*, اوردهه منه *ūrdh-muṅh*, چت *chit*: see Lazy.
Supple, نرم *narm*, لچکيلا *lachkīlā*, ملائم *mulāʾim*, چمڑا *chimṛā*.

Suppliant, Supplicating, ملتمس *multamis*, نيازمند *niyāzmand*.
Supreme, اعلا *a'lā*, برتر *bartar*, بڑا *baṛā*, صدر *ṣadr*.
Sure, يقين *yaḳīn*, واقعي *wāḳi'ī*. Surely, see Certainly.
Surly, تلخ *talkh*, کڑا *kaṛā*, چڑچڑا *chiṛchiṛā*, تلخرو *talkh-rū*.
Surreptitious, مسروق *masrūḳ*, فريب سي پايا هوا *farēb sē pāyā hū'ā*.
Suspicious, شکي *shakkī*, انديشه ناک *andēsha-nāk*, بهرميلا *bharmilā*.
Swampy, دلدلي *daldalī*. Swap, جهپ سي *jhap sē*: see Hasty.
Swarthy, سانولا *sāṅwlā*. Sweet, ميٹها *mīṭhā*, شيرين *shīrīn*.
Swift, جلد *jald*, تيز *tēz*, تيزرو *tēz-rau*, تند *tund*, بيگ *bēg*.
Symmetrical, باقرينه *bā-ḳarīna*, بااندازه *bā-andāza*.
Synonymous, مترادف *mutarādif*, هم معني *ham-ma'nī*.
Tacit, ساکت *sākit*, موني *maunī*, (implied) متضمن *mutaẓammin*.
Talkative, باتونيا *bātūniyā*, بکي *bakkī*, زيادهگو *ziyāda-gō*.
Tall, لنبا *lambā*, طويل *ṭawīl*, اونچا *ūnchā*, بلند *buland*.
Tame, هلا *hilā*, رام *rām*, حليم *ḥalīm*, (dull) کند *kund*.
Tangible, ممسوس *mamsūs*, ممکن المس *mumkinu-l-mass*.
Taper, گاودم *gāw-dum*. Tardily, آهستي *āhistē*, هولي *haulē*.
Tardy, ڈهيلا *ḍhīlā*, کاهل *kāhil*, مندا *mandā*, آهسته *āhista*.
Tart, ترش *tursh*, کهٹا *khaṭṭā*, کڑوا *kaṛwā*, سخت *sakht*.
Tasteful, مزهدار *maza-dār*, لذيذ *lazīz*, خوش ذائقه *khush-zā'iḳa*.
Tasteless, بيمزه *bē-maza*, بي لذت *bē-lazzat*, پهيکا *phīkā*.
Tawny, جهونرا *jhaunrā*, پيلا *pīlā*, بهوررنگ *bhūrā-rang*.
Technical, اصطلاحي *iṣṭilāḥī*, حکمتي *ḥikmatī*, علمي *'ilmī*.
Tedious, ڈهيلا *ḍhīlā*, بهاري *bhārī*, طويل *ṭawīl*, تهکاؤ *thakā'ū*.
Temperate, معتدل *mu'tadil*, مدهم *maddham*: see Sober.
Tempestuous, طوفاني *ṭūfānī*, تيز و تند *tēz ō tund*: see Stormy.
Temporary, چندروزه *chand-rōza*, عارضي *'āriẓī*, فصلي *faṣlī*.
Tenacious, سختگير *sakht-gīr*, (viscous) لسلسا *laslasā*.
Tender, نرم *narm*, ملائم *mulā'im*, نازک *nāzuk*: see Kind.
Tenth, دسوان *daswāṅ*. Tepid, شيرگرم *shīr-garm*, گنگنه *gunguna*.
Terrestrial, ارضي *arẓī*, خاکي *khākī*, زميني *zamīnī*, دنياوي *dunyāwī*.
Terrible, Terrific, هولناک *haulnāk*, دهشت انگيز *dahshat-angēz*.

Testy, Tetchy, چڙچڙا *chiṛchiṛā*, تنکمزاج *tunuk-mizāj*.
Tete-a-tete, روبرو *rū-ba-rū*, دوبردو *dō-bar-dō*.
Than, سي *sē*, سين *sēṅ*, سون *sōṅ* or (dakh.) *sūṅ*, كه *ki*, از *az*.
That, (pron.) وه *wuh* or (dakh.) *wah*, اس *us*, (conj.) كه *ki*, كيونكه *kyūṅ-ki*.
Thee or to thee, تجهه كو *tujh kō* or تجهي *tujhē*. Their, انهكا *unh-kā*, &c.
Them, انهكو *unh-kō* or انهين *unhēṅ*. Themselves, وي آپ *wē āp*, &c.
Then, تب *tab*, تد *tad*, تو *tō*. Thence, وهان سي *wahāṅ sē*: see Therefore.
Thenceforth, Thenceforward, تس پيچهي *tis pīchhē*, تد سي *tad sē*.
Theoretic, Theoretical, خيالي *khiyālī*, قياسي *ḳiyāsī*, علمي *ʿilmī*.
There, وهان *wahāṅ*, ادهر *udhar*. Thereabout, لگبهگ *lag-bhag*.
Thereafter, بعد از آن *baʿd az ān*. Therefore, اس واسطي *us wāsṭē*.
These, يي *yē*. They, وي *wē*, يي *yē*, انهون ني *unhōṅ nē*.
Thick, (not thin) موٿا *mōṭā*, دلدار *daldār*, (close) گهنا *ghanā*.
Thin, پتلا *patlā*, دبلا *dublā*, تنک *tunuk*, رقيق *raḳīḳ*.
Thine, تيرا *tērā*, تور *tōr*. Third, تيسرا *tīsrā*, سيوم *siyūm*.
Thirsty, پياسا *pyāsā*, تشنه *tishna*, تشنه لب *tishna-lab*.
This, يهه *yih* or dakh. *yah*. Thither, ادهر *udhar*: see There.
Thorny, كٿيلا *kaṭīlā*, خاردار *khārdār*, (arduous) كٿهن *kaṭhin*.
Thorough, كامل *kāmil*, پورا *pūrā*. Thoroughly, سراسر *sarāsar*.
Those, وي *wē*. Thou, تو *tū*. Though, حال آنكه *ḥāl-ānki*: see Although.
Thoughtful, فكرمند *fikr-mand*, انديشه ناک *andēsha-nāk*.
Thoughtless, بيفكر *bē-fikr*, بيپروا *bē-parwā*, غافل *ghāfil*.
Threefold, تگنا *tigunā*, تلڙا *tilaṛā*, سهچند *si-chand*.
Threescore, تين كوڙي *tīn kōṛī*, ساٿهه *sāṭh*. Thrice, تين بار *tīn bār*.
Thrifty, جزرس *juz-ras*, كفايتي *kifāyatī*, كم خرچ *kam-kharch*.
Through, سراسر *sarāsar*, وارپار *wārpār*, (by means of) سي *sē*.
Throughout, سرتا پا *sar tā pā*, بهر *bhar*, تمام *tamām*.
Thunderstruck, بجلي مارا *bijlī-mārā*, گاج مارا *gāj-mārā*.
Thus, يون *yūṅ*, يونهي *yūṅhī*, ايسا *aisā*, اسطرح *is-ṭarḥ*.
Thwart, آڙا *āṛā*, ٹيڙها *ṭēṛhā*, ترچها *tirchhā*: see Across.
Thy, تيرا *tērā*, تور *tōr*. Thyself, تو آپ *tū āp*, توهي *tū-hī*.
Tidy, آراسته *ārāsta*, لطيف *laṭīf*, ستهرا *suthrā*.

Tight, تنگ *tang*, چست *chust*, کشیده *kashīda*, سخت *sakht*.
Till, تک *tak* or dakh. تگ *tag*, تلک *talak* or dakh. تلگ *talag*.
Timely, بروقت *bar wakt*, برموقع *bar mauka*: see Early.
Timeserving, زمانه ساز *zamāna-sāz*, اهل زمان *ahl-i-zamān*.
Timid, Timorous, ڈرپوکنا *ḍar-pōknā*, ڈرالو *ḍarālū*.
Tiny, بہت چھوٹا *bahut chhōṭā*, ننھا *nannhā*, خورد *khurd*.
Tipsy, مست *mast*, متوالا *matwālā*, سرخوش *sar-khush*.
Tiresome, تھکاؤ *thakā'ū*, سہراؤ *sihrā'ū*, اداس *udās*.
To, کو *kō* or dakh. *kū*, کي تئيں *kē ta'īn*, تک *tak*, تلک *talak*.
Together, ایک ساتھ *ēk sāth*, باهم *bāham*, سمیت *samēt*, اکٹھا *ikaṭṭhā*.
Tolerable, سہاؤ *sahā'ū*, سہنہار *sahanhār*, (passable) بین بین *bain-bain*.
Tonguetied, زبان بند *zabān-band*, گرفته زبان *girifta-zabān*.
Tonic (giving strength), مقوي معده *mukawwī-i-mi'da*.
Too, زیاده *ziyāda*, بہت *bahut*, نپٹ *nipaṭ*, حد سي *hadd sē*.
Toothless, پوپلا *pōplā*, مرلا *murlā*. Toper, پیوکڑ *pēwakkaṛ*.
Topsyturvy, الٹا پلٹا *ultā-pulṭā*, ته و بالا *tah ō bālā*.
Torpid, ٹھٹھرا *ṭhiṭharā*, سن *sun*, بيحس *bē-hiss*, سست *sust*.
Total, تمام *tamām*, کل *kull*, سب *sab*, پورا *pūrā*: see All.
Totally, سراپا *sarāpā*, جزو کل *juz-ō-kull*, بالکل *bi-l-kull*.
Tough, چمڑا *chimṛā*, سخت *sakht*, مضبوط *mazbūṭ*, چمٹھا *chimṭhā*.
Toward, Towards, کي طرف *kī ṭaraf*, کي جانب *kī jānib*, کي پاس *kē pās*.
Tractable, حکم بردار *hukm-bardār*, نرم *narm*, حليم *halīm*: see Docile.
Traditional, زباني *zabānī*, سماعي *samā'ī*, نقلي *naklī*.
Traitorous, دغاباز *daghābāz*, بيوفا *bē-wafā*, خائن *kha'in*.
Tranquil, تهر *thir*, آسوده *āsūda*, سنسان *sunsān*, سکهي *sukhī*.
Transient, Transitory, ناپائدار *nā-pā'ēdār*, فاني *fānī*, چنچل *chanchal*.
Transparent, شفاف *shaffāf*, براق *barrāk*, صاف *sāf*.
Transverse, آڑا *āṛā*, ترچھا *tirchhā*, بينڈا *bēnḍā*, ایرا *īrā* (?).
Treacherous, بي ایمان *bē-īmān*, غدار *ghaddār*, کپٹي *kapaṭī*.
Treble, Triple, تگنا *tigunā*, تہرا *tihrā*, سه چند *si-chand*.
Tremendous, مہیب *muhīb*, هولناک *haulnāk*, ڈراؤنا *ḍarā'ōnā*.
Triangular, مثلث *musallas*, تکونیا *tikōniyā*, سه گوشه *si-gōsha*.

Tributary, خراج گذار *khirāj-guzār*, باج گذار *bāj-guzār*: see Subject.
Triennial, سه ساله *si-sāla*, تساله *ti-sāla*, تين برسا *tīn-barsā*.
Trifling (trivial), هلكا *halkā*, سبك *subuk*, اوچها *ōchhā*.
Trim, آراسته *ārāsta*, زيبا *zēbā*, لطيف *latīf*, سازباز *sāz-bāz*.
Trite, پرانا *purānā*, ديرينه *dērīna*, (common) عام *āmm*.
Trivial, هلكا *halkā*, سبك *subuk*, بيقدر *bē-kadr*, ادنا *adnā*.
Troublesome, رنجاور *ranjāwar*, بهاري *bhārī*, مشكل *mushkil*.
Truant, سست *sust*, آواره *āwāra*, هرزه گرد *harza-gard*.
True, سچا *sachchā*, سچ *sach*, راست *rāst*: see Just, Faithful.
Truly, واقعي *wāki'ī*, في الحقيقت *fi-l-hakīkat*, سچ *sach*.
Trusty, Trust-worthy, معتبر *mu'tabir*, امانت دار *amānat-dār*.
Tumultuous, هلچلي *halchalī*, آشوبي *āshōbī*, دنگيت *dangait*.
Turbid, گدلا *gadlā*, مكدر *mukaddar*, گاڑها *gāṛhā*: see Dirty.
Turbulent, دنگيت *dangait*, دنگي باز *dangē-bāz*, هڑ دنگا *huṛ-dangā*.
Tush! Tut! پهش *phish*, چهي *chhī*. Twain, دو *dō*.
Twice, دوبارہ *dō-bāra*. Two-fold, دو تها *dō-tahā*, دگنا *dugnā*.
Typical, دال *dāll*, تمثيلي *tamsīlī*. Typically, تمثيلاً *tamsīlan*.
Tyrannical, ظالم *zālim*, ستمي *sitamī*, كٹهن *kaṭhin*: see Cruel.
Vacant, خالي *khālī*, تهي *tihī*, (unemployed) معطل *mu'attal*.
Vague, غير معين *ghair mu'aiyan*, نا معلوم *nā-ma'lūm*: see Doubtful.
Vain, (fruitless) بيفائده *bē-fā'ida*, باطل *bātil* لاحاصل *lā-hāsil*.
In vain, عبث *abas*, رايگان *rā'ēgān*, برباد *bar-bād*.
Valiant, دلير *dilēr*, بهادر *bahādur*, شجاع *shujā'*, دلچلا *dil-chalā*.
Valid, قائم *kā'im*, مستحكم *mustahkim*, ثابت *sābit*: see Firm.
Valuable, قيمتي *kīmatī*, گران مايه *girān-māya*, گران بها *girān-bahā*.
Vapid, بي مزه *bē-maza*, پهيكا *phīkā*, سيٹها *sīṭhā*: see Insipid.
Variable, متبدل *mutabaddil*, متلون *mutalauwin*: see Inconstant.
Various, متفرق *mutafarrik*, جدا جدا *judā-judā*, مختلف *mukhtalif*.
Vast, Vasty, بڑا *baṛā*, عظيم *azīm*, وسيع *wasī'*, اپار *apār*.
Vaulted, گمبذ دار *gumbaz-dār*, قبي دار *kubbē-dār*.
Vehement, شديد *shadīd*, سخت *sakht*, كڑا *kaṛā*, تيز *tēz*, تند *tund*.
Vendible, بيچني جوگ *bēchnē-jōg*, چلنتا *chalantā*, رواج *rawāj*.

Venerable, مکرم *mukarram,* معزز *mu'azzaz,* بزرگ *buzurg.*

Venomous, زهري *zahrī,* زهر دار *zahr-dār,* (noxious) موذي *mūẕī.*

Venturesome, Venturous, جان باز *jān-bāz:* see Bold.

Verbal, زباني *zabānī,* منهه بولا يا اکهري *muṅh-bōlā* or *-akhrī.*

Verbally, Verbatim, لفظاً *lafẓan,* لفظ بلفظ *lafẓ ba-lafẓ.*

Verbose, طول کلام *ṭūl-kalām,* طول طويل *ṭūl-ṭawīl,* پرگو *pur-gō.*

Verdant, سبز *sabz,* هرا *harā,* سرسبز *sar-sabz.*

Verily, see Truly, Certainly. Veritable, سچ *sach,* درست *durust.*

Vernacular, ديسي *dēsī.* Vernal, بهاري *bahārī,* ربيعي *rabī'ī.*

Versed, کاردان *kār-dān,* آزموده کار *āzmūda-kār:* see Skilful.

Very, (adj.) سچ *sach,* see True, Real: (adv.) بهت *bahut,* نپٹ *nipaṭ.*

Vexatious, آزارده *āzār-dih,* دل خراش *dil-kharāsh,* دکهه داۓ *dukh-dā'ī.*

Ugly, بد صورت *bad-ṣūrat,* زشت رو *zisht-rū,* بد ڈول *bad-ḍaul.*

Vicious, Vitious, عيبي *'aibī,* شرير *sharīr,* فاسد *fāsid:* see Bad.

Victorious, جيتو *jītū,* فتح ياب *fatḥ-yāb,* غالب *ghālib,* فيروز *fīrōz.*

Videlicet, يعني *ya'nē,* جانو *jānō.* Vigilant, آگاه *āgāh:* see Cautious.

Vigorous, زوراور *zōrāwar,* قوي *ḳawī,* زبردست *zabar-dast.*

Vile, نيچ *nīch,* پست *past,* ذليل *ẕalīl,* خوار *khwār,* دون *dūn.*

Villanous, پاجي *pājī,* نيچ *nīch,* رزاله *rizāla,* حقير *ḥaḳīr:* see Base.

Vindictive, کينه‌ور *kīna-war,* انتقام يا ويل کش *intiḳām-* or *wail-kash.*

Violent, شديد *shadīd,* سخت *sakht,* تند *tund.*

Violently, سخت *sakht.*

Virile, مردانه *mardāna.* Virtually, في الحقيقت *fi-l-ḥaḳīḳat.*

Virtuous, دهرمي *dharmī,* نيک *nēk,* بهلا *bhalā,* صالح *ṣāliḥ.*

Virulent, شديد *shadīd,* سخت *sakht.* Viscous, لجلجا *lajlajā.*

Visible, ظاهر *ẓāhir,* صريح *ṣarīḥ.* Visibly, ظاهراً *ẓāhiran.*

Visionary, وهمي *wahmī,* خيالي *khiyālī,* تصوري *taṣauwurī.*

Vital, زنده *zinda,* حيات منسوب *ḥayāt-mansūb,* جاندار *jān-dār.*

Vivacious, زنده دل *zinda-dil,* دل شاد *dil-shād,* مگن *magan.*

Vivid, (bright) روشن *rōshan,* (splendid) چٹکيلا *chaṭkīlā:* see Lively.

Ultimate, آخري *ākhirī.* Unable, بي مقدور *bē-maḳdūr:* see Weak.

Unacceptable, ناپسند *nā-pasand,* نامنظور *nā-manẓūr.*

Unaccoutred, بي ساز *bē-sāz*. Unaccustomed, بي ربط *bē-rabṭ*.
Unacquainted, ناواقف *nā-wāḳif*, اجان *ajān*.
Unaffected, بيساخته *bē-sā<u>kh</u>ta*. Unanimous, ايك دل *ēk-dil*.
Unanswerable, لارد *lā-radd*. Unarmed, نهتها *nihatthā*.
Unasked, بي طلب *be-ṭalab*. Unassisted, بي مدد *bē-madad*.
Unavoidable, لابد *lā-budd*. Unauthorised, بي سند *bē-sanad*.
Unaware, Unawares, اچانك *achānak*, ايكا ايك *ēk-ā-ēk*.
Unbecoming, نازيب *nā-zēb*, بد نما *bad-numā*: see Improper.
Unbidden (uninvited), انبلايا *an-bulāyā*, بيدعوت *be-da*wat*.
Unblamable, نردوكهي *nirdōkhī*, روسفيد *rū-sufaid*: see Faultless.
Unblemished, بيداغ *bē-dā<u>gh</u>*. Unblown, ناشگفته *nā-shigufta*.
Unborn, انجنا *anjanā*, ناپيدا *nā-paidā*, (future) آينده *āyanda*.
Unbound, (a book) غير مجلد *<u>gh</u>air mujallad*: see Loose.
Unbounded, اپار *apār*, بيحد *bē-ḥadd*, غير محدود *<u>gh</u>air-maḥdūd*.
Unbridled, بي لگام *bē-lagām*. Unburnt, انجلا *anjalā*.
Uncertain, غير مقرر *<u>gh</u>air muḳarrar*, مشكوك *mashkūk*.
Unchangeable, بي تبديل *bē-tabdīl*, بي زوال *bē-zawāl*, امٹ *amiṭ*.
Unchaste, شهوتي *shahwatī*, ناپاكدامن *nā-pākdāman*.
Uncivil, بدخلق *bad-<u>kh</u>ulḳ*, كج خلق *kaj-<u>kh</u>ulḳ*, بيسيل *bē-sīl*.
Unclean, see Filthy. Uncomfortable, ناخوش *nā-<u>kh</u>ush*.
Uncommon, كم ياب *kam-yāb*, انوٹها *anūṭhā*, نادر *nādir*.
Uncompounded, غير مركب *<u>gh</u>air murakkab*, انملا *an-milā*.
Uncontrollable, بيضبط *bē-ẓabṭ*, بيقيد *bē-ḳaid*, اروك *arōk*.
Uncouth, بهونڈا *bhōnḍā*, بي ڈهب *bē-ḍhab*, بي اسلوب *bē-aslūb*.
Uncultivated, غير مزروع *<u>gh</u>air mazrū*, پڑتي *paṛtī*, جنگلي *janglī*.
Undaunted, بيباك *bē-bāk*, ساهسي *sāhasī*.
Undecided, نامقرر *nā-muḳarrar*.
Undefiled, see Pure, Clean. Undefined, نامشخص *nā-musha<u>khkh</u>aṣ*.
Undeniable, بيدريغ *bē-dare<u>gh</u>*. Under, نيچي *nīchē*, تلي *talē*.
Underhand, پنهاني *pinhānī*, مخفي *mu<u>kh</u>fī*. Undermost, زيرتر *zērtar*.
Undeserved, غير واجب *<u>gh</u>air wājib*, ناحق *nā-ḥaḳḳ*.
Undesigned, بي قصد *bē-ḳaṣd*. Undesigning, بيغرض *bē-<u>gh</u>araẓ*.

Undetermined, غير مقرر *ghair mukarrar*, شكي مزاج *shakkī-mizāj.*

Undigested, غير منهضم *ghair munhazim*, نامرتب *nā-murattab.*

Undisciplined, بي قواعد *bē-kawā'id*, بيربط *bē-rabt.*

Undisguised, بيساخته *bē-sākhta*, كهلا *khulā*, بيلباس *bē-libās.*

Undone, (ruined) خراب *kharāb*, (opened) ادهرا *udhrā*, (not done) ادهورا *adhūrā.*

Undoubtedly, بيشك *bē-shakk*, اور كيا *aur kyā*, بي شبهه *bē-shubha.*

Undutiful, ناحكمي *nā-hukmī*, (son) ناخلف *nā-khalaf*, كپوت *kapūt.*

Uneasy, بي آرام *bē-ārām.* Unemployed, معطل *mu'attal.*

Unequal, Uneven, ناهموار *nā-hamwār*, نشيب فراز *nashēb farāz.*

Unequivocal, نامشكوك *nā-mashkūk*, صاف *sāf*, غير مبهم *ghair mubham.*

Unerring, اچوك *achūk*, بيخطا *bē-khatā*, نشان انداز *nishān-andāz.*

Unexampled, بي مثال *bē-misāl.* Unexpected, ناگهاني *nāgahānī.*

Unexperienced, ناتجربه كار *nā-tajriba-kār*, ناواقف *nā-wākif.*

Unexplored, انڈهونڈها *an-dhūndhā*, ناآزموده *nā-āzmūda.*

Unfading, انمرجهاؤ *an-murjhā'ū.* Unfair, ناراست *nā-rāst.*

Unfaithful, بيوفا *bē-wafā.* Unfashionable, بيرواج *bē-rawāj.*

Unfathomable, Unfathomed, اتها *athā*, اگم *agam.*

Unfavourable, نامهربان *nā-mihrbān*, نامسعد *nā-mus'ād.*

Unfeathered, بي پر و بال *bē par ō bāl.* Unfeeling, see Cruel.

Unfeigned, ابهگلي *abhaglī*, بيحيله *bē-hīla*, بيريا *bē-riyā.*

Unfelt, غير محسوس *ghair mahsūs*, انجان *anjān.*

Unfinished, ناتمام *nā-tamām*, بي انجام *bē-anjām*, ادهورا *adhūrā.*

Unfit, نالائق *nā-lā'ik*, ناشائسته *nā-shā'ista*, ناقابل *nā-kābil.*

Unforeseen, ناپيشديده *nā-pēsh-dīda*, ناديده *nā-dīda.*

Unfortunate, بدبخت *bad-bakht*, ابهاگي *abhāgī*, مفلوك *maflūk.*

Unfounded, بي ٹهكانا *bē-thikānā.* Unfrequent, see Uncommon.

Unfriendly, غير آشنا *ghair āshnā*, نامهربان *nā-mihrbān*, روكها *rūkhā.*

Unfruitful, اپهل *aphal*, نابهرهمند *nā-bahramand:* see Barren.

Unfurnished, بيساز *bē-sāz*, بي اسباب *bē-asbāb*, ناآراسته *nā-ārāsta.*

Ungain, Ungainly, بي نزاكت *bē-nazākat*, اناڑي *anāṛī:* see Uncouth.

Ungenerous, ناجوانمرد *nā-jawānmard.* Ungenial, ناموافق *nā-muwāfik.*

Ungenteel, ناخوش خلق *nā-khush-khulk*, ناشائسته *nā-shā'ista.*

Ungovernable, Ungoverned, بي ضبط و ربط *bē-zabt ō rabt:* see Disobedient.

Ungraceful, بدسج *bad-saj,* بيڈهب *bē-dhab,* بينزاكت *bē-nazākat.*

Ungracious, بينزاكت *bē-nazākat,* ناگوار *nā-gawār,* شرير *sharīr.*

Ungrateful, ناشكر *nā-shukr,* كافرنعمت *kāfir-i-ni'mat,* بيوفا *bē-wafā.*

Unhandsome, بدصورت *bad-sūrat,* نامعقول *nā-ma'kul.*

Unhappy, ناخوش *nā-khush,* ناخوشنود *nā-khushnūd:* see Unfortunate.

Unhealthful, Unhealthy, ناتندرست *nā-tandurust,* ناموافق *nā-muwāfik.*

Unheard, انسنا *ansunā.* Unholy, نامقدس *nā-mukaddas.*

Unhurt, بي چوٹ *bē-chōt,* بيزخم *bē-zakhm,* بينقصان *bē-nuksān.*

Uniform, ايكسان *ēk-sān,* برابر *barābar.* Uniformly, برابري سي *barābarī sē.*

Unimportant, غير اهم *ghair ahamm,* سبك *subuk,* هلكا *halkā.*

Uninformed, غيرمطلع *ghair muttali',* بيخبر *bē-khabar,* نادان *nādān.*

Uninhabitable, بودوباش كرني كي ناقابل *būd-ō-bāsh karnē kē nā-kābil.*

Uninhabited, انبسا *anbasā,* نرجن *nirjan,* ناآباد *nā-ābād.*

Uninjured, بينقصان *bē-nuksān,* ناآزاررسيده *nā-āzār-rasīda.*

Uninstructed, انسكها *ansikha,* بي تعليم *bē-ta'līm,* موركهه *mūrakh.*

Unintelligible, بيسمجهه *bē-samajh,* نادانستني *nā-danistanī.*

Unintentional, Unintentionally, بيقصد *bē-kasd,* بي اراده *bē-irāda.*

Uninterested, بيسوارتهه *bē-swārth,* لاغرض *lā-gharaz,* بيسود *bē-sūd.*

Uninterrupted, اننتر *an-antar,* بلا فاصله *bilā-fāsila.*

Uninvited, بيدعوت *bē-da'wat,* بينوتا *bē-nautā,* انبلايا *anbulāyā.*

Unique, يكتا *yaktā,* اكا *ikkā,* لاثاني *lā-sānī,* طاق *tāk,* وحيد *wahīd.*

Universal, مطلق *mutlak,* كلي *kullī,* عمومي *umūmī,* جامع *jāmi'.*

Unjust, ناحق *nā-hakk,* بي انصاف *bē-insāf,* بيداد *bē-dād.*

Unkind, بي شفقت *bē-shafakat,* بيمهر *bē-mihr,* نامهربان *nā-mihrbān.*

Unknown, نامعلوم *nā-ma'lūm,* انجانا *anjānā,* انپهچان *anpahchān.*

Unlawful, خلاف شرع *khilāf-i-shar',* ناجائز *nā-jā'iz,* حرام *harām.*

Unless, الا *illā,* بغير *baghair,* اگرنه *agar-na,* مگر *magar.*

Unlike, نامشابه *nā-mushābih,* انميل *anmēl:* see Dissimilar.

Unlikely, ناغالب *nā-ghālib.* Unlimited, بيحد *bē-hadd.*

Unlooked for, ناگهاني *nā-gahānī.* Unlucky, منحوس *manhūs.*

Unmanageable, بي صبط *bē-zabṭ,* سرکش *sarkash,* بيلگام *bē-lagām.*
Unmanly, نامردانه *nā-mardāna.* Unmannerly, بي ادب *bē-adab.*
Unmarried, انبياها *anbyāhā.* Unmeaning, بي معني *bē-maʿnī.*
Unmerciful, بيرحم *bē-raḥm.* Unmindful, بيلحاظ *bē-liḥāẓ.*
Unmixed, انملا *anmilā.* Unmoved, اچل *achal,* بيرقت *bē-riḳḳat.*
Unnatural, نامطبوع *nā-maṭbūʿ,* خلاف طبعيت *khilāf-i-ṭabʿīyat.*
Unnecessary, ناضرور *nā-ẓarūr.* Unobserved, انديکها *andēkhā.*
Unoccupied, نامشغول *nā-mashghūl,* خالي *khālī:* see Vacant.
Unpalatable, بدمزه *bad-maza,* ناگوار *nā-gawār.*
Unparalleled, بي مانند *bē-mānand.* Unpared, انچهيلا *anchhīlā.*
Unpardonable, Unpardoned, غيرمعذور *ghair-maʿẕūr.*
Unperceivable, ناديدني *nā-dīdanī.* Unperceived, ناديده *nā-dīda.*
Unperishable, لازوال *lā-zawāl,* لافاني *lā-fānī:* see Eternal.
Unpleasant, ناخوش *nā-khush,* ناگوار *nā-gawār:* see Disagreeable.
Unpolished, بي صيقل *bē-ṣaiḳal,* (rude) ناتراشيده *nā-tarāshīda.*
Unpolite, بي مروت *bē-murūwat,* بدخلق *bad-khulk.*
Unprecedented, بيتمثيل *bē-tamṣīl,* بي معمول *bē-maʿmūl.*
Unpremeditated, بيپيشبندي *bē-peshbandī,* بديهي *badīhī.*
Unprepared, ناتيار *nā-taiyār,* غيرمستعد *ghair-mustaʿidd.*
Unprincipled, بدذات *bad-ẕāt,* بدگهر *bad-guhar,* بيراه *bē-rāh.*
Unprofitable, لاحاصل *lā-ḥāṣil,* بيفائده *bē-fāʾida.*
Unpromising, انهونهار *anhōnhār.* Unpropitious, بديمن *bad-yumn.*
Unprotected, بيسايه *bē-sāya,* بيوصيله *bē-waṣīla,* اسرن *asaran.*
Unprovided, بي سروسامان *bē-sar-ō-sāmān,* بي اسباب *bē-asbāb.*
Unqualified, نالائق *nā-lāʾiḳ,* ناسزاوار *nā-sazāwār.*
Unquestionable, بلااعتراض *bilā-iʿtirāẓ,* بي شبهه *bē-shubha.*
Unquiet, بيچين *bē-chain,* چنچل *chanchal,* مضطرب *muẓṭarib.*
Unread, انپڑها *anpaṛhā,* ناخوانده *nā-khwānda:* see Ignorant.
Unreasonable, بيجا *bē-jā,* نامعقول *nā-maʿḳūl,* بيٹهکانا *bē-ṭhikānā.*
Unreserved, بيتکلف *bē-takallvf,* صاف دل *ṣāf-dil,* بيريا *bē-riyā.*
Unrestrained, بيقيد *bē-ḳaid,* بيلگام *bē-lagām,* بيضبط *bē-ẓabṭ.*
Unrighteous, غيرصالح *ghair-ṣāliḥ,* بي انصاف *bē-inṣāf,* پاپي *pāpī.*

Unripe, انپکا *anpakā*, ناپخته *nā-pukhta*, نارسیده *nā-rasīda*.

Unrivalled, بینظر *bē-nazīr*, بیرقیب *bē-rakīb*, غیرحریف *ghair-harīf*.

Unruly, بیضبط *bē-zabt*, بیلگام *bē-lagām*, بیحکم *bē-hukm*.

Unsafe, ناسلامت *nā-salāmat*, باخطره *bā-khatra*, بي امن *bē-amn*.

Unsatisfactory, ناصواب *nā-sawāb*, ناساز *nā-sāz*.

Unseasonable, بیوقت *bē-wakt*, بیجا *bē-jā*, بي ايام *bē-aiyām*.

Unseasoned, بینمک *bē-namak*. Unseemly, نامناسب *nā-munāsib*.

Unseen, اندیکھا *andēkhā*, ادشت *adisht*, نادیده *nā-dīda*.

Unsettled, بیقرار *bē-karār*, بي بندوبست *bē-band-ō-bast*.

Unshod, ننگي پاؤں *nangē pā'ōn*. Unsightly, بدنما *bad-numā*.

Unskilful, ناواقف *nā-wākif*, بیهنر *bē-hunar*, نرگن *nirgun*.

Unsound, شکسته *shikasta*, عیبدار *aib-dār*, بیصحت *bē-sihhat*.

Unsparing, بیدریغ *bē-daregh*. Unstable, بیقرار *bē-karār*.

Unsteady, بیثبات *bē-sabāt*. Unsuccessful, بیمقصد *bē-maksad*.

Unsuitable, ناموافق *nā-muwāfik*. Unsullied, بي عیب *bē-aib*.

Untamed, انهلا *anhilā*. Untasted, انچکھا *anchakhā*.

Untaught, نا آموخته *nā-āmōkhta*. Untimely, بیوقت *bē-wakt*.

Until, جب تک *jab-tak*, لگ *lag*. Unto, کو *kō*, کیتئیں *kē-ta'īṅ*.

Untold, انکها *ankahā*. Untouched, انچهوا *anchhūā*.

Untoward, see Perverse. Untrue, نا راست *nā-rāst*.

Unusual, بیدستور *bē-dastūr*. Unwary, بیخبر *bē-khabar*.

Unwearied, اتهک *athak*. Unwelcome, نا پسند *nā-pasand*.

Unwholesome, ناگوار *nā-gawār*. Unwilling, نا راض *nā-rāz*.

Unwitting, انجان *anjān*. Unwittingly, نا دانسته *nā-dānista*.

Unworthy, نا لائق *nā-lā'ik*, نا سزاوار *nā-sazāwār*.

Vocal, آوازدار *āwāz-dār*, صوتي *sautī*, شبدي *shabdī*.

Vociferous, شورپشت *shōr-pusht*, غوغائي *ghaughā'ī*.

Void, خالي *khālī*, تهي *tihī*, سن *sun*, (null) باطل *bātil*.

Volatile, (winged) پرنده *paranda*, (playful) چنچل *chanchal*.

Voluntary, اختیاري *ikhtiyārī*, قصدي *kasdī*, ازخود *az khud*.

Voluptuous, عیاش *aiyāsh*, رسیلا *rasīlā* : see Luxurious.

Voracious, جوع البقر *jū'u-l-bakar*, مربهکها *mar-bhukkhā*.

Up, اوپر *ūpar*, بالا *bālā*, (out of bed) اتها *uṭhā*: see Standing.
Upon, پر *par*, اوپر *ūpar*. Upper, بالاتر *bālātar* اعلي *a'lā*.
Uppermost, سب سي بالاتر يا اونچا *sab sē bālātar* or *ūnchā*.
Upright, (erect) كهڑا *khaṛā*, (just) صادق *ṣādiḳ*: see Honest.
Upward, Upwards, اوپر *ūpar*, (more than) زياده *ziyāda*.
Urgent, ضرور *ẓarūr*, لازم *lāzim*, سخت *sakht*, بجد *bajidd*.
Useful, كام كا *kām kā*, كارامدني *kār-āmdanī*: see Profitable.
Useless, ناكارا *nākārā*, نكما *nikammā*, بيفائده *bē-fā'ida*.
Usual, رائج *rā'ij*, مروج *murauwaj*, چلني *chalnī*, جاري *jārī*.
Usually, اكثر *akṣar*, اغلب *aghlab*, بيشتر *bēshtar*.
Utmost, Utter, نهايت *nihāyat*, نپت *nipaṭ*, غايت *ghāyat*.
Utterly, تمام و كمال *tamām ō kamāl*, حد *ḥadd*, نهايت *nihāyat*.
Vulgar, (common) عام *āmm*, عرفي *ūrfī*, (mean) كمينه *kamīna*.
Uxorious, زن مريد *zan-murīd*, كرلگوا *karlagū'ā*.
Waggish, ظريف *ẓarīf*, مسخره *maskhara*, خوش طبع *khush-ṭab'*.
Wan, زرد *zard*, پيلا *pīlā*, زعفراني *za'farānī*.
Wanton, شوخ *shōkh*, لهر باز *lahar-bāz*, اچپل *achpal*, كامي *kāmī*.
Warlike, جنگي *jangī*, رزم پيشه *razm-pēsha*, لڑانكا *laṛānkā*.
Warm, گرم *garm*, تتا *tattā*, حار *ḥārr*, (ardent) سرگرم *sar-garm*.
Wary, هوشيار *hōshyār*, اگرسوچي *agrasōchī*, چوكنا *chaukannā*.
Waspish, چڑچڑا *chiṛchiṛā*, زود رنج *zūd-ranj*, گهونا *ghūnā*.
Waste, خراب *kharāb*, ويران *wīrān*, پائمال *pā'ēmāl*, اجاڑ *ujāṛ*.
Wasteful, اڑاو *uṛā'ū*, مسرف *musrif*, فضول خرچ *fazūl-kharch*.
Watchful, بيدار *bē-dār*, هوشيار *hōshyār*, چوكس *chaukas*: see Cautious.
Watery, آبي *ābī*, پنيها *panīhā*, (tasteless) پنسا *pansā*: see Insipid.
Wayward, شوخ *shōkh*, هتهيلا *haṭhīlā*, ضدي *ẓiddī*.
Weak, كم زور *kam-zōr*, ضعيف *ẓa'īf*, زير دست *zēr-dast*: see Feeble.
Wealthy, مالدار *māldār*, زردار *zardār*, دولتمند *daulatmand*.
Wearisome, تهكاو *thakā'ū*, بهاري *bhārī*. Weary, مانده *mānda*.
Wedded, بياهتا *byāhtā* (f.), بياها *byāhā* (m.). Wee, see Small.
Weekly, هر هفته *har hafta*, هفته هفته *hafta hafta*.
Weighty, وزني *waznī*, بهاري *bhārī*. Welcome, مبارك *mubārak*.

Well (adj.), اچها *achchhā*, بهلا *bhalā*, بهلا چنگا *bhalā-changā*.

Well (adv.), درست *durust*, بهلا *bhalā*, خوب *khūb*, اچهي طرح *achchhī-tarah*.

Wellbred, خوش خلق *khush-khulk*, نيك اطوار *nēk-atwār*.

Well done! شاباش *shābāsh*, زهي *zahē*, آفرين *āfarīn*.

West, Westward, پچهم كو *pachchham kō*, طرف مغرب *taraf-i-maghrib*.

Westerly, Western, پچهمي *pachchhamī*, مغربي *maghribī*.

Wet, بهيگا *bhīgā*, گيلا *gīlā*, تر *tar*, نم *nam*, نمناك *namnāk*.

What? كيا *kyā*, كون *kaun*. What, جو *jō*. Whatever, جو كچه *jō kuchh*.

Wheaten, گيهون كا *gēhūn kā*. When? كب *kab*. When, جب *jab*.

Whence? كهان سي *kahān sē*, (from what source?) كس واسطي *kis wāstē*.

Whence, جهان سي *jahān sē*, (from which source) جس واسطي *jis wāstē*.

Where? كهان *kahān*. Where, جهان *jahān*, جدهر *jidhar*.

Whereas, ازبسكه *az-bas-ki*, چونكه *chūn-ki*. Whereby, جس سي *jis sē*.

Wherever, جهان جهان *jahān jahān*. Wherefore, اس واسطي *is wāstē*.

Wheresoever, جهان كهين *jahān kahīn*. Whereupon, اسپر *us-par*.

Whether, كه *ki*, كيا *kyā*. Which? كون *kaun*. Which, جو *jō*.

Whichever, جوكه *jō-ki*. While, Whilst, جبتك *jab-tak*, جد *jad*.

Whimsical, هردم خيالي *har-dam-khiyālī*, لهري *lahrī*.

White, سفيد *sufēd*, سيت *sēt*, (fair) گورا *gōrā*, (bright) اجلا *ujlā*.

Who? كون *kaun*, كس ني *kis-nē*. Who, جو *jō*, جون *jaun*, جس ني *jis-nē*.

Whoever, جو كوئي *jō-kō'ī*. Whomever, جس كسي كو *jis kisī kō*.

Whole, (sound) مسلم *musallam*, (entire) تمام *tamām*: see All.

Wholesome, صحت آور *sihhat-āwar*, موافق *muwāfik*: see Useful.

Why? كيون *kyūn*, كاهيكو *kāhē kō*, كس واسطي *kis wāstē*.

Wicked, برا *burā*, پاپي *pāpī*, شرير *sharīr*, بد *bad*, زبون *zabūn*.

Wide, چوڑا *chaurā*, چكلا *chaklā*, پهنا *pahnā*, فراخ *farākh*.

Wild, جنگلي *janglī*, وحشي *wahshī*, دشتي *dashtī*: see Licentious.

Wilful, خود پسند *khud-pasand*, خود سر *khud-sar*: see Perverse.

Wilfully, ديده و دانسته *dīda ō dānista*: see Intentionally.

Willing, راضي *rāẓī*, راضا مند *raẓā-mand*, خوش *khush*: see Desirous.
Wily, حيله باز *ḥīla-bāz*, روباه باز *rōbāh-bāz*: see Cunning.
Windy, هوائي *hawā'ī*, بادي *bādī*, (puffed up) پهولا *phūlā*: see Stormy.
Winning, موهنا *mōhnā*, دلربا *dil-rubā*, دل كش *dil-kash*: see Charming.
Wise, عقلمند *ʿaḳlmand*, عاقل *ʿāḳil*, دانا *dānā*, زيرك *zīrak*.
Wishful, مشتاق *mushtāḳ*, آرزومند *ārzūmand*, راغب *rāghib*.
With (prepos. or postpos.), سي *sē*, (along with) ساتهه *sāth*, مع *maʿ*.
Within, بهيتر *bhītar*, اندر *andar*, بيچ *bīch*, مين *meṅ*.
Without, (adv.) باهر *bāhar*, بيرون *bērūn*, (prep.) بي *bē*, بلا *bilā*.
Wittingly, جان بوجهكي *jān būjhkē*, ديده و دانسته *dīda ō dānista*.
Witty, تيز فهم *tēz-fahm*, چتر *chatur*, ظريف *ẓarīf*: see Jocular.
Woful, غم ناك *gham-nāk*, سنتاپي *santāpī*, سوگ آور *sōg-āwar*.
Wooden, لكڙي كا *lakṛī kā*, چوبين *chōbīn*. Woody, جنگلي *janglī*.
Woollen, اوني *ūnī*, پشمي *pashmī*, پشمينه *pashmīna*.
Worldly, دنيادار *dunyā-dār*, سنساركي *sansārik*, دنياوي *dunyāwī*.
Wormeaten, كرم خورده *kirm-khurda*, گهنا *ghunā*, كيڙها *kīṛahā*.
Worse, بدتر *badtar*. Worst, بري سي برا *burē sē burā*.
Worthless, بيقدر *bē-ḳadr*, ناكارا *nā-kārā*, ناچيز *nā-chīz*.
Worthy, لائق *lā'iḳ*, قابل *ḳābil*, مستوجب *mustaujib*, بهلا *bhalā*.
Wrathful, غضبناك *ghaẓab-nāk*, خشم ناك *khashm-nāk*, كوپي *kōpī*.
Wretched, بينصيب *bē-naṣīb*, پريشان *parēshān*, كنگال *kangāl*.
Written, لكها هوا *likhā hū'ā*, نوشته *nawishta*, مرقوم *marḳūm*.
Wrong, نامناسب *nā-munāsib*, ناحق *nā-ḥaḳḳ*, غلط *ghalaṭ*.
Wrongful, بي انصاف *bē-inṣāf*, ناحق *nā-ḥaḳḳ*. Wroth, see Wrathful.
Wrought, بنا *banā*, گڑها *gaṛhā*. Wry, ٹيڑها *ṭēṛhā*, كج *kaj*.
Yclad, پهنا هوا *pahnā hū'ā*. Ycleped, نام زد *nām-zad*.
Yea, هان *hāṅ*, بلي *balē*. Yearling, ايكسالي *ēk-sālī*.
Yes, هان *hāṅ*, بلي *bālē*, آري *ārē*, تو *tau*, جي *jī*.
Yet, (conj.) تو بهي *tau-bhī*, پر *par*, (adv.) تس پر *tis-par*: see Beside.
Yon, Yonder, وه *wuh* or (dakh.) *wah*, پرلا *parlā*, پري كا *parē kā*.
Of yore, مدت كا *muddat kā*, اگلا *aglā*, قديم سي *ḳadīm sē*.
Young, جوان *jawān*, خورد سال *khurd-sāl*, نو *nau*: see Small.

Your, تمہارا *tumhārā*, اپنا *apnā*. Yourself, تم آپ *tum āp*.

Youthful, جوان *jawān*, تازہ *tāza*, قوي *ḳawī*.

Zealous, گرم *garm*, سرگرم *sar-garm*, تند *tund*, ساعي *sā'ī*.

Zigzag, ٹیڑھا *ṭēṛhā*, کج و پیچ *kaj ō pēch*, بکڑا *bakṛā* (?).

PART III.

SHORT SENTENCES OF COMMON USE.

کہاں سي آئي هو	*kahāṅ sē ā'ē hō*	Where are you from?
کدھر جاؤگي	*kidhar jā'ōgē*	Where are you going?
تم کون هو	*tum kaun hō*	Who are you?
کس واسطي آئي هو	*kis wāsṭē ā'ē hō*	Why are you come?
مجهي کچھ کہوگي	*mujhē kuchh kahōgē*	Will you say something to me?
وہ کون هي	*wuh kaun hai*	Who is he? Who is that?
ادھر آؤ	*idhar ā'ō*	Come here.
نزديک آؤ	*nazdīk ā'ō*	Come near.
جلدي جا	*jaldī jā*	Go quickly.
جلدي چلو	*jaldī chalō*	Go (or move) quickly.
چپ رہ	*chup rah*	Be silent.
حاضري لاؤ	*ḥāẓirī lā'ō*	Bring breakfast.
کهانا لاؤ	*khānā lā'ō*	Bring dinner.
روٹي لاؤ	*rōṭī lā'ō*	Bring bread.
دودھ لاؤ	*dūdh lā'ō*	Bring milk.
مصري دو	*miṣrī dō*	Give some sugarcandy.
کهانا کهاؤ	*khānā khā'ō*	Eat (your) dinner.
دودھ پيؤ	*dūdh pī'ō*	Drink milk.
چراغ جلاؤ	*chirāgh jalā'ō*	Light the lamp.
بتي جلاؤ	*battī jalā'ō*	Light the candle.
گلگير لاؤ	*gulgīr lā'ō*	Bring the snuffers.
گل لو	*gul lō*	Snuff the candle.

بتي بجهاؤ	*battī bujhā'ō*	Put out the candle.
فانوس لاؤ	*fānūs lā'ō*	Bring a shade (for the candle).
فانوس اٹهاؤ	*fānūs uṭhā'ō*	Take away the shade.
بهوليو مت	*bhūliyō mat*	Do not forget.
چا بناؤ	*chā banā'ō*	Make tea.
داهني پهرو	*dāhnē phirō*	Turn to the right.
بائين پهرو	*bā'eṅ phirō*	Turn to the left.
موٹيونكو بلاؤ	*mōṭiyōṅ-kō bulā'ō* . . .	Call the porters.
ميز لگاؤ	*mēz lagā'ō*	Lay the table.
اسباب ليجاؤ	*asbāb lējā'ō*	Take away the things.
ميز اٹهاؤ	*mēz uṭhā'ō*	Remove the table.
خبردار هو	*khabar-dār hō*	Be careful.
حكم كيا هي	*ḥukm kyā hai*	What is (your) command?
گاڑي تيار كرو	*gāṛī taiyār karō*	Get the carriage ready.
كچهه مضايقه نهين	*kuchh muẓāyaka nahīṅ*	. It is no matter.
تم كو فرصت هي	*tum kō furṣat hai* . . .	Are you at leisure?
هم كو معاف كيجيي	*ham kō mu'āf kījiyē* . .	Be pleased to pardon me.
تهوڑي روٹي لاؤ	*thōṛī rōṭī lā'ō*	Bring a little bread.
بچهونا بچهايا هي	*bichhaunā bichhāyā hai*	. Have they made the bed?
دروازه بند كرو	*darwāza band karō* . . .	Shut the door.
وي بوڑهي هين	*wē būṛhē haiṅ*	They are old.
يهه كم بختي هي	*yih kam-bakhtī hai* . . .	This is a misfortune.
ميري كتاب لاؤ	*mērī kitāb lā'ō*	Bring my book.
ميري جوتي لاؤ	*mērī jūtī lā'ō*	Bring my shoes.
تم بازار جاؤ	*tum bāzār jā'ō*	Go you to the market.
تهوڑا گوشت لاؤ	*thōṛā gōsht lā'ō*	Bring a little meat.
دق مت كرو	*diķ mat karō*	Do not plague (me).
ميري خانسامان كو بلاؤ	*mērē khānsāmān kō bulā'ō* .	Call my *khānsāmān*.
كهاني كا حكم دو	*khānē kā ḥukm dō* . . .	Order dinner.
مين باهر جاؤنگا	*maiṅ bāhir jā'ūngā* . . .	I shall go out.
ميرا كپڑا لاؤ	*mērā kapṛā lā'ō*	Bring my clothes.
تم جلد آيو	*tum jald ā'iyō*	You must come quick.

راج مستري کو بلاؤ	*rāj mistarī kō bulā'ō* . .	Call the bricklayer.
کوٹھي مرمت کرو	*kōṭhī marammat karō* . .	Repair the house.
خبر کا کاغذ لاؤ	*khabar kā kāghaz lā'ō* . .	Bring the newspaper.
يهہ وهي هي	*yih wuh-ī hai*	This is that very (thing).
وهان سبهي هين	*wahāṅ sab-hī haiṅ* . . .	They are quite all there.
وهان کوئي هي	*wahāṅ ko'ī hai*	Is any one there?
وہ پهير کهو	*wuh phēr kahō*	Say that again.
هم کل جاوينگي	*ham kal jāwēṅgē*	We shall go tomorrow.
توپ کيون چهوٹي	*tōp kyūṅ chhūṭī*	Why is the gun fired?
پالکي جلدي منگاؤ	*pālkī jaldī mangā'ō* . . .	Send for the palanquin immediately.
صاحب اٹها هي	*ṣāḥib uṭhā hai*	Is the gentleman up?
گهومکر آؤ	*ghūm-kar ā'ō*	Come round. Turn about.
ذرا آهسته چلو	*zarrā āhista chalō* . . .	Go a little more gently.
آؤ موزي اتارو	*ā'ō mōzē utārō*	Come, take off (my) boots.
گهر سي نکلو	*ghar sē niklō*	Get out of the house.
وہ بيوقوف هي	*wuh be-wuḳūf hai* . . .	He is a simpleton.
اپني هاتهہ دهوؤ	*apnē hāth dhō'ō*	Wash your hands.
اپنا منهہ دهوؤ	*apnā muṅh dhō'ō*	Wash your face.
بهت گرمي هي	*bahut garmī hai*	It is very hot.
وہ کتاب همکو دو	*wuh kitāb ham-kō dō* . .	Hand me that book.
يهہ اتفاق کب هوا	*yih ittifāḳ kab hū'ā* . . .	When did this happen?
ٹهنڈا پاني لاؤ	*ṭhanḍā pānī lā'ō*	Bring (some) cold water.
تهوڑا شربت لاؤ	*ṭhōrā sharbat lā'ō* . . .	Bring a little sherbet.
گهٹا نمود هوا	*ghaṭā namūd hū'ā* . . .	It appears cloudy.
آج پاني برسيگا	*āj pānī barsēgā*	It will rain to day.
اسکي بهت دوست هين	*us-kē bahut dōst haiṅ* . .	He has many friends.
يهہ اچها موسم هي	*yih achchha mausim hai* .	This is fine weather.
اسکي بڑي داڑهي هي	*us-kī baṛī dāṛhī hai*. . .	He has a great beard.
يهہ کيا چڑيا هي	*yih kyā chiṛiyā hai* . . .	What bird is this?
يهہ انکا تماشا هي	*yih un-kā tamāshā hai* . .	This is their fun.
وہ بڑا متوالا هي	*wuh baṛā matwālā hai* . .	He is a great toper.

انکا بڑا گناہ هي	*un-kā baṛā gunāh hai* . .	Their crime is great.
يہہ ميدان کسکا هي	*yih maidān kis-kā hai* . .	Whose field is this?
اسکا مقدمہ آج هوگا	*us-kā muḳaddama āj hōgā* .	His trial will be to day.
يهان بهت مکهيان هين	*yahāṅ bahut makkhiyāṅ haiṅ*	There are many flies here.
کتني آدمي حاضر هين	*kitnē ādmī ḥāẓir haiṅ* . .	How many men are present?
چراغ مين تيل نهين	*chirāg͟h mēṅ tēl nahīṅ* . .	There is no oil in the lamp.
يہہ فقط حيله هي	*yih faḳaṭ ḥīla hai* . . .	This is all a trick.
همکو ايک نمونه ديجيي	*ham-kō ēk namūna dījiyē* .	Be pleased to give me a pattern.
تمهاري پاس رسي هي	*tumhārē pās rassī hai* . .	Have you any string?
بادشاہ تخت پر بيٹها	*bādshāh tak͟ht par baiṭhā* .	The king sat on the throne.
اسکي آواز اچهي هي	*us-kī āwāz achchhī hai*. .	He (or she) has a fine voice.
ٹوپي اور کرتي جهاڑو	*ṭōpī aur kurtī jhāṛō* . . .	Brush (my) hat and coat.
يہہ کونسا جانور هي	*yih kaun-sā jānwar hai* . .	What kind of animal is this?
تمهاري کيا صلاح هي	*tumhārī kyā ṣalāḥ hai* . .	What is your advice?
وہ ميوہ کهانا اچها نهين	*wuh mēwa khānā achchhā nahīṅ*,	That fruit is not good to eat.
اسمين تم فايده پاؤگي	*is-mēṅ tum fā'ida pā'ōgē* .	You will find this very useful.
اپني بالونمين کنگهي کرو	*apnē bālōṅ-mēṅ kanghī karō*	Comb your hair.
تمهاري عمر کيا هي	*tumhārī umr kyā hai* . .	What is your age?
پالکي ميري پاس بهيجو	*pālkī mērē pās bhējō* . . .	Send me the palanquin.
هاتهہ دهوني کا پاني لاؤ	*hāth dhōnē kā pānī lā'ō*. .	Bring water to wash (my) hands.
ايک جوڑا کپڑا لاؤ	*ēk jōṛā kapṛā lā'ō* . . .	Bring a suit of clothes.
دوات قلم کاغذ لاؤ	*dawāt ḳalam kāg͟haz lā'ō* .	Bring the inkstand, pen and paper.
وہ گورا کون هي	*wuh gōrā kaun hai* . . .	What European is that?
وہ کسکا گهوڑا هي	*wuh kis-kā ghōṛā hai* . .	Whose horse is that?
يہہ هماري گهوڑي هي	*yih hamārī ghōṛī hai* . .	This is our (or my) mare.
يہہ کسکا گهڑا هي	*yih kis-kā ghaṛā hai*. . .	Whose water-pot is this?
تمهارا نام کيا هي	*tumhārā nām kyā hai* . .	What is your name?
وہ بهت چالاک هي	*wuh bahut chālāk hai* . .	He is very active.

يہہ زمين شور هي	*yih zamīn shōr hai* . . .	This ground is salt (barren).
اترو نهين تو گروگي	*utrō nahīṅ tō girōgē* . . .	Get down lest you fall.
يہہ روپيه ميکھي هي	*yih rūpiya mē<u>kh</u>ī hai* . .	This rupee is adulterated.
اسکي شکل بد هي	*us-kī shakl bad hai* . . .	It looks ill.
انگريزي زبان مشکل هي .	*angrēzī zabān mushkil hai* .	The English tongue is difficult.
يہہ بهت اچها هي	*yih bahut achchhā hai* . .	This is very good.
يہہ عجيب خبر هي .	*yih ājīb <u>kh</u>abar hai* . . .	This is wonderful news.
هم بهوکهي پياسي هين	*ham bhūkhē piyāsē hain.* .	* We are (I am) hungry and thirsty.
وه هشيار آدمي هي	*wuh hushyār ādmī hai* . .	He is a prudent man.
جهلمل اٹهاؤ	*jhilmil uṭhā'ō*	Raise up the venetian blinds.
برتن ليجاؤ	*bartan lejā'ō*	Take away the dishes.
يہہ درخت جلد موليگا	*yih dara<u>kh</u>t jald maulēgā* .	This plant will soon blossom.
تم هميشه غلط کرتي هو	*tum hamēsha <u>gh</u>alaṭ kartē hō*	You are always blundering.
وه بندي خاني مين بهيجا گيا	*wuh bandī-<u>kh</u>ānē mēṅ bhējā gayā,*	He was sent to prison.
اسکي دليل مضبوط هي	*us-kī dalīl mazbūṭ hai* . .	His argument is strong.
وه بڑا بي ادب هي	*wuh baṛā be-adab hai* . .	He is very unmannerly.
آسمان خوب صاف هي	*āsmān <u>kh</u>ūb ṣāf hai* . . .	The sky is very clear.
وي لڑکي شوخ هين	*wē laṛkē shō<u>kh</u> haiṅ* . . .	Those boys are pert.
اسني بڑي سزا پائي	*us-nē baṛī sazā pā'ī* . . .	He got a great punishment.
وي سب چپ رهي	*wē sab chup rahē*	They all remained silent.
اسکا دل بيقرار هي	*us-kā dil bē-ḳarār hai* . . .	His heart is unsettled.
يہہ کاغذ تر هي	*yih kā<u>gh</u>az tar hai* . . .	This paper is damp.
کون شور کرتا هي	*kaun shōr kartā hai* . . .	Who is making a noise?
تم کيا کهتي هو	*tum kyā kahtē hō*	What are you saying?
تم کيا کهاتي هو	*tum kyā khātē hō*	What are you eating?

---

* Like as in Europe the plural of the second person is commonly adopted when applied to an individual, so in Hindustani not only the plural of the second person, but also that of the first, and even of the third, is in use much substituted for the singular.

سليس هندي تو بولو	*salīs hindī tō bōlō* . . .	Speak easy Hindustani.
چلي جاؤ رخصت هو	*chalē jā'ō, rukhsat hō* . .	Go along, you are dismissed.
وهان پهر مت جاؤ	*wahāṅ phir mat jā'ō* . . .	Go not there again.
همكو كناري پر اتارو	*ham-kō kinārē par utārō* .	Put me down on the shore.
وهان كون رهتا هي	*wahāṅ kaun rahtā hai* . .	Who lives there?
سيدهي آگي چلي جاؤ	*sīdhe āge chalē jā'ō* . . .	Go straight forwards.
كچهه شراب پاني لاؤ	*kuchh sharāb pānī lā'ō* . .	Bring some wine and water.
پاني خوب ٹهنڈا كرو	*pānī khūb ṭhanḍā karō* . .	Cool the water well.
كهانا ميز پر لاؤ	*khānā mēz-par lā'ō* . . .	Bring dinner on table.
همكو بڑي فجر جگاؤ	*ham-kō baṛī fajar jagā'ō* .	Waken me very early.
آج دن پهرچها هي	*āj din pharchhā hai* . . .	It is fair to day.
آج كچهه ابر هي	*āj kuchh abr hai*	It is a little cloudy to day.
اسني اقرار كيا هي	*us-nē iḳrār kiyā hai* . . .	He has made a confession.
همكو نيند آتي هي	*ham-kō nīnd ātī hai* . . .	I am very sleepy.
وه اكثر متوالا رهتا هي	*wuh aksar matwālā rahtā hai*	He is generally drunk.
يهه ساري لكڑي اچهي هي	*yih sārī lakṛī achchhī hai* .	This wood is entirely sound.
اسني بهت دولت جمع كي هي	*us-nē bahut daulat jamʿ kī hai,*	He has amassed great wealth.
ابهي هم كام شروع كرين	*abhī ham kām shurūʿ karēṅ*	Let us now begin work.
اپني ساتهه همكو جاني دو	*apnē sāth ham-kō jānē dō* .	Allow me to go with you.
وه بڑا عاقل هي	*wuh baṛā ʿāḳil hai* . . .	He is a very wise man.
يهه خوب ميوه هي	*yih khūb mēwa hai* . . .	This is fine fruit.
يهه اچهي روٹي هي	*yih achchhī rōṭī hai* . . .	This is good bread.
ما باپ انكي مرگئي هين	*mā bāp un-kē mar-ga'ē haiṅ*	Their parents are dead.
تمهاري چهري تيز هي	*tumhārī chhurī tēz hai* . .	Is your knife sharp?
كيا يهه چهري تمهاري هي	*kyā yih chhurī tumhārī hai*	Does this knife belong to you?
اسكي دانت مين درد هي	*us-kē dānt mēṅ dard hai* . .	He has the toothach.
يهه بتي موم كي هي	*yih battī mōm kī hai* . .	This candle is of wax.
يهه پهل بڑا كهٹا هي	*yih phal baṛā khaṭṭā hai* .	This fruit is very sour.
يهه كپڑا بڑا موٹا هي	*yih kapṛā baṛā mōṭā hai* .	This cloth is very coarse.
يهه سب سي بهتر هوگا	*yih sab sē bihtar hōgā* . .	This will be the best.
يهه قلم بهت نرم هي	*yih ḳalam bahut narm hai* .	This pen is too soft.

یہہ حرف بد صورت هي	*yih ḥarf bad-ṣūrat hai* . .	This letter is ill formed.
تم انگریزي بول سکتي هو	*tum angrēzī bōl saktē hō* .	Can you speak English?
اس گھڑي کو لي چلو	*is ghaṛī kō lę chalō* . . .	Take away this watch.
هم سب کچھ جانتي هین	*ham sab kuchh jāntē haiṅ* .	We know all.
وي بهت کچھ جانتي هین	*wē bahut kuchh jāntē haiṅ* .	They know much.
گنا بڑا میٹھا هي	*gannā baṛā mīṭhā hai* . .	The sugar cane is very sweet.
اس گھر کا لوازمہ نهین	*is ghar kā lawāzima nahīṅ*.	The house is unfurnished.
وي بیخبر سوتي هین	*wē bē-khabar sōtē haiṅ* . .	They are dead asleep.
تم اس گھر کي مالک هو	*tum is ghar kē mālik hō*. .	Are you the owner of this house?
کهو تو وہ کیا کهتا هي	*kahō tō wuh kyā kahtā hai*	Tell (me) what he says.
اس ادمي کو تم جانتي هو	*is ādmī ḳō tum jāntē hō*. .	Do you know this man?
نیلام مین جاٴوگي	*nīlām mēṇ jā'ōgē*	Will you go to the auction?
وہ نیلام کا کام کرتا هي	*wuh nīlām kā kām kartā hai*	He is by trade an auctioneer.
روٴي کا گٹھر کھولو	*rū'ī kā gaṭhar khōlō* . . .	Open this bale of cotton.
اسکي ڈاڑهي بڑي هي	*us-kī ḍāṛhī baṛī hai* . . .	He wears a long beard.
تم اسکا سبب جانتي هو	*tum iskā sabab jāntē hō*. .	Do you know the cause?
چوکي لو بیٹھو	*chaukī lō baiṭhō*	Take a chair and sit down.
کون باب هم پڑهین	*kaun bāb ham paṛhēṅ* . .	What chapter shall I read?
اسکي بڑي عزت هي	*us-kī baṛī ʿizzat hai* . . .	He bears an excellent character.
مٹي سي اینٹ بناٴي هي	*miṭṭī sē īnṭ banā'ī hai* . .	Bricks are made of clay.
تم ني نیا مدرسہ دیکھا هي	*tum nē nayā madrasa dēkhā hai*,	Have you seen the new college?
کنگھي لو اور سر جھاڑو	*kanghī lō aur sir jhāṛō* . .	Take a comb and comb your hair.
یہہ باب کا آخر هي	*yih bāb kā ākhir hai*. . .	This is the end of the chapter.
گفتگو کرنا تمهین بهاتا هي	*guftgū karnā tumhēṅ bhatā hai*,	Are you fond of conversation?
گئي برس اناج بهت هوا تها	*ga'ē baras anāj bahut hū'ā thā*,	There was plenty of corn last year.

کیا قیمت هي ان چیزونکي	*kyā ķīmat hai in chīzōṅ-kī*	What is the cost of these things?
اسکو بڑي کهانسي هي	*us-kō baṛī khānsī hai* . .	She has a bad cough.
یهہ همارا وطن هي	*yih hamārā waṭan hai* . .	This is my native country.
یهہ برتن پهوٹا هي	*yih bartan phūṭā hai* . .	This bason is cracked.
اس دودهہ سي ملاي نهین هوتي	*is dūdh sē malā'ī nahīṅ hōtī*	This milk produces no cream.
تمهاري بات هم سچ جانتي هین	*tumhārī bāt ham sach jāntē haiṅ,*	I give credit to what you say.
اسکو لته کهتي هین	*is-kō latta kahtē haiṅ* . .	This is called a creeper.
وہ بیبي بڑي علامه هي	*wuh bībī baṛī ăllāma hai* .	She is an excellent critic.
وهان بڑا مجمع آدمیونکا تها	*wahāṅ baṛā majmaʿ ādmiyōṅ-kā thā,*	There was a great crowd of people.
کیا تمهین چهینا بهاتا هي	*kyā tumhēṅ chhēnā bhātā hai*	Are you fond of curds?
یهہ گهر بهت نم هي	*yih ghar bahut nam hai* .	This house is very damp.
اسکي خط کي کون تاریخ هي	*us-kē khaṯṯ kī kaun tārīkh hai,*	What is the date of his letter?
اب کتنا وقت هي	*ab kitnā waķt hai* . . .	What time of day is it?
وہ بڑا قرضدار هي	*wuh baṛā ķarẕdār hai* . .	He is very much in debt.
وي فریب سي دن کاٹتي هین	*wē farēb sē din kāṭtē haiṅ* .	They live only by deceit.
تم اسمین عیب کو دیکهتي هو	*tum is-mēṅ ăib kō dēkhtē hō*	Do you observe any defect in this?
اسني عدالتمین عذر کیا	*us-nē ădālat-mēṅ ŭẕr kiyā* .	He made his defence in court.
اس کام مین بڑي دیر هي	*is kām mēṅ baṛī dēr hai* .	There is much delay in this affair.
اس تالاب کا عمق کیا هي	*is tālāb kā ŭmuķ kyā hai* .	What is the depth of this tank?
وہ چوسربازي سي تباہ هوا	*wuh chausar-bāzī sē tabāh hū'ā,*	He was ruined by playing at dice.
هم تمهاري بات مانینگي	*ham tumhārī bāt mānēṅgē* .	I shall attend to your directions.

يہہ راہ بڑي غليظ هي	*yih rāh baṛī ghalīz hai* . .	This road is very dirty.
يہہ فوج قواعد نهين جانتي	*yih fauj ḳawā'id nahīn jāntī* . .	These soldiers are undisciplined.
وہ ايجاد بہت اچها هي	*wuh ījād bahut achchhā hai*	That is a great discovery.
هم سب حيله نكرين	*ham sab ḥīla na-karēn* . .	Let us not use disguise.
تم اس مرض كا نام كهو	*tum is maraẓ kā nām kahō* .	Tell me the name of this distemper.
اب وہ بہت لاچاري مين هي	*ab wuh bahut lā-chārī mēn hai,*	She is now in great distress.
دوسري مهيني كي پہلي تاريخ اسكي مال كي قسط پهنچيگي	*dūsrē mahīnē kī pahlī tārīkh us-kē māl kī ḳist pahunchēgī,*	A dividend on his estate will be paid the first of next month.
اسكا پيشه طبابت كا هي	*us-kā pēsha ṭabābat kā hai* .	His profession is that of a doctor.
اسكا كرني والا كون هي	*is-kā karnē-wālā kaun hai* .	Who was the doer of this?
اسني دو خوراك دوا لي	*us-nē dō khōrāk-i dawā lī* .	He has taken two doses of medicine.
گهر كي نيچي موري هي	*ghar kē nīchē mōrī hai* . .	There are drains under the house.
وہ بڑا متوالا هي	*wuh baṛā matwālā hai* . .	He is quite a drunkard.
اس جنس كا محصول لگتا هي	*is jins-kā maḥṣūl lagtā hai* .	Do these articles pay duty?
تهوڑي دن هوئي اس محلي مين لرزا هوا تها	*thōṛē din hū'ē is maḥallē mēn larzā hū'ā thā,*	An earthquake was felt lately in this part.
ابهي بهاٹها هي	*ab-hī bhāṭhā hai*	It is now ebb tide.
همني دوا اسكو دي پر اس سي فايدہ نہ هوا	*ham-nē dawā us-kō dī par us-sē fā'ida na hū'ā,*	I gave him medicine, but it had no effect.
هم ني ايك چڑيا كا گهونسلا اور اسمين چار انڈي ديكهي	*ham nē ēk chiṛiyā kā ghōnslā aur us-mēn chār anḍē dēkhē,*	I saw a bird's nest with four eggs.
همني دريا كناري بيٹهي هوئي انكو ديكها	*ham-nē daryā kinārē baiṭhē hū'ē un-kō dēkhā,*	I saw him sitting on the bank of the river.

وہ بڑي زور سي کام کرتا هي	*wuh baṛē zōr sē kām kartā hai,*	He goes to work with energy.
بوناوہ هي جسکا قد چهوٹا هي	*baunā wuh hai jis-kā ḳadd chhōṭā hai,*	Dwarf—one who is small in stature.
اسکي مال کا کون وصي هي	*us-kē māl kā kaun waṣī hai*	Who is the executor to his estate?
اس کام کرني مين کيا خرچ هوگا	*is kām karnē mēṅ kyā kharch hōgā,*	What will be the expense of doing this?
وہ کاروبار مين مشاق هي	*wuh kār ō bār mēṅ mashshāḳ hai,*	He has experience in business.
کيا يہہ عوام کي گفتگو کا طور هي	*kyā yih ăwāmm kī guftgū kā ṭaur hai,*	Is this mode of expression common?
هم ني اس خط کي نقل تمهين دکهائي	*ham nē is khaṭṭ kī naḳl tumhēṅ dikhā'ī,*	I showed you an extract from his letter.
هم انکو بيدهڑک کهہ سکتي هين	*ham un-kō bē-dhaṛak kah saktē haiṅ,*	I can speak to him without fear.
ان دونو کي شکل ملتي هي	*in dōnō kī shakl miltī hai .*	The features of these two are alike.
اس مقام مين ايک دينگي هي	*us maḳām mēṅ ēk dēṅgī hai*	There is a ferry boat at that place.
اس تالاب مين کوئي مچهلي هي	*is tālāb mēṅ kō'ī machhlī hai,*	Are there any fish in this tank?
آگ چقماق سي نکلي	*āg chaḳmāḳ sē niklē . . .*	Fire is produced by flint and steel.
ايک غول بهيڑونکا همني ديکها	*ēk ghōl bhēṛōṅ-kā ham-nē dēkhā,*	I saw there a flock of sheep.
آٹي سي روٹي بنتي هي	*āṭē sē rōṭī bantī hai . . .*	Bread is made of flour.
وہ بانسري بجا جانتا هي	*wuh bānsrī bajā jāntā hai .*	He plays on the flute.
يهان بهت مکهيان هين	*yahāṅ bahut makkhiyāṅ haiṅ,*	Here are a great many flies.
اسکو بڑي دور انديسي هي	*us-kō baṛī dūr-andēshī hai .*	She possesses much foresight.

اسني مال بهت جمع كيا	*us-nē māl bahut jamʿ kiyā* .	He has made a large fortune.
گهر كي بنياد پڑي	*ghar-kī bunyād paṛī* . . .	The foundation of the house was laid.
آينده كي بات هم نهين جانتي	*āyanda-kī bāt ham nahīṅ jāntē,*	We cannot see into futurity.
همني اسي خبر كي كاغذ مين ديكها	*hum-nē usē k͟habar kē kāg͟haẕ mēṅ dēkhā,*	I saw this in the gazette.
تم اس صاحب كو جانتي هو	*tum us ṣāḥib kō jāntē hō* .	Do you know that gentleman?
اسني علم ارض مين ايك كتاب تصنيف كي هي	*us-nē ʿilm-i-arẓ mēṅ ēk kitāb taṣnīf kī hai,*	He has composed a book on geography.
اسكي پانچ لڑكي تين بيٹي دو بيٹي هين	*us-kē pānch laṛkē, tin bēṭē, dō bēṭī haiṅ,*	He has five children, three boys and two girls.
خبر دار يهه سهل مين ٹوٹ جائيگا شيشي كا هي	*k͟habar dār yih sahl mēṅ ṭūṭ jāʼēgā shīshē kā hai,*	Take care, this will easily break, it is made of glass.
همني ايك جوڑا دستانه مول ليا هي	*ham-nē ēk jōṛā dastāna mōl liyā hai,*	I have bought a pair of gloves.
تم جانتي هو كس سي سريش بنا هي	*tum jāntē hō kis sē sarēsh banā hai,*	Do you know what glue is made of?
سوني روپي لوهي پيتل يا تانبي سي زنجير بني هي	*sōnē rūpē lōhē pītal yā tāmbē sē zanjīr banī hai,*	Is this chain made of gold, silver, iron, brass, or copper?
اپ مهرباني كركي خبر كيجيي	*āp mihrbānī karkē k͟habar kījiyē,*	Have the goodness, Sir, to inform me.
اسني اپني باپ كو بهت تكليف دي	*us-nē apnē bāp kō bahut taklīf dī,*	He has caused much grief to his father.
اس لڑكي كا مربي كون هي	*is laṛkē kā murabbī kaun hai,*	Who is the guardian of this child?
اسكو صبحكي پهرني كي عادت هي	*us-kō ṣubḥ-kē phirnē kī ʿādat hai,*	He is in the habit of walking out early.

اسکا هاتھ پکڑ لو	*us-kā hāth pakaṛ lō* . . .	Take hold of his hand.
همکو سورج نکلني سي کام کرني جاني هوتا هي يهه بڑي مشکل هي	*ham-kō sūraj nikalnē sē kām karnē jānē hōtā hai, yih baṛī mushkil hai,*	I must go to work every day at sunrise: this is a great hardship.
ڈاک گھر بند هوگا اسلئي همني جلدي چٹھي لکھي	*ḍāk ghar band hōgā, is-li'ē ham-nē jaldī chiṭṭhī likhī,*	I write in great haste to save the post.
اسني کمري مين گھستي ٹوپي اتار لي	*us-nē kamarē mēn̐ ghustē ṭōpī utār lī,*	On entering the room he took off his hat.
اسکو آگي سي اب تخفيف هي	*us-kō āgē sē ab ta<u>kh</u>fīf hai,*	She is now much better than she was.
يهان کاغذ کا بڑا ڈھير هي ليکر اور جگهه مين رکھو	*yahān̐ kāg͟haẕ kā baṛā ḍhēr hai, lēkar aur jagah mēn̐ rakhō,*	Here is a heap of papers, put them away.
چلني مين ميرا پاٴون اسکي ايڑي پر پڑ گيا	*chalnē mēn̐ mērā pā'ōn̐ us-kī ēṛī par paṛ gayā,*	I trod on his heel.
کتني انچائي اس ديوار کي هي	*kitnī unchā'ī is dīwār kī hai*	What is the height of this wall?
تم هماري اس کام مين کچھ مدد کر سکتي هو	*tum hamārē is kām mēn̐ kuchh madad kar saktē hō,*	Can you afford me any assistance in this?
وي فقط ترکاري کھاکر جيتي هين	*wē fakaṭ tarkārī khākar jītē hain̐,*	They live on herbs solely.
بنگالي مين پهاڑ بهت کم هين	*bangālē mēn̐ pahāṛ bahut kam hain̐,*	There are but few hills in Bengal.
اسني اشارہ کيا اس ارادي پر	*us-nē ishāra kiyā is irādē par,*	He gave a hint to this effect.
يهانسي گنگا ساگر تک کرايه کشتي کا کيا هوگا	*yahān̐-sē gangā sāgar tak kirāya kishtī kā kyā hōgā*	What will be the boat-hire from this place to Saugor?
يهان زمين مين سوراخ کرو	*yahān̐ zamīn mēn̐ sūrā<u>kh</u> karō,*	Make a hole in the ground here.
بهت دير هوئي اب هم گھر جاوين	*bahut dēr hū'ī ab ham ghar jāwēn̐,*	It is late, let us now return home.

اسني بڑي عزت پائي	*us-nē baṛī ʿizzat pāʾī*	He has obtained much honour.
همني بنسي سي ايک مچهلي پکڑي	*ham-nē bansī sē ēk machhlī pakṛī,*	I have caught a fish with a hook.
اس گائي کي سينگ نهين	*is gāʾē kē sīng nahīṅ*	This cow has no horns.
ايک دار الشفا وهان بنيگا	*ēk dāru-sh-shafā wahāṅ banēgā,*	An hospital is about to be built there.
تم جانتي هو کيا بجا هي	*tum jāntē hō kyā bajā hai*	Do you know what hour it is?
تمني گرني سي کچه چوٹ پائي	*tum-nē girnē sē kuchh chōṭ pāʾī,*	Had you any hurt from your fall?
همکو خيال نهين تها که تم آج آؤگي	*ham-kō khiyāl nahīṅ thā ki tum āj āʾōgē,*	I had no idea that you would come to day.
کتني دن سي تمکو يهه بيماري هي	*kitnē din sē tum kō yih bīmārī hai,*	How long have you had this illness?
يهه خيال کهانسي پيدا هوا	*yih khiyāl kahāṅ-sē paidā hūʾā,*	Whence came this idea?
يهه مهم عظيم هي	*yih muhimm-i-ʿaẓīm hai*	This is an important affair.
وه مکار مشهور هي	*wuh makkār-i mash'hūr hai*	He is a notorious impostor.
يهه مهر نهين اٹهتي	*yih muhr nahīṅ uṭhtī*	This seal makes no impression.
يهه لکڑي اگر ايک پور بڑي هوتي تو اس کام مين آتي	*yih lakṛī agar ēk pōr baṛī hōtī, tō is kām mēṅ ātī,*	Had this piece of wood been an inch longer, it would have done very well.
تم جانتي هو اسکي آمدني کيا هي	*tum jāntē hō us-kī āmdanī kyā hai,*	Do you know what is his income?
دوسري مهيني کي پهلي تاريخ تک هماري رهني سي تمهين کچه رنج هوگا	*dūsrē mahīnē kī pahlī tārīkh tak hamārē rahnē sē tumhēṅ kuchh ranj hōgā,*	Will my staying here till the first of next month be any inconvenience to you?
اس کتاب مين فهرست هي	*is kitāb mēṅ fihrist hai*	Is there an index to this book?

تم کتني دنون سي هندوستان مين هو	*tum kitnē dinōṅ sē Hindūstān mēṅ hō,*	How long have you been in India?
يہ کام ايسا نهين کہ تم غفلت کرو	*yih kām aisā nahīṅ ki tum ghaflat karō,*	This affair is not to be treated with indifference.
تمهاري بيماري کا احوال همني گئي هفتي سي سنا	*tumhārī bīmārī kā aḥwāl ham-nē ga'ē haftē sē sunā,*	I heard of your indisposition last week.
اگر تم آج کي ڈاک مين خط بهيجو تو ابهي ڈاک گهر مين بهيجني چاهيي	*agar tum āj kī ḍāk mēṅ khaṭṭ bhējō tō abhī ḍāk ghar mēṅ bhējnē chāhiyē,*	If the letter goes by to day's post, you must send it to the post-office now.
حکيم ني يہ نسخہ لکها هي	*ḥakīm nē yih nuskha likhā hai,*	The doctor wrote this prescription.
اسني هماري سامهني ايسا کها	*us-nē hamārē sāmhnē aisā kahā,*	He said so in my presence.
همارا تلفظ درست هي	*hamārā talaffuẓ durust hai*	Is my pronunciation correct?
تم اسکي کيا دليل لاتي هو	*tum is-kī kyā dalīl lātē hō* .	What proof can you give of this?
تم توشہ سفر کا کرو	*tum tōsha safar kā karō* .	Make provision for your journey.
يہ کتاب کسطرح چهاپي گئي سارا تختہ هي يا دو ورقا يا سہ ورقا يا چو ورقا	*yih kitāb kis-ṭaraḥ chhāpī ga'ī sārā takhta hai yā dō-waraḳā yā si-waraḳā yā chau-waraḳā,*	Is the work printed in folio, quarto, octavo, or duodecimo?
گودڑ سي کاغذ بنتا هي	*gūdaṛ sē kāghaẓ bantā hai* .	Paper is made of rags.
ملک اور ملکہ وهان دونو حاضر تهي	*malik aur malika wahāṅ dōnō ḥāẓir thē,*	The king and queen were both present.
ايک قلم اور ايک دستہ کاغذ عنايت کيجئي	*ēk ḳalam aur ēk dasta kāghaẓ ʿināyat kījīʾē,*	Give me a quill and a quire of paper.
يہ فقرہ اور کسي کتابسي چن ليا هي	*yih fiḳra aur kisī kitāb-sē chun liyā hai,*	This is a quotation from some other book.

اسني سب روپئي گھڑدوڑ کي بازيمين اڑا دئي	*is-nē sab rupī'ē ghuṛ-dauṛ kī bāzī-mēṅ uṛā dī'ē,*	He lost all his money at a horse-race.
باغ کي کچھ باڑ ٹوٹ گئي	*bāgh kī kuchh bāṛ ṭūṭ ga'ī.*	Some of the garden rails are broken.
کون يہ خبر لايا	*kaun yih khabar lāyā* . .	Who brought these tidings?
وي حقه پيتي هين	*wē ḥukka pītē haiṅ* . . .	They smoke tobacco.
همني مشعل جلاکي سير کيا	*ham-nē mash'al jalākē sair kiyā,*	We travelled by the light of torches.
اسني همکو ايک چهوٹي کتاب دي	*us-nē ham-kō ēk chhōṭī kitāb dī,*	He gave me a tract.
تمهارا پيشه کيا هي	*tumhārā pēsha kyā hai* . .	What is your trade?
هم خزاني مين جاتي هين	*ham khazānē mēṅ jātē haiṅ,*	I am going to the treasury.
ان موتيونکي قيمت کيا هي	*un mōtiyōṅ-kī ḳīmat kyā hai,*	What is the price of those pearls?
هم چهاتا پيچهي چهوڑ آئي هين	*ham chhātā pīchhē chhōṛ ā'ē haiṅ,*	I have left behind my umbrella.
اس کتاب کي ايک جلد هي يا دو	*is kitāb kī ēk jild hai yā dō*	Is the book in one or two volumes?
اب وي جهاز مين مندراسکو جاتي هين	*ab wē jahāz mēṅ mandrās-kō jātē haiṅ,*	He is now on a voyage to Madras.
يہ کسکام کا هي	*yih kis-kām kā hai* . . .	What is made of this?
همکو ايک ويفر ديجيي	*ham-kō ēk wēfār dījiyē* . .	Please to give me a wafer.
کيا مهينا تم پاتي هو	*kyā mahīnā tum pātē hō* .	What wages do you get?
باغکي ديوار گر پڑي	*bāgh-kī dīwār gir paṛī* . .	The garden wall is fallen down.
تمهاري گهڑي اچهي چلتي هي	*tumhārī ghaṛī achchhī chaltī hai,*	Your watch goes well.
يہ راه چندرنگر کي هي	*yih rāh Chandarnagar kī hai,*	Is this the road to Chandernagore?
هم کسطرح اسکو کرينگي	*ham kis-ṭaraḥ us-kō karēṅgē*	In what way am I to do this?

يهہ پتھر کتنا بھاري هي	*yih patthar kitnā bhārī hai*	What is the weight of this stone?
ايک کوا انسي کھودني کهو	*ēk kū'ā un-sē khōdnē kahō* .	Tell him to dig a well.
تم چاهو تو سب لو	*tum chāhō tō sab lō* . . .	You are welcome to the whole.
تمهاري خواهش کيا هي	*tumhārī khwāhish kyā hai* .	What is your wish?
تمسي يهہ هو سکتا هي	*tum-sē yih hō saktā hai* .	Are you able to do this?
هم دس روز غير حاضر تهي	*ham das rōz ghair ḥāẓir thē*	I have been absent ten days.
هم خالي زمين پر بيٹهي تهي	*ham khālī zamīn par baiṭhē thē,*	We sat on the bare ground.
کيا هم اسمين تقصيروار هين	*kyā ham is-mēṅ taḳṣīr-wār haiṅ,*	Am I blamable in this?
بيشک تم بيقصور هو	*bē-shakk tum bē-ḳuṣūr hō* .	Without doubt you are blameless.
يهہ چهري بڑي کند هي	*yih chhurī baṛī kund hai* .	This knife is very blunt.
سمندر خوب ٹهيرا هوا تها	*samundar khūb ṭhēṛā hū'ā thā,*	The sea was quite calm.
جو وه کهتا هي تم سچ سمجهتي هو	*jō wuh kahtā hai tum sach samajhtē hō,*	Do you think what he says is true?
هان هم اسکو يقين جانتي هين	*hāṅ ham us-kō yaḳīn jāntē haiṅ,*	Yes, I am certain of it.
همين جاڑا بهت لگتا هي	*hamēṅ jāṛā bahut lagtā hai*	I feel very cold.
عوام ايسا کهتي هين	*ʿawāmm aisā kahtē hain* . .	The common people speak thus.
وه اس زبان مين کامل هي	*wuh is zabān mēṅ kāmil hai*	He is complete master of the language.
يهہ سطر ٹيڑهي هي	*yih saṭr ṭēṛhī hai*. . . .	This line is crooked.
اسکي آني نه آني مين شک هي	*us-kē ānē na ānē mēṅ shakk hai,*	It is doubtful whether he will come.

وہ گونگي بہري هي	*wuh gūngī bahrī hai.* . .	She is both deaf and dumb.
وي مٹي کي برتن بناتي هين	*wē miṭṭī ke bartan banātē hain,*	They manufacture earthenware.
هم تمکو سهل سبق دينگي	*ham tum-kō sahal sabaḳ dēṅgē,*	I will set you an easy lesson.
اپني بڑي بهاي کو يہ کتاب دينا	*apnē baṛē bhā'ī kō yih kitāb dēnā,*	Give this book to your elder brother.
تم دونون سي بڑا کون هي	*tum ḍōnōṅ sē baṛā kaun hai*	Which of you two is the elder?
دو خط برابر کهينچو	*dō* ***kh****aṭṭ barābar khainchō* .	Draw two even lines.
وي سبکي سب گئي هين	*wē sab kē sab gā'ē hain* . .	They are gone, every one of them.
تمکو کوي مانع نهين جو چاهو سو کرو	*tum-kō kō'ī mānìʿ nahīṅ jō chāhō sō karō,*	You are free to do as you please.
وہ غير محتمل هي	*wuh* ***gh****air muḥtamil hai* .	That is not probable.
وہ جهاز جلد آيا	*wuh jahāz jald āyā* . . .	That vessel has made a quick passage.
يہ نادر بوٹا هي	*yih nādir būṭā hai* . . .	This is a very rare plant.
کچا چاول کهانا خوب نهين	*kachchā chāwal khānā* ***kh****ūb nahīṅ,*	It is not good to eat rice raw.
يي چيزين بالفعل کمياب هين	*yē chīzēṅ bi-l-fiʿl kam-yāb hain,*	This article is now scarce.
هم جاني سي باز نهين رہ سکتي	*ham jānē sē bāz nahīṅ rah saktē,*	I cannot avoid going.
همني سنا وي صحيح سلامت لندن پهنچي	*ham-nē sunā wē ṣaḥīḥ salāmat landan pahunchē,*	I heard of his safe arrival in London.
همين يقين نهين کہ ايسا هوا هي	*hamēṅ yaḳīn nahīṅ ki aisā hū'ā hai,*	I am not certain that it is so.
تم موٹا کاغذ چاهتي هو يا باريک	*tum mōṭā kā***gh***az chāhtē hō yā bārīk,*	Do you wish for thick paper, or thin?
انکي فعلون مين دغابازي بهري هي	*un-kē fiʿlōṅ mēṅ da***gh***ā-bāzī bharī hai,*	Their conduct was full of treachery.

يہہ خط ناگہاني پہنچا	*yih khaṭṭ nāgahānī pahunchā,*	This letter was unexpected.
تمني اور هي قسم کا بيج مول ليا هي	*tum-nē aur hī ḳism kā bīj mōl liyā hai,*	You have bought the wrong kind of seed.
جو هم کہتي هين تم اسکو قبول کرتي هو يا نهين	*jō ham kahtē hain tum is-kō ḳabūl kartē hō yā nahīn,*	Do you accede to what I propose, or not?
هم اپني گهر مين تمهاري مهماني کر سکتي هين	*ham apnē ghar mēn tumhārī mihmānī kar saktē hain,*	I can accommodate you in my house.
مين اپني خواهش بهرپور نکر سکا	*main apnī khwāhish bharpūr na-kar sakā,*	I was not able to accomplish my wishes.
آج محفل موقوف هي دو شنبي کي روز پهر هوگي	*āj maḥfil mauḳūf hai dō shambē kē rōz phir hōgī,*	To day's meeting was adjourned till Monday next.
وه خبر سنکي بهت آزرده هوا	*wuh khabar sunkē bahut āzurda hū'ā,*	The news afflicted him greatly.
اتنا مهينا هم نهين دي سکتي	*itnā mahīnā ham nahīn dē saktē,*	I cannot afford to give so much wages.
مهرباني کرکر هماري مدد کرو	*mihrbānī karkar hamārī madad karō,*	Pray afford me your assistance.
عدالتمين کهڙي هوتي هي وه کانپني لگا	*ʿadālat-mēn khaṛē hōtē hī wuh kāmpnē lagā,*	On appearing before the court he was much agitated.
همني کل ايک بڑي مچهلي پکڙي	*ham-nē kal ēk baṛī machhlī pakṛī,*	I caught a large fish yesterday.
گذري منگلکو مين ني اسکو ديکها	*guzrē mangal-kō main-nē is-kō dēkhā,*	I saw him last Tuesday.
يہہ لکها پڑها نهين جاتا	*yih likhā paṛhā nahīn jātā*	This writing is not legible.
همارا مهينا اسکيسي کم هي	*hamārā mahīnā is-kē-sē kam hai,*	My wages are less than his.
وه بيجان هوکر زمين پر گر پڑا	*wuh bē-jān hōkar zamīn par gir paṛā,*	He fell to the ground lifeless.
يہہ بوجه بهاري هي يا هلکا	*yih bōjh bhārī hai yā halkā*	Is this package light or heavy?

يهہ کمرا خوب روشن هي	*yih kamarā khūb rōshan hai*	This is a light room.
يي کوٹھرياں بہت اونچياں هين	*yē kōṭhriyāṅ bahut ūnchi-yāṅ haiṅ,*	These rooms are very lofty.
تم کتني دن وهاں رهوگي	*tum kitnē din wahāṅ rahōgē*	How long shall you remain there?
وہ بہت تهوڑي قيمت مانگتا هي	*wuh bahut thōṛī ḳīmat māngtā hai,*	The price he asks is very low.
وہ بہت موٹا هوا هي	*wuh bahut mōṭā hū'ā hai* .	He is now grown very lusty.
وهاں تمهارا جانا نہ جانا برابر هي	*wahāṅ tumhārā jānā najānā barābar hai,*	It is immaterial whether you go or not.
پہاڑ کو جنبش نهين	*pahāṛ kō jumbish nahīṅ* . .	A mountain is motionless.
اسمين طرفين کا فائدہ هوگا	*is-mēṅ ṭarafain kā fā'ida hōgā,*	This will be for our mutual benefit.
هم دوسري مهيني وهاں جاوينگي	*ham dūsrē mahīnē wahāṅ jāwēṅgē,*	We will go there next month.
هماري انگلياں جاڑي سي ٹهٹهر گئين	*hamārī ungliyāṅ jāṛe sē ṭhiṭhir ga'īṅ,*	My fingers are numbed with cold.
تمني اپني خط مين تاريخ نهين لکهي	*tum-nē apnē khaṭṭ mēṅ tārīkh nahīṅ likhī,*	You have not dated your letter.
يهہ زمين بوئي گئي هي	*yih zamīn bō'ī ga'ī hai* . .	This land is cultivated.
يهہ اصطلاح في الحال متروک هي	*yih iṣṭilāḥ fi-l-ḥāl matrūk hai,*	This term is become obsolete.
ڈر کي ماري اسکا رنگ زرد هوگيا	*ḍar kē mārē us-kā rang zard hō gayā,*	He became pale through fear.
وہ اب غريب هوگيا	*wuh ab gharīb hō gayā* . .	He is now become poor.
هم تم سي کوئي مخصوص بات کہا چاهتي هين	*ham tum sē kō'ī makhṣūṣ bāt kahā chāhtē haiṅ,*	I wish to converse on particular business.
يهہ صاف لکها هي اور بآساني پڑها جاتا هي	*yih ṣāf likhā hai aur ba-āsānī paṛhā jātā hai,*	This writing is plain and easy to be read.
انهون ني مخفي بات چيت کي	*unhōṅ nē makhfī bāt-chīt kī*	They held a private conversation.
يهہ کاغذ آگ سي سينکو	*yih kāghaz āg-sē sēnkō* . .	Dry this paper at the fire.

اس صندوق کو خالي کرو	*is ṣandūḳ-kō khālī karō* . .	Empty this box.
کون ايسي لوگونکو کام ديگا	*kaun aisē lōgōṅ-kō kām dēgā*	Who would employ such people as these?
همارا خط اپني خط مين رکهه دو	*hamārā khaṭṭ apnē khaṭṭ mēṅ rakh dō,*	Enclose my letter in yours.
همني اسکو نوکر رکها هي	*ham-nē is-kō naukar rakhā hai,*	I have engaged him as my servant.
هم پوچهکر تمکو خبر دينگي	*ham pūchh-kar tum-kō khabar dēṅgē,*	I will enquire, and let you know.
وه داناۓي مين هر ايک سي بڑا هي	*wuh dānā'ī mēṅ har-ēk sē baṛā hai,*	He excels every one in intelligence.
يي جانور فقط گهاس کهاتي هين	*yē jānwar faḳaṭ ghās khātē haiṅ,*	These animals feed only on grass.
جاؤ باغ سي تهوڑا ميوه لاؤ	*jā'ō bāgh sē thōṛā mēwa lā'ō*	Go fetch some fruit out of the garden.
اس پيچکو ريتي سي گهسو	*is pēch-kō rētī sē ghisō* . .	File this screw.
تم آگي جاؤ هم پيچهي آوينگي	*tum āgē jā'ō ham pīchhē āwēṅgē,*	You go before, I will follow.
تم يي چيزين کتني جلدي تيار کرسکتي هو	*tum yē chīzēṅ kitnī jaldī taiyār kar saktē hō,*	How soon can you furnish these things?
وي اپني مقدور بهر بهت جلد گيي	*wē apnē maḳdūr bhar bahut jald ga'ē,*	They hasted away as fast as possible.
اسکا زخم اب اچها هوا هي	*is-kā zakhm ab achchhā hū'ā hai,*	His wound is now healed.
يي چيزين ولايت سي آئين هين	*yē chīzēṅ wilāyat sē ā'īṅ haiṅ,*	These things were imported from Europe.
تمني کسواسطي ايسا کرنا اسي سکهلايا	*tum-nē kis-wāsṭē aisā karnā usē sikhlāyā,*	Why did you teach him to act thus?
هم کيون اس کام مين هاتهه ڈالين	*ham kyūṅ us kām mēṅ hāth ḍālēṅ,*	Why should we interfere in that affair?
جو وه همکو کهتا هي تمهين ترجمه کرني هوگا	*jō wuh ham-kō kahtā hai tum-hēṅ tarjuma karnē hōgā,*	You must interpret what he says to me.

اي صاحب همكو اميد هي كه جناب كو تصديع ندين	*ai ṣāḥib ham-kō ummēd hai ki janāb-kō taṣdīʿ na-dēṅ,*	I hope, Sir, I do not interrupt you.
يهه مقدمه همين تجويز كرني هوگا	*yih muḳaddama hamēṅ tajwīz karnē hōgā,*	We must investigate this matter.
يهه خبر سنكر وه بهت ڈر گيا	*yih khabar sun-kar wuh bahut ḍar gayā,*	The news very much alarmed him.
نقد روپيي پاني سي وي پانچ روپيي سيكڑا چهوڑ دينگي	*naḳd rūpiyē pānē sē wē pānch rūpiyē saikṛā chhōṛ dēṅgē,*	They allow five per cent. discount for ready money.
حساب كركي پانسو روپيي هونگي	*ḥisāb karkē pānsau rūpiyē hōṅge,*	The bill will amount to five hundred rupees.
حسابكي جمع ديكهكر همكو تعجب هوا	*ḥisāb-kī jamʿ dēkh-kar ham-kō taʿajjub hū'ā,*	I was amazed at the amount.
اسكي چيزين قيمت تجويز هوكر بيچي جاوينگي	*us-kī chīzēṅ ḳīmat tajwīz hōkar bēchī jāwēṅgī,*	His goods will be appraised and sold.
وه پكڑا گيا اور قيد هوا	*wuh pakṛā gayā aur ḳaid hū'ā,*	He was apprehended and put in prison.
همكو چاهيي آپسمين مدد كرين	*ham-kō chāhiyē āpas-mēṅ madad karēṅ,*	We ought to assist each other.
همني خبر پائي دس گهنٹي كي وقت دار العدالتمين حاضر هوني هوگا	*ham-nē khabar pā'ī das ghanṭē kē waḳt dāru-l-ʿadālat-mēṅ ḥāẓir hōnē hōgā,*	I have received notice to attend the court at ten o'clock.
تم پيڑي كو بڑهاكر تنور مين لگاٶ	*tumpēṛē kō baṛhākar tanūr mēṅ lagā'ō,*	Bake this dough in the oven.
وه ايك پيسي سي كم نهين ديتا	*wuh ēk paisē sē kam nahīṅ dētā,*	He would not abate me one *pice*.
همني بهت آدميونكو گنگا مين غسل كرتي ديكها	*ham-nē bahut ādmiyōṅ-kō gangā mēṅ ghusl kartē dēkhā,*	I saw numbers bathing in the Ganges.

جو همني كيا هي معاف كيجيي	*jō ham-nē kiyā kai mu'āf kījiyē,*	I beg your pardon for what I have done.
اسني اپني ساري كاغذونپر سياهي ڈال دي	*is-nē apnē sārē kāg͟haẕōṅ-par siyāhī ḍāl dī,*	He blotted his paper all over.
اسكو مين ني سر پر بوجه ليجاتي ديكها	*is-kō maiṅ-nē sir par bōjh lējātē dēkhā,*	I saw him carrying a load on his head.
انهون ني خط لكهكر چارون طرف خبر بهيجي هي	*unhōṅ nē k͟hatt likh-kar chārōṅ ṭaraf k͟habar bhējī hai,*	They have circulated notices.
هم يه خوب نهين سمجه سكتي	*ham yih k͟hūb nahīṅ samajh saktē,*	I do not well understand this.
تمني همارا كام درهم برهم كر ديا	*tum-nē hamārā kām darham barham kar diyā,*	You have confused my work.
جهاز كا بوجه اسي آڑهت مين ديا گيا	*jahāz kā bōjh usē āṛhat mēṅ diyā gayā,*	The cargo of the vessel was consigned to him.
همكو نچاهيي كسيكو حقير سمجهين	*ham-kō na-chāhiyē kisī-kō ḥaḳīr samjhēṅ,*	We ought not to despise any one.
تم اس نوكر كو اور مت اٹكاؤ	*tum us naukar-kō aur mat aṭkā'ō,*	Do not detain the servant any longer.
وه دو پهر پر ايك گهڑي كهانا كهاتا هي	*wuh dō pahar par ēk guṛē khānā khātā hai,*	He dines at one o'clock.
همني آج تك چوركو نه پهچانا	*ham-nē āj tāk chōr-kō na pahchānā,*	I have not as yet discovered the thief.
اسكا حكم هم رد نهين كر سكتي	*us-kā ḥukm ham radd nahīṅ kar saktē,*	I cannot disobey his orders.
تم اسكو منع كر سكتي هو كه وه پهر ايسا نكري	*tum us-kō man' kar saktē hō ki wuh phir aisā na-kare,*	Cannot you dissuade him from doing so?
اس رسي كو دهرا كرو تو كامكي هوگي	*is rassī-kō duhrā karō tō kām-kī hōgī,*	Double this string, and then it will do.
تهوڑا صبر كرو وه اب كپڑي پهنتا هي	*thōṛā ṣabr karō wuh ab kapṛē pahantā hai,*	Wait a little, he is now dressing.

اس طرح سي هم دس روپيي مهينا كما سكتي هين	*is ṯarḥ sē ham das rūpiyē mahīnā kamā saktē haiṅ,*	In this way I can earn ten rupees a month.
ايسا جلد هانكني كو گاڑي بان كو منع كرو	*aisā jald hānknē kō gāṛī-bān kō mānʻ karō,*	Tell the coachman not to drive so fast.
جو همني آگي خط نلكها يه قصور معاف كيجيي	*jō ham-nē āgē khaṯṯ na-likhā yih ḳuṣūr muʻāf kījiyē,*	Pray excuse my not writing before.
اي صاحب تمهارا حكم جلدي كيا جائيگا	*ai ṣāḥib tumhārā ḥukm jaldī kiyā jā'ēgā,*	Sir, your orders shall be executed without delay.
اگر تم پوچهو تو جو تم نه سمجهتي هو وه تمهين سمجها ديگا	*agar tum pūchhō tō jō tum na samajhtē hō wuh tumhēṅ samjhā dēgā,*	If you ask, he will explain any part which you do not understand.
يه بات انگريزي مين كسطرح بولي جاتي هي هم نهين جانتي	*yih bāt angrēzī mēṅ kis-ṯarḥ bōlī jātī hai ham nahīṅ jāntē,*	I do not know how to express this in English.
اسكي مدد اگر نهوتي تو همارا كام سرانجام نه پاتا	*us-kī madad agar na-hōtī tō hamārā kām sar-anjām na pātā,*	Had it not been for his assistance I should have failed in my purpose.
اگر وه نپكڑتا تو مين دريا مين گر پڑتا	*agar wuh na-pakaṛtā tō maiṅ daryā mēṅ gir paṛtā,*	I should have fallen into the river but for him.
اگر تم آتي تو هم بهت خوش هوتي	*agar tum ātē tō ham bahut khush hōtē,*	I should have been glad if you had come.
اگر پهر تم ايسا كروگي تو مجرم هوگي	*agar phir tum aisā karōgē to mujrim hōgē,*	If you do so again, you must be fined.
جوار بهر پور هي جهاز اب پاني پر چليگا	*jawār bhar-pūr hai jahāz ab pānī par chalēgā,*	It is high water, the vessel will now float.
اگر پهلي مين اسي ديكهونگا تو خبر دي دونگا	*agar pahlē maiṅ usē dēkhūṅgā tō khabar dē dūṅgā,*	If I should happen to see him before you do, I will tell him this.
وي اپني مقدور بهر بهت جلد گئي	*wē apnē maḳdūr bhar bahut jald ga'ē,*	They hasted away as fast as possible.

وہ اپني گهوڑي پر چڑهکر چلا گيا	*wuh apnē ghōṛē par chaṛhkar chalā gayā,*	Having mounted his horse, he rode off.
جو هم كهتي هين تم سنتي هو	*jō ham kahtē hain̄ tum suntē hō,*	Do you hear what I say?
وهان پهنچني كي ليي همين ايک پالكي اور كشتي كرايه كرني هوگي	*wahān̄ pahunchnē kē li'ē hamēn̄ ēk pālkī aur kishtī kirāya karnē hōgī,*	To go there I must hire a palanquin and boat.
همكو يهه اميد هي جلدي تمسي ملاقات هوگي	*ham-kō yih ummēd hai jaldī tum-sē mulāḳāt hōgī,*	I hope soon to see you.
كوئي يهان ايسا نهين جو همين اس مقدمي كي خبر دي سكي	*kō'ī yahān̄ aisā nahīn̄ jō hamēn̄ is muḳaddamē kī khabar dē sakē,*	Is there no one here that can inform me concerning this?
جو بات خط كي لكهني مين تم بهول گئي وه سطرونمين لكهه دو	*jō bāt khaṭṭ kē likhnē mēn̄ tum bhūl ga'ē wuh saṭrōn̄-mēn̄ likh dō,*	Interline what you have omitted in your letter.
ايک چيتي پر همني كئي گوليان لگائيان ليكن اسكي ايک بهي نلگي	*ēk chītē par ham-nē ka'ī goliyān̄ lagā'iyān̄ lēkin us-kē ēk bhī na-lagī,*	We fired several times at a *chītā*, but not one ball struck him.
اگر وه بيشتر همكو كهتا تو هم بهت خوش هوتي	*agar wuh beshtar ham-kō kahtā tō ham bahut khush hōtē,*	If he had informed me of this before, I should have been better pleased.

DIALOGUE.

Addresses at meeting.

سلم	*salām*	Peace or safety!
سلمٌ عليكم	*salāmun ālaikum*	The peace (be) on you!
بندگي عرض كرتا هون	*bandagī ārz kartā hūn̄* . .	My service to you, Sir!

In reply.

و عليكم السلام	*wa ā̊laikumu-s-salām* . . .	And on you (be) the peace!
صاحب سلامت	*ṣāḥib salāmat*	Sir, peace or health (to you)!
ميري بهي بندگي پهنچي	*mērī bhī bandagī pahunchē*	My service, also, to you!
حضرت سلامت بندگي	*ḥaẓrat salāmat bandagī* . .	Sir, health (and my) service (to you)!

At parting.

خدا حافظ	*khudā ḥāfiẓ*	God (be your) protector! Farewell!
سلامٌ عليكم	*salāmun ā̊laikum*	Peace (be) on you!

Inquiry after health.

تمهاري كيا حالت هي	*tumhārī kyā ḥālat hai* . .	How are you?
اب آپ كا مزاج كيسا هي	*ab āp kā mizāj kaisā hai* .	How do you do, Sir?
اب مزاج مبارك كيسا هي	*ab mizāj-i mubārak kaisā hai*	

In reply to inquiry after health.

دعا كرتا هون	*du'ā̊ kartā hūṅ*	I pray (for you).
الحمد لله	*alḥamdu lillāh*	Praise to God!
فضل الهي سي بهت اچها هي	*faẓl-i ilāhī sē bahut achchhā hai,*	By the divine favour (my health) is very good.

Inquiry after time.

كتنا دن چڑها هي	*kitnā din chaṛhā hai*. . .	What o'clock is it? (Asked before noon).
كتنا دن آيا هي	*kitnā din āyā hai*. . . .	
اب كتنا دن هي	*ab kitnā din hai*	What o'clock is it? (Asked after noon).
كتنا دن باقي هي	*kitnā din bāḳī hai* . . .	
كتنا دن رها هي	*kitnā din rahā hai* . . .	

In reply to inquiry after time.

دس گهنٹي	*das ghanṭē*	Ten o'clock.
دس گهڑي	*das ghaṛī*	

ساڑھي دس گھڑي	*sāṛhē das ghaṛī*	Half past ten o'clock.
اگارہ کا عمل هي	*igārah kā ãmal hai* . . .	Near eleven.
سوا گيارہ کا عمل هي	*sawā gyārah kā ãmal hai* .	A quarter past eleven.
بارہ گھڑي کا عمل هي	*bārah ghaṛī kā ãmal hai* .	Between eleven and twelve.

ميرا مجرا پهنچي	*mērā mujrā pahunchē* . .	My respects (to you)!
تمهارا کيا مقصد هي	*tumhārā kyā makṣad hai* .	What is your desire?
آپ کا کيا مقصد هي	*āp kā kyā makṣad hai* . .	What is your wish, Sir?
آپ کيا کها چاهتي هين	*āp kyā kahā chāhtē haiṅ* .	What do you wish to say, Sir?

گفتگو درميان آقا اور نوکرون وغيرہ کي	*guftgū darmiyān āḳā aur naukarōṅ ō ghaira kē,*	Dialogue between a gentleman and his servants, &c.
کوئي هي	*kō'ī hai*	*Gent.* Is any one there?
نوکر آئي هين	*naukar ā'ē haiṅ*	*Gent.* Are the servants come?
سب نهين آئي هين	*sab nahīṅ ā'ē haiṅ* . . .	*Servt.* They are not all come.
کون نهين آيا	*kaun nahīṅ āyā*	*Gent.* Who is not come?
فلانہ شخص	*falāna shakhṣ*	*Servt.* Such a one.
فلانہ شخص نهين آيا	*falāna shakhṣ nahīṅ āyā* .	*Gent.* Is not such a one come?
نهين صاحب	*nahīṅ ṣāḥib*	*Servt.* No, Sir.
وہ کب آويگا	*wuh kab āwēgā*	*Gent.* When will he come?
ساڑھي نو گھڑي کي وقت	*sāṛhē nau ghaṛī kē waḳt* .	*Servt.* At half past nine.
نائي آيا هي	*nā'ī āyā hai*	*Gent.* Is the barber come?
ديکھتا هون صاحب	*dēkhtā hūṅ ṣāḥib*	*Servt.* I will see, Sir.
نهين صاحب ابتک نهين آيا	*nahīṅ ṣāḥib ab-tak nahīṅ āyā,*	*Servt.* No, Sir, he is not yet come.
ميرا کپڑا لاؤ	*mērā kapṛā lā'ō*	*Gent.* Bring my clothes.
آپ کون سي کرتي آج پهنينگي	*āp kaun-sī kurtī āj pahnēṅgē,*	*Servt.* What coat, Sir, will you put on to day?
ميري نيلي کرتي لاؤ اور کمري انگرکھا اور ازار لاؤ	*mērī nīlī kurtī lā'ō aur kamrī angarkhā aur izār lā'ō,*	*Gent.* Bring my blue coat and waistcoat and pantaloons.

هاتهہ منهہ دهوني كا پاني لاو	*hāth muṅh dhōnē kā pānī lā'ō,*	*Gent.* Bring me water to wash my hands and face.
صابون دو	*ṣābūn dō*	*Gent.* Give me the soap.
رومال كهان هي	*rūmāl kahāṅ hai*	*Gent.* Where is the towel?
صاحب يهان هي	*ṣāḥib yahāṅ hai*	*Servt.* Sir, it is here.
ميري جراب لاؤ	*mere jurrāb lā'ō*	*Gent.* Bring my stockings.
آج آپ اپنا جوتا پهنينگي يا موزي	*āj āp apnā jūtā pahnēṅgē yā mōzē,*	*Servt.* Will you, Sir, wear boots or shoes to day?
ميري موزي لاؤ	*mērē mōzē lā'ō*	*Gent.* Bring my boots.
مسواك اور منجن ميري واسطي لاؤ	*miswāk aur manjan mērē wāsṭē lā'ō,*	Bring me a tooth-brush and the tooth-powder.
كنگهي لاؤ اور سركي بالون كي واسطي برش لاؤ	*kanghī lā'ō aur sir kē bālōṅ kē wāsṭē brash lā'ō,*	Bring me a comb and hair-brush.
ميرا رومال كهان هي	*mērā rūmāl kahāṅ hai* . .	Where is my handkerchief?
ميري دستاني لاؤ	*mērē dastānē lā'ō*	Bring my gloves.
كون سي دستاني آپ كو چاهيي هين چمڙي كي يا سوتي	*kaun-sē dastānē āp kō chāhiyē haiṅ chamṛē kē yā sūtī,*	*Servt.* Will you, Sir, have cotton or leathern ones?
چمڙي كي دستاني لاؤ	*chamṛē kē dastānē lā'ō* . .	*Gent.* Leathern ones.
سئيس كو بلاؤ	*sa'is kō bulā'ō*	Call the groom.
سئيس حاضر هي صاحب	*sa'is ḥāẓir hai ṣāḥib* . . .	*Servt.* The groom is here, Sir.
گهوڙي پر زين باندهو	*ghōṛē par zīn bāndhō* . .	*Gent.* Saddle the horse.
ميري نئي ٹوپي لاؤ	*mērī na'ī ṭōpī lā'ō* . . .	Bring my new hat.
رومال جيب مين ركها هي	*rūmāl jēb mēṅ rakhā hai* .	Have you put a handkerchief in my pocket?
چابك دو	*chābuk dō*	Give me the whip.
كهارون كو بلاؤ	*kahārōṅ kō bulā'ō* . . .	Call the palanquin-bearers.
پالكي تيار كرو	*pālkī taiyār karō* . . .	Get the palanquin ready.
گرانٹ صاحب كي گهر كي طرف جاؤ	*Grānṭ ṣāḥib kē ghar kī ṭaraf jā'ō,*	Go to Mr. Grant's.
يهہ چٹهي ليجاؤ	*yih chiṭṭhī lē-jā'ō*	Take this note.

جلد آؤ	*jald ā'ō*	Come quickly.
اخبار کا کاغذ لاؤ	*akhbār kā kāghaz lā'ō* . .	Bring the newspaper.
تهوڑا ٹهنڈها پاني لاؤ	*thōṛā ṭhanḍhā pānī lā'ō* .	Bring some cold water.
يهہ گرانٹ صاحب کا گهر هي	*yih Grānṭ ṣāḥib kā ghar hai*	*Bearer.* This is Mr. Grant's house.
نهين يهہ اور صاحب کا گهر هي	*nahīṅ yih aur ṣāḥib kā ghar hai,*	*Gent.* No, this is another gentleman's.
تم فلاني صاحب کا گهر جانتي هو	*tum falānē ṣāḥib kā ghar jāntē hō,*	Do you know such a gentleman's house?
هان صاحب مين اسکو خوب جانتا هون	*hāṅ ṣāḥib maiṅ uskō khūb jāntā hūṅ,*	*Bear.* Yes, Sir, I know it well.
دربان دروازه کهولو	*darbān darwāza khōlō* . .	Ho! porter, open the door.
خبر کرو که ايک اجنبي صاحب آئي هين	*khabar karō ki ēk ajnabī ṣāḥib ā'ē haiṅ,*	*Porter.* Give intelligence that a strange gentleman is come.
پالکي اتارو	*pālkī utārō*	*Gent.* Set down the palanquin.
چهاتا لگاؤ	*chhātā lagā'ō*	Hold the umbrella between me and the sun.
کس کمري مين گرانٹ صاحب حاضري کهاتي هين	*kis kamarē mēṅ Grānṭ ṣāḥib ḥāẓirī khātē haiṅ,*	In what room does Mr. Grant breakfast?
دالان مين يا که کهانا کهاني کي کمري مين	*dālān mēṅ yā ki khānā khānē kē kamarē mēṅ,*	In the hall or in the dining-room?
خدمتگار ايک چا کي پيالي ميري واسطي لاؤ	*khidmatgār ēk chā kī piyālī mērē wāsṭē lā'ō,*	Khidmatgar, bring me a cup of tea.
صاحب چا اور قهوه دونو تيار هين جو کچهه ان دونون مين سي پسند هو سو مين آپ کي واسطي لاؤن	*ṣāḥib chā aur ḳahwa dōnō taiyār haiṅ jō kuchh un dōnōṅ mēṅ sē pasand hō sō maiṅ āp kē wāsṭē lā'ūṅ,*	*Khidmatgār.* There is both tea and coffee, Sir, whichever you please I will bring you.

اچها پہلي ميري واسطي ايک پيالي قهوه کي لاو	*achchhā pahlē mērē wāsṭē ēk piyālī ḳahwa kī lā'ō,*	*Gent.* Well, bring me a cup of coffee first.
انڈي لاو	*anḍē lā'ō . . . . . .*	Bring the eggs.
کچه اور دوده تو لاو	*kuchh aur dūdh tō lā'ō . .*	Some more milk.
ايک چا کي پيالي لاو	*ēk chā kī piyālī lā'ō . . .*	Bring me a cup of tea.
آپ کو گاڑهي چا پسند آتي هي	*āp-kō gāṛhī chā pasand ātī hai,*	*Khidmatgār.* Do you like it strong, Sir?
هان مجهي گاڑهي چا پسند آتي هي	*hāṅ mujhē gāṛhī chā pasand ātī hai,*	*Gent.* Yes, I like it strong.
ايک انڈا چمچه مولي روٹي مکهن اور کچه مربه لاو	*ēk anḍā chamcha mūlī rōṭī makkhan aur kuchh murabba lā'ō,*	Bring an egg, spoon, radish, bread, butter and some jam.
چا دان مين کچه اور چا ڈالو	*chā-dān mēṅ kuchh aur chā ḍālō,*	Put some more tea in the tea-pot.
کيا آج مچهلي نهين ملي	*kyā āj machhlī nahīṅ milī .*	What, was there no fish to be got to day?
صاحب اچهي مچهلي آج نهين ملي	*ṣāḥib achchhī machhlī āj nahīṅ milī,*	*Servt.* Sir, there was no good fish to be had to day.
پيالي مين مصري ڈالي هي	*piyālī mēṅ miṣrī ḍālī hai .*	*Gent.* Have you put sugar in the cup?
هان صاحب مصري ڈالي هي	*hāṅ ṣāḥib miṣrī ḍālī hai ·*	*Servt.* Yes, Sir, sugar is put in.
نمک اور کالي مرچ لاو	*namak aur kālī mirch lā'ō .*	*Gent.* Bring me the pepper and salt.
ميري رکابي گرانٹ صاحب کي پاس ليجاو اور تهوڑي مچهلي اور خشکه لاو	*mērī rikābī Grānṭ ṣāḥib kē pās lē-jā'ō aur thōṛī machhlī aur khushka lā'ō,*	Take my plate to Mr. Grant for some fish and rice.
کس قسم کي مچهلي آپ چاهتي هين بهکٹهي يا تپسي	*kis ḳism kī machhlī āp chāhtē haiṅ bhikṭhī yā tapassī,*	*Servt.* Which fish do you prefer, Sir, biktī or mango fish?

تهوڑي سي تپسي مچهلي ميري واسطي لاو	*thōṛī sī tapassī machhlī mērē wāsṭē lā'ō,*	*Gent.* Bring me some mango fish.
لال مرچ لاو	*lāl mirch lā'ō*	Bring the red pepper.
كيا كون سي مرچ هي كالي مرچ يا لال مرچ	*kyā kaun sī mirch hai kālī mirch yā lāl mirch,*	What kind of pepper is this? black pepper or red?
صاحب يهه لال مرچ هي	*ṣāḥib yih lāl mirch hai* . .	*Servt.* This, Sir, is red pepper.
ايك چاپينيكا چمچه لاو	*ēk chā pīnē-kā chamcha lā'ō*	*Gent.* Give me a tea-spoon.
تهوڑا سا خاگينه اپ كهائيگا	*thōṛā sā khāgīna āp khā'iyēgā,*	*Servt.* Will you take some omelet, Sir?
نهين حقه بردار كو كهو كه حقه لاوي	*nahīṅ ḥuḳḳa-bardār kō kahō ki ḥuḳḳa lāwē,*	*Gent.* No. Tell the hukka-bardār to bring the hukka.
خانسامان كو كهو كه تفن كي وقت پانچ چار صاحبون كي واسطي سامان تيار كرو	*khānsāmān kō kahō ki tifin kē waḳt pānch chār ṣāḥibōṅ kē wāsṭē sāmān taiyār karō,*	Tell the khānsāmān to provide every thing for tiffen; I expect four or five friends.
آج آپ گهر مين كهانا كهائيگا	*āj āp ghar mēṅ khānā khā'iyēgā,*	*Khānsāmān.* Do you dine at home, Sir, to day?
هان ميري ساته پانچ چهه صاحب اور بيبيان كهاني كو كهائينگي سو تم انكي مناسب كو تيار كرو	*hāṅ mērē sāth pānch chha ṣāḥib aur bībiyāṅ khānē kō khā'ēṅgē sō tum un-kē munāsib kō taiyār karō,*	*Gent.* Yes, I have five or six ladies and gentlemen; prepare every thing suitable.
قاز اور فيل مرغ ان دنون مين اچهي ملتي هين جو آپ كي مرضي هو تو مين دو تين مول ليون	*ḳāz aur fīl-murgh in dinōṅ mēṅ achchhē miltē haiṅ jō āp kī marẓī hō tō maiṅ dō tīn mōl lē'ūṅ,*	*Khāns.* Good geese and turkeys are to be had at this season; if it is your pleasure, Sir, I will buy two or three.
هان هر ايك قسم كي تين چار لو	*hāṅ har ēk ḳism kē tīn chār lō,*	*Gent.* Yes, buy three or four of each sort.

جو بهيڑ کا گوشت اچها نملي تو گاي کا گوشت ليون	*jō bhēṛ kā gōsht achchhā na-milē tō gā'ē kā gōsht lē'ūṅ,*	*Khāns.* If good mutton cannot be got, shall I buy beef?
نهين ايک مرغ اور ايک بطک منگاو	*nahīṅ ēk murgh aur ēk baṭak mangā'ō,*	*Gent.* No, send for a fowl and a duck.
قصاي کي يهان سي گوشت لاو	*kaṣā'ī kē yahāṅ sē gōsht lā'ō*	Get meat from the butcher's.
خبردار که آج چه گهڑي کي وقت کهانا تيار هووي	*khabardār ki āj chha ghaṛī kē waḳt khānā taiyār hōwē,*	Take care that dinner be ready to day at six o'clock.
هم ابهي جاوينگي کهانا کهاني کا وقت هي	*ham abhī jāwēṅgē khānā khānē kā waḳt hai,*	I must go now, it is dinner time.
کهانا تيار هو تو لاو	*khānā taiyār hō tō lā'ō* . .	Bring dinner if ready.
کهانا ميز پر آيا	*khānā mēz par āyā* . . .	*Servt.* Dinner is on the table.
تهوڑا شوربه لاو	*thōṛā shōrba lā'ō*	*Gent.* Bring me a little soup.
شوربي کا باسن ميري واسطي لاو	*shōrbē kā bāsan mērē wāsṭē lā'ō,*	Bring me a soup plate.
يهه شوربه نهايت گاڑها هي اور بهت گرم هي	*yih shōrba nihāyat gāṛhā hai aur bahut garm hai,*	This soup is too strong and too hot.
تهوڑي مچهلي ميري واسطي لاو	*thōṛī machhlī mērē wāsṭē lā'ō,*	Get me some fish.
ايک صاف رکابي اور چهري کانٹا لاو	*ēk ṣāf rikābī aur chhurī kānṭā lā'ō,*	A clean plate, and knife and fork.
چٹني اور آچار دو	*chaṭnī aur āchār dō* . . .	Give me the *chaṭnī* and pickles.
کچهه ترکاري ميري واسطي لاو	*kuchh tarkārī mērē wāsṭē lā'ō,*	Bring some vegetables.
کچهه آلو کچهه کرمکلا کچهه پهولکوبي	*kuchh ālū kuchh karamkallā kuchh phūl-kōbī,*	Some potato, some cabbage, some cauliflower.
کچهه گاي کا گوشت لاو	*kuchh gā'ē kā gōsht lā'ō* .	Bring some beef.

تهوڑا بهیڑ کا گوشت سوأر کا گوشت بچهڑي کا گوشت هرن کا گوشت حلوان مرغ تیتر خرگوش مرغابي اور سوأر کا نمکالوده ران میري واسطي لأو	*thōṛā bhēṛ kā gōsht sū'ar kā gōsht bachhrē kā gōsht hiran kā gōsht ḥalwān murgh tītar khargōsh murghābī aur sū'ar kā namak-ālūda rān mērē wāsṭē lā'ō,*	Bring me a little mutton, pork, veal, venison, kid, fowl, partridge, hare, duck and ham.
تهوڑا اس پلأو سي دو	*thōṛā us pulā'ō sē dō* . .	Give me a little of that *pulā'ō*.
کچه اور خشکه لأو	*kuchh aur khushka lā'ō* . .	Bring a little more boiled rice.
کچه نمک اور رأي اور سرکه اور تیل لأو	*kuchh namak aur rā'ī aur sirka aur tēl lā'ō,*	Bring some salt and mustard and vinegar and oil.
اس مٹهاي سي تهوڑي دو	*us miṭhā'ī sē thōṛī dō* . .	Give me a little of that sweetmeat.
یهه کون سا میوه هي	*yih kaun sā mēwa hai* . .	What sort of fruit is this?
صاحب یهه آم هي اور یهه کیلا هي	*ṣāḥib yih ām hai aur yih kēlā hai,*	*Khidmatgār*. This is a mango, and this is a plantain.
کیا انگور اور سیب اور انجیر نهین ملي	*kyā angūr aur sēb aur anjīr nahīṅ milē,*	*Gent.* What, have you not got grapes and apples and figs?
نهین صاحب اس ملک مین کم ملتي هین	*nahīṅ ṣāḥib is mulk mēṅ kam miltē haiṅ,*	*Khidmat.* No, Sir, they are rarely to be met with in this country.
شراب لأو	*sharāb lā'ō*	*Gent.* Bring me wine.
کون سي شراب آپ کو پسند آتي هي	*kaun sī sharāb āp-kō pasand ātī hai,*	*Khidmat.* Which wine, Sir, do you prefer?
تهوڑي لال شراب میري واسطي لأو	*thōṛī lāl sharāb mērē wāsṭē lā'ō,*	*Gent.* Bring me a little red wine.
ایک بیر کا شیشه لأو	*ēk bīr kā shīsha lā'ō* . .	Bring a glass of beer.
آو موزي اتارو	*ā'ō mōzē utārō*	Come, take off my boots.
کرتي اتار لو	*kurtī utār lō*	Take off my coat.

بچھونا بچھایا ھي	*bichhaunā bichhāyā hai* .	Have they made the bed?
صاحب ابتک نہين بچھایا	*ṣāḥib ab-tak nahīṅ bichhāyā*	*Khidmat.* Sir, they have not yet made it.
چراغ لگاؤ	*chirāgh lagā'ō*	*Gent.* Set the lamp.
ھمکو بڑي فجر جگاؤ	*ham-kō baṛī fajr jagā'ō* .	Wake me very early in the morning.
گھڑي ميز پر رکھو	*ghaṛī mēz par rakhō* . .	Put my watch on the table.
کرسيان ميز کي آسپاس رکھو	*kursiyāṅ mēz kē āspās rakhō*	Put the chairs round the table.
پاني کا کوزہ پلنگ کي نيچي رکھو	*pānī kā kūza palang kē nīchē rakhō,*	Put the guglet of water beneath the cot.
پلنگ کي سرھاني پر گھڑي لٹکاؤ	*palang kē sirhānē par ghaṛī laṭkā'ō,*	Hang up the watch at the head of the bed.
کنجيان تکيي کي تلي رکھ دو	*kunjiyāṅ takiyē kē talē rakh dō,*	Put the keys beneath the pillow.
سب دريچي کھول دو پر خبردار دروازہ بند کيجيو	*sab darīchē khōl dō par khabardār darwāza band kījiyō,*	Open all the windows, but take care to shut the door.
خدمتگار سي پوچھو کہ حاضري تيار کي ھي کہ نہين	*khidmatgār sē pūchhō ki ḥāẓirī taiyār kī hai ki nahīṅ,*	Ask the servant whether he has prepared breakfast or not.
سنو تو تمھارا نام کيا ھي اور تمھاري صاحب کا نام کيا	*sunō tū tumhārā nām kyā hai aur tumhārē ṣāḥib kā nām kyā,*	Pray, what is your name, and what is the name of your master?
اس صاحب کي پاس کب سي نوکر ھو	*us ṣāḥib kē pās kab sē naukar hō,*	How long have you been the servant of that gentleman?
تمھارا وطن کہان ھي اور يہان سي کتني دور ھي	*tumhārā waṭan kahāṅ hai aur yahāṅ sē kitnī dūr hai,*	What is your native country, and how far is it from this?
تم کہان کي رھني والي ھو	*tum kahāṅ kē rahnē-wālē hō*	Where do you live?
تيري بستي يہان سي کتني دور ھي	*tērī bastī yahāṅ sē kitnī dūr hai,*	How far hence is your town?

دس دن کا راستا هي	*das din kā rāstā hai.* . . .	It is ten days journey.
تمهاري عمر کيا	*tumhārī ūmr kyā.*	How old are you?
هماري عمر بيس برس کي هي	*hamārī ūmr bīs baras kī hai*	My age is twenty years.

سوداگري کا بيان	Relating to commerce, &c.*
سرکار هنڈي ليجا اور روپيي جلد لاو	Sarcār, take the draft and bring the money. Be quick.
کيا کرني هوگا ابهي گياره گهنٹي دن هوا هي	What is there to do? It is now eleven o'clock.
جلدي جاو جو همکو وقت پر روپيي مليں دو پهر ايک کي وقت هماري پاس حاضر کرو	Be quick, that I may have the money in time. Let me have it by one o'clock.
دفتر خاني ميں جاکر بڑي سرکار سي کهو	Go to the counting house, and speak to the head sarcār.
سرکار سي کهو که بنک نوٹ ليکر هنڈي کي روپيي ادا کري	Tell the sarcār to take bank notes, and pay the amount of the draft.
روپيي ابهي فلاني کو بهيجني هوگا	The money must be sent to Mr. ——.
فلاني صاحب سي عرض کرو که تين گهنٹي کي آگي باقي روپيي ادا کريں	Request Mr. —— to order what remains to be paid in before three o'clock.

* Extracted from "The Hindoostanee and English Student's Assistant," printed at Calcutta in 1826.

تم کبھو فلانی صاحب کی باغ مین گئی تھی

Have you ever been to Mr. such a one's garden?

ای صاحب مین هر روز اُس راه جاتا هون

Sir, I go that way every day.

تم وهان اسیوقت جاؤ و الّا کچھ نهوگا

You must go there immediately, else nothing will be done.

سرکار کو ایک کشتی کرایه کرنی کی لیئی بهیجو

Send a sarcār to hire a boat.

هم آج چورنگی جاوینگی

I will go to Chowringhee to day.

چینا بازار جاکر دو گول لینٹین مول لاؤ

Go to the China bazar, and buy a pair of globe lanterns.

کون رسید کا روپیه حصول کریگا

Who will collect the bills?

آغا جان حصول کرنی مین خوب مضبوط هی

Aghājān is clever in collecting bills.

فلانی صاحب سی روپئی ملنا مشکل هی

It is very difficult to get money of such a one.

هم بازار گئی تهی چینی فی روپیه مین ساڑهی تین سیر هی

I have been to the bazar; sugar is now three and a half seers a rupee.

تهوڑی دن صبر کرکی کپڑا مول لینا بهتر هی

It will be better to wait a few days, and then buy the cloth.

ایسی آدمی کس کام کی هین وی سب کار بار مین نادان هین

Of what use are such people? They know nothing of business.

هم کار بار جانتی هین همین فریب دینا دشوار هی

I understand business—I am not to be imposed upon.

کشمش فی روپیه چھ سیر هی

Raisins are six seers for a rupee.

هزار روپئی کی مول لو

Buy about one thousand rupees worth.

بازار کا نرخ ٹهیک معلوم نهین هوسکتا

There is no understanding the bazar prices.

کلکتّي مین بازار کا نِرخ دو گھڑِي یکسان نہین رہتا	In Calcutta, the bazar rate is scarcely for two hours alike.
همنّي بیعانه دِیا هَي کل چِیزین وزن کرینگي	I made a deposite; to morrow I shall see them weighed.
خبردار تم فریب نکھانا	See that you are not imposed on.
تُمنّي اُنکو نمُونی سي مِلا لِیا هَي وهٔ سب برابر هَي	Have you compared them with the sample? Do they agree?
دو یا تِین بستّي سب سي بہتر هَین	Two or three packages are superior.
جو جو چِیزین تیّار هَین جاو اور اُنکي واسطي روَنه لي آو	Go and procure a pass for the things that are ready.
ایک کِشتّي کرکي اُنهین جهاز پر بهیج دو	Get a boat, and send them on board the ship.
اَي صاحِب کپتان کي سرکار ني کها کِه آج جهاز مین یي چِیزین لاد نسکینگي	Sir, the captain's sarcar said, the goods cannot be shipped to day.
سرکار جو کهتا هَي اُسي مت مانو هم جو کهتي اُسي سُنو	Do not mind what the sarcar says, but mind what I say.
اَي صاحِب آپ کي حُکم سي مَین جاتا هون	Sir, according to your command, I am going.
او پیادي تحوِیلدار کو بُلاو	Piyāda, call the cashier.
کِتنّي رُوپیي کل جمع هُوئي هین	How much was collected yesterday?
بازار مین کمپني کي کاغذ پر کیا بٹا هَي	What is the discount on the Company's paper in the bazar?

چهه روپيي سيکڙا کمپني کي کاغذ مول ليني مين دو روپيي چهه آني اور بيچني مين دو روپيي آٹهه آني بٹا هي	If you purchase the Company's paper of six per cent. interest, the discount is two rupees six annas; and, if you sell, it is two rupees eight annas.
يي چٹهيان ٹهکاني کي موافق بهيج دو	Send these letters as directed.
پرمٹ گهر سي وي چيزين گاڙي مين کرکي لي آو	Bring those goods in carts from the Custom house.
او دربان دفتر خاني کي سرکار سب آئي هين	Darbān, are the counting-house sarcars come?
لهار کي کارخاني مين کون کام کرتا هي	Who is at work in the iron-factory?
اي صاحب کوئي ابهي تک نهين آيا	Sir, nobody is yet come.
هر روز يهي احوال هي اِسي واسطي فلاني صاحب کا کام ابهي تک تمام نهين هوا	This is the case every day, and therefore Mr. ——'s work is not yet done.
فلاني صاحب هر روز اس کام کي ليي همين کهتي هين	Mr. —— is speaking to me daily about this work.
جب وي آوين تو انکو هماري پاس بهيج دو	When they come, send them to me.
کب تک وي ولايتي چيزين پرمٹ گهر مين پڙي رهينگيان	How long are those Europe goods to lie at the Custom house?
اي صاحب بغير چلان کيونکر اسباب خلاص کر لائي سکتا هون	Sir, without an invoice to know what they are, how can I bring them?
سب صندوقونکي کهولني اور قيمت ديکهني سي تم معلوم کر سکتي هو	By opening the boxes and seeing their value, you will be able to understand.

اَي صاحِب مَین اکیلا بسْتہ کھولْني نہین سکْتا	Sir, I cannot myself open the packages.
اَي سرکْار چلان لیکر جلْد وَہان جاؤ	Sarcar, take the invoice and go directly.
دوپہر دو کي وَقْت پرْمِٹ گھر کي صاحِب ني آکر صنْدُوق کو کھُلْوایا	At two o'clock, the custom house officer came and opened the boxes.
اَي کراني نقْل کرْکي پیادي کي حَوالي کردو	Kranee, copy these and give them to the serjeant.
لُہار کو بُلاکر صنْدُوق کھُلْواکر چلان کي مُطابِق بعْد شُمارِ اسْباب کي قِیمت درْیافت کرْکي پہر بنْد کرو	Call a blacksmith and open the boxes; compare the value and quantity of the goods with the invoice, then make them tight again.
اَي پِیادي جب اپْني تلاشِي کِي صحِیح کر چُکو تحْوِیل دار کو دو	Serjeant, when you have signed your name, give (them) to the cashier.
وَہي چلان لیکر پہر پرْمِٹ کي صاحِب کي حُضُور مین جانا ہُوا	Taking the invoice, I had to go again and shew it to the head officer.
یَہي کام کرتي کرتي چار بج گَیي تب پرْمِٹ گھر بنْد ہُوا	Having done all this, it had struck four o'clock, and the custom house was shut.
دُوسْري روز مَین ني چلان لیکر صاحِب کو سونْپ دِیا	The next day I delivered the invoice to the officer.
سب اسْباب کِي قِیمت اَور محْصُول ٹھہراکر اُسْني صحِیح کِي ۔	Having ascertained the value of the articles and the duty, he signed it.

اي سرکار هم ايک کوڑي انعام پرمٹ کي اور گهاٹ کي آدميون کو نهين دينگي	Sarcar, I will not give a kowrie to the people of the custom house or wharf.
اي سرکار تم پوليس جاکر خلاصي نامه کيون نهين لکهوا لاي	Sarcar, why did you not go to the police office and get a pass?
اي صاحب هم کيا کرين دو تين دنسي همين فرصت نهين اور کچهري مين جاني سي کام تمام نهين هوتا	Sir, what can I do? For two or three days I have not had a moment's leisure; one cannot get a thing done at once at the court.
بغير هماري جانيکي کچه نهوگا	If I do not go myself, nothing is done.
اي خداوند پانچ دن گذري که حضور ني لکها تها که کل پٹني کو چيزين روانه هونگي اور ابتک خلاصي نامه نهين ملا	Sir, I know that five days ago you wrote to Patna, that the things would be forwarded to morrow or next day, and no pass is yet obtained.
وي چيزين بغير خلاصي نامي کي بهجوا نهين جا سکتيان	How can they go? They cannot be sent without a pass.

A SHORT DESCRIPTION OF INDIA, BY WAY OF QUESTION AND ANSWER.

Selected from the مرآت الاقاليم (*mir'ātu-l-akālīm*), printed at the School-book Society's press. Calcutta, 1836.

س* هِنْدُوسْتان کَیسا مُلْک هَي

ج† ایک بڑا وسیع مُلْک هَي جو به سبب آبادي اَور حاصِلات اَور ادب اَور قاعِدي کي قدِیم سي مشْهُور چلا آیا هَي

س هِنْدُوسْتان کي حُدُودِ ارْبعه کیا هَین

ج حدِّ شِمالي تاتار اَور تبت اَور جنُوبي حدِّ بحْرِ هِنْد اَور حدِّ شرْقِي مُلْکِ برما و خلِیجِ بنگاله اَور حدِّ غرْبِي خلِیجِ عرب اَور فارِس

س هِنْدُوسْتان مین بڑي نهْرین کَون کَون هَین

ج گنگا جو سات سَي کوس بهْکر خلِیجِ بنگالي مین گِرْتي هَي اُسْمین جمْنا اَور گهاگْره پچْهم اَور برمپُوتر جِسْکو سانْپو کهْتي هَین تِبت اَور آشام سي هوکر گنگا مین مِلْتي هَي اَور پچْهم مین رُودِ سِنْدْه جِسْکو نِیلاب بهِي کهْتي هَین وُه پانْچ نهرونْسي مخْلُوط هَي چُنانْچه اِسِي جهت سي اُن مُلْکون کو جو اُسْکي چارونْطرف هَین پنْجاب کهْتي هَین اَور دکْهن مین نرْبدا اَور گاداوري

---

* س the first letter, as a contraction, of سُوال *suwāl*, question.

† ج the first letter of جَواب *jawāb*, answer.

اور کِشْنا هَي يي تِينون ندِيان پُورب طرف هوکر خلِيجِ بنگالي سي جا مِلِي هَين

س هِنْدُوسْتان مين کَون کَون پهاڑ نامِي هَين

ج کوهِ هِماله تمام جهان مين نامِي هَي کيُونکِه بُلنْدِي مين اُسکي برابر کوئِي پهاڑ نهين وهْ هِنْدُوسْتان اَور تِبت کي درْميان واقِع هَي اَور راج محلّ کِي پهاڑِي اَور دکْهن مين کوهِ گهاٹ جِسکا سِلْسِله لبِ دريا سي شرْقا غرْبا مُحاذِي هَي

س جغْرافي والون ني هِنْدُوسْتان کِي ممْلکت کوکَي حِصّه مين مُنْقسِم کِيا هَي

ج چار حِصّي مين پهْلا حِصّه وُه هَي جو گنْگا اَور اُن ندِيون کي حواشِي مين جو اُسي مخْلُوط هَين واقِع هَي دُوسْرا حِصّه سِنْدْه ندِي کي اطْراف مين اَور اُن ندِيون کي جو اُسي مِلِي هَين تِيسْرا حِصّه وُه جو گنْگا اَور سِنْدْه اَور کِشْنا کي ما بَين واقِع هَي چوتْها حِصّه وُه هَي جو کِشْنا کي جنُوب واقِع هَي

س کَون کَون صُوبجات گنْگا کي جوانِب مين واقِع هَي

ج بنْگاله اَور بِهار اَور اِله آباد اَور اَودْه اَور آگْره اَور دِهْلِي

س صُوبهٔ بنْگ مين کَون کَون شهْر مشْهُور هَين

ج کلْکته ڈهاکه مُرْشداباد

س صُوبهٔ بِهار مين کَون کَون

ج عظِيم آباد بنارس اعْظم گڈْه جونْپور غازِي پُور

س صُوبهٔ اِله آباد مين کَون کَون شهْر بهُت نامِي هَين

ج الهٰ آباد

س صُوبۀ اَوَدْھ مین کَون کَون شَہْر مَشْہُور ھَین

ج لَکْھنَو بہرایچ فَیض آباد برِیلِي گورَکْھپُور

س صُوبۀ آگْرہ مین کَون کَون شَہْر نمُود رَکْھتي ھین

ج آگْرہ اَور مَتْھرا اَور کانْہپُور

س صُوبۀ دِھْلِي مین کَون کَون

ج دِھْلِي مِیرٹ ھرْدْوار کرْنال

س سِنْدْھ ندِي کي اطْراف مین کَون کَون صُوبہ واقِع ھین

ج کشْمِیر کابُل قنْدْھار مُلْتان سِنْدْھ اجْمِیر مالوَہ

س اُن صُوبون مین کَون کَون شَہْر مَشْہُور ھَین

ج لاھَور کشْمِیر کابُل اٹک غِزْنِي قنْدْھار مُلْتان تہْھہ اجْمِیر اُوجَین
گوالِیار جَيپُور

س وَسط مین کَون کَون صُوبجات ھین

ج گُجرات خانْدیس بِرار اُوڑیسہ سرْکار دَولتآباد

س اُنکي کَون کَون شَہْر مَشْہُور ھَین

ج گُجرات مین احْمد آباد اَور کمْبي خانْدیس مین سُورت اَور برْھن پُور
دَولت آباد مین بمْبَئي اَور پُونا بِرار مین اَورنگ آباد اَور ناگْپُور اَور اِلک پُور
اَور اُوڑیسہ مین کٹک

س دکْھن کَون کَون صُوبجات پر مُشْتمِل ھَي

ج بِیجاپُور گولْکنْدہ کارْناٹک مَیسور کونْکین

س اُن صُوبون مین کَون کَون شہر مشہُور ہَین

ج بیجاپُور مین بیجاپُور گولکنڈہ مین گولکنڈہ اَور حَیدر آباد کارناٹک مین آرکاٹ اَور منڈراس اَور پانڈیچری اَور تین جور مَیسور مین سرنگاپاتام اَور ترچناپلي اَور کیلیکٹ کونکین مین گوا

س اُن صُوبجات مین کَون کَون صُوبي انگریزي عمل سي باہر ہَین

ج اُتر طرف جو کُچھ ستلج اَور سِندھ ندي کي شمال اَور مغرب کي حاشیہ مین واقع ہَي یعني کابل اور پنجاب یي سب مُلک سِکھ کي عمل مین ہَین اَور اَودھ خاص اَور سِندھ اَور دکھن مین تانجور کي چھوٹي صُوبي یي سب اپني نوّاب کي عمل مین ہَین

س ہِندُوستان کي جنسین جو سوداگري کي لائِق ہَین کیا ہَین

ج نیل روئي افیون ململ ریشم چاوَل چیني دوشالي گرم مصالح اَور جواہرات چُنانچہ ہِندُوستان کي الماس اَور زُمُرُّد اَور لعل تمام جہان مین مشہُور ہَین

س ہِندُوستان کي باشندي کِتني ہونگي

ج دس کروڑ اُسمین سات کروڑ پچاس لاکھ ہِندُو ہَین اَور ایک کروڑ ستاسي لاکھ پچاس ہزار اہلِاسلام مسیحي اَور یہُودي باسٹھ لاکھ پچاس ہزار اَور یي اکثر دکھن مین ہَین

س ہِندُوستان کي آب و ہوا کَیسي ہَي

ج اُتر اَور پچھم کي صُوبجات مین موسِمِ سرما مین سردي ہوتي ہَي مگر باقي تمام ہِندُوستان مین بجز کوہسي کي کوئي علامت سردي کي نہین

بارِش زِيادہ يا گرمِي زِيادہ اِس پهير پهار سي مَوسِمون کا تفاوُت معلُوم هوتا هَي

س اهلِ هِند کي اَوصاف کيا هَين

ج ادب و قاعِدي مين بِهتر مگر راستِي و صفاي دِلي سي عارِي يعني اُن مين اکثر آپسمين اِعتماد نہين هوتا اَور دوستِي بهِي بي غرض نہين صناعات مين چابکدست اِلا آلاتِ جرِ ثقِيل کِي صنعت سي واقِف نہين اگر اُنمين اِسطرح کا بهِي عِلم هوتا تو غالِب تها کِه تمام عالم مين صناعات کي باب مين نامدار هوتي

Translation of the foregoing " Short Description of India.'

Q. What sort of country is Hindustan ?

A. It is a very extensive country, which by reason of its population, products, manners and customs, has continued famous from antiquity.

Q. What are the boundaries of the four (sides) of Hindūstān ?

A. The northern boundary is Tartary and Tibet, the southern boundary is the Indian ocean, the eastern is the Barmā kingdom and bay of Bengal, and the western boundary is the gulph of Arabia and Persia (Arabian sea).

Q. What great rivers are there in Hindustan ?

A. The Ganges, which after flowing seven hundred *kōs* (1400 miles ?) falls into the gulph of Bengal. In it the Jumna and Gogra from the west, and Brahmapūtar, called also *Sāmpū*, coming from Tibet and Assam, fall. And, on the west is the river Sindh (Indus), also called *Nīlāb*, which is composed of five rivers : so that, for this very reason they name the countries which are about it, *Panjāb*. On the south is the Nerbada, the Godāvery, and the Kishnā; which three rivers, flowing to the east, fall into the bay of Bengal.

Q. What celebrated mountains are there in Hindustan?

A. The Himālaya mountains are well known throughout the world, because that, in respect to height, no other mountain is equal to them. They lie between Hindustan and Tibet. Moreover, there are the hills of Rājamahal; and, in the Dakhan are the Ghāt mountains, the chain of which is to the east and west over against the sea coast.

Q. Into how many parts have geographers divided Hindustan?

A. Into four parts. The first part is that which is situate on the Ganges as well as on the shores of those rivers which fall into it: the second is in the districts of the river Sindh (Indus) as well as in those of the rivers falling into it: the third part is that which lies between the Ganges, the Sindh and the Kishna: and, the fourth is that which lies to the south of the Kishna.

Q. What *Sūbas* (provinces) are situated on the sides of the Ganges?

A. Bengal, Bihār, Ilāhābād, Oude, Agra and Dehli.

Q. In the *Sūba* of Bang (Bengal) what noted cities are there?

A. Calcutta, Dacca, Murshidabad.

Q. What in the *Sūba* of Bihar?

A. *Azīmābād* (Patna), Benares, *Aāzam-gaḍh* (Azemghur), Jaunpoor, Ghazipoor.

Q. In the *Sūba* of Ilahabad, which are the most renowned cities?

A. Ilahabad.

Q. In the *Sūba* of Oude, which are the most celebrated cities?

A. Lucknow, Baraitche, Fyzabad, Bareily, Gorucpoor.

Q. In the *Sūba* of Agra what cities possess celebrity?

A. Agra, Mathura and Caunpoor.

Q. What in the *Sūba* of Dehli?

A. Dehli, Meerat, Hurdwar, Kurnal.

Q. What *Sūbas* (provinces) are situate on the sides of the river *Sindh* (Indus)?

A. Cashmere, Cabul, Candahar, Mooltan, Sinde, Ajmeer, Malwah.

Q. What celebrated cities are there in those *Sūbas?*

A. Lahore, Cashmere, Cabul, Attock, Ghizni, Candahar, Mooltan, Tatta, Ajmeer, Oojein, Gualior, Jeypoor.

Q. In the middle part, what *Sūbas* are there?

A. Gujerat, Khandesh, Berar, Orissa, Circars, Dowletabad.

Q. Of them, what cities are renowned?

A. In Gujerat, Ahmedabad and Cambay; in Khandesh, Surat and Boorhanpoor; in Dowletabad, Bombay and Poona; in Berar, Aurungabad, Nagpoor, and Ellichpoor; and, in Orissa, Cuttack.

Q. What provinces does the Deccan comprise?

A. Bejapoor, Golconda, Carnatic, Mysore, Concan.

Q. What are the famous cities in those provinces?

A. In Bejapoor is Bejapoor; in Golconda, Golconda and Hyderabad; in the Carnatic, Arcot, Madras, Pondicherry, and Tanjore; in Mysore, Seringapatam, Trichinopoly, and Calicut; in Concan is Goa.

Q. In (all) those provinces, what provinces are out of (exempt from) English sway?

A. To the north, whatever is lying on the north and west border of the Sutlej and Indus; that is to say, Cabul and Panjab, all which country is under the government of the Seikhs: Oude is a kingdom of itself: and Sinde as well as the small provinces of Tanjore in the Deccan are all under the rule of their own princes.

Q. What are the articles of commerce of Hindustan?

A. Indigo, cotton, opium, muslin, silk, rice, sugar, shawls, warm spices, and jewels, so that the diamonds, emeralds, and rubies of India are celebrated in all the world.

Q. How many are the inhabitants of India?

A. One hundred millions, of which seventy-five millions are Hindoos, eighteen million seven hundred and fifty thousand Mahomedans; and, six million two hundred and fifty thousand Christians and Jews, the latter of which are chiefly in the Deccan.

Q. What is the climate of Hindustan?

A. In the provinces of the north and west, there is cold in the winter season; but, in all the rest of Hindustan except the mountains there is no symptom of cold. The rain is excessive or the heat is excessive: by this alternation the difference of the seasons becomes known.

Q. What are the qualities of the people of India?

A. In manners and customs excellent; but, void of probity and sincerity: that is to say, there is amongst them, for the most part, no reliance on one another, and disinterested friendship exists not. In works of art they are dexterous; yet, with the construction of mechanical instruments they are unacquainted: had science of this kind also prevailed among them, it is probable they would have become famous throughout the world in what relates to the arts.

DIALOGUE IN THE DAKHNĪ OF MADRAS,

Extracted from "An Introduction to the study of the Hindostany Language as spoken in the Carnatic. Compiled for the use of the Company of Gentlemen Cadets on the Madras establishment at New-town, Cuddalore. Government Press, 1808." ("Reprinted by order of the College Board, 1843").

With notes on the variations, where they may occur, of this dialect from the Hindūstanī of Northern India.

كوئي هي	*kō'ī hai*	*Gent.* Is any one there?
نوكران آئي هين	*naukarāṅ* ā'ē haiṅ* . . .	Are the servants come?
سب نهين آئي هين	*sab nahīṅ ā'ē haiṅ* . . .	*Servt.* They are not all come.
آج جلد سوار هوؤنگا	*āj jald sawār hō'ūṅgā* . .	*Gent.* I will ride out soon to day.
گهوڙي والي كو بلاؤ	*ghōṛē-wālē kō bulā'ō* . . .	Call the horsekeeper.
گهوڙي پر زين بانده	*ghōṛē par zīn bāndh* . .	Saddle the horse.
بهوئيان كو بلاؤ	*bhō'iyāṅ* kō bulā'ō* . . .	Call the palanquin bearers.
پالكي تيار كراؤ	*pālkī taiyār karā'ō* . . .	Make the palanquin ready.
فلاني شخص كي گهر جاؤ	*falānē shakhṣ kē ghar jā'ō* .	Go to such a person's house.
دهوبي كو كپڙي ديؤ	*dhōbī kō kapṛē dē'ō* . . .	Give the clothes to the washerman.
پهنني كي كپڙي لاؤ	*pahannē kē kapṛē lā'ō* . .	Bring my clothes to dress.
كڙته صاف كرو	*kuṛta ṣāf karō*	Clean (or brush) my coat.
بتي سلگاؤ	*bāttī silgā'ō*	Light the candle.
شمع ميز پر ركهو	*sham' mēz-par rakhō* . .	Put the candle on the table.
صبان اجالا هوتيچ آؤ	*ṣabāṅ ujālā hōtē-ch† ā'ō* .	Come to morrow at daylight.
صبان بڑي فجريچ آؤ	*ṣabāṅ baṛī fajr-īch† ā'ō* .	Come very early to morrow.

* The plural form: see Shakespear's Grammar of the Hindustani, par. 87.

† The حرف تخصيص *ḥarf-i-takhṣīṣ*, adverb of identity or peculiarity in Dakhnī, corresponding to هي *hī* or ي *ī* in northern Hindustani: see Shakespear's Grammar, par. 156.

بھوئیان کہان گئے ہین	*bhō'iyāṅ kahāṅ ga'ē haiṅ* .	Where are the palanquin bearers gone?
سیدھی طرف چلو	*sīdhē ṭaraf chalō*	Go to the right.
ڈائین طرف چلو	*ḍā'ēṅ ṭaraf chalō* . . .	Go to the left.
آج جمعدار نہین آئے ہین	*āj jamadār nahīṅ ā'ē haiṅ* .	Is not the jamadār come to day?
ہرکارے جمعدار کو بلاؤ	*harkārē jamadār kō bulā'ō* .	Harkāra, call the jamadār.
جمعدار کوٹ مین رہتے ہین یا اپنے گھر مین	*jamadār kōt mēṅ rahtē haiṅ yā apnē ghar mēṅ,*	Does the jamadār live in the barracks or in his own house?
بٹلر کو بلاؤ	*baṭlar kō bulā'ō*	Call the butler.
خبردار آج چار گھنٹون کو کھانا تیار ہونا	*khabardār āj chār ghanṭōṅ kō khānā taiyār hōnā*	Take care, dinner must be ready to day at four o'clock.
مین آئے تک گھر کو مت جا	*maiṅ ā'ē tag ghar kō mat jā*	Do not go home till I come.
یک حویلی کرائے کو لیو	*yak ḥawēlī kirā'ē kō lē'ō*	Hire a house.
یک پڑوا کرایہ کراؤ	*yak paṛwā kirāya karā'ō* .	Get a boat hired.
کہان جانے صاحب	*kahāṅ jānē ṣāḥib* . . .	Where are you going, Sir?
دریا کی سیر کو	*daryā kē sair kō*	For an excursion to sea.
کیتے دن تم وہان رہینگے	*kētē din tum wahāṅ rahēṅgē,**	How many days shall you remain there?
دو یا تین روز	*dō yā tīn rōz*	Two or three days.
کس وقت تم سوار ہووینگے	*kis waḳt tum sawār hōwēṅgē,**	When will you embark?
جب کھاری چڑاؤ ہووے	*jab khārī chaṛā'ō hōwē* . .	When it is high water in the inlet.
اب تو اتار ہے	*ab tō utār hai*	It is now low water.
کچھ مضایقہ نہین رات کو پھر چڑاؤ ہوویگا	*kuchh muẓāyaḳā nahīṅ rāt kō phir chaṛā'ō howēgā,*	No matter; it will be high tide again at night.

* In Dakhnī, the second person plural of the future and aorist is similar to the first and third.

پڑوي والون کو تاکید کرو که حاضر رهین	*paṛwē-wālōṅ kō tāḳīd karō ki ḥāẓir rahēṅ,*	Give strict orders to the boatmen to keep ready.
اوڑنا بچهانا اور کهاني پيني کا اسباب پڑوي پر بهيجديو	*ōṛnā bichhānā aur khānē pīnē kā asbāb paṛwē par bhēj-dē'ō,*	Send the bed clothes, bedding, with the things for eating and drinking on board the boat.
يه سب سامان بهيج چکا هون صاحب	*yah sab sāmān bhēj chukā hūṅ ṣāḥib,*	All these things I have sent, Sir.
کيون بهي هو مين صبان جاٴونگا	*kyūṅ bhī hō maiṅ sabāṅ jā'ūṅgā,*	I will positively go to morrow.
او کون هي	*ō * kaun hai*	Who is he (or that)?
آپ کي باورچي کا بهاٴي	*āp kē bāwarchī kā bhā'ī* .	Sir, the brother of your cook.
گهوڑي والي پاس جاکر يه دانه اسکي آگي رکهکر ديکهو که او گهوڑيکو کهلاتا هي	*ghōṛē-wālē pās jākar yah*† *dāna us-kē āgē rakhkar dēkhō ki ō ghōṛē-kō khilātā hai,*	Go to the horse-keeper, place this grain before him and see that he gives it to the horse.
يه کس قسم کي جانوران هين	*yah*† *kis ḳism kē jānwarāṅ haiṅ,*	What kind of animals are these?
مرغابي هين	*murg͟hābī haiṅ.*	They are waterfowl.
تم ميري خاوند کي هاته کيتي کو بيچينگي	*tum mērē k͟hāwind kē hāth kētē kō bēchēṅgē,*‡	For how much will you sell them to my master?
تماري عقل مين اس گهر کا پيچها آگي سي خوشتر نما هي	*tumārī*§ *ạḳl mēṅ is ghar kā pīchhā āgē sē k͟hushtar-numā hai,*	In your opinion is the back of this house prettier than the front?

---

* Dakh. *he, she, that* or *it*: see Shakespear's Hindustani Grammar, p. 158.

† See Shakespear's Hindustani Grammar, p. 159.

‡ In Dakhnī, the second person plur. of the future and aorist is similar to the first and third: see Shakespear's Hindustani Grammar, par. 113.

§ See Shakespear's Hindustani Grammar, p. 158.

هرگز نهين برعكس ميري خيال مين اسكا آگا پاچهي سي بهت اچها هي	*hargiz nahīṅ bar ăks mērē <u>kh</u>iyāl mēṅ us-kā āgā pīchhē sē bahut achchhā hai,*	By no means, on the contrary in my opinion the front of it is much prettier than the rear.
كهان راجا كا بيٹا اور كهان يه شهرة	*kahāṅ rājā kā bēṭā aur kahāṅ yah shuhra,*	What connexion is there between the prince's son and this report?
تماري كيا صلح هي	*tumārī* kyā ṣalāḥ hai* . .	What is your advice?
يه سب سي بهتر هوويگا	*yah sab sē bihtar hōwēgā* .	This will be best of all.
ايكيچ هي	*ēk-īch*† *hai.*	It is all one (the same thing).
كچهه فرق نهين	*kuchh farḳ nahīṅ*. . . .	There is no difference.
تم انگريزي بول سكتي هين	*tum angrēzī bōl saktē haiṅ*‡	Can you speak English?
بهلا سليس هندوستاني تو كهو	*bhalā salīs hindustānī tō kahō,*	Well, speak easy Hindustani to me.
كهو تو او كيا كهتا هي	*kahō tō ō*‡ *kyā kahtā hai* ..	Tell me what he says.
تم كهان سي آئي هين	*tum kahāṅ sē ā'ē haiṅ*§. .	Whence are you come?
مجهي اور كچهه در كار نهين	*mujhē aur kuchh dar-kār nahīṅ,*	I do not want any more.
اگر تم اپنا كام درست نكرين تو برطرف كرونگا	*agar tum apnā kām durust na-karēṅ*‡ *tō bar-ṭaraf karūṅgā,*	If you do not do your business better, I will turn you away.
ناشته لاو	*nāshta lā'ō*	Bring breakfast.
مصري ديو	*miṣrī dē'ō*	Give me the sugarcandy.
كچهه اور دودهه تو ديو	*kuchh aur dūdh tō dē'ō* . .	Give me some more milk.

---

* See Shakespear's Hindustani Grammar, p. 158.

† See Shakespear's Hindustani Grammar, par. 156.

‡ Dakh. *ō* or *wah*, &c., instead of the Hindustani *wuh* : see Shakespear's Hindustani Grammar, p. 158.

§ See Shakespear's Hindustani Grammar, par. 113.

مین ابهي باهر جايا چاهتا هون	*maiṅ ab-hī bāhar jāyā chāhtā hūṅ,*	I want to go out directly.
وهان اندر مت جاؤ	*wahāṅ* (or *w'hāṅ*) *andar mat jā'ō,*	Go not in there.
اوترو نهين تو گر پڙينگي	*ūtrō nahīṅ tō gir paṛēṅgē**	Come down otherwise you will fall.
جهاڑ پر كاهيكو چڑهتي هين	*jhāṛ par kāhē-kō chaṛhtē haiṅ,**	Why do you climb up the tree?
اتني بات كهني سي كيا حاصل مين اسكا آدها بهي نهين سمجهتا هون	*itnī bāt kahnē sē kyā ḥāṣil maiṅ us-kā ādhā bhī nahīṅ samajhtā hūṅ,*	What is the use of talking so much? I do not comprehend one half of it.
اس كام پر خدا واسطي اتنا جهوٹ مت بولو	*is kām par khudā wāsṭē*† *itnā jhūṭ*‡ *mat bōlō,*	Do not tell me, for God's sake, so many lies about this business.
اوس بستي كا نام كيا هي	*ūs bastī kā nām kyā hai* . .	What is the name of that place?
وهان كهاني كي كچهه چيز ملتي هي	*wahāṅ* (or *w'hāṅ*) *khānē kī kuchh chīz miltī hai,*	Is any thing to be got there to eat and drink?
دهوپ كي آسري كي واسطي كچهه كهڑا كرو	*dhūp kē āsrē kē wāsṭē kuchh khaṛā karō,*	Put up something to shelter us from the sun.
كيتي گهڑي دن چڑا هي	*kētī ghaṛī din chaṛā*§ *hai* .	What o'clock is it?
پالكي جلدي منگاؤ	*pālkī juldī mangā'ō* . . .	Send for the palanquin quickly.
مزدورون كو بلاؤ اور سب چيزبست هماري ساته بهيج ديؤ	*mazdūrōṅ kō bulā'ō aur sab chīzbast hamārē sāth bhēj dē'ō,*‖	Call the porters and send all my baggage along with me.

* See Shakespear's Hindustani Grammar, par. 113.

† Dakh. *khudā wāsṭē* or *khudā kē wāsṭē*.

‡ Dakh. *jhūṭ*, in Hīndustāni most commonly *jhūṭh*; but, in Dakhnī, an unaspirated letter often occurs where it would be aspirated in Hindustani.

§ In Hindustani *chaṛhā*.

‖ In Hindustani usually *dō*.

تم کہان اوترینگي صاحب	*tum kahāṅ ūtrēṅgē ṣāḥib*	Where will you alight (stop), Sir?
چلو همکو فلاني صاحب کي پاس پهنچا ديؤ	*chalō ham-kō falānē ṣāḥib kē pās pahunchā dē'ō,*	Come, take me to such a gentleman's house.
توپ چهوٹي	*tōp chhūṭī*	Has the gun been fired?
يک جوڑا کپڑي ديؤ	*yak jōṛā kapṛē dē'ō*	Give me a suit of clothes.
ٹوپي کرته جهاڑو	*ṭōpī kurta jhāṛō*	Brush my hat and coat.
گهوڑي پر زين باندهي هي يا نهين	*ghōṛē par zīn bāndhī hai yā nahīṅ,*	Is the horse saddled or not?
سواري کا گهوڑا لاؤ	*sawārī kā ghōṛā lā'ō*	Bring the saddle-horse.
هماري ساته تمکو بهي آنا پڑيگا	*hamārē sāth tum-kō bhī ānā paṛēgā,*	You must come along with me.
تماري صاحب ابتگ اٹهي هووينگي	*tumārē ṣāḥib ab-tag* uṭhē hōwēṅgē,*	Is your master got up yet?
هو صاحب ليکن کهين باهر گئي هين	*hō ṣāḥib lēkin kahīṅ bāhar ga'ē haiṅ,*	Yes, Sir, but he is gone out somewhere.
تمکو کچه معلوم هي که کهان گئي	*tum-kō kuchh ma'lūm hai ki kahāṅ ga'ē,*	Do you know where he is gone to?
همکو ايک پياله دوده تهوڑي مصري ايک انڈا چمچه مولي روٹي مسکه اور تهوڑا مربه ديؤ	*kam-kō ēk piyāla dūdh thōṛī miṣrī ēk anḍā chamcha mūlī rōṭī maska aur thōṛā murabba dē'ō,*	Give me a cup of milk, a little sugarcandy, an egg, a spoon, a radish, bread, butter and a little jam.
ايک دن کا کرايه کيا هي	*ēk din kā kirāya kyā hai*	What is the fare per day?
سيدها آگي چلي جاؤ	*sīdhā āgē chalē jā'ō*	Go straight forwards.
پهرکر آؤ	*phir-kar ā'ō*	Come round about.
سيدهي هاته کو پهرو	*sīdhē hāth kō phirō*	Turn to the right.
ڈاوين هاته کو پهرو	*ḍāwēṅ hāth kō phirō*	Turn to the left.
جلدي چلو	*jaldī chalō*	Go fast.
ذره آهسته چلو	*ẕarra āhista chalō*	Go a little slower.
هٹکر جاؤ	*haṭ-kar jā'ō*	Make way.

* In Hindustani *ab-tak*.

كهڑي رهو	*khaṛē rahō*	Stop.
مين پهر آ ئي تگ يهانچ رهو	*main phir ā'ē tag* yahānch† rahō,*	Stop here till I return.
مين ابهي پهر آ ونگا	*main ab-hī phir ā'ūngā* . .	I will be back immediately.
آگي دوڑكر خبر ليؤ كه صاحب گهرمين هي يا نهين	*āgē dauṛkar‡ khabar lē'ō ki ṣāḥib ghar mēn hai yā nahīn,*	Run on before and enquire if the gentleman is at home or not.
رهو رهو پالكي نيچي ركه ديؤ	*rahō rahō pālkī nīchē rakh dē'ō,*	Stop, stop, put the palanquin down.
تمارا صاحب گهرمين هي	*tumārā ṣāḥib ghar mēn hai*	Is your master at home?
پالكي اٹهاؤ اور گهر كو چلو	*pālkī uṭhā'ō aur ghar kō chalō,*	Take up the palanquin and go home.
يه گٹهري گهر كو ليچلو	*yah gaṭhrī ghar kō lē-chalō*	Carry the bundle home.
هم فلاني صاحب كي يهان كهانا كهاينگي تم تين پهر كو وهان آ ؤ	*ham falānē ṣāḥib kē yahān khānā khā'ēngē tum tīn pahar kō wahān ā'ō,*	I shall dine at Mr. such a one's, come there in the afternoon.
آ ؤ موزي اتارو	*ā'ō mōzē utārō*	Come, take off my boots.
تهوڑي شراب پاني لاؤ	*thōṛī sharāb pānī lā'ō* . .	Bring some wine and water.
پاني خوب ٹهنڈا كرو	*pānī khūb thanḍā karō* . .	Cool the water well.
كهانا تيار هووي تو لاؤ	*khānā taiyār hōwē tō lā'ō* .	Bring dinner if ready.
صاف چهري كانٹا ديؤ	*ṣāf chhurī kānṭā dē'ō* . .	Give me a clean knife and fork.
تهوڑا نمك رائي مرچ آچار سركه شراب پاني گوشت اور ايك صاف باسن ديؤ	*thōṛā namak rā'ī mirch āchār sirka sharāb pānī gōsht aur ēk ṣāf bāsan dē'ō,*	Give me a little salt, mustard, pepper, (some) pickles, vinegar, wine, water, meat, and a clean plate.

* Observe this sentence, which in Hindustani might have been *mērē phir ānē tak.*

† See Shakespear's Hindustani Grammar, par. 156.

‡ Or, in Dakhnī, *daurkar;* the dental or simple *t*, *d*, or *r* being in this dialect frequently substituted for the Hindustani *ṭ*, *ḍ*, or *ṛ*.

باسن اٹھا لیجاؤ	*bāsan uṭhā lē-jā'ō*	Take away the things.
دوات قلم کاغذ لاؤ	*dawāt ḳalam kāghaz lā'ō* .	Bring the inkstand, pen and paper.
فلاني صاحب کي پاس يهه خط ليجاؤ اور جواب کي واسطي ٹهہرو	*falānē ṣāḥib kē pās yah khaṭṭ lē-jā'ō aur jawāb kē wāsṭē ṭhahrō,*	Take this letter to such a gentleman's and wait for an answer.
وہ فرنگي کون هي	*wah farangī kaun hai* . .	Who is that European?
وہ کسکا گھوڑا هي	*wah kis-kā ghōṛā hai* . .	Whose horse is that?
پکارکر بولين تو هم سنينگي	*pukārkar bōlēṅ* tō ham sunēṅgē,*	If you speak loud, I shall hear you.
آهسته آهسته اور لفظ جدا جدا بولين توهم تماري بات سمجهينگي	*āhista āhista aur lafẓ judā judā bōlēṅ* tō ham tumārī bāt samjhēṅgē,*	If you speak slowly and distinctly, we shall understand you.
همارا سلام اپني صاحب کو کهو	*hamārā salām apnē ṣāḥib kō kahō,*	Give my compliments to your master.
اس آدمي کو تم جانتي هين	*us ādmī kō tum jāntē haiṅ**	Do you know that man?
اس کاغذ کو کرسي کي تلي سي اٹھا لاؤ	*us kāghaz kō kursī kē talē sē uṭhā lā'ō,*	Bring me that paper from beneath the chair.
ديکهو آسمان کهلا هي	*dēkhō āsmān khulā hai* . .	See, is the weather cleared up?
جوتيان اچهي طرح صاف کرو	*jūtiyāṅ achchhī ṭaraḥ ṣāf karō,*	Clean (my) shoes well.
ناشته تيار هي	*nāshta taiyār hai*. . . .	Is breakfast ready?
ابهي نهين صاحب ليکن ذري وقت مين تيار هوويگا	*ab-hī nahīṅ ṣāḥib lēkin ẕarrē waḳt mēṅ taiyār howēgā,*	Not yet, Sir, but it will be ready in a little time.
کيا آج مچهي نهين ملي	*kyā āj machchhī nahīṅ milī*	What, could no fish be got to day?

* In Dakhnī, the second person plural: see Shakespear's Hindustani Grammar, par. 113.

اچھي مچھي نہين ملي صاحب	*achchhī machchhī nahīṅ milī ṣāḥib.*	There was no good fish to be had, Sir.
چادان مين چا ڈالا	*chā-dān meṅ chā ḍālā** . .	Have you put tea into the pot?
ڈالا هون صاحب	*ḍālā hūṅ* ṣāḥib*	I have put it in, Sir.
کٹھوري مين مصري رکھا	*kaṭhōrī meṅ miṣrī rakhā** .	Have you put sugar into the cup?
هو صاحب	*hō ṣāḥib*	Yes, Sir.
خوب کٹھوري مين چا اونڈيل	*khūb kaṭhōrī mēṅ chā ūṅḍēl*	Well, pour out the tea.
سامان نکالو	*sāmān nikālō*	Take away the things.
صاحب آج کيتي گنٹھون کو کھانا تيار کرنا	*ṣāḥib āj kētē ganṭhōṅ*† *kō khānā taiyār karnā,*	Sir, at what o'clock must dinner be ready to day?
ساڑي چار گنٹھون کو	*sāṛē chār ganṭhōṅ*† *kō* . .	At half past four.
کيا کيا چيزين چاهئي	*kyā kyā chīzēṅ chāhi'ē* . .	What things do you wish?
يک دست کا کباب يک ران اور مچھي ابالي هوئي دو تين طرح کي سالني ترکاري اور پنڈالوان تهوڑي پوريان اور اچھي ميوي	*yak dast kā kabāb yak rān aur machchhī ubālī hū'ī dō tīn ṭaraḥ kē sālnē tarkārī aur pinḍālū'āṅ,*‡ *thōṛī pūriyāṅ aur achchhē mēwē,*	A shoulder of mutton roasted, a leg and some fish boiled, two or three kinds of curry, vegetables and yams, some sweet cakes and good fruit.
بکري کا گوشت اچھا نہين ملا تو گائي کا گوشت ليؤن	*bakrē kā gōsht achchhā nahīṅ milā tō gā'ē kā gōsht lē'ūṅ,*	If good mutton cannot be got, shall I take beef?

* In these instances, the construction is not inverted by the use of ني *nē*, as it would have been in Hindustani, though ڈالنا *ḍālnā* is a transitive verb in a past tense.

† In Hindustani, this word would be گھنٹون *ghanṭōṅ*.

‡ In Dakhnī, the plural of پنڈالو *pinḍālū*: see Shakespear's Hindustani Grammar, par. 87.

نهين ايک مرغ اور ايک بدخ منگانا	*nahīṅ ēk murgh aur ēk badakh mangānā,**	No, send for a fowl and duck.
کس قسم کي ميوي ملي	*kis ḳism kē mēwē milē* . .	What kinds of fruit have you got?
جام آم موز چکوتري انار خربزي اور اناناس	*jām ām mauz chakōtarē anār kharbuzē aur annās,*	Guavas, mangos, plantains, shaddocks, pomegranates, muskmelons and pine-apples.
چار پانچ روز کي آگي عربستان سي آئي سو جهازان مين کچھ بادام يا فندق يا کهجور يا منقه يا کشمش نهين آئي	*chār pānch rōz kē āgē ārabistān sē ā'ē sō jahāzāṅ mēṅ kuchh bādām yā finduḳ yā khajūr yā munaḳḳa yā kishmish nahīṅ ā'ē,*	Did not any almonds or filberts or dates or raisins or currants come in the ships which arrived, four or five days ago, fiom Arabia?
آئي تهي صاحب ليکن جلد بکني سي مجهي نهين ملي	*ā'ē thē ṣāḥib lēkin jald biknē sē mujhē nahīṅ milē,*	Some came, Sir, but were so quickly sold that I could not get any.
شام کو چا اور قهوه بنانا	*shām-kō chā aur ḳahwa banānā,*	Make tea and coffee in the evening.
کيا تماريچ واسطي يا اور کوئي سرداران آوينگي	*kyā tumārēch† wāsṭē yā aur kō'ī sardārāṅ āwēṅgē,*	What, for yourself, or will any other officers come?
هو اور دو تين سردار آتي هين	*hō aur dō tīn sardār ātē haiṅ,*	Yes, two or three other officers are coming.
صاحب فجر قواعد هي آپ کتين کيتي گنٹهون کو اٹهاٶن	*ṣāḥib fajr ḳawā'id hai āp ka-taiṅ kētē ganṭhōṅ kō uṭhā'ūṅ,*	There is drill in the morning, Sir; at what o'clock shall I waken you?

* In Dakhnī, the infinitive form is very often used imperatively to denote the absolute necessity of doing the action intended: see Shakespear's Hindustani Grammar, par. 72.

† See Shakespear's Hindustani Grammar, par. 156.

پوني پانچ گنٹھون کو	*paunē pānch ganṭhōṅ kō*	At a quarter before five o'clock.
ڈوالي صاف کيا	*ḍō'ālī ṣāf kiyā**	Have you cleaned my belt?
تلوار تيار رکھا	*talwār taiyār rakhā**	Have you got my sword ready?
کرته اور پٹکه باهر رکھ	*kurta aur paṭka bāhar rakh*	Put out my jacket and sash.
گلوبند کي چپراس تيار هوئي هي	*gulūband kī chaprās taiyār hū'ī hai,*	Is the buckle of the stock ready?
ٹوپي اور طره ميز پر رکھ	*ṭōpī aur ṯurra mēz-par rakh*	Put my hat and feather on the table.
سب سامان تيار کيا هون صاحب	*sab sāmān taiyār kiyā* hūṅ ṣāḥib,*	I have prepared every thing, Sir.
اچھا بڑي فجر جو مين نهين اٹھون تو خوب طرح سي جگانا	*achchhā baṛī fajr jō maiṅ nahīṅ uṭhūṅ tō k͟hūb ṭaraḥ sē jagānā.*	Well, if I do not get up early, you must waken me properly.
موم بتي اور موم دان نکالکر فجر مجھي اٹھاني کي وقت پر سلگا	*mōm-battī aur mōm-dān nikālkar fajr mujhē uṭhānē kē waḳt-par silgā,*	Take away the candle and candlestick and light (it again) when you waken me in the morning.
صاحب پوني پانچ گھنٹي هوئي اٹھو	*ṣāḥib paunē pānch ghanṭē hū'ē uṭhō,*	Sir, it wants a quarter of five, get up.
پهلا تمبور بجا هي	*pahlā tambūr bajā hai*	Has the first drum beaten?
هو صاحب ابيچ بجني لگا	*hō ṣāḥib ab-īch bajnē lagā.*	Yes, Sir, it has just begun to beat.
اچھا کپڑي دي	*achchhā kapṛē dē*	Well, give me my clothes.
حجام آيا هي	*ḥajjām āyā hai*	Is the barber come?
ديکھتا هون صاحب	*dēkhtā hūṅ ṣāḥib*	I will see, Sir.

* The verb, though transitive and in the past tense, agrees with the nominative case understood; the construction not being inverted, as in Hindustani, by the use of the particle ني *nē*.

هاتھ مون دھوني پاني لا	*hāth mūṅ dhōnē pānī lā* .	Bring me water to wash my hands and face.
صابون دي	*ṣābūn dē*	Give me the soap.
رومال رکھ	*rūmāl rakh*	Hold the towel.
مسواك اور منجن دي	*miswāk aur manjan de* . .	Give me the tooth-brush and tooth-powder.
کنگوئي لا	*kangū'ī lā*	Bring the comb.
رومال جيب مين رکھا	*rūmāl jēb-mēṅ rakhā* . . .	Have you put my handkerchief in my pocket?
دستيان کهان هين	*dastiyāṅ kahāṅ haiṅ* . .	Where are my gloves?
ساڙي سات گھنٹون کي وقت گھوڑا تيار کراکر قواعد کي جگھ کو بھيج دي	*sāṛē sāt ghanṭōṅ kē wakt ghōṛā taiyār karākar kawā'id kī jagah-kō bhēj dē,*	Make the horse be got ready, and send it to the place of exercise at half past seven o'clock.
صاحب سلامت	*ṣāḥib salāmat*	Sir, safety* (to you).
خير و عافيت سوبدار صاحب آج کيا رپوٹ هي	*khair ō āfiyat sūbadār ṣāḥib āj kyā rapōṭ‡ hai,*	Good and health,† Mr. Sūbadār, what is the report to day?
اور کچھ نهين صاحب سب بھلي بھلائي	*aur kuchh nahīṅ ṣāḥib sab bhalī bhalā'ī,§*	Nothing extraordinary, Sir, all is right.
آج کمپني مين کيتي کاهلي هين	*āj kumpanī-mēṅ‡ kētē kāhilē haiṅ,*	How many sick are there to day in the company?
دو سپاهي يک تمبوروالا اور يک چھوکرا	*dō sipāhī yak tambūr-wālā aur yak chhōkrā,*	Two sepoys, one drummer and one boy.
کس درد سي	*kis dard-sē*	Of what illness?

---

* A respectful mode of address from a Musalman.

† A benediction much used as a respectful return to an address.

‡ An English word as introduced into military use at Madras.

§ A phrase, meaning that all is right or going on well.

ایک سپاهي کو تپ هي دوسري کو بائي کا درد تمبوروالي کو سیتلا نکلي هي اور چهوکري کا سر دکهتا هي	*ēk sipāhī-kō tap hai dūsrē-kō bā'ī kā dard tambūr--wālē-kō sītalā niklī hai aur chhōkrē kā sir dukhtā hai,*	One sepoy has a fever, the other has the rheumatism, the drummer has got the smallpox, and the boy's head aches.
ڈاکتر صاحب کچه انکي دوا فرمائي هين	*ḍāktar* ṣāḥib kuchh unkī dawā farmā'ē hain,*	Has the doctor ordered them any medicine?
هو صاحب آپي آکر انکي مرضان دریافت کرکر دوا دیا هي	*hō ṣāḥib āpē*† *ākar un-kē maraẓān daryāft karkar dawā diyā hai,*	Yes, Sir, he came himself, enquired into their complaints, and gave them physic.
آسپتري مين انکي جگه صاف هي	*āspatrī*-mei un-kī jagah ṣāf hai,*	Is their place in the hospital clean?
هو صاحب هر روز جهاڑا جهوڑي کرتي هين	*hō ṣāḥib har rōz jhāṛājhūṛī*‡ *kartē hain,*	Yes, Sir, they sweep it out every day.
کوت حوالدار هر روز کیتي دفعه انکي خبر لیني جاتا هي	*kōt ḥawāldār har rōz kētē daf'ā un-kī khabar lēnē jātā hai,*	How many times each day does the *kōt-ḥawāldār* go to enquire after them?
فجر کي قواعد کي بعد دو پهر کو اور شام کي ورسي کي آگي	*fajr-kē ḳawā'id kē ba'd dō pahar kō aur shām-kē warsē-kē āgē,*	After morning's drill, at midday, and before evening's parade.
آج کیتي جني مینگاٹ چڑي هين	*āj kētē janē mēngāṭ* chaṛē hain,*	How many men have mounted the main guard to day?
ایک جمعدار دو حوالدار تین نایک بانسلي والا اور تین سپاهي	*ēk jam'dār dō ḥawāldār tīn nā'ik bāṅslī-wālā aur tīn sipāhī,*	One jamadār, two hawaldars, three nā'iks, the fifer and three sepoys.
کوت کي گاٹ مین کیتي هين	*kōt kī gāṭ*-mēn kētē hain .*	How many are on the barrack guard?

* Borrowed from the English.

† A Dakhni form corresponding to the Hindustani آپ *āp*.

‡ A reiterative form, *jhāṛā-jhūṛī karnā,* to sweep out.

اڑدلیان مین کوئي گئي هین	*arḍalī'āṅ*-mēṅ kō'ī ga'ē haiṅ,*	Have any gone as orderlies?
کوئي کمان مین هي	*kō'ī kamān†-mēṅ hai* . . .	Are any on command?
پکهالي کیتي گهنٹون کو پاني لاتا هي	*pakhālī kētē ghanṭōṅ-kō pānī lātā hai,*	At what o'clock does the *pakhālī* bring water?
فجر کي چه اور شام کي پانچ گهنٹون کو	*fajr-kē chha aur shām-kē pānch ghanṭōṅ-kō,*	At six o'clock in the morning and five in the evening.
کمپني مین کیتي بندوقان هین	*kumpanī-mēṅ kētī bandūḳāṅ haiṅ,*	How many firelocks are there in the company?
اسي پر پانچ اچهي هین اور پندره خراب	*assī-par pānch achchhī haiṅ aur pandrah kharāb,*	There are eighty five good ones and fifteen bad.
هر ایک سپاهي کي پاس کیتي ٹوٹي هین	*har ēk sipāhī-kē pās kētē ṭōṭē haiṅ,*	How many cartridges has each sepoy?
باره باره	*bārah bārah*	Twelve each.
هر ایک سپاهي کا سامان درست هي	*har ēk sipāhī kā sāmān durust hai,*	Are the accoutrements of each sepoy good?
هو صاحب هر ایک کي پاس ایک بندوق اور ایک سنین ایک ڈبه ایک مڑتول ایک مڑوڑي ایک کانٹا اور دو پهتري ایک سنین کي ڈوالي ایک ڈبي کي ڈوالي ایک بندوق کي ڈوالي ایک سنین کي میان ایک پگڑي ایک لال کرته اور بله هي	*hō ṣāḥib har ēk kē pās ēk bandūḳ aur ēk sanīn ēk ḍabba ēk marṭōl ēk maṛōṛī ēk kānṭā aur dō phatrē ēk sanīn kī ḍō'ālī ēk ḍabbe-kī ḍō'ālī ēk bandūḳ kī ḍō'ālī ēk sanīn-kī miyān ēk pagṛī ēk lāl kuṛta aur billa hai,*	Yes, Sir; each has a firelock, a bayonet, a pouch, a hammer, a worm, a pricker and two flints, a bayonet belt, a pouch belt, a sling, a bayonet sheath, a turband, a red jacket and a breastplate.

* Plural of *arḍalī*, the duty of an orderly.

† Borrowed from the English.

کمپني کي کپڙي سب اچھي هين	*kumpanī-kē kapṛē sab achchhē hain,*	Are all the clothes of the company good?
هر ایک سپاهي کي پاس چار جوڑي اچھي هين	*har ēk sipāhī kē pās chār jōṛē achchhē hain,*	Each sepoy has four good suits.
اچھا نائک سوبدار کو بلاؤ	*achchhā nā'ik sūbadār-kō bulā'ō,*	Very well, nā'ik, call the sūbadar.
سوبدار صاحب میري گاٹ مین کیتي جوان هین	*sūbadār ṣāḥib mērī gāṭ-mēn kētē jawān hain,*	How many men, Sūbadār, are there in my guard?
کیتي پهري هین	*kētē pahrē hain*	How many sentries are there?
کهان کهان کهڙي رهتي سو مجهي بتاؤ	*kahān kahān khaṛē rahtē sō mujhē batā'ō,*	Shew me where they stand.
پهریوالون کو کیا حکم هي سو مجهي بولو	*pahrēwālōn-kō kyā ḥukm hai sō mujhē bōlō,*	Tell me the orders which the sentries have.
قلعي کي دروازي کیتي گهنٹون کو موچتي هین	*ḳal'ē kē darwāzē kētē ghanṭōn-kō mūchtē hain,*	At what o'clock do they shut the gates of the fort?
ایک چهه گهنٹون کو ایک آٹهه گهنٹون کو اور باقي بارهٔ گهنٹون کو	*ēk chha ghanṭōn-kō ēk āṭh ghanṭōn-kō aur bāḳī bārah ghanṭōn-kō,*	One at six, one at eight, and the rest at twelve o'clock.
بندوقان کیتي گهنٹون کو سلاي اور پهر کیتي گهنٹون کو اٹهاتي هین	*bandūḳān kētē ghanṭōn-kō sulā'ē aur phir kētē ghanṭōn-kō uṭhatē hain,*	At what o'clock did they ground arms, and at what o'clock will they take them up again?
ایک دفعه مین کیتي سپاهیان کهاني کو چهوڑتي هین	*ēk daf'a-mēn kētē sipāhiyān khānē-kō chhōṛtē hain,*	How many soldiers are allowed at one time to go to dinner?
رون کیتي گهنٹون کو جاتي	*rōn** *kētē ghanṭōn-kō jātī* .	At what o'clock do the rounds go?

* Borrowed from the English.

دوسري گاٹان سي كيتي گهنٹون كو رپوٹ بهيجتي هين	*dūsrī gāṭāṅ*-sē kētē ghanṭōṅ-kō rapōṭ* bhējtē haiṅ,*	At what o'clock do they send the reports from the other guards?
پهري كيتي گهنٹون كو بدلاتي هين	*pahrē kētē ghanṭōṅ-kō badlātē haiṅ,*	At what o'clock do they relieve the sentries?
باره گهنٹون كو مجهي جگاني كي واسطي ايك نائيك بهيج ديؤ اور پهر باره كي چار كو	*bārah ghanṭōṅ-kō mujhē jagānē-kē wāsṭē ēk nā'ịk bhēj dē'ō aur phir bārah-kē chār-kō,*	Send a nā'ik to waken me at twelve o'clock, and again at four.
توپ چهوٹي صاحب جوانان كهڑا كرون	*tōp chhūṭī ṣāḥib jawānāṅ khaṛā karūṅ,*	The gun has fired, Sir, shall I fall in the men?
سپاهيان كو خبر كرو كه رات كو باره كي دو گهنٹون كو كوچ هي	*sipāhiyāṅ-kō <u>kh</u>abar karō ki rāt-kō bārah-kē dō ghanṭōṅ-kō kūch hai,*	Tell the sepoys that we march to night at two o'clock.
صبان كيتي كوس چلينگي	*sabāṅ kētē kōs chalēṅgē . .*	How many coss shall we march to morrow?
كهان جانا هي	*kahāṅ jānā hai . . . .*	Whither are we to go?
كسي دهيڑ كو راسته بتاني كي واسطي تيار كرو	*kisī dhēṛ-kō rāsta batānē kē wāsṭē taiyār karō,*	Have some village cooley ready to shew the road.
صبان مقام كهان كرينگي	*ṣabāṅ muḳām kahāṅ karēṅgē*	Where shall we halt to morrow?
ايك نائيك اور چهه سپاهي سامان تياركراني اگهاڑي بهيجو	*ēk nā'ik aur chha sipāhī sāmān taiyār karānē aghāṛī bhējō,*	Send a nā'ik and six sepoys on before to prepare things.
صاحب يهان كي لوگ بڑي شرير هين حوالدار كي گاٹ بهيجا چاهئي	*ṣāḥib yahāṅ kē lōg baṛē sharīr haiṅ ḥawāldār kī gāṭ bhējā chāhi'ē,*	The people about here, Sir, are very riotous; you should send a havaldar's guard.
سب حاضر هين	*sab ḥāẓir haiṅ . . . . .*	Are all present?

* Borrowed from the English.

هو صاحب لام باندهكر كهڑي هين	*hō ṣāḥib lām* bāndhkar khaṛē hain,*	Yes, Sir, they are fallen in, in line.
حكم سنو هوشيار رهو سيدهي يا ڈاوين طرف پهرنا هي	*ḥukm sunō hōshyār rahō sīdhē yā ḍāwēṅ ṯaraf phirnā hai,*	Hear the word, attention, to wheel or turn to the right or left.
حكم پر ايكسان قدم اٹهاو	*ḥukm-par ēk-sāṅ ḳadam uṭhā'ō,*	Raise your feet at once upon the word.
فيل ملكر چلو	*fail*† *milkar chalō* . . .	March with close files.
عهدي والي اپني ڈسٹانس ركهو	*ūhdē-wālē apnē ḍisṭāns*† *rakhō,*	Officers, keep your distance.
لمبا قدم ڈالو	*lambā ḳadam ḍālō* . . .	Step out.
چهوٹا قدم ڈالو	*chhōṭā ḳadam ḍālō* . . .	Step short.
خبردار اب ترچها قدم	*khabar-dār ab tirchhā ḳadam,*	Attention now, the oblique step.
سيدهي طرف سامني بڑهو	*sīdhē ṯaraf sāmnē baṛhō* .	Forward, on the right.
كهڑي رهو	*khaṛē rahō*	Halt, stand still.
بندوقان اتارنا	*bandūḳāṅ utārnā*	To order arms.
سنينان چڑهاو	*sanīnāṅ chaṛhā'ō*	Fix bayonets.
بندوقان كهاندي پر لينا	*bandūḳāṅ khāndē-par lēnā* .	To shoulder arms.
بندوقان قينچي باندنا	*bandūḳāṅ ḳēnchī bāndnā* .	To pile arms.
پهري والي كهان كهان كهڑا كرون	*pahrē-wālē kahāṅ kahāṅ khaṛā karūṅ*	Where shall I post the sentries?
دونو بازو پر ڈيري كي آگي اور پيچهي اور بندوقانكي پاس ايك ايك پهره كهڑا كرو	*dōnō bāzū-par ḍērē kē āgē aur pīchhē aur bandūḳāṅ-kē pās ēk ēk pahra khaṛā karō,*	On both flanks, before and behind the tents, and near the arms, one each.
ورسا كيتي گهنٹون كو هوتا هي	*warsā kētē ghanṭōṅ-kō hōtā hai,*	At what o'clock is parade?

* لام *lām*, or لين *lain*, from the English military term, line.

† The English word, here adopted.

پوني چھ گھنٹون کو	*paunē chha ghanṭōṅ-kō* . .	At a quarter before six.
سيدھي طرف آنکھان پھراؤ	*sīdhē ṭaraf ānkhāṅ phirā'ō,*	Turn the eyes to the right.
بيچمين آگي آؤ	*bīch-mēṅ āgē ā'ō*	Dress up the centre.
بہت آئي پھر ذرہ دبو	*buht ā'ē phir ẓarra dabō* .	Too much; dress back again a little.
لف مين دبو	*laf*-mēṅ dabō*	Dress back on the left.
سنتر لف کي بيچمين آگي آؤ	*santar* laf*-kē bīch-mēṅ āgē ā'ō,*	Dress up between the centre and the left.
ريٹ مين مت هلو	*raiṭ*-mēṅ mat hilō* . . .	Do not move on the right.
سنتر کي دو تين جوان ذرہ دبو	*santar*-kē dō tīn jawān ẓarra dabō,*	Dress back two or three files in the centre.
بس هلو مت	*bas hilō mat*	Enough; do not move (steady).
بندوقان اتارو	*bandūḳāṅ utārō*	Order arms.
سنينان چڑھاؤ	*sanīnāṅ chaṛhā'ō*	Fix bayonets.
سلامي هاتھ	*salāmī hāth*	Present arms.
سنينان نکالو	*sanīnāṅ nikālō*	Unfix bayonets.
بغلي هاتھ	*baghlī hāth*	Secure arms.
گھوڑا دو کل پر چڑھاؤ	*ghōṛā dō kal-par chaṛhā'ō* .	Cock (your firelock).
گھوڑا ايک کل پر رکھو	*ghōṛā ēk kal-par rakhō* . .	Half cock.
کل کھينچو	*kal khaiṅchō*	Draw the trigger.
هاتھ ران کو لگاؤ	*hāth rān-kō lagā'ō* . . .	Keep your hands flat to the thigh.
سران مت هلاؤ	*sirāṅ mat hilā'ō*	Do not stir your heads.
سران اٹھاؤ	*sirāṅ uṭhā'ō*	Raise your heads.
سيدھي کھڑي رهو	*sīdhē khaṛē rahō*	Stand erect.
يہ گاؤن کسکي علاقي مين هي	*yah gā'ōṅ kis-kē ‛ilāḳē mēṅ hai,*	Who does this village belong to?

* English military terms, adopted in Dakhni.

اس چوحدي مين كوئي زميندار هي	*is chau-ḥaddī-mēṅ kō'ī za-mīndār hai.*	Is there any zemindar in this neighbourhood?
صبان كي راستي مين كچهه ندي نالي هين	*ṣabāṅ-kē rāstē-mēṅ kuchh naddī nālē haiṅ.*	Are there any rivers or rivulets on to morrow's march?
جهاڑي جنگل هي	*jhāṛī jangal hai*	Is there thicket and jungle?
پهاڑان هين	*pahāṛāṅ haiṅ*	Are there hills (or mountains)?
تلاوان هين	*talāwāṅ haiṅ*	Are there tanks?
اسكي اطراف كا ملك بنجر هي يا ساگمڑي هوتي هي	*is-kē aṭrāf-kā mulk banjar hai yā sāg-maṛī hōtī hai.*	Is the country about here waste or cultivated?
اس مين دهان بهت پيكتي هين اور دوسرا اناج كم	*is-mēṅ dhān boht pīktē** *haiṅ aur dūsrā anāj kam.*	They sow much rice here and other grains less.
صبان كي راستي مين تو بهت چكڑ پاني هوگا	*ṣabāṅ-kē rāstē-mēṅ tō boht chikkaṛ pānī hōgā.*	There will then be much mud and water on to morrow's road.
هو صاحب دو كوس تگ دهان مڑي كي ميڈان پر چلنا بعد از ايك كوس تلاؤ كي كٹي پر پيلور سوكا راسته هي	*hō ṣāḥib dō kōs-tag dhān maṛī kē mēḍāṅ*† *-par chalnā ba'd-az ēk kōs talā'ō kē kaṭṭē-par pailūr sūkā rāsta hai.*	Yes, Sir, two coss we have to march along the banks of paddy fields; afterwards, for one coss, on the borders of a tank; but beyond that the road is dry.
بيچمين هي سو ندي پاياب هي	*bīch-mēṅ hai sō naddī pāyāb hai.*	Is the river, on the way, fordable?

* پيكنا *pīknā*, explained in Persian by زراعت شدن *zirā'at shudan*, To be sown (?).

† From ميڈ *mēḍ* or ميند *mēnḍ*, Bank.

صبان کي مقام کي گاؤن کي پاس کوئي امرائي هي	*ṣabāṅ kē muḳām kē gā'ōṅ kē pās kō'ī amrā'ī hai.*	Are there any trees (groves) near the village where we shall halt to morrow?
گاؤن کي کتوال کو بلا بهيجو	*gā'ōṅ-kē kutwāl-kō bulā bhējō.*	Send for the Cutwal of the village.
يهان سي فلانه گاؤن کيتي دور هي	*yahāṅ* (or *yhāṅ*) *sē falāna gā'ōṅ kētī dūr hai.*	How far is such a village from this?
جوانان مول ليئي سو سامان کا پيسه ديئي	*jawānāṅ mōl lī'ē sō sāmān kā paisa dī'ē.*	Have the men paid for the things that they purchased?
اور تو کچھ باقي نهين	*aur tō kuchh bāḳī nahīṅ*	. Nothing more, then, remains.

PART IV.

نقلیات (*nakliyāt*), SHORT STORIES,

In the Persian and Nagari characters, with translations and grammatical analysis of some parts.

۱ نقل

ایک شخص بادشاہ کی عین قلعی کی نیچی لوٹا گیا اسنی بادشاہ کی خدمت مین عرض کی کہ جہان پناہ مجھی قزاقون نی حضور کی قلعی کی دیوار کی نیچی لوٹ لیا بادشاہ نی فرمایا کہ تو ہشیار کیون نرہا بولا کہ غلام کو معلوم نتہا کہ حضرت کی زیر جہروکھی مسافر لوٹی جاتی ہین بادشاہ نی کہا کیا تونی یہہ مثل نہین سنی چراغ کی نیچی اندھیرا

In Nagari characters.

१ नक़्ल

एक शख़्स बादशाह के ऐन क़लए के नीचे लूटा गया उसने बादशाह की ख़िद्मत में अर्ज़ की कि जहान पनाह मुझे क़ज़्ज़ाक़ों ने हुज़ूर के क़लए की दीवार के नीचे लूट लिया बादशाह ने फ़र्माया कि तू हुश्यार क्यूं नरहा बोला कि ग़ुलाम को मअ्लूम नथा कि हज़रत के ज़ेर झरोखे मुसाफ़िर लूटे जाते हैं बादशाह ने कहा क्या तूने यिह मसल नहीं सुनी चिराग़ के नीचे अन्धेरा ।

١ (१) for *ēk*, one, or *pahlī*, first, *naḳl*, story.

Ēk, one, a,
shakhṣ, person,
bādshāh, king,
kē, of,
ʻain, eye (the very),
ḳalʻe, castle, palace,
nīchē, under, beneath,
lūṭā, plundered,
gayā, went, was.
Us-nē, he,
kī, of,
khidmat, service,
mēṅ, in,
ʻarẓ, representation,
kī, made,
ki, that,
jahān, world,
panāh, protection,
mujhē, me, to me,
ḳuzzāḳōṅ, robbers,
ḥuẓūr, presence,
dīwār, wall,
lūṭ, having plundered,
liyā, took.
Farmāyā, commanded,
tū, thou,
hushyār, careful,
kyūṅ, why?
na-rahā, not remained.
Bōlā, (he) spoke,
ghulām, (your) slave,
kō, to,
maʻlūm, known,
na-thā, (it) was not,
ḥaẓrat, presence,
zēr, under,
jharōkhē, window,
musāfir, traveller, travellers,
lūṭē, plundered,
jātē, going, being,
haiṅ, are.
Kahā, said,
kyā, what?
tū-nē, thee-by, thou,
yih, this,
maṡal, proverb,
na-hīṅ, not-indeed, not,
sunī, heard,
chirāgh, lamp,
andhērā, dark, darkness.

A person was plundered beneath the very castle of the king. He made representation in the service of the king,* (saying) that, world-protection!† robbers took (and) plundered me under the wall of the castle of the (royal) presence. The king commanded,‡ (saying) that, why didst thou not remain careful? (He) spoke (saying) that, it was not known to (your) slave, that travellers are being plundered under the window of the (royal) presence. The king said, what? by thee (has) not indeed this proverb (been) heard, "under the lamp (is) darkness."

---

* He represented submissively to the king. † Your Majesty!

‡ Implying "said," when spoken of a sovereign.

Grammatical Analysis.

Ēk, a noun of number[1] (frequently used as an indefinite article): *pahlī,* an ordinal of number,[2] feminine,[3] singular, agreeing with *naḳl,* s. f.[4] nominative case singular.

Ēk (as before): *shaḳhṣ,* s. m.[5] nom. case,[6] governing the verb: *bādshāh,* s. m.[7] gen. case, governed by *kē,* a simple postposition[8] (or particle placed after a noun) governing the preceding word, and in the masculine inflected state[9] to agree with the substantive following: *āin,* s. m. here used adjectively[10] to *ḳal'ē,* s. m. gen. case, sing. inflected from *ḳal'ā,*[11] and governed by *kē,* a postposition governing the genitive case preceding, and itself in the mas. inflected state (from *kā*)[12] to agree (like the termination of an adjective) with the following *nīchē,* s. m. sing. inflected from *nīchā,*[13] abl. case, governed by a postpos. understood,[14] or used absolutely as a postposition[15] or adverb:[16] *lūṭā,* v. a. past participle,[17] mas. sing, (root *lūṭ*), agreeing with *shaḳhṣ* before described: *gayā,* v. n. past tense indefinite,[18] mas. sing. (root *jā*) governed by *shaḳhṣ; lūṭā gayā,* however, may be accounted the passive voice,[19] past tense indefinite, mas. sing. from the root *lūṭ*. *Us,* pronoun of the third person,[20] or the remote demonstrative, sing. from *wuh,* inflected by reason of the attached or sub-

---

[1] See 1st Part, Gram. par. 38. [2] Gram. par. 39.

[3] Gram. par. 3. [4] Declined like بات (*bāt*) Gram. par. 9.

[5] Declined like راجا (*rājā*), Gram. par. 9. [6] Gram. par. 53.

[7] Declined like *rājā*, Gram. par. 9. [8] Gram. par. 6.

[9] Gram. par. 6. [10] Gram. par. 11.

[11] Declined like بندہ (*banda*) G. par. 9. [12] G. par. 6.

[13] Declined like گھوڑا (*ghōṛā*) G. par. 9. [14] G. par. 57.

[15] G. par. 34. [16] G. par. 35. [17] G. par. 20.

[18] G. par. 23 and 20. [19] G. par. 31. [20] G. par. 15.

sequent particle *nē*:[1] *bādshāh*, s. m. gen. case, governed by *kī*, a postpos. fem. governing the preceding word and agreeing with the noun next subsequent:[2] *khidmat*, s. f.[3] abl. case, sing. governed by *meṅ*[4] a simple postposition: *ʿarẓ*, s. f.[5] nom. case sing. governing *kī*,[6] v. a. past tense indef. sing. fem. (root *kar*): *ki*, a conjunction of explanation:[7] *jahān*, s. forming, with the subsequent *panāh*, a compound attributive (used like the English, "Your Majesty") voc. case sing.: *mujhē*, pron. of the first pers. accus. or dat. case sing. (nom. sing. *maiṅ*),[8] governed by the following verb: *ḳaẓẓāḳōṅ*, s. m. plur. inflected (from *ḳaẓẓāḳ*) by reason of the following *nē*:[9] *ḥuẓūr*, s. m. gen. case sing. governed by *kē*,[10] a simple postpos. governing the noun which precedes and agreeing with the subsequent *ḳalʿē*, s. m. gen. case sing. as before: *kī*, postpos. governing the gen. case, and fem.[11] to agree with the following *dīwār*, s. f. gen. case sing. governed by *kē*, postpos. mas. inflected to agree with *nīchē* as before explained: *lūṭ*, v. a. the root[12] or the past conjunctive participle:[13] *liyā*, v. a. past part.[14] or past indef. tense[15] third pers. mas. sing.[16] (root *lē*), the object of the sentence (*mujhē*) being in an oblique case.[17] *Bādshāh* as before: *nē*, particle following the subject of the sentence before a transitive verb in a past tense: *farmāyā*, v. a. past tense indef.[18] third pers. mas.

---

[1] G. par. 23, note. [2] G. par. 6.

[3] Nouns ending in ت are frequently feminine: G. par. 2.

[4] G. par. 6. [5] Declined like بات (*bāt*): G. par. 9.

[6] The feminine of *kiyā*: G. par. 20, *a.* and par. 23, with the note: also par. 72; the verb being made to agree with the object of the sentence.

[7] G. par. 36. [8] G. par. 15. [9] G. note to par. 23.

[10] G. par. 6. [11] G. par. 6. [12] G. par. 18.

[13] G. par. 22. [14] G. par. 20, *c.* [15] G. par. 23.

[16] G. par. 23, note. [17] *Lūṭ liyā* may be considered a compound verb: G. par. 28, Intensives. [18] G. par. 23 and 20.

sing. (root *farmā*), the object being the following sentence:[1] *ki*, conj. as before: *tū*, pron. second pers.[2] nom. case sing. governing the verb; *hushyār*, adj. nom. case, agreeing with the person to which *tū* refers: *kyūn*, adv. of method, derived from the interrogative pron.:[3] *na-rahā*, a compound of *na*, the simple adverb of negation,[4] and *rahā*, v. n. past tense indef.[5] third pers. mas. sing. (root *rah*), governed by *tū*. *Bōlā*, v. n. past tense indef.[6] third pers. mas. sing. governed by *shakhs* understood: *ki*, conj. as before: *ghulām*, s. m.[7] dat. case sing., governed by *kō*,[8] a simple postpos. governing the dat. or accus. case: *ma'lūm*, an Arabic passive participle, which may here be considered as an adj. agreeing with the subject of the sentence or the nom. case understood to *na-thā*, verb, subst. past tense[9] mas. sing. having the simple adverb of negation[10] prefixed, and governed by the following sentence as the subject: *ki*, conj.: *hazrat*, s. f. gen. case sing.: *kē*, postpos. mas.[11] governing the foregoing noun in the gen. case, and inflected to agree with the compound following: *zēr*, prepos.: *jharōkhē*, s. m. sing. inflected from *jharōkhā* by reason of a postpos. understood:[12] *musāfir*, s. m.[13] plur. nom. case, governing the following verb: *lūṭē*, past part. mas. plur.[14] (root *lūṭ*) agreeing with *musāfir*: *jātē*, pres. part. mas. plur.[15] (root *jā*) agreeing with *musāfir*: *hain*, verb subst. pres. tense third pers. plur.[16] (root *hō*), governed by *musāfir*.

---

[1] G. par. 23, note. [2] G. par. 15. [3] G. par. 50.
[4] G. par. 35. [5] G. par. 23 and 20.
[6] G. par. 23 and 20. [7] Declined like راجا (*rājā*), G. par. 9.
[8] G. par. 6. [9] G. par. 32. [10] G. par. 35.
[11] G. par. 6. [12] *Zēr jharōkhē* may be regarded as a compound, and inflected by some postpos. understood: G. par. 57.
[13] Declined like راجا (*rājā*), G. par. 9. [14] G. par. 20.
[15] G. par. 21. [16] G. par. 32: and, *lūṭē jātē hain* may be considered as the passive voice, see G. par. 31, and the conjugation of the passive voice.

Bādshāh as before: *nē*, particle following the subject of a sentence before a transitive verb in a past tense:[1] *kahā*, v. a. past tense indef.[2] third pers. sing. mas. (root *kah*), the object being the following sentence:[3] *kyā*, pron. interrogative,[4] nom. case, here used absolutely as an interjection: *tū*, pron. of the second pers.[5] nom. case sing. uninflected though followed by *nē*, a particle following the subject before a transitive verb in a past tense: *yih*, pron. proximate demonstrative,[6] nom. case sing. agreeing with *mas̤al*, s. f. nom. case,[7] sing. governing the verb: *sunī*, v. a. past part.[8] or past tense indef.[9] sing. (root *sun*), governed by *mas̤al*:[10] *chirāgh*, s. m.[11] gen. case, sing. governed by *kē*, a simple postpos.[12] as before: *nīchē*, s. m. sing. inflected, or adv. as before: *andhērā*, s. m. nom. case, sing.[13] governing the subst. verb, *hai*, understood.

---

٢ نقل

احمد سلطان اپني فوج کو ماه بماه درماها دِيا کرتا اور اپني لشکر کي سرداروں کو دونوں وقت ساتھ کھِلايا کرتا اور محمود سلطان اُسکي بِالعکس کرتا ايک دِن اُن ميں لڑائي هوئي احمد کي فتح هوئي محمود کي شِکست لوگوں ني پوچھا اِسکا کيا سبب کِسي ني جواب دِيا کِه جِسکي ديغ اُسکي تيغ

---

[1] G. note to par. 23.

[2] G. par. 23 and 20.

[3] G. note to par. 23, and par. 72.

[4] G. par. 15.

[5] G. par. 15.

[6] G. par. 15.

[7] Declined like بات (*bāt*): G. par. 9.

[8] G. par. 20.

[9] G. par. 23.

[10] G. par. 72.

[11] Declined like راجا (*rājā*), G. par. 9.

[12] G. par. 6.

[13] Declined like گھوڑا (*ghōṛā*), G. par. 9.

In Nagari characters.

२ नक़्ल

अह्मद सुलतान अपनी फ़ौज को माह बमाह दर्माहा दिया कर्ता और अपने लश्कर के सर्दारों को दोनों वक़्त साथ खिलाया कर्ता और महमूद सुलतान उसके बिलअक्स कर्ता एक दिन उन में लड़ाई हुई अह्मद की फ़तह हुई महमूद की शिकस्त लोगों ने पूछा इसका क्या सबब किसी ने जवाब दिया कि जिसकी देग उसकी तेग़ ।

۲ (२) for *dō*, two, or *dūsri*, second, *nakl*, story.

Ahmad (proper name),
sultān, king, sultan,
apnī, own, his own,
fauj, army,
kō, to,
māh, month,
ba-māh, by month,
darmāhā, monthly pay,
diyā, given,
kartā, makes,
aur, and,
apnē, own, his own,
lashkar, army,
kē, of,
sardārōn, chiefs, officers,
kō, to,
dōnōn, the two, both,
wakt, time, times,
sāth, with, in (his) company,
khilāyā, given to eat, fed,
kartā, makes,
aur, and,
mahmūd (proper name)
sultān, king, sultan,
us-kē, of that,
bil'aks, on the contrary,
kartā, does, practises.
Ēk, one,
din, day,
un, them,
mēn, in, between,
larā'ī, fight, battle,
hū'ī, became;
ahmad kī, of Ahmad,
fath, victory,
mahmūd kī, of Mahmud,
shikast, defeat.
Lōgōn-nē, people,
pūchhā, asked, inquired,
is-kā, of this,
kyā, what?
sabab, cause, reason.
Kisī, some one,
nē (particle),
jawāb, answer,
diyā, gave, given,
ki, that,
jis-kī, of whom,
dēgh, caldron, pot,
us-kī, his, of him,
tēgh, sword.

3 P

Ahmad Sultan makes given (makes a practice of giving) to his army, month by month, (its) monthly pay; and, to the officers of his army, at both times (of eating in the day), he makes given to eat (makes a practice of giving to eat): and, Mahmud Sultan practises the contrary of that. One day, a battle became (took place) between them; the victory became Ahmad's, the defeat Mahmud's. People asked, (saying) what is the cause of this? Some one gave answer, (saying) that, "of whom is the caldron, of him is the sword."

Grammatical analysis.

Dō, a noun of number[1]: *dūsrī*, an ordinal of number,[2] fem. sing. agreeing with *naḳl*, s. f. nom. case sing.

Aḥmad, n. prop. mas. nom. case, sing.: *sulṭān*, s. m.[3] nom. case sing. governing the verb: *apnī*, pron. common or reflective,[4] gen. case fem. agreeing with *fauj*, s. f.[5] dat. case sing. governed by *kō*,[6] a simple postposition: *māh*, s. m. followed by *ba-māh*, a prepos. with the foregoing noun repeated in the Persian construction:[7] *darmāhā*, s. m. nom. case sing. though the object of the verb: *diyā*, past participle[8] of the transitive verb (root *dē*), uninflected mas. sing.: *kartā*, pres. participle or pres. indef. tense,[9] third pers. mas. sing. (root *kar*), forming with the preceding part. a compound frequentative verb:[10] *aur*, conj.: *apnē*, pron. common or reflective,[11] gen. case mas. inflected to agree with *lashkar*, s. m. gen. case sing. governed by *kē*, a simple postpos. mas. agreeing with *sardārōṅ*, s. m. dat. case plur. governed by *kō*, a simple postpos.: *dōnōṅ*, a numeral, *dō* with

---

1 G. par. 38.
2 G. par. 39.
3 Declined like راجا (*rājā*), G. par. 9.
4 G. par. 15.
5 Declined like بات (*bāt*), G. par. 9.
6 G. par. 6.
7 G. par. 8.
8 G. par. 20, c.
9 G. par. 24.
10 G. par. 28, Frequentatives.
11 G. par. 15.

the plural affix:[1] *wakt*, s. m. sing. governed by some postpos. understood:[2] *sāth*, s. m. governed by a postpos. understood, and here used as an adverb:[3] *khilāyā*, past part.[4] mas. uninflected sing. (root *khilā* which is a causal of *khā*):[5] *karta*, v. a. pres. indef. tense,[6] third pers. mas. sing. (root *kar*), forming with the preceding part. a compound frequentative verb:[7] *aur*, conj.: *maḥmūd*, n. prop. mas. nom. case sing.: *sulṭān*, s. m. nom. case sing. governing the verb: *us-kē*, pron. of the third pers. gen. case sing.[8] the affixed postpos. *kē* being mas. inflected to agree with *bi-l-aks*, an Arabic preposition followed by the article with a noun,[9] used here adverbially: *kartā*, v. a. pres. indef. tense third pers. mas. sing. (root *kar*), governed by *mahmūd sulṭān*. *Ēk*, noun of number: *din*, s. m. sing. governed by a postpos. understood:[10] *un*, pron. third pers. or remote demonstrative,[11] abl. case plur. governed by *mēṅ*,[12] a simple postpos. governing the abl. case: *laṛā'ī*, s. f.[13] nom. case sing. governing *hū'ī*, v. n. past indef. tense[14] fem. sing. (root *hō*): *aḥmad* and *maḥmūd*, n. prop. gen. case, governed by *kī*, a simple postpos. fem. to agree with the subsequent noun: *fatḥ*, s. f.[15] nom. case sing. governing *hū'ī*, v. n. past indef. tense fem. sing. (root *hō*): *shikast*, s. f.[15] nom. case sing. governing *hū'ī* understood. *Lōgōṅ*, s. m. plur.[16] (from *lōg*) inflected by reason of the following *nē*,[17] a particle: *pūchhā*, v. a. past indef. tense,[18] third

---

[1] G. par. 10.
[2] G. par. 57.
[3] G. par. 35, 34.
[4] G. par. 20.
[5] G. par. 27.
[6] G. par. 24, 21.
[7] G. par. 28.
[8] G. par. 15.
[9] G. par. 8.
[10] G. par. 57.
[11] G. par. 15.
[12] G. par. 6.
[13] Formed from the verb *laṛā-nā*; see G. par. 43: and declined like *ghōṛī*, G. par. 9.
[14] G. par. 23, and 20, c.; *hū'ī* being the fem. of *hū'ā*.
[15] Declined like بات (*bāt*), G. par. 9.
[16] Declined like راجا (*rājā*), G. par. 9.
[17] G. par. 72.
[18] G. par. 23, 20.

pers. mas. sing. (root *pūchh*), preceded by *nē* and governed by the subsequent sentence: *is-kā*, pron. proximate demonstrative,[1] gen. case sing. governed by the affixed *kā*, simple postpos. mas. uninflected, and agreeing with the following noun:[2] *kyā*, pron. interrog. nom. case:[3] *sabab*, s. m. nom. sing. governing the verb substantive, *hai*,[4] pres. tense third person sing. understood. *Kisī-nē*, pron. indefinite, (nom. *kō'ī*)[5] inflected by reason of the affixed particle *nē*:[6] *jawāb*, s. m. nom. sing. following *nē*,[6] and therefore, though the object of the sentence, governing the verb: *diyā*, v. a. past inde. tense,[7] third pers. mas. sing. (root *dē*): *ki*, conj.: *jis-kī*, pron. relative,[8] gen. case sing. with the governing postpos. *kī*,[9] fem. to agree with *dēgh*, s. f.[10] governing the verb subst. *hai*, pres. tense third pers. sing. understood: *us-kī*, pron. third pers.[11] gen. case sing. with the affixed postpos. *kī*, fem. to agree with *tēgh*, s. f.[10] nom. sing. governing the verb subst. *hai* understood, as before explained.

---

۳ نقل

دو سِپاہِي آپسمين کِسِي شہر کي کُوچي مين خانه جنگِي کر رہي تهي ايک جُلاها يِہ خبر سُنتي هِي اپني کرگهہ سي اُٹه کر اُس کُوچي مين آيا اور تماشا ديکهني لگا قضاکار ايک تلوار جو دُوسري کي سِر سي اُچٹي تو جُلاهي کي آ لِگي مثل کرگهہ چهوڑ تماشي جائي نا حق چوٹ جُلاها کهائي

---

[1] G. par. 15. [2] G. par. 6. [3] G. par. 15.
[4] G. par. 32. [5] G. par. 15. [6] G. par. 23, note, and par. 72.
[7] G. par. 23 and 20. [8] G. par. 15. [9] G. par. 6.
[10] Declined like بات (*bāt*), G. par. 9. [11] G. par. 15.

In Nagari Characters.

३ नक़ल

दो सिपाही आपस्में किसी शह्र के कूचे में ख़ान: जंगी कर रहे थे एक जुलाहा यिह ख़बर सुन्ते ही अपने कर्गह से उठ कर उस कूचे में आया और तमाशा देखने लगा क़ज़ाकार एक तलवार जो दूसरे के सिर से उचटी तो जुलाहे के आ लगी मसल कर्गह छोड़ तमाशे जाए ना हक़्क़ चोट जुलाहा खाए ।

۳ (३) for *tīn*, three, or *tīsrī*, third, *naḳl*, story.

Dō, two,
sipāhī, soldier, soldiers,
āpas-mēṅ, among themselves.
kisī, some, a,
shahr, city,
kē, of,
kūchē, lane, street,
mēṅ, in, among,
khāna-jangī, quarrel, rout,
kar, having made,
rahē, remained,
thē, were.
Ēk, one, a,
julaha, weaver,
yih, this,
khabar, news, report,
suntē, hearing (on),
hī, very, exactly,
apnē, his own,
kargah, work-place, shop.
sē, from,
uṭh, rising,
kar, having made,
us, that,
āyā, came,
aur, and,
tamāshā, sight, sport,
dēkhnē, to see, look at,
lagā, was applied, began:
ḳazākār, by chance,
talwār, sword,
jō, which, when,
dūsrē kē, of the other,
sir sē, from the head,
uchṭī, slipped, glanced,
tō, then,
julāhē kē, of the weaver,
ā, having come,
lagī, was applied, reached.
Masal, proverb:
kargah, work-shop,
chhōṛ, having left,
tamāshē, (to) the sight, show,
jā'ē, may go, (if) goes,
nā, not, un-, in-,
ḥaḳḳ, right, just,
chōṭ, blow, hurt, wound,
khā'ē, may suffer, (then) gets.

Two soldiers had remained making a rout (or quarrelling) in the street of some city. A weaver, immediately on hearing this report, having risen from his work-shop, came into that street, and began to look at the sight. By chance, a sword, which glanced from the head of the other (soldier), reached the weaver's (head). Proverb: having left the work-shop, the weaver goes (to) the sport, unjustly (without deserving it) a blow he suffers (or gets).

Grammatical analysis.

Tīn, noun of number:[1] *tīsrī,* ordinal of number,[2] fem. agreeing with *naḳl,* s. f. nom. sing.

Dō, noun of number: *sipāhī,* s. m.[3] nom. sing. or plur. derived from *sipāh* by affixing *ī,*[4] and governing the verb: *āpas-mēn,* pron. common or reflective, abl. case:[5] *kisī,* pron. indef. (nom. *kō'ī*),[6] inflected to agree with *shahr,* s. m. gen. case sing. governed by *kē,* a simple postpos. mas. inflected to agree with *kūchē,* s. m. abl. case sing. (nom. *kūcha*) governed by *mēn,* a simple postpos.: *k͟hāna,* s. m. nom. case sing.: *jang-ī* derived from *jang* (battle, fight), *k͟hāna-jang-ī* being an abstract noun, formed in the Persian way, by adding *ī*[7] to *k͟hāna-jang* (house-quarreller), fem. nom. sing.: *kar,* v. a. root[8] or past conjunctive participle:[9] *rahē,* past participle,[10] mas. plur. (root *rah*), agreeing with *sipāhī: thē,* verb. subst.[11] past tense mas. plur. governed by *sipāhī: rahē thē,* moreover, may be regarded as the pluperfect or past past tense[12] of *rah,* v. n. *Ēk,* noun of number used as an indefinite article: *julāhā,* s. m. nom. sing.[13]

---

[1] G. par. 38. [2] G. par. 39.

[3] Declined like راجا (*rājā*), G. par. 9. [4] G. par. 44.

[5] G. par. 15 and 6. [6] G. par. 15.

[7] G. par. 43. [8] G. par. 18. [9] G. par. 22.

[10] G. par. 20. [11] G. par. 32. [12] G. par. 23, *a.*

[13] Declined like گھوڑا (*ghōṛā*), G. par. 9.

governing the verb: *yih*, pron. prox. demonstrative, nom. sing. agreeing with *khabar*, s. f. nom. sing.[1] though the object to *suntē*, pres. part. mas. sing.[2] inflected[3] (root *sun*): *hī*, adv. of peculiarity:[4] *apnē*, pron. com. or reflective, gen. sing. mas. inflected to agree with *kargah*, s. m. abl. case sing. governed by *sē*, postpos.: *uṭh-kar*, past conjunctive part.[5] (root *uṭh*): *us*, pron. remote demonstrative sing. inflected (from *wuh*) to agree with *kūchē-mēṅ*, s. m. abl. sing. (nom. *kūcha*), governed by *mēṅ*, postpos.: *āyā*, v. n. past indef. tense,[6] third pers. mas. sing. (root *ā*), governed by *julāhā*: *aur*, conj.: *tamāshā*, s. m. nom. sing. though denoting the object of the sentence: *dēkhnē*, v. a. infin.[7] mas. (root *dēkh*), inflected before *lagā*, v. n. past indef.[8] (root *lag*), third pers. mas. sing. forming, with *dēkhnē* preceding, a compound inceptive verb:[9] *ḳaẓākār*, adv.: *talwār*, s. f. nom. sing. governing the verb: *jō*, pron. relative, nom. case, or adv.[10] *dūsrē-kē*, ordinal of number[11] or adj. used substantively, gen. mas. sing. governed by *kē*, postpos.: *sir-sē*, s. m. abl. sing.: *uchṭī*, v. n. past indef.[12] fem. sing. (root *uchaṭ*), governed by *talwār*: *tō*, adv.[10] correlative to *jō* preceding: *julāhē kē*, s. m. gen. sing. some postpos. or noun being understood after it: *ā*, v. n. root or past conjunct. participle:[13] *lagī*, v. n. past indef.[14] third pers. fem. sing. (root *lag*) governed by *talwār*. *Masal*, s. f. nom. sing. used absolutely: *chhoṛ*, v. a. root or past conjunct. participle: *tamāshē*, s. m. sing. inflected by reason of some postpos. understood:[15] *jā'ē*, v. n. fut. indef. or aorist[16] (root *jā*), third person sing. governed by *julāhā*

---

[1] Declined like جگہ (*jagah*), G. par. 9.
[2] G. par. 21.
[3] G. par. 74.
[4] G. par. 35.
[5] G. par. 22.
[6] G. par. 23.
[7] G. par. 19.
[8] G. par. 23.
[9] G. par. 28.
[10] G. par. 35.
[11] G. par. 39.
[12] G. par. 23.
[13] G. par. 18, 22.
[14] G. par. 23.
[15] G. par. 57.
[16] G. par. 25.

understood: *nā*, adv. forming, with *ḥaḳḳ*, s. m. following, a Persian compound adjective:[1] *chōṭ*, s. f. nom. sing. though the object of *khā'ē*, v. a. fut. indef. or aorist[2] (root *khā*) third pers. sing. governed by *julāhā*.

---

۴ نقل

اکبر نے بیربل سے پوچھا کہ لڑائی کے وقت کیا کام آتا ہے بیربل نے عرض
کیا کہ جہان پناہ اوسان بادشاہ نے کہا ہتھیار اور زور کیوں نہیں کہتا بیربل
نے کہا جہان پناہ اگر اوسان خطا ہو جاوے تو ہتھیار اور زور کس کام آوے

In Nagari characters.

४ नक़्ल

अकबर ने बीर्बल से पूछा कि लड़ाई के वक़्त क्या काम आता है बीर्बल ने अर्ज़ किया कि जहान पनाह औसान बादशाह ने कहा हथ्यार और ज़ोर क्यूं नहीं कहता बीर्बल ने कहा जहान पनाह अगर औसान ख़ता हो जावे तो हथ्यार और ज़ोर किस काम आवे ।

۴ (४) for *chār*, four, or *chauthī*, fourth, *naḳl*, story.

Akbar nē, Akbar,	*waḳt*, (at) the time,	*ãrz*, representation,
Bīrbal sē, from Bīrbal,	*kyā*, what?	*kiyā*, made,
pūchhā, asked,	*kām*, action, use (to),	*jahān*, world,
ki, that,	*ātā hai*, coming is.	*panāh*, protection,
laṛā'ī kē, of battle,	*Bīrbal nē*, Bīrbal,	*ausān*, presence of mind.

---

[1] G. par. 48. [2] G. par. 25.

Bādshāh nē, the king,	***nahīn***, not,	*hō jāwē*, should become,
kahā, said,	*kahtā*, (art thou) saying.	*tō*, then,
hathyār, arms,	*Agar*, if,	*kis*, what?
aur, and,	*khaṭā*, error, fault (in),	*kām*, action, use (to),
zōr, strength,		*āwē*, would come.
kyūn, why? how?		

Akbar asked of Bīrbal, (saying) that, at the time of battle what comes (of most) use? Bīrbal (humbly) made representation (saying) that, world-protection! (your Majesty!) presence of mind (or courage). The king said, why sayest (thou) not, arms and strength? Bīrbal replied, your Majesty! if presence of mind (or courage) should become wanting, then of what use would come (or be) arms and strength?

Grammatical analysis.

Chār, noun of number:[1] *chauthī*, ordinal of number[2] fem. agreeing with *naḳl*, s. f. nom. sing.

Akbar, n. prop. denoting the agent or subject of the sentence, and followed by *nē*, a particle:[3] *bīrbal*, n. prop. abl. case sing. governed by *sē*, a postposition: *pūchhā*, v. a. past indef. tense,[4] third pers. sing. mas. (root *pūchh*), the following sentence being the object: *ki*, conj.: *laṛāʾī*, s. f. being an abstract noun derived from the root *laṛ* (fight) or *laṛā* (cause to fight),[5] gen. case sing. governed by *kē*, a postpos. mas. inflected to agree with *waḳt*, s. m. sing. governed by a postpos. understood:[6] *kyā*, pron. interrogative, nom. case governing the verb: *kām*, s. m. sing. governed by some postpos. understood:[6] *ātā hai*, v. n. present definite tense,[7] third pers. sing.

[1] G. par. 38.

[2] G. par. 39.

[3] G. par. 23, note, and par. 72.

[4] G. par. 23.

[5] G. par. 43.

[6] G. par. 57.

[7] G. par. 24, *b*.

mas. (root *ā*). *Bīrbal nē*, n. prop. denoting the agent or subject of the sentence, and followed by *nē*, a particle:[1] *ʿarẓ*, s. f. nom. sing., but here it is used as forming, with the subsequent verb, a nominal compound verb[2] (*ʿarẓ karnā*): *kiyā*, v. a. past indef.[3] third pers. mas. sing. (root *kar*), the following sentence being the object: *jahān*, s. forming, with *panāh*, s., a Persian compound in the voc. case: *ausān*, s. m. nom. sing. answering to the previous interrogation, and governing the verb *ātā hai* understood. *Bādshāh nē*, s. m. sing. denoting the agent or subject, with *nē*, a particle:[1] *kahā*, v. a. past indef.[4] third pers. mas. sing. (root *kah*), the following sentence being the object: *hathyār*, s. m. nom. sing.: *zōr*, s. m. nom. sing.: *kyūn*, adv. of interrogation, formed from the interrogative pronoun:[5] *nahīn*, emphatic adverb of negation:[6] *kahtā*, v. a. pres. indef. tense,[7] second pers. mas. sing. (root *kah*), agreeing with *bīrbal* understood. *Agar*, conj. conditional:[8] *khaṭā*, s. f. nom. sing. forming, with *hō* or *hō-jā*, a nominal compound verb:[9] *ho-jāwe*, an intensive compound verb neuter, future indef. or aorist,[10] third pers. sing. governed by *ausān*: *tō*, adv. consequential to *agar* or *jō*:[8] *kis*, pron. interrog. inflected from *kaun*[11] to agree with *kām*, s. m. sing. governed by some postpos. understood:[12] *āwē*, v. n. fut. indef. or aorist,[10] third pers. sing. (root *ā*), governed by *hathyār aur zōr*.

---

[1] G. par. 23, note, and par. 72. [2] G. par. 28.
[3] G. par. 23, and 20, *c*. [4] G. par. 23. [5] G. par. 35.
[6] G. par. 35. [7] G. par. 24. [8] G. par. 36 and 79.
[9] G. par. 28. [10] G. par. 25. [11] G. par. 15.
[12] G. par. 57.

٥ نقل

ایک کمیني اور بهلي آدمي سي اِفلاس مین دوستي هوئي کمینه دولتمند
هوتي هي نجیب زادي سي آنکهین لگا چُراني تب وُه خفا هوکر بولا یه
سچ هي کمیني کي دوستي جیسي بالوُ کي بهیت

In Nagari characters.

५ नक़ल

एक कमीने और भले आदमी से इफ़लास में दोस्ती हुई कमीन' दौलतमन्द होते ही नजीब ज़ादे से आंखें लगा चुराने तब वुह ख़फ़ा होकर बोला यिह सच है कमीने की दोस्ती जैसी बालू की भीत।

٥ (५) for *pānch*, five, or *pānchwīṅ*, fifth, *naḳl*, story.

Kamīnē, low-bred,
bhalē, good, well-bred,
ādmī, man,
iflās, poverty,
dōstī, friendship,
hū'ī, became.
Daulat-mand, rich,
hōtē, (on) becoming,
hī, very, exactly,
najīb, noble,
zādē, born,
ānkhēṅ, eyes,
lagā, was applied,
churānē, to steal.
Tab, then,
wuh, he, that (person),
ḳhafā, angry, offended,
hōkar, having become,
bōlā, spoke, said,
sach, true,
hai, is, (it) is,
jaisī, what-like, as,
bālū, sand,
kī, of,
bhīt, wall.

With a low-bred and a well-bred man in poverty friendship became (took place). (On) becoming rich exactly (immediately), the low-bred (man) began to steal (turn away his) eyes from the noble-born (man). Then he, having become offended, spoke (saying) this is true, "the friendship of the low-bred (the base man) is like a wall of sand."

Grammatical Analysis.

Pānch, noun of number: *pānchwīn,*[1] ordinal of numb. fem.

Ek, noun of number, used as the indefinite article: *kamīnē,* adj. mas. sing. abl. case[2] (nom. *kamīna*), agreeing with *ādmī* understood: *aur.* conj.: *bhalē,* adj. mas. sing. abl. case (nom. *bhalā*), agreeing with *ādmī,*[3] s. m. abl. sing., governed by *sē,* postpos.: *iflās,* s. m. abl. sing., governed by *meṅ,* postpos.: *dōstī,* s. f.[4] nom. sing. (being an abstract noun formed from *dōst,* friend, by subjoining ī),[5] governing *hū'ī,* v. n. past indef. tense, third pers. fem. sing.[6] (root *hō*), governed by *dōstī.* *Kamīna,* adj. mas. nom. sing., used substantively, governing the verb: *daulat-mand,* adj. (formed from *daulat,* riches, by affixing *mand*),[7] nom. sing. mas., agreeing with *kamīna,* or the substantive understood: *hōtē,* v. n. pres. part.[8] mas. sing. (root *hō*), inflected and followed by *hī,* adv. of peculiarity or identity:[9] *najīb,* adj. used substantively, and compounded with the following *zāde,*[7] adj. mas. sing. abl. case, here used substantively, and governed by *sē,* postpos.: *ānkhēṅ,* s. f. nom. plur. (from *ānkh*),[10] the object to the verb *churānē: lagā,* v. n. past indef. tense[11] (root *lag*), third pers. mas. sing., governed by *kamīna: churānē,* v. a. (being a derivative from *chōr,* thief),[12] infin. mas. (root *churā*), forming, with the preceding word, the compound inceptive, *lagā churānē.*[13] *Tab,* adv.:[14] *wuh,* pron. third pers.[15] nom. sing., governing the verb: *khafā,* adj.[16] nom. mas. sing., agreeing with *bhalā ādmī* understood:

---

1 G. par. 39.
2 Declined like بندہ (*banda*), G. par. 9.
3 Declined like راجا (*rājā*), G. par. 9.
4 Declined like گھوڑی (*ghōṛī*), G. par. 9.
5 G. par. 43.
6 G. par. 23 and 20.
7 G. par. 48.
8 G. par. 21.
9 G. par. 35 and 74.
10 Declined like بات (*bāt*), G. par. 9.
11 G. par. 23 and 20.
12 G. par. 30.
13 G. par. 28.
14 G. par. 35.
15 G. par. 15.
16 Not admitting of inflection: see G. par. 4, *a.*

hōkar, v. n. past conjunctive part.[1] (root *hō*): *bōlā*, v. n. past indef. tense[2] (root *bōl*), third pers. mas. sing. governed by *wuh*, and agreeing with *bhalā ādmī* understood: *yih*, pron. proximate demonstrative,[3] nom. sing. governing the verb: *sach*, adj. nom. sing. agreeing with *yih*: *hai*, verb subst.[4] pres. tense, third pers. sing.: *kamīnē*, adj. gen. sing. mas. used substantively, and governed by *kī*, postpos. fem. agreeing with *dōstī*, s. f. nom. sing. governing the subst. verb *hai* understood: *jaisī*, adj. fem. sing. derived from the relative pronoun,[5] and agreeing with *bhīt*: *bālū*, s. m. gen. sing. governed by *kī*, postpos. fem., agreeing with *bhīt*, s. f.[6] nom. sing. governing *hai* understood.

---

٦ نقل

ایک بادشاه نی اپني وزیر سي کها که مین تین باتین کهتا هون تو تینون کا جواب ایک بات مین دي روٹي جلي کیون گهوڑا اڑا کیون اور پان سڑا کیون وزیر لي کها جهان پناه پهیرا نتها بادشاه بهت خوش هوا اور مرتبه زیاده کیا

In Nagari characters.

६ नक़्ल

एक बादशाह ने अपने वज़ीर से कहा कि मैं तीन बातें कहता हूं तू तीनों का जवाब एक बात में दे रोटी जली क्यूं घोड़ा अड़ा क्यूं और पान सड़ा क्यूं वज़ीर ने कहा जहान पनाह फेरा नथा बादशाह बहुत ख़ुश हुआ और मर्तबः ज़ियादः किया ।

---

[1] G. par. 22. [2] G. par. 23 and 20. [3] G. par. 15.
[4] G. par. 32. [5] G. par. 14.
[6] Declined like بات (*bāt*), G. par. 9.

٦ (६) for *chha*, six, or *chhaṭhī*, sixth, *naḳl*, story.

Wazīr, vizir, minister,
maiṅ,[1] I,
tīn, three,
bāteṅ,[2] words,
kahtā,[3] saying,
hūṅ,[4] am,
tū,[1] thou,
tīnōṅ,[5] all three, the three,
jawāb, answer,
dē,[6] give:
rōṭī, bread,
jalī,[7] burnt,
kyūṅ,[8] why? how?
ghōṛā, horse,
aṛā,[7] stopped, become restiff, stood still.
pān, betel leaf,
saṛā,[7] rotten, musty.
Phērā,[7] turned,
na-thā,[9] (it) was not.
Bahut, much, very,
khush, pleased, delighted,
martaba, rank, degree,
ziyāda, more, greater,
kiyā,[10] made.

٧ نقْل

ایکْ دِن نوشیرْوان نےِ وَزِیر سےِ پُوچْھا جہان مین سب چِیز پر مُقدّم کیا ہَے جَواب دِیا عَورت اَور مَوت اَور حاجت پُوچْھا کیُونْکر کہا عَورت نہوتیِ تو تُو کہان مےِ پَیدا ہوتا اَور مَوت نہوتیِ تو یِہ سلْطنت تُجْھے نہ پُہنْچتیِ اَور حاجت نہوتیِ تو مَین تیرےِ سامْھنےِ کیُون کھڑا رَہْتا

In Nagari characters.

७ नक़्ल

एक दिन नौशीर्वान ने वज़ीर से पूछा जहान में सब चीज़ पर मुक़द्दम क्या है जवाब दिया औरत और मौत और हाजत

---

[1] G. par. 15.
[2] G. par. 9.
[3] G. par. 21.
[4] G. par. 32.
[5] G. par. 10.
[6] G. par. 26 and 18.
[7] G. par. 20.
[8] G. par. 35.
[9] The adverb of negation, G. par. 35, and the subst. verb, past tense, third pers. sing., G. par. 32.
[10] G. par. 23, and 20, *c*.

पूछा क्यूंकर कहा औरत नहोती तो तू कहां से पैदा होता और मौत नहोती तो यिह सल्तनत तुझे न पहुंचती और हाजत नहोती तो मैं तेरे साम्हने क्यूं खड़ा रहता।

٧ (७) for *sāt*, seven, or *sātwīṅ*, seventh, *naḳl*, story.

Din, day,
nōshīrwān, n. prop.[1]
jahān, world,
sab, all,
chīz, thing,
par, on, over,
muḳaddam, prior, excellent,
hai,[2] is?
Diyā,[3] given, (he) gave,

ʻaurat, woman,
maut, death (s. f.),
ḥājat, necessity (s. f.).
Kyūṅkar,[4] why? how?
Na-[5]*hōtī*,[6] (if) exists not,
tō,[7] then,
kahāṅ,[8] where?
paidā, produced, born,
hōtā,[9] becomest;

salṭanat, empire, sovereignty,
tujhē,[10] to thee,
pahunchtī,[9] arrives, comes;
tērē,[11] of thee, thy,
sāmhnē,[12] (in) front, before,
khaṛā, standing,
rahtā,[9] remain.

٨ نقل

ایک کایتھ اور اُس کا غُلام دونون ایک گھر مین سوتي تھي | لالا ني کہا رام
چیرا دیکھہ تو پاني برستا هَي یا کُھل گیا | اُس ني کہا برستا هي | پُوچھا تو کِس

[1] A celebrated king of Persia.
[2] G. par. 32.
[3] G. par. 23, and 20, c.
[4] G. par. 35.
[5] The simple adverb of negation: G. par. 35.
[6] G. par. 24, and 21.
[7] The consequential conjunction: G. par. 36 and 79.
[8] G. par. 35.
[9] G. par. 24 and 21.
[10] G. par. 15.
[11] G. par. 15 and 16.
[12] G. par. 34.

طرح جانتا هَي تَين تو پڑا سوتا هَي|كها بِلّي آئِي تهِي اُس كو مَين ني ٹٹولا تها

بهِيگِي تهِي|كها چِراغ بُجّها دي كها مُنّهه ڈهانْپ كي سو رَهو اندّهيرا هو جائيگا

پهِر كها دروازه بنْد كر دي. كها بهيّا جِي دو كام همْني كِيئي ايكْ كام تُم كرو

غرض اَيسا حُجّتِي اَور سُسْت تها|آخِر نه اُٹّها پڑا پڑا جَواب ديتا رَها

In Nagari characters.

८ नक़्ल

एक कायथ और उस का ग़ुलाम दोनों एक घर म सोते थे लाला ने कहा राम चेरा देख तो पानी बरसता है या खुल गया उस ने कहा बरसता है पूछा तू किस तरह जानता है तैं तो पड़ा सोता है कहा बिल्ली आई थी उस को मैं ने टटोला था भीगी थी कहा चिराग़ बुझा दे कहा मुंह ढांप के सो रहो अन्धेरा हो जाएगा फिर कहा दर्वाज़ः बन्द कर दे कहा भया जी दो काम हम्ने किये एक काम तुम करो ग़रज़ ऐसा हुज्जती और सुस्त था आख़िर न उठा पड़ा पड़ा जवाब देता रहा।

^ (८) for *āṭh*, eight, or *āṭhwīṅ*, eighth, *naḳl*, story.

Kāyath, name of a tribe,	*dōnōṅ*,[1] the two, both,	*thē*,[3] were.
ghulām, slave,	*ghar*, house,	*Lālā*,[4] the master,
	sōtē,[2] sleeping,	*rām-chērā*,[5]

[1] G. par. 10. [2] G. par. 21.

[3] G. par. 32; and *sōtē thē* may be regarded as the present past or imperfect tense, G. par. 24, *a*.

[4] Uninflected, though acted upon by *nē*: see G. par. 5, and 4, *a*.

[5] Lit. slave of *Rāmā*, a term used in calling to a slave.

dēkh,[1] see, look,	*jāntā*,[3] knowing,	*ṭaṭōlā*,[15] handled, felt,
tō, then, indeed,	*hai*,[10] art?	*thā*,[16] was;
pānī,[2] water,	*Taiṅ*,[7] thou,	*bhīgī*, wet.
barastā,[3] raining,	*paṛā*,[11] fallen, lying down,	*Chirāgh*, lamp,
hai,[4] is,	*sōtā hai*,[12] art sleeping.	*bujhā*,[17] extinguish,
yā,[5] or,	*Billī*, the cat,	*dē*,[18] give.
khul,[6] having opened,	*āī*,[13] come,	*Muṅh*, face, mouth,
gayā, (it) is gone.	*thī*,[14] was,	*ḍhāmp-kē*,[19] having covered,
Us[7]*-nē*,[8] he.	*us-kō*,[7] it, to it,	*sō*,[20] sleep,
Kis,[7] what?	*maiṅ*[7]*-nē*,[8] I,	*rahō*,[21] remain;
ṭaraḥ, manner (in),[9]		

[1] G. par. 26, and 18.

[2] A mas. noun, though terminating in *ī*: G. par. 2, *a*.

[3] G. par. 21.

[4] G. par. 32.

[5] G. par. 36.

[6] Root of the verb, compounded with *gayā*, past tense of *jā*: G. par. 28; also, par. 23, and 20, *c*.

[7] G. par. 15.

[8] G. par. 23, note, and par. 72.

[9] G. par. 57.

[10] *Jāntā-hai*, pres. def. tense of *jān*, know, third pers. mas. sing.: see G. par. 24, *b*.

[11] G. par. 20.

[12] Pres. def. tense (root *sō*), third pers. mas. sing.; see G. par. 24, *b*.

[13] Past part. fem. sing. (root *ā*) agreeing with *billī*.

[14] *A'ī thī*, pluperfect tense, third pers. fem. sing.; see G. par. 23, *a*.

[15] G. par. 20.

[16] G. par. 32; *ṭaṭōlā thā*, pluperfect tense (root *ṭaṭōl*), third pers. mas. sing.: see G. par. 23, *a*.

[17] A transitive or causal verb, from *bujh*; see G. par. 27.

[18] G. par. 26: *bujhā dē*, however, may be considered a compound intensive verb; see G. par. 28.

[19] G. par. 22.

[20] G. par. 18.

[21] G. par. 26: but *sō rahō* may be accounted a compound intensive verb; see G. par. 28.

andhērā, dark,
hō-jā'ēgā,[1] (it) will become.
Phir, again,
darwāza, door,
band, fastened, shut,
kar,[2] make, having made.
Bhaiyā, brother, comrade,
jī :[3] life, master, Sir,
dō, two,
kām, thing, business,
ham[4]***-nē***, we,
kiyē,[5] done, have done,
tum, you,
karō,[6] do.
gharaẓ, in short,
aisā,[7] this-like, so,
ḥujjatī,[8] disputations,
sust, lazy,
ākhir, at last,
uṭhā,[9] rose, got up,
paṛā paṛā, continuing, laid down,
dētā,[10] giving,
rahā,[9] (he) remained.

---

۹ نقل

ایک مُسلمان بِیمار تھا غُلام سي کہا کِہ فلاني حکِیم کي پاس جاکر دَوا لا ۱
اُسني کہا شاید حکِیم جي اِسوقت گھر مین نہووین کہا ہونگي جا | تب
اُسني کہا اگر مُلاقات بِهي هووي لیکن دَوا ندین تد کہا رُقعہ همارا لیجا البتہ

---

[1] Fut. tense, third pers. mas. sing. of the comp. intensive root, *hō-jā*; see G. par. 28, and 25.

[2] The root, G. par. 18, or the past conjunct. participle, G. par. 22.

[3] Much used after appellatives, in a benedictive or auspicious sense; unless it be from Turkish, or some other language, in the sense of "master."

[4] G. par. 15; the plur. of *main*, often applied, as in this instance, to a single person.

[5] G. par. 23, and 20, *c*.

[6] G. par. 26.

[7] G. par. 14.

[8] Formed from *ḥujjat*, by affixing *ī*; see G. par. 48.

[9] G. par. 23, and 20.

[10] G. par. 21.

دینگي پهِر کها کِه جو اُنهون ني دَوا بهِي دِي اگر فائِدہ نکري کها اَي کم بخت یهین بَیٹها تمهِیدین بانْدها کریگا یا جایگا کُها صاحِب فرض کِیا کِه اگر فائِدہ بهِي کري تو حاصِل کیا آخِر ایکدِن مرنا بر حق هَي جَیسا اب مري تَیسا تب

In Nagari characters.

९ नक़्ल

एक मुसल्मान बीमार था ग़ुलाम से कहा कि फ़लाने हकीम के पास जाकर दवा ला उस्ने कहा शायद हकीम जी इस्वक़्त घर में नहोवें कहा होंगे जा तब उस्ने कहा अगर मुलाक़ात भी होवे लेकिन दवा नदें तब कहा हक़्क़ः हमारा लेजा अल्बत्तः देंगे फिर कहा कि जो उन्हों ने दवा भी दी अगर फ़ाइदः नकरे कहा ऐ कम बख़्त यहीं बैठा तम्हीदें बान्धा करेगा या जाएगा कहा साहिब फ़र्ज़ किया कि अगर फ़ाइदः भी करे तो हासिल क्या आख़िर एक्दिन मर्ना बर हक़ है जैसा अब मरे तैसा तब।

१ (९) for *nau*, nine, or *nauwīṅ*, ninth, *naḳl*, story.

Musulmān, a Mahommedan,	*falānē*, such a, a certain,	*dawā*,[2] medicine,
bīmār, sick, ill,	*ḥakīm*, physician,	*lā*,[3] bring.
ghulām, slave, servant,	*pās*, to the side, near,	*Shāyad*, may be, perhaps,
	jākar,[1] having gone,	

[1] G. par. 22.

[2] A fem. noun, ending in *ā*; G. par. 2, note.

[3] G. par. 18, and 26.

jī,[1] life : master, Sir,
is[2]*-waḳt*,[3] this time (at),
ghar mēṅ, house in,
na-hōwēṅ,[4] may not be.
Hōṅgē,[4] (they) will be.
jā, go.
Tab, then,
agar, if,
mulāḳāt, meeting,
bhī,[5] even, also,
hōwē,[4] should be,
lēkin,[6] but, yet,
na-dēṅ[4] (they) should not give.
Tad, then,
ruk'a, note, letter,
hamārā,[7] of us,
le-jā,[8] take,
albatta, certainly,
dēṅgē,[4] (they) will give.
Phir, again,
jō, which, when,
unhōṅ[9] *nē*, they,
dī,[10] gave,
fā'ida, benefit,
na-karē,[4] (it) should not make.
Ai,[11] O!
kam-ba<u>kh</u>t,[12] wretch,
yahīṅ, here,
baiṭhā, seated,
tamhīdēṅ, preambles, conditions,
bāndhā,[13] bound,
karēgā,[14] wilt (thou) make?
yā, or,
jā'ēgā,[4] wilt (thou) go?
Sāḥib, master, Sir,
farẓ, obligation,
kiyā,[15] made, done,
ḥāṣil, the gain, result,
ā<u>kh</u>ir, at last,
ēk-din, (on) one day,
marnā, to die, dying,
bar ḥaḳḳ, on right, on (one's) lot,
jaisā,[16] what-like, as,
ab,[17] now,
marē,[4] (one) should die.
taisā,[16] that-like, so.

---

[1] Much used after appellatives, as noticed under the eighth story.
[2] G. par. 15.
[3] Governed by some postpos. understood: see G. par. 57.
[4] G. par. 25.
[5] The adv. even, also.
[6] Conjunction; see G. par. 36.
[7] The plural in the first person substituted for the singular: G. par. 15, & 65.
[8] A compound intensive verb; G. par. 28.
[9] G. par. 15, 16, and 65.
[10] G. par. 23, and 20, c. *a.*
[11] G. par. 7.
[12] G. par. 48.
[13] A transitive or causal verb, formed from *bandh*, be bound; G. par. 27, *a.*
[14] Forming, with the preceding past participle, a compound frequentative verb; G. par. 28.
[15] G. par. 20, *c.* And *farẓ kiyā* should be regarded as a compound nominal verb, G. par. 28, in the sense of "granted," or "admitted."
[16] G. par. 14.
[17] G. par. 35.

۱۰ نقل

ايک حکيم ني اپني لڑکي کو نصيحت کي اَور بعد اُسکي لڑکي سي پُوچھا
که مَين ني جو جو کها وه سب تُو ني سمجھا بولا كه کيا اُسني کها كه تُو
ابتک کهان تها جو تُو ني ميري بات نه سُني يه کهني لگا كه مَين اِس فکر
مين تها كه ميخ جو گاڑتي هَين اُسکي مِٹّي کَون ليجاتا هَي

In Nagari characters.

१० नक़्ल

एक हकीम ने अपने लड़के को नसीहत की और बअ़द उसके लड़के से पूछा कि मैं ने जो जो कहा वुह सब तू ने समझा बोला कि क्या उसने कहा कि तू अबतक कहां था जो तू ने मेरी बात न सुनी यिह कहने लगा कि मैं इस फ़िक्र में था कि मेख़ जो गाड़ते हैं उसकी मिट्टी कौन लेजाता है।

۱۰ (१०) for *das*, ten, or *daswīṅ*, tenth, *naḳl*, story.

Laṛke, boy,
naṣīḥat, instruction,
kī,[1] made,
baʿd,[2] after,
us-kē, that,
jō jō,[3] what what, whatever.
sab, all,
samjhā,[4] understood?
Bōlā,[4] (he) spoke, said.
Ab-[5]*tak*,[6] till now,

---

[1] Past participle, or past indef. tense (root *kar*), fem. sing. governed by the nom. sing. fem. preceding: G. par. 20, *a*. c., and par. 23, with the note.

[2] G. par. 34.

[3] G. par. 15, note to page 27.

[4] G. par. 20, and 23

[5] G. par. 35.

[6] G. par. 34.

kahāṅ,[1] where?
jō,[1] when,
sunī,[2] heard, heardest.
Kahnē lagā,[3] began to say,
fikr, thought,
mēkh, peg, nail,
gāṛtē,[4] driving down,
miṭṭī, earth.
kaun,[5] who?
lē-jātā,[6] taking away.

---

١١ نقل

ایک بڑے آدمي كي يہہ خو تهي كه جب اپني نوكرون پر خفا هوتا تو انهين خوب مارتا پهر بعد دو چار گهڑي كي هر ايک كو پانچ پانچ مات مات روپئي ديتا ايكروز اسني اپني آدميون كو مارا ايک ني انهه آدميونسي كها كه تم جو هميشه مار كهاتي هو كيا تمهين اور كهين نوكري نهين ملتي انمين سي ايک بول اٹها كه تم ني يهه مثل نهين سني دودهيل گائي كي دو لات بهي بهلي يعني دودهه والي گائي اگر لات ماري تو برا نماني

In Nagari characters.

११ नक़्ल

एक बड़े आदमी की यिह खो थी कि जब अपने नौकरों पर

---

[1] G. par. 35.

[2] Past indef. tense (root *sun*), fem. sing. governed by *bāt*, s. f. preceding: see G. par. 23, note, and par. 72.

[3] A compound inceptive verb: see G. par. 28.

[4] Pres. participle, mas. plur. governed by some such noun as *lōg*, people, understood.

[5] G. par. 15.

[6] A compound intensive verb, formed by the addition of *jātā*, going, to the root *lē*, take; see G. par. 28.

ख़फ़ा होता तो उन्हें ख़ूब मार्ता फिर बऽद दो चार घड़ी के हर एक को पांच पांच सात सात रूपिये देता एक रोज़ उस्ने अपने आद्मियों को मारा एक ने उन्ह आद्मियों से कहा कि तुम जो हमेश: मार खाते हो क्या तुम्हें और कहीं नौकरी नहीं मिल्ती उन में से एक बोल उठा कि तुम ने यिह मसल नहीं सुनी दूधेल गाए की दो लात भी भली अपने दूध वाली गाए अगर लात मारे तो बुरा नमाने।

॥ (११) for *igārah*, eleven, or *igārawīṅ*, eleventh, *naḳl*, story.

Baṛē, great,
ādmī, man,
khō, custom, habit,
jab, when,
naukarōṅ, servants,
par, on, at, over,
khafā, angry, offended,
hōtā, becomes,
unhēṅ, them,
khūb, good, well,
mārtā, strikes, beats.
Phir, again, then,
baʿd, after,
dō chār,[1] two (or) four,
ghaṛī[2] (a division of time so called),
har, every, each,
pānch pānch,[3] five, five,
sāt sāt,[3] seven, seven,
rūpiyē, rupees,
dētā, (he) gives.
Rōz, day,
unh, those,[4]
tum, ye, you,
jō, who, which,
hamēsha, always,
khātē, eating, suffering,
tumhēṅ, to you,
aur, other, else,
kahīṅ, somewhere,
naukarī, service,
na-hīṅ, not,
miltī, is met with, is got,
bōl, having spoken,
uṭhā, rose,

---

[1] In such indefinite expressions of number, it is usual to say, "two (or) four," where the English would say "two or three."

[2] A space of twenty four minutes.

[3] In a distributive sense; see G. par. 41: so, "*pānch pānch*, each, five, &c."

[4] The pronoun aspirated; see G. par. 16.

dūdhēl, milch,
gā'ē, cow,
lāt,[1] kick, kicks,
bhalī, good.

ya'nē, that means, that is,
dūdh-wālī, milk having,

burā, bad,
na-mānē,[2] should not regard.

---

۱۲ نقل

اِمیر تیمُور جب ہِند مین آیا ا تب یِہ بات کہِي اِکہ مَین نے لوگون
سي یُون سُنا ہَي اجو ہِند مین راگ خُوب ہوتا ہَي کِسِي گوَیّي کو بُلاؤ
تو مَین سُنُون ایکٔ اَندھِي گاین بڑِي لسّان بادشاہ کِي خِدمت مین آن
حاضِر ہُوئِي اَیسا گائِي اجو اِمیر تِیمُور سُنکر بہُت خُوش ہُوئِي اَندھِیکو پُوچھا
تیرا نام کیا ہَي کہا دَولت بادشاہ نے کہا کیا دَولت بِھي اَندھِي ہوتِي ہَي
جَواب دِیا جو اَندھِي نہوتِي تو مُجھ لنگڑي کي گھر کیُون آتِي اِس جَواب سي
اِمیر بہُت راضِي ہُوا اَور انعام جو دِیا چاہتا تھا اُسي دو چند دِیا

In Nagari characters.

१२ नक़्ल

अमीर तीमूर जब हिन्द में आया तब यिह बात कही कि मैं ने लोगों से यूं सुना है जो हिन्द में राग ख़ूब होता है

---

[1] A feminine noun, which, though used here in a plural sense, does not take the plural form, because it is preceded by a numeral: G. par. 61.

[2] A verb, indef. fut. or aorist, third pers. sing. (root *mān*), with the simple adv. of negation prefixed; and, the nom. case understood, which may be such word as *kō'ī*, any one.

किसी गवैये को बुलाओ तो मैं सुनूं एक अन्धी गायन बड़ी लस्सान बादशाह की ख़िदमत में आन हाज़िर हुई ऐसा गाई जो अमीर तीमूर सुनकर बहुत ख़ुश हुए अन्धीको पूछा तेरा नाम क्या है कहा दौलत बादशाह ने कहा क्या दौलत भी अन्धी होती है जवाब दिया जो अन्धी नहोती तो तुझ लंगड़े के घर क्यूं आती इस जवाब से अमीर बहुत राज़ी हुआ और इन्आम जो दिया चाहता था उस्से दो चन्द दिया।

۱۲ (१२) for *bārah*, twelve, or *bārahīṅ*, twelfth, *naḳl*, story.

Amīr Tīmūr, n. prop.
hind, India,
āyā, came,
lōgōṅ, people,
yūṅ, thus,
jō, which, that, when,
rāg, music,
khūb, good, fine,
hōtā hai, is becoming, is;
kisī, some,
gawaiyē-kō, singer,
bulā'ō, call, send for,
maiṅ sunūṅ, I may hear.

Andhī (f.), blind,
gāyan, female singer,
baṛī lassān, very good voiced,
bādshāh, king, emperor,
khidmat, service,
ān,[1] having come,
hāzir, present, ready.
Aisā,[2] this-like, so,
gā'ī, she sang,
sunkar, having heard,
bahut khush, much pleased,

nām, name.
Daulat, fortune.
Bhī, even, also.
Jawāb diyā, (she) gave answer,
tujh, thee,
langṛē, lame,
rāzī, satisfied, pleased,
in'ām, present, favour,
chāhtā, wishing, intending,
us-sē, from that,
chand,[3] what quantity, as much.

---

[1] The past conjunctive participle (root *ā*), instead of the regular form, *ā*: G. par. 22.

[2] From the demonstrative pron. *yih*, this, with the adjunct, *sā*, like: G. par. 14, *a*.

[3] G. par. 41.

۱۳ نقل

ایک صرّاف اشرفیونکا توڑا لیي جاتا تھا | اُسي دیکھ کر ایک رهمار کا
جي للچایا | وہ اُسکي پیچھي لگچلا تھوڑي دور جاکي اُسني چاہا کہ توڑا
چھین لي اِس مابین مین کئي ایک آدمي آگئي اُنھون ني اُسکي
مُشکین باندھ لین اَور کوتوال کي یہان لي چلي | کِسي ني اُسي دیکھ
کر کہا | کہ تُو جب اِدھر سي گیا تھا تب تو تیرا یِہہ حال نہ تھا | اِتني
دیر مین تُو ني کیا کِیا جو باندھا گیا | اُسني کہا میري وہي نقل هَي

مکھي بیٹھي شہد پر پنکھ گئي لپٹائي ،
ہاتھ ملي اَور سر دھني لالچ بري بلائي ،

In Nagari characters.

१३ नक़्ल

एक सर्राफ़ अश्रफ़ियों का तोड़ा लिये जाता था उसे देख कर एक रह्मार का जी ललचाया वुह उस्के पीछे लग्चला थोड़ी दूर जाके उस्ने चाहा कि तोड़ा छीन ले इस मा बैन में कई एक आदमी आ गए उन्हों ने उस्की मुश्कें बान्ध लीं और कोत्वाल के यहां ले चले किसी ने उसे देख कर कहा कि तू जब इधर से गया था तब तो तेरा यिह हाल न था इत्नी देर में तूने क्या किया जो बान्धा गया उस्ने कहा मेरी वही नक़्ल है।

मक्खी बैठी शह्द पर पंख गए लिपटाए। हाथ मले और सिर धुने लालच बुरी बलाए।

١٣ (१३) for *terah*, thirteen, or *terawīṅ*, thirteenth, *naḳl*, story.

Ṣarrāf, money-changer,
ashrafiyōṅ,[1] ashrafees,
tōṛā, a bag,
liyē,[2] having taken,
jātā thā, was going.
Usē,[3] him, it, that,
dēkh-kar, having seen,
rahmār, footpad,
jī, life, soul,
lalchāyā,[4] was tantalized:
pīchhē, in the rear, after,
lag,[5] being applied, near,
chalā, moved, went.
Thōṛī, little,
dūr, distance,
jākē, having gone,
chāhā, wished, attempted,
chhīn, having snatched,
lē,[6] he might take,
mā-bain,[7] interval,
ka'ī, some,
ka'ī ēk, some few,
ā-ga'ē,[8] came suddenly.
Unhōṅ[9]*-nē*, they,
mushkēṅ bāndh,[10] having tied his arms behind,
līṅ,[11] took,
kōtwāl, magistrate,
yahaṅ,[12] to the abode,
lē, having taken (him),
chalē, moved, went.
Idhar,[13] here, thither,
gayā thā, wast gone,
ḥāl, state, condition,
itnī,[14] this-much, so much,

---

[1] Plural of *ashrafī*, a large gold coin so called.

[2] G. par. 22, note. [3] Accus. or dat. sing. from *wuh*: G. par. 15.

[4] Past indef. tense of the neuter verb, root *lalchā*, apparently derived from *lālach*, avarice: G. par. 30.

[5] Root of a verb, forming, with the next following, a compound intensive; G. par. 28: or, it may be regarded as an adv.; G. par. 35 and 34. [6] G. par. 25, *a*.

[7] A compound of two Arabic words, meaning "that which (is) between"

[8] A compound intensive verb: G. par. 28.

[9] G. par. 15 and 16.

[10] *Mushkēṅ bāndhnā*, to fasten the elbows of a man behind him, to pinion.

[11] Past indef. fem. plur. (root *lē*), governed by *mushkēṅ*, s. f. nom. plur.

[12] G. par. 34. [13] G. par. 35.

[14] Fem. of *itnā*; G. par. 50; and agreeing with *dēr*, s. f.

dēr, delay, space of time,
kiyā,[1] done, hast done?
bāndhā gayā,[2] bound gone.
Wah-ī,[3] that very.
Makkhī, a fly,
baiṭhī, seated, sat,
shahd-par, honey-on,
pankh, (its) wings,
ga'ē, went, continued,
lipṭā'ē,[4] clinging :
hāth (its) hands,
malē,[5] (it) may rub, rubs,
sir, head,
dhunē,[5] (it) may beat, beats,
lālach, avarice,
burī, bad,
balā'ē[6] (for *balā*), evil.

---

۱۴ نقل

ایک شاعر نے کسی تونگر کی تعریف کی اور کچھ نپایا پھر ھجو کی تو بھی تونگر نے کچھ نکہا | دوسرے روز شاعر اسکے دروازے پر جاکے بیٹھا | تونگر نے کہا اے شاعر تو نے تعریف کی مین نے کچھ ندیا پھر ھجو کی مین نے کچھ نہ کہا اب تو یہان کیون بیٹھا ھے | اسنے جواب دیا کہ آرزو میری یہ ھے کہ تو مر جاوے اور مین مرثیہ کہون

In Nagari characters.

१४ नक़्ल

एक शाइर ने किसी तवंगर की तअ़रीफ़ की और कुछ नपाया फिर हजो की तौ भी तवंगर ने कुछ नकहा दूसरे रोज़ शाइर उसके दर्वाज़े पर जाके बैठा तवंगर ने कहा ऐ शाइर तू ने

---

[1] G. par. 20, c. and 23. [2] Passive voice, been bound; G. par. 31.

[3] Or *wuh-ī*, the demonstrative pron. with the adv. of peculiarity, *ī*, affixed.

[4] Past part. plur. mas. of the neuter verb, *lipṭā*, cling, stick.

[5] Fut. indef. or aorist, third pers. sing.

[6] The *ē* seems here added, for the sake merely of rhyming with *lipṭā'ē*.

तअरीफ़ की मैं ने कुछ न दिया फिर हजो की मैं ने कुछ न कहा अब तू यहां क्यूं बैठा है उसने जवाब दिया कि आर्ज़ू मेरी यिह है कि तू मर जावे और मैं मर्सियः कहूं।

۱۴ (१४) for *chaudah*, fourteen, or *chaudawīṅ*, fourteenth, *naḳl*, story.

Shā'ir, poet,	*tau*, then,	*na-diyā*, gave not,
kisī, some,	*bhī*, also, even.	*ab*, now,
tawangar, rich (man),	*Dūsrē*, the second, next,	*yahāṅ*, here.
ta'rīf, praise,	*rōz*, day (on),	*Ārzū* (f.), desire, wish,
kī, made;	*darwāzē*, door,	*mar*, having died,
kuchh, any (thing),	*jāke*, having gone,	*jāwē*,[1] mayest go,
na-pāyā, found (or got) not.	*baiṭhā*, sat:	*marsiya*, elogy,
Hajō, satire;	*ai*, O!	*kahūṅ*,[2] may say (or) speak.

---

۱۵ نقل

ايک روز بادشاه مع شاهزادي شکار کو گئي جب هوا گرم هوئي تب بادشاه اور شاهزاده دونو اپني اپني لبادي کو ايک مسخري کي کاندهي پر دهر ديئي بعد اسکي بادشاه ني هنسکر فرمايا اي مسخري تيري اوپر ايک گدهي کا بوجه هي يهه بات سنتي هي مسخري ني جواب ديا اي جهان پناه بلکه دو گدهي کا

In Nagari characters.

१५ नक़्ल

एक रोज़ बादशाह मअ शाहज़ादे शिकार को गए जब हवा

[1] *Mar-jāwē*, a compound intensive verb; see G. par. 28.

[2] Fut. indef. or aorist, first pers. sing.: G. par. 25.

गर्म हुई तब बादशाह और शाहज़ादः दोनो अपने अपने लुबादे को एक मसख़रे के कान्धे पर धर दिये बअ़द उसके बादशाह ने हंसकर फ़र्माया ऐ मसख़रे तेरे ऊपर एक गधे का बोझ है यिह बात सुन्ते ही मसख़रे ने जवाब दिया ऐ जहान पनाह बल्कि दो गधे का।

١٥ (१५) for *pandrah*, fifteen, or *pandrahwīṅ*, fifteenth, *naḳl*, story.

Maʿ,[1] with, along with,
shāhzādē, prince,
shikār, hunting.
Hawā, (s. f.) air,
garm, warm, hot,
dōnō,[2] both, the two,
apnē apnē,[3] each his,
lubādē, outer coat,
maskharē, buffoon,
kāndhē, shoulder,
dhar, having placed,
diyē, gave.
Baʿd uskē, after that,
hanskar, having laughed,
farmāyā,[4] commanded, said,
ūpar, over, upon,
gadhē, ass,
bōjh, load.
Jahān-panāh,[5] world-protection!
balki, but, moreover.

---

١٦ نقل

ایک شخص کسي بخیل سي دوستي رکهتا تها| ایک روز اُسني بخیل سي کها| که اب مَین سفر کو جاتا هُون اپني انگوٹهي مُجهي دي که مَین اُسي اپني ساتهه رکهُون| اور جب اُسي دیکهُون تب مُجهي یاد کرُون یهه کلام بخیل

---

[1] An Arabic preposition, causing the following noun to be inflected.

[2] G. par. 10.

[3] By the repetition here individuality is denoted: G. par. 83.

[4] Used respectfully instead of *kahā*, as applied to a king.

[5] Addressed to a sovereign, like as "your Majesty" is often applied in English.

ني سنكر جواب ديا كه اگر تو مجهي ياد ركها چاهتا هي تو جب تو اپني انگلي
خالي ديكهيگا تب مجهي ياد كريگا اور كهيگا كه مين ني فلاني دوست سي
انگوٹهي مانگي تهي اسني ندي

In Nagari characters.

१६ नक़्ल

एक शख़्स किसी बख़ील से दोस्ती रखता था एक रोज़ उसने बख़ील से कहा कि अब मैं सफ़र को जाता हूं अपनी अंगूठी मुझे दे कि मैं उसे साथ रखूं और जब उसे देखूं तब तुझे याद करूं इस कलाम बख़ील ने सुनकर जवाब दिया कि अगर तू मुझे याद रखा चाहता है तो जब तू अपनी उंगली ख़ाली देखेगा तब मुझे याद करेगा और कहेगा कि मैं ने फ़लाने दोस्त से अंगूठी मांगी थी उसने नदी।

١٦ (१६) for *sōlah*, sixteen, or *sōlahwīṅ*, sixteenth, *naḳl*, story.

Shaḵẖs, person,
baḵẖīl, miser,
dōstī, friendship,
rakhtā, holding, having.
Ab, now,
safar, journey,
apnī, thy own, thy,
angūṭhī, ring,
mujhē, to me, me,
sāth, (in) company, with,
rakhūṅ, may hold, keep,
yād, memory,
yād karūṅ, may remember.
Kalām, speech,
sunkar, having heard,
rakhā chāhtā,[1] wishing to keep,
unglī, finger,
ḵẖālī, empty, bare,
dōst, friend,
māngī, asked,
na-dī,[2] gave not.

---

[1] A compound desiderative verb, *rakhā chāhnā*, to wish kept, or to wish to keep: G. par. 28.

[2] G. 20, *a. c.*, and par. 23.

۱۷ نقل

ایک بخیل مسجد کی طرف واسطی نماز کی جاتا تها اثنای راه مین اس کو یاد آیا که چراغ گهر کا نبجهاکر نہین آیا هون وهان سی پهرا اور دروازی پر آ لونڈی سی پکارکر کہا چراغ کو گل کر اور دروازه مت کهول که کهسیگا لونڈی نی کہا ای صاحب اپنی راه جو آئ گئی جوتا نه گهسا هوگا بولا ای عقلمند لونڈی اندیشه مت کر که مین ننگی پاون آیا هون اور بغل مین جوتی کو لایا هون

In Nagari Characters.

१७ नक़्ल

एक बख़ील मस्जिद की तरफ़ वास्ते नमाज़ के जाता था अस्नाए राह में उस को याद आया कि चिराग़ घर का बुझाकर नहीं आया हूं वहां से फिरा और दर्वाज़े पर आ लौंडी से पुकारकर कहा चिराग़ को गुल कर और दर्वाज़ः मत खोल कि घिसेगा लौंडी ने कहा ऐ साहिब इतनी राह जो आए गए जूता न घिसा होगा बोला ऐ अक़्लमन्द लौंडी अन्देशः मत कर कि मैं नंगे पाओं आया हूं और बग़ल में जूते को लाया हूं।

۱۷ (१७) for *satrah*, seventeen, or *satrahwīṅ*, seventeen, *naḳl*, story.

Masjid, mosque,	*namāz*, prayer.	*yād*, memory (in),
ṭaraf,[1] side, towards,	*Asnā-ē*,[2] in the midst of,	*yād āyā*,[3] came in memory,
wāsṭē,[1] for the sake,	*rāh*, road, way,	

[1] G. par. 34. [2] G. par. 8.

[3] A compound nominal verb: G. par. 28.

chirāgh, lamp,
bujhākar,[1] having put out;
wahāṅ,[2] there,
phirā, (he) turned back,
darwāzē, door,
ā, having come,
laundī, slave girl,
pukārkar,[1] having cried out,
gul kar,[3] extinguish,
mat,[4] not, do not,
khōl, open,
ki,[5] because,
ghisēgā,[6] (it) will wear.
Ai ṣāhib, O master, O Sir,
itnī,[7] this much, so much,
jūta, shoes.
Aḳlmand,[8] wise, sensible,
andēsha, thought, care,
nangē, naked, bare,
pā'ōṅ, feet[9] (on),[10]
baghal, armpit,
lāyā, brought, carried.

---

१८ मनु

एक दिन अकबर बादशाह ने बीरबल से कहा कि तू मुझे चार मनुष ला दे सूर्बीर कायर लज्जावान और निलज्ज बीरबल दूसरे दिन भोर ही एक रंडी को साथ अपने बादशाह के सोंहीं ले गया शाह ने पूछा लाया बोला महाराज उपस्थित है यह कह बीरबल ने उस रंडी को बादशाह के साम्हने ले आ खड़ा किया बादशाह ने कहा अबे मैं ने चार जना बुलवाये थे तू एक को लाया और तीन कहां हैं निवेदन किया महाराज इस में चारों के गुन हैं आज्ञा की बखान कर बोला कि जिस काल यह अपने सुसराल में रहती है मारे लाज के अच्छी भांति गला

---

[1] G. par. 22.
[2] G. par. 35.
[3] A compound nominal verb: G. par. 28.
[4] Adverb of prohibition: G. par. 35, and 77.
[5] G. par. 36.
[6] G. par. 25.
[7] G. par. 50.
[8] G. par. 48.
[9] G. par. 5, *a*. note.
[10] G. par. 57.

खोलकर बोलती भी नहीं और जिस बिरियां कहीं ब्याह में गालियां गाती है तो बाप भाई स्वामी ससुर और सब कुटुम के लोग बैठे सुना कर्ते हैं पर यह किसी की कान नहीं कर्ती और जब अपने स्वामी के पास बैठती है तो रात को अकेली घर के कोठे में भी नहीं जाती और कहती है मुझे जाते डर लगता है फिर जिस समय किसी से इस की आंख लगती है तो आधी रात की अंधेरी में अकेली बे हथियार जार के पास निधड़क चली आती है और चोर गवार भूत परेत से नहीं डर्ती यह बात सुन बादशाह ने प्रसन्न हो बीर्बल को पारितोषिक दिया और कहा तू सच कहता है।

१८ for *aṭhārah*, eighteen, or *aṭhārawīṅ*, eighteenth, *naḳl*, story.

Manush, man.
sūrbīr, hero.
kāyar, coward.
lajjāwān, modest.
nilajja, shameless.
bhōr, dawn of day.
ranḍī, woman.
sōṅhīṅ, before.
upasthit, present.
sāmhnē, before.
abē, holla!
janā, person.
bulwāyē, ordered to be called.
nibēdan, representation.
ājnā, (f.) command.

bakhān, explanation.
kāl, time.
susrāl, father-in-law's house.
mārē, stricken, by reason.
lāj, modesty.
bhānti, manner.
galā, throat.
biriyāṅ, time.
byāh, wedding.
gāliyāṅ, indecent songs sung at weddings.
swāmī, lord, husband,
sasur, father-in-law.

kuṭum, tribe, family.
kān, shame.
akēlī, (f.) alone.
kōṭhē, apartment.
samai, time.
andhērī, darkness.
hathiyār, arms.
jār, paramour.
nidhaṛak, fearless.
ghabār, dust (?).
bhūt, ghost.
prēt, goblin.
prasann, pleased,
pāritōshik, a complimentary present.

१८ नक़्ल

चार जना अपने गांव से निकले ब्राह्मन राजपूत बनिया और नाई और किसी किसान के खेत पर जा लगे गन्ने उखाड़ उखाड़ फांदियां बांधने और चूसने उस खेतवाले ने देखा और अपने जी में बिचारा कि ये चार और मैं अकेला जो कुछ कहता हूं तो ये मुझे बिन ठोंके न रहेंगे इस से कुछ जुगत किया चाहिये यह बात मन में ठान वह उन के पास आ रामराम कर बोला कि सुनो जी ब्राह्मन हमारा गुरु राजपूत भाई बनियां महाजन तीन मनुष के गांडे खाने की तो चिंता नहीं भला इस नाई ने क्या समझके मेरे खेत में हाथ डाला इस का तुम्हीं न्याव करो यह बात सुनकर वे चुप हो रहे तब इस ने नाई से गन्ने छीन लिये और उसे जुतियाकर निकाल दिया फिर किसान कहने लगा कि सुनो भाई ब्राह्मन गुरु तुम भाई हमारा तुम्हारा द्रव्य एक है इस बनिये ने क्या बूझ के मेरा खेत उजाड़ा भला इस का तुम्हीं बिचार करो जो तुम हम इस के यहां से रुपये लेंगे तो क्या यह अच्छा ब्याज छोड़ देगा इस बात को भी सुन वे कुछ न बोले तद तो इस ने उसे भी धौलियाके गांडे छीन निकाल दिया निदान इसी भांति से उस ने हर एक को निकाला और अच्छा धन बचाया इस बात को सुन अचरज कर एक ने अपने मित्र से कहा यह क्या अंधेर है कि चार जने पर एक जन प्रबल रहे उस ने पूछा यह क्या बात है मुझे समझाके कहो उस ने उन का वृत्तांत कह सुनाया तब उस का हितकारी बोला क्या तुम ने यह कहावत नहीं सुनी जो इतना अचरज करते हो कि जुग फूटा और नई मारी गई ।

१९ for *unīs*, nineteen, or *unīswīṅ*, nineteenth, *naḳl*, story.

Janā, person.
gāṅw, village, town.
baniyā, trader.
gannē, sugar-canes.
ukhāṛ, having plucked up.
phāṅdiyāṅ, bundles.
chūsnē, to suck.
khēt-wālē, field-owner.
ṭhoṅkē, having beaten.
jugat, contrivance.
ṭhān, having settled.
rām-rām, words used as a salutation.
jī, Sir! master!
guru, spiritual guide.
mahājan, banker, trustworthy person.
gāṅḍē, sugar-canes.
nyāw, justice, decision.
chhīn liyē, took away.
jutiyākar, having beat with a slipper.
dravya, property, thing.
būjhkē, having thought,
ujāṛā, has wasted.
byāj, interest.
dhauliyākē, having thumped.
bhānti, manner, mode.
bachāyā, saved, preserved.
achraj, wonder.
andhēr, darkness, incomprehensible thing.
prabal, predominant.
brittānt, circumstances.
chinhārī, acquaintance.
jug phūṭā aur nard mārī ga'ī, the pair (at the game of *chausar*) is separated and the piece is stricken (taken. A proverb, inculcating the value of unanimity).

---

२० नक़ल

एक कायथ ने गाने बजाने के संसर्ग में किसी गवैये से यह कविता सुनी इश्क़ क्या शै है किसी कामिल से पूछा चाहिये तभी से वह चित्त के ढूंढ ढांढ में था कि एक गोसाईं इसें मिला इसने दंडवत कर उस से पूछा कि महाराज इश्क़ क्या वस्तु है मुझे दया कर बताइये इस की बात सुन उस ने कहा बाबा मैं ने तो अपने गुरु देव के मुख से यों सुना है इश्क़ उसी की झलक है ज्यों सूरज की धूप जहां इश्क़ तहां आप है क़ादिर नादिर रूप।

२० for *bīs*, twenty, or *bīswīṅ*, twentieth, *naḳl*, story.

Kāyath, name of a tribe.	*kāmil*, learned (man).	*dandawat*, obeisance.
gānē, singing (v. noun).	*tab-hī*, that very time.	*vastu* or *bastu*, thing.
bajānē, playing on music.	*siddh*, accomplished (man).	*dayā*, kindness, favour.
sansarg, meeting, assembly.	*ḍhūnḍh ḍhānḍh*, search.	*bābā*, Sir!
gawaiyē, singer.	*gōsā'īṅ*, a devotee so called.	*dēv*, a god, a divinity.
kabitā, poetry, verse.	*isēṅ*, to this. (The nasal added, like as in *tumhēṅ*).	*jhalak*, refulgence.
shai, thing.		*dhūp*, glare, shine.
		ḳādir, mighty.
		nādir, wonderful.
		rūp, form, figure.

*ʿIshk us**-*ī kī jhalak hai jōṅ sūraj kī dhūp:*
jahāṅ ʿishk tahāṅ āp hai ḳādir nādir rūp.

Love is the refulgence of that very (Being), like as sunshine (is) of the sun: wherever (is) love, there is He Himself; the almighty, all-wonderful Form!

Or,

Love? 'Tis a ray, from Him it streams,
Like as the sun darts forth its beams:
Love? Where is love, there Him you see;
Almighty and all-wondrous He.

* This *us*, like the Arabic *hū'a* (*he*), refers to God, as He who really and universally is.

PART V.

HINDUSTANI COMPOSITION.

*Cases of Nouns.**

Of the house.	House†-*of*‡ (*kā, kē* or *kī*).
To the boy.	Boy-*to* (*kō* or *kē ta'īṅ*).
From the horse.	Horse-*from* (*sē*).
From the cat.	Cat-*from* (*sē*).
By deceit.	Deceit-*by* (*sē*).
O friend!	*O* (*ai*) friend!
O boy!	*O* (*ai*) boy!
At the door.	Door-*at* (*par*).
On the mouth.	Mouth-*on* (*par*).
On the road.	Road-*on* (*mēṅ*).
In the heart.	Heart-*in* (*mēṅ*).
In the hand.	Hand-*in* (*mēṅ*).
In the road.	Road-*in* (*mēṅ*).
Up to the house.	House-*up-to* (*tak* or *talak*).
With sand.	Sand-*with* (*sē*).
With (in company with) the dog.	Dog-*with* (*kē sāth*).

* See 1st Part, Gram. par. 4, 5, 6, 7, 8, 9.

† The Substantives, Adjectives, and Verbs, will generally be found under the particular heads in the Vocabulary.

‡ The Hindūstānī words are to be placed according to the order of the English, observed on this column.

Near the door.	Door-*near* (*kē pās*).
Near the village.	Village-*near* (*kē nazdīk*).
Along with the boys.	Boys-*along with* (*ke sāth*).
From among the people.	People *among* (*mēn*) from.
Over the head.	Head-*over* (*kē ūpar*).
Beneath the ground.	Ground-*beneath* (*kē nīchē*).
In the midst of the city.	City-*of midst-in* (*kē bīch*).
Towards the sky.	Sky *towārds* (*kī ṭaraf*).
For God's sake.	God *for the sake of* (*kē wāsṭē*).
For this reason.	*This* (*is*)-*for the reason* (*wāsṭē*).
For the sake of the destitute.	Destitute *for the sake of* (*kī khāṭir*).
For the sake of a friend.	Friend *for the sake of* (*kē li'ē*).
Like (in the manner of) every man.	*Every* (*har ēk*) man-*like* or -*in the manner of* (*kī ṭaraḥ*).
Before the horse.	Horse-*before* (*kē āgē*).
Behind the house.	House-*behind* (*kē pīchhē*).
In the presence of the judge.	Judge-*in presence of* (*kē sāmhnē*).
In front of the house.	House *in front of* (*kē āgē*).
Within the city.	City-*within* (*kē andar* or *kē bīch*).
According to that.	*That* (*us*) -*according to* (*kē muwāfiḳ*).
With respect to him.	*Him* (*us*) -*with respect to* (*kī nisbat*).
The boy's father's horse.	Boy-of father-of horse.
The girl's mother's maid.	Girl-of mother-of maid.
The merchant's brother's daughter.	Merchant-of brother-of daughter.
On the back of the horse.	Horse-of back-*on* (*par*).
Near the friend's house door.	Friend-of house-of door-*near* (*kē pās*).
Under the wall of the house.	House-of wall-*under* (*kē talē*).
Betwixt the leaves of the book.	Book-of leaves *betwixt* (*kē darmiyān*).

Among the houses of the village.	Village-of houses-*among* (*kē bīch*).
For the sake of learning science.	*Science learning* (*ʻilm sīkhnē*) -*for the sake of.*
Towards the door of the mosque.	Mosque-of door-towards.
Instead of the book.	Book-*instead of* (*kī jagah*).
Instead of the bread.	Bread-*instead of* (*kē ʻiwaẓ*).
In exchange for gold.	Gold-*in exchange of* (*kē badlē*).
Thus far (hitherto).	*Hitherto* (*yahāṅ-tak*).

*Substantives with Adjectives.**

Elder brother.	*Elder* (*baṛā*) brother.
Younger (little) sister.	*Younger* (*little, chhōṭī*) sister.
A very rich man.	*Very* (*baṛā*) rich man.
Good men.	*Good* (*bhalā*) men.
So much space.	*So much* (*itnā*) space.
All the chamber.	*All* (*sab*) chamber.
A little book.	*Little* (*chhōṭī*) book.
Such a gentleman.	*Such a* (*falānā*) gentleman.
Of all the people.	All *people* (*lōgōṅ*) -of.
In great calamity.	*Great* (*baṛī*) calamity-in.
With much happiness.	*Much* (*bahut*) happiness-with.
By a bad business.	*Bad* (*burā*) business-by.
At midnight.	*Mid* (*ādhī*) night-*at* (*kō*).
A very virtuous lady.	*Very* (*bahut*) *virtuous* (*nēk*) lady.
A very good boy.	*Very good* (*bahut achchhā*) boy.
A very wise person.	*Very wise* (*baṛā dānā*) person.
To such people.	*Such* (*aisē*, plur. mas.) people-to.
A few days ago.	*Few* (*thōṛē*) days-from.
On last Tuesday.	*Last* (*guẓrē*) Tuesday-*on* (*kō*).
The least part.	*Least* (*sab-sē chhōṭā*) part.

* See 1st Part, Gram. par. 11, 12, 13, 14.

A very low price.	*Very* (*bahut*) *low* (*thōṛī*) price.
Very high rooms.	Very high rooms.
In the highest rooms.	*Highest* (*sab sē ūnchī*) rooms-in.
The greatest power.	*Greatest* (*sab sē baṛā*) power.
Of every moment.	*Every* (*har-har*) moment-of.
On the right foot of the mare.	Mare of *right* (*dāhnē*) foot on.
From low rooms.	*Low* (*nīchī*) rooms-from.
In muddy water.	*Muddy* (*gandē*) water-in.
Several times.	*Several* (*ka'ī*) *times* (*bār*).
On the subject of the new book.	*New* (*na'ī*) book *on the subject of* (*kī bābat*).
Very large eyes.	*Very large* (*baṛī baṛī*) eyes.
What sort of flowers?	*What sort of* (*kaisē*) flowers.
Together with a littleish dog.	*Littleish* (*chhōṭē-sē*) dog-*together with* (*kē sāth*).
Hundreds of thousands of cities.	*Hundreds of thousands* (*lakhōṅ**) cities.
In the first chapter.	*First* (*pahlē*) chapter-in.
The second woman.	*Second* (*dūsrī*) woman.
Twenty fourth year.	*Twenty fourth* (*chaubīswāṅ*) year.
In the twentieth year.	*Twentieth* (*bīswēṅ*) year-in.
Fairer than the girl.	Girl-*from* (*sē*) fair.
The fairest boy.	*Fairest* (*sab sē gōrā*) boy.
In very hot water.	*Very hot* (*bahut garm*) water-in.
Along with blackish dogs.	*Blackish*(*kālē-sē*)dogs-with(*sāth*).
To a poor man like me.	*Me-like* (*mujh-sē*) poor-to.
Along with both the boys.	*Both* (*dōnō**) boys *along with* (*kē sāth*).

Nouns and Pronouns.†

I and my brother.	I *and* (*aur*) my brother.

* See Gram. par. 10.

† See 1st Part, Gram. par. 15, 16.

My dog's name.	My dog-of name.
My sister's house.	My sister-of house.
I, thou and he together.	I, thou and he *together* (*ikaṭṭhē*).
We all three.	We *all three* (*tīnōṅ*).
In our books.	*Our* (*hamārī*) books-in.
With us both.	*Us* (*ham*) both-*with* (*kē sāth*).
To thy father's servant.	Thy father-of servant-to.
On your mare's foot.	Your mare-of foot-on.
They and their three dogs.	They and *them-of* (*unh kē*) three dogs.
That horse near my mare.	That horse my mare-*near*.
This maid servant of your mother.	This your mother-of maid servant.
This boy's mother.	*This* (*is*) boy-of mother.
Near these fragrant flowers.	These fragrant flowers-near.
To these but not to those.	These-to *but* (*par*) those-to *not* (*nahīṅ*).
He himself and they themselves.	He *himself* (*āp*) and they *themselves* (*āp*).
Those soldiers' turbans.	*Those* (*un*) soldiers-of turbans.
Who is that stranger?	That stranger *who* (*kaun*) *is* (*hai*).
Whose book is this?	This *whom-of* (*kis-kī*) book is.
Where is your honour's house?	*Your honour* (*āp*) -of house *where* (*kahāṅ*) is.
Whose clothes are those?	Those whom-of clothes *are* (*haiṅ*).
What is the name of that village?	That village of name *what* (*kyā*) is.
What is that for?	That *what for* (*kāhē kō*) is.
What do you, Sir, command (say)?	*You Sir* (*āp*) what commanding (*farmātē*) are.
What you wish that do.	*What* (*jō*) you *wish* (*chāhō*) *that* (*sō*) *do* (*karō*).
Whatever officer or soldier.	*Whatever* (*jō kō'ī*) soldier *or* (*yā*) officer.

Whoever this may be.	*Whoever* (*jō kō'i*) this *may be* (*hōwē*).
With whomsoever he met.	*Whomsoever-with* (*jis kisī-sē*) *met* (*milā*).
On the back of some one.	*Some one* (*kisī*) -of back-on.

*Pronouns, Nouns, Verbs, &c.**

Beat that dog.	That dog-to *beat* (*mārō*).
Open the door.	*Door* (*darwāza*) *open* (*khōlō*).
Bring the palanquin.	Palanquin *bring* (*lā'ō*).
Give this book to him.	This book him-to *give* (*dō*).
I am here.	I *here* (*yāhāṅ*) *am* (*hūṅ*).
We are standing.	We standing are.
Thou art going.	Thou *going* (*jāta*) *art* (*hai*).
Ye are coming.	Ye *coming* (*ātē*) *are* (*hō*).
He is my friend.	He my friend is.
She is my sister.	*She* (*wuh*) my sister is.
They are my father's servants.	They my father-of servants are.
Where are your horses?	*Your* (*tumhārē*) horses where are.
This is my book.	This my book is.
That is in our books.	That our books-in is.
Are those your horses?	Those your horses are?
What is the name of that village?	*That* (*us*) village-of name what is.
Who is that person?	That person *who* (*kaun*) is.
Whose hat is this?	This *whose* (*kis-kī*) hat is.
What has been that has been.	*What* (*jō*) *been* (*hū'ā*) *that* (*sō*) been.
Why do you do so?	You *why* (*kāhē-kō*) *so* (*aisā*) doing are?

* Besides the paragraphs before referred to, see 1st Part, Gram. par. 17 to 33, as well as the Syntax, par. 52 to 83.

Of what is this the key?	This *what-of* (*kāhē-kī*) key is?
Whatever he says is true.	*Whatever* (*jō kuchh*) he says *that* (*sō*) true is.
He is abusing himself.	He *self-to* (*apnē ta'īn*) *abuse* (*gālī*) giving is.
The soldier went with his officer.	Soldier *his own* (*apnē*) officer-with *went* (*gayā*).
He beat his brother.	*He* (*us-ne**) *his* (*apnē*) brother-to beat.
They (respectfully for he) are sleeping.	*They* (*āp*) *sleeping* (*sōtē*) are.
They were talking amongst themselves.	They *themselves-amongst* (*āpas-mēn*) *talking* (*bāt kartē*) were.
Of what place are they people?	They *where-of* (*kahān-kē*) people are?
I called him.	*I* (*main-nē*) him-to *called* (*bulāyā*).
But he came not.	*But* (*lēkin*) he *not* (*nahīn*) came.
I know nothing.	I *any thing* (*kuchh*) knowing not.
But what I have said.	*But* (*magar*) what *I* (*main-nē*) said have.
He minds not my word.	He my word *minds* (*māntā*) not.
But abuses me.	*But* (*balki*) *me-to* (*mujhē*) *abuse* (*gālī*) gives.
If he go then he will see.	*If* (*agar*) *he go* (*jāwē*) *then* (*tō*) he will see.
I indeed was not present.	I *indeed* (*tō*) present not was.
What care indeed has he?	*Him-to* (*us-kō*) *indeed* (*tō*) what care is.
At the time of beating him.	Him-to *beating* (*mārnē*†) -of the time.

* See Grammar, par. 23, note, and par. 72.

† Infinitive used as a gerund or verbal noun: see Gram. par. 19.

An eatable thing.	*Eating* (*khānē**) -of thing.
Never do so.	*So* (*aisā*) ever not *to do* (*karnā†*).
Having seen this she went away.	This having seen she *went away* (*chalī ga'ī‡*).
They are gone to him.	They him-near *gone* (*ga'ē*) are.
That woman had been beaten.	That woman *beaten* (*mārī*) *gone* (*ga'ī*) was.
I have done eating.	I *having eaten* (*khā*) *have done* (*chukā§*).
I had wished to teach him.	*I* (*maiṅ-nē*) him-to *taught* (*sikhāyā*) *wished* (*chāhā*) *had* (*thā§*).
They were in the habit of coming to me every day.	They *every day* (*har rōz*) me-near *come* (*āyā*) making were.§
I could not find how to get across.	I *across* (*pār*) *going* (*jānē*) not *find* (*pā*) *could* (*sakā*).
He wished to come with me.	He *me-with* (*mērē sāth*) *to come* (*ānē*) wished.
I have bought this horse.	*I* (*maiṅ-nē*) this horse-to *have bought* (*mōl liyā hai§*).
Ten men were killed with him.	Ten *men* (*jawān*) him-with killed went.
If you had remained here, you would have seen him.	*If* (*agar*) you here *remain* (*rahtē*),‖ *then* (*tō*) him-to *see* (*dēkhtē‖*).

---

* Infinitive used as a gerund or verbal noun : see Gram. par. 19.

† The infinitive used in an imperative or prohibitive sense : see Gram. par. 73.

‡ A compound verb : see Gram. par. 28, 10th.

§ A compound verb : see Gram. par. 28, 4th, 8th, 9th, 1st.

‖ The indef. present used in the sense of the past conditional : see Gram. par. 24, note.

I saw that woman coming.	I that woman-to *coming* (*ātē*)* *saw* (*dēkhā*).
In going along, I saw.	*In going along* (*chaltē hū'ē**) I saw.
Immediately on hearing this.	This *hearing exactly* (*suntē*-hī*†).
Immediately on hearing so much speech.	*So much* (*itnī*) speech *hearing* (*suntē*) *exactly hī*†).
After it became evening.	Evening *become* (*hū'ē*)* *after* (*ba*'*d*).
I used to converse with him.	I *him-with* (*us-sē*) *converse used* (*bāt kartā thā*).
(If) I go, then what?	(If I) *go* (*jā'ūṅ*) *then* (*to*‡) what?
Pray be seated.	*Sit* (*you*) (*baiṭhiyō*§).
Be pleased, Sir, to say.	*You Sir* (*āp*) *say* (*kahiyē*§).
What should we wish? (What is needed?)	What *should we wish* (*chāhiyē*§).
You must get away hence.	*We* (or *they*) *should wish* (*chāhiyē*) *that* (*ki*) you here-from *having issued* (*nikal*) may go.
It is necessary to obey the orders of government.	*Government* (*sarkār*) -of order *performed* (*ba-jā layā*‖) *it is requisite* (*chāhiyē*¶).
I cannot (shall not) go there.	I there not *going-of* (*jānē-kā***).
This is not a thing that can be.	This *being-of* (*hōnē-kā***) thing not.
Your coming here is of no use.	Your here *coming* (*ānā*) *any use* (*kuchh kām*) -of not.

---

* See Gram. par. 75. † See Gram. par. 35, page 61.

‡ Gram. par. 79. § Respectful imperative: see G. par. 26, *a*.

‖ See Gram. par. 28, 8th. ¶ See Gram. par. 26, *a*.

** See Gram. par. 73.

There is no use of your coming here.	*Your here coming* (*tumhārē yahāṅ ānē*) -from any benefit not.
That gentleman has departed hence.	That *gentleman* (*ṣāḥib*) here-from *going* (*rawāna*) *become* (*hū'ē*).*
What do you, Sir, say (command)?	*The presence* (*ḥaẓrat*) what *commanding* (*farmātē*) are?
I (the devoted servant) have (has) a representation (to make).	*Devoted servant* (*fidwī*) -of one *representation* (*ʿarẓ*) is.
Give to each one.	One one†-to give.
Divide and place them by fours.	Four four-*by* (*sē*) *having divided* (*bāṅṭkar*) place.
The three (all three) came together to me.	*The three* (*tīnōṅ*) *having met together* (*milkar*) me-near came.
That person had taken up the book.	*That person-by* (*us shakhṣ-nē*) book *taken-up* (*uṭhā'ī*) was.
Those people bought the books.	*Those people-by* (*un lōgōṅ-nē*) books *bought* (*mōl līṅ*).
Allow me to go with you.	*Self-with* (*apnē sāth*) us-to *to go* (*jānē*) give.‡
Their parents are dead.	*Mother father* (*mā bāp*) them-of *having died* (*mar*) gone§ are.
This house is unfurnished.	This house-of *furniture* (*lawāzima*) not.‖
He has the toothach.	His tooth-in pain is.
This cloth is very coarse.	This cloth *very* (*baṛā*) coarse is.
This will be the best.	This all-from *better* (*bihtar*) will be.
Is your knife sharp?	Your knife sharp is.

* See Gram. par. 65.

† See Gram. par. 41.

‡ Gram. par. 28, 6th.

§ Gram. par. 28, 2nd.

‖ Gram. par. 77.

Does this knife belong to you?	*What* (*kyā*) this knife yours is.
Can you speak English?	You *English* (*angrēzī*) speak able are.*
85 We know all.	We *every thing* (*sab kuchh*) knowing are.
They are dead asleep.	They *senseless* (*bē-khabar*) sleeping are.
Are you the owner of this house?	You this house-of *owner* (*mālik*) are.
Do you know this man?	This man-to you knowing are.
Will you go to the auction?	*Auction* (*nīlām*) -in you will go.
90 Do you know the cause of this?	You this-of *cause* (*sabab*) knowing are.
Take a chair and sit down.	Chair *take* (*lō*) *sit* (*baiṭhō*).
What chapter shall I read?	*What* (*kaun*) chapter I *shall read* (*paṛhūṅ*).
This is the end of the chapter.	This chapter-of end is.
What is the cost of these things?	What price is these things-of.
95 This is my native country.	This my *native country* (*waṭan*) is.
This house is very damp.	This house much moist is.
What time of day is it?	Now *how much* (*kitnā*) time is.
Tell me the name of this distemper.	You this distemper-of name say.
There is much delay in this affair.	This *affair* (*kām*) -in great delay is.
100 Do you know that gentleman?	You that gentleman-to knowing are.
Have the goodness, Sir, to inform me.	*You Sir* (*āp*) kindness having done information *make* (*kījiyē*†).
Take hold of his hand.	Him-of hand having seized *take* (*lō*).

* Gram. par. 28, 3rd.

† Gram. par. 26, *a*.

What is the height of this wall?	*How much* (*kitnī*) height this wall-of is.
He gave a hint to this effect.	*He* (*us-nē**) hint made this intent-on.
5 Make a hole in the ground here.	Here ground-in hole make.
Do you know what hour it is?	You knowing are what *sounded* (*bajā*) is.
Whence comes this idea?	This idea where-from produced become.
The sky is overcast.	*Sky* (*āsmān*)-on cloudiness become is.
Is this the sort you wanted?	You this sort-of wishing are.
10 He wears spectacles.	He (they) spectacles applying is (are).
I (or we) have bought a score of sheep.	*We* (*ham-nē**) twenty sheep bought are.
What did you give for that seal?	*You* (*tum-nē**) that seal-of what given.
Sow this seed in the garden.	This seed-to garden-in *sow* (*bō'ō*).
Send a servant.	One servant-to *send* (*bhējō*).
15 Give me a sheet of paper.	One *sheet* (*takhta*) paper us-to give.
Where can we get straw?	Dry *grass* (*ghās*) where *shall we get* (*pawēngē*).
He committed suicide.	*He* (*us-nē**) self-to self *killed* (*mārā*).
Where shall we get timber?	We *timber* (*shahtīr*) where shall get.
Who brought this intelligence?	Who this *intelligence* (*khabar*) brought.
20 They smoke tobacco.	They *hukka drinking* (*pītē*) are.

* Gram. par. 23, note.

He gave me a tract.	*He* (*us-nē**) us-to little book *gave* (*dī*).
Please to give me a wafer.	Us-to one *wafer* (*wēfar*) *please give* (*dījiyē*).
On hearing the news he was much alarmed.	This *intelligence* (*khabar*) *having heard* (*sunkar†*) much fear (he) went.‡
The bill will amount to five hundred rupees.	Account *having made* (*karkē†*) *five hundred* (*pānsau*) rupees will be.
I was amazed at the amount.	Account-of *amount* (*jam*ᵃ, f.) having seen† us-to wonder became.
His goods will be appraised and sold.	Him-of things price *having been ascertained* (*tajwīz hōkar†*) *sold* (*bēchī*) will go.
He was apprehended and put in prison.	He *seized* (*pakṛā*) went,§ and *imprisoned became* (*ḳaid hū'ā*).
Do you think what he says is true?	What he saying is you true *thinking* (*samajhtē*) are.
Yes, I am certain of it.	Yes, we it-to certain knowing are.
I feel very cold.	Us-to *cold* (*jāṛā*) much applying is.
It is doubtful whether he will come or not.	Him-of *coming* (*ānē*)‖ not coming-in *doubt* (*shakk*) is.
Give this book to your elder brother.	*Own* (*apnē*)¶ great brother-to this book to give.**
Which of you two is the elder?	You both-from great which is.

* Gram. par. 23, note.

† Gram. par. 22.

‡ Gram. par. 28, 2nd.

§ Gram. par. 31.

‖ Gram. par. 19.

¶ Gram. page 26 and par. 66.

** Gram. par. 73.

They are gone, every one of them.	They *all-of* (*sab-kē*) all gone are.
Do you wish for thick paper or thin?	You thick paper wishing are or thin.
Do you accede to what I propose or not?	*What* (*jō*) we saying are you this-to acceptance making are or not.
I was not able to accomplish my wishes.	I *own* (*apnī**) wish *complete* (*bhar-pūr*) not make could.
To day's meeting was adjourned to Monday next.	*To day* (*āj*) meeting *stopped* (*mauḳūf*) is *Monday-of day* (*dō shambē kē rōz*) again (it) will be.
I cannot afford to give so much wages.	*So much* (*itnā*) pay we not give can.†
Pray afford me your assistance.	Kindness *having done* (*karkar*‡) our help make.
On appearing in court he was much agitated.	*Court* (*ādālat*)-in standing becoming (on) exactly to tremble began.
I caught a large fish yesterday.	We§ yesterday one great fish *seized* (*pakṛī*).
I saw him last Tuesday.	Past *Tuesday-on* (*mangal-kō*) *I* (*maiṅ-nē*§) him-to saw.
This writing is not legible.	This *written* (*likhā*) read not goes.‖
How long shall you remain there?	You *how many* (*kitnē*) days shall stay.
The price he asks is very low.	He very little price *asking* (*mang-tā*) is.

---

* Gram. par. 66.

† Gram. par. 28, 3rd.

‡ Gram. par. 22.

§ G. par. 23, note, and par. 72.

‖ Gram. par. 31.

It is immaterial whether you go or not.	There your *going* (*jāna**) not going alike is.
Enclose my letter in yours.	Our letter (your) own letter-in *place* (*rakh*) give.
Had it not been for his assistance, I should have failed in my purpose.	Him-of assistance if not becomes, *then* (*tō*) our business *accomplishment* (*sar-anjām*) not finds. †
I should have fallen into the river but for him.	If he not seizes,† then I river-in *fall* (*gir paṛtā*).†
I do not know how to express this in English.	This word English-in *what manner* (*kis ṭarḥ*) spoken going is, we not know.
I had no suspicion that he had done this.	*Us-to* (*hamēṅ*) *suspicion* (*gumān*) not *that* (*ki*) *he* (*us-nē*) so done is.
Sarkār, are all my things ready?	O *sarkār* our all things ready are.
Sir, the *sarkār* has taken money for them; no doubt they will be here by two o'clock.	*O sir* (*ai ṣāḥib*) *sarkār* rupee *taken* (*lē-gayā*) is; and things two watch two-in *certainly* (*al-batta*) here will arrive.
When the things come, send them immediately to Nya Ghaut.	When things *may come* (*āwēṅ*) then *that very* (*us-ī*) *moment* (*dam*) new quay-in having sent to give.
It is now high water; I cannot wait longer.	*Now-exactly* (*ab-hī*) ebb-tide near is, we *more* (*aur*) patience not *make able are* (*kar saktē haiṅ*).
The goods you, Sir, have purchased, are, I think, dear.	What *goods* (*asbāb*) *you, Sir* (*āp-nē*) purchased *me near* (*mērē nazdīk*) great *dear* (*girān*) are.

* Gram. par. 19.

† See Gram. par. 24, note.

House rent is very dear in Calcutta.	Calcutta-in house-of hire great dear is.
I would have gone there, but was fearful it would be late before I arrived.	We there going were, *but* (*lēkin*) this fear-from *that* (*ki*) there *arriving-till*(*pahunchnē tak*) *delay will be* (*dēr hōgī*) not went.
I know not if many or few were there.	We not knowing are, *that* (*ki*) there *few* (*thōṛē*) were or many.

---

* State of Hindūstān in the time of Sultān Mahmūd Ghaznawī and of his house (*khāndān*).

A thousand years after the (*commencement of the*) *Christian era* (*sana Isawī*), Mahmūd Ghaznawī, having made invasion on Hindūstān twelve times, brought Multān, Lāhaur, Dihlī, Mathurā, and Canauj *into subjection* (*taht-mēṅ*). *Afterwards* (*ba'd us-kē*) *he demolished* (*kharāb kiyā*) the idol-houses of Sōmnāt and Nagarkōt and of wheresoever he went; and spoiled the idols. Fifty thousand Hindūs were killed in the defence of *the temple* (*mandir*) of Sōmnāt. *At length* (*ākhiru-l-amr*), when (their) *power availed not* (*bas na-chalā*), then all the Hindūs, *having agreed together* (*muttafiķ hōkar*), said that we *will give* (*dētē haiṅ*) eight crores (of) rupees *on this condition* (*ba-īn shart*) that they (or you) *should not destroy* (*mismār na-kījiyē*) the image. He not *assenting* (*ķabūl na-karkē*), commanded that that image *should be sawn asunder* (*āra-sē chirī jāwē*); *so that from its interior* (*chunānchi uskē pēṭ-sē*) precious jewels, that in worth and value were more than those rupees, issued. In the house of Sultān Mahmūd Ghaznawī the *sovereignty* (*saltanat*) *remained* (*ķā'im rahī*) *during* (*tak*) one hundred (and) eighty-five years: afterwards, it *became annihilated* (*nēst ō nābūd hō-ga'ī*) by Sultān Shihābu-d-dīn Ghaurī.

---

* Here, the position of the Hindūstānī words is not always pointed out.

State of the Afghān *sway* (*tasallut*) in Hindūstān *after the extinction* (*nēst ō nā-būd hōnē kē baʿd*) of the *Ghaznawī family* (*ghaznawī khāndān*).

In the first place (*pahlē*) Shihābu-d-dīn Muhammad Ghaurī, *having ravaged* (*takht ō tārāj karkē*) the Ghaznawī empire, became *absolute in sway* (*mutasallit*) over Hindūstān. Afterwards, during three hundred (and) forty two years, *several* (*ka'ī ēk*) different families exercised the sway: among them, Kutbu-d-dīn, *a Turkish slave* (*Turkī ghulām*), that by the revolution of fortune had become *the adopted son* (*mutabannā*) of Muhammad Ghaurī, is *of all most celebrated* (*sab-sē mash'hūr*). He gave great *extension* (*wus'at*) to *the provinces of the people of Islām* (*ahl-i-islām kē mamālik*); *to wit* (*yaʿnē*), having become victorious over the Hindū Rājās, he made Dihlī *the royal residence* (*pā'ē takht*).

Account (*bayān*) of *the Tīmūr dynasty* (*saltanat-i-tīmūrī*).

In the year one thousand three hundred and ninety seven *of Christ* (*ʿīsawī*) Tīmūr Shāh, having made invasion on Hindūstān, arrived in Dihlī. There, *having put to the sword* (*tah-i-tēgh karkē*) two hundred thousand men, *he desolated the country* (*mulk-kō wīrān kar ḍālā*), but kept it not in his possession; yet, a hundred and twenty seven years after, his great grandson's grandson, Bābar Shāh, *becoming* (*hōkar*) victorious over the princes of Dihlī, *seized* (*lē lī*) the empire.

Akbar his grandson was just and wise. He made Candahār (*kandhār*), Cashmīr, Gujarāt, Sindh, Bengal and *Orissa* (*uṛēsa*) comprised in *one same* (*ēk hī*) empire. After him Jahāngīr and Shāhjahān *enjoyed the sovereignty* (*bādshāhat kī*), and, Aurangzēb, that is Aalamgīr, who reduced all the *ṣūbas* of Hindūstān under his rule. From his time, *however* (*magar*), the Moghal power became weak; and, Bahādur Shāh, after him, enjoyed the sovereignty, and Jahāndār Shāh and Farrukhsiyar and Rafī'u-d-darjāt (*rafī'u-d-darjāt*) and Muhammad Shāh, in whose time Nādir Shāh, emperor of Persia, having made *invasion* (*yalghār*) on the empire of Hindūstān, *overthrew* (*tah ō bālā kar ḍālā*) the Moghal dominion. After him, Ahmad Shāh and Aalamgīr (*ālamgīr*) Sānī and Shāh Aalam (*ālam*) *exercised the sovereignty* (*bādshāhat kī*).

The cause of Nādir Shāh's coming into Hindūstān.

Among the nobles of Dihlī was great discord. He who possessed the rank of *wazīr*, in the year 1722 *of Christ* (*īsawī*) *wrote* (*likh bhējā*) to Nādir Shāh (saying)* that, *now is the opportunity* (*waḳt ḳābū kā hai*); *remove* (*uṭhā dō*) Muhammad Shāh from the throne. *Accordingly* (*chunānchi*), he came into Hindūstān, and was victorious. He slew two hundred thousand people. *Having discovered* (*daryāft karkē*) the design of the nobles, he removed not Muhammad Shāh from the throne; but, having taken from him eighteen crores (*karōṛ*) fifty *lacs* (*lākh* of) rupees, and *having seized* (*ḳabẓa karkē*) on the *provinces* (*mamālik*) of the west side of the Sindh river, in the year of Christ 1741, he (Nādir Shāh) went to his own country. He was a great tyrant; so that, in the stopping of some riot at the time of a fair, suddenly a person discharged a ball, which went near him (Nādir Shāh) and did not hit; nevertheless, having become enraged, he gave command to the soldiers that a general massacre *should take place* (*hō*). This command he gave *at the second watch of the night* (*dō pahar rāt kō*, twelve o'clock); and, *by the second watch two ghaṛis* (*dō pahar dō bajē kē amal tak*, forty-eight minutes after twelve) of the next day, more than a hundred thousand people were slaughtered. From his time, the Moghal sovereignty *became void of a reality* (*bē ḥaḳiḳat hō gaī*), *that is to say* (*yaʿnē*) every *commander and governor* (*amīr umarā*), *becoming* (*ban*) each himself a master, sat, and *were* (*hō ga'ē*) rulers *with absolute sway* (*bi-l-istiḳlāl*).

---

* See 1st Part Grammar, par. 78.

How and when the people of England obtained *entrance* (*daḵẖl*) into Hindustān.

In the year 1600 of Christ, they first began to come *in the way* (*ṯaur par*) of commerce. Before them, the Portuguese and Dutch and French were possessing *factories* (*kōṭhī*) in Hindūstān. *After some length of time* (*baʿd chand muddat kē*), the English, *for* (*kē li'e*) the protection of their factor and merchandise, by permission of the *Nauwāb*, *sent for* (*bulāyā*) their soldiers, and prepared a fort (*ḳalʿā*). Afterwards, the *Rājās* of Hindūstān, having become weak from the oppression of the Nauwāb Sirāju-d-daula, Nabob of Murshidābād, gave advice to the English, (saying) that do you *expel* (*ḵẖārij karō*) him from his provinces, and we are your assistants: so that, in the year 1757 of Christ, the English *defeated* (*shikast dī*) the army of the Nabob, and received from Shāh Aalam (*ʿālam*) the office of the *dīwān-ship* (*dīwānī*); that, *by means of it,* (*us-kē ba-mūjib*) they brought Benares and the *sūba* of Bihār and Urēsa into their *subjection* (*taḥt*). In that very time, Asafu-d-daula, the Nabob of *Oude* (*awadh*) *gave up to them* (*un-kē sipurd kiyā*) the city of Benares: and, in the year 1793 of Christ, the kingdom of Tīpoo Sultan in Carnatic (*karnāṭak*) came to (their) hand. *In short* (*gharaẓ*) *by some means* (*kisī ṣūrat sē*) the English people *by degrees* (*rafta rafta*) acquired the entire dominion.

STORY.

Some one said to a wise man, that *such a person* (*falān ādmī nē*) has reviled you. Having made a little consideration, he said, hear (me) friend: *who* (*jisnē*) reviled me, *as it were* (*gōyā*) he threw an arrow *in the rear* (*pīchhē*), *that* (*sō*) touched me not; but, thou, *having taken up* (*uṭhākē*) the arrow, *hast thrust it into me* (*mujhē chubhāyā*): well, what advantage is there to thee in that?

STORY.

There was *extreme* (*nihāyat*) friendship between a camel and an ass. By chance a journey *became necessary* (*dar pēsh hū'ā*) for the two. In the midst of the way, a river occurred. The camel entered into the water: the water was up to his belly. He began to say, O friend, come hither, the water is little. The ass said, it is true, it is *up-to* (*tak*) thy belly, it seems little to thee; but, it will be up to my back; *I shall be drowned* (*ḍūb jā'ūṅgā*).

STORY.

A thief went to steal a horse *at the abode of some one* (*kisī kē yahāṅ*). By chance he was caught. The *owner of the horse* (*ghōṛē-wālē nē*) said to him, if thou wilt teach me to steal a horse, then I *will set thee at liberty* (*tujhē chhōṛ dūṅ*). The thief consented. Having gone he loosened the *foot-rope* (*pā-band*) of the horse. Having given the bridle, he *mounted* (*sawār hū'ā*); and, *immediately on mounting* (*chaṛhtē hī*) said, see, (in) this manner they steal. *On the very saying this* (*yih kahtē hī*), he made the horse run. Riders made much *pursuit* (*pīchhā*) of him, but *overtook* (*pāyā*) not.

APPENDIX.

FORMS OF LETTERS AND NOTES,

Taken from the "Taleem Namuh," lithographed at Bombay in 1835.

Letter from one friend to another. خط ایک دوست کا دوسري دوست کو

محبت و دوستي کي گلذار رفاقت اور آشنائي کي چمن کي بهار يار جاني دوست غمخوار فلان سلمه الرحمان

دوست اخلاصمند فلان سلام و محبت کا هديه خيرخواهي اور دلکي چاه کا تحفه آگي رکهکي ضمير يگانيت تاثير پر روشن کرتا هي که جس دن سي يه دوست آپ کي پاس سي جدا هوکي يهان آپا هي خدا جانتا هي که هر گهڑي فراق کا درد اٹهاتا هي خدايتعالی اپني فضل و کرم سي ايسا سبب کري که تم هم جلدي ملين اور خوشي سي ايک ساته بيٹهين پهرين چلين اب عرض يه هي که ان دنون مين اس مخلص کي فرزند کي شادي کي تياري هي سو آپکي ذات کي بغير خوش اور گوارا نهين لگتي شفقت فرماکي دو هفتون کي فرصت کرکي ضرور تشريف لاکي شادي کي مجلسون کو رونق بخش هونا اگرچه تصديع هي سچ ليکن دوستون کي خوشي کي واسطي قبول کرنا لازم هي اور آپ کي فرزند کو بيٹا هوا اسکي خبر سنکي دل بهت شاد هو رها هي مبارک هووي اور خالق بي نياز اسکي عمر زياده کري اور آپکي زير سايه پرورش پاوي عجب هي که اس خوشي کي خبر اس مخلص کو لکه نه بهيجي اسطرح دوستون کو بهولنا مناسب نهين اميد که اب اس مخلص کو دل سي فراموش نجانکي يه خط پهنچتي هي تشريف لانيکا قصد کرنا که يه مخلص هميشه آپکا احسانمند رهي زياده کيا تصديع والسلام

Muḥabbat wa dōstī kē gūlzār, the rose-bowers[1] of love and friendship, *rifāḳat aur āshnā'ī kē chaman kē bahār*, the vernal pride of the parterre of sociality and kindness, *yār-i jānī dōst gam-khwār*, the

---

[1] The plural is adopted by way of shewing greater respect.

dear, grief-dispersing friend, ***fulāṅ, sallamahu-r-raḥmān,*** such a one, whom God preserve!

Dōst-i ikhlāṣmand, fulān, the sincere friend, such a one, ***salām o muḥabbat kā hadīya, khair-khwāhī aur dil-kī chāh kā tuḥfa āgē rakhkē,*** having placed before (you) the gift of salutation and love, the offering of good wishes, and of the desire of his heart, ***ẓamīr-i yagāniyat tāṣīr par rōshan kartā hai,*** is representing to (your) unison-impressed mind, ***ki jis din sē,*** that from what day, ***yih dōst āp kē pās sē judā hōkē,*** this friend having become separated from you, Sir, ***yahāṅ āyā hai,*** is come here, ***khudā jāntā hai,*** God is knowing, ***ki har ghaṛī firāḳ kā dard uṭhātā hai,*** that every hour he is suffering the pain of absence. ***khudā'ē ta'ālā apnē faẓl o karam sē aisā sabab karē,*** may God the most high of his goodness and graciousness make such a cause, ***ki tum ham jaldī milēṅ,*** that you and we may soon meet, ***aur khushī sē ēk sāth baiṭhēṅ phirēṅ chalēṅ,*** and with happiness together may sit, walk and ramble. ***Ab arẓ yih hai ki in dinōṅ mēṅ is mukhlis kē farzand kī shādī kī taiyārī hai,*** now the petition is this, that in these days is the preparation for the wedding of your sincere friend's son, ***sō āp-kī ẕāt kē ba-ghair khush aur gawārā nahīṅ lagtī,*** (and) that proves not pleasant and agreeable without the being (there) of you, Sir, ***shafaḳat farmākē,*** having granted the indulgence, ***dō haftōṅ kī furṣat karkē,*** having made the leisure of two weeks, ***ẓarūr tashrīf lākē shādī kī majlisōṅ kō raunaḳ-bakhsh hōnā,*** (it is) a matter of necessity, having done us the honour of coming, (for you) to be the ornament of the assemblies of the wedding. ***Agarchi taṣdī* hai sach,*** although it is an inconvenience indeed; ***lēkin dōstōṅ kī khushī kē wāsṭē ḳabūl karnā lāzim hai,*** yet for the sake of the happiness of friends it is indispensable to accede. ***Aur āp kē farzand kō bēṭā hū'ā,*** and a son (is) become (born) to your son, ***us-kī khabar sunkē dil bahut shād hō ṛahā hai,*** having heard the news of that, (my) heart has continued much delighted. ***Mubārak hōwē***, may he be fortunate, ***aur khālik-i bē-niyāz us-kī ûmr ziyāda karē***, and may the all-independent creator increase his life, ***aur āp-kē sēr sāya parwarish pāwē***, and may he (the child) find nourishment under the shadow of you, Sir! ***âjab hai ki is khushī kī khabar is mukhliṣ kō likh na bhējī***, it is wonderful that (they) did not write and send intelligence of this happiness to this sincere friend. ***Is-ṯarah dōstōṅ kō bhūlnā munāsib nahīṅ***, to forget friends in this manner is not proper; ***ummaid ki ab is mukhliṣ kō dil sē farāmōsh na-jānkē***, (his) hope (is) that now not considering this sincere (friend) forgotten from the heart, ***yih khaṯṯ pahunchtē hī***, (on) the very arriving (of) this letter, ***tashrīf lānē kā ḳaṣd karnā***, to form the design of doing the honour to come; ***ki yih mukhlis hamēsha āp-kā iḥsānmand rahē***, that this sincere friend may remain for ever obliged to you, Sir. ***Ziyāda kyā taṣdī'***, (to say) more what irksomeness (to you): ***wa-s-salām***, and the salutation!

The friend's answer. دوست کا جواب

دوست نواز محب صادق یار دلدار رفیق موافق فلان سلمه الله تعالي

مخلص فلان اشتیاق ملاقات اخلاص آیات کا دل مین اتنا بهرا هي که
زبان کو طاقت نهین که بیان کري اور قلم کو قدرت نهین که لکهي خیر سلام
سنت السلام کي مراتب ادا کرکي اپني حقیقت ظاهر کرتا هي که تمهارا خط
خوشي اور خورمي کي وقت وارد هوکي دل و جان پر بهت سي تازگي لایا اور
اسکي مطالعه سي فرحت و شادماني کي روشنائي کا سرمه آنکهون کو لگا
اور فرزند ارجمند کي شادي کي خبر معلوم کرکي آپکي مرضي موجب
مخلص ني شادي کي تجمل کي مجلسون مین سر افراز هونیکا اراده کیا هي
انشاء الله تعالي جتني جلدي هو سکي سو کرکي آن پهنچتا هي اور یه
مخلص آپ کي یاد دل سي فراموش نهین کرتا گئي اٹهوارٔي مین فرزند
پیدا هوني کي تهنیت کا خط روانه کیا هي سو البته پهنچا هوگا یا آج کل
تمکو پهنچیگا و السلام بالاکرام

Dōst-nawāz, the friend-comforter, ***muḥibb-i ṣādiḳ***, faithful attached, *yār-i dildār*, ally possessing (my) heart, *rafīḳ muwāfiḳ*, fellow traveller (in all things) accordant, *fulān*, such a one; *sallamahu-l-lāh ta'ālā*, whom may God, the most high, preserve!

Mukhliṣ fulān, the sincere (friend) such a one, *ishtiyāḳ-i mulāḳāt ikhlāṣ-āyāt kā dil mēṅ itnā bharā hai*, the desire of a meeting with the model of sincerity has so filled (his) heart, *ki zabān kō ṭāḳat nahīṅ*, that ability is not to the tongue, *ki bayān karē*, that (it) should explain (it), *aur ḳalam ko ḳudrat nahīṅ ki likhē*, and power is not to the pen that it should write (it). *khair salām*, well, salutation (?). *Sunnatu-l-islām kē marātib adā karkē apnī ḥaḳīḳat ẓāhir kartā hai*, having performed the ceremonies of the law of Islām, he sets forth his narration, *ki tumhārā khaṭṭ khushī aur khurramī kē waḳt wārid hōkē*, that your letter having arrived at a time of joy and happiness, *dil ō jān par bahut sī tāzagī layā*, brought much refreshing to (his) heart and soul, *aur us-kē muṭāla'ā sē*, and from the perusal of it, *farḥat ō shādmānī kī rōshnā'ī kā surmā āṅkhōṅ kō lagā*, the collyrium of the brightness of joy and gladness was applied to (his) eyes, *aur farzand-i arjamand kī shādī kī khabar ma'lūm karkē*, and having learned the intelligence of the marriage of the worthy son, *āp-kī marẓī mūjib*, by reason of your pleasure, Sir, *mukhliṣ nē shādī kē tajammul kī majlisōṅ mēṅ sar-afrāz hōnē-kā irāda kiyā hai*, the sincere (friend) has formed the intention of becoming honoured in the assemblies for completing the marriage. *Inshā'a-l-lāh ta'ālā*, if God the most high wills, *jitnī jaldī hō sakē sō karkē ān pahunchtā hai*, as much haste as he can, that having made, he is (about) arriving. *Aur yih mukhliṣ āpkī yād dil sē farāmōsh nahīṅ kartā*, and this sincere (friend) makes not the remembrance of you, Sir, forgotten from (his) heart, *ga'ē aṭhwāṛē mēṅ farzand paidā hōnē kī tahniyat kā khaṭṭ rawāna kiyā hai*, in the week passed he sent a letter of the joyful event of a son being born, *sō albatta pahunchā hōgā yā āj kal tum-kō pahunchēgā*, that must certainly have arrived or will in a day or two arrive to you, *wa-s-salām bi-l-ikrām*, and the salutation with honour!

Method of writing notes. چتهیان لکهني کي ترتیب

حضرت مربي صاحب سلمت

کل شام کو بندہ آپکي خدمت مین پهنچا تها لیکن آپ باهر تشریف لیگئي تهي اور آج تین چار خط سورت و بنگالي کو لکهني تهي اس لیي فرصت نه هوئي خدا کرتا هي تو بعد مغرب خدمت مین حاضر هونگا زیادہ کیا عرض

Ḥaẓrat, the presence, *murabbī*, patron, *ṣāḥib*, lord, master, *salāmat*, safety, health!

Kal shām kō banda āp-kī khidmat mēn pahunchā thā, yesterday in the evening (your) servant had arrived to wait on you, Sir, *lēkin āp bāhar tashrīf lē-ga'ē thē*, but you were gone out; *aur āj tīn chār khatt sūrat ō bangālē kō likhnē thē*, and to day there were three or four letters to write to Surat and Bengal; *is liyē furṣat na hū'ī*, for this reason leisure was not: *khudā kartā hai*, (if) God is doing (if God grants), *to baʿd maghrab khidmat mēn ḥāẓir hūngā*, then after sun-set I will be present in (your) service. *Ziyāda kyā ʿarz*, more why the representation? (what need to represent more?).

بهائي صاحب بهت مهربان سلمت

نیازمند ني گلستان کي کتاب آپکي فرماني سي شیخ آدم کو دي تهي سو چهه مهیني هوئي اب تک انهون ني پیچهي نهین بهیجي مهرباني کرکي انکو تاکید دینا که جلدي روانه کرین والسلم بالاکرام

Bhā'ī ṣāḥib, Mr. (my) brother, *bahut mihrbān*, extremely kind, *salāmat*, safety or health!

Niyāz-mand nē gulistān kī kitāb āp-kē farmānē sē shaikh ādam kō dī thī, (this) indigent (person) at your commanding had given the book of the gulistān to Shaikh Adam, *sō chha mahīnē hū'ē ab tak*

unhōṅ nē pīchhē nahīṅ bhējī, that (book) six months past till now they (he) has not sent back, *mihrbānī karkē un-kō tākīd dēnā ki jaldī rawāna karēṅ*, having done (me) the favour (it is necessary) to give injunction to them (him) that they forward it immediately. *Wa-s-salām bi-l-ikrām*, and the salutation with honour!

برادر عزیز القدر سلامت

شیخ داؤد تمهاري کتاب گلستان پرسي نقل کرتي هين اور قريب تمام هوني کي آئي هي انشاء الله تعالى اس هفتي مين تمكو واپس بهيجينگي والسلام

Barādar-i āzīzu-l-ḳadr salāmat, brother honourable in rank, safety!

Shaikh dā'ūd tumhārī kitāb-i gulistān par sē nuḳl kartē haiṅ, Shaikh Dā'ūd is making a copy from your book of the gulistān, *aur ḳarīb tamām hōnē kē ā'ī hai*, and it has come near to being finished; *inshā'a-l-lāh ta'ālā*, if God the most high wills, *is haftē mēṅ tum-kō wāpas bhējēṅgē*, in this week they will send (it) back to you: *wa-s-salām*, and the salutation!

دوست کرم بخش سلامت

کل عربستان سي جهاز آئي انمين جدي کي حاکم ني مکي شريف کا کچهه هديه مرسول کيا تها سو تبرک جانکي اس مين سي آپ کي واسطي بهيجا هي زياده والسلام

Dōst-i karam-bakhsh salāmat, liberality-imparting friend, health!

Kal ārabistān sē jahāz ā'ē, yesterday ships came from Arabia, *un mēṅ juddē kē ḥākim nē makkē sharīf kā kuchh hadīya marsūl kiyā*, in them the governor of Judda had sent some present of the honoured Mecca, *sō tabarruk jānkē us mēṅ sē āp kē wāsṭē bhējā hai*, having thought that a blessing (I) have sent some of it for you, Sir, *ziyāda wa-s-salām*, more (what need?) and the salutation!

مہربان کرم بخش سلامت

یہہ غریب شخص ناصر خان که رام داس کي یہان نوکر هي اسکو پانچ
روپئي مهیني کي ملتي هین سو عیال داري کي سبب بس نهین هوتي
اب وهان حوالدار کي جگهہ هي اسکا مهینا سات روپئي اگر سفارش کرین تو
وہ جگهہ اسکو ملیگي اور اپني بال بچون سمیت آپ کي حق مین دعا
کرتا رهیگا تس پر یہہ مخلص بهي آپکا احسانمند هوگا و السلام

Mihrbān-i karam-bakhsh salāmat, liberality-imparting friend, health!

Yih gharīb shakhṣ nāṣir khān ki rām dās kē yahāṅ naukar hai, this poor person, Nāsir Khān, who is a servant at the residence of Rām Dās, ***us-kō pānch rūpa'ē mahīnē kē miltē haiṅ***, he gets five rupees a month; ***so 'iyāl-dārī kē sabab bas nahīṅ hōtē***, they are not enough for the purpose of house-keeping; ***ab wahāṅ ḥawāldar kī jagah hai***, now there is the place of ***ḥawāldār***, ***us-kā mahīnā sāt rūpa'ē***, its month (pay) seven rupees, ***agar sifārish karēṅ to wuh jagah is-kō milēgī***, if they will make recommendation then that place will come to this (person), ***aur apnē bāl bachchōṅ samēt āp kē ḥakk mēṅ du'ā kartā rahēgā***, and along with his children he will (ever) continue making prayer on behalf of you, Sir, ***tis par yih mukhliṣ bhī āp-kā iḥsānmand hōgā***, moreover this sincere (friend) also will be grateful to you. ***Wa-s-salām***, and the salutation!

GRAMMATICAL TERMS,

Borrowed from the Arabic, and generally applied to the Hindūstānī by the Munshīs or Muhammadan native teachers in India.

Words admit of three principal divisions: namely,

اسم *ism*, Noun. فعل *fi'l*, Verb. حرف *ḥarf*, Particle.

The Noun may be of various kinds: namely,

اسم خاص *ism-i-khāṣṣ*, Noun proper; as, يوسف *yūsuf*, كلكته *kalkatta*.

اسم عام *ism-i-ām*, Noun common; as, گهوڙا *ghōṛā*, كتاب *kitāb*.

اسم صفت *ism-i-ṣifat*, Noun adjective; as, اچها *achchhā*, برا *burā*.

اسم ضمير *ism-i-ẓamīr*, Pronoun personal; as, ميں *main*, تو *tū*, وه *wuh*.

اسم اشاره *ism-i-ishāra*, Pronoun demonstrative; as, يه *yih*, وه *wuh*; the first of which is called اسم اشارهٔ نزديک *ism-i-ishāra-i-nazdīk*; and, the latter, اسم اشارهٔ بعيد *ism-i-ishāra-i-ba'īd*.

اسم استفهام *ism-i-istifhām*, Pronoun interrogative; as, كون *kaun*, كيا *kyā*.

اسم موصول *ism-i-mauṣūl*, Pronoun relative, as, جو *jō*, جون *jaun*.

اسم جواب موصول *ism-i-jawāb-i-mauṣūl*, Pronoun correlative; as, سو *sō*, تون *taun*.

اسم ضمير مشترک *ism-i-ẓamīr-i-mushtarik*, Pronoun reflective; as, آپ *āp*.

اسم مبهم *ism-i-mubham*, Pronoun indefinite; as, كوئي *kō'ī*, كسي *kisī*, كچه *kuchh*.

اسم فاعل *ism-i-fā'il*, Name of the Agent; as, لكهني والا *likhnē wālā*, كرنيهارا *karnē-hārā*.

اسم مفعول *ism-i-maf'ūl*, Participle Past; as, مارا *mārā*, or مارا هوا *mārā hū'ā*.

اسم حاليه *ism-i-ḥāliya*, Participle Present; as, مارتا *mārtā*, or مارتا هوا *mārtā hū'ā*.

اسم ظرف زمان *ism-i-ẓarf-i-zamān*, Adverb of Time; as, اب *ab*, كب *kab*.

اسم ظرف مكان *ism-i-ẓarf-i-makān*, Adverb of Place; as, يهان *yahāṅ*, ادهر *udhar*.

اسم عدد *ism-i-ădad*, Noun of Number; as, ايك *ēk*, دو *dō*, سو *sau*.

For Gender, a Noun common, Noun Adjective, Participle or Verb may be—

مذكر *muẕakkar*, Masculine; as بيٹا *bēṭā*, دولها *dūlhā*; or,

مؤنث *mu'annaṡ*, Feminine; as, بيٹي *bēṭī*, دلهن *dulhan*.

For Number, Nouns of various descriptions, as well as Verbs, may be

واحد *wāḥid*, Singular; as, ايك كتا *ēk kuttā*, ايك گهوڑي *ēk ghōṛī*; or,

جمع *jam'*, Plural; as, دو كتي *dō kuttē*, بهت گهوڑيان *bahut ghōṛiyāṅ*.

A Noun common, moreover, may be معين *mu'ăiyan*, Definite, or غير معين *ghair mu'ăiyan*, Indefinite; the first being often distinguished by the use of some demonstrative pronoun, and the latter by that of the indefinite pronoun: yet, this circumstance can frequently be ascertained from the context only. And, such Nouns masculine as admit of change of termination in the singular may be termed منصرف *munṣarif*, Inflected; so, گهوڑي كو *ghōṛē kō*, from گهوڑا *ghōṛā*.

As to Case (حالت State), a Noun may be in the—

حالت فاعلي *ḥālat-i-fāĭlī*, Nominative case; as لڑكا *laṛkā*, بات *bāt*.

حالت مفعولي *ḥālat-i-maf'ūlī*, Accusative case; as, لڑكون كو *larkōṅ kō*.

حالت جري *ḥālat-i-jarrī*, Dative or Ablative case; as, مرد كو *mard kō*, پيالي سي *piyālē sē*.

حالت اضافت *ḥālat-i-iẓāfat*, Genitive case; as, لڑكي كي ما *laṛkē kī mā*.

حالت ندا *ḥālat-i-nidā*, Vocative case; as, اي بهائي *ai bhā'ī*, او لڑکو *ō laṛkō*.

An Adjective in the Comparative degree is termed—

اسم تفضيل *ism-i-tafẓīl;* as, زياده اونچا *ziyāda ūnchā*: and,

اسم مبالغه *ism-i-mubālagha*, in the Superlative degree; as, سب سي بڑا *sab sē baṛā*.

A Pronoun personal, admitting variation for number and case, may be—

First personal, ضمير متكلم *ẓamīr-i-mutakallim*; as, مين *maiṅ*, هم *ham*.

Second personal, ضمير مخاطب *ẓamīr-i-mukhaṭab*; as, تو *tū*, تم *tum*.

Third personal, ضمير غائب *ẓamīr-i-ghā'ib*; as, وه *wuh*, وي *wē*.

The Verb may be—

فعل لازمي *fi'l-i-lāzimī*, Verb Intransitive; completing in itself the action intended, without reference to any other object; as, مين آيا *maiṅ āyā*, وه دوڑا *wuh dauṛā*.

فعل متعدي *fi'l-i-muta'addī*, Verb Transitive, requiring something additional to which the action passes; as, لڑکا گهوڑيکو مارتا هي *laṛkā ghōṛē-kō mārtā hai*, مين ني گهوڑا دوڑايا *maiṅ nē ghōṛā dauṛāyā*, اسني کها که مين يه مقدمه تجويز کرونگا *us-nē kahā ki maiṅ yih muḳaddama tajwīz karūṅgā*, He said (I will) he would consider the subject.

فعل معروف *fi'l-i-ma'rūf*, Verb Active; as, مين لکهتا هون *maiṅ likhtā hūṅ*.

فعل مجهول *fi'l-i-maj'hūl*, Verb Passive; as, وي ماري گئي *wē mārē ga'ē*.

فعل متعدي بالواسطه *fi'l-i-muta'addī bi-l-wāsiṭa*, Causal Verb; as, لکهانا *likhānā*, دلوانا *dilwānā*.

فعل مرکب *fi'l-i-murakkab*, Compound Verb; as, ڈال دينا *ḍāl dēnā*, لکه سکنا *likh saknā*, بات کرنا *bāt karnā*.

فعل معاون *fi'l-i-mu'āwin*, Auxiliary Verb; as, هونا *hōnā*.

A Verb, too, may be—

مثبت *muṡbit*, Affirmative; as, لکهنا *likhnā*; or,

منفي *munfī*, Negative; as, نه لکهنا *na likhnā*.

The Form of a Verb is termed صيغه *ṣīgha.*

The Infinitive of a Verb, مصدر *maṣdar* or صيغهٔ مصدر *ṣīgha-i-maṣdar.*

The Tense, زمان *zamān*, of a Verb may be—

Past Indefinite, ماضي مطلق *māẓī mutlaḳ* ; as in مين ني خط بهيجا *main nē khatt bhējā.*

Past Proximate, ماضي قريب *māẓī ḳarīb* ; as in تم ني اپني خط پر مهر كي هي *tum nē apnē khatt par muhr kī hai.*

Past Remote or Pluperfect, ماضي بعيد *māẓī ba'īd* ; as in هم خالي زمين پر بيٹهي تهي *ham khālī zamīn par baiṭhe thē.*

Past Continuative or Imperfect, ماضي استمراري *māẓī istimrārī* ; as in وي سب همكو تاكتي تهي *wē sab ham-kō tāktē thē.*

Past Conditional, ماضي شرطيه *māẓī sharṭiya*, or
Past Optative, ماضي متمني *māẓī mutamannī* } as in اگر وه آتا تو مين اسكو كتاب ديتا *agar wuh ātā tō main us-kō kitāb dētā.*

Past Dubious or Past Future, ماضي متشكي *māẓī mutashakkī* ; as in مين ني خط بهيجا سو اسكو پهنچا هوگا *main nē khatt bhējā sō us-kō pahunchā hōgā.*

Past Conjunctive, ماضي معطوفي *māẓī ma'ṭūfī* or ماضي معطوفه *māẓī ma'ṭūfa* or ماضي معطوف عليه *māẓī ma'ṭūf ālaihi* ; as in اسكو يه بات پوچهكر اسكا جواب ليكي مجهي كهو *us-kō yih bāt pūchhkar us-kā jawāb lēkē mujhē kahō.*

Present Indefinite, حال مطلق *ḥāl-i-mutlaḳ* ; as in وي جانتي *wē jāntē* : frequently, however, this form of the verb, with a conditional conjunction or adverb of wishing expressed or understood in the same sentence, is termed Past Conditional or Past Optative, as before described.

Present Definite or Present Present, زمان حال بلا شك *zamān-i-ḥāl bilā shakk* ; as in مين يهان رهتا هون *main yahān rahtā hūn.*

Present Dubious or Present Future, زمان حال متشكي *zamān-i-ḥāl mutashakkī* ; as in وه آتي هوگي *wuh ātī hōgī.*

Future, زمان مستقبل *zamān-i-mustaḳbil* ; as in وي آئينگيان *wē ā'ēngiyān.*

In the Subjunctive or Aorist form, a verb is termed فعل مضارع *fi'l-i-muẓāri'* (so named, because sometimes imparting a future and sometimes a present sense); as in وہ آوي تو مين جاؤن *wuh āwē tō main jā'ūn* (if he shall come then I shall go), or خدا چاهي سو كري *khudā chāhē sō karē* (what God wills, that He does).

The Imperative is called امر *amr*, or امر صيغه *ṣīgha-i-amr*; as in بول *bōl*, بولو *bōlō*: the Respectful Imperative may be termed امر تعظيمي *amr-i-ta'ẓīmī*; as in بوليي *bōliyē*, آپ دیجیي *āp dījiyē*: and, when strict injunction is intended, امر تاكيدي *amr-i-tākīdī*; as in ميرا كها مانيو *mērā kahā māniyō*, اسكي بات مت سنيو *us-kī bāt mat suniyō*.

The Persons in Verbs, like as in the personal pronouns, are—

First person, متكلم *mutakallim*.
Second person, مخاطب *mukhāṭab*.
Third person, غائِب *ghā'ib*.

A Particle, حرف *ḥarf*, may be—

Preposition or Postposition, حرف جر *ḥarf-i-jarr*; and this may be simple, مفرد *mufrid*; as كا *kā*, كو *kō*, سي *sē*, مين *mēn*, پر *par*, تك *tak*; or compound, مركب *murakkab*; as, كي تئين *kē ta'īn*, كي پاس *kē pās*, كي اوپر *kē ūpar*, كي واسطي *kē wāsṭē*, كي ليي *kē li'ē*, كي طرف *kī ṭaraf*, كي خاطر *kī khāṭir*, كي طرح *kī ṭarah*.

Conjunction, used to conjoin sentences, حرف جمله *ḥarf-i-jumla*, and this is of various descriptions; so,

حرف شرط *ḥarf-i-sharṭ* (conditional); as, اگر *agar*, جو *jō*.
حرف جزا *ḥarf-i-jazā* (retributive); as, تو *tō* (then).
حرف استثنا *ḥarf-i-istiṣnā* (exceptive); as, ليكن *lēkin*, پر *par*, مگر *magar*.
حرف استفهام *ḥarf-i-istifhām* (of interrogation); as, كيون *kyūn*, كسواسطي *kiswāsṭē*.
حرف سببي *ḥarf-i-sababī* (of cause or reason); as, كيونكه *kyūnki*, اسواسطي *iswāsṭē*.

حرف بيان *ḥarf-i-bayān* (of explanation); as, كه *ki*, جيساكه *jaisāki*, چنانچه *chunānchi*, مثلا *maṡalan*.

Conjunction, used to link together sentences or words, and this may be—

حرف عطف *ḥarf-i-āṭf* (copulative); as, اور *aur*, و *wa*: or,

حرف ترديد *ḥarf-i-tardīd* (distinctive); as, يا *yā*, خواه *khwāh*, كه *ki*.

Adverb, and this may be—

حرف تشبيه *ḥarf-i-tashbīh* (of comparison); as, جيسا *jaisā*, گويا *gōyā*, مثلا *māṡalan*.

حرف قبول *ḥarf-i-ḳabūl* (of assent); as, هان *hāṅ*, هون *hūṅ*, بلي *balē*.

حرف نفي *ḥarf-i-nafī* (of dissent or negation); as, نهين *nahīṅ*, نه *na*, اهان *ahāṅ*, اونهون *ūṅhūṅ*.

حرف نهي *ḥarf-i-nahī* (of prohibition); as, مت *mat*.

حرف تخصيص *ḥarf-i-takhṣīṣ* (of peculiarity); as, هي *hī*, or ي *ī*.

Interjection, and this may be—

حرف ندا *ḥarf-i-nidā* (of addressing or calling); as, اي *ai*, او *ō*, اجي *ajī*, اري *arē*, ابي *abē*.

حرف تعجب *ḥarf-i-ta'ājjub* (of wonder or applause); as, واه *wāh*, واه واه *wāh-wāh*, اچها *achchhā*, خوب *khūb*.

حرف تاسف *ḥarf-i-ta'assuf* (of grief or sorrow); as, آه *āh*, هائي *hā'ē*, وائي *wā'ē*.

The particle ني *nē*, used after the name of an agent before a transitive verb in a past tense is sometimes termed علامت فاعلي *ālāmat-i-fā'ilī*.

THE MILITARY WORDS OF COMMAND,

English and Hindūstānī, in Nagari and Roman Characters.*

इस्टांड आट ईज़	Stand at ease.	चैन से खड़े रहो	*chain sē khaṛē rahō.*
आटन्शन	Attention.	हुश्यार हो जाओ	*hushyār hō jā'ō.*
आइज़ रैट	Eyes right.	दहनी नज़र	*dahnī naẓar.*
आइज़ लिफ़्ट	Eyes left.	बाईं नज़र	*bā'īṅ naẓar.*
आइज़ फ़िरन्ट	Eyes front.	साम्हने नज़र	*sāmhnē naẓar.*
टू दी रैट फ़ेस	To the right face.	दहने फिरो	*dahnē phirō.*
टू दी लिफ़्ट फ़ेस	To the left face.	बाएं फिरो	*bā'ēṅ phirō.*
टू दी रैट अबौट फ़ेस	To the right about face.	दहने से आधा चक्कर फिरो	*dahnē sē ādhā chakkar phirō.*
टू दी लिफ़्ट अबौट फ़ेस	To the left about face.	बाएं से आधा चक्कर फिरो	*bā'ēṅ sē ādhā chakkar phirō.*
रैट या लिफ़्ट हाफ़ फ़ेस	Right *yā* (or) left half face.	आधा दहने या बाएं फिरो	*ādhā daknē yā bā'ēṅ phirō.*
फ़िरंट	Front.	साम्हने	*sāmhnē.*
रैट या लिफ़्ट अबौट थिरी क्वाटर्ज़ फ़ेस	Right *yā* (or) left about three quarters face.	दहने या बाएं से तीन हिस्से चक्कर फिरो	*dahnē yā bā'ēṅ sē tīn ḥiṣṣē chakkar phirō.*

---

* Extracted from the "Ungrézee Lushkuree Kuwaed," translated into the Urdū language by Lieutenant Arthur Hogg, and published by T. Astell, at the British Library, Calcutta, 1837; to which work the reader is referred for explicit information on the Exercises of the English Army.

रियर	Rear.	पीछे	*pīchhē.*
हाल्ट	Halt.	ठहरो	*ṭhahrō.*
फ़र्वर्ड	Forward.	आंगे बढ़ो	*āgē baṛhō.*
मार्च	March.	चलो	*chalō.*
हाल्ट दरस हाल्ट दरस अप	Halt dress. (or) Halt dress up.	ठहरकर बराबर हो जाओ	*ṭhaharkar barābar hō jā'ō.*
इस्टेप औट	Step out.	लंबा क़दम रक्खो	*lambā ḳadam rakkhō.*
इस्टेप शोर्ट	Step short.	एड़ी अंगूठे के पास रखकर धीरे क़दम चलो	*ēṛī angūṭhē kē pās rakh-kar dhīrē ḳadam chalō.*
मार्क टैम	Mark time.	अपनी जगह खड़े हो. कर क़दम पीट्ते रहो	*apnī jagah khaṛē hōkar ḳadam piṭtē rahō.*
रैट कलोज़ कुवैक मार्च	Right close, quick march.	दहनी तरफ सरको जल्दी चलो	*dahnī ṭaraf sarkō jaldī chalō.*
इस्टेप बयक मार्च	Step back, march.	पीछे हटो चलो	*pīchhē haṭō chalō.*
चेंज फ़ियट	Change feet.	क़दम बदलो	*ḳadam badlō.*
टू दी लिफ़्ट उ,बलीक मार्च	To the left oblique, march.	बाएं तिर्छा क़दम चलो	*bā'ēṅ tirchhā ḳadam chalō.*
टू	Two.	दो	*dō.*
कुवैक मार्च	Quick march.	जल्दी चलो	*jaldī chalō.*
डबल मार्च	Double march.	दौड़कर चलो	*dauṛkar chalō.*
इस्लो मार्च	Slow march.	आहिस्त: क़दम	*āhista ḳadam.*
दरस	Dress.	बराबर होजाओ	*barābar hō jā'ō.*
बै दी रैट फ़र्वर्ड दरस	By the right forward dress.	दहने देख आगे बढ़कर बराबर हो जाओ	*dahnē dēkh āgē baṛhkar barābar hō jā'ō.*
बै दी रैट या लिफ़्ट बयकवर्ड्ज़ दरस	By the right *yā* (or) left backwards dress.	दहने या बाएं देख पीछे हट बराबर हो जाओ	*dahnē yā bā'ēṅ dēkh pīchhē haṭ barābar hō jā'ō.*

रैट वील	Right wheel.	दह्ने खूंट पर साम्हने से चक्कर खाओ	*dahnē khūnṭ par sāmhnē sē chakkar khā'ō.*
लिफ़्ट वील	Left wheel.	बाएं खूंट पर साम्हने से चक्कर खाओ	*bā'eṅ khūnt par sāmhnē sē chakkar khā'ō.*
अंदीरैट बयक्वर्ड्ज़ वील	On the right backwards wheel.	दह्ने खूंट पर पीछे से चक्कर खाओ	*dahnē khūnṭ par pīchhē sē chakkar khā'ō.*
रैट या लिफ़्ट शोल्डर्ज़ फ़र्वर्ड	Right *yā* (or) left shoulders forward.	दह्ना या बायां कांधा घुमाओ	*dahnā yā bayāṅ kāndhā ghumā'ō.*
रैट अब्लीक	Right oblique.	दह्ने तिर्छा क़दम चलो	*dahnē tirchhā ḳadam chalō.*
हाल्ट फ़्रिंट	Halt front.	ठहरकर साम्हने हो जाओ	*ṭhaharkar sāmhnē hō jā'ō.*
रैट या लिफ़्ट हाफ़ टर्न	Right *yā* (or) left half turn.	आधा दह्ने या बाएं मुड़ो	*ādhā dahnē yā bā'eṅ muṛō.*
फ़्रिंट टर्न	Front turn.	साम्हने मुड़ो	*sāmhnē muṛō.*
इस्पुर्ट आर्म्ज़	Support arms.		
इस्लोप आर्म्ज़	Slope arms.		
कार्री आर्म्ज़	Carry arms.		
शोल्डर आर्म्ज़	Shoulder arms.		
रियर रांक तेक उपन आर्डर	Rear rank take open order.	पिछली सफ़ खुलो	*pichhlī ṣaf khulō.*
रियर रांक टेक क्लोस आर्डर	Rear rank take close order.	पिछली सफ़ मिलाओ	*pichhlī ṣaf milā'ō.*
रैट टर्न	Right turn.	दह्ने मुड़ो	*dahnē muṛō.*
रैट या लिफ़्ट अबौट टर्न	Right *yā* (or) left about turn.	दह्ने या बाएं से आधा चक्कर मुड़ो	*dahnē yā bā'eṅ sē ādhā chakkar muṛō.*
इस्क्वाड	Squad.		

रैट वील	Right wheel.	दहने घूमो	*dahnē ghūmō.*
बै दी रैट या लिफ़्ट या सिंटर मार्च या कुवैक मार्च	By the right *yā* (or) left *yā* (or) centre march *yā* (or) quick march.	दहने या बाएं या बीच से चलो या जल्दी चलो	*dahnē yā bā'ēṅ yā bīch sē chalō yā jaldī chalō.*
टू दी रैट या लिफ़्ट क्लोज़	To the right *yā* (or) left close.	दहने या बाएं सरको	*dahnē yā bā'ēṅ sarkō.*
स्टेप बयक मार्च	Step back march.	पीछे हट्कर चलो	*pīchhē haṭkar chalō.*
फ़र्म फ़ोर डीप	Form four deep.	चार की क़तार बन जाओ	*chār kī ḳaṭār ban jā'ō.*
रियर फ़र्म फ़ोर डीप	Rear form four deep.	पीछे चार की क़तार बन जाओ	*pīchhē chār kī ḳaṭār ban jā'ō.*
रैट फ़र्म फ़ोर डीप	Right form four deep.	दहने चार की क़तार बन जाओ	*dahnē chār kī ḳaṭār ban jā'ō.*
लिफ़्ट फ़र्म फ़ोर डीप	Left form four deep.	बाएं चार की क़तार बन जाओ	*bā'ēṅ chār kī ḳaṭār ban jā'ō.*
लिफ़्ट फ़ेस	Left face.	बाएं फिरो	*bā'ēṅ phirō.*
बै सब्डवयज़्न्ज़ रैट वील	By subdivisions right wheel.	आधी कम्पनी के दहने खूंट पर साम्हने से चक्कर खाओ	*ādhī kampanī kī dahnē khūṇṭ par sāmhnē sē chakkar khā'ō.*
बै सब्डवयज़्न्ज़ अन दी लिफ़्ट बयक्वर्ड्ज़ वील	By subdivisions on the left backwards wheel.	आधी कम्पनी में बाएं खूंट पर पीछे से चक्कर खाओ	*ādhī kampanī mēṅ bā'ēṅ khūṇṭ par pīchhē sē chakkar khā'ō.*
बै सब्डवयज़्न्ज़ लिफ़्ट वील इन्टो लैन	By subdivisions left wheel into line.	आधी कम्पनी से बाएं खूंट पर साम्हने से सफ़ में चक्कर खाओ	*ādhī kampanī sē bā'ēṅ khūṇṭ par sāmhnē sē ṣaf mēṅ chakkar khā'ō.*
रैट या लिफ़्ट फ़ेस	Right *yā* (or) left face.	दहने या बाएं फिरो	*dahnē yā bā'ēṅ phirō.*

हाल्ट फ़िरंट दरस	Halt front dress.	ठहरकर साम्हने फिर्.	*ṭhaharkar sāmhnē*
हाल्ट फ़िरंट दरस अप	(or) Halt front dress up.	कर बराबर हो आओ	*phirkar barābar hō jā'ō.*
रैट एंड लिफ़्ट फ़ेस	Right and left face.	दहने और बाएं फिरो	*dahnē aur bā'ēṅ phirō.*
रैट कौंटरमार्च	Right counter-march.	दहने कावा देकर फिरो	*dahnē kāwā dēkar phirō.*
कम्पनी अन दी सिंटर रैट वील	Company on the centre right wheel.	कम्पनी बीच पर दहने पाव चक्कर मारो	*kampanī bīch par dahnē pā'ō chakkar mārō.*
कम्पनी अन दी सिंटर लिफ़्ट वील	Company on the centre left wheel.	कम्पनी बीच पर बाएं पाव चक्कर मारो	*kampanī bīch par bā'ēṅ pā'ō chakkar mārō.*
कम्पनी अन दी सिंटर रैट अबौट वील	Company on the centre right about wheel.	कम्पनी बीच पर दहने आधा चक्कर मारो	*kampanī bīch par dahnē ādhā chakkar mārō.*
कम्पनी अन दी सिंटर लिफ़्ट अबौट वील	Company on the centre left about wheel.	कम्पनी बीच पर बाएं आधा चक्कर मारो	*kampanī bīch par bā'ēṅ ādhā chakkar mārō.*
फ़ार्म कम्पनी	Form company.	कम्पनी बन आओ	*kampanī ban jā'ō.*
लिफ़्ट सबडवीज़न लिफ़्ट हाफ़ फ़ेस कुवैक मार्च	Left subdivision left half face, quick march.	बाएं आधी कम्पनी आधा बाएं फिरकर जल्दी चलो	*bā'īṅ ādhī kampanī ādhā bā'ēṅ phirkar jaldī chalō.*
फ़ार्म सबडवीज़नज़	Form subdivisions.	आधी कम्पनी बन आओ	*ādhī kampanī ban jā'ō.*
लिफ़्ट सबडवीज़न रैट अबौट थिरी क्वार्टरज़ फ़ेस कुवैक मार्च	Left subdivision right about three quarters face, quick march.	बाएं आधी कम्पनी दहने से तीन हिस्से चक्कर फिरकर जल्दी चलो	*bā'īṅ ādhī kampanī dahnē sē tīn ḥiṣṣē chakkar phirkar jaldī chalō.*
लिफ़्ट सबडवीज़न लिफ़्ट हाफ़ टर्न डबल	Left subdivision left half turn, double.	बाएं आधी कम्पनी आधा बाएं मुड़कर दौड़ो	*bā'īṅ ādhī kampanī ādhā bā'ēṅ muṛkar dauṛō.*
कुवैक	Quick.	जल्दी	*jaldī.*

लिफ़्ट सबडिवयनज़ मार्क टैम रैट हाफ़ टर्न	Left subdivisions mark time, right half turn.	बाईं आधी कम्पनी अपनी जगह खड़ी हो क़दम उठाओ आधी दहने मुड़ो	*bā'īṅ ādhī kampanī apnī jagah khaṛī hō ḳadam uṭhā'ō, ādhī dahnē muṛō.*
थिरी फ़ैलज़ अन दी लिफ़्ट रैट टर्न लिफ़्ट वील	Three files on the left, right turn, left wheel.	तीन क़तार बाईं कमर पर दहने मुड़कर बाएं घूमो	*tīn ḳaṭār bā'īṅ kamar par dahnē muṛkar bā'ēṅ ghūmō.*
वन टू या थिरी फ़ैलज़ टू दी फ़िरंट	One, two *yā* (or) three files to the front.	एक या दो या तीन क़तार साम्हने को बढ़ो	*ēk yā dō yā tīn ḳaṭār sāmhnē kō baṛhō.*
सिक्शनज़ या थिरीज़ रैट या लिफ़्ट शो. लडरज़ फ़रवरड कुवैक मार्च फ़रवरड	Sections *yā* (or) threes right *yā* (or) left shoulders forward, quick march, forward.	टोली या तीन तीन सिपाहियों की टो. ली दहना या बायां कांधा घुमाके जलदी चलो साम्हने बढ़ो	*ṭōlī yā tīn tīn sipāhiyōṅ kī ṭōlī dahnā yā bāyāṅ kāndhā ghumākē jaldī chalō sāmhnē baṛhō.*
सिक्शनज़ या थिरीज़ अन दी रैट या लिफ़्ट बयकवरड्ज़ वील कुवैक मार्च	Sections *yā* (or) threes on the right *yā* (or) left back-wards wheel, quick march.	टोली या तीन तीन सिपाहियों की टो. ली दहने खूंट पर पीछे से चक्कर खाओ जलदी चलो	*ṭōlī yā tīn tīn sipāhiyōṅ kī ṭōlī dahnē khūṅṭ par pīchhē sē chakkar khā'ō jaldī chalō.*
रैट या लिफ़्ट शो. लडरज़ फ़रवरड	Right *yā* (or) left shoulders forward.	दहना या बायां कां. धा बढ़ाओ	*dahnā yā bāyāṅ kāndhā baṛhā'ō.*
रैट या लिफ़्ट वील इन टू लैन	Right *yā* (or) left wheel into line.	दहने या बाएं खूंट पर साम्हने से चक्कर खाओ	*dahnē yā bā'ēṅ khūṅṭ par sāmhnē sē chakkar khā'ō.*
फ़िरंट फ़रम कम्पनी या सबडिवयन या सिक्शन	Front form company *yā* (or) subdivision *yā* (or) section.	पूरी या आधी कम्पनी या टोली बन जा. ओ	*pūrī yā ādhī kampanī yā ṭōlī ban jā'ō.*

बन दी लिडिंग फैल टू दी रैट फ़रम कम्पनी	On the leading file to the right form company.	पहिली क़तार पर दहने से कम्पनी बन जाओ	*pahilī kaṭār par dahnē sē kampanī ban jā'ō.*
बन दी लिडिंग फैल टू दी रैट अबौट फ़र्म कम्पनी	On the leading file to the right about form company.	पहिली क़तार पर दहने से पिछली तरफ़ कम्पनी बन जाओ	*pahilī kaṭār par dahnē sē pichlī ṭaraf kampanī ban jā'ō.*
हाल्ट लिफ़्ट वील इन टू लैन	Halt, left wheel into line.	ठहरकर बाएं खूंट पर साम्हने से सफ़ में चक्कर खाओ	*ṭhaharkar bā'ēn khūnṭ par sāmhnē sē ṣaf mēn chakkar khā'ō.*
टू दी रैट फ़र्म कम्पनी	To the right form company.	दहनी कमर तक कम्पनी बन जाओ	*dahnī kamar tak kampanī ban jā'ō.*
लिफ़्ट शोल्डरज़ फ़रवरड	Left shoulders forward.	बायां कांधा घुमाओ	*bāyān kāndhā ghumā'ō.*
सिक्शनज़ रैट	Sections right.	टोलियां दहने	*ṭōliyān dahnē.*
फ़र्म दी रालीएंग स्क्वेर	Form the rallying square.	जमअ होने का चौखूंटा बन जाओ	*jam' hōnē kā chaukhūnṭā ban jā'ō.*
दी स्क्वेर विल मार्च टू दी फ़्रिंट या रियर या रैट या लिफ़्ट	The square will march to the front *yā* (or) rear *yā* (or) right *yā* (or) left.	चौखूंटा साम्हने या पीछे या दहने या बाएं चले	*chaukhūnṭā sāmhnē yā pīchhē yā dahnē yā bā'ēn chalē.*
इन्वरडज़ फ़ेस	Inwards face.	भीतर फिरो	*bhītar phirō.*
परीपेयर टो रिज़िस्ट कावलरी रडी	Prepare to resist cavalry. Ready.	सवारों की मुदाफ़अत को मुस्तइद रहो	*sawārōn kī mudāfa'at kō musta'id rahō.*
रीडयूस दी स्क्वेर	Reduce the square.	चौखूंटा खुल जावे	*chaukhunṭā khul jāwē.*
रियर रांक टेक उपन आर्डर	Rear rank, take open order.	पिछली सफ़ खुलो	*pichhlī ṣaf khulō.*

रियर रांक टेक क्लोस आर्डर	Rear rank, take close order.	पिछली सफ़ मिल आओ	*pichhlī ṣaf mil jā'ō.*
दी बटेलैन विल आद्वेंस	The battalion will advance.	पल्टन आगे बढ़े	*palṭan āgē baṛhē.*
दी बटेलैन विल रीतैर	The battalion will retire.	पल्टन हटे	*palṭan haṭē.*
परीपेयर तू चार्ज	Prepare to charge.	हम्ल: करने पर तैयार हो	*ḥamla karnē par taiyār hō.*
चार्ज	Charge.	हम्ल: करो	*ḥamla karō.*
फ़राम दी रैट या लिफ़्ट आफ़ कम्पनीज़ बै फ़ैलस तू दी फ़िरंट	From the right *yā* (or) left of companies by files to the front.	हर एक कम्पनी की दहनी या बाईं कमर से क़तार क़तार साम्हने चलो	*har ēk kampanī ki dahnī yā bā'īṅ kamar sē ḳaṭār ḳaṭār sāmhnē chalō.*
कम्पनीज़ रैट या लिफ़्ट टर्न लिफ़्ट या रैट वील	Companies right *yā* (or) left turn left *yā* (or) right wheel.	दहने या बाएं मुड़ो बाएं या दहने घूमो	*dahnē yā bā'ēṅ muṛō bā'ēṅ yā dahnē ghūmō.*
फ़राम दी परापर रैट या लिफ़्ट आफ़ कम्पनीज़ पास बै फ़ैलस टू दी रियर	From the proper right *yā* (or) left of companies pass by files to the rear.	हर एक कम्पनी की अगली दहनी या बाईं कमर से क़तार क़तार पीछे चलो	*har ēk kampanī ki aglī dahnī yā bā'īṅ kamar sē ḳaṭār ḳaṭār pīchhē chalō.*
लिफ़्ट या रैट टर्न रैट या लिफ़्ट वील	Left *yā* (or) right turn, right *yā* (or) left wheel.	बाएं या दहने मुड़ो दहने या बाएं घूमो	*bā'ēṅ yā dahnē muṛō dahnē yā bā'ēṅ ghūmo.*
पास बै फ़ैलस टू दी रियर रैट फ़ेस रैट वील	Pass by files to the rear, right face, right wheel.	क़तार क़तार पीछे चलो दहने फिरो दहने घूमो	*ḳaṭār ḳaṭār pīchhē chalō dahnē phirō dahnē ghūmō.*
दी बटेलैन विल आद्वेंस बै वींगस	The battalion will advance by wings.	पल्टन पहलू पहलू चले	*palṭan pahlū pahlū chalē.*
लिफ़्ट वींग { हाल्ट / मार्च }	Left wing { halt, / march. }	बायां पहलू { ठहरो / चलो }	*bāyāṅ pahlū* { *ṭhahrō,* / *chalō.* }

रैट वींग { हाल्ट, रडी, प्रज़ंट, लोड, मार्च }	Right wing { halt, ready, present, load, march. }	दहना पहलू { ठहरो, घोड़ा दो पाए पर चढ़ाओ, शस्त लो, टोंटा भरो, चलो }	*dahnā pahlū* { *ṭhahrō, ghōṛā dō pā'ē par chaṛhā'ō, shast lō, ṭōnṭā bharō, chalō.* }
लिफ़्ट वींग { हाल्ट, वग़ैरा }	Left wing { halt, *wa ghaira* (&c.). }	बायां पहलू { ठहरो, वग़ैरा }	*bāyāṅ pahlū* { *ṭhahrō, wa ghaira.* }
दी बटेलैन विल रीटैर बै वींग्स	The battalion will retire by wings.	पलटन पहलू पहलू हटे	*palṭan pahlū pahlū haṭē.*
रैट या लिफ़्ट डवीज़न टू दी फ़्रिंट	Right *yā* (or) left division to the front.	दहना या बायां तुमन साम्हने बढ़े	*dahnā yā bāyāṅ tuman sāmhnē baṛhē.*
रीमेनिंग डवीज़न्ज़ रैट या लिफ़्ट शोल्डर्ज़ फ़र्वर्ड	Remaining divisions right *yā* (or) left shoulders forward.	बाक़ी तुमन दहना या बायां कांधा घुमाओ	*bāḳī tuman dahnā yā bāyāṅ kāndhā ghumā'ō.*
फ़रम लैन अन दी फ़र्स्ट डवीज़न	Form line on the first division.	पहिले तुमन के बरा-बर सफ़ बन जाओ	*pahilē tuman kē barābar ṣaf ban jā'ō.*
टू सिंटर सबडवीज़न्ज़ टू दी फ़्रिंट	Two centre subdivisions to the front.	बीच की दो आधी कम्पनी साम्हने बढ़ें	*bīch kī dō ādhī kampanī sāmhnē baṛhēṅ.*
रीमेनिंग सबडवीज़न्ज़ रैट या लिफ़्ट शोल्डर्ज़ फ़र्वर्ड	Remaining subdivisions right *yā* (or) left shoulders forward.	बाक़ी आधी कम्पनी दहना या बायां कांधा बढ़ाओ	*bāḳī ādh kampanī dahnā yā bāyāṅ kāndhā baṛhā'ō.*
फ़रम लैन अन दी टू सिंटर सबडवीज़न्ज़	Form line on the two centre subdivisions.	बीच की दो आधी कम्पनी के बराबर सफ़ बन जाओ	*bīch kī dō ādhī kampanī kē barābar ṣaf ban jā'ō.*

रैट एंड लिफ़्ट शोल्डरज़ फ़रवरड	Right and left shoulders forward.	बाक़ी आधी कम्पनी दहना और बायां कांधा बढ़ाओ	*bāḳī ādhī kampanī dahnā aur bāyāṅ kāndhā baṛhā'ō.*
फ़रम लैन टू दी रैट	Form line to the right.	दहनी तरफ़ सफ़ बन जाओ	*dahnī ṭaraf ṣaf ban jā'ō.*
रैट वींग लिफ़्ट शोल्डरज़ फ़रवरड	Right wing left shoulders forward.	दहना पहलू बायां कांधा बढ़ाओ	*dahnā pahlū bāyāṅ kāndhā baṛhā'ō.*
लिफ़्ट शोलडरज़ फ़रवरड फ़रवरड	Left shoulders forward, forward.	बायां कांधा बढ़ाओ आगे बढ़ो	*bāyāṅ kāndhā baṛhā'ō, āgē baṛhō.*
रिटैर बै कम्पनीज़ या सबडवयज़नज़ फ़राम दी लिफ़्ट या रैट इन रियर अफ़ दी रैट या लिफ़्ट	Retire by companies *yā* (or) subdivisions from the left *yā* (or) right in rear of the right *yā* (or) left.	कम्पनी यां आधी कम्पनी में बाईं या दहनी कमर से बाईं या दहनी कमर के पीछे हटो	*kampanī yā ādhī kampanī mēṅ bā'īṅ yā dahnī kamar sē bā'īṅ yā dahnī kamar kē pīchhē haṭō.*
कम्पनी या सबडवयज़न रैट अबौट फ़ेस	Company *yā* (or) subdivision right about face.	कम्पनी या आधी कम्पनी दहने से आधा चक्कर फिरो	*kampanī yā ādhī kampanī dahnē sē ādhā chakkar phirō.*
रीटैर फ़राम बोथ फ़लैंक्स बै सबडवयज़नज़ इन रियर अफ़ दी सिंटर	Retire from both flanks by subdivisions in rear of the centre.	आधी कम्पनी में दोनो कमर से बीच के पीछे हटो	*ādhī kampanī mēṅ dōnō kamar sē bīch kē pīchhē haṭō.*
रैट या लिफ़्ट सबडवयज़न रैट अबौट फ़ेस	Right *yā* (or) left subdivision right about face.	दहनी या बाईं आधी कम्पनी दहने से आधा चक्कर फिरो	*dahnī yā bā'īṅ ādhī kampanī dahnē sē ādhā chakkar phirō.*
दी बटलैन विल मोफ़ इन कालम अफ़ डवीयज़नज़ या सिक्शनज़ फ़राम दी रैट अलोंग दी रियर	The battalion will move in column of divisions *yā* (or) sections from the right along the rear.	पलटन कम्पनी या आधी कम्पनी की क़तार बनकर दहनी कमर से सफ़ के पीछे चले	*palṭan kampanī yā ādhī kampanī kī ḳaṭār bankar dahnī kamar sē ṣaf kē pīchhē chalē.*

लिफ़्ट फ़ेस लिफ़्ट वील	Left face left wheel.	बाएं फिरो बाएं घूमो	*bā'eṅ phirō bā'eṅ ghūmō.*
रैट फ़ेस	Right face.	दहने फिरो	*dahnē phirō.*
रैट वील	Right wheel.	दहने घूमो	*dahnē ghūmō.*
फ़रम कलम आट क्वाटर डिस्टैंस अन दी रैट या लिफ़्ट सिंटर कम्पनी	Form column at quarter distance on the right *yā* (or) left centre company.	बीच की दहनी या बाइं कम्पनी पर पा. ओ खुली क़तार बने	*bīch kī dahnī yā bā'īṅ ḳampanī par pā'ō khulī ḳaṭār banē.*
थिरीज़ रैट एंड लिफ़्ट शोलडरज़ फ़रवरड	Threes right and left shoulders forward.	तीन तीन की टोली दहना या बायां कांधा बढ़ाओ	*tīn tīn kī ṭōlī dahnā yā bāyāṅ kāndhā baṛhā'ō.*
थिरीज़ लिफ़्ट शोलडरज़ फ़रवरड	Threes left shoulders forward.	तीन तीन की टोली बायां कांधा बढ़ा. ओ	*tīn tīn kī ṭōlī bāyāṅ kāndhā baṛhā'ō.*
फ़रम इसक्वेर	Form square.	चौखूंटा बन जाओ	*chaukhūṅṭā banjā'ō.*
हाल्ट रैट अबौट फ़ेस	Halt, right about face.	ठहरकर दहने से आधा चक्कर फिरो	*ṭhaharkar dahnē sē ādhā chakkar phirō.*
फ़रम इसक्वेर अन दी रैट या लिफ़्ट कम्पनी कम्पनीज़ रैट या लिफ़्ट शोलडरज़ फ़रवरड	Form square on the right *yā* (or) left company. Companies right *yā* (or) left shoulders forward.	दहनी या बाईं कम्पनी पर चौखूंटा बन जाओ सब कम्पनी दहना या बायां कांधा बढ़ाओ	*dahnī yā bā'īṅ kampanī par chaukhūṅṭā ban jā'ō. Sab kampanī dahnā yā bāyāṅ kāndhā baṛhā'ō.*
परीपेयर फ़ौर काव. लरी रिडी	Prepare for cavalry. Ready.	सवारों की मुदाफ़अत को तैयार हो तै. यार	*sawārōṅ kī mudāfa'at kō taiyār hō. Taiyār.*
नीलैंग रैंक्स रिडी पर्ज़ंट	Kneeling ranks, ready. Present.	ज़ानू गिराई सफ़ तैयार हो शस्तकरो	*zānū girā'ī ṣaf taiyār hō. Shast karō.*

लोड	Load.	टोंटा भरो	*ṭōnṭā bharō.*
रीफ़र्म कलम	Reform column.	क़तार फिर बन जाओ	*ḳaṯār phir ban jā'ō.*
अन दी टू सिंटर सबडिवीज़नज़ फ़र्म स्क्वेर	On the two centre subdivisions form square.	बीच की दो आधी कम्पनी के पीछे चौ. खूंटा बन जाओ	*bīch kī dō ādhī kampanī kē pīchhē chaukhūnṭā ban jā'ō.*
हाल्ट फ़्रंट	Halt front.	ठहर्कर साम्हने फिरो	*ṭhaharkar sāmhnē phirō.*
हाल्ट रैट एंड लिफ़्ट फ़ेस	Halt, right and left face.	ठहर्कर दहने और बाएं फिरो	*ṭhaharkar dahnē aur bā'ēṅ phirō.*
रीफ़र्म लैन	Reform line.	सफ़ फिर बन जाओ	*ṣaf phir ban jā'ō.*
हाल्ट फ़्रंट ड्रेस	Halt, front dress.	ठहर्कर और साम्हने फिर्कर बराबर हो जाओ	*ṭhaharkar aur sāmhnē phirkar barābar hō jā'ō.*
फ़र्म डबल कलम आफ़ सबडिवीज़नज़	Form double column of subdivisions.	आधी कम्पनी की दुहरी क़तार बन जाओ	*ādhī kampanī kī duhrī ḳaṯār ban jā'ō.*
फ़र्म स्क्वेर टू डीप अन दी टू सिंटर कम्पनीज़ रीमेनिंग कम्पनीज़ रैट एंड लिफ़्ट शोल्डर्ज़ फ़र्वर्ड	Form square two deep on the two centre companies. Remaining companies right and left shoulders forward.	बीच की दो कम्पनी पर दो की क़तार का चौखूंटा बन जाओ बाक़ी कम्पनी दहना और बायां कांधा बढ़ाओ	*bīch kī dō kampanī par dō kī ḳaṯār kā chaukhūnṭā ban jā'ō. Bāḳī kampanī dahnā aur bāyāṅ kāndhā baṛhā'ō.*
दी स्क्वेर विल मार्च टू दी फ़्रंट या रियर या रैट या लिफ़्ट फ़ेस	The square will march to the front *yā* (or) rear *yā* (or) right *yā* (or) left face.	चौखूंटा साम्हने या पीछे या दहनी या बाईं की राह से चले	*chauḳhūnṭā sāmhnē yā pīchhē yā dahnī yā bā'īṅ kī rāh sē chalē.*

बै सब्डिवीज़न्ज़ अन दी रैट एंड लिफ़्ट बैकवर्ड्ज़ वील	By subdivisions on the right and left backwards wheel.	दहने और बाएं खूंट पर आधी कम्पनी में पीछे से चक्कर खाओ	*dahnē aur bā'ēṅ khūṇṭ par ādhī kampanī mēṅ pīchhē se chakkar khā'ō.*
फ़रम लैन	Form line.	सफ़ बन जाओ	*ṣaf ban jā'ō.*
रैट एंड लिफ़्ट शोल्डर्ज़ फ़रवर्ड	Right and left shoulders forward.	दहना और बायां कांधा बढ़ाओ	*dahnā aur bāyāṅ kāndhā baṛhā'ō.*
चेंज फ़िरंट टू दी रियर उपन दी सिंटर	Change front to the rear upon the centre.	पलटन के बीच पर पिछली तरफ़ सामने हो जाओ	*palṭan kē bīch par pichhlī ṭaraf sāmhnē hō jā'ō.*
थिरीज़ रैट एंड लिफ़्ट शोल्डर्ज़ फ़रवर्ड	Threes right and left shoulders forward.	तीन तीन की टोलियां दहना और बायां कांधा बढ़ाओ	*tīn tīn kī ṭōliyāṅ dahnā aur bāyāṅ kāndhā baṛhā'ō.*
रैट एंड लिफ़्ट कौंटर मार्च	Right and left counter march.	दहने और बाएं से कावा देकर फिरो	*dahnē aur bā'ēṅ sē kāwā dēkar phirō.*
फ़रम उपन कलम इन फ़िरंट अफ़ दी रैट कम्पनी	Form open column in front of the right company.	दहनी कम्पनी के आगे खुली क़तार बन जाओ	*dahnī kampanī kē āgē khulī ḳaṭār ban jā'ō.*
रीमेनिंग कम्पनीज़ रैट फ़ेस	Remaining companies right face.	बाक़ी कम्पनी दहने फिरो	*bāḳī kampanī dahnē phirō.*
हाल्ट फ़िरंट दरस	Halt front dress.	ठहरकर सामने होकर बराबर हो जाओ	*ṭhaharkar sāmhnē hōkar barābar hō jā'ō.*
रैट वील इन टू लैन	Right wheel into line.	दहने खूंट पर सामने से चक्कर खाओ	*dahnē khūṇṭ par sāmhnē sē chakkar khā'ō.*
फ़रम उपन कलम इन रियर अफ़ दी रैट या लिफ़्ट कम्पनी	Form open column in rear of the right *yā* (or) left company.	दहनी या बाईं कम्पनी के पीछे खुली क़तार बन जाओ	*dahnī yā bā'īṅ kampanī kē pīchhē khulī ḳaṭār ban jā'ō.*

रीमेनिंग कम्पनीज़ रैट या लिफ़्ट फ़ेस	Remaining companies right *yā* (or) left face.	बाक़ी कम्पनी दहने या बाएं फिरो	*bāḳī kampanī dahnē yā bā'ēṅ phirō.*
फ़रम लैन टो दी रिवर्स फ़्लेंक	Form line to the reverse flank.	रिवर्स कमर तक सफ़ बन जाओ	*rivars kamar tak ṣaf ban jā'ō.*
बै सक्सिसिव डवीज़नज़ रियर वींग टू दी फ़िरंट	By successive divisions. Rear wing to the front.	पै दर पै कम्पनी से पिछला पहलू सामने हो	*pai dar pai kampanī sē pichhlā pahlū sāmhnē hō.*
बै डबल फ़ैलज़ फ़राम दी सिंटर रियर वींग टू दी फ़िरंट	By double files from the centre. Rear wing to the front.	कम्पनी के बीच से दुहरी क़तार में बढ़कर पिछला पहलू सामने हो	*kampanī kē bīch sē duhrī ḳaṭār mēṅ baṛhkar pichhlā pahlū sāmhnē hō.*
टू सिंटर सिक्शनज़ औटवरडज़ वील	Two centre sections outwards wheel.	बीच की दो टोली दहने और बाएं खूंट पर सामने से चक्कर खाओ	*bīch kī dō ṭōlī dahnē aur bā'ēṅ khūṅṭ par sāmhnē sē chakkar khā'ō.*
फ़रम इस्कुवेर अन दी फ़िरंट कम्पनी	Form square on the front company.	अगली कम्पनी पर चौखूंटा बन जाओ	*aglī kampanī par chaukhūṅṭā ban jā'ō.*
फ़रम इस्कुवेर अन दी रैट या लिफ़्ट सिंटर कम्पनी रैट या लिफ़्ट वींग रैट अबौट फ़ेस	Form square on the right *yā* (or) left centre company. Right *yā* (or) left wing, right about face.	बीच की दहनी या बाईं कम्पनी पर चौखूंटा बन जाओ दहना या बायां पहलू दहने से आधा चक्कर फिरो	*bīch kī dahnī yā bā'īṅ kampanī par chaukhūṅṭā ban jā'ō. Dahnā yā bāyāṅ pahlū dahnē sē ādhā chakkar phirō.*
सिक्शनज़ औटवरडज़	Sections outwards.	टोलियां दहने और बाएं खूंट पर बाहर चक्कर खाओ	*ṭōliyāṅ dahnē aur bā'ēṅ khūṅṭ par bāhar chakkar khā'ō.*
फ़िरंट टरन सिक्शनज़ औटवरडज़	Front turn. Sections outwards.	सामने फिरो टोलियां दहने और बाएं खूंट पर बाहिर चक्कर खाओ	*sāmhnē phirō. Ṭōliyāṅ dahnē aur bā'ēṅ khūṅṭ par bāhir chakkar khā'ō.*

फ़ार्म स्क्वेर अन दी सिंटर	Form square on the centre.	बीच की कम्पनी पर चौखूंटा बन जाओ	*bīch kī kampanī par chaukhūṇṭa ban jā'ō.*
वींग्ज़ इनवर्ड्ज़ टर्न	Wings inwards turn.	दोनो पहलू भीतर मुड़ो	*dōnō pahlū bhītar muṛō.*
स्क्वेर अन दी सिंटर	Square on the centre.	बीच पर चौखूंटा बन जाओ	*bīch par chaukhūṇṭā ban jā'ō.*
रैट वींग रैट अबौट टर्न	Right wing, right about turn.	दहना पहलू दहने से आधा चक्कर मुड़ो	*dahnā pahlū dahnē sē ādhā chakkar muṛō.*
डबल	Double.	दौड़ो या दौड़कर चलो	*dauṛō yā* (or) *dauṛkar chalō.*
फ़ार्म कलोस या कुवाटर दिस्तेंस कलम अन — कम्पनी रैट या लिफ़्ट इन फ़िरंट	Form close *yā* (or) quarter distance column on — company. Right *yā* (or) left in front.	किसी कम्पनी पर मिली या पाओ खुली क़तार दहनी या बाईं कम्पनी साम्हने होकर बन जाओ	*kisī kampanī par milī yā pā'ō khulī ḳaṭār dahnī yā bā'īṅ kampanī sāmhnē hōkar ban jā'ō.*
हाल्ट फ़िरंट ड्रेस	Halt front dress.	ठहरकर साम्हने फिरकर बराबर हो जाओ	*ṭhaharkar sāmhnē phirkar barābar hō jā'ō.*
फ़ार्म कलम अन — सिंटर कम्पनी	Form column on — centre company.	बीच की किसी कम्पनी पर चौखूंटा बन जाओ	*bīch kī kisī kampanī par chaukhūṇṭā ban jā'ō.*
फ़ार्म कलम आट क्वारटर डिस्टेंस रैट या लिफ़्ट इन फ़िरंट अन — कम्पनी	Form column at quarter distance, right *yā* (or) left in front on — company.	किसी कम्पनी पर पाओ खुली क़तार दहनी कम्पनी साम्हने होकर बन जाओ	*kisī kampanī par pā'ō khulī ḳaṭār dahnī kampanī sāmhnē hōkar ban jā'ō.*
रीमेनिंग कम्पनीज़ थिरीज़ रैट या लिफ़्ट शोल्डरज़ फ़रवर्ड	Remaining companies threes right *yā* (or) left shoulders forward.	बाक़ी कम्पनी तीन तीन की टोली बनकर दहना या बायां कांधा बढ़ाओ	*bāḳī kampanī tīn tīn kī ṭōlī bankar dahnā yā bāyāṅ kāndhā baṛhā'ō.*

क्लोज़ टू दी फ़िरंट	Close to the front.	साम्हने को मिल जाओ	*sāmhnē kō mil jā'ō.*
दी कलम विल मार्च टू दी रैट या लिफ़्ट फ़लेंक रैट या लि. फ़्ट फ़ेस क्वीक मार्च	The column will march to the right *yā* (or) left flank. Right *yā* (or) left face. Quick march.	क़तार दह्नी या बाईं तरफ़ चले दह्ने या बाएं फिरो जल्दी चलो	*ḳaṭār dahnī yā bā'īṅ ṭaraf chalē dahnē yā bā'ēṅ phirō. Jaldī chalō.*
बै सिक्शन्ज़ रैट या लिफ़्ट	By sections right *yā* (or) left.	टोलियां दह्ने या बाएं	*ṭōliyāṅ dahnē yā bā'ēṅ.*
कलम टू दी रैट या लिफ़्ट वील	Column to the right *yā* (or) left wheel.	क़तार दह्ने या बाएं खूंट पर साम्हने से चक्कर खाओ	*ḳaṭār dahnē yā bā'ēṅ khūṅṭ par sāmhnē sē chakkar khā'ō.*
रैट या लिफ़्ट वील	Right *yā* (or) left wheel.	दह्ने या बाएं खूंट पर साम्हने से चक्कर खाओ	*dahnē yā bā'ēṅ khūṅṭ par sāmhnē sē chakkar khā'ō.*
कौन्टर्मार्च बै सब्डविज़न्ज़ रौंड दी सिन्टर	Countermarch by subdivisions round the centre.	बीच के गिर्द आधी कम्पनी से कावा देकर फिरो	*bīch kē gird ādhī kampanī sē kāwā dēkar phirō.*
रैट या लिफ़्ट सब्डविज़न्ज़ रैट अबौट फ़ेस	Right *yā* (or) left subdivisions right about face.	दह्नी या बाईं आधी कम्पनी दह्ने से आधा चक्कर फिरो	*dahnī yā bā'īṅ ādhī kampanī dahnē sē ādhā chakkar phirō.*
रैट सब्डविज़न्ज़ रैट अबौट टर्न	Right subdivisions right about turn.	दह्नी आधी कम्पनी दह्ने से आधा चक्कर मुड़ो	*dahnī ādhī kampanī dahnē sē ādhā chakkar muṛō.*
फ़िरंट टर्न फ़ार्वर्ड	Front turn, forward.	साम्हने मुड़कर आगे बढ़ो	*sāmhnē muṛkar āgē baṛhō.*
दी कलम विल उपन फ़राम दी फ़िरंट	The column will open from the front.	क़तार अगली कम्पनी से खुल जावे	*ḳaṭar aglī kampanī sē khul jāwē.*
दी कलम विल उपन फ़राम दी रियर	The column will open from the rear.	क़तार पिछली कम्पनी से खुल जावे	*ḳaṭār pichhlī kampanī sē khul jāwē.*

डीपलोए ऑन दी फ़्रिंट कम्पनी	Deploy on the front company.	अगली कम्पनी से बराबर सफ़ बन जाओ	*aglī kampanī sē barābar ṣaf ban jā'ō.*
डीपलोए ऑन दी रियर कम्पनी	Deploy on the rear company.	पिछली कम्पनी से फैलकर सफ़ बन जाओ	*pichhlī kampanī sē phailkar ṣaf ban jā'ō.*
डीपलोए ऑन दी फ़्रिंट कम्पनी	Deploy on the front company.	अगली कम्पनी से बराबर फैलकर सफ़ बन जाओ	*aglī kampanī sē barābar phailkar ṣaf ban jā'ō.*
रीमेनिंग कम्पनीज़ थिरीज़ रैट शोल्डरज़ फ़रवरड	Remaining companies. Threes right shoulders forward.	बाक़ी कम्पनी तीन तीन की टोलियां बनकर दहना कांधा बढ़ाओ	*bāḳī kampanī tīn tīn kī ṭōliyāṅ bankar dahnā kāndhā baṛhā'ō.*
रीमेनिंग कम्पनीज़ शोल्डरज़ फ़रवरड	Remaining companies shoulders forward.	बाक़ी कम्पनी कांधा बढ़ाओ	*bāḳī kampanī kāndhā baṛhā'ō.*
शोल्डरज़ फ़रवरड	Shoulders forward.	कांधा बढ़ाओ	*kāndhā baṛhā'ō.*
कम्पनीज़ — पेसेज़ टू दी रैट या लिफ़्ट वील	Companies — paces to the right *yā* (or) left wheel.	कम्पनी कई क़दम दहने या बाएं खूंट पर सामने से चक्कर खाओ	*kampanī ka'ī ḳadam dahnē yā bā'ēṅ khūṅṭ par sāmhnē sē chakkar khā'ō.*
वील बयक इन टू लैन	Wheel back into line.	सफ़ में पीछे से चक्कर खाओ	*ṣaf mēṅ pīchhē sē chakkar khā'ō.*
चेंज फ़्रिंट ऑन — कम्पनी रैट या लिफ़्ट थरोन फ़रवरड	Change front on — company right *yā* (or) left thrown forward.	दहने या बाएं पहलू के आगे बढ़ने से किसी कम्पनी पर वज़ा बदलो	*dahnē yā bā'ēṅ pahlū kē āgē baṛhnē sē kisī kampanī par waẓ' badlō.*
रीमेनिंग कम्पनीज़ — पेसेज़ टू दी रैट या लिफ़्ट वील	Remaining companies — paces to the right *yā* (or) left wheel.	बाक़ी कम्पनी कई क़दम दहने या बाएं खूंट पर सामने से चक्कर खाओ	*bāḳī kampanī ka'ī ḳadam dahnē yā bā'ēṅ khūṅṭ par sāmhnē sē chakkar khā'ō.*

दरस अप	Dress up.	बराबर हो जाओ	*barābar hō jā'ō.*
चेंज फ़िरंट अन दी रैट या लिफ़्ट कम्पनी रैट या लिफ़्ट थरोन बयक	Change front on the right *yā* (or) left company right *yā* (or) left thrown back.	दहनी या बाईं कम्पनी पर दहने या बाएं पहलू के हटने से वज़अ बदलो	*dahnī yā bā'īṅ kampanī par dahnē yā bā'ēṅ pahlū kē haṭnē sē waẓ' badlō.*
रीमेनिंग कम्पनीज़ रैट अबोट फ़ेस — पेसेज़ टू दी रैट या लिफ़्ट वील	Remaining companies right about face — paces to the right *yā* (or) left wheel.	बाक़ी कम्पनी दहने से आधा चक्कर फिरो कई क़दम दहने या बाएं खूंट पर चक्कर खाओ	*bāḳī kampanī dahnē sē ādhā chakkar phirō ka'ī ḳadam dahnē yā bā'ēṅ khūnṭ par chakkar khā'ō.*
रैट या लिफ़्ट वींग रैट अबोट फ़ेस कम्पनीज़ — पेसेज़ इनवरड्ज़ वील	Right *yā* (or) left wing right about face. Companies — paces inwards wheel.	दहना या बायां पहलू दहने से आधा चक्कर फिरो कम्पनी कई क़दम भीतरी खूंट पर चक्कर खाओ	*dahnā yā bāyāṅ pahlū dahnē sē ādhā chakkar phirō. Kampanī ka'ī ḳadam bhītrī khūnṭ par chakkar khā'ō.*
कम्पनीज़ — अन दी रैट या लिफ़्ट बयकवरड्ज़ वील	Companies — on the right *yā* (or) left backwards wheel.	कम्पनी कई क़दम दहने या बाएं खूंट पर पीछे से चक्कर खाओ	*kampanī ka'ī ḳadam dahnē yā bā'ēṅ khūnṭ par pīchhē sē chakkar khā'ō.*
फ़रम लैन अन दी सिंटर कम्पनी कम्पनीज़ इन फ़िरंट रैट अबोट फ़ेस	Form line on the centre company. Companies in front, right about face.	बीच की कम्पनी से बराबर सफ़ बन जाओ सामने की कम्पनी दहने से आधा चक्कर फिरो	*bīch kī kampanī sē barābar ṣaf ban jā'ō. Sāmhnē kī kampanī dahnē sē ādhā chakkar phirō.*
कम्पनीज़ अन दी रैट बयकवरड्ज़ वील	Companies on the right backwards wheel.	कम्पनी दहने खूंट पर पीछे से चक्कर खाओ	*kampanī dahnē khūnṭ par pīchhē sē chakkar khā'ō.*

अड्वेन्स इन डैरिक्ट इश्लोन अफ़ कम्पनीज़ फ़राम दी रैट या लिफ़्ट	Advance in direct echellon of companies from the right *yā* (or) left.	तिर्छी कम्पनी बन्कर दहनी या बाईं कमर से आगे बढ़ो	*tirchhī kampanī bankar dahnī yā bā'īṅ kamar sē āgē baṛhō.*
कम्पनीज़ रैट या लिफ़्ट शोल्डर्ज़ फ़र्वर्ड	Companies right *yā* (or) left shoulders forward.	कम्पनी दहना या बायां कांधा बढ़ाओ	*kampanī dahnā yā bāyāṅ kāndhā baṛhā'ō.*
सब्डिवीज़न्ज़ या सिक्शन्ज़ रैट या लिफ़्ट	Subdivisions *yā* (or) sections right *yā* (or) left.	आधी कम्पनी या टोलियां दहने या बाएं	*ādhī kampanī yā ṭōliyāṅ dahnē yā bā'eṅ.*
रीफ़ार्म लैन	Reform line.	सफ़ फिर बन जाओ	*ṣaf phir ban jā'ō.*
फ़ार्म लैन अन दी लीडिंग डवीज़न	Form line on the leading division.	अगली आधी कम्पनी या टोली से सफ़ बन जाओ	*aglī ādhī kampanī yā ṭōlī sē ṣaf ban jā'ō.*

CORRECTIONS.

Page line

11, 19 — for ड read ड़

12, 29 — for तश्राला़ read तश़्राला़

31, 8 — for *layē* read *lāyē*

32, 25 — for *dīyē* read *diyē*

45, 13 — for هرا read هوا

61, 6 — for مثلاً (*mislān*) read مثلاً (*masalan*)

115, 19 — for گھیون *ghyauṅ* read گھیوں *ghē'ūṅ*

118, 18 — for *nīnāyā* read *nināyā*

120, 2 — for *bichchū* read *bichchhū*

121, 26 — for چرا *chirā* read چڑا *chiṛā.*

127, 14 — for بشت read پشت

138, 8 — for *kŏkh* read *kōkh*

142, 5 — for *ra sha* read *ra*sha*

143, 3 — for *nākrā* read *nāḳrā*

160, 16 — for *mōtiyā* read *mōṭiyā*

166, 9 — for گھیون *ghyauṅ* read گھیوں *ghē'ūṅ*

168, 6 — for *fil* read *fīl*

Page line

174, 21 — *kēwār* read *kēwāṛ*

217, 19 — for *sa ī* read *sa*ī*

220, last — for *hār* read *hāth*

225, 17 — for *chīknā'ī* read *chiknā'ī*

257, 30 — for *khaṣṣiyat* read *khāṣṣiyat*

296, 28 — for *wāḳī** read *wāḳi**

314, 14 — for *ṭhanḍī* read *ṭhanḍā'ī*

321, 5 — for *mīlānā* read *milānā*

331, 24 — for *ṭa n* read *ṭa*n*

339, 4 — for تکنا read ٹکنا

352, 21 — for يقبن read يقين

352, 31 — for *barā* read *baṛā*

358, 15 — for *agmanā* read *āgmanā*

362, 15 — for معيب read مہيب

363, 13 — for *ba-tadrij* read *ba-tadrīj*

377, 29 — for *ghaliban* read *ghāliban*

380, 16 — for سوخ read شوخ

385, 4 — for نابعدار read تابعدار

386, 6 — for *bharmila* read *bharmīlā*

402, 28 — for *achchha* read *achchhā*

406, 29 — for *bhatā* read *bhātā*

410, 7 — for *hum* read *ham*

433, 2 — for عمر read عمر

Page line

440, 1 & 2 — dele the words after هيَ

444, 1 & 2 — dele the words after Kishnā

448, 5 — for جمعدار read جمعدار

450, 13 & 22 — for ‡ substitute §

455, 28 — for ڈالنا *ḍālnā* read ڈالا *ḍālā*

469, last — for 31 read 30

471, 26 & 30 — for 32 read 31

471, 31 — for 31 read 30

476, 9 — for inde . read indef.

476, 24 — for 32 read 31

477, 6 — for उषृटो read उषृटी

478, 30 — for 32 read 31

483, 8 — for कमीन॰ read कमीनः

484, 30 — for 30 read 29

485, 26 — for 32 read 31

486, 19 — for गोशार्वान read गोशीर्षान

486, 23 & 26 — for 32 read 31

487, 21 — for 32 read 31

488, 14 — for दता read देता

488, 21 — for 32 read 31

489, 15 & 24 — for 32 read 31

495, 1 — for उगृषं read उगृषें

499, 20 — for 30 read 29

500, 21 — for 31 read 30

506, 5 — for डर read डंर

507, 9 — for जिंता read चिंता

507, 10 — for डाला read जाला

507, 23 — for कँ read कतें

508, 24 — for का read की

523, last — for 31 read 30

543, 23 — for Astell read Ostell

544, 19 — for उ ्लीक read उब्लीक

545, 20 — for पिछ्ल। read पिछ्ली

546, 10 — for प।छे read पीछे

551, 23 — for *ādh* read *ādhī*

552, 25 — for बटलैन read बटेलैन

553, 6 — for बाइ read बाईं

556, 10 — for दो read दी

557, 28 — for सिफ़्ट read सिफ़्त

558, 16 — for दकर read देकर